THE VANITY FAIR DIARIES

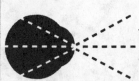

THE VANITY FAIR DIARIES

1983-1992

TINA BROWN

THORNDIKE PRESS
A part of Gale, a Cengage Company

GALE
A Cengage Company

Farmington Hills, Mich • San Francisco • New York • Waterville, Maine
Meriden, Conn • Mason, Ohio • Chicago

Copyright © 2017 by Tina Brown.
Thorndike Press, a part of Gale, a Cengage Company.

ALL RIGHTS RESERVED
Thorndike Press® Large Print Popular and Narrative Nonfiction.
The text of this Large Print edition is unabridged.
Other aspects of the book may vary from the original edition.
Set in 16 pt. Plantin.

**LIBRARY OF CONGRESS CIP DATA ON FILE.
CATALOGUING IN PUBLICATION FOR THIS BOOK
IS AVAILABLE FROM THE LIBRARY OF CONGRESS.**

ISBN-13: 978-1-4328-4507-0 (hardcover)
ISBN-10: 1-4328-4507-1 (hardcover)

Published in 2017 by arrangement with Henry Holt and Company

Printed in Mexico
1 2 3 4 5 6 7 21 20 19 18 17

To Ed Victor (September 1939–June 2017)

Champion and beloved friend

CONTENTS

CONTENTS

HOW I GOT THERE

Sunday, April 10, 1983

I am here in NYC at last, brimming with fear
and insecurity. Getting in late last night on British Airways, I suddenly felt the enormousness
of New York City, the noise of it, the speed of it,
the lonely obliviousness of so many people trying to get ahead. My London bravado began to
evaporate. I wished I was with Harry, who I
knew would be sitting at his computer in front
of his study window, in Kent, furiously pounding
away about Rupert Murdoch.

I am staying at the Royalton Hotel on West
Forty-Fourth Street, opposite the Algonquin
Hotel. It's a bit of a fleapit but in walking
distance to the Condé Nast HQ at 350 Madison
Avenue. The man at the desk seemed half-
asleep when I checked in and there was no one
around to haul my bag to the elevator. All the
way in from JFK in the taxi, a phone-in show
was blaring a woman with a rasping German
accent talking in excruciating detail about blow

jobs. The instructions crackling from the radio to "tek it in the mouth und move it slowly, slowly up und down" got so oppressive I asked the cabdriver what the hell he was listening to. He said it was a sex therapist called Dr. Ruth who apparently gives advice on the radio and has an enormous following.

As soon as I woke up I rushed to the news-stand on the corner to look for the April issue of *Vanity Fair.* The second edition is even more baffling than the first one I saw in London in February.

So begin my *Vanity Fair* diaries, scribbled over the years in blue school exercise books late at night after dinners, or on planes to London, or in a book-lined aerie overlooking the Atlantic Ocean in Quogue on Long Island, or in the small hours of the morning when I couldn't get back to sleep after a midnight bottle feed of one of my two children. When, in 2015, I started to look into the diaries again, my intention was to use them as a refresher for a book I was thinking of about the Crazy Eighties. But the more I read the more I realized I had already written one.

The writer of a memoir or a history knows from the outset where the story is going and how it will end. The diarist doesn't have a clue what's around the corner. All one can know about is the past and, with any luck, the onrushing present. That's a feature of the form, not a bug. What you lose in omniscience and perspective you gain in heedless immediacy and suspense.

Opening the volumes I was amazed to rediscover how madcap those days and years were — how chancy, how new, how supercharged. And I found that the recklessness of the telling — so many instant insights as often to be regretted as vindicated — was the way to surf the eighties, at the speed those years were lived.

Let me forewarn. These were years spent amid the moneyed elite of Manhattan and LA and the Hamptons in the overheated bubble of the world's glitziest, most glamour-focused magazine publishing company, Condé Nast, during the Reagan era. Please don't expect ruminations on the sociological fallout of trickle-down economics. My *Vanity Fair* did its share of investigative reporting on the crimes and cruelties of politics and policy. But as day-to-day, night-to-night experience, this was the gilded, often egregious eighties as lived at the top. Today, when most of the time I yearn to be under my duvet at night bingeing on Netflix's latest noir heartpounder, I am blown away by the sheer number of dinners, galas, and cocktail parties I attended as editor in chief of *Vanity Fair.* The social energy of the eighties in New York was ferocious. When did I sleep? (It turns out to have been an asset that I am allergic to alcohol. Most of these accounts of dinner parties probably wouldn't have happened if I'd had a glass in my hand.)

By the time I became editor in chief of *Vanity Fair* in January 1984, Ronald Reagan was on a glide path to reelection. He had made an improbable journey from radio announcer to midlevel movie star to union leader to television host to two-term governor of California to president of the United States.

Reagan's ascent to the White House marked the definitive end of one era — that of the turbulent 1960s and its threadbare seventies endgame — and the supersonic launch of another gilded age. Tax cuts for the wealthy in 1981 unleashed animal spirits on Wall Street. There were new buzz-words like "junk bonds" and "arbitrage." Go-getters in suspenders, their eyes ablaze with the thrill of winning, thrived in an orgy of mergers and acquisitions. As Senator Daniel Patrick Moynihan put it when asked to define the eighties, we "borrowed a trillion dollars from the foreigners and used the money to throw a big party."

The Reagan White House set the social pace of the most visible stratum of American high life. With her huge coiffed movie-star head and tiny, svelte body in ruby-red Adolfo suits, Nancy Reagan was the reigning star of John Fairchild's Seventh Avenue and society bible, *W,* the oversized fashion monthly that was sister of his powerful retail newspaper *Women's Wear Daily.* The Reagans filled the East Room and the State Dining Room and the pages of *W* with A-listers, B-listers, and *Hollywood Squares* C-listers. Nancy's devoted gay "walkers" — social escorts from the world of fashion and decorating — always stood ready to ditch their Bel Air and Park Avenue circles for the heady whirl of formal dinners and luncheons in the executive mansion.

The American media world for which I was headed in the early eighties was enjoying an era of blockbuster confidence. The gatekeepers to what was not yet called "content" — the studio heads, network chiefs, major-label music honchos, Hollywood agents — were stars themselves. In publishing, paying outlets for writers and photographers — cash-cow newspaper chains, prosperous publishing houses, ad-stuffed magazines — were legion. There were twenty-five hundred new magazines launched between 1979 and 1989. To be the editor of *Time* or *Newsweek* was to be a demigod.

Meanwhile, pop culture was all about the shiny surface — high voltage, high volume. Even porn became high gloss. On television, *Dynasty* was big: big hair, big money, big ratings. The slick tire-squealer *Miami Vice,* whose heroes drove Ferraris in sequences spliced with rock video montages and were unafraid to wear pastel tees with white linen suits, made its debut on September 16, 1984. "Material Girl," the monster hit song in which Madonna celebrates affluence and scorns romance, came out a few months later. In the video, her hard-edged Marilyn Monroe impersonation has the unapologetic ersatz fabulousness that defined female glamour in the eighties. In New York, the decade's biggest signifier would turn out to be a building, not a person: Trump Tower, the very definition of ersatz with its fool's-gold facade, its flashy internal waterfall, its dodgy financing.

More broadly, these were the years when America began lurching toward serious economic inequality. Those big tax cuts for the rich combined with big cuts in social spending squeezed America's vaunted middle class at both ends.

In the New York of 1984, it was either the sedan or the sidewalk. Martin Amis's *Money* was published in January 1984, and Jay McInerney's *Bright Lights, Big City* in August, and both captured the mood — doomy, self-destructive, even hopeless, but at the same time soaringly ambitious. The big artists were Keith Haring, Jean-Michel Basquiat, Kenny Scharf: graffiti-making urchins who were plucked from the streets like fairy-tale paupers and made princes of the galleries and salons. And as the sidewalks were filling with the homeless, the adjacent streets were filling with stretch limos — a moment that would be nicely captured, as so many were, by Oliver Stone's *Wall Street,* which came out in 1987, right after the October stock market crash of that year. Oscillating between these worlds, New York City often felt on the brink. My diaries are full of moments when the uneasy sense of precariousness intrudes.

In April 1983 when the entries begin, I was professionally listless after four years as a successful magazine editor in London.

To recap, I was twenty-five in 1979 when I was invited to edit *Tatler,* a famous (if fading) monthly in London. This was an outlandish break for someone who had never edited anything, much less a magazine that trailed clouds of glory with a 270-year pedigree that included contributors such as Jonathan Swift, the author of *Gulliver's Travels.* By 1979, however, *Tatler* had become a skinny, shiny sheet, its circulation barely ten thousand. Its new owner, Gary Bogard, an Australian real estate entrepreneur unknown to London's intelligentsia, had offered the job of resuscitation to pretty much every credible editor in town, without success.

At the time I was a freelance writer contributing frisky commentary to the leftish weekly *New Statesman,* which, under its great editor, the squash-faced Anthony Howard — known as "Fetus Features" by my fellow contributor Christopher Hitchens — was an older, more droll British cousin to *The Nation* or *The New Republic.* Howard had recruited me when I was an undergraduate at Oxford, and his literary stable also included Julian Barnes, James Fenton, and Martin Amis, whose pieces often ran under a pseudonym, Bruno Holbrooke.

In addition to the *New Statesman* (or the Staggers, as we called it), I was writing for *The Telegraph Sunday Magazine,* mostly light stuff about London social trends. I also wrote for *Punch,* the venerable humor magazine, which at one point assigned me to dance for a set on a tabletop in a G-string at a bar in Hackensack, New Jersey, and tell the magazine's aging readers what the life of a go-go dancer was like. That was when I began to reflect on how great it would be to be the one assigning the pieces instead of being assigned.

In the spring of 1979 Nigel Dempster, the influential *Daily Mail* gossip columnist and wag who was now advising Gary Bogard in his ambitions to turn the waning *Tatler* into a bona fide glossy, noticed my pieces. He told Bogard to forget about established names and go for youth.

It didn't take long for me to discover that I loved being an editor.

As a movie producer's daughter, I'd inherited a feel for what it takes to wrangle a story. My father, George H. Brown, was one of a happy, now vanished breed of Gentleman Film Producers who worked on contract for the Rank Organization at Pinewood Studios — the hub of the British film industry, headquartered in a converted country house estate twenty miles west of central London at Iver Heath. The Gentleman Producer prided himself on the high-low mix of his oeuvre: a broad comedy today, a costume drama tomorrow, a refined detective story the day after.

Dad produced over thirty feature films in his fifty-year career, from vintage dramas such as *Sleeping Car to Trieste* (1948), *Hotel Sahara* (1951), and *Desperate Moment* (1953) to light comedies such as *School for Secrets* (1946), *Vice Versa* (1948, with his best friend, Peter Ustinov), and *The Chiltern Hundreds* (1949) to character pieces such as the BAFTA-winning *Guns at Batasi* (1964, starring Richard Attenborough and the ingenue Mia Farrow, recruited at the last moment when the original star, Britt Ekland, ran off with Peter Sellers).

Large, blond, and ebullient in his well-tailored suits, my father filled a room with his commanding height and broken nose. At Pinewood he met Bettina Kohr, the exotic-looking brunette who became my mother. She had worked as the assistant to Laurence Olivier on his adaptations of *Henry V* (1944)

17

and *Hamlet* (1948, the first British film to win Hollywood's Best Picture Oscar). She was a hilarious wit and a voracious reader. They stayed married for fifty years.

Throughout my childhood the Brown family lived in the idyllic Buckinghamshire hamlet of Little Marlow. Our brick-fronted Georgian house had large bay windows, like Dickens's Old Curiosity Shop. There was a tumbledown apple orchard at the back, and purple blooms of wisteria flourished around the windows and doors. Opposite the house was a broad meadow circled by majestic lime trees, where the yell of soccer and the plop of cricket provided the metronome of passing time.

I was born in 1953, five years after my brother, Christopher. An extremely nervous fair-haired little girl — known then as Cristina — I was desperately shy, wailing for my mother at other children's parties.

Mum had chosen to become a full-time wife, devoted to her husband's life and business and to us. Christopher and I would have hated losing her exclusive involvement in our happy world. She was our partner in crime, the divine muse and clever mimic who dreamed up stories, saw through phonies, and headed off bores. Every morning of lower school she drove me to Rupert House in Henley-on-Thames, crammed into her bright red three-wheel bubble car. I was proud of how different she looked from the other mums waiting outside for their charges at four o'clock. Next to all their careful bouffants and boringly decorous pearls she was statuesque and striking, with her raven hair pulled back in a bun and her dangly turquoise earrings. Her diva looks radiated dangerous glamour.

In our house at Little Marlow there was a wild love of stories and a passion to find, hear, read, see, and tell them. My father was always in search of a "cracking good yarn" to bring to the screen. The Sunday papers were a story quarry. So was the pile of books and scripts we took on family vacations. While we were at school Mum would be at her portable typewriter, pounding out potential film "treatments" for Dad, sparked by the novels that arrived in a box once a week from the Harrods lending library, culled from her perusal of *Books and Bookmen* and *The Listener.* As soon as I was a sentient being I was included in the discussions of how to get a story "done" — the chase, the seduction, the patient persistence required to carve vivid characters and narrative lines from a writer's original material and bring it to the screen. My father did a lot of that. When he was on deadline, locked in the dining room with a screenwriter, Christopher (himself a future film producer) and I knew better than to interrupt.

And then there were the parties. Our parents loved playing host. Propinquity to Pinewood made our Buckinghamshire home into the unlikely soundstage for their rolling postproduction festivities, with a cast of rising starlets, operatic art directors, tragic comediennes, moody directors, on-the-make leading men, the odd literary lion, and whichever squat Turkish financier had put up 20 percent of the production money. They would roll up in their Bentleys and Jags for the wrap parties in our big, beamed living room with French windows that opened out onto the lawn. During the holiday season you could spot the latest James Bond or the star of a *Carry On* comedy lying contentedly inebriated under the Christmas tree. Like the ingredients of my father's lovingly concocted summer sangria, the social mix was full of interesting flavors. I once watched my mother introduce the elderly literary legend Dame Rebecca West — a neighbor who shared Mum's passion for murder investigations — to the double entendre specialist TV comedian Benny Hill. The great lady of letters bent down and examined him as if he were a vivisected newt.

My parents, like their peers in the Bucks Beverly Hills, had one foot in show business and the other in the local squirearchy, reflected in their choice of our schools. I attended a series of turreted academies with horsey debs and *Country Life* Camillas. My shyness faded by middle school and I became a ringleader. I'd usually do well for a year or two, garnering alphas in English and history and spending long hours in my huge owl spectacles, transcribing Shakespeare's sonnets into my journal with an Osmiroid italic-nibbed fountain pen. Then I'd suddenly stage a rebellion.

My crimes were never then-cool modern subversions like smoking hash or hiding copies of Helen Gurley Brown's *Sex and the Single Girl*. They were always crimes of attitude. I was bounced from Godstowe, a frowning single-sex day school on a Buckinghamshire hill, for writing an end-of-term play in which Godstowe was blown up and replaced by a public lavatory. I was bounced, too, from Oakdene, a starchy boarding establishment in Beaconsfield I was sent to next for two brief but eventful semesters.

My parents were always magnificent in these disciplinary altercations. They showed up looking confident and serene, and listened with wonder to the tale of their daughter's unrecognizable delinquencies. "How very sad it must be for you to have failed with this unusual girl," my father gently told the mono-bosomed headmistress, Miss Havard, before loading up the car with my trunk and speeding us off to the refuge of Little Marlow, my mother staring proudly ahead.

My final foray was Hampden House, an exclusive girls' school in Great Missenden. Somehow, in a considerable feat, my parents got me a place there without admitting I had been expelled from Oakdene for calling Miss Havard's bosom in a discovered diary an "unidentified flying object."

At most boarding schools of the era, few of the 250-girl school population, many of them daughters of earls and honorables, attempted to go on to university. Most chose instead to learn china mending at Sotheby's or attend finishing school in Switzerland. But what Hampden House, once the family home of John Hampden, a Roundhead hero of the English Civil War, lacked in academics it made up for in atmosphere, stimulating my passion for history and drama. This time the play I wrote — and produced and directed — was about Henry VIII and his six wives.

True to form, I quickly found a way to blow the temporary acclaim. One of Hampden House's odder regulations decreed that we had to wear two pairs of underwear: one of white cotton and, over it, a voluminous pair of gray flannel overknickers. Plus, we were forbidden to change our underpants more than three times a week. The year was 1968, and one cold spring afternoon, I led fifty marching girls across the lacrosse field, waving placards that read END KNICKER MADNESS and chanting "Knickers out out out!

Knickers in in in!"

But it was me who was out. Soon my parents were once again loading my belongings into the trunk of the car for the one-way journey back to Little Marlow.

In despair, my parents sent me to Beechlawn Tutorial College in Oxford, a "crammer" for a floating population of foreigners and hopeless rich girls who had dropped out of real school but wanted to try for Oxford or Cambridge anyway. Girls were billeted around the town of Oxford in faculty-approved digs and sent here and there to individual sessions with tutors. (I was lodged at a convent where the nuns forced you to read over dinner, which was absolutely fine with me.) My tutor, the excellent Alison Holmes, made me double down on my English literary studies, as storytelling and criticism were where I excelled. In March of 1971, when I was all of seventeen, Mrs. Holmes decided I was ready for the entrance exam to Oxford. It's remarkable that with such a checkered academic record I somehow got in, but British academia was very different then. The trio of condescending dons who decided your fate at the all-important interview wanted only to know if you could think. Oxford would take care of the rest.

The telegram arrived for me six weeks later in Paris, where I was on a student exchange trip, learning French while tearing around to

23

discos every night in the beat-up Citroën of a friend of my host family. It read, PLEASED TO INFORM OFFERING PLACE AT ST ANNE'S COLLEGE OXFORD STOP.

I went up to St. Anne's six months later, in October of 1971, to "read" (i.e., major in) English. St. Anne's was still all-female in those days, of course, and disappointingly un-medieval in its architecture. I instantly envied what the boys had, the spires of Magdalen and Christ Church and Brasenose and all that *Brideshead Revisited* scenic bliss.

But St. Anne's in the seventies was the most intellectually exciting of the women's colleges. The great novelist Iris Murdoch adorned its English faculty. So did the incomparable teacher Dorothy Bednarowska, an Anne Bancroft brunette whose deeply hooded eyes, elegant black-stockinged legs, and crackling asperity riveted us. "Mrs. Bed" served her students sherry and smoked slim, sophisticated cigarettes that accumulated quivering towers of ash as she applied her relentless rigor to the texts of Dickens, Thackeray, and George Eliot. She demanded relentless rigor in return. Her forensic deconstruction of Dr. Lydgate's frailties in *Middlemarch* was a tour de force of literary castration. I worshipped her. She taught me not only the joy of deep textual study — critical for an editor — but also the edgy pride of being at an all-women's college. From our first tutorial I never again pined for what the boys had.

Instead, I dived into all the glories that Oxford could offer in student drama, journalism, and Zuleika Dobson romance. I was swept off my feet in sophomore year by Martin Amis, then a twenty-three-year-old literary lothario who had graduated by then but still had deep roots in Oxford. He was small and Jaggeresque, his chief charms his voice, a rich, iconoclastic croak, and the blond hair that curled onto the collar of his velvet jackets. Martin and I met at a London literary party, where we broke the ice by chatting about the current issue of the *New Statesman.* I remarked that I had a particular passion for the work of the Staggers contributor Bruno Holbrooke. It was a longer evening than I expected after that.

At Oxford, I wrote and produced a play — *Under the Bamboo Tree,* about a love triangle — that was chosen for the Edinburgh Festival and the London Fringe and won the Sunday Times Student Drama Award. And I signed on as a writer for the (now unfortunately named) student magazine, *Isis.* It was edited by one of my closest friends, then and now: Sally Emerson, later an acclaimed novelist, who married her Oxford boyfriend, Peter Stothard. (Two decades later he became editor of *The Times,* then of the *Times Literary Supplement.*)

At *Isis* I discovered that journalism was a wonderful excuse to satisfy the curiosity I possess in abundance. If you read or hear something that pings your antennae, you have license to pick up the phone and launch a barrage of intrusive questions. Until that moment I had imagined myself as a novelist or a playwright. But tracking down real people and learning the truth about them now seemed much more exciting than making stuff up. And I learned that there is no fun in the world greater than the frenzy of closing a magazine on deadline.

A boyfriend at Wadham College, Stephen Glover, who in 1986 would go on to cofound *The Independent,* drove me to Somerset one day to interview a son of my literary hero Evelyn Waugh for an *Isis* series on distinguished Oxford alumni. Auberon Waugh, known as Bron, was himself a prolific, acerbic, lethally funny literary critic, novelist, and columnist for *The Spectator* and *Private Eye.* Physically he resembled his father: he had his little potbelly, sandy pate, and rimless glasses. But I loved him for his wit, and for a decade after our meeting we conducted a prolific, romantically charged pen friendship. He introduced me to half the literary names of London, including Nigel Dempster, and he invited me to a lunch then considered as cool as an invitation backstage at a Dylan concert: the biweekly *Private Eye* hackfest upstairs at a Soho pub, the Coach and Horses. My *Isis* account of that lunch, in which I made as much fun of the *Eye* staff as they did of the politicians they sometimes invited, launched me as an enfant terrible of the British media. The *Eye* got its revenge by referring to me ever after as "the buxom hackette," but the piece, and my subsequent contributions to the Staggers, caught the eye of the most important editor working in Fleet Street.

Harold Evans, known to almost everyone as Harry and as of 2004 to Buckingham Palace as Sir Harold, reigned for fourteen years as the fearless, crusading editor of the UK's most admired quality newspaper, *The Sunday Times.* One of his achievements was creating a model for investigative journalism, the anonymous Insight team, celebrated among much else for exposing the top British spy, Kim Philby, as a Russian agent as well as the malfeasance of the drug company that created the great Thalidomide disaster. (In 2002, readers of the *Press Gazette* and the *British Journalism Review* would vote Harry the greatest British newspaper editor of all time, which has made it even harder for me to win an argument.)

Lunching with him one day, Pat Kavanagh, the influential (and stunningly beautiful) literary agent, thrust some clips of my *New Statesman* articles and my *Isis* piece on *Pri-*

vate Eye into Harry's hand. "Read these," she commanded.

I didn't hear anything for weeks. *The Sunday Times* was in the thick of investigating the defective design of a DC-10 that had killed 346 passengers. Then, one afternoon, I got a call from the office of Mr. Evans and was asked to come around to the paper's headquarters to see him. The fact that the mighty Mr. E had read my insignificant jottings (on a train journey to Manchester, he later told me) and actually wanted to meet me was, to me, heart-stopping.

I arrived at the gray fortress of great journalism on Grays Inn Road near King's Cross ten minutes early. His secretary, the redoubtable Joan Thomas, told me to wait outside. Mr. Evans, she said firmly, was working on the front page and could not be disturbed. An hour ticked by, and then another. She suggested I come back the next day but I said no, I'd rather wait. When she went to the bathroom I surged through Harry's office door, determined to get my shot. Overcome by my own impudence, I froze. Amid a platoon of shirtsleeved editors grouped around a high layout table, my future husband was sketching out the front page. Looking up from the layouts, a pair of dazzling blue eyes met mine. "Don't bother me now, love," he said. (He has said it a lot since.) It's fair to say that as I backed out of the room, I fell in love with his professional absorption.

I soon started writing for *The Sunday Times.* Less than a year later, when our affair bloomed in 1977, I chose to stop. Harry was still married and our affair was a *scandale.* Then came the call from *Tatler.*

All my lit-crit writer friends from Oxford thought I should decline the offer to undertake the revamp of *Tatler.* They thought that society magazines were inherently, irrevocably uncool. But I saw opportunity. Poring over musty bound volumes of old issues, I dreamed of a magazine that would combine the literary sharpness of the original eighteenth-century coffeehouse *Tatler* with the social exuberance of the Jazz Age iteration, overlaid with modern irreverence. Plus, it would be my own show. I could give an outlet to all the talent I knew was out there, much of it undiscovered. And, as I would realize only later, the timing was perfect.

The same month I took over the editorship of *Tatler,* in June 1979, a new prime minister took over 10 Downing Street.

After a long Labour government malaise climaxing in the "winter of discontent" of 1978–79, when every trade union went on the warpath, Margaret Thatcher's ascendance and the Tory victory unleashed a thrusting upward mobility. It gave a new lease on life to the fraying upper middle classes. And there was another windfall for *Tatler*'s editorial fortunes and business prospects: Lady Diana Spencer's emergence, rise, and conquest of Prince Charles and the British public. It was the twentieth century's biggest social story since King Edward VIII traded the throne for Mrs. Simpson in 1936.

Lady Di's world was *Tatler*'s world. She was nineteen; most of our staffers were only a few years older. Her life's trajectory resembled that of many of my classmates at Hampden House. We were able to write about her world with insider-y insolence. *Tatler* became the go-to shop for every nuance of the royal romance. The Di story would be to *Tatler* what O. J. Simpson later was to CNN.

Editing *Tatler* with no experience, I often felt like William Boot, the hero of Evelyn Waugh's peerless Fleet Street satire *Scoop,* in which Boot, the timid, clueless country life correspondent of Lord Copper's newspaper, the *Daily Beast,* is mistakenly sent to cover an inexplicable war in Africa.

By now I was living with Harry. Our Ponsonby Terrace house was nestled in a quiet Regency street behind the Tate Gallery. Ancient ivy festooned the old brick wall around the small back garden. I spent a lot of time creaking up and down the four flights of stairs to my study. On Fridays we would take off for serene writing weekends at a country cottage in Brasted, Kent. (Eventually, in 1981, when his divorce came through, we got married. The impromptu ceremony took place at Grey Gardens, the East Hampton home of the journalist Sally Quinn and the *Washington Post* editor Ben Bradlee, with a small gaggle of writer friends in attendance — on my side, *Vogue*'s Joan Buck, *New York* magazine's Marie Brenner, and Nora Ephron; and on Harry's side, his *Sunday Times* mate Anthony Holden, the *Observer*'s theater writer, John Heilpern — Joan's British husband — and the *Sunday Times'* gangly Northern Ireland correspondent David Blundy with his young daughter, Anna. Ben Bradlee hung a boom box in the bushes to play Handel's *Water Music,* and Sally supplied a picnic wedding feast from Loaves and Fishes in Sagaponack.)

Back at Ponsonby Terrace my illustrious husband offered me more and better on-the-fly editing tutorials than anything I could have obtained in a magazine training class. It was as true then as it is now that if you ask him a question about journalism, you are liable to get a seminar. When it came to *Tatler*'s page layout, I needed one. At home one evening when I was fretting over how to present a scoopy story about Princess Margaret and her social arbiter the Hon. Colin Tennant, he gave me a crash course in page design. He projected a photo of a crowded dance party in Mustique on our sitting room wall, zoomed in on Princess Margaret and her dancing partner, Tennant, and drew a rectangle around them in pencil on the peach wallpaper. The couple were now the vivid focus. My first lesson in picture cropping and my first double-page spread. I sometimes wonder if those red pencil marks are still there beneath the new owner's wallpaper.

Tatler had a staff of just twelve and a miserly budget of a hundred thousand pounds a year. Our editing motto was: If you don't have a budget, get yourself a point of view. Of necessity I wrote a good many of our pieces myself, including a spiky monthly guide to London's eligible bachelors, which for obvious reasons appeared under a pseudonym, Rosie Boot. "What about an exciting émigré for a change?" reads a 1981 Rosie Boot entry. "Gregory Shenkman is half-Russian but wholly available and in a city overrun with effeminate one-shave-a-day men is refreshingly hairy."

My early staff hires were young Turks with an abundance of attitude. They were critical to our success. All but one of those I will mention ended up crossing the Atlantic to join me at *Vanity Fair,* and their names will recur often in the pages ahead. Let's call the roll.

Nicholas Coleridge, twenty-two, fresh out of Eton and Cambridge and an internship at *Harpers & Queen,* was the staff ideas-and-attitude kid. He had turbocharged social energy and wrote wicked, sharply observed pieces about the precocious world in which he nightly socialized. (He later rose to be president of the whole of Condé Nast International.)

Miles Chapman, twenty-seven, was the cranky, bitterly funny copy chief. When he arrived at *Tatler* he wore Rupert Bear sweaters and rimless glasses but soon shed fifteen pounds, dyed his hair inky blue, and became an avatar of gay style. He had a genius for the critical details — headlines, blurbs, captions — that define a magazine's voice. His own absurdly over-refined accent was manufactured from an adolescence listening to classical music commentary and poetry recitals on BBC Radio 3 while hiding from an unpleasant stepfather in the bedroom of a humble semidetached house in Surrey.

Michael Roberts, *Tatler*'s fashion editor, stolen from the style pages of *The Sunday Times,* was the art-school graduate son of a black father posted to England after the war who left Michael's mother, a secretary, pregnant. He wore the same oversized black cashmere roll-necks all year round and smoked long menthol cigarettes. Aloof, feline, with a smile of disarming sweetness when he sensed a target for satire, he was as clever with copy as he was with clothes. He led a vagabond life, rarely cashing a check, his own ineffable chicness often held together with safety pins, a fashion statement in itself.

Only one person could track where Michael was and what he was up to — his assistant, Gabé Doppelt, the petite daughter of rich South African parents. She was nineteen and in charge of classified ads when I arrived — an undemanding job, since there weren't any — until I noticed that she was the queen of Get Shit Done, a role she played not just for me and Michael but for Anna Wintour when she joined her as her right hand at *Vogue* in New York in 1987.

A vital need in start-up chaos is a managing editor. I poached the preternaturally competent and diplomatic Chris Garrett from an ailing fashion magazine to crack the whip on *Tatler*'s deadlines and budget.

Finally, Sarah Giles. A society girl with a champagne personality who at the time was an exotic travel agent, Sarah was like something out of the Happy Valley set in Kenya in the 1930s, where some of her aristocratic forebears had indeed partied up a storm. She had no familiarity with matters editorial, but on a hunch I made her our features editor. She couldn't and didn't edit or write, but she had a talent I've considered crucial at every entity I've run: she could produce. She had a killer eye for a story and would beat the doors down to obtain access for a writer to get it done. The jingle of her dachshund's chain (she always brought him to the office) followed by her booming laugh were the first sounds I heard when I got into the *Tatler* office in the morning.

Was it a coincidence that much of the talent at *Tatler* was comprised of rebels against the British class system? I tend to think it was the source of much of its energy and irreverence.

Tatler was soon giving our primary competitors, *Harpers & Queen* and *Vogue,* a run for their money. Thanks to Michael Roberts's connections from his work at *The Sunday Times,* top-of-the-line photographers shot for us for next to nothing — Norman Parkinson, the society portraitist with the handlebar mustache; kinky, outrageous Helmut Newton; raffish David Bailey, who, because *Tatler* couldn't afford the airfares, once drove me to Paris in his litter-strewn jeep for a cover shoot with his ex-wife Catherine Deneuve; Derry Moore, now the 12th Earl of Drogheda, whose impeccable taste gave us ravishing portfolios of beautiful houses and rooms.

The *Tatler* team was wildly competitive. British *Vogue* was the grandest galleon of the glossies and always got unquestioned access to the highlights of the social and fashion season. Its duchess-like editor, Beatrix Miller, used to small-wave people she was tired of talking to out of her office with a "That's all" reminiscent of Miranda Priestly in *The*

Devil Wears Prada. At lunchtime she would adjourn to the restaurant Apicella near Vogue House and accept obeisance from passing luminaries.

Tatler's cover story on Princess Caroline of Monaco was a gratifying triumph over our lordly rivals at *Vogue,* who thought they had her in the bag. As it happened, Michael Roberts was a close friend of Manolo Blahnik, not yet the cult figure he became in *Sex and the City* but already the sophisticated Chelsea cobbler at Zapata, where all the smartest girls bought their shoes. After repeated nos from formal channels, a tip-off from Manolo got *Tatler* in the game. The word was that Her Serene Highness was personally coming into Zapata to try on a pair of gold sandals. I wrote a personal note requesting a cover shoot and Michael Roberts had my request slipped into the box she would open to try them on, thus circumnavigating her ferocious gatekeepers. Within weeks we were both on our way to the rosy portals of the Rainier palace in Monte Carlo for the shoot.

Tatler's finest hour was the wedding of Prince Charles and Lady Diana in July 1981. I had first met the princess-to-be in 1980 at the American embassy, during her engagement to Charles. She wore a dress of white organza and blue sequined chiffon that revealed her pale young shoulders, her neck circled by the sheen of a pearl choker fastened with a diamond clip. Her skin was apricot velvet, her eyes huge blue pools of feeling. She was very young and very hesitant, always blushing before she spoke, then contributing lighthearted small talk that broke the ice with simplicity and charm. As both writer and editor, I tracked her for all the years that followed, till lunch in New York with me and Anna Wintour, during the summer of 1997, two months before she died. She had come for a charity auction of her dresses at Christie's. By then she had long been an accomplished superstar, the hesitancy replaced by self-possession. She was a media goddess, turning every head as she strode across the Grill Room of the Four Seasons restaurant in three-inch heels and a dazzling green Chanel suit. But her conversation at lunch was all about loneliness.

There was no foreboding of that in the summer of 1981. The royal wedding was a national expression of joy. *Tatler* flooded the zone in the months leading up to it with every angle, past, present, and future. Among the blizzard of pieces on her early life, Nick Coleridge contributed an extended caption masterpiece about Di's flatmates. It began, "There are still a few girls left in Britain who haven't been to bed with Jasper Guinness and all of them are friends of Lady Diana Spencer." Beneath the passport-sized photo of a discreetly smiling country girl named Virginia

Pitman, we ran this blurb:

Since leaving Hatherop Castle School, a spell behind the counter at Asprey's has been followed by a Cordon Bleu cooking course and Cooking for Directors in the City. Her goldfish, Battersea, which is cosseted between plastic weeds from Harrods, is a perennial conversation piece.

"The goldfish," said Miles Chapman on receipt of the copy to edit, "is fucking genius." *Tatler*'s newsstand numbers soared. We had taken the circulation from ten thousand to one hundred thousand and become the third big British glossy, alongside *Vogue* and *Harpers & Queen.* We were in profit and prospering, a grown-up monthly coffee-table magazine with perfect binding, fat advertising, and a voice that made news. One of the innovations Miles had come up with was a line on the spine of the magazine that summarized a mood. The one for the 1981 end-of-year holiday issue was "Deeper, Crisper, Breaking Even." As a marker of how we'd become an authority on the Big Story I was asked to co-anchor the NBC *Today* show's royal wedding coverage from London with Jane Pauley and Tom Brokaw.

When the excitement was over, Gary Bogard made a big decision. He sold *Tatler* to Condé Nast Publications for a million pounds. It was Condé Nast's first new maga-zine title in Britain in twenty-five years. The sale was final in April of 1982. We decamped from our latest Covent Garden honky-tonk outpost and took up residence at the ultimate glossy status address: Vogue House, in Han-over Square.

It was the right move at the right moment. Yet the sale of *Tatler* to Condé Nast, however important for the magazine's solidity, de-pressed our spirits. Gary Bogard had been the best owner anyone could wish for. Behind his reserve, he had a keen aesthetic sense, maverick business skills, a love of quality, and a love of me. The *Tatler* team had been ragtag renegades, flamethrowers at the black-tie balls. Now we were part of the establishment, lodged with all the other British Condé Nast publications and run by the ultimate Mayfair backslapper and man about town, Bernard Leser — a very different animal from Bog-ard, our beloved and clever outsider. My scrappy publisher, Tina Brooks, who had sold ads with furious upstart passion, was removed by Condé Nast in favor of a country squire wannabe in a tweed trilby hat who went fish-ing on weekends.

Within eighteen months of the new Ameri-can ownership the core members of my team and I were getting bored. We felt we had slowed down. We heard little from the mighty American company that had bought us outside of occasional quick visits from its small, nervous chairman, S. I. Newhouse Jr. — known as Si — who would give me ten minutes when he came through London on art-buying trips. Oh, and we kept hearing about a big glamorous project in the works in New York: the relaunching of the company's former flagship, *Vanity Fair,* whose heyday was the 1920s.

I felt the rise of envy at what such a magazine, reconceived, could be. To anyone who considered themselves, as I did, a magazine romantic, *Vanity Fair* represented the last word in literary prestige, social glamour, and visual ravishment. Flippant, knowing, and debonair, *Vanity Fair*'s voice — the most precious and elusive quality a magazine can offer its readers — was forged by its celebrated editor Frank Crowninshield, known to all as "Crownie," whose appointment in 1914 was the inspired pick of Condé Montrose Nast (1872–1942), the dashing Casanova and publishing entrepreneur whose philosophy was "class not mass."

In my twenties I was given a coffee-table book that collected *Vanity Fair*'s iconic portraits, and I lusted for the sophisticated New York it represented. Its pages shimmered with photographs by Man Ray, Cecil Beaton, Edward Steichen, and George Hoyningen-Huene and glowed with rich color plates by Matisse, Picasso, Gauguin, Covarrubias, and

Rockwell Kent. The seductiveness of the images, the lapidary sheen of the prose in Crownie's *VF* spoke to me like the rising strains of Gershwin's *Rhapsody in Blue*. (I especially loved the wit of Crownie's annual In and Out gallery, titled Hall of Fame, which nominated celebrities of the time for fame or oblivion.)

Like Keats and Shelley, *Vanity Fair* died young. By 1936, when Hitler marched into the Rhineland, the voice that had defined the magazine's classic nonchalance had become its downfall. It was no longer the time for such airy contributions as a profile of Mahatma Gandhi titled "Lord of the Loin Cloth" or a picture of Mussolini next to a monkey, with the caption "In all of Italy / there's no old meanie / who can make a monkey / of Mussolini." To ride the zeitgeist successfully you have to know when it's turned. A fast-paced new weekly titled *The New Yorker,* edited by the rough literary beast Harold Ross, had burst into bloom and was stealing Crownie's best talent. *Vanity Fair* got skinnier and skinnier until Mr. Nast dealt it a hammer blow even more mortifying to Crownie than outright closure: he folded it into *Vogue.*

For almost half a century *Vanity Fair* had slept, immured in a magazine mausoleum. Then, as the 1980s got under way, Condé Nast Magazines — now part of the publishing conglomerate of a New Jersey newspaper family, the Newhouses — spurred by Si, decided to bring it back to life. Its rebirth was heralded by a blaze of marketing hype beyond anything the magazine world had ever seen.

Many would later argue that the excellence and ubiquity of that marketing campaign were bound to trip up the new *Vanity Fair*. All through 1982 the drumroll built ever more inflated expectations. Advertisements for the new *Vanity Fair* blazed from every major billboard. One showed the dancer Twyla Tharp leaping into the air over the single word "Breakthrough." Another — perhaps the most notorious in the history of *Vanity Fair* mistakes — had a bare-chested John Irving, author of *The World According to Garp,* attired in red wrestling togs. The Irving image was splashed over the hubristic statement "No Contest," followed by *Vanity Fair*'s logotype and the words "Coming in March 1983."

At the time of *Vanity Fair*'s relaunch, Si Newhouse, fifty-six, and eight years into holding the reins of power he took from his father, had been on an acquisition and start-up tear. Short and nebbishy, he had a charmingly awkward persona that concealed a big ambition: to establish Condé Nast as the most prestigious magazine company in the world.

Within a year of his father's death in 1979,

Si, in rapid succession, bought the most important publishing house in America, Random House, whose imprints included Alfred A. Knopf, the prestige literary house; oversaw the successful start-up of a pioneering health and fitness magazine, *Self;* and bought and revamped *Gentleman's Quarterly,* better known as *GQ.* And he was always on the lookout for more.

Si was the aesthete in the Newhouse family. He combined an eye for business opportunity with a passion for art, design, and high gloss. Intellectually insecure, he relied on the self-confident baron of taste and flair he had inherited from his father's circle: Alexander Liberman, Condé Nast's editorial director. Liberman — Russian-born, like Alexey Brodovitch, his brilliant rival at Carmel Snow's *Bazaar* — was a well-known, if secondary, painter and sculptor, but he was revered for his panoptic control of every title at Condé Nast. He was everything that Si was not and wanted to be: a tall, slim, effortlessly cultured *homme du monde* with a small, elegant mustache and a poet's swept-back mane of salt-and-pepper hair.

Alex became S. I. Newhouse Jr.'s mentor, introducing him to the world of art and fashion and café society over which he reigned with his stylish Russian wife, Tatiana, who made chic, much-copied hats for Saks. Alex was politically astute and, as an aficionado of turbulence, schooled in survival. His father, an economist and lumber specialist, had managed to be an adviser both to the tsar in prerevolutionary Russia and, afterward, to Lenin. Alex's early life in St. Petersburg and Moscow was fraught with terror and violence. When Lenin died, the Libermans fled to Paris, where Alex first met Tatiana and helped the family's stricken finances by working as a graphic artist and designer on the news magazine *VU*. They thrived there in the city's fashionable creative milieu. Alex would later leverage his early connections there to take excellent pictures of the greatest artists of the school of Paris at work — Chagall, Picasso, Matisse. (The photographs were shown at the Museum of Modern Art in 1959 and published as a book that is still a classic, *The Artist in His Studio*.)

But it was the pace, glamour, and opportunity of Manhattan, where the family fled again in 1941 after the Nazis occupied Paris, that suited Alex best of all. He loved the self-invention of New York and, perhaps because he had so many painful memories, the American refusal to look back. He was swiftly hired for the design desk of *Vogue*, where he caught the ever-alert eye of Mr. Nast himself. He rose and rose after that to become, at Condé Nast Publications in 1962, "the tsar of all the Russias."

Normally, the hiring (and firing) dynamic

between Alex and Si worked uncannily well. Si loved quality, for sure, but only if it sold well. And Alex, though an artist by taste and temperament, knew how to protect and extend his power base. Yes, in the swinging sixties he had wooed Diana Vreeland away from Carmel Snow's *Bazaar* and championed her throughout the eight creatively glorious years of her editorship of *Vogue.* But in the early seventies, when ads began to slide and the elitist irresponsibility of the previous decade was superseded by recession and earnest feminism, Alex readily agreed with Si that Vreeland had exceeded her sell-by date and it was time to deliver the coup de grâce. Her departing words were "Alex, we have all known many White Russians, and we've known a few Red Russians. But, Alex, you're the only Yellow Russian I have ever known."

The revival of *Vanity Fair* in 1983 was as much a passion project for Si as it was for Alex, but for different reasons. Si had long idolized a magazine that was not for sale: *The New Yorker.* Under its revered second editor, William Shawn, it had for thirty-five years been the jewel in the crown of American publishing — not only the highest-quality, the most influential, and the most admired of literary magazines but also the most successful. For two decades, the prosperity and prestige of *The New Yorker* had made the young Mr. Newhouse sigh.

But by 1982, *The New Yorker* was starting to lose ground, its readership aging every year. The cartoons were keeping it alive while the famously lengthy articles, unbroken by photographs or illustrations or display type, were moldering unread in the accumulating pile of issues in the wicker baskets by subscribers' beds. To Si this looked like an opening. If he couldn't have *The New Yorker,* maybe *The New Yorker* could be bested by a revived *Vanity Fair.* He looked around for a launch editor who had the cred to take it on, and Bob Gottlieb, his intellectual guru, whom he had picked to run Knopf, suggested Richard Locke, the nerdy, introverted deputy editor of *The New York Times Book Review,* known for his highbrow taste.

Alex, meanwhile, saw *VF* as an opportunity to burnish his own place at the intellectual high table. At Condé Nast his power base was *Vogue,* where he had the last word on everything. He dominated its editor in chief, Grace Mirabella, and her features editor, the gossipy sixty-nine-year-old culture baron, Leo Lerman, but he resented that he and his art were not taken seriously enough, trivialized, he believed, by his oversight of *Vogue.* Hiring Locke from the Gray Lady would be a step in the right direction.

As the new *VF* moved toward the deadline for its first issue, the pre-launch hype was building to a climax and premium ad pages were selling briskly. Granted, we in London occasionally heard rumors of editorial chaos from friends at Condé Nast in New York. Manuscripts and proposals were piling up unread; some talented staffers had been hired, but few had any experience with what it takes to put out a glossy commercial magazine; Locke himself seemed paralyzed with indecision. Of course, any start-up, especially one on the scale of the new *VF,* tends to be a scene of frenzy and conflict. But the truth is that the competing visions — of the marketing department, of Si and Alex, of Richard Locke — never came into alignment. All they had in common was that they were derivative of something better.

Which brings us to a fateful, rainy afternoon in early February of 1983.

A heavy envelope arrived at the offices of *Tatler* on the fourth floor of Vogue House. It bore a New York postmark and contained the freshly minted, still unreleased, eagerly awaited first issue of American Condé Nast's *Vanity Fair.*

I summoned Miles, Michael, Gabé, and Sarah to page through it with me, expecting to revel in wonders that would raise our own editorial game. But as we looked at it in silence, we were, as Brits like to say, gob-smacked. *VF*'s editors had a free hand to hire anyone in the world — any writer, any photographer, any designer. And *this* is what they'd done with such largesse? This flatulent, pretentious, chaotic catalog of dreary litterateurs in impenetrable typefaces? A forty-page safari through a new Gabriel Márquez novel? When the first issue broke, the scorn of the response was unanimous. *Time, The New York Times,* and the *New Republic* all put the boot in. The *New Republic*'s acerbic Brit, Henry Fairlie, nominated the twelve-page Ralph Lauren ad spread as the only appealing feature he could find. Everyone trashed the cacophony of the graphics.

The entire management of Condé Nast Magazines was mortified. A party at Newhouse's home for the staff to celebrate the publication was over and done within thirty minutes. Richard Locke went into what the staff called "bunker" mode, cowering in his office. Liberman feared that this failure could be pinned on the editorial director — i.e., himself — and started looking for a new editor to clean up fast.

Meanwhile, in London I had grown increasingly restless at *Tatler.* In one of those reckless, abrupt moves I seem to be prone to making, I sent UK Condé Nast managing director Bernard Leser and Si Newhouse my letter of resignation.

My husband was also now free. In 1981 Rupert Murdoch acquired *Times* newspapers from the Thomson organization. Unwisely, Harry left his successful power base at *The*

Sunday Times, run as an entirely separate newspaper, to edit its august but ailing sister paper, *The Times.* He was soon in a noisy showdown with the new owner. On acquisition, Murdoch had made five promises to *The Times* board and the British government to respect the historic political and editorial independence of *The Times.* Within twelve months he had broken every one. In 1982 Harry earned twin journalistic distinctions: Britain's Granada Television voted him editor of the year, and Murdoch fired him.

In the meantime, my parents had left England, too, decamping to their house in the south of Spain to enjoy the bougainvillea.

Harry started considering invitations to teach from US universities. I'd been feeling the lure of America for some time. I loved our London life together but I knew that if he was willing, I would give it all up in a heartbeat to live in New York City. The year after graduation from Oxford I had spent a thrilling three-month sojourn there, freelancing from a death therapist's sublet in Chelsea. (I wrote a play about the experience, *Happy Yellow,* that was produced at the London Fringe in April 1977.) I wanted to go back to Manhattan — and conquer it. New York was the big time, the wider world, the white-hot center, and that's where I, a girl of the arena, wanted to be.

One evening in the spring of 1983, a call for me came through from the United States to our Ponsonby Terrace refuge. It was from Alexander Liberman. I had met this famous corporate charmer only briefly, the year before, on a visit to New York with Michael Roberts for the American fashion collections. Why was Mr. Liberman calling me now?

The strains of Gershwin's clarinet again began to rise in my head. A tortured, perilous courtship for the editorship of *Vanity Fair* was about to begin.

1983
DANCE WITH ME

Sunday, April 10, 1983

I am here in NYC at last, brimming with fear and insecurity. Getting in late last night on British Airways, I suddenly felt the enormousness of New York City, the noise of it, the speed of it, the lonely obliviousness of so many people trying to get ahead. My London bravado began to evaporate. I wished I was with Harry, who I knew would be sitting at his computer in front of his study window, in Kent, furiously pounding away about Rupert Murdoch.

I am staying at the Royalton Hotel on West Forty-Fourth Street, opposite the Algonquin Hotel. It's a bit of a fleapit but in walking distance to the Condé Nast HQ at 350 Madison Avenue. The man at the desk seemed half-asleep when I checked in and there was no one around to haul my bag to the elevator. All the way in from JFK in the taxi, a phone-in show was blaring a woman with a rasping German accent talking in excruciat-

51

ing detail about blow jobs. The instructions crackling from the radio to "tek it in the mouth und move it slowly, slowly up und down" got so oppressive I asked the cabdriver what the hell he was listening to. He said it was a sex therapist called Dr. Ruth who apparently gives advice on the radio and has an enormous following.

As soon as I woke up I rushed to the newsstand on the corner to look for the April issue of *Vanity Fair.* The second edition is even more baffling than the first one I saw in London in February. The cover is some incomprehensible multicolored tin-man graphic with no cover lines that will surely tank on the newsstand. Some stunning photographs — they can afford Irving Penn and Reinhart Wolf, which made me pine with envy, and they don't disappoint — but the display copy is nonexistent, so it's not clear why they are there. There's a brainy but boring Helen Vendler essay next to an Amy Clampitt poem, a piece headed (seriously) "What's Wrong with Modern Conducting?" and a gassy run of pages from V. S. Naipaul's autobiography. All this would be fine in the *Times Literary Supplement,* but when it's on glossy paper with exploding, illegible graphics, it's a migraine mag for God knows whom. Plus I learned today the Naipaul extract cost them seventy thousand dollars! That's nearly a whole year's budget at *Tatler*!

The question is, how long can Richard Locke survive as *VF*'s editor?

Leo Lerman, the old features legend at *Vogue,* heard I was in town and called me at the Royalton early this morning. He twittered on about last night's screening, then asked me to think of a piece to write for *Vogue,* so that's a relief. It means that leaving *Tatler* in the UK so abruptly hasn't alienated the US Condé Nast powers as I feared.

Tuesday, April 12, 1983

What a strange place the Four Seasons restaurant is. I went there for my lunch with Alex Liberman. It's at Fifty-Second and Park Avenue and supposed to be the big power spot. So antiseptic and colorless. Why do power people want to go there? The booths are widely spaced, which I suppose is nice as people can't overhear each other. It was designed by the famous architect Philip Johnson but has no personality at all, except a big Hollywood fountain in the Grill Room next to where we ate.

Alex was already at the table when I arrived, looking urbane with a trim David Niven mustache and navy knitted silk tie. He was ultra-charming and clearly in courtship mode, which was exciting. I suppose not many people dive out of Condé Nast Publications unless they are fired, and he was clearly

53

puzzled that I had wanted to leave *Tatler* so quickly after Condé Nast bought it. I didn't want to say it was because the whole scrappy news tempo of *Tat* had been slowed down by Condé, that I hated Vogue House's faux-gentility thing, with all those B-listers running around the publishing floor failing to sell ads. Still, when you are in NYC you realize how small the whole London operation really is. You feel the New York Condé Nast HQ is the big American machine firing on all cylinders. In London we always felt we were the center of the world, which feels silly from here. Still, fuck it. I remind myself that our little team at *Tat* was top class and we would never have put out anything as overblown and humorless as the vaunted issue of the new *Vanity Fair* with their engorged budget! I thought there would be more social fencing around with Liberman over lunch but he came right out with it. The first thing he said was "How do I pin you down? What do you want? We need you on *Vanity Fair*!" Weeks of speculation and there it was, if enigmatic. This was before the crab cocktail. I tried not to let him see my excitement.

Si Newhouse himself then unexpectedly showed up. He came bustling over from another booth. He was immediately disarming, looking at me with rueful happiness and saying, "I'm so glad to see you! I nearly called you at the Royalton but then I wondered what sort of reaction I'd get." Amazing, given he owns it all.

I reeled back to the hotel and waited for Miles Chapman, who's over here, too, from *Tatler*. I asked him to take me to a *Town and Country* gala at Sotheby's for the oldster snapper Norman Parkinson. I was so wiped out that I wanted to go to bed but needed to show support for Parks, who shot so many great covers at *Tat*. I told Miles about what just happened and he was immediately wildly excited, planning his own move to New York if we pull it off. By the time we got out of the taxi we had already dreamed up a new *Vanity Fair* front-of-book section called the Smart Set, named after the 1920s mag that competed with *VF* in the old days.

At the dinner I was seated next to *Town and Country*'s famous editor Frank Zachary, whom I adored. He is something of a legend here, having once been the editor and art director of the fabulous 1950s mag *Holiday*, which specialized in all those glorious society escapism pictures by Slim Aarons. It was Zachary who brought Cartier-Bresson aboard. I love his squashed nose and old-fashioned Walter Matthau–ness and the way he hitches up his trousers: "Gad, Gad, is that really so? That's terrible," he says when you tell him something that interests him. "Tell me more." I got him talking about working with the visual genius Alexey Brodovitch. He told me Brodovitch was destroyed when Carmel Snow died in 1961 and they wanted to make *Bazaar* commercial. I am so envious of those great magazine days.

Parkinson was a delight as always, tall as a guards officer with his dashing white mustache, capering around the floor with his favorite rich ladies, totally reinvented by the patronage of Zachary and Hearst Magazines, Condé's biggest competitor, to whom he is passionately loyal. He jived and twisted with Gloria Vanderbilt and a succession of foreign countesses. Recklessly, I said to him, "I think *Vanity Fair* is after me." He showed consternation. "Don't expect me to follow you to Condé, darling," he said. "Good luck."

Also on the dance floor were Nancy Reagan's viperish, portly walker Jerry Zipkin, plus Betsy Bloomingdale, her best friend from Bel Air who has the wind-tunnel look of a recent face-lift, and God help us, the Baron and Baroness di Portanova, with whom I made such satirical hay at *Tatler,* so I avoided them. Zachary mumbled with the enjoyment of the real social anthropologist, "This do is like some terrible double issue."

Wednesday, April 13, 1983

Estée Lauder's eldest son, Leonard, who runs the Lauder company and seems to be the real powerhouse at the business now, asked me to breakfast (a strange time to meet) at the Plaza's Edwardian Room. I remember my first sight of Estée three years ago, when I went up to her office on the thirty-seventh floor of the General Motors Building to do a *Tatler* piece. She was so teeny-tiny, wearing a Givenchy print dress and matching royal-blue hat, but she really is a bit of a phenomenon. It takes a woman to invent miniature pressed perfumes you can put in your handbag at dinner. What will they do when she's gone? Maybe Leonard is looking for a new "face."

Still zonked from jet lag, I nearly overslept. It was ironic given how long I pursued anyone and everyone in the Lauder company to buy ads in *Tatler* that Estée's son and president of the company (his wife, Evelyn, apparently is vice president, a real family affair) seems to now be chasing me. Leonard is a tall, suave suit of about fifty, with banjo-shaped eyes, enormously charming. I thought he was going to ask me to write Estée's biography. (Such a great story of striving émigré hardship, but they would never let the true one be told.) Then I suddenly realized he was wooing me to join the Lauder company. He mentioned "heading up their British branch" or suggesting to them a company they might buy and I could run. "If, for example, Burberry were to be on sale, we'd be interested in that," he said. I was incredulous. I am a journalist. I wouldn't have a clue about how to run a chain of shops that specializes in raincoats. In America, success in one field seems to make people think you can do anything. Maybe I will be offered a job as a brain surgeon next.

Everyone comes at you with such velocity here. Now that Estée's beloved husband and business guru, Joe Lauder, has died, I feel sorry for her. She's the inventor of it all, but you can see the company repositioning for the future and easing her into the background. "If you are interested in working with us," Leonard said, "we would get to know you, you would get to know us, and we could teach you about our corporate culture." Corporate culture. That's not a phrase I've heard before. I have to admit, I love the feeling of being at the heart of the media and money capital of the world. It's high-stakes and frightening, which is pretty sexy.

Leo Lerman asked me to dinner with his boyfriend, Gray Foy. He hobbled down the steps of the restaurant leaning on his walking stick, with Gray holding him up like an eighteenth-century manservant. And with Gray's full crown of flowing silver hair, it was a glorious period combo. Joan Buck came with the *New Yorker* cartoonist Willie Hamilton, who I thought was hilarious. Plus the wildly chic beauty and jewelry designer Paloma Picasso, the daughter of Picasso and

Françoise Gilot, who was more amusing than I anticipated.

Leo is clearly thrilled at the rude reception to *VF*, as he's moldered at *Vogue* running the features department for so long and has such a love-hate relationship with Liberman.

The Condé Nast politics suddenly took an interesting turn when Leo whispered that Alex and Si had told him at the Four Seasons yesterday that there were "plans afoot to build a bridge" and bring Leo from *Vogue* onto *Vanity Fair!* "As features editor?" "No. As editor in chief!" My heart stopped, though I tried not to show it. Maybe that overture to me was really about working for Leo. Returning to the Royalton as soon as I could afterward to think about this stunning development, I decided after a long, hot bath that maybe an interim ed — which Leo surely must be — is not such a bad idea. Leo is about a hundred years old and has never edited a magazine, let alone turned around one so troubled. He's always been relegated to culture queen at *Vogue*. Also I realize how few people I know here — only two writers — Joan, and Marie Brenner, the magazine journalist from San Antonio who was living in London with the *Times* London bureau chief, Johnny Apple, and is now back here. She's a wonderful friend to have: big voice, big laugh, big energy, radiates warmth. But otherwise, I don't have any network of writers and editors to staff up a turnaround like I did in London, though knowing Marie certainly helps. Maybe I could play some contributing role for a bit and get to learn the lay of the land. Leo would be less antagonistic to me than the snooty Richard Locke. Perhaps I could be called international editor or something for a year. Or maybe not . . .

Alex and Si have apparently told Leo to keep all this to himself, but here he was telling me, probably to warn me to keep out of his way. Condé Nast is like ancient Rome with all the politics and secrets, everything revolving round Si as Emperor Augustus.

A good part of dinner was taken up with Gray and Leo's noisy character assassination of Arianna Stassinopoulos [later Huffington]. Gray described how, even though she had only met him twice, she threw a birthday party for him with a three-piece orchestra and a Greek choir. "My dear," squawked Gray, "there was a fiddler behind every tree, scraping away. And the guests, in the middle of August! She had called them from far and wide — they came by butterfly wing, yak, and canoe!" Gray suffers from asthma, which I think he hypes up as his cover not to get a job and live off Leo. He's clearly someone to watch your back around. When the ultra-charming Willie Hamilton had left the table, he pitched into him: "What a snob that man is," he raged, "like a self-mounted butterfly!"

Leo looked proud. "Oh, he cuts through it all, does this one," he said, patting Gray's knee as if he was the mischievous young Turk he probably once was thirty years ago. "Don't cross up Gray, anyone! He'll kill you, that's all!" I felt put on notice. They hobbled off to a waiting limo. Leo's dome head, black astrakhan hat, and white beard give him the air of a camp Tolstoy or a boho Santa (not sure which).

Thursday, April 28, 1983

I didn't call Liberman because my courage is fading and I didn't know what to say. Then, I got a message from Richard Locke's office to come in and see Locke — clearly under instructions from Liberman — at the Condé Nast office at 350 Madison Avenue. It's a whole building next to a preppy men's store, Brooks Brothers, with a newsstand in the lobby full of Condé Nast magazines. The meeting was extremely uncomfortable. I found Locke abrasive and hostile.

There was a huge knights of the round table desk in his office, behind which he looked very anxious and bespectacled, like a school prefect awaiting the results of election for head boy. The smell of disaster clung about him. There was a funereal feel to the people I passed in cubicles. When I suggested an idea he said it was either already in the works or not "right" for *VF*. Alex had asked me to call him afterward to report but I didn't, as I don't want to be charmed into coming to work for Locke. When Alex learned I had left the building, he called me again at the Royalton and asked me to come in.

Going to see Alex was an enlightening experience of what I now understand as "corporate culture." He works from a cool white room on the fourteenth floor of the Condé Nast building. His PA is a refined youth with a Tibetan head-shave who asked me if I'd mind waiting for five minutes. The whole atmosphere was one of serenity and calm, very different from the executive floor of London Condé Nast, which is all Connaught Hotel–y, with posh female secretaries everywhere you turn. Bernie Leser's great catchphrase in London was "My door is always open," but once you were through the open door, he was continuously interrupted by squawk-box inquiries. He would then spend a lot of time telling me his flight schedule. ("I change in Paris to see the Cartier people and fly on to Rome for a meeting with Mr. Valentino," etc.)

By contrast Alex's management style, when he wants you, is that he has all the time in the world. When he asked me to lunch he offered me four consecutive days and whenever I suggested times for an appointment, he always said yes, he was free. It's like a spider in the center of a web. Spinning and spinning and reeling you in on silken thread.

After five minutes, Alex's door opened and out trouped five identical youths, also with cropped Tibetan head-shaves. They were followed by Liberman himself, exuding ironic sprightliness. He raised his shoulders and gestured at the departing troupe. "*GQ* magazine," he explained, "they want my opinion. Well, we have a problem. We are selling too many copies."

[Rising sales can mean losing money if the advertising rates have not been set to cover the cost of production.] He laughed rustily. "You can't win, it seems!"

The Liberman desk is clean except for a pristine-looking date book. He listens intently with his hands crossed in his lap, as if he is interested only in me and my problem. "So, tell me how it went with Richard Locke?" I told him — what did I have to lose? — that I couldn't work as an executive for Locke, that we had different ideas on what would make a magazine work. He shifted irritably in his sleek office chair. "Well, quite frankly, Tina, it may be that Richard has no alternative but to listen." I felt that this was the moment when I could have Richard's job, but I hung back. Partly guilt, poor bastard, partly fear. My stomach churns for the small familiarity of *Tatler*. We talked some more and Alex suggested I make a proposal about "what I need to make this work. We need you." I should have grabbed it, but couldn't. It's accelerated too quickly (isn't this what I wanted?). Also, what does *needing me* really mean? As editor in chief? Or as some conniving editorial implant? If the second, no.

Instead of coming back the next day to talk as he asked, I jumped on the night flight at JFK and came back to London. Harry thought I was foolish to be so elusive and advised me to call Alex. So I did and apologized for skipping out for a "family emergency" and told Alex I had thought about it, and could offer a consultancy in June and July for ten thousand dollars plus a hotel. (Harry thought that seemed a good way to test the waters.) Alex showed no irritation and was as infinitely courteous as ever. When he beat me down a bit on the money he used the phrase "whatever makes you happy" while making me less so, but after fleeing without explanation I felt I had to accommodate him. He was pleased I would come in June but anxious to know if I could come back in September. This made me nervous. I said "possibly." I detected faint vexation then.

Today I learned he has offered the editor in chief job to Leo, who accepted immediately. I have mixed feelings. Not panic because there is no way Leo can do the *VF* job successfully. But it is possible I have blown it — giving up *Tatler* too soon, annoying Bernie Leser at

London Condé, fencing around with Alex too much, and now Leo may suddenly decide I am a threat. Am annoyed with myself that I choked. Harry said he would have been happy to move to NYC. Obviously, Alex's style is to dangle rather than offer jobs to avoid rejection and now it's too late. There might be no magazine at all in six months if Leo edits it. I feel I have been pathetic. No man would have fled town with a prospective editorship on the table. It wasn't so much the job itself that scared me as New York. I could be eaten alive in a place where I don't know anybody or know where the alliances are.

Nothing to do but keep Leo friendly. I called him to congratulate him and he sounded dead keen to have me come and help. Alex, too, called and asked if I could get there by May 23 and I said yes, if I could clarify my precise role and my title (I don't want to get tarred by being too overtly attached to a bad magazine). Now my engines are revving. Leo and I could be a good combo. He has a big following, as much for his literary taste as the famous parties he threw in the fifties and sixties, attended by divas of stage and page. Plus his Rolodex expands beyond his own circle of culture mavens and he's always been great at wheedling tidbits out of good writers for *Vogue*'s People Are Talking About section.

Sunday, May 8, 1983

Came back from the country to find that thanks to Pat Kavanagh's negotiations, Condé Nast has agreed to my terms about being called international editor, and that *The Sunday Times* has bought my introduction to my anthology of *Tatler* pieces, *Life as a Party.*

Hoping I will now be less confused about the competing things I want to do. I gave up *Tatler* to write more and now here I am about to jump into the maelstrom. I want to have a baby with Harry but am afraid it will take away my work drive and he is so caught up in his. And then where would I be? Harry will be shut in a room writing *Good Times, Bad Times* [his account of life editing *The Sunday Times* and *The Times* and his battle with Rupert Murdoch] and I will just wind up bringing him cups of tea. (Hah! How he would love that!) It's raining. The garden in Kent is dense and vivid. I wish I could take it with me, a portable oasis.

Tuesday, May 24, 1983
NYC

My first day in the office at *Vanity Fair* as a consultant. It was incredibly exciting hailing a yellow cab on a beautiful spring morning outside the Surrey hotel (a definite upgrade from the Royalton, I must say) and riding down to the Madison Avenue HQ of Condé Nast Publications! All the clouds in my head have cleared. Knowing it's for a limited amount of time makes me confident and less scared of biting off more than I can chew.

But boy, it's a sick scene in the offices of *Vanity Fair* on the fourth floor. No wonder two bouquets awaited me. One from Alex, one from Leo. The scene is far weirder than I had imagined and Leo is far, far older when sighted at an ideas meeting cupping his ear to hear better and surrounded by a claque of sycophants he's brought down from *Vogue* and sullen staffers he's inherited from Locke. Most of the things he suggested to write about had appeared somewhere else and even I know that.

Now I understand why they wanted me here so fast. In this month's *New Criterion*, the art critic Hilton Kramer, just the kind of name who matters to Alex, has written a killer critique of *VF:* "Stale, predictable, devoid of charm or enchantment," he calls it. "From the caricatures of David Levine and the graphics of Andy Warhol to the animadversions of Gore Vidal and the incontinent blather of John Leonard, everything about the new *Vanity Fair* has the look and sound and feel of something shopworn and secondhand." Jesus.

I've been given my own office a long way from the main desk pool where I'd rather be.

Liberman came down to see me, in his spry persona ("Welcome, my dear!"), then "Confidentially to you, I have cleaned up the art department" (i.e., fired Lloyd Ziff, a gifted, laid-back Californian with a big reputation. He'd been driven out of his mind by Locke's clueless indecision and Alex redoing all his layouts). "So! We will talk!"

I caught sight of Alex again later in the day concentrating hard in the art department, with a jeweler's loupe in his eye, studying pictures. I loved seeing this, as it's the first time I had viewed him in art-director mode and could sense his happiness and oblivious concentration. So much more interesting than corporate charmer.

I went over to Lloyd Ziff's office and found him still there, slumped in a chair. Alex has brought in Ruth Ansel from *House & Garden* as *VF* creative director and switched out Lloyd to fill her job. "So," Lloyd said bitterly, "the boot has now been shuffled to the other foot. Ruth Ansel, a beautiful person who I love, is coming down here — but how can I go from doing the layouts for *Vanity Fair* to moving pretty pictures of houses around?" I will say for American Condé, they have so many star art directors. Ruth, like Lloyd, has worked with amazing people like Bea Feitler, the famous art director at *Rolling Stone* (she came to *VF* and died just before the first issue), and was very close to Diane Arbus.

Leo looks very pale and waxy. He pants around, giving me sly deadeye looks as well as the odd shaft of campy warmth. He plays the editorial meetings very grand, with only grand names suggested to do grand pieces. Steven Aronson has a book called *Hype* coming out and I suggested we do a big piece by *VF*'s sharpshooter critic, James Wolcott, defenestrating it. Leo recoiled at the idea of the magazine even noticing Aronson's book, on the basis that Aronson bitched up Diana Trilling and she's one of the Ladies (and his close friend). I think Wolcott is highbrow enough to take on both Aronson and the rise of hype, but Leo didn't.

I was relieved to find a familiar Brit face in the writer Anthony Haden-Guest and bought him a sandwich in the diner nearby. He seemed incurious about what I was doing there, perhaps because so many people have come and gone at *VF*, or because he's just one of life's magazine nomads, peddling his sentences for as long as the gig lasts.

Wednesday, May 25, 1983

Depressed. After Leo enthused about my Smart Set front-of-book mock-ups yesterday and suggested I show them to Alex, my appointment with Alex was postponed as Leo had obviously thought about it overnight and decided he wanted to be there, too. It was rescheduled for the three of us on Thursday. Now that I am here, Alex is going to insist I work through Leo, which is right, but only if he's genuinely collaborating. I spent last night in the hotel listening to the whine of police sirens as I don't have anyone to see. So far, every writer I have suggested for the magazine, Leo's said "Fix up lunch for the three of us," which is a real drag as I'm used to having my own direct relationships with writers. Plus, why lunch? All so slow and heavy. And anyway, his diary seems to be perennially full. It will all take forever and I am used to just getting on the phone. I feel sorry for him. He looks at me with awful suspicion, like a manic, whiskery prawn, convinced I am Alex's spy. He's been tortured for so long, I guess now that he's finally got some power of his own he's terrified of it being taken away from him. It's disappointing, though. I thought I was going to be deputed to lead the talent to a promised land for him and he would look good and we'd have fun. I miss Harry! I think of him chained to his word processor in Kent, cranking out the memoir, and wonder how I am going to get through the separation.

Thursday, May 26, 1983

I am finding it fascinating to see the Leo/Alex relationship at work. When Alex arrives in the afternoon you see Leo stiffen with terror. He is immediately transformed from a cantankerous grand old man into a petulant little boy, while Alex clearly thrives on messing with his head. Today he comes down to Leo's office and looks at the board of mini layouts of the next issue in silence, then starts shuffling all the little cards around the board, with Leo watching in agony. Glancing sideways at him, Alex says, "Eighteen pages of Paul Theroux to start, Leo?"

"It's really a very striking read," whimpers Leo.

"But eighteen pages, dear friend? Come, Leo, you know you will have a space problem. We will have to take out the Calvino story!"

"No," wails Leo, "not Calvino!"

"Well, Leo. You will have a space problem."

Then Alex turns around and his veiled black eyes bat opaquely at me, head nodding slightly like a sinister marionette. "Let us ask Tina's point of view!" Sensing danger, I express ignorance of this particular issue and its contents.

Today we had the meeting to look at the layouts I'd mocked up for the Smart Set idea. Alex didn't like it. "Americans have no humor," he explained. "There is no society here. These pages are brilliant but they savor of Diana Vreeland, which was poison to readers. No, I could more readily see these pages appearing in *Vogue*." At first I felt paranoid like Leo. Alex is going to take my best ideas back to *Vogue*! But as I think about what he said, I realize he is right. Here in America people come from nowhere, everywhere, and get to the top. So different from England, where the establishment is everyone who went to either Oxford or Cambridge and the same six schools. I loved the Smart Set name because I was ironically referencing the old *Vanity Fair* heyday under Frank Crowninshield. But no one will get that except magazine buffs and it will just come over as snobby. It was interesting to hear the legendary Diana Vreeland referred to not as the Goddess but as reader "poison." Alex, I realize, may have all the cultural sheen of the artist, but he's very commercial. I felt new respect. I asked him, in front of Leo, if he could confirm what I had raised in our negotiations — that I have a set number of pages I am commissioning (so I don't have to always go through Leo). He responded in what I am beginning to sense is the Condé Nast way, with the counteroffer of something that sounded very flattering but was both unnecessary and a distraction. "Tina must have an assistant," he said. Leo started to look agitated again. "Really not necessary," I said. "Can we count on you, my dear?" Alex said, putting his hand on my shoulder and easing us both out the door.

Feeling glum, I took a taxi this evening to

dinner at Marie Brenner's apartment on West Twentieth Street in the Chelsea district. So great that I got to know her in London and now have her as a friend here. After the Byzantine politics of 350 Madison Avenue, it was a relief to mix with other journalists on my wavelength.

Marie's apartment on a quaint tree-lined block has a London/Islington feeling. Her baby girl, Casey, is sweet and round and happy. Her writer husband, Jonathan Schwartz, is bearish, an expert on Frank Sinatra. The other guests were the *WSJ*'s David McClintock, who wrote *Indecent Exposure,* the page-turner about intrigue at Columbia Pictures, and a small, sprightly, silver-haired film producer named Dominick (Nick) Dunne, who is the brother-in-law of Joan Didion. He has a wonderful mellow voice and told funny, observant stories full of juice about Hollywood and Park Avenue. Seems he was a success in movies, then became an alcoholic and lost it all, including his marriage. One feels he could have been a priest.

By the second course we were firm friends. He's working on a novel based on a society murder in the Woodward family where the former showgirl shot her husband and a high-powered cover-up stopped it from coming to trial [*The Two Mrs. Grenvilles*]. I asked if he'd thought about writing for magazines. He said he'd never thought about doing nonfiction before. Marie joined us on the sofa for coffee. The emotion of the night ratcheted up when Dominick suddenly revealed to me something terrible — his daughter, Dominique, was murdered. She got involved with an increasingly controlling man, a chef at LA's fashionable Ma Maison restaurant. He throttled her. For three days before she died, Dominick sat by her hospital bed, looking at her bruised neck. Now he's going out to LA for the murder trial. Marie told him he should think about keeping a diary. It might be a solace, a way to process the pain. I said if he did, it's something I'd love to publish in *Vanity Fair.* His face lit up as if I'd just thrown him a lifeline. He said he didn't know how to begin to write an article. I suggested what I always do to encourage first-timers: Just write as if in a letter to me, pour it out and we'll help knit it together; not to worry about structure. I asked him to come in to meet Wayne Lawson, one of the *VF* senior editors I inherited from Locke, who worked with him at the *NYT Book Review.* Wayne is a true craftsman of copyediting, relaxed, ego-free. He has a deceptively colorless appearance down to his horn-rimmed glasses, but I've found he has acute sensitivity to a sentence. We have him in the wrong job at the moment, managing things rather than engaging his good literary judgment. Nick promised he'd follow up. He seemed buoyed up when he left the dinner, as if he'd glimpsed some redemption from all his suffering.

Monday, May 30, 1983

The office seems such a cauldron of politics. I volunteered to write what Leo likes to call a *feuilleton,* about Henry Kissinger's series of sixtieth-birthday parties. Stayed back at the hotel to write it up, reminding me what toil it is to write anything. Harry came in like a visiting whirlwind for the weekend, which was such a relief, and he showed me some of his latest pages of *Good Times, Bad Times.* The book has great narrative pace. The undercurrent of class warfare between the old guard at the *Times* and Harry's meritocratic energy that jostled them makes for great drama.

Henry K has been superfriendly to Harry since he edited his memoirs, ostentatiously supportive during the Murdoch horrors (while, of course, playing both sides and staying equally close to Murdoch). Even though Henry K is a rumbling old Machiavelli, I can't help admiring his incredibly sharp wit and the fertile insights he tosses out. The birthday parties were an amazing parade of international power players. I was the youngest by thirty years and would never have been asked without Harry. The most interesting of them was Henry and Nancy's own reception in their soberly distinguished apartment at the River House, where Henry seemed truly the person he really is, the foreign policy superwonk surrounded by academics and foreign-affairs buffs and banking nerds. It was a total contrast to the money-and-froth fest upstairs hosted by the Wall Street tycoon John Gutfreund and his over-the-top trophy wife, Susan. The Gutfreunds' apartment is a minimalist sky lab over a 360-degree vista of glittering skyline. When we walked in there was a Brazilian millionaire and his arm-candy wife, Mrs. Johnny Carson, and little Stavros Niarchos, who was squiring a very tall German princess in silver shoes. When short of conversation we admired the aquatic Monets sprinkled around. After Susan Gutfreund did her florid toast, Henry returned it with: "Those of you who came to lunch today must realize that it was held in the slum quarters of River House, though we have applied for a grant under an urban renewal scheme. Huh. Huh. Huh . . ."

It's taken me three days to write a thousand words about all this, which is absurd. Have been wrestling to find an idea to knit my observations together and stop it from being just a social piece. Today I finally came up with the concept of applying shuttle diplomacy to Henry's different social identities — i.e., commuting between Park Avenue high life, Washington power, and academia. Hope

Leo likes it. He seems to resent me as an editor, but perhaps if I write for him we can recover some of the old rapport we had when he was at *Vogue*.

Wednesday, June 1, 1983

I had lunch with the writer Emily Prager and liked her so much. I read her excellent new book *A Visit from the Footbinder* and thought she ought to be writing for *VF*. She has a sweet, tough little face and dazzling smile.

New York women are so much more confident than we are in London. They really are ahead of us in what they expect, what they assume, what they aspire to do. They seem so much better on their feet and in meetings. American girls' schools, I think, are much better at teaching girls how to speak in public and handle themselves in a public setting. I am terrified of speaking in public, still. I agonize too much. I dread it when American hosts and hostesses bang the glass and start going round the table soliciting instant insights, the way they do. I always feel as if I am dreading the teacher coming to me next and yet when others are talking I often think — I had something so much better I could have offered up. So why didn't I?

Emily talked a lot about how hard it is for writers to get on TV. She said when her book came out Simon & Schuster's PR said, "TV is for experts. Don't talk about the novel itself, be an expert on Chinese foot-binding." She did it so well, apparently, some viewers thought she was doing a how-to presentation and wanted to try it. She was dear-departed *Tatler* writer Henry Post's great friend and told me how awful it was watching him weakened and devoured by AIDS. I told her Henry's death was the first time I ever heard of the disease, when it was still called GRID.

Everything in the magazine Leo is producing at the moment is so irrelevant and precious. I raised the notion of an AIDS story with him but he seemed terrified to touch it.

This evening I went to a dinner party for the Brit socialite Jane Bonham-Carter at the investigative journalist Ed Epstein's Upper East Side apartment. I find the cityscape at night so thrillingly materialistic. And yet a dinner like this with Ed and his friends can be cozy. When I mix like this with writers and journalists I start to think I could be perfectly happy living here as long as I could escape the city on the weekend. In London we felt we'd explode unless we went to the woods and fields of Brasted on the weekend. But to the frantic pace of New York, London is a millpond.

The new, swaggery Texan editor of *Newsweek,* William Broyles, was at the dinner with his wife, Sybil, who was his art director at *Texas Monthly.* They are a sexy alpha pair.

Broyles is going through at *Newsweek* what Harry went through at the *Times*. The thousand and one old-guard pessimists who try to block his ideas all the time on one side, and on the other, the restless, tetchy owner, Katharine Graham, who's obviously falling out of love with him but can't afford to sack another editor after she just got rid of her last one, Ed Kosner, who happened to be very good. Harry says she plainly had a crush on Broyles, who has a bit of the Ben Bradlee he-man appeal, but not Ben's sophisticated political skills in handling Kay. Bill would have made a wonderful editor for *Vanity Fair*. I wonder why they never thought of him. Too virile perhaps. Sybil said they both didn't realize how great their team was in Texas until they left it. (Like me at *Tatler*.)

Ed Epstein told me that two weeks ago at a dinner party, Si Newhouse said the new editor of *Vanity Fair* was Tina Brown and someone called Renata Adler as well. (A novelist, I am told.)

It shows that (a) Si doesn't know what the fuck is going on on the *VF* floor and (b) no wonder Leo is paranoid.

Thursday, June 9, 1983

I took Emily Prager in to see Leo and get a piece from her. Much to my embarrassment he treated me and my guest the way Bea Miller treats the succession of mortified matrons who run her features department at British *Vogue* when they wheel in some social nonentity to meet her and be a contributor. He took very little notice of poor Emily, taking calls continuously, cross-talking crassly with his ET-like assistant, and made Emily go over all her ideas again rather than the one we were there to talk about. He kept squawking, "We must have more names in it!" as if the point of the piece was the names she would drop rather than the fact she was writing it. I felt extremely pissed off, as she was clearly not happy, and I feel I have burned a contact I was trying to encourage. Still, he liked my Kissinger squib. I asked for the byline to be anonymous as I feel if I write something it ought to be more substantial.

Now I am on the way to the American Booksellers Association convention to scout *Vanity Fair* serial extracts (I think Leo wanted me out of the office) and meet up with the wonderful, exuberant literary agent Ed Victor, who is in from London. He's American but lives there and is such a big bear of a man his friendship will be a welcome relief. I also loved the notion of going to Dallas and seeing a bit more of the United States rather than just the hothouse of Condé Nast.

The oven-breath of Texas heat hit me so hard I gasped when I got off the plane. The enormous black-windowed limo Condé Nast uses seemed to take forever to get to the hotel, and when I stepped into the big glitzy conference lobby the temperature changed to meat-locker cold. The lobby was seething with publishing folks with badges. A woman from Harlequin Books in a huge floppy white hat was saying, "So I said to Pocket Books, they can shove it!"

Ed Victor is in his element, leaping around his hotel room in a T-shirt that says "My lawyer can beat your lawyer."

Saturday, June 11, 1983

America is so wildly foreign. This ABA event could put a writer off writing books forever. Ed Victor took me to what was touted as an A-list publishing party hosted by Pocket Books for the old forties movie star Lana Turner at the Adolphus Hotel. "All the crowned heads of publishing will be there," said Ed, my Virgil through this whole experience. "There is no way we're going out to that ranch for the *New York Review of Books* party." The big publishing star of the moment seems to be Dick Snyder, the CEO of Simon & Schuster. Ed told me that Snyder's secretary, Nancy, once told an agent, "Mr. Snyder doesn't wish you bad. And he doesn't wish you good. He just wishes you don't call him no more." He arrived fashionably late surrounded by a praetorian guard of glamorous editors and PR people. Snyder is very short, with tiny legs, a flushed, scowly face, and a mouth that appears to be on a rubber band. He talks in rattling absolutes. Ed told him Harry is writing a book about Rupert Murdoch. "You can't interest me," fired back Snyder. "Nobody gives a shit about Murdoch in this town. He's just the purveyor of bad journalism and nobody cares about that either." It's amazing to me how low the credibility of Leo's *Vanity Fair* has sunk. Editors and publishers roll their eyes or make snotty comments or handicap the odds of it closing. A lesbian publicist buttonholed me for some time with a story of despair about the death of the woman's movement. Certainly Gloria Steinem doesn't seem very full of crusading zeal anymore. I caught sight of her willowy figure and aviator glasses at the party. In a group of other women who surrounded her I heard her say, "We must become the men we wanted to marry." I loved that.

Everyone was there for Lana Turner but after an hour she still hadn't appeared. Ron Busch of Pocket Books came over, looking ashen and sweaty. "Everyone's asking where Lana is," he said. "I can only say where I hope she is. In the shower having a vaginal douche." (We are clearly a long way from Bloomsbury Square.) Owen Laster, a literary agent friend of Ed's, was determined to hang on. "I have to see her," he said, "I don't care

how rough she looks." A gourd-faced publisher on the terrace said he'd once waited
for three hours in vain for Lana Turner. Ron
had to go up to her room and threaten to
make her pay her own airfare and expenses if
she didn't come down immediately. She
finally descended, lifted, tucked, and coiffed
into chapel-of-rest perfection and escorted
by a six-foot-two, thirty-year-old armpiece.
"Nobody talks to me like that," she apparently snarled at Busch when he entered her
room, but just as the party was thinning out,
she got herself downstairs and made one
circuit stalking through the crowd, saying to
each guest, "Don't listen to a word from that
jackass." Humbled, Busch offered her a rose
she ignored. "I guess I'll have to eat shit all
night," he told Ed.

I thought a lot about Lana Turner during
Ed's raucous Tex-Mex dinner afterward at
the Café Cancun. What she'd been saying or
going through in the room before she came
down. Who the escort was — was he paid
for? The drinking, the loneliness. I'm glad
she did come down or she'd just hate herself
even more the next morning. I want to get a
piece done on her for *Vanity Fair* that uses
her as a prism for all the glamour stars who
age without pity. Dominick Dunne would be
great on this.

Bruce Harris, the head of Crown Publishing Group, joined us late for dinner.

There was much talk about how popular their author Jean Auel is. "My author" was a refrain that kept coming up. You are just an author here, it seems, unless you make the bestseller list, then you become "our author." Bruce Harris was so solicitous of Auel that he was almost as late as Lana Turner. "Bantam didn't send the limo for Auel," he said. "She's our Margaret Mitchell," said Bruce. "And forty-one weeks on the bestseller list. For that I send a limo."

Laster was still musing about Lana Turner. "She just stormed past Ron Busch," he said wonderingly. "It was like *Portrait in Black.*" In their hearts you feel American publishers will always revere a movie star more than an author.

At one a.m., spacey with jet lag, I finally headed for my room at the Adolphus. I caught sight of "our author" Lana Turner walking unsteadily into the elevator in front of me, her black bugle beads flashing.

Friday, June 10, 1983

Things have improved and regressed by turns. On Wednesday I was lunched by Alex Liberman at La Grenouille, the very elegant, flower-filled East Side restaurant that is his favorite haunt for romancing people he wants to hire. The waiters all treated him as if he was God and there were rapid French pleasantries about Alex's wife, Tatiana, and the best things on the menu that day. Oscar de la Renta was at the next table, like a sleek panther with shiny black hair and eyes, gossiping with Bill Blass.

It became clear that the lunch was Alex's attempt to turn me into "his" person, which I found discomforting. Irritated though I am by Leo's refusal to trust me, I don't want to be another backstabbing Condé Nast courtier either. I think Alex is secretly a very worried man. Wrong as Leo is for *VF,* he is a loss to *Vogue,* where he was Alex's trained circus animal. Alex could wind up losing his power base. At lunch he told me his worries that Leo is bringing too many "fags," as he called them, to the magazine. He became quite vehement about it, and talked a lot about "the fag networks who controlled the art scene." By which he meant, I suspect, the critics who don't afford him the proper respect in their reviews of his own work. He also said in different ways that Leo has no taste and can't write. If he thinks that, why did he wield cultural power at *Vogue* for so long? Leo is an omnivorous reader. The sad thing is that when he was at *Vogue,* I found Leo wonderful to work for. He was so appreciative of good writing and had read so much of it. He knew good sentences and he relished them.

I didn't want to say that some of Alex's own

contributions to *VF* have been its biggest problem. All that dated, kinetic splashiness on the page and thrown-around type he does. It feels quite wrong for a magazine that's supposed to be about words as much as pictures. The layouts in *VF* need to be clean, strong, and classical, without this distracting frenzy. More Brodovitch, less Liberman!!

I noticed that his attention span is actually short. And that his eyes are so black I wonder if he's on medication. He has the habit of checking out for a few seconds and staring enigmatically into the distance. Sometimes his nostrils widen as he stifles a tiny yawn. I sensed he was just a bit bored with having to romance me, though we began to connect when we talked about his past on the great French news magazine *Vu* in the thirties, and how much he loved the pace of current affairs. I began to see that he's a frustrated newsman in a company that's all about luxury. Even though his past and his friendships with artists like Braque and Picasso are so fascinating to me, he doesn't want to talk about it. I'd love to hear about his and Tatiana's flight from the Nazis that brought him to New York, but he won't go there. He's just as fascinated by what's happening on page one of the *New York Post,* which he loves for its tabloid energy. I also feel the magazines for him are really just a game, that his real interests are with his own work. Moving the

Condé Nast chess pieces around is just a way to limber up his strategic skills before going back to drill away at huge slabs of rock, or hurl paint at a canvas in his studio.

In the evening Ed Epstein took me to a party at the great magazine editor Clay Felker's apartment, where he lives with the writer Gail Sheehy. Huge thrill because I am obsessed with Clay as an editor of genius. His *New York* magazine was so alive, so audacious. It defined the seventies and invented so many writers, from Gloria Steinem to Tom Wolfe. When I was living in New York for the three months after Oxford I became addicted to it. It created a longing in my stomach to see the next issue and race to the newsstand when it came out.

Clay has very pale, watchful eyes, thin, sandy-blond hair, and a certain ruthless disregard until you say something that interests him and provokes a barrage of questions. Gail is a vivacious redhead with a torrent of ideas. Everyone at the party was so famous but unfortunately I had never heard of them. I said to Shirley MacLaine, "What do you do?" She gave me a manic, hostile stare and went on talking to Ed Epstein about how he should research a book about flying saucers. I couldn't believe, once it was pointed out who he was, the excessive copiousness of Kurt Vonnegut's hair, or the extreme pushiness of his photographer wife, Jill Krementz.

I felt I would scream if I heard about another book in progress or a new TV show someone's writing.

I hadn't seen Clay in four years, when I first met him with Harry and he still had *New York* mag. Now the best editor in America doesn't have a magazine. He, too, ran into a buzz saw called Rupert Murdoch. I could sense his unhappy restlessness. How much he yearns to have his vehicle back to tell stories. Every observation he made about media, people, what was happening in the room was a great feature idea. I was happy that he said *Tatler* was the best mag he had seen in a decade. "You must write now, about all this." He gestured around the room. The natural editor. Still recruiting. If he was running a magazine now I would work for him in a heartbeat!

Saturday, June 11, 1983

Awful day. Leo, after ostentatiously being fond of me before my lunch with Alex and in front of Si, was back to cutting me out again and ignoring my suggestions. It's unfair and ridiculous. I am just trying to get better pieces for him. I went out to drink with Trey Speegle, a smart Texan designer in the art department. We talked about *VF* and what it needed and I think he's very much on my wavelength. Nick Dunne came in and I took him to La Goulue as it was my turn to conduct a romance. I like him so much. He talked about his successive stages of grief, guilt and rage and the feeling of suspended time as he sat beside his daughter's life-support system day after day. But he also talked about the grotesque humor that strikes in the middle of tragedy, how the priest had double-booked his daughter's funeral with a wedding and all the celebrity mourners of Dominique had to wait around outside while confetti was thrown as the honeymoon couple left. And how his sister-in-law, Joan Didion, was closing a piece for *The New York Review of Books* and wouldn't get off the phone when they needed to communicate with the cops. He seems to me such a natural writer. You can teach people structure and how to write a lead. But you can't teach them how to notice the right things. I just hope he gets it on the page, or we can interview it out of him. We walked out of La Goulue into dazzling summer sunshine and walked up Madison Avenue, he to his shrink, me to the Surrey hotel. On the way we ran into Andy Warhol and Baby Jane Holzer, who hailed Nick. Both these legends looked utterly bleached out. Like negatives walking side by side along the street. Nick and I then stopped at Books and Company and browsed the seductive, shiny new book table. It was such a perfect afternoon.

In the evening I went out to dinner with Willie Hamilton and we laughed about that Leo evening. He took me to a party on the roof of what seemed to be the very edge of Manhattan, with a ladder leading to another asbestos roof where you could look out at New Jersey and the lonely beauty of the Statue of Liberty. It was so breathtaking. The host was a trendy glassblower or something, with a Japanese wife. All the men had the new Edward Steichen chiseled look of slicked-back hair and wide trousers. There was a very superior architect who had been at a recent dinner with a lot of other architects at Si Newhouse's house, where he and Victoria had shown *The Fountainhead,* which he seemed to think was very gauche. Then of course the talk turned to *VF* and he said, "I told Si he should model it on *Tatler,*" and said all his friends in the advertising world think Leo will bury it.

I couldn't sleep all night. Here I am about to slink back to England, leaving *VF* to its doom. Maybe I should think again.

Saturday, June 25, 1983

It's so hot. Everyone seems to have a place to go on the weekends. I wish someone would invite me! I miss Harry so much and think longingly of the garden at Brasted and the cool walk through the woods behind.

Leo doesn't ask me to features meetings or if he does, he rejects everything I suggest. Doesn't he understand I could save his job? I feel I am really wasting my time here and have to cut my losses.

I am supposed to be seeing Alex next week before I leave New York, but it seems wise to go and see Si and tell him I can't be a consultant or any part of this magazine as it is. I either have to edit it or split. I feel I have to say this to Si directly because you can never tell with Alex how the message will be relayed. After all, he is implicated in the disaster that it is.

I realize I blew it last time when they came to me to recruit me after Locke, but I wasn't ready then, and now I am. I'm not afraid of it anymore. I know I could do a better job than anything I am seeing coming out of that art room. It's time to be ballsy or forget about it.

Si met me at the elevators on the fourteenth floor, looking even more rumpled and perplexed than usual. In his unadorned office there's a wire paperback rack such as one sees at airports, full of books from the imprints he owns — Random House, Crown, Knopf. On the floor were a row of Condé Nast magazines as if he had been staring at them to see which one of them to keep. He drew up a chair next to me, my side of the desk. I was so nervous. But I took a deep breath and told him that when my consultancy is up next week I don't want any further arrangement with *Vanity Fair*. He frowned with concern and asked why. I said I believed it was on the wrong track, and didn't want to be associated with it. I said Leo had done a great job of hiring people but leadership must come from the top and he can't provide it. I said *VF* needs a dramatic change of direction to revive it. And readers are going to be disappointed with what they see.

His lower lip jutted further than usual. "I am very concerned by what you say," he said. "Alex and I don't want old ideas served up in an old way."

"That's what you are going to get," I said mulishly.

"Isn't there any way we can ease the collaboration?" he said. "So that you and Leo —"

"No," I replied.

"But the timing" — he faltered — "Leo has just become editor. He needs time."

"The magazine can no longer afford that time," I said. "The only thing I can do for you when you are ready is be the editor."

He looked exasperated, as well he might. "But, Tina, you never seemed interested in editing it when we talked to you."

"I wasn't," I said. "But I don't want to see it fail."

I felt this was a very serious moment from

which there would be no turning back.

"I will do a good, jazzy job for you, Si, if you want me," I said, looking at him very directly now.

He shifted around in his chair. "This is, this is — where will you be? Here or in London?"

"London," I said, adding, "I am seeing Alex on Monday. And will tell him all this."

More shifting around. "Well, I'm, I'm glad you are seeing Alex. If you write a book, maybe Random House . . ."

I rose and we shook hands, with him still looking puzzled.

I felt elated when I walked out of there. I feel I recouped all the loss in pride I have experienced hanging around waiting for Leo to be in a good mood while he fucks it all up.

I went back down to my desk and responded coolly when Leo asked me to step in. He sensed something was up because he immediately said, "Let's now discuss all you will do for us when you are back in London."

"There's nothing to discuss," I said. "My consultancy ends here."

"But aren't you coming back and forth?"

"No."

"So no international editor?" he said with a sly smile.

"That's right."

"So who am I going to ask when I need all

those wonderful British writers you brought in?"

"Try British *Vogue,*" I said. He looked uneasy and I was about to feel sorry for him, but then I saw the glint in his eye and realized he was gloating. He feels he has won, for now.

Saturday, July 23, 1983

Today I was summoned to Alex's house in Connecticut, rather than wait to see him in the office on Monday. In readiness for the meeting I paged through Barbara Rose's biography of him as an artist and was impressed. It's fashionable in art circles to call Alex a lightweight, but whether you like the colorful abstract canvases or not, he's clearly a serious talent, possessed of an intellectual vigor that would make him worthy of consideration without any of his social or publishing connections. At ten o'clock this morning a limo from Berkshire Livery slid up to the Surrey hotel to drive me out to the Liberman retreat at Warren. Everything worked wonderfully, including the summer downpour. It cut out the possibility of such social decoys as "Tatiana will be happy to lend you a swimsuit." Si would, I know, have told Alex that I had been to see him and meant business. I realized I had to make clear to Alex that Leo can't edit the magazine because he doesn't have any point of view about what it ought to be. I would soft-pedal that though in favor of the less subjective fact that even if he is doing a good job, the perception is so bad in the advertising community that it doesn't matter. As Marie Brenner's husband, Jonathan Schwartz, put it, "People have one thing to say about *Vanity Fair*. Toilet."

Armed with this determination, I felt self-confident and free. I dressed very English in a long-sleeved navy silk Saint Laurent shirt with a white collar and a navy skirt with oyster stockings and low-heeled pumps. I was going to drop the flirtatious charm of La Grenouille, however, and become, as Gloria Steinem put it so well, the man you want to marry.

When I pulled up to the house I was floored at first by how beautiful it is. Clean, classic white clapboard brimming with geraniums, glorious piles of books everywhere, and bronzes lurking among lush ferns and plants. Alex was dressed off-duty but looked as stylish as ever in a check shirt and old workman pants, his manner cordial but with a small undertow of irritation. I think if I had waffled about being unsure again he would have dispatched me back on the three-hour drive without any lunch. But he sat me down on the sofa and I pitched right in. He was immediately engaged, direct and real without all the courtly affect of the city. I felt the pleasure of a muscular mind talking to me as a peer, on a serious professional footing, instead of with urbane condescension to a skittish girl.

I told him everything I believed. That *VF* would be down the drain by the end of the year if it kept going like this. That I had come to New York with the belief that Leo could, with help, be the right appointment, but now I realized he was an impediment to its success because he cannot think conceptually. He is afraid of team spirit because he is threatened by anyone good. And finally, he can never produce a magazine that is anything more than received opinion. "It should be a sound, not an echo," I said a bit loftily. Alex smiled.

Tatiana descended at last wearing huge violet glasses and what seemed a straw flower pot on her head. This was the first time I had met her, though of course I had heard about her tyrannies and harsh immediate judgments that dispatch supplicants to hell. Though in the early pictures she is clearly dramatically beautiful, there's a real drag-queen look to her now. She spoke in hoarse, sweeping statements, as I had been told she would. "Why doesn't Princess Anne get her chin fixed?" "The Falklands War? It was pure public relations." "*Vanity Fair.* Hah! Visually, it is nothing. It WAS a good magazine, once."

"Why?" barked Alex, bristling. "Why was it good?"

"It knew what it was doing," she said with deadly emphasis. "We all used to read it."

"Forgive me," said Alex, "all your class liked it because it was a smart, superficial, thin little magazine that endorsed all their snobberies." I realize he had started to hate the legend of the old *Vanity Fair* that got in his way so much.

"Non!" declared Tatiana fiercely. "Because it was VERY good. And VERY beautiful to look at. In Paris we used to eagerly await its arrival."

It sounded as if they were talking about a wholly new topic, but could it really be they never discussed *Vanity Fair* before? In interviews he always says they never discuss his day job, but I assumed that was just pretense to look discreet.

Whichever it was, I knew that she would play a key role in Alex's opinion of me.

After lunch looking over that heavenly garden, he took me out in his pickup truck to see his sculptures. "What am I to do?" Alex said as we bumped along. "You would make a brilliant editor of *Vanity Fair,* but I have a human problem."

"I understand," I replied. "But Leo is the only person who doesn't see himself as an interim appointment. He could be cast as a savior in a difficult time who then made way for a new regime."

"Si is coming here tomorrow," said Alex. "Confidentially, we are looking for a new editor of *GQ*. Fairchild is bringing out a new men's glossy called *M* which has all Fairchild's brilliant journalistic stamp on it. What do you think of Bob Colacello for *GQ*?"

"Excellent," I said. (Bob was editor of *Interview* with Andy Warhol and said to be a star.) "But" — I was determined not to be diverted — "that also raises the question of *Vanity Fair*. If Colacello is brought in to turn *GQ* into an upscale men's feature magazine, *Vanity Fair* needs a very clear position in the market."

"I know," said Alex. And I longed to know if his secret wish now was just to kiss off *Vanity Fair*. After all, if it really fulfilled its potential, it would threaten the primacy of *Vogue*. I think he is torn between a personal desire for it to fail and a professional desire not to have his successful record blotted at the end of his career and lose his mystique with Si.

He took me to the warehouse full of huge, orange, iron constructions being welded by his team of four. They looked, I realized, like abstract cannons. In his studio the paintings were equally huge, the workshop of a much younger man, you would think, judging by the energy it must take to fill these canvases.

On the table were hundreds of layouts for the magazines that he supervises: *Vogue, House & Garden, Glamour,* and *Vanity Fair.* It is clear that he is the real editor of all of them. Unless he can relinquish his grip on *VF,* no editor can make a success of it.

But I felt I had broken through to Alex today and now we were real friends with mutual respect. We sat in the garage on folding chairs and he recapped where we were.

"How much of all this did you say to Si?" he asked. I felt he was probably going to present my perceptions of Leo as his and see what Si made of them.

My own feeling is, they will do nothing for now. How can they? But I was pleased to hear two days later that at ten a.m. Si had wanted to see Leo, I am sure to hear what he has in the works and judge for himself whether it's the old potatoes I outlined.

We parted with a warm embrace. "I expect nothing, Alex," I said.

"But if I do something dramatic you won't run away again?" he asked with a smile.

"No, you have my commitment. But I cannot wait too long," I said.

Rushing back in the rain through the Connecticut lanes in the limo, I felt my heart sing. I know that whatever happens now, I have established myself as a fighter in Alex's eyes, which any perusal of his paintings shows is what he admires.

Saturday, August 6, 1983
Spain

Waiting. Have run away again, this time to Spain, to stay with Mum and Dad and try to go back to the play about a Nigel Dempster figure named Quentin Wasp I abandoned months ago. Finding it so hard and the harder I try the more I dream of a phone call summoning me back to America. I am so baffled and intrigued and longing for the outcome.

It's good to be with Mum and Dad. They've cultivated a fun new life here in Salto de Agua in the hills of Málaga, looking down at the Mediterranean. Mum has adopted three stray dogs and five disreputable-looking cats. There's always a party going on on the patio at night.

Harry is incommunicado at Brasted on the last straits of *Good Times, Bad Times.* It's going to be explosive. He's pulled no punches describing Murdoch's eroding his editorial base at *The Times* by lies, bullying, and suborning the disaffected old guard at the same time he was urging Harry to get rid of them.

Thursday, September 8, 1983
London

The Kraken wakes. A telegram arrives from

Alexander Liberman, asking me to call him. Trembling, I dial the number, but it turns out to be more of the same. "It is Si's and my dream," he says, "that you edit *Vanity Fair*." (Pause.) "But I cannot dismantle the status quo. So I have to ask you to work through Leo and make suggestions, which I will then endorse." Thanks, but no thanks, Alexovich! I politely tell him that I am currently far too tied down in London and hope we could be in contact again soon. Even the mention of that snaky compromise makes me feel nauseated. A letter then arrives from Leonard Lauder. "I hear you've done some wonderful things for *Vanity Fair*," he writes, urging me to be back in touch. It proves to me that Condé Nast is still using my name to sell ads. It's galling, but I have given up on it and switched my sights back to London. I can get something to run here.

Saturday, September 10, 1983

The suspense about *VF* is now making me a basket case. I went to see wonderful Dr. Tom Stuttaford for sleeping pills and he was at his tweedy best. I told him about all my mixed-up longings. "Hmm," he said. "I never did understand your infatuation with America. I tried it once and wouldn't dream of making it a habit." He removed his fountain pen and wrote a new prescription with an inky flourish. "Here's my diagnosis, Tina. Buy a large house in the country, have a couple of babies, and just accept you are complicated." In other words, just go off and be a wife.

Monday, September 19, 1983

Harry got an invitation to go to Duke University in North Carolina as a visiting professor. Could be a nice interlude. It will greatly refresh him and get him away from Murdoch's gloomy orbit. I can buy some Dr. Scholl's sandals and take an American history course, which I have always wanted to do. Plus, we would then be snugly based in the US of A if *Vanity Fair* happens and I get called like Agrippa to leave the plow.

Tuesday, September 20, 1983

Auberon Waugh took me to lunch at L'Escargot in Soho. We are both so much better with each other by letter. When we actually meet, he chain-smokes in a tortured way, his gingery, schoolboyish face screwing up with regret. He's always difficult, but was particularly so today because of the looming shadow of Harry's impending book. He knows I know he is gearing up to savage it in *The Spectator* or the *Daily Mail* or one of his other multiple outlets. It was hopeless to try to defang him. I think Bron was as depressed by our lunch as I was. He clearly misses the old Oxford days when he was my hero and I his muse. And so do I in a way.

Then tonight, ye gods! Leo Lerman phoned, asking me to write a piece about something, anything, for *Vanity Fair*. I asked him who was on the next *VF* cover and he said Francine du Plessix Gray! That's truly a desperate move on so many levels. First, unabashed nepotism to put Alex's stepdaughter on the cover, however good a writer she may be. Second, it shows he is still stuck in that suicidal choice of black-and-white Irving Penn nostril shots, which are a death knell to the newsstand. Why would Alex let him do it? I guess he's just milking the mag to give more and more promotion to friends and family and enhance at least the personal power base.

Friday, September 30, 1983

Asked to do a million things but don't care about any of them. I miss the *focus* of an issue to get out. Deadlines are a great antidote to insecurity. And I miss my beloved *Tatler* gang.

I had an abysmal lunch with Bernie Leser, probably deputed by Si to keep in touch. He had just come back from the America's Cup and, no doubt just to discomfit me, banged on about watching the last race with his old

Aussie chum Rupert Murdoch.

Then he told me my successor at *Tatler,* Libby Purves, had quit. "We accepted Libby's resignation as editor of *Tatler* because we realized that she didn't have your two most important attributes." Pause. "Your looks and your lifestyle." What? That's what he attributes to my turning around a magazine? I truly cannot imagine any man being told such a thing. Put me in a bad mood all day.

Friday, November 4, 1983

Good Times, Bad Times finally hit the stores. It has been a press atom bomb, with front-page coverage every day.

The revelations of Rupert's conduct flouting his guarantees to the board of *Times* newspapers provoked a flurry of parliamentary questions in the House of Commons, so Harry had his press conference there, which sent the book straight to number one on the bestseller list. It's getting fabulous reviews, hooray!

After the presser, we drove home with Anthony Holden, who has been in his element stirring up all the hacks in the Blue Lion pub. He said he overheard Arthur Brittenden, the *Times* PR man, say, "Of course everyone knows Harry Evans is a compulsive liar." Holden said to him, "How sad that the man who was once a respected journalist has become the mere trumpet-piece of News International!" We killed ourselves laughing over "trumpet-piece."

W has interviewed me about *VF*'s travails for a piece that is coming out in ten days. They asked me what I thought of it and I decided to be candid to send a little spark Si's way.

Wednesday, November 9, 1983

I am writing this in a room in a hotel in Moreton-in-Marsh, Gloucestershire, where I have come to do a follow-the-hunt piece for the *Daily Mail.* I felt like a bit of traditional old England after the last few weeks with all Harry's book press raging.

It was a lovely day here in the autumn sunshine. So refreshing not to be talking about *Times* newspapers or angsting about *Vanity Fair*! Lady Northampton, one of the women hunting, is divine. A tough, saucy blonde living in my dream house, a rosy-colored manorette with a huge sitting room looking out on her acres bounded by stern iron gates, and the prettiest, sweetest little girl bouncing around, who I wish was mine. Dashing on her horse through country lanes with her fat snood and tight breeches, Rosie Northampton seemed to me the most care-free woman in England. The *Daily Mail* of course wants some slasher piece about snobs on horseback. But mostly the people hunting were relaxed, courteous country people, not all aristos by any means. The men were gallant, raising their hats at the slightest provocation, the women dignified and strong. Their hunting-speak wafted back to me as they paused to pat their steeds.

"I've just come back from the Quorn. Frightful country."

"So difficult, it was nose to brush all the way."

Rosie's two black Labradors slept in the biggest basket I have ever seen, coiled together like sighing, silky serpents. Maybe Dr. Stuttaford is right. We should just buy a big country house and raise children.

Friday, November 18, 1983

With Harry off promoting his book and me upstairs in my tiny book-lined study at Ponsonby Terrace, all is calm again. I received a lovely prebirthday letter from Bron Waugh, saying that all my conflictedness arises from being married to a "fellow stormy petrel." He counseled, "Your place is front row at the ringside, occasionally being splattered with blood." I.e., forget about Rosie Northampton fantasy. Knowing he is right, I thanked him.

Monday, November 21, 1983

Milestone. I am thirty today. The big Three. Or the big Zero. Harry bought me some beautiful pearls. We went out to dinner, just us, in our old Greek Street haunt, since I hate birthday parties when they are mine. I feel gloomy about hitting this number. As if it's time to really deliver and stop rattling about. I am the same age as Clare Boothe Luce was when she took over as managing editor of *Vanity Fair,* but that seems a dream that's fading. Alex Liberman has asked Michael Roberts to come over to NYC and help bring some attitude to the visual pages. Good to have him as a source to know what's going on.

Tuesday, November 22, 1983

I have to get back to New York! Went as Harry's consort to an absurd dinner party hosted by the ambassador to the Organisation for Economic Cooperation and Development (whatever that is), Edward Streator, and his wife, Priscilla. It was in honor of (57 Varieties) Jack Heinz's seventy-fifth birthday, and for some bizarre reason the ambassador toasted him and me (perhaps Harry had revealed I turned thirty). Afterward when the women were banished, I sat in a corner with the impossibly chic Belgian Dominique de

107

Borchgrave, who told me that Lady Aliki Russell remained traumatized by my reference to her in *Life as a Party* as a "frisky pachyderm."

"But she keeps writing to say how much she enjoyed the book," I said.

"Precisely," said Dominique triumphantly, her painted nose rising out of a roll-necked lamé silk dress. Then she pitched into how "demented" Princess Michael of Kent is. "She pounced on Peter Hall at the National Theatre last week after the Jean Seberg play and said please don't ask me to anything as bad again. And Peter said, 'Ma'am, you can be sure of that!' And as for her husband, NO, I don't feel sorry for Prince Michael. It has been my honor or should I say my *horreur* to sit next to him four times this past year. The man offends my womanhood!"

I could not escape this cascade because I was pinned against the flocked wall with a very small coffee cup. She raged on. "Have you watched Robert Lacey's television program *The Aristocrats*? Robert Lacey is so common. And such a fiend! He asked my friend the Marchesa di Frescobaldi what she'd do if her son marries a peasant on the estate! Excuse me! What can she say, except *'je m'excuse de répondre,'* et cetera et cetera! The Westminsters came out of it the worst. They are so middle class, they live like my concierge, yet the money and land they control is quite demented!"

Wednesday, November 23, 1983

Leo's arrived in London. I finally risked tea at the Ritz, a very stilted affair where we were both so ill at ease that Leo doused the stamp sandwiches in milk. He looked so old and flustered and is in a rotten situation. He asked me if I could write for the magazine and I just evaded it with talk of holiday plans. I felt sad when I left, wishing he'd let me help him when I could.

Thursday, November 24, 1983

Went to a very uptight lunch the Kissingers threw at the Connaught for their friends here, who are wonks and diplomats and establishment oldies like Marcus Sieff, who owns Marks and Spencer. I feel Henry is in a lot of pain from Seymour Hersh's devastating book, *The Price of Power.* He looks tormented. Nancy appeared under strain, too, but was able to maintain social banter better than he. She has the habit of assuming that everyone present knows world leaders as well as they do. "So we thought we'd try a new French restaurant and François Mitterrand came up with a great suggestion. You know François?" or "The trouble with Helmut

109

Schmidt is he's so unpunctual you can't go in to dinner until he arrives." Or the best, "What I couldn't get over was not the Pope surviving the assassin's bullet but surviving an Italian hospital, but you know what the Pope's like!"

Henry kept up a steady and remorseless interrogation of the Tory MP George Walden about why Mrs. Thatcher had taken leave of her senses and denounced the US invasion of Grenada. He told a story about how he had taken on a commission to report on Latin America for Reagan. "How can a former secretary of state refuse a president's request? But I felt so bad about it that Nancy and I left a dinner party early and I came home and put a call through to Gerald Ford, a man of total common sense. But before he could come back to me, the White House came through and I said, 'Mr. President, are you sure you want me to do this? I must tell you of my grave reservation.' He said, 'I am sure.' Then as I put down the phone, Gerald Ford came on, he said, 'Henry, this is a tar baby. No way should you touch it.' I tell you I am going to get off this commission on January sixteenth and I have made it clear to the White House that I will have nothing whatever to do with implementing any of the recommendations."

The underlying truth, of course, is Sy Hersh's book. Henry is determined not to let

Sy hound him out of public life, and yet it has nearly hounded him into taking on the wrong thing. "One civil war is quite enough to be involved in in a lifetime," he added bitterly.

It must be very difficult for Nancy K, though he still has his sense of humor. "Nowadays the only thing I send in advance is paranoia," he said.

Friday, December 9, 1983
Treasure Beach Hotel, Barbados

Beach time in Barbados. I suddenly got a call from . . . Alex Liberman. He tracked me down here to invite me to have lunch with him and Si in New York on December 15. Harry urged me to go and not dither around and so I said yes right away as if it was no trouble, even though it means leaving him and the Christmas vacation to go to New York for two days and I don't have anything to wear.

Now H and I are getting some peace while it lasts. The cicadas are whirring, there is a fruit punch beside me, and I am lolling on a beach bed while Harry swims his thousand and one lengths in the pool. I have just read a bad novel by Gore Vidal, but it's hard to concentrate. I know this is a short respite before I leave Harry, get on the plane to New York, and find out if my life is going to change forever.

Thursday, December 15, 1983

Arrived in New York yesterday ready for — and steeled against — another exhausting round of finessing and compromise from Alex and Si.

The day started very early, waking up at the Algonquin Hotel feeling extremely nervous. It seemed the right place to stay for such an important literary mission. I had arranged a breakfast meeting with a lawyer, John Breglio, recommended by Harry's friend Bob Yoakum. I had hoped for an intimidating macho man, but perhaps his low-key style is better for Condé Nast. He did give me one piece of very good advice. Which was not to be fazed by ambiguity, but to be as direct as possible. And turn any questions back at them. If for instance they again ask me what I think of Leo, I should parry with, "What do YOU think of Leo?" and "What are YOUR plans for the editorship?"

Thus armed, I set off an hour early for Si's town house on East Seventieth Street, determined to beat the Christmas traffic and relax over a coffee in a nearby diner. I picked up an outfit at Bergdorf this morning — a black Chloé dress with wide shoulders and high heels, but it suddenly felt as if it reeked too much of "interview" uniform, when Si is always so casual. Instead I wore the outfit I flew out to Barbados in, an old Lady Di–like ensemble I bought in a shop in Windsor, a calf-length navy tartan skirt, long boots, and a navy sweater with a deep V in the back that now displays Barbados tan. I hoped I was looking breezily English, rather than quietly hysterical.

Thus disguised, I pressed the doorbell of a pale gray concrete facade that looked like a cross between a museum and a modern church. A security guard lurked outside. The door was opened by a black housekeeper. Inside, the overall impression I got was art gallery. Everything seemed to be in hallowed beige and the walls displayed iconic abstract art I have seen on Museum of Modern Art postcards. Some I recognized as Alex's. I was sent upstairs to the library, where I could hear voices. It was Si and Alex, already characteristically together and early. I looked first at Si, who appeared genial and refreshed. Gone was the protruding lip and furrowed brow of the hot summer day when I told him I couldn't work for Leo. No, Si was in happy chipmunk mode, with brushed hair, tanned face, and even a tie — bright blue. I hoped I was responsible for this new aura of humor and hope. That morning I had just read in *The New York Times* that Random House's book on Barbara Hutton, extracted in *VF,* had been withdrawn for being almost entirely fallacious. And it's only two months since the billion-dollar Newhouse tax case hit the paper. But he showed no sign of angst about these. I have come to realize that when you are worth as much as he is, there is no such thing as bad news, except, perhaps, losing it all.

Then I looked at Alex. I have spent so much time plumbing his mental processes that I am almost fond of him. He looked a little frailer, but courtly as always. Si got me a Coke from the bar and we sat down for small talk. My mental bravado about how self-confident I would be now evaporated and I felt both shy and stilted. Alex made the conversation work by telling me how delightful my "compatriot" Michael Roberts is. "You remember his parody of Diana Vreeland, Si? He has done something about the Queen with a look-alike. Quite frankly, I think it is a hoot!" "Don't talk to me about fakes," said Si, perched on a square stool like a happy elf. "Have you read about the Barbara Hutton stuff? What they don't say about it is that the bits that weren't wrong were plagiarized!" He laughed his little spluttery laugh. I was intrigued, as I always am by the workings of this curious Condé Nast game, that Alex and he hadn't discussed the Hutton business before. A silence fell. I asked Si if he had ever had to withdraw a book before. "Only a cookbook some years ago," he said. "In one of the recipes it forgot to say that the can of condensed milk should be opened before it was put in the saucepan and it exploded all over some poor woman's kitchen!" He laughed so helplessly that his eyes watered and he went pink and suggested we all go down to the dining room. Alex gave his small, tight smile.

In the dining room there was more art dominating all the walls. And a table exquisitely set with Mexican silver plates. Alex looked around at all the colorful abstract blobs. "How charming!" he said. "Is this Victoria's handiwork? I see Christmas everywhere!"

"Yes, the angels were Victoria's idea," said Si, although I couldn't see any angels in the whirling splashes and circles around us. The housekeeper served us with a delicious savory and another silence fell. I glanced sideways at Alex, who was looking at his plate with his thin profile to me, inscrutable. Clearly determined to let Si take the lead.

"Well, Tina," Si said at last. "I hope you don't feel *Vanity Fair*'s prospects are as hopeless as you told *Women's Wear Daily* recently?"

Shit! I forgot about that piece. "I haven't seen that," I said. "I hope —"

"It was a full page," said Alex. "A very nice piece apart from those comments."

Si laughed. "Yes, you said it had no future. Is that your opinion?"

"Is it yours?" I said, remembering John Breglio's advice.

"Well," said Si, "I can only speak from the business standpoint. At the beginning there was a great deal of interest. A great deal. Then we had problems. Then Leo came in and I think he has silenced the magazine's intellectual critics, but then these are probably not the magazine's constituency anyway. We've put in a new publisher, David O'Brasky, who was responsible for the business success of *New York* magazine, and I think he will sell more advertising. But . . ." He trailed off.

"And editorially?" I said. He deferred to Alex, who wiped his mustache with a dab and looked at me, asking me to speak. I ignored Breglio's advice this time. "I think the magazine has failed to find its identity," I said, aware of how amorphous this sounded. "I think there is good stuff in it, but it isn't breaking through. And what's more, I think at this stage its incremental improvements can't win back interest and excitement." To soften the notion that the editor and by inference Alex, too, had failed, I added, "I think it's almost irrelevant now what's IN the magazine unless the PERCEPTION of the magazine can be changed." Si was nodding through the second half of this. Alex spoke at last. "Unfortunately," he said, "*Vanity Fair* has lacked the necessary leadership from the beginning."

"Clearly," I said boldly. "I think I could make a difference to that."

There was another pause. I pushed it further and looked at Alex.

"What do you have in mind?" I said.

"You," he replied, gazing at me full-on.

Bull's-eye! They were offering me the job! I stared back at him. It had been such a long, agonized slow dance, I now felt light-headed.

"What would be helpful," said Si, suddenly leaping to the details, "is if you could spend a few months working with Leo to save his face." From this moment everything sped up. I never had the chance to say "I accept." All was now business.

"Perhaps," I said. "I could take three or four members of staff and work ahead on another floor."

"That wouldn't work," said Alex, always practical once decisions had been made. "I fear, Si, we will have to bite the bullet. Leo has created a void around himself. He won't listen to anyone." (Except Alex!) "He is so paranoid that all the people he hires are left to do nothing because he must do it all. He will be too bitter and make it impossible for Tina to be effective."

"That's a pity," said Si. "Isn't there any way?"

"I had one idea," I said. "Editor emeritus."

Si started to laugh. "I can't live with that," he said. "An editor emeritus who's only been there for seven months! What about some kind of literary editor?"

"No, Si," said Alex. "Leo will be commissioning things and making commitments Tina will be stuck with." (Amazing now that he had switched sides how pragmatic and helpful he had become.)

"Well, we have to come up with something," said Si. "We can't have Leo diving out of there exuding malice. This move will cause reverberations in worlds where the magazine wants to retain links. Could he be some kind of consultant to *Vanity Fair*?"

"Or the whole group!" said Alex on the wings of a new brain wave.

"That's good," said Si. "Leo Lerman, who we borrowed from *Vogue,* is now going back to —"

"The company as a whole!" said Alex quickly, perhaps suddenly seeing Leo stomping into *Vogue,* where he has just brought in Anna Wintour as number two in the role of creative director (from where she will likely succeed Grace as editor), and is already feeling new blood livening things up. Anna, for sure, would show Leo the door.

"Put his name under mine on the corporate masthead!" said Alex, adding with a burst of faux generosity, "Put his name OVER mine on the masthead if you wish! Why should we be petty at this point?"

"I would be very happy to consult Leo," I said. "And with his flair for houses and food I am sure *House & Garden* and *Gourmet* . . ."

Now we all felt happy. "I'll pay Leo's salary for the rest of his life and give him two trips a year to Europe," Si said.

The two of them looked at each other.

"We'll have to talk to Leo," Si said.

"Don't look at me," said Alex, laughing rustily.

"I am not looking at you," said Si. "I will do it when I get back from my vacation on January first."

Alex dabbed at his mustache again, put down his napkin, and looked at me with his mouth a tight O of sophisticated amusement.

"He wanted YOU to travel if I remember," he said to me.

"International editor?"

Si laughed again and shook his head.

"I take your word for it that Leo wouldn't have you around," he said, "but it's funny that someone you see at a social level who seems so benign should be so . . . difficult professionally."

"He made mincemeat of me in the summer," I said, starting to relax. "He saw me off."

"This frail old man," Si repeated wonderingly. I glanced at Alex and saw him flinch a bit. He is in his midseventies. Here's another reason why he now wants Leo out. Leo is giving old age a bad name around Condé Nast. To be so extravagantly unfit is an eyesore in Alex's clean-desk world. His own hospital tests are enough of an intimation of mortality without Leo hobbling around. He said, "Linda Rice, our marvelous production lady who adores Leo, even she said to me, Alex, it is not possible. He cannot see the mini layouts on the board! It takes so long to unpin everything constantly!"

Poor Leo. This was an upsetting story. I couldn't do this if he'd been nicer to me in the summer. Still, I want it done elegantly and will try to recover the friendship.

By two thirty it was all over. Si raised the issue of salary. "I feel comfortable with a hundred and thirty thousand dollars," he said, but fell agonizingly silent when I said I wanted a two-year contract.

"We don't give ANY editors contracts," he said at last. Alex sat there looking detached. The whole issue seemed to amuse them both. Perhaps for sinister, devious motives or because no one else has asked them for a contract or because they find me entertaining all around. I gracefully abandoned this with the determination to get Breglio to win the point for me. [Note: He did.] We arranged to meet for lunch on January 2. I shall begin as editor in chief on January 3. There will be no time to go back to London first. I will have to come straight from Barbados.

Si picked up a tote bag full of books. "Can I give you a lift?" he said to me.

"Should we be seen together?" said Alex, the automatic conspirator.

"I will walk," I said, and when Si left the room I embraced Alex, who suddenly seemed somewhat emotional. "Thank you," I whispered, "for understanding that I couldn't work with Leo."

"Impossible. Impossible, my dear," he said. What is the old fox planning? To use me to hire a staff, turn *VF* around, and grab the credit? Perhaps because so much of his life as an émigré has been about improvisation I am learning he operates on a daily expediency basis more than a long-term plan. It would have been smarter really to announce Leo as moving into the consultant role, then announce me, but now that he's going with the flow he just wants to see it happen.

After the lunch I felt in a daze. I tried to call Harry in Barbados from a pay phone but couldn't reach him. I have to break it to him that I won't be going with him to Duke, but I can't demur about the job again. I know he will want me to accept. I walked past the festive holiday windows to Books and Company on Madison Avenue but didn't really see the new books that were stacked up on the table.

I felt a crazy calm for the first time in many months, unwilling to let all the implications rush in: I will not be going back to London. I am moving to America. I am going to be editor in chief of *Vanity Fair.*

1984
ALL IN

I have arrived in New York from Barbados for the big announcement. Already I feel the joy of being taken over by a revving media machine. At ten a.m. Si Newhouse reached me in my room at the Algonquin to ask me to look at the draft of the press release. He had clearly written the announcement himself because it was endearingly amateurish — "So hats off to Leo for a job well done!" — with its explanation that Leo had requested a return to writing and general editing.

I'm going to miss Harry horribly. Even though it means now he'll be spending weeks at Duke without me, he's thrilled I got the job. It's as if he just snapped into *Sunday Times* editor mode and assigned me to the New York bureau. After emotional hugs he went home to rent out Ponsonby Terrace.

When I got into New York yesterday afternoon, I raced over to Saks and bought a black Ted Lapidus suit and white shirt for the press shots (alternative was a pile of sarongs from Barbados or the tartan Lady Di number. The Chloe number I bought in December was just a mistake). Plus it's freezing.

Si in an old black sweater was very warm and welcoming, at the 350 Madison office, and Alex was avuncular, too. A cool-looking photographer was waiting in his office.

"Not too much contrast," Alex told him expertly as the photographer led me away to a view from a window on the top floor where I would be pictured looking alert for duty. I was then sent off to see Pam Van Zandt, the personnel director.

I had expected "human resources," as they call the job here, to be occupied by some plump homespun figure like we had in London. But PVZ, as she is known, is a streamlined blonde with a low, confidential voice and steely blue eyes that show their whites when she discusses "termination" procedures. (They say "letting go" here when they mean "sacked.") She prepared me for the great unveiling with thrilling efficiency.

My work visa? Step this way. I walked into a room where five lawyers were sitting around a table discussing my problem. One of them fired questions at me. The other fired solutions. A third whipped out forms that I had to sign for working papers. Insurance? Tax, savings plan? Limo account? Over here! I even got a free pass to a gym. It was like

Lexington Public Library
(859) 231-5500
www.lexpublib.org

10/11/2022 04:29:24 PM

100010857XXXX

Title: Me
Item Number: 0000225879717
Due on 11/08/2022

Title: Apollo 13
Item Number: 3333000584146
Due on 10/18/2022

Title: Primary colors
Item Number: 3333000418873
Due on 10/18/2022

Title: Front of the class
Item Number: 3333000306557
Due on 10/18/2022

Title: She's so lovely
Item Number: 0000226828671
Due on 10/18/2022

You saved 82.95 using your local library.

checking into a health spa. I expected to be handed a toweling robe and led quietly toward the scales. Best of all was PVZ coming up with an apartment for me to see on East Fifty-Second Street. It is currently being used by Italian *Vogue,* who are moving out at the end of January.

Next was lunch with Alex at the Four Seasons. We talked about first steps with the magazine. I told him I wanted to get right away from *Vogue*'s look, and (since that's his handiwork) I used the reasoning that because he had so little confidence in the *VF* material thus far he's been forced to jazz it up with noisy typography, but now that the material will be strong it should have a clean, classical look.

When Si came over from another table for coffee, I heard Alex say, "The problem with the art department is they have had so little confidence in the material they've had to jazz it up too much." Si gave his industrious frown, registering perhaps his perplexity at Alex's gifts for disassociation.

Now I am back at the Algonquin, nursing the Secret. I haven't told a soul in case it leaked. I was too exhausted to go out so I ordered a baked potato from room service and was blown away by the exorbitant price. The Algonquin's literary legend is clearly a thing of the past. The famous wood-paneled Oak Room, where I once quaffed cranberry juice with S. J. Perelman and Harry on our honeymoon as a piano tinkled, was full of Japanese tourists with cameras.

Thursday, January 5, 1984

D Day. The news of my appointment clearly stunned the *VF* staff. They all knew Leo was on shaky ground but didn't expect this change so fast, or that it would be me named in the job, as I have been out of sight for six months. I have had meetings with a parade of shell-shocked editors and staff writers to get to know them properly. Some, like Wayne, I knew already from the summer, but now the dynamic is different. Elizabeth Pochoda, who was a senior ed when I was there before, has already gone, which, even though she is smart, is a relief, as she was a part of the Locke lobby and it gives me space to hire someone else. Anthony Haden-Guest told me he will be leaving in a month for *New York* mag, perhaps sensing I was someone who would demand commitment. Most welcoming faces were the art department, Ruth Ansel and her deputy, Charles Churchward; relieved, I think, not to be torn anymore between the warring Alex and Leo. One great person I am glad is here is Bob Colacello, who's very affable behind huge black-framed glasses. I could immediately see why he succeeded as editor of *Interview*. I liked every single idea he put up and understand now, too, why Alex has been considering him for *GQ*.

It feels extremely strange to walk past the secretive staff cubicles to the editor in chief's office at the end of the gangway and realize it's now mine. It still has the Richard Locke penumbra of the dark oversized furniture and — a relic of Leo's needs — its own loo, which I am not unhappy to inherit. In another Condé Nast magic-wand moment, an office designer arrived today and asked me how I wanted the space changed. I asked for a horseshoe desk, a round meeting table, a couch, and a wall of corkboards for covers.

My first issue will be April 1984, so with seven weeks to go to press there is very little time. I was crushed to discover that Dominick Dunne's account of his daughter's murder that I urged him to write last summer finally came in six weeks ago, and so is just going to press in the March issue before mine. It's every bit as brilliant as I hoped. The man is a real writer. I wish I could save it for April instead of having it appear in the last desperate issue of Leo's, which has twelve ad pages in it and a weird vampy cartoon of a flapper with a cigarette holder on the cover.

I asked Alex for an editorial budget, but he seemed vague about the matter, telling me I had to "do what I must to get it right." I immediately asked Nick Dunne to come in and talk about a contract. My goal is to hire five or six terrific magazine writers who can become definitive *Vanity Fair* voices, not keep using all the rented bylines who have gone stale elsewhere. Nick was ecstatic. Like a warm, leaping leprechaun. My first hire!

We need to whip up something fast for April, and there is no time to do anything except a piece that has attitude and voice or buy in something already written. I had a drink with Michael Roberts at the Algonquin. He's ecstatic I have arrived. Feels *VF* is desperate for some of *Tatler*'s humor after the last two months dealing, as he put it, with "all the sad-sack bluestockings," who are holdovers from the Locke regime.

We brainstormed on what we could do for the April cover. As it'll be Oscar season, we settled on "Blonde Ambition," about the current crop of striving starlets, and will get Helmut Newton to photograph them to add some visual edge. The magazine desperately needs a shot of old-style glamour after all the months featuring glowering intellectuals. Perfect subject, too, for Nick Dunne, who can riff on Hollywood glamour of the past as well as the present.

The good thing is that my summer stint gave me so many insights and I know my way around the office. Like attending summer school before the real thing. I want to get everyone out of lurking in their cubicles. I had a features meeting with four of the editors, which was very strange because no one argued. I am used to the rowdy *Tatler* staff combating everything I say. Here they took assiduous notes, which I found disconcerting. That's going to have to change.

Friday, January 6, 1984

Staff parade continues. The writer Stephen Schiff is a Locke hire I definitely want to keep. He's a curly-haired, quietly funny movie critic from *The Boston Phoenix,* where he was a finalist for the Pulitzer Prize in criticism. He said, "Sometimes I'd look around and think I would NEVER be old enough for this magazine. Leo's editorial policy seemed to be, catch them before they die." He noted shrewdly re Alex that if you had an idea that was any good, it somehow seemed to find its way not into *VF* but into *Vogue.* Schiff has done some very stylish pieces for the mag and is someone who can definitely increase his tempo. Coming from newspapers, he can write at speed. As well as longer movie essays, I am going to give him a back-of-the-book place to do a Short Schiff column with smart bites handicapping good movies. The magazine is all one stately rhythm at the moment, with no short takes and no places to graze at the back and front.

Nick Dunne is already hitting the phones

on Blonde Ambition. He's found a fabulous-sounding new actress called Daryl Hannah who's making a mermaid comedy.

Next weekend when it's all quiet I am going to get Ruth Ansel and Charles Churchward to come in and we will start redesigning the mag front to back.

Monday, January 9, 1984

Clay Felker keeps sending me candidates for jobs on the mag. He is being very supportive, if exhausting. In fact, supportive New Yorkers are now one of my biggest hazards. Every time I go out, some media big-shot comes over and stabs me in the chest with a big meaty finger and says,

"What YOU should do is hire Norman Mailer." "What YOU should do is clear out all those deadbeats under Leo Lerman." I call it the New York finger. I was invited to lunch by the literary agent Morton Janklow at the Four Seasons yesterday. He has huge headlamp eyes behind intimidating glasses and so wore me out with all the high-octane helpful suggestions and iconic bylines he represents; I wanted to lie down afterward with a compress.

Clay's latest recommendation is to hire a seasoned ed called John Walsh to be my executive editor. I am so used to effete fashionistas and literary types from *Tatler* world that I found Walsh a bit startling. He's a loud, bluff, aging flower child with a sports background, white eyelashes, and a cowboy hat. He obviously has a lot of flair and experience, but was a bit overwhelming. Kept assailing me about what my "vision" of the new *VF* might be. I felt something of a credibility problem with him. Mine. I realized how insubstantial and British I must seem to him with only *Tatler* under my belt compared to his bulging résumé. However, by the end of our exchange I had clearly passed some test because he downed his Dubonnet in a gulp (we were at the bar at the Regency) and said, "Hell, now I'm getting excited. The other jobs I have been offered are bigger but this one I could give my whole energy to." Felt a rush of success when he said that, but still need to ponder if I can handle him.

Tuesday, January 10, 1984

I have loved my first week!

The work ethic and energy here are so different from England. It holds you up with invisible hands and makes you feel buoyant when you get out of bed. I notice the difference especially when I call London to talk to writers and I hear the rain in their voices — "Hull-o," with a downward intonation. It makes my spirit sag. I called Martin [Amis] today to ask him to do a piece about a new

131

West End play and he said, "Do I have to see it?"

I like many of my inherited staff. Tracy Young is the best surprise. She has a hard, brittle wit. I have asked her to edit the new diary section at the front where her attitude can run free. In three days I've tried to allot each staff member to a specific job as most seemed to be just floating around, unsure of what they are supposed to be doing, or sitting in corners, plotting. I am mostly working off instinct of what they can do as I have no real time to find out. I've got the literary girl Friday April Bernard off her high horse by giving her the arts section redesign to do. Suzanne Stephens has learned she's not doing architecture crit anymore. (Criticism per se in a monthly never makes much sense to me. It's all out of date or striving to be forward-looking without any information.) I read today that the movie director Michael Cimino is doing a remake of *The Fountainhead,* so I diverted Suzanne into doing a feature on the Howard Roarks of today. I have Horst doing classic *VF* portraits in black and white of newcomers like Michael Graves and Richard Meier with smart copy by Suzanne. The new *VF* has to be, above all, great looking, and the photographers Condé Nast has hanging around are so extraordinary that there shouldn't be a bad page in the magazine. The pictures have got to be allowed at last to breathe without type all over them.

Wayne Lawson seems like the secret weapon to promote. He is very likable with his laconic southern belle act and deliberately colorless facade that masks a wicked sense of humor. He has been negotiating with the Hollywood literary agent Swifty Lazar for Diana Vreeland's memoirs. Swifty asked for fifty thousand dollars! Harry told me they were only worth ten thousand, and, amazingly, Swifty accepted it. It felt like a victory for the new regime.

Condé Nast has given me a temporary secretary. She's an industrious mouse with a completely round face and round glasses, like something out of *Little Women*. She is being worked so hard by me that her glasses mist up and her little cheeks are scarlet as she taps away furiously.

Wednesday, January 11, 1984

Pam Van Zandt's apartment for me didn't come through, as Italian *Vogue* stayed on, so I contacted an agent advertising rentals in the *Daily News*. I have a rush of desire to live somewhere modern. I had always imagined myself living in a New Yorker–y brownstone walk-up, but I am over old-world touches. I want to be the opposite of who I was in London. I want to live in a glass box with white sofas that looks down on the electric

133

throb of the city. I am so dying to get out of the Algonquin, with its sleepy switchboard and jostling lobby, that I picked the first apartment the agent sent me, a sublet in a black glass tower with curved corners at the Northwest corner of Second Avenue and Sixty-Sixth Street.

Harry came in from London and we met the real estate agent in the lobby of the glass tower on my lunch hour. The agent wore a porkpie hat very straight on his head and a raincoat and said his name was Hershey Schwartz. The sublet he showed us in the So-low Tower (as it's called) is somewhat preposterous. An overfurnished glitz bowl with ultrasuede pillars and fairy lights in the rubber plants. Two beds, two bathrooms. I have never seen a bedside table crammed with so many speaking alarm clocks and whirring coffee machines and Fabergé pill pots. Still, the selling point for me is the enormous health club on the top floor with a skylit swimming pool surrounded by windows, where you can gaze out on the glamour and the glitter of the spires below. And we only took it for six months.

The owner is a Blanche DuBois blonde called Mrs. de Voff. When she opened the door, she was wearing a negligee, which she kept unbuttoning to show her new silicone breasts.

"I am very proud to be renting your apartment, Mrs. de Voff," I said.

At this point Harry had to rush off to catch a plane to Durham. Once he'd gone, Hershey Schwartz demanded I give him a five-thousand-dollar up-front deposit — in cash. "Anything can happen in New York," he kept saying. "You could meet a man tomorrow who offers you a fifteen-hundred-dollar three-bed penthouse and you drop me cold." So I went to the bank on Third Avenue, came back with the cash, and counted out the notes into Schwartz's porkpie hat.

Thursday, January 12, 1984

It's snowing! Just got back from an amusing dinner at Dick and Shirley Clurman's for the *New York Times* social writer Charlotte Curtis. Dick was chief of foreign correspondents at *Time* but retired now, and Shirley works for Barbara Walters at ABC. They keep themselves aloft in the New York scene by giving wonderful dinner parties. I found Charlotte Curtis unbearable. What a bogus grandee she is, a coiffed asparagus, exuding second-rate intellectualism. She didn't ask me one question about *VF* or any damn thing. Still, I always love hearing Shirley yak on in her cigar-brown voice. She reminds me of Olive Oyl in Popeye. She and Dick have been such loyal friends to us, eternally generous with their support and their connections.

Shirley's always awash with luscious high-powered gossip, and Dick is curiously endearing the way he masks his own shyness by banging a glass at dessert and demanding everyone give up some insight or news. One point of discussion was Henry Kissinger's reaction when told by phone call, while inspecting the layout of his new house in Connecticut with Oscar de la Renta, that Seymour Hersh had leaked his entire South America report to *The New York Times.* Henry drove straight back to the city in a murderous rage.

"But you know," rasped Shirley, "if I had to choose a best friend for a desert island, between Sy and Henry I would choose Sy, even though he's a killer, because he's sexy and divine and I just love that juicy, funny little way he has."

"If Henry heard that," rumbled Dick, "he'd never speak to you again."

"I know," said Shirley. "But let's face it, how many great minds can one deal with in a busy life?"

Friday, January 13, 1984

Real estate disaster! Fucking Hershey Schwartz, the agent with the porkpie hat, has disappeared! When the rental contract didn't appear I called the office number on his card only to learn he's never worked there. He has vanished with my five thousand bucks! Feel so dumb. He cleaned us out! Feel furious, too, that Condé Nast doesn't look after overseas arrivals better. Harry went ballistic that I was so careless in not checking Hershey out. Big flaming marital row about the porkpie hat transaction just when I was already late leaving for the office.

I called the police station. After much hanging on the phone a laconic voice on the other end made it clear I was a dope to have handed over cash to someone I had never met before. Also that it's a scam that happens all the time and I should come in and fill out forms. Mrs. de Voff sounded distressed but just referred us back to the agency who said Hershey Schwartz didn't work there. I told PVZ, who was coolly sympathetic and got Condé to advance me another — much smaller — deposit. I feel abused and suddenly poor from this rip-off instead of festive and rich on my new salary. Why is everything in New York so fraught?

Saturday, January 14, 1984

I am worried about Michael Roberts, who is now officially our style director. At *Tatler* he was always in the center of things in the art department and I was in and out working with him all day. Fashion is so much part of Alex's wheelhouse that I sense Michael is under his scrutiny and so does Michael, who is like a cat with his fur bristling when Alex comes down. I sense Alex finds Michael's ideas rarefied for America. He hasn't hit his stride yet. But then he's only just arrived! I am moving him nearer to me and he's now working on some Olympic-themed fashion pages for May. My biggest worry right now is the thinness of material in-house for the makeover in April.

Sunday, January 15, 1984

Went into the office when all was quiet to work on the *VF* redesign with Ruth Ansel and Charles. It was bliss. We started front-to-back throwing out all the clutter and pretentiousness and choosing new typefaces. Created a Vanities section at the front to be a mixture of Talk of the Town–type short literary pieces and *Tatler*'s front-of-book section with its flavor of social observation. I've put a strip I call Night Table Reading in the front, where we ask interesting people to talk about books, and a Flashback page to summon up the old *VF* for nostalgia freaks. Have mixed sophisticated black ink drawings with photos and added a smart slender black rule between the items.

I am particularly proud of the Contents page. I brought it much further to the front as there's nothing more annoying than searching through ads (when we finally get some) while looking for what's in the magazine. A Contents page has to immediately establish a magazine's voice and attitude and mix, but so often it's just treated as a humdrum info list rather than the reader's first experience of the tone.

Next to the articles list I chose thumbnails of the great photos inside, with three striking small images to run down the side. These three picture choices also show off at a glance the mix of lightness, substance, and surprise that defines (or will) the overall magazine. I had Miles, who's in from London so I can introduce him to PVZ and hire him, run up dummy pages to get the feel right. It enabled Ruth to design with real copy to see if it really worked in the space. The copy describing each story will be written run-on style with boldface breakout words that allow Miles to do fun, allusive things with the phrasing; e.g., for a snippet about screenwriter hell in Hollywood, "Muse, get me **rewrite**." Finally, we slapped a big, bold **APRIL** over the top of the page.

After Contents and the Vanities section, the feature pages now follow in a racy, unbroken run with strong, clean type and crisp, uncluttered use of the pictures. Looks so much braver. We had joyous fun, only stopping to gorge on pizza.

With the office quiet on Sunday I could ransack the art department drawers. I had come to suspect they might be filled with treasures I haven't been shown. And lo, what did I find? An astonishing portfolio of pictures of the new American comedians by Annie Leibovitz, who has a *VF* contract I now learn. It has, apparently, been sitting around for months. Peewee Herman with a pair of underpants on his head! Eric Bogosian distorted longwise in a fun house mirror! Gilbert Gottfried hanging with head invisible under a lampshade in a Hollywood hotel room. They are absolutely glorious and I will rush them into the April issue with the perfect headline of "April Fools"! (It was gratifying to see Miles's Cheshire cat smile at this.) For wonderful counterpoint I also found a moody Deborah Turbeville portfolio of crumbling Roman villas in Capri I can run with a piece that Bruce Chatwin has offered on Capri's literary exiles, Axel Munthe and Curzio Malaparte. These two features feel immediately right for the mix I want to waste no time in showing — edgy modernity and pop culture from Annie combined with dreamy literary excellence from Bruce. The missing component is news, but we will get there.

Now I am back home in my new whirring, blinking apartment. I went up to the roof tonight just to gaze at the electric power of Manhattan's skyline. My new home.

I am in bed with a cup of tea, slogging

through a pile of manuscripts. Harry has gone to Duke. He called to say his first lecture was SRO, and he sounded happy. I miss him, but also feel content.

Tuesday, January 17, 1984

Wow! Tonight was the launch of *Good Times, Bad Times* in New York and the wonderful Clurmans threw Harry a book party at Mortimer's restaurant on the Upper East Side. It was so high powered the energy threatened to lift the lid off the restaurant. Shirley had ordered huge white balloons with "Good Times, Bad Times" printed on them and at the end of the party we released them over Manhattan and watched them float away into the freezing night.

There was an incredible media turnout — from *The New York Times* especially. The editor, Abe Rosenthal, was much grittier than I expected, but seemed to have huge respect for Harry. So did the chairman, Punch Sulzberger, who was more grave and reserved. Si turned up in bashful chipmunk mode, accompanied by a young chipmunk clone who is apparently a cousin who edits one of Donald Newhouse's newspapers. Alex came early and was a little aloof because this is not his crowd. I was astonished at the outsize panache of Pat Buckley, a close friend of

141

Shirley's, a great American goddess with big white shoulders, voluminous blonde hair, and dancing diamond earrings. Bill Buckley did a pale, sexy, contact-lens stare at me. What a fascinating, magnetic phenomenon they are. Shirley Clurman was in overdrive, hurling us at every new face. "This is Norman Podhoretz. The bravest man in the United States. This is Mr. Blustein, whose first name I always forget. Harry, he may be hustling you, on the other hand, he could have money. Tina, dear, you should meet Iris Love . . . Irene Selznick . . . Marietta Tree. Harry, be nice to Aileen Mehle, who will write about this party in her Suzy column. Morley Safer. Harry, this is definitely A-list. Punch Sulzberger never goes to book parties." And on and on. In all the ego fest I didn't find a cozy mooring except with Marie Brenner, now separated from Jonathan Schwartz with a new doctor boyfriend.

Wednesday, January 18, 1984

Today Alex came down and startled me by saying, "Tina. Please don't be offended. But I hear from Si that you dined in the Four Seasons last night."

"No," I said, mystified.

"He says you were sitting upstairs," he said.

"Ah, lunch!" I beamed. "Yes, I was lunching there with Grace Mirabella."

"And you were upstairs."

"Yes." Pause.

"My dear, you were in Siberia," he said. I stared at him.

He chuckled. "Very much the wrong table. Si was very concerned. He called me first thing this morning. He told me it's very bad for your image and the magazine's for you to be seated there. We must find you a social secretary to look after you."

Thursday, January 19, 1984

The snow continues. I am now trying to put the revamped April magazine together in earnest. It comes out the middle of March and there is not much time before we have to go to press. Alex rattled me by coming down and redoing some layouts when I was at lunch, and that's something I cannot let him do. It was a feature on the great French photographer Jacques Henri Lartigue by Joan Buck. I was in heaven when I found the pictures in the ever-yielding art department drawer last week. I have always adored Lartigue since Harry framed one of his smaller pictures for me as a Valentine's present (the one of a strolling patrician man in a rakish flat cap arrested midstride on the Normandy sands as he ponders two women in long white dresses; I call it Proust on the beach).

I didn't even know Lartigue was still alive

143

(and living in Paris, about to be ninety), but *VF* has these ravishing unseen pictures of the women he has loved, chosen especially for us. The layouts Alex did were actually great but there isn't the room in the issue to run at this length. So when I came back I cut it down again, and also threw out his overblown type treatment, which I cannot have any more of and was ruining the simplicity of the spreads. I was determined to make a fight of it, aware that right away, early on, I had to send the message loud and clear about who is now editing this magazine.

Alex returned at four o'clock and stood with his hands behind his back, staring down at the layout table. I joined him there. He bristled and looked at me. "I see you have eliminated the best pictures," he said. There was a gathering silence in the art department. Ruth and Charles said nothing. They had experienced this scene before. I summoned my resolve. "Adding another three spreads of Lartigue is a waste of space," I said. "I have so much great stuff to get in this issue."

"But where's the glory?" he replied with sudden impatience. "My dear, a magazine must know how to waste space. You have no glory in this issue." He turned to walk away, then pivoted and surprised us all. "Well," he said with his most opaque black stare, "perhaps you are right. Perhaps these sacred monsters have had their day." Watched by the still-silent art department, he walked stiffly out.

There was much celebration in the office at this power victory. But oddly, I didn't feel happy myself. I talked to Harry on the phone. He questioned my instant rejection of the idea. "Lartigue is a photographic scoop. Perhaps it makes more of a statement to run them long. Maybe two extra spreads. Think about it."

Back home, I made myself a grilled sandwich and took it up to the roof. That view of Manhattan's lights always fills me with such awe and aspiration; it helps me think. I love Lartigue. Why am I fighting it? The pictures he sent us may be some of the last he chooses, and they are about love. Perhaps Alex is right. Where is the glory in the magazine? I remembered something else he said to me a few days ago when he came and sat in my office for no apparent reason. It was almost plaintive. "I feel I am not being used enough." Was he asking me to let him bring me his skill, not for power reasons but for real creative contribution? He is so stunningly talented, and yet his gifts are also shapeless. They need to come up against a point of view that disciplines them. He realizes this, I think, especially after the first year of *VF* when he dominated and failed. And then I also thought about his comment about how a magazine must know how to "waste space." I am still living in *Tatler* world, where every page was a budget issue and the pace was more comic-book kinetic. I understood suddenly what he meant. There also needs to be languor sometimes in a glossy magazine, visual theater, the sweep of a great photograph not as illustration but to be savored for its own luxurious sake. He was right. I will give Lartigue another six pages. I can't wait to tell him tomorrow that I have reversed myself.

Friday, January 20, 1984

Still snowing. I waited for Alex to come down for our eleven a.m. meeting, impatient now to tell him about Lartigue. But he didn't appear. Finally at two I called his office and they told me he is snowed in in Connecticut. I felt very upset. I suddenly really missed him, I realized, and wanted terribly to share this lightbulb moment. At five p.m. I finally called him at his home and told him he was right about Lartigue. There was a silence. Then the rusty laugh. "Well, my dear. It is your magazine and you must make the decision."

"I have," I replied. I felt suddenly tearful. A rite of passage had been navigated between us and I needed to let him know. "I love working with you, Alex," I said. Another pause.

"Me too, my dear," he replied. "Me too."

Monday, January 23, 1984

This afternoon I met with James Wolcott, who's on the *VF* writing staff. I was prepared to dislike him since he gave *Good Times, Bad Times* a perfunctory and negative review. He is pale and raffish with small suspicious eyes and exudes vague, downtown hostility. But after a brief and inconclusive interview in which we cautiously circled each other, I read his parody of Renata Adler's new book and it is utterly brilliant and hilarious. It reminds me of Jonathan Meades at *Tatler;* it's so anarchic and intelligent. He's clearly capable of something really good. I shall continue his contract and give him a column so he can show off at length. He's too talented to lose, even if I can't win him round.

Saturday, January 28, 1984

So happy it's Saturday. My first quiet day to savor time alone. Harry stayed at Duke this weekend. I am going through piles of *VF* submissions that have been sitting around for months and I feel like Mrs. Thatcher "doing her boxes." I've always loved the routine aspects of editing, the poised pencil, the swift identification of the lines that have to go, the insert that will make it sing, the rewarding moment when you see that the whole thing should start on page nine and flip the penultimate paragraph to the top of the piece, and all you want to do is call the writer immediately and tell him or her why. The trouble is that as a writer myself I feel obsessed with getting back to people quickly, as I know only too well that after submitting a piece to the editor you sit there waiting for response with curdling hopes. You can tolerate the first day's wait, even half the second, but by the end of day two there's a pain in your stomach and by three and four deep misery and rage are setting in. Writers can handle fast rejection. But they cannot stand the slow no. Whenever I receive copy I feel there's a time bomb in my bag.

The last two days were draining. Anthony Haden-Guest is half out the door to *New York* magazine to work for Ed Kosner, and I never know if he's feeding them our ideas. We had a heated exchange when I thanked him for a recommendation and he told me that the Kosners were angry he gave it to me; i.e., he's discussing what he's doing for us with *New York* mag. "It's all right," he said, in his strange glaucous way. "They know I am still working for you."

"So does Si Newhouse know," I shrieked. "*VF* is paying your salary!" An unfortunate and crass explosion on my part that I regretted. He stormed out, flushed, and I leaned against the wall in my office with a palpitating heart. I just made an enemy for nothing, but I am tired of people who aren't all in. There is so much whispering in the corridors from the old Locke gang and everyone in the media seems to want us to fail. I am getting jumpy and overwrought.

Monday, January 30, 1984

Like so many people in New York publishing, the president of Condé Nast is an outsize figure. He oversees all the publishers and ad sales of Condé titles. Whereas Bernie Leser in London was a tycoon wannabe, Bob Lapham is a big, fat operator on a much more impressive scale, a three-hundred-pound pelican full of salty Madison Avenue asides and loquacious insights into the working and financing of the company. We had lunch in a stuffy French restaurant in midtown, Le Périgord, with much flowery Gallic paraphernalia. But as soon as Lapham got into his favorite subject — the previous year's catastrophe at *Vanity Fair* — we both thawed out and I started to find him hilarious.

"Locke said he wanted approval of *Vanity Fair*'s publisher," Lapham said, swirling his vodka in a wineglass. "So every candidate I had, I had to run past Locke. So I bring in candidates and soon we've gone through Henry, through George, through Jim, until finally I say to Si, 'I've run out of candidates. Locke doesn't like any of them.' So Si says, 'Wait, there was that tall guy.' I say, 'Corr?' He says, 'Yeah, Corr.' Now, Joseph Corr was a guy who was rather well read. He knew quite a lot about litter-ature. He just knew nothing about selling advertising! I say, 'Okay, you have Corr.' And that's how we got this goon. Sure, he was an attractive person. He'd been in the US Army. He used to call the sales force 'my troops.' And one thing's for sure. It was Gallipoli every day in there. Whoever heard of an editor with powers to veto the publisher? One guy I hired to be publisher, Locke changed his mind about before his first day, and I had to fire him before he started."

Why, I asked him, had Locke exerted such powers over Si?

"They talked books together," Lapham said. "The two guys" — he nearly said "little guys" — "used to sit in swivel chairs talking about litter-ature."

Tuesday, January 31, 1984

Had such a fun evening. I got the art department and Assistant Editor April Bernard to stay late and we did a workshop on the new arts pages at the back of the book, designing the spreads first and tailoring the copy to fit, working like a chain gang, cutting, snipping, and pasting. Ruth is disheveled and cosmopolitan and old-world hip, with big shawls and an air of past Italian lovers. Charlie has a slightly crooked chin and short crinkly hair like a 1930s muscle man. He is still in post-traumatic shock over some of Alex's and Leo's illustration cover choices before I got there. "Here's this drawing that looks like an abstract rip-off of the Jolly Green Giant that Alex likes. Here's this Avedon portrait that's going to sell on the newsstands. We're going to mock up both, of course, close our eyes, and choose the wrong one for March. Okay? That's what it used to be like."

One regular feature I am introducing adds culture to the middle as well as the back of the book — a spread that shows a painting chosen by a writer who deconstructs it for the reader. It's great to toss in a classical image in a run of contemporary pages. For the first issue I've got Anthony Burgess writing about Thomas Gainsborough's *Mr. and Mrs. Andrews,* gloating prettily over their domain, which is a glorious pace changer in a fast mix. Another addition is to break up long-running text spreads with dropped-in single images and a leg of snappy copy, we're titling Spotlight. The great usefulness of a Spotlight is we can change up the mood of a fatiguing reader with a picture that offers a quick flash of something else. If it's a long, gray business story, we can stick in an image of drop-dead glamour by Helmut Newton. A big, high-minded art piece with paintings can be pace-changed with a strong black-and-white portrait of some hard-charging business head. And so on.

There was a great spirit when we finally disbanded, leaving scissors and paste and cut-up magazines all over the art table.

It seems to me that half the ill will created against the magazine has been from the overpaid "consulting editors" recruited by either Locke or Leo to be on the alert for good material but who hang around the office, then trash it when they go out to dinner. Jonathan Lieberson is one of these. Very brilliant and sophisticated (he's the son of the legendary music mogul Goddard Lieberson, whose name means nothing to me but apparently should). He is beloved by the editor of *The New York Review of Books,* Bob Silvers, but full of condescension about our chances of success. He has a lupine beard, slightly crossed eyes, and a pretentious drawly voice. He immediately started telling me I wouldn't be allowed to edit the magazine because of Alex and he would like to play the role of "in-house critic," reading all the copy that comes in and giving me his "considered opinion." That sounds like being the editor to me but without any responsibility and taking a not insignificant check to go with it. So I thanked him profusely and said I couldn't wait to start while having no intention of letting him.

I went for a drink at the Algonquin with Wallace Shawn, the editor of *The New Yorker*'s son, who I have been told wants to write. I loved his creaky voice and twinkly, creased-up eyes. He's like a small, anxious hippo, so full of quotable insights. "America has no memory," he explained. "Nothing LEADS to anything in New York."

Wednesday, February 1, 1984

Mag progressing to my first deadline. I'm on the way back to NYC on the train from DC after going to Sally Quinn and Ben Bradlee's Welcome to America party for me and Harry. Their new house in Georgetown is truly heaven. It is huge and gracious but not excessive, and Sally has done it up with relaxed good taste. Comfortable creamy sofas, salmony walls, a study painted to look like wood. It's like being in Somerset in the heart of Washington. I felt my spirit ache for a settled home like we had in London, and so did Harry.

The guests were a great many forceful and effusive DC power women, and chiseled anchor people from Sunday morning TV shows I don't yet watch. I liked meeting Ted Kennedy, who looked gaunt and lean after a season drying out, and also a very droll, intelligent Ivy League guy, Michael Kinsley, who swears he was at Oxford with me (must ask Sally) and who got kicked out of *Harper's*. Mort Zuckerman, the fast-talking Boston real estate tycoon and owner of *The Atlantic* mag, who was always trying to hire Harry to edit it when we were in London, came with his new girlfriend, Amanda Burden. She's a charming sparrow-faced blonde who clearly longs to be looked after, which assuredly Mort will never do. The nicest part was afterward, when we went out with Ben and Sally to a local steakhouse for supper. I love Ben. There is truly something big and beautiful about his spirit wrapped up in the macho persona. He gave me a torrent of great ideas about *VF*. I was stunned to find he is related to Frank Crowninshield (he is Benjamin Crowninshield Bradlee!) and knew him when he was thirteen. "It was impossible to overestimate the man," he said. "He had taste, he had discernment. He was never afraid of hiring the best people."

Thursday, February 2, 1984

Back in NYC and shattered to find that Clay Felker's new weekly newspaper the *East Side Express* has folded! It was a wonderful, snappy, vibrant thing, and his backer — some guy who manufactures pet food (Leonard Stern of Hartz) abruptly pulled the rug out from under him yesterday lunchtime. Today the bailiffs were in and everyone got fired. I phoned the three brightest and offered them jobs. The awfulness of this event brought back the memories of Murdoch and *The Times*. I think of the pale emptiness of Clay's eyes in the summer over dinner, and I think of the pleasant hopeful warmth in him when we lunched at the Algonquin over a month ago, talking about his frisky new paper. This latest failure is his spiritual death.

John Heilpern said he went to the office and Clay had shut himself in his room to hide from the TV cameras. Gail Sheehy showed up begging him to fight on, just as I had done with Harry versus Murdoch, and perhaps as wives and girlfriends always do. Clay, John said, was slumped, expressionless, unable to speak. He didn't return my call. It's so awful because the paper was full of vitality and risk and great ideas. Clay could make a shopping list compelling.

Newspapers and magazines take time. It's hopeless to go into business with amateurs instead of people who understand publishing. Clay keeps putting his trust in soulless rich people who throw him under the bus, but bona fide publishing companies find him too threatening to hire. It's very difficult to lose your power perch midlife. You rack up enemies and baggage, and threaten the mediocrities mostly running the media companies who could give you what you want. So you are left with a mercurial money man like Mr. Pet Food, who probably thinks it will bring him power and social cachet but isn't willing to pay for it . . . I am so glad Harry has never done that. He's lucky to have his writing and teaching. He's very happy at Duke, which Clay would never be. What can Clay do now? New York is so pitiless, it has kissed him off: "Clay's toast." "He bombed." I remembered Wallace Shawn. "America has no memory. Nothing LEADS to anything in New York." *VF* has a miserable twenty ad pages for April! Will I also soon be toast?

Michael called from LA. He and Helmut and Nick Dunne are on the Blonde Ambition shoots. He said it's pissing with rain and the first blonde didn't go well. Michelle Pfeiffer turned up at the restaurant with brown hair! We had all assumed she looked like she does in *Scarface*.

Friday, February 10, 1984

Two weeks to press day. Thanks to Marie Brenner I have a fantastic new PA, Sarah Lewis, stolen from Ed Kosner. She is subtle, gamine in appearance, with a quiet intelligence and organizing skills that are making an impact already. She will help smooth troubled waters, too, with office relationships. I have one problematic relic of the ancient regime, Linda Rice, the production editor who still sees Alex as her real boss and has been complaining to him about our deadline crunches. I went ballistic and said if she had a problem she should bring it to me. This created frost between me and Alex, with whom I now have such a collaborative amity. "I find we have a Richard Locke situation developing," he told me in a chilly phone call, "where I am not allowed to speak to your staff." I soothed him down but the day was soured and it made me unhappy. I feel terribly lacking a managing number two who can pull all the thousand details of the new sections and staff problems together for me. I was so ratty all day, disaffected groups started to gather in corners.

Harry urged me to go see Pam Van Zandt, as political situations can escalate and turn nasty. Thank God I did. I discovered that both Alex and Linda had also requested appointments with her. I love going to see PVZ. If I was a corporate manager I would model myself on her — the cool eyes, pale hair, soft dresses, and attentive calm behind her clean desk. I told her about Linda and she immediately agreed that I should now get my own editorial production and management executive and she had thoughts already of whom we could attract. Then she asked how it was going generally. "The great treat," I said, knowing she was seeing him later and also because it was true, "is the joy of working with Alex. I am learning so much. I find him extraordinary." She looked astonished, as she is so used to the tension between editors and Alex. Then she flipped open her talent binder and we focused on whom we could hire.

Later, when Alex came down to see me after his meeting with her, he was back to his old warmth. "I love your sensibility, my dear," he said. "The magazine is going to be a triumph and it is all you." Now, thank God, Linda is back in her box, and she told PVZ she is "crazy about me" and that I resemble Vreeland in the sixties, but I am not going to be persuaded. I told PVZ I am nonnegotiable about wanting her removal. There will be other speed bumps and Linda has proven that she will run to Alex when there are problems.

The mock-up of the new front-of-book section, Vanities, is looking great. In fact Alex is right, now that I see pages pasted in the dummy, the mag is starting to be transformed. Helmut Newton's pictures of the Hollywood blondes are so strong and sexy. I am splashing the mermaid starlet Daryl Hannah on the cover, wearing a black blindfold, with the arch cover line Blonde Ambition. She's holding an Oscar statuette in each hand like a glitzy version of blind justice, which adds another level of double entendre as the fate of the mag weighs in the balance. Nick

Dunne's piece is delicious candy. He brings Chandlerish texture by throwing movie backlight on the actresses. "There is a mythology of the great blonde movie stars, and I happen to enjoy it. I thrill to the lore that Louis B. Mayer, the most powerful man in Hollywood, destroyed the suicide note of Paul Bern to protect MGM's investment in Jean Harlow. I still want to believe that Lana Turner was discovered at the soda fountain of Schwab's drug store on the Sunset Strip." Then we have Annie's fantastic pictures of Keith Richards and Patti Hansen with Philip Norman's juicy book extract about Keith, and the glorious Lartigue portfolio. It lacks hard reporting, but no time to achieve it for the first issue.

Friday morning was the big day when I had my first "print order meeting" with all the Condé Nast brass. It takes place upstairs on the management floor, and the circulation director assesses the sales potential of the impending issue. I stood at a lectern in the top-floor conference room as all the suits filed in. I was full of excitement until I saw that Leo was one of them. He glowered at me all the way through and threw me off completely, so I didn't present well. Si, who I haven't seen in a month, sat there in his sweatshirt looking, as always, deceptively sleepy. But at the end of the meeting Peter Armour, the circulation director, at the end of the table announced like an auctioneer, "My recommendation is to increase the newsstand order of the April 1984 issue by twenty-five thousand." They all filed out. Si stayed and sat next to me. He flicked through the April dummy hesitantly, pausing at certain spreads. "It's full of life," is all he would say. Who knows what the public reaction will be?

Sunday, February 12, 1984

Deadline upon us. Friday evening we put the last-minute headlines and blurbs on before the April issue closes. Tracy and I sat in my office and banged out the blurbs on the Vanities section. Tracy wrote the blurb on the opening page — "Stepping out, stepping up, stepping on toes, *Vanity Fair* laughs up its sleeve."

"How about laughs up its *ravell'd* sleeve?" I said, and we fell about laughing at this arf-arf *Macbeth* allusion ("Sleep that knits up the ravell'd sleeve of care") and rushed to read it out to the group of editors celebrating Wayne's birthday in his cubicle. When I said "ravell'd," Wayne fell about laughing, too. But we are probably all just literary snobs who've drunk the Kool-Aid of our inside jokes. Charles Churchward, whose instincts I always trust, said he didn't know what the fuck ravell'd meant and nor would anyone else.

I took the mock-up of the Helmut Newton

cover pic of Hannah in the black blindfold pasted onto a dummy copy of a magazine down to the newsstand in the lobby and stuck it next to the garish lineup of its competitors. People rushing out of the building at five kept staring at me hovering around the rack and pacing back and forth. Hmmn. Am I right to use the pic that covers her eyes? It goes against all newsstand rules of needing eye contact with the reader. On the other hand, its racy S and M flair announces a risqué new day for *Vanity Fair*. After five minutes of obsessing at the rack, I decide to go with it.

Now am in the nerve-racking limbo between going to press and coming out mid-March and already into the crash of the May issue without knowing how the revamp will be received and being able to adjust mistakes. I am decided on hiring John Walsh as my features ed. David Halberstam and Jonathan Schwartz warned me off him, but Bradlee, Bill Broyles, and Felker all raved, and those are good recommenders. Plus, just when I was dithering, he wrote me a really smart memo. My stock shot up in the office when he came in, maybe because his snow-white beard and white eyelashes made them briefly think I'd hired Ernest Hemingway. He started bombarding me with ideas as soon as the contract was papered, his suggestions punctured by wild baboon-like giggles that betray a promising strand of irresponsibility. "I'm on the case," is his catchphrase. One of the cases he's on, however, is Tracy Young's, who he keeps insisting everyone tells him is bad news. "I hear she's a badmouth and her Rolodex doesn't go above Thirteenth Street," he told me late at night on the phone.

Tuesday, February 14, 1984

We all wait nervously for reaction. For distraction, I felt like dressing up. With nothing more I could do to the April issue as it prints, I put on a long black velvet Bruce Old-field dress and pearl choker and went off to the New Yorkers for New York gala at the Waldorf. I was seated next to the famous magazine writer Gay Talese, who has a weary, worldly face.

"Find me a better magazine writer in this new generation than I am. That's all!" he barked. He launched into an encomium about Harold Hayes, the legendary *Esquire* ed who is still around, he says. "I'd write for you if you had Hayes," he said. "We all would."

Steve Brill, the ed of the monthly mag *American Lawyer,* which I adore for its clean, wide format and investigative muscle, and Clay Felker were at the next table. Clay and Gail have invited us to dinner, just the four of us at his apartment on Monday. But now

Clay said, "My cook's gone to Argentina so we have to go out, and Kay Graham is joining us." Clearly he's dreaming of Kay's money already, but she will string him along and not give him a cent. Gay said to me, "I think you'll make it at *Vanity Fair.* You step into two fuckups before you, with no past. Whatever mistakes and prejudices you've accumulated in England, you're a fresh face here. You'll do it." Handicapping my success or failure, it seems, is an irritating New York game.

Sunday, February 19, 1984

Monday is President's Day and Harry is in Chicago. I took myself off to the Don CeSar hotel in St. Petersburg, Florida. I first sighted its pretentious pink porticos rising out of the best beach in Florida on a boat trip with Harry once and have dreamed of it ever since. It's got everything I currently want: a limitless white beach to walk on, total anonymity, a hot whirlpool massage, and a great big warm swimming pool. I had such a pulverizing last three days in the city before I left that I wondered, hurling my white pants and swimsuit into a bag, whether I could bear the journey. My other bag contained the manuscript of Norman Mailer's new book that just arrived for possible serial, *Tough Guys Don't Dance,* and a box file full of

163

submitted pieces. I got into St. Pete at one a.m. yesterday and saw how worthwhile the effort was immediately. I have been rattled by office politics. It seems that John Walsh is right and Tracy is getting into a disaffected corner with the production ed, Linda Rice, creating vibes I don't like.

I lay in the sun all day and fell into a doze replete with warmth and Caesar salad. I read an odd, brilliant manuscript by a writer Alex knows, Gregor von Rezzori, who wrote *Memoirs of an Anti-Semite*. He has a haunting voice and I definitely want him in the mag. His lofty, émigré style is reminiscent of Nabokov. I am going to ask him to reproduce Humbert Humbert's drive across America for us for a summer issue.

Monday, March 5, 1984

Got back from Florida refreshed and fired Linda Rice. Gotta clean house. A few days away made me determined to remove negative elements from the office. I made sure I had Si's support for it first. I asked to go up to see him. He looked nervous when I walked in, as he always is when he is not sure what it's about. I said, "Si, is there some kind of corporate problem about uh, letting go Linda Rice?"

"Problem?" he said.

"Yes," I said. "There seems to be a miasma

of embarrassment hanging over the subject of her employment."

"If you need to fire Linda, fire Linda," Si said, looking amused. (Hang on, I thought we said "letting go" around here.) "Do you have a problem with firing people, Tina? I wouldn't have thought you did."

"No," I replied. "And I feel I should start firing a few who are making problems."

"All at once or one by one?" I felt he was teasing me now.

"I will let you know," I said.

I immediately went downstairs and kissed good-bye to Locke's golden girl Moira Hodgson. She writes well but her resentful politesse has been getting on my nerves.

Tuesday, March 6, 1984

Michael Roberts is suddenly on his former fashion star form. We agreed we should start his fashion pages with a bang, and he has delivered brilliant Olympic Games–themed pictures for May. I love seeing him in the art department pondering the spreads with his cigarette aloft, like an elegant camel. He has stealthily begun to glitz up the dowdy atmosphere in the office with his multicolored dress rails hung with designer "frocks," bangles, stiletto shoes, and the inevitable signature wrappers of half-eaten chocolate bars. Yesterday morning a jabbering Greek

165

lady burst into the art department, pointing at Michael. It turned out she was the overnight cleaner whom Michael, by mistake, had locked in the fashion closet all night.

My new friend and hopefully contributor to *VF* is the marvelously funny and intellectually exuberant Australian art critic from *Time,* Robert Hughes. He did the famous BBC TV show *The Shock of the New* and has a robust iconoclasm that's been missing from my life since London. We had a riotous lunch in the Four Seasons with Bob getting drunker and drunker. He said New York for him would never be by the sea. "Who was the architect who built that great French letter of concrete around it all?" he roared, and relished my descriptions of Locke-land that had preceded me. "Only the Brits can think the right level of malignant thoughts a magazine requires, and provide an antidote to all the upbeat American gush." At the end of our lunch Alex and Si came over from their table, Alex, at his most foxy, to see Bob as he is so important to his artist world. Si asked Bob what he thought of the new Jasper Johns show. Bob promptly poured rivers of eloquent scorn on Johns, not caring, it seemed, that Si has spent a great part of his fortune on buying his paintings. When Alex drew Bob aside, Si turned to me and said, "Do you know an English author called Kenneth Rice? He's just written a book about George V." (He meant Kenneth Rose.) "It's really very good."

"Why is it good?" I asked. Si looked startled by my question.

"Well . . . George V was really a very dull man, but this book makes him seem interesting."

Wednesday, March 7, 1984

Still waiting for the April issue. America is so enormous it takes a week for the trucks to rumble across the country distributing it. At night I sometimes think of them speeding along ribbons of open highway with all our energy and hopes on the back. I had a great evening with Annie Leibovitz, who came over with Ruth. She told me some of the stories of the wild days at *Rolling Stone*. It turns out Annie has an apartment in the same building as me, though hers is on the thirty-ninth floor so she has the glorious astronaut's view, and of course it isn't stuffed with all the paraphernalia of Mrs. de Voff's humming electronic brothel that I currently live in. The other night Harry opened a closet door in the bathroom and a cascade of porn magazines rained down.

Annie is such an Amazon. Tall, funny with a big brash laugh, but also so highly strung that her nerve endings are at the tips of her fingers. She's off drugs now and said, "I love living here and being alone. I'm learning to

167

live with myself." She told me she leaves the windows open so the wind rushes in and freezes her all night. When she talks about her work, she is so intense, her eyes go serious and driven behind her oversized aviator glasses. She wants to do her best work ever for *VF* and she will. I recognize her demons and salute them. We are going to have a wonderful time.

Sunday, March 11, 1984
Apt. 2A, 120 Central Park South

I have moved! The de Voff apartment got too much to bear. I began to feel I would open the fridge door and find frilly lingerie and cuckoo clocks. Condé Nast found me this pristine two-bedroom rental, and I am so happy to escape. You can see the horses and carriages through the big picture window overlooking the park. The parquet floor is made to dance on. It is clean and stark and yet cozy. I am blissfully happy to be here and can't wait to show Harry when he's next in from Duke.

Mum and Dad arrived to stay with me. Mum found NYC absolutely thrilling and understood for the first time why I must be here, in the center of the world. Dad seems preposterously British in New York but wonderfully solid to lean on. Apparently some man outside Bloomie's accosted him with "Wally! I haven't seen you since we both worked at the deli!" On seeing Dad's furious colonial mustache bristling at him, he backed off. While I was at work they kitted out the new apartment for me, trailing around department stores and returning with giant parcels of sheets and towels and cutlery. Mum said that when they adjourned with the parcels to a diner for lunch, Dad ordered broiled flounder and a cup of tea. It was so lovely to sit up with her while Dad was asleep, cackling over stories from Spain like the old days.

Had a terrific drink tonight with Tom Wolfe, who is tall and thin like a candle in his white suit, with a dryness suddenly illuminated by joyous shafts of pure malice. Was hoping to have the mag to show him but still no copy. I told him I was having dinner with Martin Amis. "Ah, the rising novelist of thirty-four? Funny how you are a hardened thief at thirty but a rising novelist at thirty-four." Outside it was pouring rain and we lingered over our drink at Le Périgord. He told me he is finishing his new novel about New York and the "masters of the universe" of Wall Street. "Isn't it going to run over twelve months in *Rolling Stone*?" I asked. "That's the reigning myth," he said. [*The Bonfire of the Vanities* did run there.] He liked the idea I have of a column for *VF* called Reputations.

"I could write about a living author posthumously," he said, with sparkling eyes. "Bernard Malamud, for instance." I enjoyed myself so much I was twenty minutes late for Martin, whom I'd arranged to meet at the mafioso-style bar in the theater district, Barbetta. When I got there, Martin had gone, piqued to be kept waiting. But I finally got hold of him at his hotel and we had dinner. I hadn't had a conversation with him for two and a half years. He has become graver and more ironically severe than ever. Remembering the old rules of London about "not trying too hard," I tried at first to modify my liberated Manhattan directness, then thought fuck it, why should I? Still, after a glass of wine, Martin is as funny as ever. He said he ultimately hates New York because of the "unembarrassable" ads and the fact that "you're not allowed to think anyone's odd." We dissolved into competing impersonations of Al Pacino in *Scarface*. "FOCK YOU. Don't FOCK with me. Are you a man with BOLS, huh? See my BOLS? Don't FOCK with me!" Many puzzled looks around us as we repeated this over and over again with screams of laughter that were like old times.

Monday, March 12, 1984

The early copy of my April issue arrived! I see only the flaws but it's pretty great. Fresh, racy, a lot of literary spark. Needs some "bottom," as my father would say, but it's a vast improvement, especially in design. The front-of-book section is sprightly but a bit brittle in tone. The pagination leap from Keith Richards to the Gainsborough painting is great pacing. Love the Daryl Hannah cover. Fret over the lack of news grit but must be patient. It's very, very different from its portentous predecessor and I hope is not rejected. Its major success is the successful uniformity of tone.

Miles has arrived for good! PVZ has installed him at a hotel on Madison and Fifty-Second while he looks for an apartment. He said it's full of overweight Irish girls wearing T shirts saying IRA FREEDOM FIGHTER but that must be because of St. Patrick's Day coming up. His arrival was good timing. Tonight I invited the whole staff around to the apartment for a housewarming drink and a toast to the issue. It was wonderful for morale, especially as Si came, too, which made everyone feel he believed in *VF*. I had framed some Japanese rock-and-roll illustrations we are running in the mag and hung them that morning, and they had pride of place on the sitting room wall in the otherwise pictureless apartment. I felt so happy. The brand-new clean-of-clutter apartment, the snow in Central Park, the feeling of affectionate bonds between the finally gelling staff, the issue out but not yet seen and critiqued. I asked the contributing eds, too — Wolcott, whom I now like enormously, and Schiff, who is still the biggest kindred spirit. We have promoted Wayne to executive ed so I can bring in Pamela McCarthy from *Esquire* to be the managing editor. As soon as she walked in for the interview I knew this was who I wanted. She's a Taurus to her toes. Calm, smooth, organized, experienced. A sense of humor. Exudes good judgment. Felker recommended her and I am beyond grateful. The perfect foil to my own Scorpio volatility. I felt my stomach unclench when I realized how much she will help my whirling dervishness and get control of all the moving parts.

Friday, March 16, 1984

Oh happy day! Si and Alex have the early copies of April and say they love it. Let's hope the readers do. What if I have drunk my own Kool-Aid like Richard Locke? I feel sorry for him anew, one puts so much blind love into these pages. My office has been painted peach with a peach carpet and a quotation mark–shaped desk that is so much more what I want than that disgusting coffin-like reliquary Leo hid behind. I saw him today at the Four Seasons, looking like a piece of poisonous pastry. Alex has been away for two weeks but came back looking happy and relaxed.

He is obviously pleased because Si is pleased. He's getting good feedback from his own circle he showed the early copy to.

There was a nerve-racking moment when Si asked to see the first pass at the May dummy and I had my heart in my mouth over the Garry Wills piece about Rupert Murdoch's designs on the *Chicago Sun-Times*. I know Si and Murdoch are friends, but when Si got to the three Chicago spreads deep in the book he stopped and said, "Why'd you put Murdoch so late? Why not open with it? It's got impact. And I LIKE your doing this. It has great news value." This made my day.

Wednesday, March 21, 1984

I spoke to advertisers at a luncheon at the Four Seasons to pitch them our turnaround. We showed them slides of the new issue as there are not enough copies printed yet to give out. I was B-plus. I should have ad-libbed, not read my speech. I wish I could get better at public speaking. Si was at my table and didn't say much afterward, which confirmed my sense that I had muffed it. We still have pitifully few ad pages. Their reaction was positive, but still with a "wait and see" attitude that could bury us if they don't get on board soon.

Had dinner with Mort Zuckerman. He's a great gossip and clearly loves the access his real estate wealth gives him to the media world, and who can blame him as it's a hell of a lot more amusing. He said that Nora Ephron should hand over the screenplay of *Heartburn* to somebody else and "let her anger with Carl Bernstein go." I don't think I agree.

Thursday, March 29, 1984
Boca Raton, Florida

Waiting for Harry to arrive for romantic weekend. Commuter marriages are a strain. We miss each other all week but when we reunite it's sometimes like the Dorothy Parker short story "The Lovely Leave" and it all blows up into some cranky fight. So we needed this special time.

The office is gradually becoming the happy club that *Tatler* was. It's pleasing to see Miles looking glamorously chiseled in his suspenders and dyed silver hair and being his old snarky self. When I debated having a party to celebrate the revival of the old *VF* Hall of Fame at the end of the year he suggested, "You could do it in a huge iron lung."

He is especially amused by the entertainment editor Daphne Davis I recklessly hired from *WWD* without consulting anyone. She is a clever, diminutive Minnie Mouse with a tiny little voice. I brought her on in desperation to handle the increasingly aggravating

174

calls from PRs and agents who control the Hollywood stars we need for covers. She is proving quite good at it, or at any rate is the only member of our highfalutin staff who actually likes schmoozing with PRs and setting up photo shoots. But she has her eccentricities. She lies in wait at the elevator to pitch me stories when I go to lunch. Yesterday she leapt out squeaking, "You know I am totally loyal to you. I want to play Chou Enlai to your Mao Tse-tung!" Miles especially loves this story.

Saturday, March 31, 1984

The first issue of my *VF* is on the newsstands at last! I love the way it looks, sexy and strong and clean! First anecdotal reactions — good, very good, especially for the design, but I am rattled by the flood of mail — two-to-one offensive. From Ohio, more in sorrow than in anger: "Why have you trashed this magazine?" From Chicago, "Go back to Britain. This reads as if you have got a stick up your ass." First media reviews have been mildly positive. All praise the layout changes. Some say it's too lightweight, which is not unfair. Reporters are calling me with needly questions. One airline-mag blonde who came in opened with "The one thing everyone agrees on is that you're very tough." I said, "Thank you." I keep checking newsstands and surreptitiously moving the mag to the front, but won't know any sales data for another ten days. Still, Si seems cheerful and that's the main thing. I have to rush on with the next issue and hope to build momentum.

Ruth and Charles in the art department can't get their act together and make decisions. Ruth is so brilliant, but she doesn't know how to close the circle in a conversation. She goes to lunch with the famous photographer Arnold Newman and comes back with "He's interested in doing stuff with us." When Michael Roberts goes to lunch with talent he comes back with two ideas in the bag. It's tricky because I don't want the American staff to resent Miles and Michael, who know so much more about how I like to work. Which is CLOSING. I also imported John Heilpern to run the arts pages. Makes me a bit nervous to hire the husband of a friend as good as Joan (and another Brit), but there is no one better as a cultural critic. Plus I had to fire two more of the old guard this week. Duncan Stalker, a talented young editor whom I tried to win over, but he's always upstairs with Leo, bad-mouthing the new era. There was another I wanted to let go but found she is in the throes of a sex-change op, which seemed bad timing.

Entertainment Tonight came to film me in the office and I was feeling so glum with all the staff problems and anxiety about the reader reaction to April that I mistakenly ran off at the mouth and now am in terror they will run the damning segment. Usually I bang on about America the Beautiful, but this time I heard myself say, "At first I thought I had to go carefully so as not to offend the aunties in Ohio, but now I feel if they don't want to read us, too bad." What was I thinking?

"Ohio," John Heilpern said as we sat, with freezing feet from the ice storms raging outside, waiting for the curtain to rise on *Death of a Salesman,* "is a pretty fucking enormous place to kiss off, Teen. In fact most presidents have found they can't win an election without it." We both fell into a depressed silence as Dustin Hoffman did his hopelessly unconvincing Willy Loman, a foregone hit before it reached the boards. Unlike the muted smiles of British audiences at the National Theatre if a play has had good reviews, here if there's a celebrity actor in the part, the whole audience goes batshit when he or she appears onstage, applauding at every other line and standing up yelling for encores.

Before the lights even dimmed the man behind me said, "They tore the walls down in Washington."

I had a drink with Pam Van Zandt, who continues to fascinate me. "The thing about Si," she said, "is that he's eighty percent okay. And then he'll do something absolutely crazy, totally screwy that you can't understand." I thought of how Si's eyes sometimes slip sideways and he assumes an expression of deep deviousness, like a pensive Hapsburg hanging in the Prado. She is probably right.

Our publisher at *VF,* David O'Brasky, took me to the Ogilvy & Mather ad agency on Madison Avenue to do a show-and-tell on the new look of *VF.* O'Brasky is an ebullient butterball out of *The Producers* with his Noo Yawk accent and Madison Avenue history, selling ads, it seems, for every magazine that's ever mattered. Larry Cole, the boss at O & M, picked up *VF* and flicked through in a matter of seconds, shut it, and said, "Yeah, so what we're saying is, this is a total revamp, a new magazine, right? What numbers do you have to back up that this is what anyone wants?" O'Brasky did his spiel about demographics and audience polls but Cole looked at him with small, unimpressed eyes. "It looks better," he told me, "easier to read. My only real criticism is this." He stabbed his finger at my favorite picture in the Lartigue spreads, a society woman from Saint-Paul-de-Vence in a turban and huge dark glasses. "That" — he stabbed — "is retro. Who cares about this now? She's what, this lady, eighty now? And who's interested in somebody almost dead? This" — he pointed at the cover of Daryl Hannah — "I like. It's contemporary." To ensure I got the point he did it again. "This"

— at Lartigue — "retro, dead, old, I don't like. This" — Daryl — "today, contemporary, I like." Had I been right to concede to Alex? Yes, no regrets and screw Larry Cole. I still believe the Lartigue brings something wonderful and refined to the pages, especially when combined with the fresh glamour of Now. Cole didn't seem to understand that blending the two was the whole point of *VF*'s mix and flavor. I thought again of Wallace Shawn. "America has no memories."

Saturday, April 7, 1984

The promotion marathon for the new issue keeps going. Some people are waiting to say they like the new *VF* until someone else does. I am getting good feedback from writers and editors who seem to understand the combination of high-low culture (that Clay said he loved) but there's also a sense of puzzlement. I realize my approach to editing is much more European. *The New York Times* clearly thinks serious equals self-important, that it has to earn its gravitas in subject matter rather than in treatment and point of view. Compared to the London quality papers it's visually dull and devoid of surprise. One TV interview I did spent the whole air time trying to discover if the new *VF* was a fashion magazine, a movie magazine, or a literary magazine. I told them it was a mix of all of them. I did an interview every day last week and saw an advertiser for dinner with O'Brasky every night. I am getting fond of his thick-skinned enthusiasm and rubbery, unrejectable face. There is something touching about him, reinforced by the fact I learned that at Yale he had always wanted to write for the college magazine, but they kept on making him sell ads. Eventually he accepted his lot, but he still feels the buzz of editorial and wants to be a part of it. CBS news came to film me at the *VF* office in my new Ted Lapidus suit. Jane Pauley aggressed me on the NBC *Today* show about why I thought the new *VF* would work. I looked wan in a washed-out beige dress I will never wear on the air again. They showed clips of the royal wedding coverage I did with Pauley in 1981 in London. I was astonished at how old-fashioned my Camilla Parker Bowles electric-rollered waves looked and at how uninhibited I was calling Diana "Hey Big Spencer" because of her height. It all seemed light-years away.

Alex has been coming down again more, which I love. He was amused by Daphne Davis, who got overexcited when he started laying out some Drew Barrymore spreads. "You look just like John Barrymore but with more class, Mr. Liberman!" she squealed. "Douglas Fairbanks Jr., actually," he said. Then turning to me, asked, "Who is this small, charming person, Tina?" He seems in a good mood when he sails in, back erect like a ballet master.

As part of the pitch tour, O'Brasky made me have dinner with the founder of one of the major ad agencies whose accounts we don't have, Backer Spielvogel Bates. Carl Spielvogel and his wife, Barbaralee Diamonstein (seriously, you can't make it up), looked as if they had been married forever but it transpired it was only three years. I got a clue when she said, "Carl is the best in the world at copy lines, squash, and S-E-X." She, I realized immediately, was the key to the account, but I also realized with a sinking heart it might be a price too high to pay, since she has writing aspirations. She looks like an avid, bejeweled soufflé with great acquisitive black eyes darting around the table. "Barbaralee doesn't miss a deal," Carl said, dotingly, his hairline glowing amber from its recent roots retouch. "You know something?" he said, turning his sage nose toward me, "twenty years ago I used to know the name of every doorman, every parking garage guy on my block. Now I don't know any of them. You know why? It doesn't matter anymore." Barbara's a big fan of Arianna's and kept saying Mort Zuckerman should marry her. He certainly couldn't find anyone smarter or more amusing in his circle. I couldn't wait to crawl home to bed.

As soon as the rest of my furniture arrives I guess I am going to have to start having dinner parties. I realize new things about New York all the time. You have to be seen to be social. And if you don't go out, you have to be KNOWN for not going out. I saw this when I had lunch with Bob Gottlieb, the editor in chief of Knopf, who is such a legendary literary figure around town. He has made himself Famous for Never Having Lunch. So I went to his office for the revered sandwich. I found him, as everyone describes, a taller version of Woody Allen, self-consciously idiosyncratic (he sat on the floor), as if he is working overtime on being famously eccentric. Everything in New York is about personal marketing.

Monday, April 9, 1984

It was bliss having lunch with Norman Mailer today. His big, warm, wide face and profligate brilliance filled up my heart all afternoon. We talked about politics — "Jesse Jackson! What a jive-ass!" — and prison, where his old nemesis Jack Henry Abbott is still incarcerated in a federal penitentiary. Norman and Jason Epstein and George Plimpton campaigned for Abbott's release in the early eighties on the basis of the book he wrote, *In the Belly of the Beast,* only for Abbott to immediately stab a bartender once he was out.

Norman said that Abbott is like a cat who's been so badly treated it scratches, bites, and rejects until all you want to do is kill it, then suddenly rolls over and is so cute you love it. He said he adored being photographed swimming by Annie Leibovitz last summer because the picture gave him "tits." He talked about the days he and Arthur Miller had shared the same brownstone in New York, when Mailer was writing *An American Dream* and Miller *Death of a Salesman.* "I must say when I saw the play I was amazed at how good it was for such a dull guy." Norman and Bob Hughes are the two most charismatic men in America, the big alpha boys they don't make anymore.

Tuesday, April 10, 1984

O'Brasky has been pushing me to my limits, meeting with stone-faced advertisers. I am sick of being distracted from editorial by the endless quest to get ads. Newsstand report came in. April sales are up, thank God, not hugely, but 8 percent over March. Everyone seems to love the visual clarity and Nick Dunne's Blondes cover story with its insidery, laid-back voice. I feel the lack of hard news edge, but am working to get it. The movie *Splash* is a hit, so even if Daryl Hannah's blindfolded, we had the right cover star, a zeitgeist omen I hope. May issue has now gone to press and I am not sure about it.

We had lunch with Calvin Klein, whose ad pages we desperately want. He was another pretend low-key person, very soft-spoken, saying he was just interested in the creative direction when you know he makes all the commercial decisions. He's very anti the new *GQ* now that Alex has gone in the opposite direction of Colacello and hired a bearded he-man and former *Penthouse* ed, Art Cooper, to make it straight. Calvin didn't reveal his hand about what he thought about *VF* now. I can see he's going to make me work for it.

I preferred his archrival Ralph Lauren, who was at lunch the next day. He was also low-key but more watchful and shrewd. He said he thought Condé Nast made a terrible mistake under Locke, stuffing the doomed launch issue with too much of the wrong kind of advertising (i.e., Calvin Klein underpants), implying this was another reason he had pulled his ads out before I got there. O'Brasky during all this was at his most hopelessly ingratiating and getting it all wrong. Ralph looked at him with slow, blank eyes when he asked him how he was running his Seder this Passover. "Wild West style, Ralph, I'd guess?" O'Brasky beamed. "Mine, I run like a sales conference." When he went to the bathroom, Ralph asked me, "How did you get stuck with him?" The good news, however, was that he was enthusiastic about the new direction and committed to buying pages from the August issue onward, which was a real victory.

Thursday, April 19, 1984

We have been trying to find a summer rental in the Hamptons and think we have discovered something wonderful.

The more I live here the more I have a childlike longing for the crash of waves on the beach. I love New York, but its brutal onslaught never lets up. I asked Sarah Lewis what the nearest Hampton was to the city and she suggested a quiet village east of Westhampton. I called the broker to make some appointments, and H and I rented a car and drove out in torrential rain to view them. As soon as we were on the road I felt so happy. As we approached the outskirts of Quogue I was taken back to my childhood weekends with Mum at granny's house at Elmer Beach in Sussex, the jubilant barefoot walks in the rain, stopping to throw stones in the stormy, gray Atlantic, coming into our tiny flat on top of the roof, where we kicked off our wet, sandy shoes and brewed the tea. So consoling. So secretive. So unadorned.

We disembarked at a fusty little broker's run by the Piries, a mother-and-daughter team. I loved Quogue village immediately as there is very little there, just clusters of white clapboard and cedar-shingled houses, a charming colonial Presbyterian church, a ribbon of road over a bridge to the beach lined with wind-tossed oak and maple trees. The broker kept saying it all looked so much better in the sunshine, but to me it was perfect that it rained, like England.

We parked our car and got in the Piries' beat-up Ford. The houses and condos they showed us were all disappointingly contemporary, with pointy roofs and sharp-angled frames and interiors full of things we'd never want, like "wet bars" and billiard tables. There was one just about okay on the bay and we were about to take it when old Mrs. Pirie said, "There is this other house I haven't shown you, I doubt you'll like. Very old-fashioned." Our ears immediately pricked up. "Not in good shape, but it's on Dune Road on the beach. The washing machine," she added dubiously, "may very well have to be replaced."

"Take us there!" we cried.

One-sixty Dune Road. As soon as we saw it we fell in love. A shingled cottage nestling behind the dune with dormer windows and wild beach grass leading down to where the waves pounded. It reminded me of Cornwall at high tide. And Elmer, Elmer, Elmer. I could see my childhood coloring books, hear the kettle whistling on the stove. When we opened the back door and walked up the gray wooden stairs to the big, embracing living room, it felt as if this was our house, waiting for us to claim it. Owned by the same family, the Clarholmes, since it was built in 1928. It had the time-warp feel of a Somerset Maugham play, with card tables set up for a game of backgammon, a Bakelite radio, an old mahogany desk in the corner, a framed gold-prospecting certificate from 1928. To get out on the deck you had to struggle with a small wooden door that opened to a glimpse of ocean on the other side of the dune. There was a maritime feel to the wood-paneled walls trimmed with rope, and a bookish charm to the cozy bedrooms with iron bedsteads and fading lampshades. It is total and utter heaven. When the Piries left the room, Harry and I threw ourselves into an ecstatic embrace and when they returned instantly started negotiating. We found we had competition from another couple who were deciding the next day. So even though it's a staggering fourteen thousand dollars for the summer, we immediately offered a thousand more, to be FedExed on return to the city. We hurtled back on the Long Island Expressway in the rain, feeling euphoric, as if we were explorers who had truly landed at last. We've already started to scheme about how we can raise the money to buy it if it's for sale.

The May issue is out. I feel it's thin. The Olympic cover of the model in the silver sheath leaning backward into a huge hoop is beautiful but too refined. America needs gutsier. Garry Wills's piece on Murdoch's takeover of the *Chicago Sun-Times* is strong but limited in appeal, and I love Julian Allen's illustration of Rupert as Al Capone, but the piece doesn't quite land the plane. It needed a muscly investigative journalist rather than an essayist like Wills. Mailer's *Tough Guys* extract is a literary scoop, but I fret for juicier elements. What is good is the sustained strength of the redesign. Alex did an inspired layout for John Cheever's letters, taking a portrait of Cheever in a group at Yaddo and circling his face with a splashy red circle that's so eye-catching. Am very proud, too, of the contents page, which delivers in every way we hoped. But after initial interest in our revamp I don't feel people are talking about it. Literary memoirs and eye-catching contents pages are not enough. New York has checked us out and moved on. We have to make some news.

I love some of the pieces we have coming in for the June issue. I wheedled Jan Morris, the British writer who had a sex change and used to write for Harry at *The Sunday Times* as James, to do a piece about Boy George.

She has taken the hackneyed "androgyny" idea and writes instead about "intersex," "the spell of the ultimate chimera, the creature that bridges in its own being that most obvious and unbridgeable of gulfs, the gulf between M and F." She talks about the day when the "messy and graceless business of coupling to produce children" is done, replaced by "an unnoticeable implant, an untasteable tablet." And urges us all to "throw off the chains of gender" like Boy George.

Annie has done a wonderful close-up portrait of Boy holding a carnival mask. Session was a bit fraught. Michael Roberts originally wanted to do him as a June bride, and flew to Toronto for the shoot with a trunk full of wedding veils. Then Boy changed his mind, Annie went ballistic, and Michael ended up siding with Boy. But all came out good. It's a haunting photograph. They did a portrait of his makeup box too — very effective.

Thank God Pam McCarthy has arrived, like Mary Poppins, to clean up our production process and crack the whip on the budget. The June issue, though good, needs a big visceral narrative lead. The fashion cover approach is not working. *VF* needs deep dives into personalities. It's harder than I thought to get it. I have been consumed with just running the mag day to day and dragging myself to see advertisers with O'Brasky. I've had too little time on the creative input and it feels

189

anemic. I have to focus on robust reporting and cultivating strong investigation. Now that Pam's here I can hand all the management stuff off to her and spend all my time with the writers.

Another distraction is I have to do a lot of legend maintenance. Today, at Alex's prodding, I took the famous old photographer Horst P. Horst out to lunch at the Isle of Capri. He sat in a corner with crab-like posture and tinted glasses and a tight little smile. He seemed still aggrieved that forty years ago Mr. Condé Nast didn't take him as seriously as Steichen. He's photographed seven first ladies and complained about how when he did Nancy Reagan recently Grace Mirabella showed up, and Leo also appeared and got in the way and hissed that she was the worst actress ever. "I said, baby, who needs you. I am trying to make a picture here." Still, out of it I got a glorious portfolio for the September issue of Dietrich in black lace gloves and a killing picture of Janet Flanner examining a *New Yorker* cover with a lorgnette. I do see that it's important to keep the legend quotient happy, as long as they are mixed with the young Turks. (This. Old, I don't like. This. Young, contemporary, I like.) He also asked if he could photograph me. Which would be sort of great to have.

At O'Brasky's insistence I had lunch with Leonard Lauder to gin up the Lauder ad buys. He was in a surprisingly frank mood. "I worry," he said, "that one day I will wake up and be a jar of face cream. Tina, I am so good at what I do, I live every minute of my life in a directed way. Yes, I go skiing and I'm wired into a hundred different worlds in this town. But I'm worried about getting stale. I joined the board of the Aspen Institute because I thought it would refresh me — the life of the mind, writers, thinkers, but then I can only see how badly it's run. I start to stick my oar in, tell them how they can make a profit. Next thing is I'm organizing everybody." I told him that what he should do one day is throw a spanner in the works of his schedule, stand everyone up, break appointments. I didn't say, check into a hotel with the sexiest, most gorgeous woman you know, because I had the sense suddenly of where this declaration of spiritual deadness might possibly all be leading . . .

After lunch I took the train to DC to stay with Ben and Sally for Kay Graham's dinner party for us. Sixty people for sit-down in her dusty-cantaloupe dining room that used to be her children's playroom. Clare Boothe Luce was there! She went through the May issue with me. She has a perfect straight nose and a silver crown of hair and eyes that are dancing periwinkle blue. She sat on a slipper chair in a creamy pearl-studded dress with a white fur stole, and people came to pay court. I could feel her sharp critical mind as she asked pertinent questions. "What's this?" "Why this?" I wonder if it made her nostalgic for her own *VF* glory days, hard to tell. At dinner I was seated next to Kay's son, Donald Graham, who is big and straightforward and a really good egg. He teased me about not knowing anything about America. "Where's Arkansas, Tina?"

"Where's Stow-on-the-Wold, Donny?" I countered.

"I don't have to sell magazines there." He laughed.

"Arkansas is not my target audience either," I replied.

"So you kissed off Arkansas, eh? Well. That's a gamble I respect!"

Clay Felker was at my table, but sadly has become jealous of *VF*, as he is bound to feel with his own prospects dashed. He kept giving me the needle about what I didn't know about America, too, but unlike with Donny it wasn't good-natured. I suddenly got sick of it and shouted across the candles and flower arrangements, "How much weight did you lose at the fat farm, Clay?" It was the right approach. He shut up after that.

It was lovely afterward with the Bradlees

just hanging out. "I drew Justice O'Connor as a dinner partner," Ben said. "That was a bucket of mirth." Harry had drawn Pamela Harriman, and Sally was all over him to penetrate the sexual mystique. "She hung on my every word," was all my clearly hopelessly captivated husband could come up with. Sally described the Republican senator she had sat with as "a flaming cavorting asshole." I kept laughing about that when we went up to our room. "Cavorting" is such a deliciously underused word.

Thursday, April 26, 1984

A drink with Martin, who is passing through, made me realize how much I miss Englishness. I had a sudden pang for Oxford days when we lay in the little single bed in my St. Anne's room in the Woodstock Road, doting on Larkin's sentences in "The Whitsun Weddings." *I thought of London spread out in the sun / Its postal districts packed like squares of wheat.* My ideal place to live would be Transatlantica, an island that combined English irony, country lanes in summer, the National Theatre, and a real pot of tea they never seem to be able to make here, with American openness, lack of class barriers, willingness to give away money to good causes, and the view of Manhattan from the Rainbow Room at the top of Rockefeller Center. I miss the pleasing streak of delinquency in the English character.

The change of the seasons from brutal cold to sudden heat made me think of the sweet decorum of our London patio in the spring, the rhododendron bushes drowsy with raindrops. I long for the English countryside in ways I never did when I lived there. I suddenly see the great country houses that gave us so much irreverent copy at *Tatler* as a rich national resource, custodians of passing time. Here, time is to be spent, like money; time is to be killed, time is to be forgotten. Everything is a race against time. Trying to beat it is the pressure at your throat. I dream of London's manageable scale, its compactness, its conversation. America is too big, too rich, too driven. America needs editing.

Last night I had an hour in my office with Schiff explaining to me why he hasn't written anything after trips to London, Paris, and Hollywood for *VF*, because he's still "thinking the piece through." Sometimes it's hard to give writers the love.

The real agony of editing is not the bad piece versus the good piece. That's easy — kill one and publish the other. It's the borderline piece that is the source of woe. The piece that's perfectly good, inoffensively unexceptional, just okay, usually written by someone who's an almost friend or an iconic name or a writer who just didn't give their best this time but might well in the future. I have no fear of rejecting the bad and prefer to do it fast. But borderline pieces bring out the worst in me. Out of weakness I sometimes first assent, then think better of it, then am tormented by something I truly want to put in its place, then, as more of the really good surges in, ultimately eject it, making an enemy forever and wishing I'd had the discipline to just let it hide there among the good stuff as an investment in the future.

I went to see the Shirley MacLaine show with Daphne Davis as my date. "Why doesn't Tracy Young think more positive?" she piped as we stood in line for the tickets. "Why doesn't she get out of that 1968 butch costume and get herself into a skirt? Why doesn't she move on in life? Can't she understand this is a business? I did my boot camp at *Women's Wear Daily*! I know what life in this town means!"

Alex took me to La Grenouille to lunch. I always feel this is his natural habitat; surrounded by freshly cut flowers, French-speaking waiters he converses with as if he'd known them for many years, and film stars still of the vintage to wear dark glasses to lunch. Now that I have come to love him I felt the pleasure of his pleasure and the poignancy when he said, "Tatiana loves it here. It is sort of like second family, we have come here for so long." I had hoped, once again, to draw him out about his fascinating émigré past, which he never speaks about, but as always I was disappointed. Alex lives determinedly in the present. The great legends who have been his friends rarely pass his lips. He's the opposite of a name dropper, unlike so many around him who knew no one very interesting but drop their names all the time. When I put my hand on his shoulder I was startled by how thin it felt. Only his ramrod posture keeps the aging process from shrinking him. "How is Leo?" I said. "He is wearing thin," he said with his usual impeccable visual accuracy. "There was never much, you know, just froth. But now that, too . . ."

I used to imagine the Chekhovian end of them locked together and this is indeed what is happening, but it has more pathos than in my forward projection a year ago. They are wearing thin together, the indomitable silver fox and his court jester.

Tuesday, May 1, 1984

I have been horribly sick. Nausea, dizziness, the doctor says it's stress. That crazy round of advertising meetings was a killer. I feel a kind of delayed drop after taking the job in such a whirlwind and leaving London without any backward look and now it's catching up to me. I am spending an early evening in bed.

My new curtains go up on Thursday, but meantime the early summer dusk behind the sheer net Mum put up to block onlookers reminds me of early summer nights watching the gentle rippling of the net curtains in my childhood bedroom at Little Marlow. I can see the trees of Central Park turning green behind them.

Harry has accepted Zuckerman's job offer of president of Atlantic Monthly Press, which is based half in NYC and half in Boston. It will be good for him to have his own creative outlet again. It's been two years since we lived in the same place for any length of time. I really feel I need him with me now and can't wait. But also am apprehensive about the force of his personality in this small space. I have forged a lot of independence here and have paid for all of it with my own money. Will he like being in my town? And will I like having him here?

Monday, May 14, 1984

I took advice from Walter Anderson, the editor of *Parade,* who has been incredibly supportive, and assigned Gail Sheehy a series of profiles of the political candidates. I like her psychological approach and her obsessive shoe-leather reporting. Her first piece is of the Colorado senator Gary Hart, and it's going to make news. She gets into his born-

197

again background and repressed nature and reveals his long relationship with a Native American spiritual adviser, Marilyn Young-bird. No one is writing about candidates in the personal way that Gail can for us. I think she could carve out a new direction on political profiles. Pam McCarthy has really got stuck in as managing editor and is saving my life and everyone else's. I have a strong sense of her control to fall back on and it allows me to be creative with discipline behind me.

Bob Colacello had a birthday dinner hosted by the oil magnate's wife, São Schlumberger. Guests were Barry Diller, who said he loved *Vanity Fair* because he only reads magazines in taxis, the novelist Jerzy Kosinski, the retailer Gerry Stutz, Bill Buckley, and Steve Rubell, who used to own the disco Studio 54 until he was caught not paying taxes and was sent to prison, from where he's just emerged. He has an ingratiating people-pleaser grin and is the best imaginable dinner partner since he combines the two most fascinating topics in the world for any magazine editor, high society and prison. He told me how inside he violated a cardinal behind-bars rule when he leaned over and switched off a TV channel in the rec room. The next thing he knew he was hanging ten feet from the ground on a door hook. He was there so long without anyone finding him that the search sirens went off. "At first I used to phone all my famous friends outside," he said, "then I found I couldn't cope. The only way I could make it work for me was to cut off the outside world and make prison my world. Then I was okay. Except for needing air. I had to get on the roof and have air whenever I could. Even if my lawyer was there waiting for me and it clashed with my time on the roof I'd have to get up there." Now he and his partner Ian Schrager have bought the Royalton Hotel ("I had a lot of cash"), which sure needs a face-lift, as I can testify, and they are going into the "boutique hotel" business, which he says is the next big thing. Wonder if it will work. He seems such a kinetic creature of the night to me.

Even though he's so genial, I felt an edge of resentment about those who had come through for him and those who had not. "I protected a lot of people," he said. I could feel a raw killer instinct beneath the charm. He said Halston had "gone under from self-indulgence," perhaps one of those who melted away. I remember Halston's black turtleneck sweater surging ahead of me at Diana Vreeland's opening at the Costume Institute at the Met when I was at *Tatler*. Halston was king of the world then. He would be a good story I must assign now, seen as instant history before anyone else defines his rise and fall.

June issue is out and getting a mildly appreciative reaction. People seem to feel *VF* keeps improving. But it's not enough. Feel we are still cruising on the design improvements and the photographs. We need the muscle of revelation I am in overdrive trying to get. An interesting sighting on Tuesday in Le Cirque where Shirley Clurman took me to lunch. (She was in great form dissecting the Kissingers. "Have you noticed their dining room is an exact replica of the State Department's?") Richard Nixon was there at a corner table for six. On his left an immaculate blonde in a pink Bill Blass suit and a big white Ascot hat. She was applying fresh lip gloss as her husband and the other wives hung on Nixon's every word. Nixon's felonious rubber nose looked almost endearing after its long respite from cartoon life. It's fascinating and oddly cheering about American democracy that the passage of years allows anyone to resurface, no matter how vilified (the upside of No Memory). I have never been to Le Cirque before and hadn't realized what full-blown musical theater it is — all the ladies who lunch in red capes and big, gleaming earrings eating pink fish. Syrio, the maître d' with the creased smile, unfurls a crisp white napkin like a bullfighter. I was so struck with the scene that I asked Ruth Ansel to assign an artist to recreate it for the August issue, and she assigned Julian Allen, who has captured it beautifully. I wrote up the text tonight to run unsigned alongside it.

Monday, May 28, 1984

Just back from Henry Kissinger's surprise sixty-first birthday party at the River House, billed as "knock-out knockwurst," which turned out to be bulbous Germanic sausages and sauerkraut. It was pouring with rain as it was a year ago when we all — the same group multiplied by twenty — convened for his sixtieth at the Pierre. I really have no right to be at the Henry fests, it's only Harry they want. I sat between the CBS correspondent Mike Wallace and Norman Podhoretz, with Jayne Wrightsman's unflinching coiffed hair on the other side of him, and Mica Ertegun, Ahmet's chic, decorator wife, on the other side of Mike. Podhoretz, with his hard, pitiless nose and humorless skunk's eyes, fascinates me. He is so conceited and arrogant, I find it endearing. He has an utter uninterest in being anything but right, snuffling with impatience as he shovels up his sauerkraut. He and Mike Wallace argued across me about the General Westmoreland $120 million libel case against CBS. [CBS made a documentary that proved Westmoreland had contributed to the public reaction to the Tet offensive during the Vietnam War by manipulating intelligence about enemy strength in order not to embarrass LBJ.] Podhoretz assured me Westmoreland would win because he deserves to.

"You wait till you see our brief. It will knock you out," said Wallace.

"Yeah, I'm on your case. I wrote a book about Vietnam, remember? Messenger the brief over to me tomorrow."

"And, Norman, read it."

"Yeah. I'll not only read it, I'll have OTHERS read it."

"And let's not forget how much this case means to our profession," said Wallace.

"Libel? Yeah, well, as it happens I support the side of the argument that works against me professionally. I'd prefer to operate under stricter libel restraints if it curbed the flagrant abuse of facts in our society."

This ping-pong continued most of the dinner. Whenever Mike brought up a statistic, Podhoretz corrected him. Note to self. Must assign a Mike Wallace profile. My instinct is CBS will win and then Mike will be a hero. (Maybe even a cover.)

I was enchanted to find Alex was there escorting Tatiana, terrifying in her giant gentian glasses. He looked touching to me, standing erect in front of the windows that looked out onto the mist over the East River. I probably irritated Tatiana by raving about her daughter Francine Gray's new novel, *Lov-*

ers and Tyrants. So well does it catch the two of them, it obviously concerned and embarrassed Alex. "You know, we were upset when we first read it," he said. "That was Francine's view of us for a time. She has changed, but that was her view." I wished I hadn't brought it up. Pat Buckley was there laughing her voluptuous laugh and Barbara Walters in a white Grecian-style dress and Susan Gutfreund, noticeably toned down since last year. It's funny how I always dread going out and then get so much out of it when I do. Social life is the trigger for all the best stories I have ever got, or at any rate, it helps me secure, or conceptualize, most of them. Ed Epstein told me that when Clay Felker was editing he would walk by each desk at lunchtime and say, "Why aren't you out?" It's essential if you are an editor to do so, and being an introvert by nature, I remind myself of this each time.

Friday, June 1, 1984

Bill Attwood, old friend of Harry's in the newspaper business, called to tell me he had heard from a close friend of Donald Newhouse that the Newhouses were fed up with losing money and very annoyed about the Murdoch piece. It threw me off my stride. Could Si have been duplicitous? Or could it just be Donald? Yet the night before I had in

203

fact been at a benefit dinner at Donald and Sue's before a dance display for disabled kids and they were both so nice to me. I am choosing not to believe Attwood's rumors of displeasure.

Tuesday, June 19, 1984

Life still tense at the office. We saw Mort Zuckerman last night flushed from buying *US News and World Report.* In a way it's a complication. Having just taken on the Atlantic Press, his book publishing business, Harry doesn't know if Mort now wants him to edit *US News* instead — Mort keeps suggesting he does but he's such a tease. He seems obsessed with Harry, which I find appealing. He's in love with journalism and being around journalists, which is understandable given how boring real estate is. Of course, a news magazine would excite Harry more, but I fear Mort would be a highly strung press baron. I doubt he understands that great editors can't be controlled and I don't want Harry moving to DC, where *US News* is based. Now that we have settled in together I would so hate his abrupt departure again!

New York is in constant motion with its opportunities and its changing landscapes. Makes you long for the stasis I used to rail against in London. The dinner we saw Mort at was for Gore Vidal, who was fuming at me about Wolcott's review of his new book, *Lincoln.*

"He's a very good writer who unfortunately can't read," Gore said. "I just wish he'd stick to TV, which he knows about, and stop screwing around with writers like me." He's very square in the face now, Gore, and walks with a high-stepped pussycat walk. He was nonetheless cordial when he stopped hissing to me about Wolcott, which was a relief because I have seen him when he is not. Mort told me he's now deeply in love with Gloria Steinem. He has good taste in bright women who at least are age appropriate. Si has returned from his European tour in a good mood, except we now have to cut editorial costs. Condé is so erratic about budgets. First Alex refusing to give me one, then suddenly imposing one, then changing it midyear. I sat for three hours with Pam McCarthy doing a slash-and-burn cut, which brought some of my dithering about personnel into sharp focus.

Thursday, June 21, 1984

The relentless David O'Brasky dragged me to see Perry Ellis, the third of the fashion big three, to solicit their ads. This time Dick Shortway, Si's trusted corporate confidant and spy, came with us, probably so he could suggest the leverage of *Vogue* in the background as additional pressure. Shortway has a genially pitted salesman face and Ronald Reagan square-shouldered suit, worn with the flash of a gold ID bracelet. David was looking especially anxious and plump. His tiny legs were pumped into his seersucker pants like inflated sausage-shaped balloons.

Having already met the quietly flamboyant Calvin Klein and the watchful, cool Ralph Lauren, I was interested in Perry Ellis. He's the rising yuppie of the trio, a Virginian better bred than the other two, with a sportswear line that seems to be on fire. They are all fiercely competitive, Ralph I think most with Perry because of the class angle.

The three of us got to the Ellis headquarters on Seventh Avenue at two p.m. Inside the offices, everything was the new high-key low-key. The inevitable ravishing petite Japanese assistant wearing soft ballet pumps. Small cakes and biscuits were on trays outside for the staff (Perry is known to "do" tea), and canvas easels on trolleys stood around with swatches of fabric pinned on colorful combinations of Ellis's famous college knitwear. Chairs so delicate that O'Brasky nearly swiveled out the door when his thighs sank on the seat. We sat around facing Ellis, lawyer and boyfriend Laughlin, and his backer. Ellis himself has an ageless prettiness. Very light blue eyes, light southern voice, tousled wavy hair, rumpled khakis; perfect really. His business partner was also midthirties, with a frosted blond crop, rimless glasses, and stubble. He just watched and said nothing. Michael Roberts said Perry and Laughlin sometimes take a Balducci's picnic bag to Fire Island for dinner and watch the sunset.

I was surprised at how Ellis led the negotiation, kicking off with elaborate, smart praise of *VF* — its wit, edge, taste, intelligence, etc. etc.; then, as we sat there waiting for the payoff: "My question is, how much is intelligence worth in terms of the advertising dollar? I worry about the MIX as well." My heart stopped, but he meant the advertising mix, it seemed, and in doing so fingered an O'Brasky weakness — accepting the occasional cheesy ad, which lowers the glossy tone and puts off the chic brigade. But who are we to turn them away when these precious folk won't commit? O'Brasky talked too much, shifting from ham to ham. At moments of acute nerves he refers to Si as "the little short guy on the fourteenth floor, the one who pays our bills." Shortway looked sly.

"Now look, Perry," he creaked, "we know that what you care about is book position. Now as you know, this book is getting hot. Right now, these positions are yours to buy. Six months from now, they won't be. You could be trying to buy into the book and find that Ralph and Calvin are there where you want to be!" Overplaying of hand! Perry immediately bridled. "You've just put your finger on my worries, Dick," he said. "The sense of indiscriminate acceptance of ANYONE'S ad pages." (Boy, these three are competitive.) And so it went on, getting down in the end to the buzz-cut partner negotiating for discounts. Still, much jubilance going down in the elevator. We scored.

Now I am sitting in our dream rental at Quogue consumed by excitement. It is just possible we may be able to buy the house! It is for sale for $125,000, the complication being that the price doesn't cover the land it stands on. That belongs to John Post of the old Quogue family, signified by the road to the beach, Post Lane. We would have to separately rent the land. Still, that doesn't daunt us as much as it probably would most Americans, as renting land is pretty common in the UK, and surely worth it for the haven it would give us. I'd like to be able to do it with my own *Tatler* money and a mortgage.

Last night we drove to East Hampton to have dinner with Mort Zuckerman and Gloria Steinem, just the four of us. Mort is living in the guesthouse while his own is rebuilt. It startled me to see what an enormous mansion his new house is becoming for just him. Why does anyone need a house this size? The guesthouse is enchanting. Much, much nicer in my view than the monsterama in progress; so intimate and romantic.

I am in awe of Gloria but feel she under-estimates me. More bristly than sisterly, I have to say, though I like her laconic sense of humor. Mort is obviously intimidated by her, which he enjoys.

There is something immensely likeable about Mort. An idealism, despite the cutting brain, he tries to hide with slight facetious-ness that makes him vulnerable. He's obvi-ously half-terrified of spending 183 million bucks on *US News* and who wouldn't be. The numbers are insane.

How rich and fast-paced life has become. Ed Victor walked into my office in a burst of good cheer and told me that at the ABA the editor in chief of Crown had told him he would pay in the region of 250K for a novel by me! The catch is, I have no time to write it. Ed said, "I hope you're still keeping a di-ary. I see it as my retirement pension."

Wish I did have time to write a book. I've always thought my "outer life" was research for the day when I'd just withdraw and write about it. The only reason I go out is observa-tion greed. Churning through the cast of New York society, I see it as the ever-moving slipstream of a novel.

At Billy and Jane Hitchcock's dinner in Gracie Square the careless beauty of the rich was never clearer. Amanda Burden's slim, fragile shoulders in a red chiffon spaghetti-strapped dress and biscuit-colored legs. Bill Hitchcock's big jaw and opinionated mustache. But the New York establishment is much, much duller than the British. Everyone is so bland, the pleasantness is grinding, the absence of irony or eccentricity crippling. Maybe I am just a cultural misfit.

Ran into the *Harper*'s editor, WASPy, sardonic Lewis Lapham, who said to Harry, "Have you caught the New York disease?" "What's that?" "MONEY madness," Lapham said (he's writing a book on the subject), "fiddling with your calculator all the time, doing little sums on scraps of paper, knowing you will never have quite enough. It's the sickness of the town." How did he know?

Thursday, July 12, 1984

Kathleen Tynan brought in a very promising and entertaining writer from the *New Republic,* Leon Wieseltier. Has wild hair and great sardonic delivery. He told me that he had tried to connect with Richard Locke, but found him a "state-of-the-art literary asshole." He has the wit, I think, to write a *VF* column. He wants to do so under the pseudonym of Vox, which I will give a try though I don't much like pseudonyms.

Nick Dunne is working on a piece that will make a lot of waves in LA and Washington. It's about the murder of Alfred

Bloomingdale's mistress Vicki Morgan. Alfred paid her a monthly stipend of eighteen thousand dollars to cater to his various perversions. Nick and I have been totally fascinated by this story since we saw the item about the murder. It lifts a lid on Nancy Reagan's air-kissy social circle and the way this affluent, pampered Bel Air crew really operates. (Betsy Bloomingdale, Alfred's wife, is Nancy's closest friend. Alfred was the department store heir and founder of the Diners Club.) We all first heard about Vicki Morgan when she sued the dying Alfred for $5 million palimony and there were those vivid, soap opera scenes of her trying to get into the hospital. Icicle Betsy cut off the corporate checks and banned her from seeing Alfred before he died. That cast Vicki into penury and she shacked up with Marvin Pancoast, a cracked, devoted loser she'd met in a bout in a mental hospital. She bullied Pancoast and made him her slave until he couldn't take it anymore and beat her to death with a baseball bat. Or so it's been reported. Of course, the tension of the story is in whether or not Betsy had Vicki bumped off, especially since it was leaked that Vicki had sex tapes of Alfred.

One rumor strand suggests Betsy used Pancoast to do her dirty work. Or perhaps Pancoast didn't do it at all. He took the fall and was promised a payout later. (It seems more likely it was a crime of passion on the part of

Pancoast, thinking he was putting Vicki out of her misery about her downward mobility, but there's plenty of reasonable doubt to make a great, page-turning society yarn.)

These kinds of questions anyway are what allow Nick to riff on decline and fall. He's just as turned on by the melancholy details of a life on the skids as he is by high life on a roll. He has been there and he has tasted it and he never forgets how it felt. He understands Vicki Morgan's pain and is instinctively on her side against high-and-mighty Betsy. He starts sniffing the air like a journalistic truffle dog when he sees the Morgan murder covered only on page five or six in the *Los Angeles Examiner,* with hardly a mention in the *LA Times,* where Betsy has influence.

I need three more Nicks! A *VF* formula that works is beginning to finally suggest itself. Celeb cover to move the newsstand, juicy news narrative like Vicki Morgan, A-list literary piece, visual escapism, revealing political profile, fashion. If we nail each of these per issue it's gonna work.

Sunday, July 15, 1984

Copy flooding in now for the September issue, and it's tense. So many on deadline and all need a tremendous amount of work. Vicki Morgan piece is going to need a huge makeover from Wayne. Thank God Nick accepts

Wayne's very radical interventions on structure and flow and needed additions. When I leave for lunch I see them knee to knee at Wayne's cubicle and know all will be right with the world. It's always such a relief when we have a great news narrative in an issue. Without that core I end up overassigning B features in desperate hope to conceal the lack of that One Great Thing. The rest of the September mag can now be Horst's great pics, a profile of Bobby Kennedy's son Joe who's entered politics, a charming feuilleton by John Guare about a famous Penn still-life called *Theater Accident,* Alison Lurie's terrific short story, and Michael's glorious fashion spreads.

Michael excelled himself this month with a style spoof shot by Tony Snowdon of a country house murder plot using Tom Cruise as the model. I just noticed today that in the last picture of a slinky blonde in a silk evening dress there is a pair of legs in socks and walking shoes sticking out upside down from an Egyptian urn. "Was it the countess who turned out these exquisite corpses? Or were they all — in the end — fashion victims?" Michael's caption copy reads. He's so inventive. God knows what anyone will make of it. He's been off this week with Bill King shooting a Paloma Picasso cover with an outsize scent bottle held up by a butler's hands. It's very chic but probably very uncommercial, and we have no fall back. I guess the fuchsia silk gloves she's wearing and huge pink rock on a pearl necklace have a lot of glamour, which will please the fashion advertisers at least. Michael has now forged his own quiet power base inside the art department, effectively redoing all their layouts on his stuff when they go out to lunch and then waiting for me to arbitrate. He vanishes when he hears Alex is coming down.

Monday, July 16, 1984

Am in overdrive trying to buy 160 Dune Road! Legally so complicated with it just being the house without the land. Harry is going to meet with the owner, John Post, in Boston. I said, find out how many kids he has, because if a lot we will for sure end up with the land at a later date. One thing I have learned about wealthy families is the kids always fight about money. If there are more than two kids, one of them is sure to be in financial trouble, or marry someone who is, and persuade the others to sell. And we will be happily waiting. We couldn't afford it now anyway, so doing it in stages couldn't be better. The owner, Mrs. Clarholme, said to be the widow of a gold miner, wants to sell all the furniture in the house, which delights me, as I lust for that Bakelite radio.

The New York Times today attributed to

Gail Sheehy's Gary Hart piece Mondale's reconsidering him for the veep ticket. That's influential. We are finally showing the news chops. It made all the waves we hoped. Last weekend we went to dinner at Nora Ephron's at Bridgehampton with the director Sidney Lumet, the gossip columnist Liz Smith, the writer Ken Auletta, and the agent Binky Urban. Nora looked pale and slightly frail, but much less neurotic now that she has hooked up with the screenplay writer Nick Pileggi. Lumet was very loud and theatrical but enthralling when cornered on his own subject, i.e., making movies, particularly on the difference between English and American actors. Americans, he says, find it harder to get the texture and range because of the paucity of material. "The muscles you flex, after a training period of *Hamlet* and *Faustus* is irreplaceable," he said. "Good material changes you." He said Mamet's amazing new *Glengarry Glen Ross* is probably the one good play of the last five years. "Isn't it extraordinary how three great American plays, *Iceman, Salesman,* and *Glengarry* are all about salesmen?" Made me want to rush off and do it as an essay for him to grade. Or maybe — what am I thinking! — an essay for Schiff.

Flight, flight! I'm on the plane back to London.

Maybe it was the hot madness of summer but the office was combustible. Feuds erupting in every corner. Flacks on the phone to me day and night railing about all our apparent misdemeanors with the pampered movie stars they represent. When he did his country house fashion shoot, Michael Roberts apparently had promised Tom Cruise a cover, which he's not supposed to do without talking to me. Pat Kingsley, a raspy-voiced Hollywood PR fury from the influential PMK company, had just discovered that not only was Tom not on the cover but he's dressed in a Sherlock Holmes cape in a fashion spread very much on the magazine's inside in Michael's spoof. "This has cost the movie company fifty thousand dollars a day," she shrieked. "You've lost me a client! You'll never get another cover star from PMK!"

"Let's not get rash!" I screamed back. "I wouldn't want you to take up an untenable posture."

Her reply can only be characterized as $%&!@***.

Then Daphne Davis got into the mix. She spends all her time cozying up to the PRs on our behalf, so now she was at my elbow to vent her spleen against Michael because he always goes direct to the stars who like him and cuts out the PRs, which makes Daphne jealous and furious. "No one will work with Michael ever again," she howled. "Everyone knows he's a voyeur and a weirdo. I know Robert De Niro won't work with him."

"Let him refuse!" I flailed, longing only to get on the train to Quogue and pretend it's 1910 in America. "This magazine doesn't need Robert De Niro. Robert De Niro needs this magazine!"

"This is New York 1984! These PRs control everything now!"

"To hell with the PRs!" I screeched. "PRs are the scum of the earth!"

Daphne went yellow. "All PRs?"

"Well, some of them," I conceded.

This scene took place just as I was leaving the office and sent my nerves jangling like skeletons in a house of horrors. Earlier in the week the excellent ed Peter Buckley had tried to resign over a redesign of the masthead he felt disadvantaged him; John Heilpern was calling from the Beverly Hills lounge every two hours in a frantic state about the apparent no-show of Jessica Lange for an interview; and just as we were struggling to get Nick Dunne's piece into shape three days late, Si suddenly realized that by putting Paloma Picasso and her scent bottle on the cover, we were going to drive away every single other cosmetic advertiser. He demanded we pull the story and the cover. Holy moly! Alex was in Connecticut, Ruth was on Fire Island, and Michael was now in Hawaii shooting an extracurricular Levi's ad. I had no problem pulling the story, which I never much liked, but had zero cover images as backup and was so pissed with Si's late-in-the-hour fawning to advertisers. I considered making a fight of it but a Paloma scent bottle didn't seem the issue to go to battle on. I finally found a compromise that Michael hated, of course, when I told him. A different picture of Paloma WITHOUT the scent bottle, elegant enough to stand but lacking the comedic style of the white butlered hands holding it up. Si let me put her on the cover with no reference to the perfume story, and Miles, Bob Colacello, and I spent three hours trying to glam up cover lines that would make the image less bland. "Plus! Martina's muscles, Penn's patent pump . . ."

"Horst's hemorrhoids," offered Bob. But then Miles came up with an inspired, completely meaningless cover line that I found thrilling even if no one understands what the fuck it means. "Sophisticated Boom-Boom!" he suggested. Hooray. Sophisticated Boom-Boom is what *VF* is all about, damn it. I took the issue up to Si and in case he tried to get me to remove the new cover line told him in a nonnegotiating voice that I had no idea what the line meant but I liked it. He just nodded gravely and said nothing. Then, "You should do a piece on Paloma's sister. She's not sophisticated at all. She's a real peasant." But he pleased me by calling down later and telling me what "an impressive advertising picture September has."

Mort is begging Harry to edit *US News* now that Harry's ceased to be interested in it. Reverse bait-and-switch! Now that we have the house in Quogue, leaving at three p.m. on the train on Friday has become the thing we look forward to most in the world, so who needs commuting to DC? It's such a wonderful summer ritual, setting off from Penn Station on the Long Island Rail Road, changing at Jamaica, and gazing out the window all the way to Westhampton. That lonely sound of the train's honky warning as it rounds the bend. The ticket collector wears a boater and comes to each seat with sodas and chips. We always see the same people, editors and publishers with bags of manuscripts, spinsters with novels retreating to cottages in Sag Harbor.

I've had the mortgage accepted for Quogue as long as the lease is for at least fifteen years. Harry went to Boston to meet the mysterious Mr. Post at the St. Botolph Club. He owns all that stretch of Quogue beach land where we are. It was clear to H what Post wanted to know — were we acceptable, quiet WASP types rather than glitzy arrivistes who give wild beach parties? That's why I wanted Harry to go alone, as I felt *VF* might sound way too fast-track. Harry wore his London *Times* air and knitted Savile Row tie and (I am sure) was at his most engaging. He didn't give me enough of a picture of Post except that he's tall and thin and flinty (and does have lots of kids). He got on well with him. Post offered to put together a package we could scrutinize and agreed, verbally anyway, to a twenty-four-year-and-up lease! We know it's a great buy, even if it all turns sour in the end. That takes me to fifty-four and Harry to seventy-nine and by then, who knows, some other cash may have arrived.

I see America as a lucky dip. It's crazy not to keep one's eye on the prize all the time, it just keeps moving. Quogue is so much more than a house to us. It has spiritual meaning. We found it in the middle of the rainstorm, or it found us. It has a special atmosphere that will keep us sane. The station at West-hampton on Monday morning is full of wives dropping off sporty-looking guys in khaki chinos and blazers for their week back in the city. The kids hang around waiting to kiss their fathers good-bye. Why aren't I that kind of wife? Looks pretty nice to me. Or does until I step off the train into the hot, ham-burger breath of Penn Station in the city, the belly gasp of the striving week ahead after two days of sun and relaxation, and I feel my adrenaline spike. This is one of the best, best things about life in New York, these hell-for-leather contrasts!

Sunday, August 5, 1984

London! I fell in love with England all over again even though it was a crazy week finally doing the house things I put off for six months. The cats have been living at Brasted like the Duke and Duchess of Devonshire, and clearly didn't appreciate the moment of truth when I arranged to have them adopted by the window cleaner at his seaside bungalow. But we can't put off renting it anymore. The new tenants are way more demanding than the cats. Their agent calls constantly and says, "Mr. and Mrs. Higgins feel the pelmets are dirty and the shower is not up to snuff."

The strange thing about being back in London, though, is why we ever thought we needed Brasted to escape to. London is a country village where I keep running into friends. I had a lovely tea with Gabé Doppelt in Brown's Hotel and caught up on all the *Tatler* gossip. I saw Pat Kavanagh having her highlights done at Michaeljohn. I went to Herbert Johnson's and bought Dad a Panama hat that came in a bright red hat box for his birthday. I sashayed around Bond Street knowing exactly where I would get the classic silk shirts and jackets I love from Roland

Klein, the new red heels from Katrina, my pearl earrings mended at David Morris. I went to see my new nephew at Chris and Diana's house. The declivity in the back of Benjamin Brown's head is just like Chris and Dad's. Diana is a besotted mother. I am longing for my own bundle of hope just like him.

It immediately seemed a world away when I landed back in NYC. Big blowup with John Heilpern because I don't like his Jessica Lange piece after all the agony it took to secure it. I can't pretend I like something when I don't. The piece has too much him, not enough her, and he doesn't want to revise it at all or report additional material, which pissed me off. It was so difficult telling him and he seemed to deliberately make it harder and more personal. He's morose at the best of times but now it's got really dark. I felt the resentment of a man being criticized by a woman. Miserable to deal with because I admire and love him.

One bright spot was Roy Blount calling up and saying he had Bill Murray in the lobby. Bill had read a profile of me in *Ambassador* magazine and wanted to check me out! They came in together and loafed around in my office for an hour, Murray being extremely hilarious. He was obviously hoping to find me as frisky and effervescent as my interview, but after the Heilpern altercation I wasn't in great form and was likely a disappointment.

Things came to a head at the office yesterday and we had some rock and roll, which was inevitable, and now we can get it right.

Tracy is clearly so disaffected I told her she should start to look for another job. I have tried to turn her around but I can't. I know I shall miss her asperity. She was taken by surprise but shouldn't have been, as reports of her bad-mouthing are multiple inside and out.

When I told PVZ I'd asked Tracy to start looking, she asked in that soothing tone, "Do you want me to have a conversation with her?" "Yes, I'd love you to have a conversation with her," I said, thinking how useful it would be to have her do some fireside chat with Tracy that would extract happier co-operation until she leaves. The next day PVZ called and said, "I had a conversation with Tracy and she will be gone by Tuesday." Wow. The way PVZ exits people with their "package" (it sounds almost Christmassy) is so polished that they almost feel they got promoted instead of fired.

I called in Wayne after these ructions and asked him for his support. He had been close to Tracy and wasn't helping, but now I think he realizes that unless we get on board with the new mag it's hopeless. The numbers still aren't good enough for us to waste time on internal politics. All this was pretty horrible and made me wish I was a writer instead of an executive with all the fraught people management. I also feel lighter-hearted though. I have to build my own team and can't screw around anymore with holdovers.

Michael Roberts swanned in with the light in his eye that announces good pictures. All his hours watching TV on his own have paid off, as he caught an interview with the Olympic relay team and had the brain wave of using them in a shoot with Bill King. He somehow reached one of them poolside and got them to agree — four hunky members of the swim team, discreetly naked, holding Raquel Welch aloft in a Busby Berkeley formation. So upbeat and commercial.

Meanwhile the Jessica Lange saga continued. Having had the drama with the piece, now the pictures blew up. Bill King got sick and couldn't do Jessica, so I had to pull Annie Leibovitz off a David Mamet shoot, which made her furious. She insisted that the only way she would do it was against a white seamless background on a white horse, and Michael had better fucking call every stable in town.

Losing Tracy meant I no longer had any caption writer, which meant deploying Miles to rewrite Wayne's captions. (As brilliant as Wayne is on structure and line-editing of a big piece, he is no good at captions. His caption on Annie's wonderful picture of Harold Ramis holding his daughter upside down on a sand dune read, "Ramis, holding his daughter upside down on a sand dune.") Miles loves it when I ask him to pitch in, especially when it means humiliating someone else. He took one look at the rejected Ramis headline "Ramis' Second Act" (snore) and wrote "Grossbuster" over it in swaggering Magic Marker. At that moment Michael called to say there was a problem getting the horse into the elevator at the studio, after trotting it very happily down Eighty-Sixth Street. All was calming down when O'Brasky started to play musical chairs with his own staff and fired Kitty Mountain, his production executive who lives with ex-*VF* publisher Joe Corr, which O'Brasky felt meant she wasn't on his team. All these comings and goings then led to a rumor on the street that I had been fired myself, and my phone was suddenly red hot with press inquiries. Si called to reassure me. Next day I went up to see him and asked if we could schedule more regular meetings. But as always when he suddenly senses need on the other side of the desk, he went cold on me. "I don't think that's really necessary," he said, looking down at his yellow pad to indicate the meeting was over.

The office is much cooler without Tracy, but I need to find another wit. My hopes are all pinned on Bill Zehme, a writer from

Chicago who sent something in over the transom and I pounced on it in the slush pile I took home for the weekend because he so clearly has a voice. If his next piece is as good as his first two, I will offer him a contract.

Tuesday, August 14, 1984

Thank God Alex is back from Connecticut. I have missed the maturity of his judgments. He backed up my queasiness about Helmut Newton's new fashion spreads. Much though I love Helmut's kinkiness, these were just too S and M for a mainstream mag, and I am sick of his telling me I am too bourgeois to appreciate them. Alex voted against the Raquel cover, declaring it was too tacky, which was a bit crushing. Is this more warfare against Michael Roberts? Jessica Lange on a horse, he said, had "more nobility." He's wrong. So I told him I would "defer" the decision.

I told him, which I knew would please him, how Si had come down to look at the October issue, said nothing, then gazed up at the framed Covarrubias illustrations from the thirties on my wall and said of one of them, "What a cover!" minutes after telling me how the mag I am editing is bombing in "C and D" markets, i.e., nonurban, bicoastal outlets.

"I doubt Covarrubias would have gone down well in C and D markets either," I said gloomily to Alex. He laughed.

"Nostalgia has been the trouble with this magazine all along," he said. "Always remember Crowninshield's *Vanity Fair* was a failure."

Meanwhile, last time I saw Barbaralee Diamonstein at the Four Seasons she said, "Congratulations on a fatter book."

"You mean, more ads?" I said. "Yes, we're pleased."

"NO." She rolled her eyes, the all-knowing media seer. "A MUCH fatter book. Aren't Condé Nast buying you-know-what?"

Another flaming rumor of our demise, that Si is buying *Connoisseur* and folding *VF* into it. (Yet another new rumor: he's buying *Interview* and ditto.) Was cheered up when *New Republic* literary ed Leon Wieseltier paid a visit from DC and went on about how girls' shoes are an index to good sex and reminded me of the pink high heels I was wearing when he first came in to see me.

Monday, August 27, 1984

I am on the Jitney back to NYC after Ben Bradlee's birthday party at Grey Gardens in East Hampton. I had forgotten how vivid Sally had made the house, the chintz sofas and curtains, the white wicker and flowers. It was odd to think that it's three years since the operatic interlude of our wedding in their garden.

227

Mort Zuckerman came with Gloria Steinem, whom I liked much more than the last time, talking separately from the men. In fact it was an evening when I felt much warmer to the women in general. Nora Ephron, Sally, Lorne Michaels's wife, Susan, and Gloria. We stood in a corner and talked, for some reason, about exhibitionists. "A girlfriend of mine went through a phase where guys in suits were always jerking off at her on the subway," Susan Michaels said. Gloria was just passing the group and immediately stopped. "Maybe I should stick around here," she said, in her low, ironic voice. "Maybe this group is interesting."

Nora said she had a friend who for a long time was always followed by dwarves. "That's funny," Gloria said, "I had a period when I kept going on talk shows and finding I was on with a celebrity dwarf. One time we were all asked what our biggest problem was, and the dwarf said — his career! Can you imagine a female dwarf saying that?"

It was so much nicer to be with this crowd than it was the night before we got married in 1981. I remember walking along the East Hampton beach with Harry in a love cloud, so happy we had each other in the midst of a smug media power elite who all knew one another and understood the same references and jokes. I still see this East Coast media crowd as pretty pleased with their insider status, but so are we now, I suppose, or on our way to be, and perhaps since we arrived as uptight Londoners it's not surprising we had to earn the right of acceptance. I felt happy because so many people there seemed to have read the last issue of *VF* and be talking genuinely about the details of articles.

Of course the chintz glory of Grey Gardens made me itch to get started on decorating Quogue. On Saturday night, Ed and Carol Victor came over for supper and we picnicked in front of the fire as the sky went pink beyond the dormer windows. I want to build a wonderful deck and make it more private with beach pines, and put up a beach hut and build a pool and add on a study and make it all light and white and fresh like Sally has. Have to write a book to pay for it.

Mort now seems to be offering Harry the editorial director job at *US News*. It's head spinning. Harry's just got up to speed as editor in chief of Atlantic Monthly Press, where he's been signing up books, and commuting to Boston, and now Mort wants him to do the two jobs and triangulate between Boston, New York, and Washington. Insane, but Harry, being insane himself, will probably do it.

Another rabid week in the *VF* hotbox. Charles Churchward is pushing a hip Japanese artist who wants to do street-life scenes and fads for us. We all sat around and had a "fad" meeting for ideas. Miles, white with flu and his usual premenstrual tension, said, "NO one does break dancing anymore. It's ROSARIES everyone's into."

Charles said thoughtfully, "We have to think of a fad that will last till February because Yosuki takes three months to finish an assignment."

"Then it's not a fucking fad, is it?" Miles grumped.

Michael Roberts has suddenly become overtense and fed up with being in NYC and told me he may leave at Christmas to go back to London. He hates the weather. He's sick of Alex as an uncertain, competitive force. He feels alienated by the American obsession with product and performance. He said he also feels black in New York in a way he didn't in London. Taxis often won't stop for him. He was shown the service entrance when he went to a fancy apartment recently, which understandably really pissed him off. I took him out to see the new Prince movie and dinner afterward at Un Deux Trois. I told him Harry and I only cope with NYC by subscribing to *Country Life* and looking at ads for pink stone houses in Gloucestershire. When Harry joined us later, Michael seemed genuinely thrilled. Perhaps it reminded him of happy early life at *The Sunday Times* in London. New York life is so harsh. I hadn't thought about how much it means to Michael to be able to confide his angst with the people from his old life he most trusts. I feel closer to both him and Miles in New York than I did in London. We share the past and every so often it needs to be reaffirmed. I still keep expecting Michael to lash out with his old scorpion sting, but the hardness of the experience here is solidifying his own strength and the feline mind games are reducing. The next day in the office he looked up from a fashion sketch he was doing — his tall frame stooped over the layout table — with a smile of childlike warmth.

Sunday, September 2, 1984

Summer is fading, fading, fading. I dread the renewed velocity! Joan Buck made a good observation on the phone. That in the first year you live in New York the city tries to do you in. That's exactly how I feel. Getting the cable guy to show up takes Herculean bilateral negotiations. All deliveries, it seems, are scheduled when they only know for a certainty you won't be in to receive them. Just when I got settled into the apartment, scaffolding goes up in front and a lung-corroding, evil-smelling paint is slapped on, giving us both sore throats and stinging eyes. I sometimes think my rubber plants will attack me in the middle of the night. And I feel broke all the time despite earning so much money.

I know it's hugely unwise to buy the house on a land lease, which will make it a depreciating asset. I just love it so much and want to stay in Quogue forever.

Si is coming to dinner on Thursday. I've asked him with Robert Hughes and John Guare and then ten people afterward for brandy and coffee. I have made it lightweight and colorful now that I see Si's longing to be with bohemian people. His own friends all seem fairly inexcusable. Roy Cohn, for God's sake? Si seems to love thugs who give him a frisson of toughness. I am sure all the weird preponderance of modern art represents an oddity of Alfred Bloomingdale proportions. He is the only person apart from me and Michael who likes our cover of Paloma Picasso sneering out of a vicious pink gash of a mouth (which is fortunate, since he is the only person who matters). "I think it's great poster art," he told me in that shy, curiously chubby voice. But he probably just likes women who give him a hard time.

I am making a study of the merely rich versus the really rich. There is really nothing weirder than the latter . . . In his own way Si is just as ruthless as Rupert and the warmth he exudes when he feels like it is mostly transactional. There is a very cold detachment underneath that could make the inconceivable become the doable very quickly if it presented him with a solution.

Monday, September 10, 1984

A very productive week, albeit tough. PVZ
urged me to stop hemming and hawing and
reduce staff. She flipped open a folder with
all the salaries in it and we went down the
roster. We discussed tactics, football-huddle
style, then separated and charged into the
game. First, Pat Towers. PVZ got her to admit
how unhappy she is and airplaned her into
Vogue Features. Next Suzanne Stephens. I
told her I wanted to convert her from full-
time staff to writing contract. I think it actually is what she wanted and she waxed happy.
Next, Daphne Davis. The ditziness is out of
control and she wants my attention all the
time. The recent discovery that she has a large
private income made me feel less bad about
telling her I had too many staff and not
enough pages. It seems to go a lot better
when I make it economic, not about performance. She took it like a soldier. The only
one that went badly was Suzanne's assistant,
and that's because PVZ delegated her deputy
to have the conversation. We had agreed the
assistant would get a job at *House & Garden,*
but the HR deputy instead told her she would
have to "rove" around Condé Nast. Hysteria
ensued with me feeling like Klaus Barbie
until PVZ managed to magic the job back
from *House & Garden.* Because of our friendship, I asked Pam McCarthy to talk to John

233

Heilpern about moving from an executive job to a writing contract but fear he will demand I fire him just to torment me. He's so talented but refuses to take any direction when it doesn't work. I hope our friendship survives.

There was a lot of wobbliness in the staff at so many departures, but it was a huge relief to feel *VF* finally has the people I want and it needs. H and I went downtown to Bob and Victoria Hughes's for dinner. They had the languorous Brit writer James Fox, the book editor Shelley Wanger with boyfriend David Mortimer, Peter Duchin, the society band leader, and Brooke Hayward, the Hollywood princess and writer. Bob was in wonderful form, bounding around in a striped shirt and red suspenders, cooking the salmon he'd caught in Alaska. Victoria is beautiful, young, and an ex–art student I would guess who fell in love with him, which God knows is easy to do. Bob told me the intriguing fact that Si is crazy about electric trains. On Saturday mornings, Bob said, Si can be seen browsing around SoHo, looking at art and wearing a huge leather coat, with his driver crawling behind. The driver, says Bob, has been known to pull up at a deserted parking lot and take out an electric train set, which Si proceeds to operate by remote control. Can it be true? It's too delicious if it is. Bob absolutely shares my perception of the marvel of Alex. "He is extraordinary, isn't he?" he said. "He used to keep old Sam Newhouse — a Velázquez dwarf with a will of steel, by the way — under control in a way that no one else could. I once said to Alex, how do you keep him so cowed? And he said, 'Well, you know, I find it very easy. Sam is a man who feels the need to change his tie every day.' " "And you know," continued Bob, "he was right. The Velázquez dwarf appeared one day in a wide Mr. Fish tie, the next in a bow tie, but Alex has worn the same Savile Row knitted tie in a variety of dark colors for thirty years. That's confidence. He spent the last three decades knocking up enormous sculptures and managing the most voluminous social life in New York. Did you know he was a champion skier at a time when skis were twenty feet long?"

I drank it all in, adding it to my rich picture of them all. I found Peter Duchin hard to take and wonder why Bob is so enamored of him. Too much name dropping at deafening volume. Every name that came up he had to show he knew some inside information about. I had my small triumph, however, when he said, "Wayne Lawson? Doesn't he play tenor saxophone? I know him well." Hah! No you don't, chum! I DID like Shelley Wanger, though. She is subtle and thoughtful and sophisticated and her boyfriend, David Mortimer, is refreshingly low-key, too. Also liked Bob's agent, Lynn Nesbit, with her short, chic hair and glistening tanned neck. She and Duchin pounded the conversational ball back and forth over the salmon. The next day James Fox called me up and said in his attenuated voice, "I didn't understand a word of what anybody said last night. What is this New York chat all about?"

Next night was our own dinner for Si and Victoria and I was relieved the Hugheses didn't bail, and in fact showed up early, looking well groomed, which was a very nice gesture on their part, realizing that having my boss to dinner was important to me. Five minutes before the guests arrived, I saw that the dinner table was too small and the engaging out-of-work thespian who came to cook from Chelsea Foods did a brilliant switch with the kitchen table. The dinner was a howling success. John Guare talked to me about the Goodman Theatre and the Chicago movement. "In two years' time it will be somewhere else," he said. "The magic moves on." That thought about the transience of magic stayed with me. I want to bring the magic to *Vanity Fair* and it's hard to know at this point whether I will succeed. Si was warm and relaxed but seemed older in the presence of his wife, who on second meeting seemed less likely to be wearing exotic underwear. The only time Si got really animated was when I touched on the daily domestic struggle of New York life.

"Struggle!" he erupted, as I wiped down the sleeve of his jacket that he had unfortunately dipped into a boat of lemon sauce. "Struggle! Every day is a struggle! It's a fight for survival! Not to get killed! I come from a privileged environment but I saw the example — every day! Struggle!" He relapsed into relative calm after that, leaving me to wonder what on earth had gone on behind closed doors in his youth. He left early as always and the last people to go were Michael Roberts and Bob Colacello, who sat on the sofa reminiscing about working with Truman Capote at *Interview.* I heard Colacello wail, "Truman was such a liar! We'd send him to Miami and the next thing we'd hear was he had been sighted at Dallas airport!"

By Friday, the strain of all this boss entertaining wiped me out. H left for London to see his kids so I left the city for Quogue on the seven p.m. Jitney with Miles. He's been a lovely guest this weekend, wandering about in his pajamas and coming in from the beach with shells he suggested for my new color scheme. "Ticking would be a good idea. This is a ticking shell." We walked along the beach on Friday night under an enormous moon, talking about the *VF* office, and he rebuked me when I said, "I feel so sorry for Daphne Davis. She has no life."

"Perhaps," said Miles. "She has a wonderful aunt. People construct different emotional realities for themselves. Think of Quentin Crisp and his bonkers room. He's happy. Everyone has different ways of coping."

He's right, of course, and my remark was both bourgeois and patronizing. I asked him if he will go back to London anytime soon. "I think not," he said as we trudged along the sand in the moonlight. "I think I may have left London for good. But that doesn't mean I'll ever absorb America. Fenimore Cooper will never mean anything to me. But it doesn't mean I'll ever go back."

I sometimes feel there's a bravery, even nobility, to people who leave their own country for some other dream. It makes you so vulnerable. There is a bit of my own expatriate heart that's frozen, not here, not there, a lonely thing.

Friday, September 14, 1984

Just realized in horror I missed Mum's birthday yesterday. Something I have never ever done before. When I called her she pretended not to mind but I could tell she feels she's losing me. I felt upset thinking of her in the house in Spain with the cats, wondering why I was silent. We were always such bfs. Our special time after she picked me up from school and we had tea together in the kitchen unloading my day. I think of the jangle of her coin bracelet when she came in from dinner and climbed immediately to my room to kiss me good night in a warm whiff of Je Reviens.

Mum, I miss you and will never forget your birthday again. I wrote a note telling her how much I love her.

Tuesday, September 18, 1984

Life is unmanageable. My oven has a cock-roach in it. I am trying to give a dinner party for Alex and spare men keep dropping out. I feel I must be especially nice to him as Si keeps calling down with negative stats from his damn reader research, which focus-groups every page of the mag and finds, surprise surprise, that people are more interested in movie stars than they are in the book reviews. H and I are both knocked out by the New York pace. Last night we were both so tired after pulverizing days, we came home at nine and fell asleep without eating. Nicole Wisniak, the editor of the French luxury vanity mag *Egoïste* that the chic crowd all adore, came in from Paris seeking a retainer, which everyone says I should give her. She lectures me and puts the magazine down one minute while telling me how *fantastique* it is the next. My light relief is the new extrovert doorman who keeps bursting into song when I pass. Tonight he fell to his knees, singing, "Officer Krupke, I'm down on my knees!"

Saturday, September 22, 1984

I am in flight to LA for my first *VF* trip to Hollywood. Gotta get some good movie-star covers and see what's popping on the West Coast after so long holed up in long-knived Manhattan. The dinner for Alex and Tatiana had all the wrong mix. Tatiana is a barking dinosaur. Harry charmed her, fortunately. I had asked Patrick McCarthy, the editor of *WWD,* to join us with the German film director Volker Schlöndorff, who I thought would spew high Kultur, but Volker dropped out, or rather, more aggravating, said he couldn't show up till ten. Then he showed up at eight, beaming that he was able to make it after all, thus throwing out all my schemes of who sat with whom, and in the hasty relocation of placements everyone was sitting with the wrong person. Volker was sitting too far away from Alex and Tatiana, with whom he had much in common, and cocky, brash Patrick McCarthy obviously bored Alex, who regarded him as a mere midmanagement fellow. I realized in a blinding flash, seeing him with Tatiana after so long, that Alex is probably gay or, at any rate, somewhere on the borderline in the Edward, Prince of Wales genre, i.e., in the lifelong thrall of one woman who can sustain a Mrs. Simpson–like dragqueen fascination. Maybe that's the secret in those dark, fathomless eyes . . . Bob Hughes told me that Alex had once said to him, "Do you think Si is morally weak?" which is generational code for a sexuality question that also very likely betrays his private attitude toward himself. It explains some of Alex's opaqueness and the violence of his art. He flings all that fury that he may be "morally weak" against a canvas, and probably weeps into the lap of Tatiana when he's done. Anyway, despite this interesting fictional insight, the dinner party was hell.

So was the rest of the week, thanks to David O'Brasky, who can be tone-deaf as to how to get business. We went to a hugely embarrassing lunch with the Philip Morris account, who want to pull out their spreads, as they only came in with ads in the first place because of warm relations with David's predecessor in the job, Joe Corr. However, O'Brasky still kept trashing the previous *VF* regime, resolutely oblivious to the increasing stone face of the William Morris exec. Even the choice of lunch venue was all wrong, a very tight private room with a shut door and no air, from which you could still hear the extremely noisy Italian restaurant beyond. It felt like *The Last Supper.*

Before we got there, O'Brasky told me all the cigarette brands Morris could give us, then said, "And there's a new one — Parliament, they're working up for the end of 1985." So when the boss man said at the end of David's rabid sales pitch, "Well, Parliament you will certainly be a candidate for," it was obvious — to me anyway — that that was Madison Avenue parlance for "You're not going to get Benson and Hedges or anything else this year, chum. Line up for the never never." I felt like emptying the red wine over O'Brasky's head for blowing it so monumentally and not even realizing it.

On top of that was another wan attempt at a pitch at a dinner at the Diamonstein-Spielvogels' Park Avenue apartment in honor of our mutual friend the Duke professor Joel Fleishman. Their insanely grandiose apartment is poised over Manhattan like an airborne Versailles. The table was set with silver place mats you could see your face in. Every time I looked down I stared forlornly up my own nostrils. In the dining room the acoustics were so bad it was like conversing in a swimming bath. Carl Spielvogel sat at the end of the table, a stuffed pelican pontificating about his latest bout of foreign travel to China, Bali, and the Soviet Union. A football field away, Barbaralee sat opposite him, oozing cultural self-esteem. I hyped VF's new success like crazy and pretended fascination with every one of Carl's early "nailing the account" stories, but he didn't take the bait. At the end of dinner he threw the conversation open. Harry, who had contained himself till now, leapt in with some ill-timed remark about the bizarre US obsession with deficit reduction, talking forty times too fast as everyone stared at him, pickled in pomposity. Then a handsome figure dressed in liberal beige who runs the New York transport office delivered a great sonorous speech about how he had been in Europe all summer brooding on how Reagan's grossly unfair policies had somehow produced the biggest US boom in memory. Let them eat place mats.

To cap it off, as I fled the city on Friday on the four p.m. train to Quogue with Harry, the lawyer came on to say that the mortgage for 160 Dune Road had been denied. It was crushing news, just when we had got to the signing of the land lease. On Saturday night we had to go through dinner with John Post, who is currently staying at his beach house next door to us. I felt sure his hard Yankee stare could penetrate that we didn't have a way to pay for 160, but we proceeded with a full-force charm offensive to buy ourselves time. All of this madness has brought H and me so close. We have found our spiritual home in the US together and at the same time, and that at last eliminates our twenty-five-year age difference. The feeling I always had in England that there was this other married life he had before me that I could never compete with has vanished. We are in everything together now.

Yippee! I love Beverly Hills! I love the climate, the smells, the palm trees, the shiny surfaces of Hollywood people. I feel I will end up here, that it's where I ought to be. I have avoided the movie world ever since childhood made me jaded but now feel the glossy pull again . . .

Maybe Hollywood feels less judgmental than NYC, where the hammer is always about to fall on some frail career. Here, you can write your own story. Careers are reinvented every day. I have felt a growing hunger for chancier people, and to talk to the directors, writers, producers, actors of my early youth.

I went with Horst to see the "superagent" Swifty Lazar at his Trousdale house, perched on the hills overlooking the flat roofs and the sparkling swimming pools of the people he represents. Swifty is tiny and bald and hairy in the wrong places. From the back his bald head and ancient baby's neck look like crinkled foreskin. Just to be perverse, Michael Roberts wants to photograph him for a fashion feature. Swifty perched on a coffee table with his tiny legs swinging, holding forth about stars having no clue how to entertain anymore. "Warren Beatty? Lives in a hotel suite. Al Pacino? Lives in a truck. I don't know what's the matter with them.

They don't have a chef. They don't buy art. Debra Winger? What can I say? Never shaves under her arms."

I felt the warm familial glow of all the vanished bullshit artists of Dad's world in my teens. Our new LA editor, Caroline Graham, bullied the financier Selim Zilkha and his wife into giving me a dinner at another hilltop dream house in Bel Air. Caroline is a gold-dust hire. I found her at a dinner party at Kay Graham's house on Martha's Vineyard (she's the wife of Kay's son William) the summer we got married and filed her away for future hire. She's a gorgeous reedy blonde with a great Rolodex and a wicked social eye. She's now repping us in LA and she's proving, like Sarah Giles, A-plus with wrangling because she's so irresistibly charming. I was seated next to the grizzled screenwriter Robert Towne, who's a darkly funny guy. Towne said he wants to do a piece on being "serviced," the concentric rings of agents, business managers, plant doctors, men Fridays who keep the talent from taking responsibility for themselves. He is trapped and bemused by an outrageous custody battle at the moment. "Psychiatrist assholes who've never met me keep standing up in court and testifying about whether or not I have the right to see my kid . . . That's because my wife is a hostile, whacked-out drunk laying all the weirdness on me she can think of." The British film director Tony Richardson on my other side looked down at him with a small smile. "It's your fault, Robert," he said. "You don't pay attention. It's the same when you're making a movie. You should always be in control. The worst thing that can happen to you is the money people telling you not to worry. That way spells disaster. People telling you not to worry your pretty head about cost. Fastest way to lose control."

That spoke to me, I must say, about the way Condé Nast keeps the editors away from the P&L, which seemed great at first but then becomes a source of vulnerability.

I loved all the cross chat from movie people with the lights of the sprawling city of LA sparkling beyond us, the warmth of the air out on the terrace, and — what you rarely hear at NYC dinner parties — music playing in the background. The soundtrack of *The Big Chill.* (Soundtracks seem to be big in LA. Mozart is the soundtrack to *Amadeus.*)

I felt I had been in a dreamy bubble for three days when I got home and immediately felt guilty because Harry had been busy trying to rescue the mortgage on Quogue before the signing day, and the only way to get it on time was to bite the bullet and ask Mort Zuckerman to guarantee a loan, which, bless him, he did. Citibank then gave us a check and we drove like lunatics to the closing on Friday with our lawyer and the vendor, Mrs.

Clarholme, to whom we had been posing as affluent upper-class landowners. When we got there we found the plot had thickened unbelievably. Our own lawyer, a red-faced local idiot named Mr. Morgan, had made an offer himself on the house for more money, which is why things had fallen apart! The drunken clown had got greedy when he saw how cheap the house was and delayed all the lease agreements needed for the mortgage approval. But we rumbled his cheesy game and signed.

After the stress of the day we drove in stunned silence with the keys to 160 Dune Road and entered what is now OUR HOUSE. In the shiplike upstairs living room every dormer window was pink from the sunset. The dune had a lunar look, the grass ruffled by a little breeze. The distant hoot of the Long Island Rail Road car sounded like a ghost train. We walked up the overgrown strip of sand for our first sight of the foaming, frosted waves and were overwhelmed by feelings of happiness and peace.

I felt a wonderful union with Harry, more perfect than any I have felt before in the tumult of the last few years. It's funny. When you marry, everything tells you this should be the moment of commitment. But actually in the turmoil of our jostling careers, for me that moment is now. I realize I haven't really felt married till the day we signed for the house. I have been putting off that moment in the turbulence of the move to America. As we stood on the dune together, looking out at the sea, I knew once and for all that my vivid, loving, courageous husband is the only man I want to share the breadth and hope of this long, white beach with. I want our child to be conceived here, I want this to be our special place where I can be with Harry always. His love has always kept me together and now he has sealed it with a perfect house where I can dream beside him for the rest of our days, no matter what's happening beyond its four walls.

Columbus Day: Monday, October 8, 1984

The end-of-year issue of *VF* is going to bed! The Hall of Fame idea has worked a treat. We nominated ten people as the year's tops with fabulous pictures by Annie (we dumped the idea of casting another ten into oblivion as people these days are so thin-skinned and monthly mags sit around too long with umbrage mounting). The key is not just the choice of person and the portrait but the "nominating" copy that goes with it to explain why they deserve inclusion. "Because he, because she, because because . . ." It has to be the crispest, most polished house style. Much harder to do than it looks, and I recruited a collaborative wit circle that included Miles, Jim Wolcott, Schiff, John Heilpern (yes, he came back in), and Bob Colacello in brainstorming sessions to get the captions right. Such a fun process. Working with Annie on this made me see what an amazing perfectionist she is. Most hardworking photographer alive. She spends hours in the art department with Ruth, arguing over the picture edit. She will travel halfway around the world to get one more angle she didn't get at the time. With Annie, the shoot is never over and it's never good enough. "It would be so much better if he'd taken his shirt off/if she'd slicked back her hair/if I could have shot it in the morning/evening/if we'd done it in the rain." It leads to irate phone calls, fighting the expenditure or the deadline as she darkly vows, "I will pay for it myself. If I fly through Frankfurt I can get back the same night. I will get an ad to pay for it. Let's just kill the shoot." Until one of us (usually me) gives in.

Harry has been in NYC this week before he goes to DC for the *US News* editorial director job. (No, he couldn't resist the siren call of news.) I can see why a man loves to come home to a welcoming wife. It was fun (and sexy) to be the returning husband for a few days. And poignant because it was our last week together before he goes off to DC. It feels so wrong to be separated again now. After an early dinner we snuggled in bed and watched George H. W. Bush murder Geraldine Ferraro in the VP debate. I want to root for a historic woman but it was agony. Her performance reminded me of how I blew my first speech to advertisers; she looked down all the time, wore her reading glasses, and came off like a suburban schoolteacher addressing a parent-teacher meeting.

We had a dinner party at the apartment that was successful in spite of itself. The ed of *Time,* Ray Cave, whose wife is the ed of *People,* Pat Ryan, Lewis Lapham (editor of *Harper's,* what a star), Arianna Stassinopoulos, Derry Moore (passing through from London), and the First Amendment lawyer Floyd Abrams and his wife. At twelve fifteen Ray and Lapham were in full cry arguing about which covers would or wouldn't go down in Sioux Falls. I saw the chef staring menacingly through the door at us. Slipping quietly into the steamy galley, I asked him what his problem was.

"My problem is, I wanna go," he said. "My problem is it's twelve fifteen and I wanna get my shit out of here. Tell them I have to move my shit."

"Your shit," I squeaked, "will have to wait! That's the editor of *Time* magazine sitting in there and you will just have to wait to move your shit!"

I slunk back to the table, where Mrs. Abrams had just launched into her description of serving in the Israeli air force, with the chef still in my eye line, glaring at me and chewing gum. In the end he burst through with his backpack, slammed the door, and left. They all stopped talking and looked up. But stayed on till two in the morning arguing about the nature of celebrity. (Money in motion, Lewis Lapham called it, which I liked.)

Monday, October 15, 1984

I went with H to DC to settle him in and felt like a mother taking her child back to boarding school. I feel very glum because we have become so intertwined living together in New York. I hate him doing this job but recognize he must have something big of his own. I'd love him to have stayed in the publishing gig, but, typically, Mort has lost interest in the book company now that he's bought *US News.* I don't want to return to the lousy commuter marriage we had when H was at Duke. Still, whatever pain it causes me, the pleasure of seeing him back in a news context is gratifying. I suddenly wish I was in DC, too. I had the subversive thought of how nice it would be to get a big fat Condé Nast writing contract and live in one of those sweet Georgetown terrace houses off N Street with gardens and room for cats, instead of battling the wild beast of NYC alone.

There was a fiftieth birthday party for David O'Brasky at La Reserve. I wish I could have set it to music. An all-cast song with the title "Hot Book." Because that was the refrain of all the toasts — that David was the king of the Hot Book, the man who had worked in the best places at the time when it was good. Most of the Condé publishers and ad sales men were there. I ran into one of ours, Tom Florio, who I see every morning sliding out of the elevator wearing mirrored shades, looking like one of the Sharks out to kill a Jet. Tonight he was dapper in a suit. "I'm a guy in a hurry," he said to me, which felt even more like a line from a musical. O'Brasky was so pleased with all the attention that his face swelled up like a Halloween pumpkin. His friends had done up a huge board titled "The Days of David O'Brasky," comprised of all the magazines he's worked for — *Esquire, New York, Prime Time, VF* — with his name circled at the top of the mastheads. Looking at the great covers of the magazines he has worshipped from the wrong side, I felt the undertow of heroism (and pathos) that went into all the effort and mistakes. For me it was an American magazine education, hearing the Madison Avenue war stories from the bashed and boozy faces who had made the rounds selling space for Harold Hayes and Clay

252

Felker and Arnold Gingrich, singing their ballad of the Hot Book.

Monday, October 22, 1984

Holed up in bed last night and watched the second and final presidential debate between Reagan and Mondale.

Reagan improved on his doddering performance in the first debate, but he still has cascades of wrinkly melted plastic neck and that maddening oldster vagueness. In his closing statement he wandered off into an endless, rambling, baffling soliloquy about how he was once asked to write a letter to be put in a time capsule to be opened a hundred years from now and how he was driving down the California coast on the Pacific Highway and wondering what people would think a hundred years from now and how we have terrible weapons that can destroy civilization but maybe we won't and how we have a rendezvous with destiny and how George Bush is the finest vice president ever and . . . Finally the moderator was merciful enough to interrupt gently and say time was up.

Mondale seems a decent, intelligent, slightly boring fellow who would make an excellent prime minister of Norway. Needless to say, his command of the details of policy is clearly superior, but he "lost" anyway. All it took for Reagan to win the debate was a one-liner, obviously prepared in advance and delivered with movie-star panache. When one of the panel of journalists predictably brought up the fact that Reagan is already the oldest president in history and might not have the stamina to do the job in a crisis, he did one of his genial head shakes and said, "I will not make age an issue of this campaign. I am not going to exploit, for political purposes, my opponent's youth and inexperience." That's the only thing anyone will remember about this debate. All Mondale could do was laugh helplessly along with everybody else. He knew it was over.

Thursday, October 25, 1984

Closed my first *VF* Christmas issue. Huge sweat but I love it. We've done a great back-of-the-book holiday reading section with pieces by William Styron, Jerome Robbins, Sidney Lumet, Jessica Mitford, and Jim Wolcott. The Hall of Fame is fantastic. Copy we slaved over a bit arch but I still like it. "It was a year when America checked out of the Betty Ford Center and was proud, proud, proud. Aging was hip (Bardot, Steinem, Loren, and MacLaine turned fifty) but aged was hipper (Vreeland, Eudora Welty, and Ronald Reagan). And though the president said that the country wasn't hungry, Texaco ate Getty, Chevron ate Gulf, Mobil ate Superior, and the Arabs ate crow." Best Annie pics are of Aaron Spelling in bed, Springsteen against a sheath of fire, and the black-and-white-attired decorator Andrée Putman against a wall of checkered tiles. Also the sulky, Elvisy Donald Trump "because he's a brass act. And he owns his own football team. And he thinks he should negotiate arms control agreements with the Soviet Union."

Had a drama with the Joan Collins *Dynasty* cover, which featured her with a gun at her head and a line saying, "But darling you know I am bulletproof." Unfortunately her boyfriend Jon-Erik Hexum blew his brains out on the set of a soap opera with a pistol that was loaded with blanks. Thankfully we hadn't gone to press — memo to self, gun covers are a lousy idea anyway — and instead we went with something much better. "She Rhymes with Rich," after Barbara Bush's great comment about Geraldine Ferraro. Stephen Schiff has done a sparkling essay about the *Dynasty* era to go with it. Plenty of mags would put Joan on the cover, but not with Schiff's smart deconstruction of what *Dynasty* says about America. I think readers are now understanding the mix can include anyone we happen to find interesting, high or low, and any topic that illuminates the zeitgeist. The unevenness of content is beginning to settle down into something fully baked, glamorous but substantial. What unites it is the voice and the clear visual identity.

I hate Harry being in DC! I feel rage that he has jeopardized our lovely intimacy. But I can't blame him as I always choose career, too, and then regret it. I'm less noble about dealing with it than he is. Zuckerman loaned us his DC town house on Volta Place for the weekend. On Sunday we had breakfast in the garden there in the glorious fall sunshine and it felt just like Ponsonby Terrace in the old days and made us both feel mopey. Contact with the rich is ineffably spoiling. One night on Volta Place and I was longing for the same big fluffy towels and membrane-thin fluttering white sheets and the cook on hand to do a delicious dinner.

Tuesday, November 6, 1984

Reagan won reelection. Landslide and no surprise. It's a TV era and Mondale had zero performance skills. People who can't communicate should not even contemplate going into politics. Most of Reagan's voters would probably be better off under a President Mondale, but that didn't matter. I had Marie watching the returns at the Georgetown house of Averell and Pamela Harriman, with Democratic old guarders Ed Muskie, Evangeline Bruce, and co so she could record the rout of the liberal establishment close up. It was a death watch, she said, as if the make-the-world-better–ites sitting watching the returns under the van Gogh painting of white gardenias had just been mown down all at once by flashing new Buicks.

Tuesday, November 13, 1984

Social energy even more ramped up by the Reagan reelection. The White House calls the shots of what's in and what's out. *Time* magazine has done a cover story on the new concern with "civility." Credits the new mood to all the mink coats at the inauguration and the $210,000 new chinaware at the White House.

We are seeing the invasion of DC by California and Park Avenue, the fusion of *Women's Wear Daily* values with *Washington Post* power watching, a cast of characters who see everything through the lens of Hollywood and Le Cirque. It's perfect fodder for a magazine called *Vanity Fair.* I have been experiencing the endless round of black-tie dinners and openings as a trivial sidebar to the main event. But now it seems at this moment they *are* the main event, central to understanding how the money moves around and why. It could all collapse and we will see it as some fin de siècle gallery of grotesques and wish we had been more attentive.

This evening I attended Mica Ertegun's black-tie dinner in honor of the opera singer

Beverly Sills at the Metropolitan Club. Hosted by Ungaro and some new perfume. The Metropolitan Club was so baroque, glittering with gilded ceilings, great heavy knotted gold chairs, and enormous flower arrangements fit for the death of a Hapsburg monarch. And the clothes! The gleaming swaths of pearls, the peacock-blue taffeta winged shoulders, the frothy stand-up collars. I found myself nose to nose with Betsy Bloomingdale, flat as an ironing board in a scarlet and cobalt velvet harlequin dress, her crinkly eyes betraying nothing of her recent Vicki Morgan travails or of Nick's searing piece. Bianca Jagger is still more beautiful than anyone. Ahmet Ertegun wheezed away about some S and M bar in Manhattan he enjoys where no one is dressed from the waist downward. Mica, with her lacquered hair and perfect neat mouth, seems to have made a career out of the enigma of their marriage. It's all too fascinating to ignore and we need it to come alive in our pages. Norman Mailer was there, swashbuckling away about how journalism becomes daunting as you fear your ability to see, hear, and react freshly is replaced by a desire to shore up, consolidate, and plumb deeper. Is this another way of saying "selling out"? Wouldn't the young Mailer have defenestrated this dinner? Easy to be sucked in.

On the way out, my eyes met the glassy

stare of Leo Lerman on the way in and I stared right back.

1985
TEN THOUSAND NIGHTS IN A COCKTAIL DRESS

Thursday, January 10, 1985

A new year, new determined goals. I am discontented with the next issue. British whimsy like Michael's fashion feature on the rise of the "Urban Turban" is fun, but it's feeling all dessert, no entrée. AND I WILL SOLVE THIS.

I have a platonic ideal of what the mix in *VF* should be — that sweet spot between aspiration and news hunger — but achieving it is a crapshoot. To add beef I assigned a macho literary essay on the anniversary of the fall of Saigon to Pete Hamill, but it somehow feels like a refugee from an old *Esquire.*

My lodestar for a great mag is big, tall *Nova* (the British monthly glossy of the seventies edited by the excitable Yorkshireman Dennis Hackett). Its clean, fierce graphic design and its confrontational covers were masterpieces of editorial point of view, with "talking headlines" splashed over images that grabbed you as you passed the newsstand. I still remember the one of a gurgling baby centered under the logo with harsh black lettering beneath: "The Perfect Baby or the Biggest Threat Since the Atom Bomb?"

Hackett once said to me that you have to be able to throw a magazine on the floor opened to any page and instantly know what magazine you're looking at and who the reader is. That's already true of *VF*. It has quickly found a strong, vital identity in voice and in visuals. The house style (a blending of me and Miles and Schiff and Wolcott) is very much there. But not the consistent, essential element of a satiating story, the one that tells you, the reader, who you are or who you want to be.

Friday, March 8, 1985

Boom! Si bought *The New Yorker*! He paid $142 million, a sum that gives me a stomach-ache. The staff there are all fretting and fussing and crying into their lace handkerchiefs. They should be so lucky. I know firsthand how much Si worships that magazine and reads every word. Apparently someone there took our current Annie cover of naked Jerry Hall in tumbled sheets and replaced her head with an image of the *New Yorker*'s mascot, Eustace Tilley. There are rumblings Si may remove William Shawn as editor and install

Bob Gottlieb from Knopf, but again I can't believe it. Si reveres Mr. Shawn, as he always calls him, as a kind of literary shaman, a divine force who conjures imperishable words out of writers, words that often end up as Random House books, which I guess is part of his full-circle vision of his publishing empire. What does it mean for us? Si has a new love is what it means, which is unsettling.

Wednesday, March 20, 1985

My industrious hire from *The Sunday Times* in London, James Danziger, showed his worth as features ed of *Vanity Fair* by getting us a shoot with the Reagans at the White House through his and their Hollywood friend Doug Wick. We needed this scoop so bad, there was no chance we could fuck it up. So I recruited Harry Benson, the excitable Scottish photographer with toilet-brush hair who talks so much and works so fast that he has managed to get six presidents to give up human moments. "I'm better with Republicans," he told me. "Democrats are always a wee bit tricky." Also got Chris Buckley to write the piece to go with it about their marriage, which should be delicious.

My heart was beating so fast that I hardly noticed the august surroundings as we were ushered into a visitor's waiting room at the

White House. I was terrified there would be a last-minute cancellation. The press aide informed us that the president and Mrs. Reagan were due at a state banquet they were hosting for Argentine president Raúl Alfonsín but would pause for a swift formal portrait in the Map Room. As soon as the aide had departed, Benson produced a boom box from his bag and unscrolled a white background to create a portable studio. I thought the idea sounded really hokey when he told me, but he clearly knew what he was doing.

At six forty-five we heard the familiar mellow burr of the approaching commander in chief accompanied by the light social laughter of Nancy Reagan. They entered the Map Room dressed in their elegant best for the black-tie function: Nancy in a slinky jet-beaded Galanos gown, Ronnie in a Fred Astaire–fit tux, with patent crenellated hair and cordial, twinkly blue eyes. Benson immediately hit the switch of the boom box and flooded the room with the old Sinatra classic "Nancy (With the Laughing Face)." Reagan paused for a moment, looking first at us and then at Nancy with one raised eyebrow, Clark Gable style.

"I love this song, honey," she said. "Let's dance." The president replied with a line that might have been written for any number of vintage B movies: "We can't keep the president of Argentina waiting, Nancy."

"Oh, Ronnie," she teased, grabbing him by his broad shoulders, "let him wait!" She kicked back her leg (click-whirr click-whirr click-whirr, went Harry Benson's camera), and, perhaps in a paradigm of their easy marriage, the president stopped resisting and took his wife in his arms. For the next fifteen minutes they fox-trotted blithely around the Map Room to more Sinatra oldies on Benson's cassette player, exchanging the gossip of the day with each other as if no one else were there. I watched in silence, I could hardly breathe.

"A kiss!" shouted a now-ecstatic Benson, juggling three cameras. "Mr. President, give your wife a kiss!"

They moved closer. Their eyes closed. Their lips came together for the iconic moment that my happy heart knows is going to be flashed on TV screens over and over when it comes out. And then the Secret Service moved in and they were spirited away.

Now the pictures are spread on the *VF* light box in the office. I feel they are gold dust. The gaiety of this cover will be not just the Reagan kiss, but the kiss of life for *Vanity Fair.* The mood of the pictures is pure optimism. I've never much liked Reagan, but when I look at these pictures I have to admit he has the gift of instinctive collusion between imagery and national mood. And Nancy is critical to it. She is his joy gene. Coming out of the Carter recession, America needs this simple exuberance. Did they discuss it first? Benson never said he was bringing a boom box, so it must have been spontaneous. Their duality never fails to pick up the rhythm of what the public needs.

Tuesday, March 26, 1985

In LA for Swifty Lazar's famous annual Oscar party at Spago. Hand it to Swifty, he does know how to rope in the celebrities and, more impressive, when he's the host they actually behave. He domesticates the menagerie and they attend under his terms or not at all.

He loves every bit of it. Especially the great theatrical moment when the valet parking rises to a crescendo and the paparazzi bulbs start flashing as the stars start pouring into Spago from the award ceremony. He had so many famous faces there in the gyrating room. Andy Warhol with a tiny camera taking pictures, Michael Caine, Raquel Welch, Dennis Hopper, Linda Evans, Sally Field, who made a comically emotional Oscar acceptance speech about how we LIKE her, we really LIKE her, and Jackie Bisset, with Alexander Godunov swirling around air-kissing. Barry Diller was crammed up against the bar. "It's important to stay till just past midnight," he told me. "That's when the bullshit all

265

somehow metastasizes and you see Oscar night at its best." I read this morning that Shirley MacLaine cut me, but I didn't notice. The producer Ray Stark told me Swifty's germ phobia apparently means he has to spray with disinfectant everyone who enters his house. He said that Mary Lazar is the only woman Swifty could find to marry who was exactly room temperature.

Tuesday, April 2, 1985

The *New York Times* reporter Alex Jones slagged off *VF*'s prospects in *The New York Times* last week so I asked him to lunch. Was prepared for combat but really liked his Tennessee charm.

We had three coffee refills, which I hope affects the next round of coverage.

Our office has become a bear garden of socialites. The artist Richard Merkin, who came in to tout a new illustration, added to the turmoil this afternoon. I walked into the art department and he was perched on the edge of the layout table, shouting into the telephone.

"Have you seen this photograph of Jerry Zipkin on a camel?" I asked him, since he was sitting on the photo shoot of Iris Love's trip up the Nile with the San Francisco socialite Ann Getty and co. "Loved him. Hated her," Merkin replied, and went on shouting. Iris, a fizzy blonde archaeologist, is the love interest of Liz Smith and there will be hell to pay if I don't publish her piece. Trouble is, picture's great, copy not. Liz was a great friend of Leo and has not yet forgiven me for replacing him. Reinaldo Herrera appeared in a new cashmere overcoat, carrying a bag of pretzels. He's now a contributing editor thanks to Bob Colacello. Although he's such a courtier to the ladies who lunch, he still has news flair from his days as a talk show host in Caracas. He's out every night of the week with his wife, Carolina, the fashion designer. Half his ideas are flimflam. But the other half are things I want and he's a great barometer of who's rising and falling in the global social action. Also has a fund of new preposterous characters for us to profile and photograph. Today he starts baritone complaints about how he can't get pictures of grand houses into the mag unless the owners can be sure every other house will be grand. I tell him I can't design the magazine around his ridiculous friends. Besides, I remind him, we are soon to publish a lavish spread on the turreted palace of Princess Gloria von Thurn und Taxis, aka Princess TNT, the over-the-top German socialite Bob Colacello is obsessed with. "The Thurn und Taxis are mad," says Reinaldo, chomping on a pretzel. "Let me tell you that there are people you and I know who would simply get up and leave the room when the Thurn und Taxis walk into it."

Nick Dunne turned up to talk about stories, which added to the static because he and Reinaldo are so competitive. He tells me a Park Avenue hostess was carried out of Mortimer's at one a.m. the other night, as was Isabel Eberstadt. "It was exactly like a scene from *The Damned,*" Nick says.

Like me he is utterly fascinated and appalled by the Andrew Crispo murder case, in which a young male model was found shot and buried wearing a black leather mask following an S and M session with the creepy art dealer Crispo. It confirmed to me some of the darker currents I feel when I go to swell dinners, an underside of New York decadence. So glad Nick is on the von Bülow case. The second trial of Claus is coming up, accusing him of the attempted murder of his heiress wife, Sunny, at their Newport home by administering an overdosed insulin injection. It has left her in a coma for the rest of her life. It looks like Claus von Bülow let his wife die. At any rate, he is another dark bastard and I'd love to see him nailed. Stephen Schiff showed up to turn in his Wallis Annenberg profile. He handed me her husband's shockingly juicy divorce deposition. "Here," he said. "A treat."

Went to Brit writer Jon Bradshaw's publishing party at Elaine's and asked Tom Wolfe if he'd consider writing about the Crispo case. Would be so excellent if he would. "No writer who touches this subject can escape the mire," he says. "The filth rises over their heads. It's a serious, big subject." Which is Tom's polite, southern way of saying it's not for him.

Evening ended at a dinner party at Diane von Furstenberg's apartment with her new boyfriend, the suave Italian writer Alain El-kann. Also there, two architects, Michael Graves and Peter Marino, and Kitty Hawks, whose parents were the film director Howard Hawks and the famous social beauty Slim Keith. She reminds me of Jordan Baker in *The Great Gatsby.* Diane is obviously mad about Alain. She occasionally shot him deadly, sensuous looks over the giant tulip bowl.

The apartment was a bit suffocating with its love seats, framed ancient wallpaper, and God knows what mythic art hanging on the hectic walls. The talk was all about the erstwhile style writer of the *Times,* John Duka, and his conversion to the EST cult [Erhard Seminars Training — a two-weekend, sixty-hour, intensive consciousness seminar]. Marino said, "Isn't John Duka selling trousers at Bergdorf now?"

"He's doing PR for their menswear, yes," says DVF, who's always loyal to people who have given her good press.

"I am so pleased," said Kitty. "Such a much better career for him than that pathetic column in the *Times.*"

"Selling trousers is better than a column?" says Alain, with a small ironic smile. "Not a bookshop? Not even a stationery shop?"

"It will all pass," said Michael Graves, looking melancholy. "Like those sixteen hundred Moonie people who got married in Madison Square Garden."

I say, "That's a great story. I'd love to know what happened to those marriages."

"The same thing that happened to all our marriages," yawned Kitty Hawks.

Thursday, April 4, 1985

The Iris Love up-the-Nile saga built to a shuddering climax when she called this morning to say she wouldn't accept Sharon DeLano's editing of her piece. This is rich, given the gibberish it was when turned in and what a skillful rework Sharon has been able to do. Sharon is a great editing hire, recommended to me by the art critic John Richardson. She was on *The Movies* mag, which folded, and before that *The New York Review of Books.* She's very different from the rest of the *VF* crew. Grew up in a small ranching town in Oregon, got a master's degree, and in the early seventies drove across the country to New York in a VW bus. Before

The New York Review she had a job at a crappy publishing house in Union Square next to Max's Kansas City and proofread for *Kiss* and *Screw*. Apparently Silvers hired her for the *Review* within minutes of the interview because of the utter confidence of her literary opinions.

Sharon is living proof to me of the value of hiring on instinct and life texture rather than résumé. She has formidable intellectual rigor. Most of her writer contacts come from hanging out with Susan Sontag and a bunch of opera queens who took her to *Parsifal* and offbeat art movies. She has a fierce, graying, Louise Brooks bob, always wears black, and stomps around in scuffed cowboy boots. Iris Love picked the wrong adversary.

Ten minutes after I put the phone down on Iris, Sharon marched into my office at her most truculent, saying she was done with making nice to this crazy old bat just because her girlfriend writes a gossip column. In fact I had already decided the night before that her Iris edit was actually too light. All the asp-kissing stuff (as Sharon dubbed it) about the charming, fascinating socialites who went on the cruise has to come out. I told Sharon to deliver that message and, as predicted, Liz Smith got on the horn to give me the full Texan bawl-out. I am now as fed up with them all as Sharon. I called Iris on speaker with Sharon in the room and told her I thought Sharon had done an excellent edit, and Iris should accept her cut of five hundred words. "Let me know by two p.m. if you accept the edit, otherwise, alas, we have to cancel the piece." I went out to lunch only to find a bunch of messages from the Le Cirque mafia on return. Iris, I realized, had just shot herself in the foot by calling Ann Getty and her sidekick, the shipping millionaire Alecko Papamarkou, to complain about me, only to find they then insisted that (a) the copy had to be read by Lord Weidenfeld, who put the trip together, and (b) every person in her snapshots had to be called for permission to use them.

Perfect! Maybe I can now pull the whole pesky story, except this got Liz back on the phone. For all the bluster, the last thing Iris wanted was the loss of face that would come with having the piece killed. I placated Liz by telling her that I was very happy to publish Iris if she'd accept the edit. Then I called George Weidenfeld about the pictures, waxing astonished that Iris didn't seek permission from the people on the cruise to use private snapshots. "Call Ann Getty and tell her that," said George, "and I am sure she will understand." (Of course she will, because they all really want their pics used in *VF* but have to pretend they are furious.) This was doubly good because Ann has been in a rage with us since our front-of-book piece on her million-dollar curtains. This gave the opportunity for détente.

I called Ann full of dismayed solicitude and we both agreed that Iris is beyond the pale. She agreed to let us publish the pictures. All's well that ends well. Iris accepted the edit; we got photo permission and brought Ann Getty back on our side as well.

Friday, April 5, 1985

More social monstering.

Tea with the Houston grande dame Lynn Wyatt at the Carlyle.

Lynn is a platinum-blonde Texan Barbie doll with a wonderful, full-throated laugh. Her conversation really boils down to a series of very positive interjections. "You do it!" "Here's to you!" "And how!" It's hard to know how she can bear to be married to Oscar Wyatt, who has the mean-eyed conviviality of the old wildcatter he is. The last time I saw him at a gala, his huge body was squeezed uneasily into a dinner jacket, ready to spill out and sabotage her elegance at any minute. Still, he's paying for it all, as he never ceases to remind you (and her). "Oscar can tell exactly what carat a diamond is just by looking at it," Lynn told me.

Today she wears a wide-shouldered brown Saint Laurent suit jacket and miniskirt topped by an outsize head of flicked-up hair.

273

I am after access for pics of her new ranch in South Texas where Oscar has installed an airstrip for his 747. She tells me that Plácido Domingo had come for Easter with his three children and they shot coyote.

She has just returned from the Arctic Circle with her son Steve, who went to shoot polar bears. She and Oscar had tried living in an igloo. It's hard to imagine anyone the size of Oscar in an igloo, especially in a Stetson. "Tina, it's cold in an igloo," she says as we sip the Earl Grey. "Don't let anyone tell you different. And you have to eat seal meat so it sits in your stomach. I wore cashmere underwear, but Tina, it was cold." She promises to ask Oscar about the pictures of the ranch (who I fear will say no, as he hates publicity as much as she loves it) and begs me to come back to Houston.

The place is full of copy, I must say. We need to do a special issue on Texas. A good source would be the fashionable florist Leonard Tharp, whom I met at one of Lynn's dos during *Tatler* days. "I've done minny minny wonderful parties here," he told me. "I try and advise clients to break out of their rut. I've always thought it so awful to come into a party, look at the flowers, and say, Who died? But then why shouldn't a funeral be festive and fresh? And why can't a party have all the poetry of a funeral? I've had to explain this minny minny times."

Sunday, April 7, 1985

After this round of social frenzy I am worrying about the future of the mag. Went up to see PVZ, whom, even though she is really a corporate spy, I still value enough to use as a sounding board. She was sitting at her clean desk, looking as smooth and flawless as Scandinavian furniture. Her low, confidential voice makes you want to tell her everything.

I talk to her about my worries over Si's commitment long-term to *VF.* The ads are still not coming, even though the readers are. He said he would give it time, but will he? It's a year since my first issue. I can feel his attention turning away to *The New Yorker.* Will he feel it's a better bet to build that up and lose his ardor for *VF?* The rumors keep swirling he will fold *VF* and combine the two. He's very impetuous, I notice. When he gives up on something or someone, the light goes out of his eyes and it's all over. PVZ listened and listened like a shrink but at the end just gently told me to keep doing my job.

Tuesday, April 16, 1985

My landlord at 120 Central Park South has turned into a mafia don. First there was the time the water got turned off for two days and he refused to speak to anyone but me with the comment "Tell Tina Brown Jonny

275

Guerrero don't deal with no intermediaries."
I want to move if I can find someone to take
over the lease. Now in a new fit of Queens
queeniness, he won't allow the letting agency,
Feathered Nest (and they have sure feathered
theirs with their extortionate rates), to show
the apartment unless I am personally there.
The CPS doorman keeps turning interested
viewers away when I can't get there in time.
Jonny G. left this message with my office this
morning: "Tell Tina Brown she just gotta sit
there and let the parties in. Tell her, yeah, it's
an inconvenience. But she just gotta live with
it." Kiss my ring.

Wednesday, April 17, 1985

Leonard Lauder is very different on a business call than over dinner. Gone is the courtly
gent reminiscing about spotting me early at
Tatler. Now it was all firing circulation and
"demo" questions at breakneck speed.
(Lunch was over in forty minutes.) His banjo
eyes flickered with irritation as our ad director, Doug Johnson, O'Brasky's freckly deputy,
oversold the front-of-book ad position.
"What's your point?" Leonard barked at one
point. Doug has logorrhea, is the problem.
He means well, but it all just pours out with
no punch line. Prospects for ads, I'd say,
dubious.

Miles Chapman has been in England and

returned very confused and obviously longing to move back. The AIDS epidemic is truly
freaking him out and who can blame him.
He calls it the Terror. Photographers, writers,
actors, fashion folk are dying every day. He is
always at funerals. Having dragged him here
to be an editor, I feel responsible for him. He
asked me seriously how I thought he was doing at the office. No one writes captions and
blurbs and contents pages with the same flair
that he does — you have to have been raised
like Miles on the British tabloids with all their
disreputable energy to understand how critical a four-line blurb or a pull quote is in making a page have a voice. I told him, honestly,
that the work was wonderful but he has to
dial back the hostility toward everyone else.
He listened intensely as if he wanted me to
lay it on. It was pouring rain outside and I
felt his loneliness. So I asked if he wanted to
go to a screening and have dinner. Over dinner he told me the pros and cons of leaving
New York. He said he'd consulted the *I Ching,*
which had said, "An evil environment connected with a deep relationship will eventually yield a rebirth," i.e., tough it out! He'd
made a pros and cons list on a scruffy piece
of *VF* paper.

London pros. "One or two people who love
me. Nice flat. Quite rich. A real social life."
Cons. "Dullness, smallness. Sameness."

New York. "Horrible flat. Dead broke.

AIDS. No friends."

I saw with a pang that he is looking older. A kind of weary archness has set in, and a pale, unhappy glare. His knowledge of human nature is so deep and pessimistic, but no one makes me laugh like Miles. I looked at him sideways during the screening we went to and his head was back, his eyes dancing with intelligent scorn, and I felt so much affection. We have been through so much together, from the joyful *Tatler* days to the harsh foreign terrain. I know why he misses England. Harry and I were paid half as much then as we are now and never talked about money. Now that's all we seem to talk about. Money here gets into the blood like a disease. An unsettling itch that colors everything.

Like me, Miles is now caught between two worlds and may never be happy in either. I should probably start accepting and planning for the fact that it will not be long now before he returns to London.

Thursday, April 18, 1985

My last night tomorrow at Central Park South. I found a renter.

Now that the apartment is dismantled I feel a bit wistful. I do love the view of the park, but I'm on too low a floor and it's horribly noisy, especially on the weekends. The scream of police sirens addles my brain. The street outside is always full of tourists jingling around on those poor carriage horses, and the mafia don constantly raising the rent is sending us broke; so it's so long, Central Park South.

Saturday, April 27, 1985

I love my new apartment! It's at 300 East Fifty-Sixth Street, modern glass building with doorman and fancy fountain, which is a bit over the top and something I would never have imagined living in, but it's spacious and full of light and has its own dry cleaner. (Yep, that's my value system now.) I worked like a slave to get it all ready for when Harry came up from DC and he was thrilled. Mostly because he now doesn't feel there are tourists from Central Park staring at his naked torso when he walks by that window facing the street. I love having my own writing den, which is an airy half-room off the kitchen.

Maybe it's all the new nesting, but I realize I am craving a baby. A totally impractical thought. In a family mood, I called Mum over the weekend and asked her to come over from Spain. Time to draw the chairs close to the fire and contract the circle. I feel guilty about neglecting her and Dad. We were always so close and now she has a brittle front with me that is hiding pain. I miss family love, close-ness, and impromptu invitations, reflective hours between the magazine's hard-edged propulsions into limelight.

Tuesday, April 30, 1985

Drama. I had to go to the White House to get approval for the shots of the Reagans that we took six weeks ago for the June cover that is now heading to the close. We'd heard nothing from them since the shoot, and no one ever said we'd give them picture approval. We have let a few advertisers take a peek at them to get them juiced up to buy into the otherwise skinny June issue, and maybe one of them tipped off the White House. Suddenly, Nancy Reagan's office was placing calls to us, saying they needed to see them ASAP. I ignored their requests, natch. Then last night on the way home I got a message to phone the office because Si was at home "awaiting my call." Sounded ominous and it was . . . "Tina, I just got a call from Jerry Zipkin."

(So Nancy's wired and nosy walker is the one who heard about the shoot, got her worried, then offered to intervene.) "He says," Si continued, "that the first lady is very concerned about the photos she did for *Vanity Fair* and that she has been told by you she can't approve them. Get them over to her right away." Huh? Whatever happened to editorial independence? I was staggered. No asking me to think about it, just do it, and said in that tone of voice he has that means don't argue. I started to tell him that we never do that and that we are about to go to press with no other cover options. But he cut me off. "FedEx those layouts to the White House, NOW. We'll figure out the production problems later."

Fuck.

I called Pam and told her we had to send the layouts. Then I called her back and said not to. This morning, I put on a precautionary Reagan-red suit with a Chanel bag and got into the office at eight a.m. and went up to see Si with the layouts. I was momentarily startled when I walked in because he looked as if he was about to undress. In fact he was removing the crumpled sweatshirt he wears for his dawn arrivals only to replace it with office attire later on. He removed a wide blue tie from his drawer and proceeded to tie it around his neck. I briefly wondered what it would be like if we did the whole thing backward and he was left standing there naked. Not a happy thought! I told him I was going to take the spreads to the White House this morning myself rather than FedEx them. I said, "Let's decide now what we will agree to. How about just dropping the center spread where she's twirling around?"

"We will drop all of it if necessary," said Si grimly. "You don't monkey with the White House." I tried the commercial angle.

"We have already shown selective advertisers who are buying into the issue," I said. "We will look really bad with them if they buy in because of it and we yank them from the issue. Plus a press flak storm." (Hint: How will this play re *The New Yorker* vows of independence?)

He was clearly preparing to go out for a breakfast. He picked up his book bag. "Take all the layouts and make sure she likes it," he said. "Or drop it."

"And the June issue, which doesn't have a cover?" I said sullenly, following him to the elevator. I was, by this time, feeling really disappointed and pissed off with his craven behavior.

"Right now you have a problem with the White House," he said. "The June issue is your next problem. And don't let Mrs. Reagan think there is a time pressure."

I raced off to the DC shuttle in the steaming heat. It was even hotter in Washington. When I reached the gates of the White House with that intimidating forest of TV camera crews parked on the lawns and the august, postcard pillars rising up before me like a mirage, a lot of my bravado started to melt away. I sat in the stuffy antechamber to the press office for two hours. What if Nancy really hated the pictures? I guess her husband is the leader of the free world and he doesn't need the aggravation of some frisky social photo shoot he did in an absent-minded moment for a mere glossy magazine.

Jennefer Hirshberg, Mrs. R's press secretary, came out eventually. She was probably still feeling jumpy after the shit storm over the Reagans' appearance on the anniversary of V-E Day at the cemetery near Bitburg, which turned out to have forty-nine members of the Waffen-SS buried there. (Michael Deaver, usually so brilliant on PR prep work, is still living it down.)

Hirshberg asked me to unveil the layouts. I did a lot of schmoozing and flattery and presell before doing so. About how they showed the wonderful warmth of an iconic marriage that made them so accessible to Middle America, etc., which is nothing but the truth. It's hard to persuade people who are smart to do something that's really against their own interests, but these pictures, I do firmly believe, are fantastic PR for the Reagans. So I ignored Si's admonitions about not saying there was a time issue and told her it was on its way to the printer so we could of course only make small adjustments, but if only we had known they wished to see them earlier, of course, that would not have been so!

She scrutinized the layouts with a pained, doubtful look. I had laid a lot of flattering dummy copy on the top because they only said picture approval, right? We have Christopher Buckley's piece to go with it in copyediting. It's funny and sly and gorgeous as he always is, but you never know if they will like it. At the deep-kiss cover shot Jennefer Hirshberg drew in her breath sharply, then gasped at the dancing, leg-kicking sequence inside. Clutching the spreads, she vanished into the first lady's office for one hour. As the minutes ticked by I was becoming resigned and thinking glumly of what else we could scratch up for the cover. She returned finally, still looking gloomy, sat down, and started to criticize the display type's "tone" and ask for changes. That was funny because the display type was all fake! I "reluctantly" agreed. "Mrs. Reagan is very disappointed," she told me. Which really blew my mind, frankly. The pictures are so joyous and wonderful, Harry Benson at his most inspired. They celebrate what is maybe the ONLY thing everyone can agree is good about the Reagans, which is the genuine love between them as a couple. Could Nancy really be disappointed? She's an old Hollywood showgirl who knows what's appealing and what isn't to an audience. She looks wonderful in the pictures and she loves showing the world the president of the United States is her adoring slave. I suspect that Jennefer Hirshberg was just trying to save face, and the whole incident was probably instigated by Zipkin, to show he can whisper in the first lady's ear. Since the cover image of the kiss was what seemed to grieve

Hirshberg the most, I decided to be diplomatic and offer a switch with the inside picture. The kiss was wonderful for newsstand but the leg-kick cover is pretty great, too, and it means people will have to buy it to see the smooch. Plus, it gave Hirshberg a win that would make her feel happier. Sighing and shaking her head, she finally agreed to all.

I called Si from the phone booth at the airport. He was benign and chuckling now and I probably got points for decisively getting a problem off his back. Alex was even happier. "Darling, you are a genius! Your charm has worked yet again."

I am so happy the magazine has what I think will be a winning cover that could help turn our fortunes around. But I also felt good about triumphing over the mischief of the odious Jerry Zipkin, an important message to send. Had he seen he could go over my head to Si and get results, he would become the go-to person to kill every controversial social story, which would be lethal. Si, however, has totally dived in my estimation. In a moment of challenge, he had no balls at all.

Wednesday, May 1, 1985

Last night was a fascinating insight into how New York fund-raising is done at a certain level. We Brits are a nation of freeloaders and tightwads compared to the US. At *Tatler*, I got so sick of stately homeowners always pretending to have no money, a flinty tradition adopted first during the French Revolution to avoid the fate of their too-ostentatious peer group across the channel. Unlike in NYC, there isn't enough new money sloshing around in London to foment significant or lasting philanthropic influence. Asking for money is such an un-British thing. It goes with so much demurring and apologizing and polite coughing that the results are minimal. Most people seem to see donating to a cause as something someone else should do, a bit like going to (increasingly empty) church. "Charity events" are mostly just a luxury brand temporarily cozying up to a cause that might win a photo op with Princess Di.

I find it excruciatingly embarrassing myself to ask people for money, but clearly, now that I am a New Yorker I have to get over it. Norman Mailer has been on me to help him fund-raise for PEN, the literary organization that supports free speech. Since I will do anything for Norman, I had to say yes and the cause is certainly something I care about.

I love the way Norman is such a man of the arena. He's a grizzled, unabashed action junkie, so responsive and alive to the cross-currents of news. He makes everything he touches important just because he is part of it. Most writers are hermetic and self-involved. Norman is self-involved, too, but it's on such a grand, noisy scale that he sweeps all before him. I feel I want to write down everything that comes out of his mouth. He needs a Boswell to follow him around. When we were extracting *Tough Guys Don't Dance* in the mag last year he barreled into my office, sat down with legs akimbo, and announced — perhaps because this was his train of thought as he advanced with his battered book bag down the editorial aisle toward my open door — "I've never met a beautiful woman who wasn't angry." We passed a happy hour discussing why.

It wasn't hard for him to rope me into this reception for PEN. It was held at the vast Park Avenue apartment of his latest conquests, the mega-rich Reliance Insurance tycoon Saul Steinberg and his trophy wife, a slim brunette bombshell called Gayfryd. The apartment is a thirty-room palace, flaunting Louvre-standard old masters every time you turn a corner. Am used to seeing apartment art that's aggressively abstract and minimalist, but clearly Saul wants to make a statement that he's a Park Avenue Medici, because everything is oversized and over the top. It's like a set for Valhalla. The huge dining chairs had ruffled backs. Gayfryd (what's that Viking name about?) Steinberg is what Nick Dunne would call a cupcake, but she seems determined to show she is now a literary salonista. Saul is a stout, genial guy, a savvy Fred Flintstone whom she clearly didn't choose for his looks but who has redeeming intellectual ebullience. The two of them are now the center, it seems, of the new eighties money. "Saul likes his art very strong," Gayfryd told me, with her intense stare, as I gazed at the walls. In the sixteenth-century feast scene, there is a man throwing up. In the Renaissance courtyard, a dog is cocking its leg, and in the Dutch master it's a scene of rape and pillage. Is this a metaphor for the aggression of Saul's business tactics or just a fuck-you to his fancy friends?

Saul kept gesturing and mouthing to guests across the room as Norman stood center stage, stout chested, legs planted firmly apart, thumbs stuck in his pants, speaking brilliantly and extemporaneously about free speech and writers locked up for defending it.

When Norman was done, Saul came into his own. Preening like a ringmaster, he surveyed the circle of high-roller guests and declared: "Okay, my friends, who's going to buy some tickets to these great literary evenings?" A business face from the back yelled, "For you, Saul, ten K." Claudia Cohen, whose family owns Hudson News, lip-glossed into the ear of her glistening new husband, Ronald Perelman, and he burst out, "And Saul, ten K from me!" Within ten minutes Saul had raised a hundred thousand dollars for something he surely cares not a whit about, and the bidders care less. The assembled guests then dispersed into the chambers and antechambers and porticos and parterres of the apartment to knock back their drinks. Considering many of them were writers of the most deadly kind — John Gregory Dunne, Gay Talese, John Irving, Kathleen Tynan, and Mailer himself — it was pretty trusting of Saul to let them loose in his inner sanctum. He clearly has no idea that writers are the most disloyal, gossiping, satirical crowd of any and will dine out on the absurdity of his apartment for weeks to come, not to mention write about it mercilessly. But writers, of course, are also always ready to sell out for a free drink, and thus more than happy to show up and down his champagne. "I can raise up to a million in an hour," Saul told me cheerily, "more than that, it gets a little tougher."

Wednesday, May 8, 1985

Jerry Zipkin's face up close is like a huge inflated rubber dinghy, balanced on top of a short, Humpty-Dumpty body. Bob Colacello sat me next to him at his birthday dinner at Mortimer's, hoping to broker a rapprochement, I suppose. Zipkin's famous "wit" is mostly about combining outrage with theatrical emphasis. "Do I like him?" he wails in

289

answer to a question about some mutual acquaintance. "No! I don't like him." (Heavy pause.) "I ADORE HIM. Which planet have you been living on? Hello? Don't you KNOW I am the godfather of his oldest girl?" etc. The rest of his conversation is mostly free-associating names and anecdotes that have no punch line except another name and another anecdote. Over the course of the evening, he trashed Lally Weymouth, Francine du Plessix Gray, and Diana Vreeland. He had swollen gums from some dental problem, so occasionally he stopped in full flood to give a small cry of pain when hot chicken paillard connected with a sensitive point. He said he also has an allergy that has made his cheeks swell. I had an image of the rubber-dinghy face blowing up to the point that only his sharp little teeth remain. He launched into how Alex Liberman had been unfairly blamed for driving Diana Vreeland out of *Vogue* a few years back. "He had to do it! It came down from on high! You should have seen the way she ran through the cash! The limo was a thousand dollars a day! The suite at the Plaza Athénée in Paris! The red velvet tablecloths! I screamed it whenever I heard her phony version of how she was canned . . . Hello? Tina, she deserved to go!"

Gossip is a kind of addiction like overeating or drinking. His need for new, stinging nuggets of human trivia is unassuageable, the motor that propels him. What does it say about Nancy Reagan that he's her best friend? Insecurity perhaps about her California-ness and about not being Hollywood royalty like many of her friends. She could have any fascinating writer or artist or Nobel laureate as a confidant in the White House, but that would only add to her self-doubt. It must be a soothing diversion to hear this river of small, hilarious defamations collected each day especially for her. Plus she must glean a ton of usable information about donors and deals that she takes back to Ronnie.

By the second course he was spewing on about Mort Zuckerman, "I don't see his point."

"He's a very brilliant man," I reply. "He made all his own fortune at a pretty young age."

"Oh, I am sick of hearing about money," said Zipkin, who talks about nothing else. "Who's got it and who hasn't. SO WHAT! We are all rich. It's just that some of us are richer than others."

Bob turned the talk at his end to a story he's currently writing on another social queen bee, Marylou Whitney, and the Kentucky Derby. It's part of our new oral history–style series called "Voices," which is actually turning out well, as Bob is great at getting telling quotes. They all confide in him and he gets newsy stuff.

"Don't sell Marylou short!" Zipkin shouted. "Don't sell her short! That should be the title of your piece, Bob. She has to be ready to pick up at a moment's notice wherever Sonny Whitney wants to be, and get the cooks and the butlers and houses ALL working for their arrival. There's the HUGE place at St. Augustine. Another HUGE place at Saratoga, and then there's the apartment and I don't mean some dinky little pied-à-terre, this has terraces and the whole nine yards, then there's the HUGE place in Mallorca and the HUGE place in the Adirondacks. And when they entertain, it's dinner for 150, and at ten p.m. you turn over your card and there's ANOTHER TABLE NUMBER for a second course. Think of it! Make no mistake, Marylou has a tough time! Sonny wants everything JUST SO."

William F. Buckley, on my other side, turning to this outburst late, commented sleepily, "Sonny Whitney is senile now. But he was senile at Yale." The cake came out and everyone sang "Happy Birthday" to Bob.

I reeled out of there at eleven with a headache, dying to regale Harry in DC. Still, I am glad I went for Bob, of whom I am now deeply fond. Mixing with totally pretentious people all the time, he actually has no pretensions himself. I will never forget the day he responded to a snotty put-down about one of his pieces by Jonathan Lieberson: "Jonathan, I never said I was Flaubert."

Friday, May 31, 1985

My heart nearly stopped.

Vanity Fair has had a near-death experience . . .

I was leaving the office for the ABA book fair in San Francisco, followed by a West Coast ad swing, when Pam McCarthy told me she was very worried because HR is continually stalling on our junior staff replacements. I called PVZ, and given the good relationship we have forged, I hoped she would be frank with me about *VF*'s future, but she was evasive. "Pam, we need to hire these people," I said. There was a pause. "I wouldn't feel comfortable about anyone giving notice to join *Vanity Fair* right now," she said. "What do you mean?" I said, though I did know what she meant. "I don't know, Tina, I just think you should seek an interview with Si when you get back."

Bombshell. But it all made horrible sense. He has been unusually absent from calling me in the last couple of weeks. And now it was Memorial Day weekend and I couldn't call Si or anyone to confirm or deny it. I left for SF feeling ill. The June issue with the Reagans on the cover has been a triumph — flying off the newsstand and reproduced in every paper. Seventy thousand on the newsstand so far, up 10,000 over last month. The kiss pic all over the morning shows. Just as I predicted and more so. After the ABA I am supposed to be going on *The Merv Griffin Show* to talk about it. We are just picking up steam, and now Si is going to fold us? And what's worse is we have the incredible other pieces in the works that could maintain momentum.

With all of this racing through my head, I now called Doug Johnston, our ad director, who was still in NYC. To my horror he told me that on Friday Steve Florio, the president of *The New Yorker,* had called him to offer a job there, at Si's suggestion. Why the hell didn't he tell me? Doug apparently had asked Si what this meant re *Vanity Fair* and Si, the steely bastard, replied, "Don't look a gift horse in the mouth."

"Doug," I said. "You're there, I'm here. You've got to go in at six tomorrow when Si's in his office undefended and get in his face and do the sales pitch of your life! You keep telling me the ads are coming. Convince him of that!" In reply Doug started telling me all the brands that are about to say yes to buy pages, his messianic zeal rising as he began to see he might also be able to grab David O'Brasky's publisher job off him if Si gave us a reprieve. "Don't tell *me,* Doug," I screamed. "I KNOW we can win. It's Si you have to sell!" At the very least I wanted to trouble Si's luxuriously empty dawn with the realities of the street, not to mention the jobs of all our staff that are about to go south. I then called the old cavalier *servante* of Condé Nast ad sales, Dick Shortway, to enlist his help. I have continued to try to befriend him as I know he has sway with Si, since he's been at Condé for God knows how long. I woke him up, forgetting it was three hours later in NYC, but told him this was a crisis I needed his help to solve. "Tina," he wheezed, "I am going to get in there at crack of dawn and confront him head-on." Finally I woke up the art department. I asked Charles Churchward to ready the paste-ups of Helmut Newton's brilliant pics of Claus von Bülow and, for contrast, the wonderful Mary Ellen Mark photo spreads in the next issue with the Jay McInerney piece on the writer Paul Bowles living in literary exile in Tangier. Such quality surely has to find an audience soon! Then I booked a return flight home first thing in the morning, and was in agony all through the flight back.

I reached Doug when I landed at JFK. He sounded buoyant. He had spent forty minutes pitching our impending success story and told Si there was no way he wanted the *New Yorker* job because *VF* was the place to be. He said Si listened and nodded and listened and nodded. And then after pausing said,

"Stay with it, Doug."

Bull's-eye! Freckle-faced Doug Johnston is the General Patton of the hour. Dick Shortway was also full of genial self-congratulatory chuckles about what he claimed was his own critical role in staving off the death blow. Good old Shortway. But I didn't believe it until I saw Si myself.

I went straight to the office from the red-eye and called upstairs to say that I wanted to come see him. Sitting behind his desk, he looked up and smiled and came around to my side of the desk to sit down, which is always a good sign. "I'm going to give you a new publisher, Tina," he said. (*Sacrebleu!* O'Brasky out! Just as Doug hoped . . .) "And a specific time frame of two years. That should be enough to see whether the enthusiasm of readers can be converted into revenue."

I phoned O'Brasky and he sounded dejected but was very noble, saying the more important thing was to save *VF*. I hope he got a huge check.

Doug told me later that Si told O'Brasky, "David, I have decided to make a long-term commitment to *Vanity Fair.*" "Fabulous, I am thrilled," said O'Brasky. "You haven't heard the second part of the story. You're not part of it. I want your resignation." O'Brasky was in and out of there in six minutes (and probably right on to a waiting PVZ with her "conversation" and her "package"). Poor O'Brasky. He fought valiantly for *VF* in his own way. His whole stock-in-trade is the Mel Brooks–like ebullience, the short, plump legs in the business suit pumping along Madison Avenue. But he was also a throwback to an era of martini lunches and backslapping that seems a thing of the past when so many clients are high-toned fashion emperors with Japanese girls at reception wearing silent ballet slippers. I don't think Doug is exactly Pierre Bergé, but he's not as hopelessly miscast as David O.

I asked Si if he would have lunch with me soon out of the office and not at the Four Seasons. He looked shy. But I wanted to make him say yes to ensure I could really keep him on track, that this was not some impetuous Band-Aid. Because when Si says two years he always means six months.

Tuesday, June 4, 1985

Rotten, miserable day. When I had my weekly meeting with Si today in his office he wasn't particularly warm. In fact he was awkward and standoffish and it hardly felt like renewed commitment. Not at all the burst of enthusiasm about the future I had expected. He looked nervous and hot and pale, probably already regretting being railroaded into giving *VF* a second chance. I looked deeply into that asymmetrical face that can be so charming when the shy smile lights up. I am getting sick of the Condé Nast atmosphere of an insecure royal court. It struck me not for the first time as I returned his shifty gaze that he's untrustworthy. Yesterday's unthinkable becomes tomorrow's action plan with him.

Alex, ever the courtier who reflects the king's mood, wasn't friendly either . . . I detected little darts of malice in our usual healthy creative tension. I think he is annoyed that he was left out of last week's drama and I didn't enlist his aid. Maybe that's why Si suddenly went cold about it all. Alex had sowed doubts about his decision as payback. He dismissed Michael Roberts's very strong Matt Dillon cover on which he's holding a Hamlet-like skull as "poison." Alex always hates Michael's stuff. But I decided to take no notice of him. Fuck it, if we are going to get closed down, I may as well follow my own instincts. I finished writing some rollicking display type on the Gloria von Thurn und Taxis story with Miles and we did a sizzling contents page together.

Wednesday, June 5, 1985

It was pouring rain today, which I always love. It reminds me of the English summers of my childhood. All those school trips to Wimbledon in soaking uniforms. Excursions to Eton to the fourth of June celebrations with languid cricket when I was lusting after Julian Summer in sixth form, and we ended up eating the chicken and champagne picnic with his parents out of the back of the car under sodden umbrellas when the clouds burst, as they always did . . .

I got caught in the downpour with Ed Victor, who was in town from London. We ran from the Algonquin to the nearby coffee shop, then spent a lovely hour catching up on London lit gossip over fattening muffins. Back at the office I went into overdrive in a features meeting about fall stories and then had lunch at the Four Seasons with Anna Wintour, whom I have only seen sporadically in the last year. She can come off as chilly but when the dark glasses come off she's candid and confiding. She's clearly bored with being the second chair at *Vogue,* waiting for the sainted Grace Mirabella to go, and is hungry to run her own show. She said she'd love to do the editor in chief job at British *Vogue.* Bea Miller's headed for retirement after twenty years and Anna is full of ideas for how she could shake it up. Will be hard to follow Bea. She's such an icon. Discovered Grace Coddington and David Bailey and Bruce Weber and so many and came up with a strong copy background as well as fashion, whereas Anna's background is all visuals. Anna would find British Condé very damp and debby after New York. But she'd bring some American drive to the building and to the mag which now looks tired. I asked how her husband David would feel about her going and she said he's okay with commuting to London as long as it's only a couple of years. It's a smart strategy. Right now her talents here are enabling Grace to keep her job, whereas in London she can show off her flair and prove executive chops.

Just before I went to lunch, one of Si's notes came down on yellow legal paper in his wobbly madman's scrawl. It featured — a joke, which is most unusual in Hamsterland. It must have been an olive branch, as he's extended once before when he made up with a small gesture. It was a letter from some friend of Roy Cohn's offering us via Si a short story about the sex life of gay sailors. Si's note said, "Be warned. If *VF* doesn't want this, then it's sure to run in *The New Yorker.*" I said not only would I publish it, but I wanted the movie rights and asked him if he wanted to come to my toast for Doug Johnston's appointment as publisher at home tonight. He came on the phone immediately, very giggly, not able to come but full of warm cheer. It was a big relief after yesterday's treatment and a very festive evening at our apartment for Doug, with all the *VF* staff, who of course knew nothing about the fact that we'd been on the verge of folding.

The editors are getting to be tight-knit. David Kuhn, the new arts ed, has an incredibly keen instinct for a story. He's a Harvard boy who came from editing a little magazine for a nonprofit called American Council for the Arts. I decided to hire him immediately when I met him. He has great high energy, which is welcome after Heilpern's British rain clouds in the job, and I've got tired of people who were the cogs at big places. When you run a small magazine with no budget you have to do everything, which means much more resourcefulness, much more scrappy attack. I have given Kuhn the whole back of the book to run and told him to get a new section ready in two weeks. It didn't seem to daunt him at all.

Sarah Giles is doing really well transplanted here. None of the editors who work on copy can understand what she does, but glossy magazines always need at least one editor who goes out and brings things back, who hears what's happening, what's opening, what people are talking about in different worlds. Sarah isn't literary per se, but she has very good relationships with writers. She hangs out with talents like Bruce Chatwin and the urbane, bitchy old taste baron John Richardson and gets them to work for us. And she's insanely competitive on behalf of the mag. Nothing makes her upper-class nose twitch more than the sense that someone else might get the story first. I also think being new to town like me, she is more fascinated by the mores of America than Americans themselves are. She was in great form tonight, bounding around with her shrieking laugh, chain-smoking, and knocking back the white wine.

PVZ came, which was great of her, and we exchanged conspiratorial glances about the averted disaster. Nick Dunne burst in with his usual opening line, "Have I got news for you!" (in this case a new tip from the ongoing trial of Claus von Bülow). Helmut Newton's pictures of Claus dressed in black leather are extraordinary. News is a departure for Helmut. I could see he was getting bored out of his mind doing fashion photography for *Vogue.* He doesn't know it, but he's a natural journalist — sees and hears and understands everything and has an opinion about all of it. Plus his celebrity is another access card in certain circles, and sinister, suave von Bülow absolutely plays to Helmut's fascination with society kinkiness.

Nick's writing in this story has exhilarating energy that's fueled by his deep hatred of lawyered-up "jury pleasers" who remind him of the murderer of his daughter. He captures not just Claus and the divided family and the intricacies of the case, with fantastic direct quotes from all, but the whole seedy, rich Newport world Claus and Sunny inhabited.

And only Helmut could persuade a man on trial for murder to look in his closet and choose an S and M–flavored black zip-up leather jacket. He looks positively satanic. Teaming him and Nick produces something wonderfully sexy — the magazine piece as movie of the week — fast paced literary journalism from Nick and noirish visual flair from Helmut.

Very happy Jim Wolcott came to the party. He was wary of me in the first days of the mag, but I can feel the thaw and I love it when he comes in and hangs out in my office in his grungy leather jacket, free-associating about the books and movies he's read and seen. He's got such an extraordinary critical brain. Am going to give him a column, Mixed Media, that spans all his compulsive cultural food tasting. Went out to dinner with Miles and felt happy to walk up Second Avenue with him, to the small funky restaurant Les Sans Culottes. He looks much better. He's cut his hair. He loves working on the main features with me instead of just the front-of-book Vanities section, where he felt marginalized. He's proud of himself, I think, for toughing it out here and I am proud of him, too.

Tuesday, June 11, 1985

The von Bülow drama is drawing peacefully

303

toward a close. A leak to Liz Smith that he posed in black leather created such a press storm, I realized we had to dump the movie-star cover of Dillon and slap Claus on (which pained me, because it will upset Michael and give a win to Alex when he didn't deserve it, but it's the right journalistic decision). Michael showed up and started haunting the office with his deadly silent look, knowing that a possible cover kill of Dillon was in the works. Things have not been going well lately with him even before this. Alex has been grumbling about "too many spreads of naked youths dancing around," and PVZ keeps calling to say he isn't cashing his paychecks. He seems to be of no fixed address. Gabé thinks he's currently staying in the basement of Anna Wintour's house on MacDougal Street. Was just weighing all this when Helmut called me from Monaco, frantic that — whatever the circulation department thinks about alleged sexagenarian murderers being uncommercial — I MUST go with his Claus cover. He's right. It would be crazy not to do it with so much interest in the piece. I went back to the Claus pics and found the only one in color that really works as a cover — Claus and his mistress Andrea Reynolds in the Park Avenue apartment, he in tux and effete tapestry evening slippers, she in a red silk negligee that gives an intriguing whiff of luxe sexuality. After a heated powwow in the art department with Ruth and Miles we did the cover lines. Headline: FATAL CHARM, underline. "Claus von Bülow CAUGHT by Dominick Dunne. SHOT by Helmut Newton." It was just pasted down in time to flash to the suits at the August print order meeting, where the Hamster said nothing but looked quite thoughtful.

Afterward I tried to find Michael to talk him through why I had to dump the Dillon cover, but his assistant said he had left — for Paris.

Wednesday, June 12, 1985

The Reagan dancing cover continues to sell like crazy. The press has been so phenomenal, it's putting the magazine at the center of the news cycle.

Condé Nast president Bob Lapham asked me to lunch, which shows I am on the rise. He's such an old-fashioned company man of a certain era, the very opposite of bohemian Si. He took me to the stuffy, Frenchified Le Périgord restaurant on Fifty-Second Street again and studied the wine list, girth bulging out of his white cuffed shirt, his big nose shiny with corporate savoir faire.

Bob told me one story about Si that made me feel a surge of affection for him. (Si, that is.) Apparently one morning Bob went up to see him and "tried to cheer up the little guy by telling him a joke." Apparently Si looked up from his desk and said, "Lapham, is this a joke?" "Yes," said Bob. Si went back to his yellow pad. "I haven't got time," he replied. That's the kind of social privilege you only get when you're worth over a billion dollars.

Thursday, June 13, 1985

September issue now in the works is going to be a good one. For the cover we have a toss-up between Dustin Hoffman looking smart and dangerous and an enigmatic Yoko Ono as a whatever-happened-to story. Two notoriously difficult people have both said yes, and now I am going to have to annoy one of them. The big Hollywood agent Mike Ovitz delivered me Hoffman personally when I was last there, and I am probably way more scared of him than I am of Yoko.

The art department chaos is an ongoing problem. I adore Ruth's taste, and her depth of visual education. She can talk to photographers better than anyone I know. She spends hours on the phone with them, doing deep dives that enrich their pictures. But she also works entirely according to her own mysterious clock. Charles, on the other hand, on whom she completely depends, is really buttoned up, and I like his attack. He's great at the first-pass layout at great speed and brings a news edge. There are times when Ruth's layouts are too grand and stately. Both of them have extremely good copy judgment. For some reason art directors are often better judges of stories than editors are, perhaps because they are reading them with fresh eyes and no agenda. But they constantly feud. And reinforce each other's dysfunctions. Today they both scheduled for the exterminator to come to each of their apartments at ten a.m. and thus both missed the features meeting. When Ruth arrived in a swirl of pashmina I was fit to explode. Then she showed me her wonderfully elegant layout of the French writer Marguerite Duras's photos for the profile of her and I found myself melting. Ruth understands how to let a classic picture breathe and own the page. "Do you think anyone will want to read about Duras?" I asked, in a moment of self-doubt. "What, this brilliant little French gnome?" cried Ruth, gazing adoringly at the picture. "Are you kidding? How could you NOT want to read about her?" I would hate to lose her love of quality.

Sunday, June 16, 1985

How quickly the summer is flying by. The nursery serenity of Quogue makes me feel calm. Joan Buck came out to stay, looking as chic as ever in Chanel sunglasses and pleated designer chinos. She was full of gallows

307

humor, that huge belly laugh that's so at odds with her haute couture persona echoing around the porch.

My brain wave about hiring a student for the summer to cook is proving unbelievably great. It's bliss arriving on the train on Friday afternoon. The summer weekend begins as soon as we step into the parlor car at Penn Station and board the Long Island Rail Road. Finding Kelly the student already in the Quogue kitchen with delicious hot-bread smells and the radio on is throwback heaven. After dumping all our bags full of books and manuscripts we go straight out to the dune and lean against the wooden balustrade of the steps as the sun sets and gaze at the roll-ing, mighty Atlantic Ocean. God, how I love it. The evocative wail of the train on its return journey from East Hampton makes me feel I am in the middle of an O. Winston Link photograph, far from the high-rolling mad-ness of my *Vanity Fair* week.

Friday, June 28, 1985
TWA Flight 842, San Francisco to New York

I am in flight back from another advertising pitch in SF. I think it was pretty successful this time, largely because Dick Shortway came and added his heavyweight silver pom-padour and gold ID bracelet to Doug's low-key presence on the sales calls.

The socialite Denise Hale had a dinner for me. I had met her at the apartment of the realtor Alice Mason and she seemed like the right person to ask to host a dinner to drum up our advertising in SF. She's the wife of the store magnate Prentis Cobb Hale of Carter Hawley Hale and, according to Bob Colacello, has a rich background of Serbian émigré glamour. She came through for me with a dinner for twenty at L'Etoile. Caroline Graham, Dick Shortway, Doug, and I went first for a drink at her house, which drips with Chinese porcelain, silk taffeta curtains, eighteenth-century furniture, and a Degas hanging in the loo. Denise, I started to realize, is a bigger monster perhaps even than the reigning queen of Park Avenue, Nan Kempner. She bangs on in a thick Serbian accent about her dogs and how she must get silver frames for their photographs. She won't allow any cigarette smoking in the drawing room because the smell will linger in her green velvet walls. Prentis is really heavy furniture, with a dull, calculating mind and rat-trap mouth — clearly the checkbook. She doesn't have a spare room, she said, because "Prentis is afraid I will invite my friends." Great. She told stories about how she would do store checks for Prentis in disguise and if one of the salesgirls wasn't attentive enough, she'd get her fired. Even more delightful.

After reading the police report on Claus

von Bülow and how Daisy Fellowes used to rent his house in Belgravia for ten-day orgies, I am much more alert to the surprising and sometimes sinister secrets of the rich. I got a whiff of something I didn't like in the Hales' marriage. I felt lightheaded with exhaustion as we set off for L'Etoile, Denise squawking, "Forget about hairdos in this town — your false eyelashes go POOF at the first gust of wind!" Denise explained she always prefers to have dinners for people she hardly knows. "It's so much less of a strain than worrying about the comfort of friends."

As I tottered on my heels along the carpeted corridor to my suite at the Fairmont Hotel at the end of the evening, I heard the music from behind the door of the room next door. It was the mournful clarinet of Acker Bilk, playing the old hit "Stranger on the Shore" — one of Mum's favorites when I was growing up. I suddenly had an image of our big, beamed living room at Little Marlow with the French windows open in summer. I saw my small, blonde eight-year-old self spying through the door at Mum and Dad, nursing their gin and tonics on the dark green velvet Knole sofa, serenaded by the same clarinet. Mum always amused Dad so much. He loved steering her out of a first-night party with the valedictory cry of "I can't take her anywhere!" They had a Reagan-like marriage, entirely engrossed in each other for fifty years. Remembering that image of them together now, I felt my heart expand.

Sunday, June 30, 1985
Quogue

The summer's moving so fast and I clutch at it, longing to make it last forever. On Friday it was Harry's birthday. I got in from SF at six p.m. and sped from the airport to Quogue minutes before Ed and Carol Victor and Shirley Clurman came to a celebratory supper — delicious clams and chicken cannelloni served by Kelly the cook. I bought Harry a beautiful George Tice photograph of a summer porch and we had a close and loving weekend. Now I am sitting at the pine desk in the living room, listening to the deep pounding of the sea with a contentedly burning face. We have made the roof terrace look delightful with white table and chairs, geraniums, and a blue-and-white-striped umbrella. Harry's in his den watching baseball. I love to recede into my nursery world and swim backward in time with the waves.

Saturday, July 6, 1985

Harry has gone back to DC to be on a panel on libel. *US News* is proving another Zuckerman quicksand. At Harry's suggestion the new editor is Shelby Coffey, but it's clear

Mort wants to be the editor himself, constantly phoning staff and courting senior executives to put his oar in. Harry, as editorial director, is redesigning the magazine and is supposed to be Shelby's sounding board, but thanks to Mort, it's such a muddy chain of command.

I think Mort likes chaos, but Harry and he seem to have forged some deep brotherly bond that I can't quite fathom.

The editor-owner relationship is such a thorny business. I expend so much psychic space, myself, on Si maintenance.

I am staying here for the day to write an "editor's letter" to create an adjacent page at the front that advertisers keep asking for. I hate it. It's impossible to get the right voice when you have to speak for a publication. Whatever you do it turns into eight hundred chirpy words reeking of clichés about a "telling narrative" or an "insightful profile." I have made various attempts to reinvent the form, which have defeated me. Writing doesn't improve by not doing it. I am rusty and dull and uneasy.

Miles has rented a sweet, tiny apartment by a small marina near us in Westhampton. I was touched to see a glimpse of his life alone. The washing neatly folded in a corner, a copy of Anthony Powell's *A Dance to the Music of Time* on the table. He's put on weight and has started to pad about on pedantic feet. I feel we are all aging. I want to give up the glamour struggle myself and hide under long, loose silk shirts.

Thursday, July 11, 1985

Feel very emotional for some reason. Oddly blue and on the edge of tears. Doctor says I am depressed and gave me a pill.

Going to SF was great for flushing out more Californian contributors. Tonight I had a drink with a new young writer, Bret Easton Ellis, whose novel *Less Than Zero* I read in galleys and admired for its dialogue and reporting skill. That's the nicest part of my job. Being able to spirit a fresh face off a dust jacket into the bar at the Algonquin, and have the license to badger him with questions. The supercool brat on the back of the book is actually a thoughtful, sensitive, tender-eyed young man with an attractive vagueness and a head full of ideas. He loved my suggestion to hang out with one of the new so-called brat pack actors and examine how much they have been created by hype and how much by talent. Another good writer, Amy Hempel, came in, eyes shining with luminous commitment, and said she'd like to write about earthquakes. An idea came to me on the West Coast to do a whole issue that is the Pop-Up Book of California, and now all these terrific writers are coming forth and creating it with me. Another of them, David Thompson, came on the phone from SF excited about doing the profile of Robert Towne and a sketch of Mulholland Drive.

An editor's job is to make people say yes to something they hadn't thought they could do. I love getting to know writers and listening to what turns them on, which is often the direct opposite of what we had originally started to talk about. So often what they are actually known for doing doesn't reflect what they *should* be doing.

I'm sick of people writing about the "buzz" I "create" with *Vanity Fair.* Buzz sounds like something grafted on, something fake and manufactured. It's a put-down, a dismissal of impact, a way to minimize ability to identify stories people want to read and talk about. They call it "buzz." I call it engagement. I feel a nagging sense this "buzz" bullshit would not keep being said about a male editor.

Monday, July 15, 1985

The Dustin Hoffman cover for September suddenly collapsed as we were about to go to press with everything else. It was supposed to be timed with the release of the CBS TV movie version of *Death of a Salesman* until we discovered, quite by accident, they have postponed the airing till January. I went into overdrive raiding every drawer in the art dep. I wished I'd gone ahead with Yoko. Now we've had to throw together one on Anjelica Huston, who's sizzling at the moment in *Prizzi's Honor*. Fortunately Marie Brenner was on the plane to LA and Annie Leibovitz was about to leave to do a Hall of Fame shoot, and I begged and cajoled them into crashing the new cover story, getting a last-minute five-day production extension. So just when we were getting ahead with the fall, it's a dive back into mayhem. Still, it's a very good issue.

Wednesday, July 17, 1985

We had the whole *Tango Argentino* group in today to talk about a photo shoot. The genius of the show is the cast of real, authentic Argentinian tango dancers scoured from local cabarets and TV shows there. The show is touring and I went to see it with Sharon DeLano and am so obsessed by it, went back to see it again. I told Ruth to call Paloma Picasso in Paris and get her and her husband Rafael Lopez-Sanchez, who's one of the *Tango* collaborators, to pose together for the opening shots. The entire office has been taken over by babbling Argentinians. In the middle of the bedlam Marie kept getting on the phone, saying she couldn't get the Anjelica piece done in time because she had said

315

nothing of interest, and I kept telling her Failure Is Not an Option and to think of some angle to frame it, while on the other line from Tuscany was the disgraced Tory peer, Lord Lambton, ostensibly to talk about writing about his exile there for the October Englishman Abroad assignment, but he really just wanted to flirt and waste my time. The British issue, timed with the Washington country house exhibit at the National Gallery [*The Treasure Houses of Britain*], is now colliding with the California issue and neither of them have covers, unless I can get on a plane and do a big Princess Di piece. I keep hearing from my old London sources that Di and Charles are fighting like cats and dogs and Di has become a crazy diva, but no one has nailed it with anything but nuggets. With the old *Tatler* Rolodex I can probably do the piece if I go myself (plus I miss writing). In the middle of all this, with nausea still high, I had a sudden shattering thought. What if I'm pregnant?

Saturday, July 20, 1985

As soon as I wrote the words above I knew it was true and marvel at how dopey I could be not to understand the weird symptoms I have been having lately. How daft of the doctor, too, to give me antidepressants without ascertaining that first. It's amazing how calmly and naturally this news has overtaken me. Moments of truth come slowly. I think my subconscious has known, accepted, and nurtured this fact for some weeks.

I AM SO HAPPY. My first panicked worry was that I could never handle motherhood and the mag in current mode. But now that I know it's going to happen, I suddenly see it as THE PERFECT TIME. A rash of new appointments is cleaning out the leftover doldrums of transition people. The sullen picture editor was the last person who needed to go, and that I achieved yesterday when I couldn't stand her resentful stare anymore. I called Mum in Spain about the baby and she was totally freaked out. "I am coming immediately!" she yelled. "Immediately!" I could tell she was as confused as I was by the implications but also thrilled, and convinced I couldn't possibly have a baby in America with her in Spain. Yesterday, Harry arrived from DC to drive out to Quogue, and when I told him he stopped the car and showered me with kisses. He was ecstatic, unambiguously so, unlike me, and then we drove out to the beach in a kind of stunned silence, trying to reconfigure a picture of the future. He has immediately decided it will be a boy who will turn out to be H. L. Mencken, and now my still-invisible news is referred to by Harry's new nickname of "Menckers."

Walking along the beach at my paradise, I

317

felt more serene than I have for years. "Cow-like and floral," as Sylvia Plath once wrote about pregnancy. Symbolically, my writer's block disappeared and after lunch I sat down at my typewriter and rewrote my editor's letter in an hour, in a personal voice, discarding the corporate crap I had been laboring on. I feel a burst of confidence, as if Menckers had fortified me with a surge of tiny life.

Wednesday, July 24, 1985

Bloody difficult few days, exacerbated by the morning sickness. After all the aggro to get the alternative cover done with Anjelica, CBS called to say that *Salesman* with Dustin Hoffman was now back on for late August, i.e., the September issue. I decided I now preferred the Anjelica cover, so to hell with them and we proceeded with high speed.

On top of this Michael Roberts seems to have drifted off for good. He'll probably suddenly magically reappear as he used to do at *Tatler,* but meantime I need a style editor or covers will look like crap. Spoke to Alex and he said he might give us André Leon Talley, who has been working with Grace at *Vogue.*

Yesterday was my lunch with Si at the Four Seasons. He talked about his inability to find someone to edit British *Vogue.* He asked me if I would help with the search. What about Anna? I said. It would be a new playground for her while she waits for Grace to leave here. He looked thoughtful at that. Sometimes the obvious solution is under your nose. I guess Alex is not pushing her because he doesn't want to lose her from *Vogue* here. Si was in a friendly and relaxed mood, exuding baffled good nature. I always love hearing his offbeat take on things. He hated *Prizzi's Honor,* found it shallow and tiresome. He talked about William Shawn at *The New Yorker,* how "seductive" he is, full of "unexpected insights." I told him how much I liked his son Wallace, how strange he looks, how full of original observations. "Where do they come from," mused Si, screwing up his funny little hamster face, "these funny little people?" It was, in itself, a *New Yorker* cartoon.

As we drove back to the office in his limo, he looked out the window and we talked about Oxford and Cambridge, how they still provide the network of the ruling class in Britain. He said there was no such network in the US. (Not Harvard and Yale?) "You know," he said, "there's no such thing as real power in America."

"What do you mean?" I said to his profile, which was still gazing out of the window. I realized he was really thinking out loud. "Well," he said, "the president has no power. Congress can thwart him. And media power . . . I'm supposed to have media power . . . but I can't get arrested!"

"Of course you have power," I said, "but you sometimes choose not to exercise it." "But how could I exercise it?" he said, turning toward me as we cruised toward the building he owns. "Say I wrote a memo to the magazine editors telling them only to plug Random House books . . . they'd, they'd just take no notice. Or say I gave Random House a list of books by authors I told them to buy . . . well, it wouldn't last five minutes." We were now out of the car, walking past a newsstand stacked with all the magazine titles he owns. He stopped to wait for the elevator. "As for *The New Yorker,* well, I find it very hard to get William Shawn on the phone." With that he disappeared with hunched shoulders and creased, reflective face into the express elevator to the fourteenth floor. He is a character out of Thurber, a great antihero.

The final results came in for the Reagan cover and newsstand sales are up 33.6 percent compared to the same month last year. More important, subs are soaring, from 164,870 in June '84 to 317,735 in June this year. This is incredible and a relief, as I am so anxious for Si to find his faith rewarded.

Friday, August 2, 1985

Just back from London, where I went to report the Princess of Wales story, as we really need a hot cover for October, and Di is coming to Washington at that time for a White House dinner. I stayed at the Ritz and had a wonderful week. Has London changed and become reenergized in the Thatcher revival, or is it that I have a refreshed perspective after a year and a half in the New York combat zone? "Am I the places or the places me?"

I bounded around all the Di sources I could schedule, racing first to lunch with Mark Boxer, who is still as Byronically handsome as ever with his cricketer's stride and irreverent drawl. He's doing wonderfully well as editor of *Tatler,* though I never expected he'd want to do the job after such an august career as an editor and caricaturist. I still think his greatest talent is his lethal pen-and-ink satires of London society. He gave me great stuff about Charles and Diana. Then it was on to dinner with Derry Moore (photographers always notice the most), lunch with Nigel Dempster, a dress fitting at Bruce Oldfield's Beauchamp Place boutique that was a disguised gossip download, and (by far the most productive) lunch with Lord Lichfield at San Lorenzo to remind me of the flavor of all Di's haunts. Ended the trip with a dinner Ed Victor threw for Stephen and Natasha Spender. Stephen Spender was particularly amusing. He has such wonderfully malicious nostrils. "When I went to a bookshop in

Houston," he told me, "I paid with an American Express card, and the man at the till said, 'Ah, Stephen Spender, I've heard of you. Aren't you a near-celebrity?' " He added as a vague afterthought, "I suppose I half made his day!"

But what of the poor Princess of Wales? There's so much gossip. It seems all that shy, youthful exuberance of hers is being transmuted into the stifled feelings of a caged butterfly, entirely unaware of the mechanism of her own extraordinary appeal. She knows how to use it instinctively but is utterly uninterpretive of her life and fate, which is hardly surprising given how young she is. Patrick Lichfield told me that her intense unhappiness is expressing itself in volatile rages that exhaust Prince Charles, and have started to really concern the Queen and Prince Philip. The more she becomes a star on the world stage, the more Charles feels overlooked and withdraws into his melancholy inner life. Now that he doesn't have to pretend to be the world's hot bachelor, he is reverting to his real self, a lonely, eccentric figure haunted by self-doubt. He thought he was signing up for a passive, sweet-natured young girl who would produce him the heir and the spare and not interfere in any way with his glum, dutiful life and off-duty pleasures with the blondes of his past, like Lady Tryon and Camilla Parker Bowles, but that's not how it's turning out. The world is mad for Di.

Derry said that what Charles can't stand is Diana's total absence of intellectual curiosity and her obsession with clothes. Gone is the spun moonbeam dress and blushing devotion I saw at the American embassy in 1981. Now it's designer shoulder pads and a frosted bearskin hairdo. Dynasty Di. Nigel said she spends hours studying her press clippings almost as if she's trying to figure out the secret of her own mystique. Like Jackie O she shops continuously to relieve the tension. When she's at Balmoral she apparently spends hours cut off on her Sony Walkman, dancing on her own to Dire Straits and Wham! Meanwhile Charles reacts to the public lack of interest in him by depending on a raft of sycophantic gurus like Laurens van der Post and Dr. Miriam Rothschild, an authority on fleas who invented a seed mix of wildflowers known as "farmer's nightmare," which Charles has sown around his High-grove acres. It's been reported that Diana drove out his trusted private secretary, Edward Adeane, but according to Patrick Lichfield and Derry, Adeane left because he couldn't stand the motley band of mystics and self-sufficiency freaks acting as the prince's unofficial advisers.

No one is more dismayed about this apparently than Diana, who signed up to marry the royal James Bond. And Charles thought he was getting a jolly Sloane Ranger, not a highly strung superstar. Derry told me a lovely anecdote I shall include of a trip Charles apparently made to a friend's house to study the garden. He complimented the Italian hostess on her perfect English. "My father believed in educating girls," she said, laughing. "I wish," said Charles gloomily, "that had been the philosophy in my wife's family." Diana is both brilliantly instinctive and dispiritingly dim. She left school at sixteen to become a child's nanny, which all her set did, and she can hardly be blamed for it. She is a very young twenty-four and he's a very old thirty-six. It's no wonder she is turning more and more to café society who live colorfully in between those worlds. Mark Boxer told me about a fund-raiser Diana went to recently on the arm of Bruce Oldfield. When Charlotte Rampling's cool husband, the musician Jean-Michel Jarre, asked her to dance, Diana lit up. "Everyone within twenty yards got the fallout from her mood that night," Mark said. "She was suddenly aware of everything she was missing."

I have great material here for a cover story. Although bits and pieces have been leaking out of all this, no one has truly put together the parlous state of the Wales marriage, so it was well worth the trip.

I am at Quogue, sitting at the dining room table, working on my Di piece I am going to call "The Mouse that Roared." Loving being at the typewriter again. The piece is writing itself and going to get some traction, I think.

The mag is finally getting very good. The California copy has started to come in and some of it is first class, especially David Thompson's essay on Mulholland Drive. Annie Leibovitz was justifiably pissed about the cover credit on her Dustin Hoffman cover that is now running in November. She said the fashion stylist's byline was the same size as hers. Given that Dustin is wearing a black polo-neck sweater, the credit STYLED BY SHIVA FRUITMAN is indeed pretty ridiculous. "Who is this asshole Shiva Fruitman anyway?" mumbled Annie. I wish I knew, but Mr. Fruitman has now become the source of much in-house hilarity. "Styled by Shiva Fruitman," Wayne murmurs when I pass him in the hall.

I went to Ralph Lauren's show and was fascinated by the ancient blonde sitting in the best seat on the aisle, wearing clanky spectacles on a chain and a gold lamé shirt. It turned out to be *Vogue*'s senior fashion editor, Polly Mellen, whose eccentricities I had heard about but never seen. She sits there squawking and clanking and making extraordinary little facial "moues," every so often giving a tiny round of applause and mouthing "triumph, triumph" when a cashmere cardigan dress sails by. My own clothes are beginning to strain against me as El Bun grows. I don't know how long I can put off the dread maternity wear.

Friday, August 23, 1985

Mum and Dad are here from Spain! They are so thrilled about the baby and the tension of distance melted away, releasing all kinds of tangled suppressed familial emotion into a happy, uncomplicated stream. It's been lovely having them in the apartment this week, coming home to find that all kinds of little domestic jobs I have put off doing have been expertly done (the joy it must be to have a stay-at-home wife!), and seeing the pleasure they take in Quogue.

It was a good idea to make my first ed's letter a rollicking manifesto on our circulation rise. Harry has been telling me for ages to write about how well we're doing now since we can't get anyone else to do it. He made the cunning point that people believe what they see in print even if it happens to be in your own publication. I remember now how the *Daily Mail* editor David English was always doing that. "Another big win for the *Daily Mail*! Soaraway success as circulation tops a mill!" etc. And did we ever question it? No! Because we read it in the *Daily Mail*! I now find with mounting amusement that this indeed turns out to be the case with my editor's letter. People have been calling me ever since the September issue came out, congratulating me and advising we are now "very likely going to make it." Weirdly, it even seems to apply to the Newhouses. Si called me at home to say how much he liked the editor's letter and its message, "so attractively put," he spluttered. Jonathan Newhouse at *The New Yorker* told Doug Johnston that Si's brother, Donald Newhouse, told HIS brother (the Hamster bush telegraph) "that *Vanity Fair* is a winner." Since Donald has been, I suspect, a private adversary for a long time, this represents a turnaround indeed.

Sunday, August 25, 1985

Last night was Ben Bradlee's sixty-fourth birthday party at Grey Gardens. Sally freaked me out by demanding, in her witchlike way, "Is that a maternity dress?" of my, I thought, brilliantly ambiguous loose silk Roland Klein sheath. There was a big Hamptons film contingent. I sat between the director George Stevens Jr. and the columnist Ken Auletta, opposite two more directors, Alan Pakula and Sidney Lumet. Harry's end was the literary group. He sat between Sally Quinn and Nora

Ephron with the novelist E. L. Doctorow. We both felt very much part of the Hamptons community now. Everyone is talking about the early leakage of my Di piece and there was a debate about whether I should ever have described Prince Charles as "pussy-whipped from here to eternity." I took a poll around the party to see how people felt about the term. Auletta thought it was a mistake. Ben said on no account would he ever agree to let the term appear in *The Washington Post,* a family newspaper. Lumet, however, said, "Why not? It's as American as apple pie." We ate Mexican food, and Norman Lear and Peter Stone made funny toasts. I was pleased to see little Quinn cycle by on his tricycle, looking well. I longed for the birth of Menckers, who's making me extremely sick at the moment.

Monday, September 2, 1985

It's the end of Labor Day weekend and our euphoric summer — makes me melancholy to feel the change in the light and fall in the air. Except on Monday something fantastic happened. The *VF* piece by Geraldine Fabrikant for *The New York Times* that has been long in the works finally appeared as the cover of the Business News section! I'd been dreading yet another "rumored to be folding" piece, which would have meant kissing off the slowly building ad pages. (Last week Calvin Klein called from a restaurant and booked a run of six, and Ralph Lauren wants a regular position at the front.) The *Times* piece ran with a fabulous picture and headline. "New success for magazine. Vanity Fair's slick new formula" — with charts illustrating the growth in circulation and that ads are up 41 percent through the first nine months of this year. Great quotes from advertisers testifying that *VF* is now a working success with a new audience. (There was even a positive quote from the usually baleful Clay Felker, saying, "It has found its own glitzy, fashiony cultural niche. It will be a success.") As soon as I saw the headline I knew it was the single most important thing to happen all year, bona fide turnaround time. The phones were red-hot all day. Last night at Zuckerman's end-of-summer buffet in East Hampton, the set who have been so skeptical were all over me. Ed Victor told me he went to a dinner and heard Sidney Lumet say, "Oh yeah. *Vanity Fair*'s turned around. It's *The New Yorker* that's in trouble." Gotta laugh since I have had eighteen months of people telling me we were going to fold into *The New Yorker* any minute.

Knowing this was the week when I was smelling of roses, it seemed the right moment to break the news of the baby to all. First I told Pam McCarthy and Sarah Giles, who told me everyone in the office had guessed a week ago. Both were so genuinely thrilled it touched me. Then I told PVZ, who immediately saw it in corporate terms. "I am delighted a top executive is experiencing pregnancy," she said. "It gives us a chance to see what we can do for our maternity program." Then on Wednesday I went up to see Si. He was looking tired and hassled behind his big desk. "Yes, Tina, what is it?" "I find I am expecting a baby," I said, "but I just want to say it won't make any difference to my commitment to my job." He flushed and beamed with the sweetest undisguised pleasure. "I'm very happy for you, Tina," he said, "I hope you get as much pleasure from the experience as I have from mine." And he got up and came around the desk awkwardly to shake my hand in a very warm way. Alex, whom I told next, kissed me and cried, "Darling! More brilliance! It's yet another triumph for you!" Miles was the next big surprise; he was so moved he nearly cried. He dropped everything and kissed me and told me it was the most important thing in life. "It's the only bad thing about being gay, not being able to," he said, touchingly. (If it is indeed a boy I will ask him to be godfather, I resolved then.) Nick Dunne came into my office, shut the door, and hissed, "I know your story and I am in heaven! I nearly cried when I heard!"

And Marie Brenner sat me down for an in-the-know diatribe on obstetrics, pediatricians, the importance of ignoring all baby manuals, and boycotting exercise classes. So I was walking on air by the end of the week.

On Thursday night Harry and I went to a drinks party for John Mack Carter of Hearst and Si gave me a little pat as he went out and said, "I am so pleased about you." "About the *Times* piece?" "No," he replied sotto voce, "about the baby." And I realized I was seeing what a strong believer in family he is and how he sees me now as part of it. Somehow America does seem much freer and more relaxed about pregnant women in the workplace, or maybe it's that babies make a woman less intimidating. I realize already what extra strength and solidity a child will give me, what a different connection to other women with kids. Babies show the best of us. I was enchanted at a Diane von Furstenberg dinner last night when a handsome furniture designer called Dakota Johnson whipped out a picture of his baby and the director Paul Schrader did the same. Dick Snyder's wife, Joni Evans, told me Dick believes women with children are unemployable. Nice. I feel guilty about my irritation with Marie and Caroline Graham when they have to bail out of work to be with their children. I understand now how important it is to enable women to both work and have a child. All my endless planning (wait till thirty-four, then give up the job and have a baby) was ridiculous. I will never be happy unless I can do both.

Meanwhile, the repercussions of journalistic edge keep confronting me with the furious profile subjects I run into at dinner. Arnold Glimcher, the art dealer, aggressed me at the Victors for what he called "an anti-Semite tone to the Julian Schnabel piece." (Wha?) And I forgot when I merrily started to chat with Paul Schrader at DVF's dinner that Stephen Schiff had just trashed him in the current issue. With temporary amnesia I said, "I think we just did something about you in the mag, Paul." "Shall I refresh your memory?" he said. "Basically it described how I am a piece of shit who should never have got behind a camera. Shall I go on or do you remember it now?" "*C'est la vie,* Paul," said DVF sleepily, adding with seductive mischief, "There are plenty of people who agree with that anyway." It was one of the last dinners in her palatial apartment before the set is struck and she goes off to Paris with her debonair Italian lover, Alain Elkann.

One surprise yesterday morning was a furious, unsolicited call from the editor of *Women's Wear Daily,* Michael Coady. "You are out of control! Out of control!" he screamed. "Your Diana piece is a fucking disgrace! Pussy-whipped! How could you even think of using that word in a magazine!" How very strange Americans can be.

Anna Wintour got the job at British *Vogue.* Must be the best news Grace Mirabella's heard all year.

Tuesday, September 3, 1985

The baby news has been a wonderful thing for my relationship with Mum and Dad, opening up channels of tenderness. I felt blue when they left for the airport today, as always three hours before they needed to because of Dad's obsession with punctuality, insisting on three passport checks and a label on everything in sight. Seeing him standing in the bedroom in his underpants and doing all the packing, wrapping things in tissue and swathing shoes in vests and bras, made me feel full of nostalgic affection.

Thursday, September 5, 1985

Bob Colacello took me downtown to see the Azzedine Alaia show at Palladium on Fourteenth Street, Ian Schrager and Steve Rubell's hot new venue redesigned by Arata Isozaki. I had never been to Palladium before so I wanted to check it out.

Maybe my pregnancy made me just not in the mood, but I always see these avant garde outings as the emperor's new clothes. We herded through the ear-splitting noise and gloom, falling down ill-lit steps and jostling through paint-daubed house of horror sets seething with ragged-haired glitter people in vermilion lipstick. It all felt to me like the charnel house of the damned, with lost souls milling about under outsize chandeliers that used to hang at Studio 54, surrounded by in-your-face canvases by Kenny Scharf, Keith Haring, and Jean-Michel Basquiat. The show was just a load of itchy oversized sweaters worn as miniskirts, rip-off Moroccan robes, bruise-colored leggings, menstrual-red chiffon skirts. I didn't reveal to Bob how much I hated it but I felt sorry for the haggard crowd who feel obliged to be wearing this stuff soon.

Tuesday, September 10, 1985

So much creativity at work, my head is buzzing like an overheated radio. I had lunch with Reinaldo Herrera to brainstorm an Italian special issue; there is so much to do there in the world of style. He's a thundering snob but at the same time has huge enthusiasm. His impeccably pressed jeans, Savile Row shirts, and bellowing Venezuelan voice are a useful passport for *VF*'s nocturnal spy in the drawing rooms of NYC.

As usual I had to sift through the chaff of his noisy espousals of such bad ideas as photographing famous wine growers, but we did end up with a cool idea to do "Children of la Dolce Vita," photographed by Toscani, a portfolio of Italian style obsession that he can help set up because he knows them all. Then I had a hall of fame meeting with Jim Wolcott, Sharon DeLano, Ruth Ansel, and Jane Sarkin. Jane is a great new hire. Colacello recommended her from *Interview,* where she was an assistant. She is small and intense with a passionate work ethic. She also loves the whole ambience of stars and their handlers, who drive me crazy because I have no patience. She got great training in this from Bob and Andy Warhol at *Interview.* I have put her into the newly formed role of "celebrity wrangler" and have thrown her the whole raft of controlling flacks to run, which hopefully she'll do without Daphne Davis's drama.

We spread Annie's portraits across the floor of my office to write the captions, and sat there in a sea of chocolate wrappers and Coke cans. Jane had produced two very good last-minute inclusions for Annie to shoot, which greatly classes up the mix of chosen people — Congressman Tip O'Neill and the heart specialist Dr. Jarvik. "Jarvik's hot," Ruth said.

"Is he married?" said Jane. "No," said Ruth.

"Jane Jarvik," murmured Jane. "My mother would love that."

Just in from one of the most amusing dinner parties I have ever been to in NYC. Harry's on his way to London and I so wished he hadn't missed it. It was the first bash of the fall hosted by Alice Mason, the society realtor and political fundraiser who made her name in the sixties and seventies getting people not in the social register into Park Avenue co-ops. She's such an odd duck with her glaucous look and total absence of conversation. But she does have a flair for a guest list. We all were crammed into her rabbitwarren dining room on East Seventy-Second Street and seated at erected card tables. *VF*'s new success designated me a great seat at Alice's table next to the aggressive takeover king, Carl Icahn, along with the creamy TV anchor Diane Sawyer, mag magnate Malcolm Forbes, the TV writer Norman Lear, and the gossip columnist Aileen Mehle, aka Suzy. It was like a pop-up book of Reagan-era money. At one point Malcolm said about someone, "He sold the company for maybe sixty million, which was a lot of money in those days." Icahn and Forbes locked horns about the principle of corporate raids, with Suzy on Malcolm's side — she's on the board of Revlon, which is fighting off an assault by the gimlet-eyed Ron Perelman, who, as it happened, was sitting at the next table.

Icahn is a giant of a man, with a big, humorless nose, very close-together eyes, and a foghorn voice. "Listen, don't get me wrong," he honked at Malcolm across the table. "There's no halo around me. I'm in this game for the money, okay? It's like a drug. I see the challenge, the fat cats sitting on the assets, and then I get in there and I'm in there to win. After I win, then I get depressed. I tell you, I go in there and I see these blue-ribbon boards, sitting on the assets, mismanaging companies, paying themselves fat-cat salaries with golden parachutes built in, and I just fire 'em all. And you know what, the profits for ACF are up forty percent. I fired a hundred and seventy-five top executives. You know why? Because I couldn't figure out what they did all day. Have a drink with any of 'em and you'd like 'em a lot. But so what? These CEOs, these blue-ribbon boards, all they got is charm, all they got is politics."

"Well," said Malcolm genially, "with all this dough flying around I feel impelled to mention the Princeton fund, of which I am a paid-up member of the charm school board." But Icahn charged on.

"These guys, they can't manage the companies they're supposed to oversee. They're just bleeding it white and they paint me as the villain, when I come in and offer a good price for the shareholders. Why shouldn't the shareholders vote on whether I get it? They want to sell. They're only shareholders to make some dough for themselves."

"That's nice. You're in there for the little guy," Malcolm said with a twinkle. "No," roared Icahn. "I am in there to collect. But I'm telling you these fat-cat boards got no right to rob their shareholders." Aileen Mehle was by now the picture of ruffed, bosomy consternation and could no longer contain herself. "Mr. Icahn," she huffed, "I am on one of your so-called blue-ribbon boards at Revlon and —"

"Revlon!" shouted Icahn. "I wouldn't buy one share of it. It's not even worth the forty-seven bucks a pop that Perelman is offering."

Suzy's cleavage flushed. "And that's where you are wrong, Mr. Icahn! I happen to know that Revlon is a very fine company, a well-run company, and the shareholders can throw us out at the next shareholder meeting if they don't think we are doing a good job . . . but we are elected by them and we know that this Perelman assault must be repelled!"

"And you are prepared to bankrupt the company to do it!" Icahn jabbed his meaty forefinger. "Take a poison pill! The whole system is nuts!"

"This is a takeover," interposed Norman Lear. "I am taking over this table. I am going to take one thought and follow it to the bitter end. Tell us what's wrong with the system, Carl."

"It's the corporate culture. All these WASPy guys who talk through their teeth. These boards are a threat to the whole country. If the steel industry had had a takeover threat to deal with, there would still be one today." By this time Suzy was ready to come to blows. Icahn yelled at her, "Don't patronize me! Okay? Just don't do it!" It was an uncomfortable moment, a disconcerting glimpse of the psyche of a man who wants not to tease the establishment but annihilate it. At one point he growled, "Listen, there are some good CEOs out there. Like Marty Davis of G and W."

"And no one can say he got there on charm," said Norman Lear, who had watched most of this in fascinated silence. Norman is great company. He described California to me as "paradise without a vocabulary." Mort Zuckerman joined our table to listen. "What have I missed?"

Malcolm said, "Mr. Icahn was explaining his motive for corporate takeovers; it seems he is something of a crusader on behalf of vulnerable stockholders," but having missed the fray, Mort was more interested in making eyes at Diane Sawyer. When we rose for coffee, I collided with Norman Mailer, who was wonderfully warm. "You've never been more beautiful," he said, rocking about like a happy koala bear. "You've really hit your look. Stay pregnant. It suits your spacey face."

"Spacey!" I exclaimed. "But I am keen-edged and alert!"

"I know," he said. "That's why spacey-face works so well." I got into the elevator with Helen Gurley Brown and Arianna just in time before the doors closed on us. Helen pressed the button. "We're all going to Cuba," she said.

Monday, September 30, 1985

Hurricane Gloria hits! The press had been full of the warnings and we had Quogue battened down. We holed up in the city, where the office was closed for the day. It was cozy going to bed and hearing the winds howling and rattling against the windows of the apartment block. I was woken up at six a.m. by the phone ringing. "Hallo, is that Hurricane Tina?" said the Voice.

"Who is this?" I yawned.

"It's Rod from the *Daily Mail!*" (or rather the *Die-ly Mile*). "You obviously haven't seen the papers today." Turns out my just-out Princess Di piece has exploded all over the tabloids in London. The *Daily Mail* front page read, "Astonishing attack from American magazine on the Royal marriage." And then, in true *Daily Mail* style, went on to plunder my piece for every news angle and recast it as

340

a cause for Middle England's outrage. The next day the *Mail* went on to do a double-page spread about my own marriage in the same terms, casting Harry as "pussy-whipped" like Charles with me as "the Joan Crawford of publishing" like Di. It was pretty clever actually. Made me nostalgic for guffawing British sub editors who expend so much talent on worthless ends. I see David English's own hand in it, he's so good at take-downs. The paper also quoted the palace with a furious rebuttal, and as the hurricane raged around Manhattan, I spent Friday morning doing telephone interviews and issuing statements. Today Sarah Giles landed from London, bearing a sheaf of tabloids, and we read them over brunch at Mortimer's with mounting incredulity and mirth. The royal couple are going on BBC TV to rebut it, which is a first and proves beyond a doubt we got it right. The palace only denies things when they're true. It's making big news here, too. I have done a round of TV and it will consolidate us as a news machine. The rule of three — the Reagan kiss, the Claus von Bülow, now this, three stories that have taken us over the top.

Tonight Harry and I went off to the *Manhattan,inc.* party. I like the editor, Jane Amsterdam, a lot. She's kicking ass with her mag. She's also tremendously elegant and real at the same time. I thoroughly approved of her black velvet Saint Laurent suit with diamanté buttons and diamanté bag and shoes. The chicks are winning! In her mag she's handling hotter stories and exposing more dirt in the business sector than most of her male contemporaries. Good for her! In this era of conspicuous consumption, Wall Street CEOs and media moguls are getting the kind of play previously afforded rock stars and Jane knows how to take 'em down.

I am now the size of a tank. How can it be that also pregnant Anna Wintour seems to have only a neat couture bulge under a long Chanel jacket while I am now the size of a helium balloon? She's due two months before me, too — in January! She says she's going off to do the *Vogue* job in London in February, almost as soon as she drops the baby. I told her she should hire Gabé to be her right hand in Features. Gabé is bored out of her mind at *Tat* even though she loves Mark Boxer.

Tuesday, October 1, 1985

I had a dinner at Café des Artistes for Sarah Giles with the hoary mag writers Carl Bernstein and Jon Bradshaw. Carl and Bradshaw were really condescending about *VF,* comparing it to their old grand journalism days. I let them have it, telling them they were both self-satisfied oldsters who don't get out and hustle anymore, and are always telling me what's a great idea but then have no energy to report it. Maybe I am getting my revenge for all those months of everybody patronizing me, especially lofty male media heavies.

André Leon Talley has signed on to *VF* as style editor. Michael Roberts, it seems, is back at *Tatler* working for Mark Boxer. It would certainly be hard to miss André Leon Talley if he also disappeared. He is a six-foot six-inch black fashion plate in TV frame Chanel sunglasses and usually swathed in long cashmere shawls. His daily uniform is a gray cavalry twill Chanel jacket with gold buttons, specially made for him by Karl Lagerfeld, he claims. It looks so witty when writ as large as he is. As does the oversized burgundy box calf Hermès Kelly bag (these are all André's words, he's a human fashion caption) that he carries around with God knows what in it. Apparently he was raised in North Carolina by a grandmother who taught him how to appreciate luxury. He's already transformed his end of the office. The fashion department has no cubicles, but he's marked his end with a tiny teetering gilt and pastel-velvet boudoir chair that I haven't seen him, or anyone else, sitting on yet.

He has some great fashion ideas. Fiftieth anniversary of Clare Boothe Luce's *The Women* coming up and he wants to re-create their immaculate wardrobes and maquillage as modern fashion spreads by Herb Ritts.

The pages of *Vanity Fair* came alive with the Broadway opening of *Tango Argentino* last night. I am so happy we noticed it early on its bright, blazing summer tour. The show was sublime, still with its cast of real, unglamorous Argentinian tango dancers, ravaged women with hectic rouge, crumpled gigolos, and portly middle-aged husbands with magic feet. It was like being in the thick of a smoky nightclub in Buenos Aires where the dancing just happens to be extraordinary.

The cosmopolitan flavor continued at the *VF* office the next day. Marie-Paule Pellé, the *House & Garden* design editor who has been brought in from Paris by Alex as heir apparent to the editor Louis Gropp, came in jabbering in French; Beatrice Monti, wife of Gregor von Rezzori, showed up and jabbered in Italian; and the *Tango Argentino* crew jabbered in Spanish. Paloma's husband Rafael Lopez-Sanchez and their writer friend, Javier Arroyo, who co-wrote the piece for *VF* about the show's genesis, appeared flushed with first night success. Javier is part of the Paloma/Rafael circle in Paris that also includes the two original creators of the show, Hector Orezzoli and Claudio Segovia. I felt I had spent the day at a foreign airport without ever reaching my destination.

Tuesday, October 15, 1985
San Michele, Tuscany

Harry spirits me away! I am sitting at the writing desk of our room at San Michele. The hotel is even more delicious than I'd hoped — an old monastery with a Michelangelo facade, Etruscan sarcophagus in the hallway, the cloisters transformed into a long dining area with open archways looking down over Florence. I love the terra cotta walls and sailcloth blinds and lampshades, the armchairs patterned with roses. I want this color scheme everywhere I live!

Yesterday we went into Florence on the bus and saw the museum of the Duomo and the Uffizi Palace and lunched on mouthwatering pizza and salad at a café in the square, reading our books. (I brought a cache of cultural cramming: Vasari's *The Lives of the Artists,* Clark's *Civilisation,* which I haven't read since I was fifteen.) Also been reading a fascinating book, *Royal Feud,* about the Duchess of Windsor and the Queen Mother. It tells the story of their intense thirty-year enmity over Edward VIII's abdication and confirms all my suspicions of the sainted Queen Mum. She really is an intractable old battle-ax, ruthless, narrow, and a cruel snob. She should have been grateful that Edward's obsession with Wallis saved England from a Nazi sympathizer (as Edward was) on the throne. Not to acknowledge the duchess even at the end was such a malicious act. It also seems to me, reading this, that the Queen Mother's craving for the limelight (which is what it was and is) has all been to compensate for a private life of utter sterility. When I last saw Colin Tennant he told me that she had been in love with his father and he jilted her.

"Why did you like him?" Colin asked her. "He bullied me," she replied. Here was a strong, sexually driven woman who never met her match and then had to subdue the fire to marry the fairly pathetic stammering Bertie, and did everything she then could to kick him up the ladder to the throne. (I never believed her supposed "chagrin" that he would endure the stress of being king. She was desperate for it.) Intuitive history is a very amusing game. I'd like to do a biography someday. Maybe of her.

Friday, October 18, 1985

We drove to Cetinale near Siena and had lunch with Lord Lambton, who's written a piece for us on his wonderful house. Have long been fascinated by Lambton, the reprobate peer who had to resign from the Heath government in 1973 — he was secretary of defense — after being photographed in bed with two hookers smoking cannabis. Always seemed so Byronic and dark.

Pulling up to the house, which is four hundred years old and once belonged to Pope Alexander VI, I was reminded, if I needed to be, about the delightful access a magazine provides. It gives you a license to satisfy curiosity without the rent of social obligation.

Cetinale dominates a hill seven miles west of Siena. A large golden rectangle with a long, straight avenue of cypress trees at the back. Six dogs rushed out to bark at us followed by a shy Italian girl with a baby. Then Lord Lambton appeared at a top window and we waited for him to come down.

He was much taller and older than I had expected. His face all cracked and craggy, scarecrow frame slightly stooped, languid voice. Eyes full of malicious fun behind dark-tinted glasses, a strong, sarcastic mouth. Mad, bad, and dangerous to know, all right.

The shabby comfort that Lambton wrote about in his October *VF* piece has, in real life, overtones of seediness like himself. The entrance hall, with a sofa shoved against the family portrait, is cluttered and dark, the sitting room — my favorite detail is the fat stone cherub slung on a messy table — is slightly dirty. The shades are all askew on the lamps, and ancient copies of the *Daily Mail* lie heaped on a table along with books of horror stories.

The full ashtrays are the relics of his after-lunch cigars. No sign of his aristocratic mistress, "Mrs. Ward," as he calls her. He slumped down in the sofa, very civil and friendly, occasionally drifting off behind his dark tinted glasses in moments of deep introspection. "Frightfully efficient, your magazine," he said. "Never come across so much professional courtesy in my life." I told him about the flap over my Diana story in case he missed it.

"Mrs. Ward read it before the rumpus," he said, "and found it very interesting and sympathetic. Trouble was it was probably rather too well informed." He'd also read *Royal Feud* and picked up on what a shit Mountbatten was.

"I am planning a book about him myself," he said. "He's actually a man I rather admire but he was quite incapable of telling the truth. He lied about everything all the time, and you know, once you start it's frightfully difficult to stop. My theory is, he was obsessed by his illegitimacy and invented all kinds of rubbish about himself to cover it up." We had lunch in a conservatory painted from top to toe with a faded mural. His secretary joined us, a pretty, silent blonde girl with whom he probably enjoys recreational humiliation. I asked him what he had thought of our Claus von Bülow piece. "Very, very good," he said. "He brought it with him, you know, when he came to stay in July." (Really?)

"Did Andrea come, too?" I asked.

"Yes, isn't she frightful?" he replied. "She was wearing the most extraordinary clothes. It must have been a hundred and two degrees and she was in some tight, ruched blouse, jewelry, and stockings. You know, Claus was never a great friend of mine, I just knew him a bit. So when he said he wanted to come for the weekend I didn't mind. I mean one isn't going to drop someone when something like this happens. (Pause.) Do you think he did it?"

"Yes I do," I said.

"I wonder," said Lambton. "When he came to stay I thought I would clear the air. So I said, 'Look here, Claus.' " (At this he burst into wild laughter.) " 'Look here. If you didn't kill Sunny, what do you think happened?' And you know, he didn't have an answer, which seemed pretty odd after God knows how many years." (More wild laughter.) "But you know, Claus was always someone one felt a bit sorry for. Before this tragedy he had another one. All his hair fell out when he was quite young, and he had a hair transplant that didn't quite work and looked exactly like pubic hair. Frightful, poor fellow. And then the joke went around about him that he'd slept with his dead mother."

"It's not very funny, that joke, is it?" I said, increasingly appalled.

This seemed to amuse Lambton very much and he laughed so much he coughed and choked. "No, it's not very funny, is it? Not very funny at all." A cook served us pastrami followed by stuffed peppers. Lambton flipped the pastrami onto his plate with his fingers. Harry decided to try to get him on politics. Lambton was careful to say nothing about Mrs. Thatcher and made no comment when Harry pitched into monetarism and other current canards, no doubt because Tony himself is very much on the right wing of the Tory party. After lunch he took us outside and walked us around the garden, pointing out the drought-devastated olives, the bullet holes on the facade of the house where there was a shootout with the SS in the war. The garden was a tumbling miracle of color and secret arbors. There was such a lovely smell of rosemary. Amazingly, he doesn't speak a word of Italian — "I'm tone-deaf, you see" — so God knows whom he talks to. He's up at five every morning working on his novel, about a haunted abbey. Perhaps he wants a novel to match his own sinister appearance.

Lambton clearly took a shine to me, saw I appreciated his sense of humor. I could see him watching me behind his shades like a horny reptile. The fact that I am pregnant and have my husband with me just added to his perverse interest.

H and I left him waving gauntly at us amid

a sea of frenzied dogs. We spent the afternoon replaying the best bits of the visit as we loafed around among the skinny towers of San Gimignano. It seems that in the fourteenth century a tower was not just a lookout post but a status symbol for the nobles, just as it is in today's Manhattan. All Donald Trump and Edgar Bronfman require is some boiling oil to repel the takeovers and life would be pretty much unchanged.

Monday, October 28, 1985

Walked through the door of the *VF* office to instant static. Michael Coady from *WWD* yelling down the phone about what he said was an impending hatchet job I had commissioned about him. "And you know I've always defended you. Even using the word 'pussy-whipped' in that Diana piece — that was too much. People are saying you are out of control!" But the good news is that the October "Mouse that Roared" issue sold over a hundred thousand on the newsstand, which is fifteen thousand more than September. I guess I have kissed off Princess Di as an ally, if she ever was one. I am so often compared to her in appearance, and yet we couldn't be more unalike in every other way except we both require absolute control, we both are shopaholics, and we both hide deep passions under chocolate-boxy looks (which I am

351

swiftly losing in my elephantine condition).

This morning Harry got the unsettling news his *Times* deputy, Charlie Douglas-Home, died of cancer last night. Harry was very upset, even though Charlie was no friend of his in the Murdoch showdown.

It's strange how those calamitous events at *The Times* remain for me the events not of a career debacle but of a crime. I remember in the days when Rupert's henchmen were trying to force Harry out I felt I was witnessing a murder with Charlie as an accessory. As the underperformer in an illustrious family, Charlie just wanted to be editor of *The Times* so much it was easy for Rupert, so brilliant with character deduction, to exploit that weakness. In many ways, Charlie was as much a victim of Murdoch as Harry was. And now, poor Charlie is dead and *The Times*, with all its political influence, and *The Sunday Times*, which Harry made a cash cow, is Rupert's to do with as he will.

Tuesday, November 12, 1985

Princess Di wowed DC, she really did. I got multiple reports of the magic of it all. Her whirl across the dance floor in the East Room of the White House in the arms of John Travolta in the midnight-blue velvet Victor Edelstein dress — epic. She sat between the president and Baryshnikov. Every face-lift from Park Avenue to Bel Air was on the guest list. Misha Baryshnikov told me he was struck by the "extraordinary transparency of her skin against the tight blue dress, the deep blue eyes, so much more beautiful than any photograph or on TV." It's always been about the coloring with Di. The pale peach skin, the moonstone eyes. Ballet nut that she is, I am sure she would have much preferred to dance with Misha, but he had a knee injury and couldn't. It was brilliant of Nancy Reagan therefore to tap Travolta on the shoulder after dinner for an "excuse me" to lead the princess in a dance. Once again the Reagans know how to create the iconic pictures. Those ten minutes on the dance floor were instant history, glamour for the ages. Washington is such a dowdy town, a center of power but not fashion. Senatorial wives trundle around in their Escada suits and sparkly brooches on the lapel. Diana's combination of refinement, beauty, and youth was the corrective, the lift, a Bel Air White House needs. And for the Waleses, whose marriage seems to be in the tank, this iconography was a global tonic. Chris Hitchens told me that the next day he saw the princess looking "pale and ill," descending the embassy stairs with Charles as if they had just had a nasty row, but the language of gesture, the images now lighting up every publication in the world, will live so much longer than that.

Monday, November 25, 1985

Just in from a soiree for the cabaret pianist Bobby Short. Some diamond-studded socialite crooned at me, "My dear, you have certainly found your audience and it's me! *Vanity Fair* is a society movie magazine. You don't remember what they are, but you're it." She's half-right. But it's more the *VF* attitude to fame and the mix of stories that ensnare the reader with juxtaposition. We give intellectuals movie star treatment and movie stars an intellectual sheen and the same is true of the audience. Brainy people in our pages seem more glamorous and movie people seem more substantive. I love putting madcap Princess Gloria von Thurn and Taxis in the same issue as Schiff's profile of the editor of the *National Review*. Both of them are hidden stars in their own worlds, but combined in a magazine that has Dustin Hoffman on the cover, they confer fascination on each other. It's funny how sometimes the mix takes on a life of its own and goes off the cliff. The January issue is suddenly so full of people with bald heads, I had to kill three of them today.

At dinner I was seated beside Bobby Short, whom I very much enjoyed. His South of

France villa is called Villa Manhattan, which I thought was a wonderful title for a play, and he did come up with some great lines in his hoarse, punctilious voice. "Chicago! Well, it seems to have so much. The right clothes, the right jewels, the right food. But in twenty minutes it can turn into a cattle town. Los Angeles, well, I liked Los Angeles. I lived there for eighteen years. But it was a long time between thrills. New York! My God, the opulence. Once upon a time all you had to do to get attention was wear a brown tuxedo — no more!"

When he talked about how hard he works and how tired he gets of playing and smiling, it felt like the hidden core of him revealed. I remember the film director Marek Kanievska once said to me — just before I left *Tatler* and was in my between-life crisis, feeling stressed out about all the demands of an editor — "But you can't give up now! That daily battle is what makes you you, and me me. I'm a shy person, very inward looking. But I go out on a crowded set with people and cajole and hassle and scream to get it done." I thought about what Bobby Short said tonight — that I have "arrived." I know that arriving will never be an option for me.

Thursday, December 5, 1985

Now I understand why Frank Crowninshield

wrote that famous *VF* essay "Ten Thousand Nights in a Dinner Coat." New York's pace hots up to a burning crescendo this time of year. Exhausted faces with strained eyes and upturned collars hurtle between restaurants, dinner parties, and cocktails. Tonight I dine at the apartment of the department store supremo Geraldine Stutz. Lunch was Denise Hale with twenty-four guests at Le Cirque. The office is wild, stuffed with visiting foreigners and overenthusiastic socialites assailing me with new ideas. Now that I have made half of New York a contributing editor, I am paying the price. The phone lines are burning up with connections from Palm Beach, Tuscany, Los Angeles, and Washington, demanding to speak only to the editor in chief. At Denise's lunch I commissioned everyone at the table, but then again it was a pretty good lineup. John Richardson, Alex Gregory the publisher and aesthete, the film aficionado Rex Reed. Reinaldo, looking ashen from late nights, was at the next table and clearly wished he was at ours. Richardson has grown a mustache since I last saw him and is as lethal as ever, this time about the Washington National Gallery's president, J. Carter Brown. "He's the worst kind of early settler," said John. "Acquisitive, tight, opportunistic, thrusting, but all with an impeccable overbred manner and that terrible mirthless laugh." Jesus. I am told and believe that John has a cache of ruthless pen portraits of the likes of Wallis Simpson he will at some point unleash on the world, hopefully in *Vanity Fair*. He and Alex Gregory engaged in a delicious argument about Braque's horrible middle period when he only painted still lifes for rich people's dining rooms, and went on to how Chagall wasn't any good after 1914.

"My theory is that no one was any good after 1914," said Rex Reed, which was a good try but he knew he was outclassed as the three art mavens swept on.

Mort Zuckerman showed up and we had a long chat. I told him he should move *US News* to NYC as he clearly hates the travel (and I would get Harry back!). He said he was going to do that eventually, so I said, "What's wrong with now? You have three empty skyscrapers and you're sick of com-muting." He proceeded to enthuse feverishly about the idea, but then one of the enjoyable things about Mort is that you can get him excited about anything or anybody for five minutes. He went on and on about Harry's brilliant redesign of *US News* that has trans-formed the look of it but never says it to Harry himself. Ultimately, it's not going to work for Harry there unless there is some clarity of command.

With the baby coming I'm trying to finish February and prepare March and April and May at the same time, and all the cover stories keep going down like ninepins. I nearly screamed when Javier Arroyo came into the office to discuss his "politics of couture" piece and wanted to engage in social small talk. I cut him off at the pass. "Javier, I want you to go to Cadaqués in January instead and do 'The Last Days of Salvador Dalí,' " I said briskly.

"You know," mused Javier, "I saw a peecture of Dalí in Espanish paper last week with three pipes up his nose and I thought of you immediately." (How nice to know I have that effect on people!)

"Dalí, he wait to die until he sees Halley's Comet," continued Javier, confirming to me he knows so much good detail I want him to WRITE THE GODDAMN PIECE. And I will get him to do so. At lunch John Richardson said it was the best art story that hasn't been done, so if Javier doesn't do it I will try to twist John's arm to do some real reporting. ("Arianna should do that story," said John, "instead of trying to write about Picasso, about which she knows so much less than me.")

One welcome visitor in all this was dear Gabé from London. She's going to leave *Tatler* and work at British *Vogue* for Anna Wintour, which is great for both of them. I felt a twinge of regret. I should have brought her to NYC for us instead. I took her to dinner at Mortimer's with Miles and Jane Sarkin. Jane has some of Gabé's qualities — tough, loyal, tiny, huge sense of humor, and the courage of a lion under pressure. I wanted to hug Gabé when she said in her demure little voice, "T, did you know that Lord Dufferin's bum collapses once a month now and he has to have it sewn up?"

Last night was the hyperglamorous Costume Institute party at the Metropolitan Museum. Condé Nast takes four tables and I was seated next to Si. That morning he called me up to his office and gave me a fourteen-thousand-dollar raise, a strangely arbitrary amount. I didn't have the courage to say I thought the turnaround warranted more. He glowed at me, beatific behind his overlarge desk. "What you've done is nothing short of a miracle," he said with shy warmth. "It's just amazing."

I took Nick Dunne with me to the Met because Harry was in Washington and fashion isn't his scene anyway. Nick was the perfect commentator escort. "Wanna talk to Irene Selznick for three hours?" he asked when her familiar irate face under a pageboy haircut hoved into view.

I borrowed a silver velvet evening coat from Jackie Rogers to wear over a thin black silk full-length evening sack she made me to hide the bulge. A professional makeup artist came to do my face, which I didn't much like, but it made me feel suitably glam. I loved the excess and finery and ostentation of it all, teetering past Egyptian mummies and fading frescoes in our silly heels, herding into an elevator in a clash of perfumes and rustle of silks, disembarking into the darkened *Costumes of Royal India* show to oohs and aahs over outsize gold mannequins swathed in glittering silks and jewel-encrusted turbans, with the appreciative murmur of visiting Indian high society and the excited chatter of Gayfryd Steinberg and her posse. The walkers were out in force — the mincing gait of socialite Peter Schub with Lynn Wyatt on one arm and bouffante Judy Peabody on the other. Reinaldo Herrera in a tux has the inverted A waist of the society man par excellence, escorting on his left hand his lofty, expensively coiffed mother, on his right, Carolina, his Eva Peron–like wife. After dinner we wandered into the Temple of Dendur, where Peter Duchin was pounding the piano and a million candles lit the drafty spaces where the B group, who didn't get seated, sparkled and networked and hustled. As Nick said, the bravery. This is what I appreciate most about the city at night, the life force of New York aspiration, wanting, wanting to be seen. The erratic flames of the myriad glowworms — the striving fashion assistants, makeup artists, art gallery gofers, photography apprentices, gossip stringers, all the glamour wannabes dressed up with their "looks" in place. How they danced. How they gestured and waved and admired one another's glad rags, cutting like flamboyant tugs through the sea of jaded vessels such as the SS *Jerry Zipkin* and the SS *Barbara Walters*. This is the moment when the social energy of the city — in Diller's word — metastasizes, when individual crassness and need are absorbed into the bedazzled, glory-seeking hum of "Look at me! I'm alive!"

Monday, December 16, 1985

I just hosted the *VF* office holiday party in the apartment. Seventy festive staff members streamed in from every department, everyone enjoying everyone else without a deadline hanging over them. But at the end I felt blue. Everyone made plans and went merrily off into the night at eight thirty. But with Harry in DC as usual I was left alone. I am so fed up with him being there instead of here with me. A healthy reminder, I suppose, of why a profession, however fulfilling, should never be mistaken for a life. And also how happy I am to have the beating heart of this baby in me, who will in three months be every cure for loneliness.

Sunday, December 29, 1985

Back from our Christmas break at La Samanna in St. Martin. It was a too-short week in the low-key solace offered by the seaside cottages. Richard Avedon was there, as was Peter Ustinov, who reminisced about working with Dad, and Bill Murray and Sam Spiegel, yet I didn't feel socially invaded. Just sat around in all my pregnant enormity with my hair in a wet knot, which was so rare for me. At night the candlelit dark was soft and the food good, we both wound down. The big mistake was to come home via Palm Beach, where I wanted to meet Nick Dunne and Helmut Newton, who had teamed up to do a Palm Beach social story. As soon as we walked into the Breakers it was a hideous reversal of the past week. Ghastly pachyderm people milling around the pretentious spaces doshed up in observance of a strict dress code, great impersonal outdoor canteens staffed with sullen hamburger chefs, a pokey bedroom suite with a TV spewing out hotel entertainment to match the brain rot milling around in the overbearing lobby. Harry bought a bottle of whiskey and proceeded to down it in misery. Helmut's ironic despair was almost as great as mine, except he will do pictures that reflect it. I do love Helmut. Sitting in the Breakers bar in his linen "jecket," red tie, and white pants, he was absurdly, effortlessly chic. He talked of fleeing Nazi Germany at seventeen, heading for China and Australia, and of his life in Monaco: "You know there is no one to talk to but I like my terrace." I was struck all over again at the huge displacement of the émigré Jews and how much it has influenced their outsider powers of observation. Somewhere beneath the mystery and sexual irony of Helmut's work one senses a bleak soul searching for an explanation. There's an almost cosmic indifference to his shrug.

I think of him now, courtly, contrary, rigorously demanding to the point of bullying when he doesn't get his own way, gazing around the Breakers bar with a look of glinting intent.

Tuesday, December 31, 1985

New Year's Eve alone in my apartment. The office closed at one. Harry back in DC, so I wandered home. Got into my old sweatpants and wound down into morose self-communion about what I want from the year ahead. My fascination with New York success is beginning to pall. I look out of my Venetian blinds at the lighted irregular egg cartons of the apartment blocks across the street. I think with affection and a certain maternal protectiveness of my *Vanity Fair* staff alone in their own small apartments before whatever festivities they have in mind, or possibly, as with me, none. I see boyish Charles in his art director–ish minimal space, waiting for the coffee to brew, Ruth in a shapeless smock, staring around her tasteful apartment, still unfinished because she can never decide on the colors and fabrics, Sharon downtown in Chelsea, reading under a bedspread with a glass of wine, Miles watching reruns of *Masterpiece Theatre* on PBS, Wayne's thin shoulders bent over a corner desk, giving one last read to a piece, Elisabeth Biondi, our new picture editor from Germany, still shaken up after her mugging on Christmas Eve, restlessly trying one cassette then another. All of us wondering what the New Year will hold after so many months of joined, excited effort. There will always be something magical to me in creative collaboration and the bonds it forges. I silently wish them all Happy New Year.

1986
WE ARE THREE

Monday, January 27, 1986

Oh my God! I am a mother!

George Frederick Evans, named after my dad and Harry's, was born two months early at two o'clock on Sunday morning. I am so not ready for this and in my cocky, breezy, I-am-superwoman way, I never dreamed anything bad could happen with our baby. I am humbled by the awful swift cycle of events and feel there is an admonition in it. This is life. This could have been death. I have only seen my son for five minutes in the incubator. He is four and a half pounds. Trying to conjure up a maternal bond but actually feeling as if I have been in a car crash. But then, this morning, shuffling slowly in my gown with an IV attached, I went to visit him in the preemie unit with Harry.

He is so perfect and pink with a serious round head and crinkly nose and his little chest fluttering up and down like a frightened robin. He has a respiratory infection, which they say will improve. I felt the stirrings of longing then. The worst of this whole experience has been the sense of being cheated of the natural path of motherhood, the time to adjust.

It started on Saturday evening at ten o'clock. Mum and Dad were here. Another lucky thing. We had spent a freezing-cold morning out looking at nursery furniture and then afterward went to the movies to see *Out of Africa.* In the afternoon I felt tired and heavy but put it down to the flu. We ordered in Chinese food and were all watching TV in my bedroom when I felt a gush of blood between my legs. I was hemorrhaging badly. Harry rushed and phoned Dr. Sullum. He said, "Get to Mount Sinai Hospital and I'll meet you there." Harry called the ambulance and, when that failed to show, a limo. Both arrived at once. But the ambulance driver said he wouldn't take me to Mount Sinai, it was beyond his jurisdiction. It was New York–Presbyterian or nothing. By this time I was so distraught, terrified of losing the baby. An argument raged back and forth between the ambulance driver and Harry as I continued to bleed. Harry decided I better go to New York–Presbyterian even without Dr. Sullum to meet me, as Sullum has no affiliation there. We then hurtled off in a manic convoy, me in the ambulance, Harry and the parents in the limo, and were disgorged all at the same time at the neonatal unit of New York–Presbyterian. I was rushed in on a stretcher. Sullum had recommended a high-risk obstetrician but omitted to say that she lives in New Jersey. They put me on a sedative and warned me that if the placenta separated it would be an instant Caesarian. Harry sat beside me, holding my hand, trying not to cry. My doctor, a sturdy black lady with a big, confident smile, finally arrived. She looked at the monitors and immediately decided to operate. The next time I saw her she was in her cap and gown. They shot me up. When I came to in a hospital room I could see outside the window that it was all white, a snowstorm in the night. I looked up at the TV screen suspended from the ceiling and saw a space shuttle, the *Challenger,* in position for a flight. A nurse came in and said, "You have a baby boy."

It was all so unreal, so utterly unlike what I had hoped for or planned. Now we wait and pray that the fluttering creature in the warm light box will make it and be the sturdy little boy, the little Harry of our dreams. Please, God, please let him be all right.

Thursday, January 30, 1986

My life seems to have drained away. My darling baby had two days of getting steadily worse till yesterday, when his oxygen needs began to decrease. Then he got jaundice and I couldn't bear to see more tubes and plasters all over his tiny, struggling body in the incubator. But today, the improvements continued and I felt so shattered by the emotion of it all, I just sat in front of his glass container in the preemie unit and cried. This evening, to my joy, he is breathing on his own and he took my breast milk through a tube and sucked on a pacifier. With some of the tubes and bandages off him I could take a good look and I know now that he's really beautiful and distinctive. He has nice small ears and Harry's purposeful mouth and chin, a long, athletic torso and legs, as if he may become tall. Tonight, I opened the porthole and sang to him and he opened his eyes for the first time and looked me full in the face with intense blue eyes. Then he gave a sweet smile. I go over the last few weeks again and again, remembering how I broke my resolution to slow down and got tense and overtired. I can hardly bear to think what might have happened if he had been born in St. Martin. Or if the hemorrhage had happened when Harry was in DC and I was on my own. As it is, God was watching over me. In the end, to be brought to New York–Presbyterian was the best possible mistake. The neonatal is the best in the city and my obstetrician, whom I met for the first time in the emergency room and whom I would likely never have found on my own, turns out to be the very type of obstetrician I was looking for. I consulted a series of patronizing, inattentive, desultory male doctors. She is, by contrast, strong, practical, commanding, and punctilious. I feel total confidence in her. So although we are not out of the woods yet, I know George Frederick, my little Hanoverian prince, is in good hands.

What will my baby become? Will he become the joy of my life and mine of his? I like to think of him hanging tough in his container, working up the muscles he needs to pull through. If it had been a girl, I think I would have fallen apart altogether, feeling she was more vulnerable even than he is now.

Now Harry needs almost as much looking after as Georgie. He is wrecked by the experience, remembering all the pain of the premature son he lost in his first marriage to Enid. Tonight he's gone back to DC, which is as well, to take his mind off it. I want to enter a new period of calm in which all the energy goes into loving Georgie. The world is upside down. When I opened my eyes on Tuesday morning, I saw the *Challenger* shuttle explode before our eyes on TV. The crew had become so real to me. I cried and cried.

Two weeks or more has passed and my baby
is still in the hospital. But he's graduated to
the last room and is in an open bassinet,
thank God. We have been through so much
anxiety I feel as if life is pallid limbo. I work
from home, using the phone from my bed, as
stitches in my stomach from the Caesarian
are still extremely painful. The editors come
over for meetings. But between these visits I
don't think of *VF* much. I've discovered the
complete irrelevance of the office. I see the
folly of having not checked out of work much
sooner. At four thirty every day I go back to
the hospital and help the nurses feed G or let
the nurses help me. There is now only one
important fact in my life, whether or not the
scrappy, warm bundle will burp after his
bottle, or whether like a snuffling puppy he
will prefer to snuggle against my chest, making squeaking noises and failing to get rid of
his wind. Motherhood is the only surefire
head emptier I have yet encountered. My
deep depression in the hospital has given way
to manic anxiety mixed with the flutterings
of desperate hope. Bradycardia has kept G in
the hospital, and episodes of apnea when he
horrified us with spells of going dusky blue
in my inept arms. Before he moved, he was
in a horrible room with sixteen babies to

three nurses, glaring lights, banging pedal trash cans, and one nasty militant nurse who poisoned the atmosphere by constantly moaning about how much she hated working in the unit. Night after night, she banged around the poor sleeping babies, waking them up, addressing the fraught backs of their parents in their yellow gowns with her rantings. I wanted to fucking kill her. "I'm sorry, am I in your way?" Mum asked her witheringly when she pushed against the back of her chair. "Yes, you're in my way," she replied sulfurously, but there is nothing we can do because all the power to make life difficult is hers. A friend of Marie's, Barbara Liberman, sent me a premature-baby book and it's been a huge solace, as well as a revelation that I cannot kid myself about. There could be complications. Eyes and ears are at risk. Problems with motor skills. Developmental delays. I am so lucky he doesn't have cerebral palsy. He may turn blue again and I have to know what to do. It's likely, I have to accept, that he may not be 100 percent okay. But I am now just grasping how lucky we are that he's as good as he is. His weight is now five pounds, and the occasional bradycardia happening with more and more time in between.

With my neurotic moralizing streak I see what's happened as a punishment for a surfeit of thoughtless success. So you think you're going to romp through motherhood, too, huh? Try this on for size! Remember pain and grief and failure? Here's a refresher course.

My love for Harry has flowered into a desperate need for him. And he seems to feel the same way. We cling to each other like greedy castaways. I realize how much this baby is an expression of my love for him. And we lie together and cry and cry because we'd so hoped for it to happen in a different way.

The baby nurse, Juanita, has moved in to await G's homecoming. She came from the Fox Agency, where I stipulated that I wanted a warm, experienced middle-aged lady, not some posh Brit Norland nanny, or an on-the-make au pair. Mum interviewed her and said she thought she would be right. Very quiet, kind, and efficient Filipina. Able to look after me, too, when Mum goes home and H is in DC. She has to share the room with Georgie. When I started preparing the nursery today I felt glimmers of maternal excitement.

On Friday Marie Brenner, Jim Hoge's wife, Sharon, and Shirley Clurman gave a "surprise" shower for me at Mortimer's on the same date it had always been planned for, except of course, the surprise was the early birth, not the party. They had assembled a great bunch of girlfriends: Annie Leibovitz, Sarah Giles, Ruth and Pam from the office, Adele Guare, Kathleen Tynan, Norris Mailer, and Liz Smith, whom I now adore. Perversely, our dust-up seemed to win her over. Glenn Bernbaum did a long table festooned with chocolate hearts since it was Valentine's Day, and they all brought the sweetest little romper sets and blankets and quilts. Four of them bought me a glorious crib, which is being delivered tomorrow.

In fact, with all the flowers arriving and warm messages I am feeling at last the big beating heart of New York City that lies beneath its harsh exterior. There was so much kindness and affection in the room, and it felt personal, not professional for a change. I feel as if childbirth is a secret society. It seemed as if every woman there had a story of something that had gone wrong. The "have it all" propaganda in "woman's page" journalism has excessively played down the hazards of getting and being pregnant. A story in that, I am sure.

Georgie is now much better after a day on the new feed, alert when we arrived and deliciously pink. My little snow pig! I put him to my breast for the first time and he flailed around, sucking everything in sight, then took a strong nibble and looked so happy and animated. Then, when there wasn't enough milk I moved him to his new formula and he glugged all that down and did a huge burp, smacking his chops and gazing happily around. I told him a story of how he's a Quogue baby, and how all Quogue babies arrive two months early so they can be big in time for summer and be carried out to the Magic Dune. He smiled sagely and drifted off to sleep to the sound of his musical pillow. I love him so much and feel a surge of excitement at the fun he's going to be; now I can glimpse that jolly little person struggling to emerge.

Tuesday, February 25, 1986

Georgie's coming home tomorrow! I went to the hospital to start getting briefed on it all. There are so many medical issues to attend to, I am glad I have a professional baby nurse. I am a little afraid of his homecoming in case he has a relapse and there are no doctors there to help.

Harry and I went out to our last dinner as childless parents, or so it felt, with Jane Amsterdam and John Larsen, a pure fun foursome after all the tension. We rolled in at eleven, still laughing and blaspheming about the cast of characters we'd been talking about, when Harry suddenly remembered that Juanita was in the nursery for tomorrow's baby homecoming. "Shh!!" H said. "Don't forget you're a mummy now."

Wednesday, March 5, 1986

Today the pediatrician weighed Georgie in at

six pounds, eight ounces. Over a pound in a week! The little champ is pulling through. It's beautiful and strange having him home. The worst of preemie birth is how it interferes with mother-baby bonding. I feel a kind of unrequited love when I peer into his crib and see his pink, open face. My favorite face of all is his prefeed face, when he works his mouth like a little bird searching for worms. Then, when his bib is tied around his neck he looks about him with an expression of happy anticipation. Pure, guileless trust that makes me want to squeeze him to death. After his feed I rest his sweet, hay-smelling head against my chest and rub his back. Having Juanita to help has been wonderful, she is so professional, but I am now also finding that she saps my confidence as a mother a bit, always better than me at the careful doses of Mylanta he needs at intervals through the day and night. I can't do nights if I am to continue working from home, but it makes me jealous of their intimacy. After so long in the hospital, will he just think I am another nurse? Since he has fed from a bottle since birth, he and I are now both pretty useless at breastfeeding. I wanted the cozy closeness of breastfeeding. I get the closeness in other ways. I love to hold him on my chest or stomach and let him fall asleep, calmed by my breathing. Juanita says I am setting up trouble for myself, that he will be too hard to deal with when I cuddle him at night, but I am ignoring her. The pediatrician said I must look into his face and talk to him a lot, when I really just want to hold him. I still feel almost shy with him, convinced he doesn't understand I am his mother.

Looking at the other babies, I was aghast at their raucous prizefighter faces. In his white wool cardigan and knitted bonnet Georgie was like a Victorian Christmas card. This Friday is his real due date, so his weight is just what it ought to be if he'd come to full term.

Harry is wonderful with him. He sings him songs from his own past I have never heard before. Childbirth pulls so much from unconscious memory. Like me, he most loves "Happy Face" before he feeds, and "Mournful Face" when he can't burp.

Tuesday, March 11, 1986

I love working from home now, not having to contort myself into a high-heeled hellion. An interview with me in *The Sunday Telegraph* arrived, written by a smart, beady Oxford journalist, and I was depressed by its depiction of me in my suit and pearls with hair like a "tossed salad" and a "newsreader's smile." Ugh. Why do I work so hard and spend so much money to create this wholly fallacious picture of myself? Being at home and out of the insane materialism of the New York social scene has been so refreshing. Tonight is the tenth anniversary of Mortimer's, and the world and her walker are out knocking back champagne and shrieking their insincerities even as I write, while I have dined alone on a lamb chop and spent the evening trying to find out if Georgie preferred his Humpty-Dumpty mobile or his musical elephant. I feel so happy.

On Sunday I had a row with Juanita. I can't stand the way she always, always tells me I am doing something wrong when I am with G. I am a hopeless cook and a hopeless housewife, but it really hurts me to have her constantly implying I am incompetent as a mother, too. Her role is to help me be one, not compete with me for Georgie's approval. I now want to kill her every time I hear her playing his musical elephant, which has been our special toy. I told her to back off and she then went and cried for two hours in the bathroom. Then I heard her listening to tapes of the last baby she worked with screaming and babbling, probably as some kind of consolation, but it also felt weird and creepy. I think I need someone less invasive, but don't want in any way to disrupt G.

Doug Johnston came over for an office update. It jostled my bliss. The June ads now coming in are six pages fewer than last year, largely, I suspect, because some of his sales staff are dropping the ball. He's bizarrely unconcerned for some reason, telling me he has "two years to turn it around." Why on earth does he believe that? "Doug," I said, "Richard Locke was told he had two years. So were Joe Corr, David O'Brasky, and Leo Lerman. Don't you think that's an unwise assumption?" Anyone who trusts Si to be patient is crazy.

Wednesday April 9, 1986

The world is gearing up for Arianna Stassinopoulos's wedding next week to Michael Huffington, a Texas oil guy. The bridesmaids are Barbara Walters, Lucky Roosevelt, and Ann Getty. Mort Zuckerman is an usher. It's a writer's field day. Jackie Rogers is making me a skinny black top and long white skirt.

Georgie is increasingly delicious. He is now doing strenuous push-ups in his crib. Harry's Elgar trick is his best pacifier. G's round eyes go even rounder, his breathing becomes concentrated, his face assumes a rapt look as Harry waltzes him around the room in his snuggly to *The Enigma Variations.* So far there are no more signs of problems from the early birth, God bless him.

Sunday, April 13, 1986

Arianna's wedding [on Saturday, April 12]

was a diary classic. The whole world seemed to have assembled at St. Bart's Church as if for a royal occasion. The bride and groom were preceded down the aisle by a sound boom (which Harry at first thought was a cross) held aloft by a prancing sound man. Arianna herself looked amazing, a cross between Callas and Queen Alexandra. Galanos had made her a skintight, high-throated white lace gown with a coronet of orchids, and her hair was scraped back to reveal the regal nose. She was anorexically slim. To get to this size she must have lived on nothing but communion wafers for a month. The groom is a mystery really. A tall glass of water with a weak smile.

Since the service preceded Ann Getty's dinner dance, all the guests were dressed to the nines, each row bursting with taffeta and silk. Aileen Mehle was in her Belle Watling getup of two thousand bows on her head and a giant skirt. The starlet Leigh Taylor-Young was wearing a flouncing salmon tulle ball gown. Reinaldo Herrera, after saying for weeks that he refused to wear a dinner jacket because it made him feel he was in *Prizzi's Honor,* gave in and wore one but watched with heavy consternation as the service swerved from High Church to Greek Orthodox, with crowns held aloft over the bride and groom. "What will the psalms be in? Aztec?" muttered Henry Kissinger. Zuckerman trudged up and down the aisle, cracking gags as he performed his usher duties. "I'm available for bar mitzvahs, too," he hissed at Howard Kaminsky, the Random House publisher and CEO. The tiny figure of Arianna's old flame from London, the *Times* columnist Bernard Levin, ambled by, flanked by two taffeta Amazons, one of whom was Princess Michael of Kent. Anne Getty looked shapely and unconstrained in a yellow silk dress that looked good with her cloud of abundant titian hair. Barbara Walters carried off her unfortunate lavender bridesmaid dress extremely well. Afterward, a total of nearly eight hundred went on to the reception at the Metropolitan Club. There was a big posse of predinner floaters who seemed not to have seats. Most of these were Arianna's old friends. The receiving line went on till ten p.m. Harry caught sight of Anna Murdoch, who fled across the room. Rupert was more poised. He broke out of a group he was in and bounded over to greet Harry. They conversed cordially about the state of Fleet Street and the triumph of Rupert breaking the print unions at *Times* newspapers with his new printing plant at Wapping, a feat Harry genuinely admires and almost forgives the rest of it for. It's ironic. The union strikes that killed so many brilliant editions of *The Sunday Times* were the misery that made the Thomson family sell to Rupert in the first place. Perhaps it needed his brutal expediency to end the impasse. [The carnivore liberating the herbivores, as Murdoch later put it.]

At dinner I was at a great table, between Henry Kissinger and William Safire, along with Barbara Walters, Dick Snyder, Lally Weymouth, George Weidenfeld, and Princess Michael. George Weidenfeld spent much of the evening in plump reverie, puffing on his inevitable cigar. I'd love to have got inside his head. He has long been Arianna's sponsor from the days in London when she and I, as girl-about-town graduates from Cambridge and Oxford, respectively, used to go to his wonderful publishing salons on Cheyne Walk. As a combination of sophisticated cosmopolitan intellect and émigré Viennese huckster, he's always been a champion of unconventional upward mobility, especially when allied to a beautiful girl. It was his genius idea to have Arianna play the Greek card and write her biography of Callas in 1980 (which Harry extracted on the front page of the *Sunday Times* Review section, launching her author career). At the wedding he must have been thinking, *Look how we've pulled it off.* Only three years ago Arianna, looking for new horizons, was working the party circuit in New York and George was about to go broke at Weidenfeld and Nicolson. But their two-pronged seduction of Ann Getty means that both he and Arianna have landed in a giant pot of honey; he's wooed Ann into underwriting his publishing company and become her business partner, and Arianna has an influential new best friend and a new husband oozing with money from Texan oil.

George's speech was an encomium to Arianna, slightly marred by its strong commercial thrust promoting her forthcoming book on Picasso. Arianna herself gave longest and most profuse thanks to Ann Getty. At one point, according to Marie, Mrs. Huffington was seen pounding down the street away from the Metropolitan Club pursued by a solicitous Mrs. Stassinopoulos, who, after much gesticulating, persuaded her to return to the wedding party. Mrs. Huffington's umbrage could have been on any number of counts — the placing, the toasts, the cameras. In the receiving line, Arianna broke away to give love to Charlotte Curtis, which will ensure good coverage in *The New York Times*.

Wednesday, April 23, 1986

Getting to know Pace Gallery's Arnold Glimcher has yielded dividends. He has acquired a great art scoop (now ours) with the sketchbooks of Picasso, after years of courting the heirs. There are 175 in all, some owned by Paloma, some in private hands. When I expressed instant interest in publishing extracts, he asked me up to the Pace Gallery to view them. I found turning the pages strangely moving and exciting. Their very irregularity of size and shape reflects the inspiration of the moment. My particular fave is number sixty-six, a pocket-sized red moiré volume brought from the Biarritz branch of Mappin and Webb on Picasso's honeymoon with Olga in 1918. It holds seventeen different studies of her in Cubist undress. In great Alex tradition I am going to give it a twenty-two-page run. And of course have the very best *VF* writer to go with it in John Richardson, who knew Picasso and has so much knowledge. I found all this especially thrilling because the original *VF* was one of the first to publish Picasso in America. In a last inspired bit of chance I asked Alex if he had a great Picasso photograph to open and of course he does, from his book, the wondrous *Artist in His Studio.*

With this as the cultural capstone, the May issue is strong. Cher is on the cover in a great Annie close-up with her hands pressed to the steeple of her long face. Ian Jack's done a rich profile of Benazir Bhutto, who may be poised to be the leader of Pakistan (incredible to me when I think of how I used to see her hanging around the Oxford Union).

I lunched with John Richardson, who, unsurprisingly, was in full cry about Arianna's wedding. Michael Huffington, he insisted, is gay and also a born-again Christian — twice. "It's bad enough to be a born-again Christian once, but twice is too much," he said. "I dread to think what happened in between."

Georgie Porgie has caught a cold and every snuffle is like an arrow piercing. I worry so much about his health. We took him to Quogue for the first time last weekend. The alterations are wonderful! A huge farmhouse kitchen replaces the pokey two rooms that existed there before. Georgie's nursery isn't ready yet, so I put his crib in my study in front of the window looking out on the dunes, and it was so joyful to see him trying to stand up and look out. Harry sang to him all the way down in the car, to comfort him. I want more babies! Tons of them! A girl called Daisy and yet more!

Friday, April 25, 1986

Today when I woke up at seven I found myself between sleep and waking, thinking about Wallis Simpson, the Duchess of Windsor, and the irony of her fate, her lifetime of trapped penance for winning the man she loved at the expense of his abdication from the throne. I turned on the TV and a newsflash came up that she has just died. So bizarre. Harry is always saying I am psychic and perhaps I am, because a month ago I reached out to Wallis's great friend Aline, the

384

Countess of Romanones, whom Reinaldo brought to us, to tee up a piece about the duchess's last days. Fortuitously it's just about ready now to crash into the closing June issue with a cover flash. The piece is full of insider details. To me the most telling is the story about the duchess's sense of being snubbed by the royals yet again, just before the funeral of the Duke of Windsor. Wallis offered the Queen the use of her hairdresser, Alexandre from Paris, and was rejected. The duchess, after all these years, clearly didn't have a clue. She had no idea how deeply inappropriate such an offer would seem. The Queen would no more want Alexandre to pouf up her changeless, immobile shampoo-and-set than she would consider going to the Palladium with Steve Rubell for a nightcap.

Saturday, April 26, 1986

Park Avenue mores up close — some tips. To convey the precious bonds of friendship: when Reinaldo complains he has a bad back, two aspirins in an envelope dropped off at his town house by Pat Buckley's driver with a copy of Anita Brookner's new novel.

To note with regret a friend's absence from a house party — a half-eaten cake for Mortimer's owner, Glenn Bernbaum, delivered by Bill Blass's driver with a note. "We missed you this weekend, here's your piece. Enjoy."

Oscar de la Renta is an expert at these small, personal obeisances. So is Jerry Zipkin, of course. His thank-you presents are a legend of personal curation and inventiveness. A bunch of flowers after a weekend in the country sent by your secretary is not going to pass muster. Everything has to be strenuously personal, or, in the case of Pat Buckley, colorfully offbeat. Jayne Wrightsman, apparently, gave the Kissingers a tractor for Christmas for their house in Connecticut. She also buys four sets of Bulgari earrings at twenty-five thousand dollars a throw for each of her girlfriends. But few are in this league. Oscar, I am sure, is brilliant at not spending a bean. His are all tokens of high-concept creativity whipped up by his design staff.

Unlike everyone else, I really don't feel charmed by Oscar. Today he came on the phone and yelled at me because of Bob Colacello's great piece on John Fairchild and his sway over "society" in *Women's Wear Daily* and *W.* Bob wrote that Oscar leaked everything to *Women's Wear* to buy himself immunity from bad press. He got this direct from John Fairchild. Oscar, it seems, thought he was going to get special protection in *Vanity Fair* because he's such a close friend of Alex. "I am *totally* furious," he fumed at me. "I am such a friend of Condé Nast, and I have been treated like dirt. All my friends are calling me to say this piece is totally derogatory." (Glad they are all reading it.) "On top of which you say that Geoffrey Beene has a turnover of a hundred and seventy-five million and mine is twenty million, which frankly makes you ridiculous. I have nothing against Geoffrey Beene. He is a talented designer. It's just that his business is not twenty times bigger than mine! Mine is twenty times bigger than his. With my fragrance I am four hundred million! Everyone knows I am bigger than Beene!"

"Look, Oscar," I said, "if we have printed an incorrect figure, I would very much like to run a correction once we have checked it out. If we have been inaccurate, I can rush the correction into the July issue."

"What is the point?" he fumed again. (Artfully. He's not about to give me real figures to print.) "I am telling you, I would be calling Alex but he's left for Connecticut. And I tell you something else. When I see that cheap little nobody Bob Colacello he better get out of my path because I will knock him down."

I had a sudden memory frisson at this moment of my first meeting with Oscar four years ago in a freezing New York December when I was editor of *Tatler.* My mission, of course, was to try to get his advertising. Over lunch I could see Oscar sensed my need, and his amber eyes seemed to slant with cruelty as he deliberately withheld the favor. He has not perceived me as important enough, figuring he has Alex above me all sewn up. At the Saks lunch, I also learned that he is one of the only designers who refuses to let Saks advertise him in *VF.* (Why would he do that? Some umbrage whose cause is mysterious. Loyalty to Leo? Seems unlikely.) Now he just discovered that in the case of *VF,* Alex, in fact, does not call the shots.

"You know, Oscar," I said, "all this grieves me very much because I have always been very friendly toward you. In fact, only this week I killed a photograph of you with Annette Reed at a house party of Ahmet Ertegun that might have embarrassed you. And yet, I never hear from you. Ever since I have been in New York, you have never called me once." I also reminded him he's never advertised, and therefore has no leverage. He saw the blunder instantly. "You know, you are *totally* right," he said.

"Tina, I like you so much and you know I am always telling Alex what a brilliant thing he did bringing you from England. Somehow, the months flew by, my private life in total disarray . . ."

Now that I've got the conniving bastard where I want him, I am taking him to lunch May twenty-eighth to nail his business. I even followed the fine art of Park Avenue friendship and sent him over a copy of the sketchbooks of Picasso with a florid note inside. This was one of the more enjoyable power plays in NYC. Meanwhile, "I am bigger than Beene!" has become a new office catchphrase to replace "Styled by Shiva Fruitman."

Sunday, April 27, 1986

The Countess of Romanones called from Acapulco and said she had only just heard about the Duchess of Windsor's death. She is supposed to escort the duchess's body to Frogmore — on the grounds near Windsor Castle — on Tuesday. "I can't get through to the Lord Chamberlain from here, or British Airways," she said, implausibly. "Can you please send him a telex that I am on my way, and make me a reservation on the Concorde on Tuesday? I would be so terribly grateful. Also, if you wouldn't mind, can you ask Carolina Herrera if I could borrow a good black outfit for the funeral? Mine has white buttons, which might be all right — it wouldn't be in Spain, so I am not sure. I've got a black straw hat. You can tell Carolina, of course, that I'll mention that it's her dress at every appropriate moment." (I wonder which moments that would be. At the burial site?) When I transferred her over to Sarah Giles to deal with the blather, it became clear why the countess wanted us to do the bookings. She also expected us to pay! I guess the phone line to BA became cloudy when they asked for Aileen's Amex number. It was a typical response, somehow, from a friend of the Duchess of Windsor. The world's greatest clotheshorse and freeloader would have understood a dress borrowed from a designer and an air ticket scored from Condé Nast. In fairness, the duchess's estate had made no arrangements for how the round-trip would be paid, and Buckingham Palace is not exactly famous for picking up bills, especially when it came to Wallis. Still, it seemed shabby not to do so. And made the duchess's lonely end even more poignant. Is there anyone left who is not hustling? Georgie Frederick Evans, to whom I addressed this question, gave one of his extremely skeptical, nose-wrinkling smiles.

Wednesday, May 7, 1986

Robert Hughes was in noisy form about Arianna's wedding press. "It's frightening to think of George Weidenfeld fashioning this broad-shouldered Excocet beauty and aiming her at the bowels of Manhattan," he roared over lunch at the Four Seasons. He talked about the new book he's writing on the history of Australia called *The Fatal Shore* and asked me how I feel Americans see Australia. I said they see it as a more uncouth Texas. "It's so unlike Texas," Bob said. "The optimistic view of space that America has is completely untrue of Australia. Here, people feel the further west you went, the freer you were. In Australia, the further west you went, the deadlier it was. Space didn't mean freedom. It meant huge, invisible prison walls that separated you more from England. The distances in Australia are so . . . discouraging. But what I do still love about the place is the absence of euphemism. They've remained impervious to psychobabble and bullshit and jargon in a way I still find deeply refreshing. The concept of public relations is still comparatively new." It was so good to talk to Bob after two days of Fashion Week.

Ralph Lauren's show this morning was all about the marketing of a WASP daydream, an unabashed homage to Savile Row. He is a genius, I have decided, especially when you see him come out to take his bow, a small work fanatic from the Bronx, born Ralph Lifshitz, who made his way up from the tie counter at Brooks Brothers, driven by his fantasy of American blondness. And the blondes on his runway were amazing indeed — tousled Amazons in tweeds, all-American Sloane Rangers with a Hollywood gloss, snarling haughtily in their towering heels. The crowd was a clashing babble of the best people. Moving through it, inexorably, were the only people who really matter — the sober, taciturn figures of the men from Saks and the other stores, rotating from show to show with expressionless faces, looking out for the dress that will move units.

I have come to love this frivolous week in spring when creativity and commerce come together. In fact, I realize more and more, I love New York City, period. London seems to get smaller and smaller to me, as if it had swallowed Alice's "Eat-me" cake. I am beginning to feel that the vision of England I want to return to is increasingly the American vision. And I can create the best of both places here. Maybe Ralph Lauren is shrewder than he even knows. And what does my darling Georgie say to this? I will go wherever he wants and thrives! Today I bought him a wonderful feather duster to tickle his tummy on the changing table.

Sunday, May 18, 1986
Quogue

I am sitting in my brand-new den in front of the big window looking out on the dune. To enhance this working paradise I ordered a fabulous pine desk I saw at Marie Brenner's house from a warehouse in New Orleans. It's a six-and-a-half-feet-wide kitchen table with drawers, so I can spread right across instead of never having anywhere to put my overflow papers. In my extravagant way, I ordered two, one for here and one for New York, and they arrived in an enormous truck (like those days as a child when I kept ordering things from mail-order catalogs that showed up in huge containers at Little Marlow, to Mum and Dad's consternation).

This afternoon when I crept in to look at G napping, he looked so beautiful and happy it made me cry. The quality of his childhood sleep reminded me of my own. In my best memories of then, it was always summer nights like this. My favorite time was the dusk of seven o'clock, when I'd run about the lawn with Christopher, barefoot. Walking along the Quogue shore and seeing the two-year-olds with their buckets and spades made me proud and excited about Georgie's own happy life to come. But also anxious, anxious for him to turn out to be okay after all he's been through. The pediatrician says he is slow to lift his head from the crib and we are taking him to physical therapy. Harry sings him special songs and talks to him long and seriously, which he loves. I wish I could put the clock back to six months before his birth and change the outcome. I wish I knew if he will be all right.

Monday, May 19, 1986

I had a drink with Warren Beatty at the Ritz-Carlton. It was set up by Caroline Graham. She seems to know everybody, either through her school connections, her Kay Graham daughter-in-law connections, or her hot girl with David Frost in the seventies connections. She told me Warren was curious about me. I've never tried to meet him before, but now we're anxious to get a cover done for his new movie, *Ishtar.* The joy of being so far ahead on covers is that it gives us time to chase and negotiate.

I thought he'd stand me up but, even so, had raced to Bergdorf's to buy a slinky black top and turquoise jacket to impress the world's most seductive man. In fact, he confirmed the meeting several times throughout the day, each time adjusting the time a bit.

When he emerged out of the elevator at the Ritz he looked not so much a movie star as a disheveled intellectual in horn-rimmed glasses, tousled hair, and amorphous tweedy jacket. Only the unserious nose was reminiscent of Warren Beatty. The waiter tucked us into a table set for dinner, and under better lighting I could get a real look. His hair comes bouncing off his crown in a distinctly lightweight way. And his voice is light and Californian. It doesn't have the film-star timbre of Jack Nicholson. A very pretty waitress asked us what we wanted to drink. Beatty immediately registered her. "Are you the one who wants to go to NYU?" he asked. "Yeah, it's me." "I hope" — a magical smile — "you are really studying hard." Someone waved across the dining room. He took off one pair of glasses and put on another and said hi to Alan Jay Lerner. Then he put both pairs away and smiled at me myopically. That's when I got the movie-star charisma. The crow's-feet around the worn eyes all spring to attention, full of charm and irony. "Well, Tina," he said, "why are we having this drink? I only agreed to it because I really like Caroline. But, you know, I don't want to be interviewed." We dodged around that one for a bit. "How do you feel about David Thompson's piece on California in this month's issue?" I asked. Warren said nothing, but took his face into a sequence of silent reaction shots that were more expressive than anything he could say. They ranged from incredulity to pity, despair, hilarity. "If I really knew you I would tell you what I think," he said when he was done. "And it would be all about embarrassment for the guy who wrote it. But tell me, Tina, do you have any brothers or sisters?" A phone was brought to our table. He said into the mouthpiece, "Let me make a suggestion that may sound off the wall. Why don't you do this for no fee? I mean it could really work to come across as someone who's doing this for no money? Uh-huh. Uh-huh. It was just a thought." Hangs up. "Are your parents still alive, Tina?" I told him I thought he should do some memorable pictures with Annie Leibovitz. "What's memorable? I don't like what she does to people. She'd make me take my shirt off."

"Helmut Newton."

"I don't like all his whips and chains. What about the guy who's been photographing Jack [Nicholson] for you?"

"Herb Ritts?"

"Yeah. Does he take pretty pictures?"

"He's good," I said, and responding to the flirtatious gleam creeping into his eyes: "But I don't like using him because he doesn't let the editor in chief come to the cover shoots."

"Are you telling me you'd have to be on this shoot?"

"Yes," I said.

"Do I look as if I am fighting that, Tina?"

I brought the new June issue to show him, which probably wasn't such a great idea because it's more lightweight than May was. It has the great piece on the Duchess of Windsor, yes, but he probably wouldn't care about that. He's always trying to seem a political savant but I am not entirely sure he qualifies, though he's certainly smart . . . said he thought von Bülow on the cover was a big mistake and "only skimmed it," which I don't agree with and don't believe.

We talked about the need to satirize the rich at this moment. He brought up *Shampoo,* which, we agreed, is just the kind of film people want right now. "Who could write a sharp movie about the rich now?" (Me, I thought.) "Maybe Fran Lebowitz," he said, in that darting, table-hopping way. "I see her hanging out at some odd functions, looking mildly uncomfortable."

"Is she too much in the rich's thrall?" I pondered. He pushed his glasses up his nose and looked interested. "That's what you want for this subject," he said. "Someone who swam along with the rich, worked their way through it to the edges, rejected it, and now half hankers for it, even knowing what it means." Maybe he is very insightful, I thought, despite the tiny attention span.

In another mental table hop he started talking about my resemblance as an editor to Diana Vreeland. "Wasn't she fantastic?" he said. "Wasn't she just great? Shall we call her up and tell her?" The waiter brought the phone and he dialed her number without looking it up. Then he was spelling out his name to her foreign maid until Vreeland came on the line. He turned on the charm full blast. It was as if he was positioning himself to reseduce the old fashion diva at the other end of the line and was going to give it all he got. "Diana?" he said. "It's Warren. I'm sitting here in the Jockey Club with Tina Brown and we're just saying how wonderful you are." (Pause.) "Yes, wonderful. Well, if you've got laryngitis and can't speak, just listen. You're wonderful. And I am going to come and see you in two days. Yes! Because you're wonderful!" Charm, tenderness, intimacy oozed out of him.

Then he hung up and was on to why Ann Getty should be the mayor of San Francisco, how David Gergen is underrated, how Mort Zuckerman has a chance of being important "if he plays it right."

I circled inexorably back to the prospect of a *Vanity Fair* cover story and the photo session with Herb Ritts. "You know what you are, Tina?" he said. "You're a closer. I have a friend in the hamburger business who taught me that expression." He walked me out to my car, making me wait to let him guess which one it was. "So your husband's in Washington half the week?" (Pause.) "Which half?" And then, "How do we progress this now?"

"I'll call Herb Ritts," I said.

"No, no. I didn't mean the *pictures*. Look, anytime you want to waste some time . . . no interviews."

Saturday, May 24, 1986

Gregor von Rezzori's piece arrived, retracing Humbert Humbert's journey across America with Lolita. It's forty years since Nabokov wrote the original. "It was as if Humbert had been married to Lolita for a quarter of a century and then decided to have a look at where she came from," Gregor writes. Then he takes off on his darkly amusing reflections, contrasting the brashness of today with the different brashness of then. There was no girl-child accompanying Gregor, of course, or he'd be in handcuffs instead of celebrating with me about how well it turned out at the Four Seasons. I slightly wish I had asked Martin to write it as he's such a Nabokov junkie, but he would probably have asked if it was necessary to do the drive. Anyway, it's perfect for the August issue and I am now rushing it in.

Monday, May 26, 1986
Memorial Day

Back from the ABA in New Orleans on a plane jam-packed with sweating, partied-out publishers. When I got to my seat I found Faber and Faber's Matthew Evans sitting in it. We both had the same seat number. The stewardess demanded he leave the plane. He refused. (I hid during this altercation as I didn't want him to recognize me and it would have made the conflict even more embarrassing.) I was convinced I was going to be turfed off the plane, which made me frantic as I needed to get back to G and was already tired and hot and pissed off. They finally found me a seat at the back, where I palpitated in sardine intimacy for the rest of the flight with two beer-breathed book packagers while I continued to hide from Matthew behind a *Wall Street Journal.*

399

In a deft piece of family publishing synergy Harry is now coming out with the Picasso sketchbooks as a book for Atlantic Monthly Press, which he still half runs for Mort. He hosted an ABA party for Paloma Picasso. We had lunch with the preposterous Princess Michael of Kent, who looked about fifteen hands high in an orange silk wrap dress. She has developed a mad, false laugh and a new Lady Bracknell voice for dealing with inferiors. "Row-eena," she gushed at the cowed debutante she totes around as her "lady-in-waiting," "where is the Dom Perignon? It was sitting outside but those fooools have taken it away! Find it!" (Mad false laugh.) "Isn't the service quite diabolical? Do shut the kitchen door, Rowena. I hate to stare into a kitchen!"

After the party we went out to dinner with Paloma and Ed Victor and Sarah Giles and Leonardo Mondadori, who is publishing the sketchbooks in Italy, and we had so many laughs. Howard Kaminsky, the short, comical publisher of Random House, is a wisecrack a minute. I see why Si likes him. He took a party out on a boat to see the alligators and asked the guide if he gave "good swamp."

Wednesday, June 11, 1986

I finally had my kiss-and-make-up lunch with Oscar, who is still "*totally* offended" but off the war path. He told me all about his son,

Moses, whom he found in a trash can in the Dominican Republic and adopted. I was touched. A nicer side of Oscar at last.

The September issue is a real pain in the ass, with stories going down like bowling pins. But one great thing is that the Reagans have agreed to sit for our feature, "Staying Married Is the Best Revenge," as have the Buckleys, Joan Didion and John Gregory Dunne, and the Libermans. Harry Benson came up with another great idea tonight. The Thatchers! Dynamite!

I have finally decided to get the last twenty pounds of baby weight off with a trainer coming to torture me three times a week. He's a bespectacled eunuch with huge thighs called Richard who says "Good job!" and "Go get 'em" as I wrestle with push-ups and sit-ups and bends.

Si and Victoria took us out to dinner at Arcadia with Jane Kramer of *The New Yorker.* Si was at his most relaxed and genial, coming out with some memorable Si-isms. When I asked him why he liked Vienna so much, he said, "Because it's so . . . boring. People always answer the phone there on the second ring and they never put you on hold." Victoria is, I realize, very much like Si. She loves going to their Florida house because there is no staff. "I put my foot down and said we only buy the house if there is no art and no servants! Then I know if I put something down, it will still be there next time I look."

Jane complained to Si about the latest willfully tedious three-parter in *The New Yorker*. But Si defended it, revealing as he did that he had read all three parts, which, he said, with a beatific smile, "all hung together with a subtle homogeneity when read all together." The irony is, he may be the only person left who has done so, including, I suspect, William Shawn.

Thursday, June 12, 1986

The Dunne-Herrera combo has brought in a great scoop on Imelda Marcos in exile. She is said to have lost most of the fortune her husband scammed as president of the Philippines, but who knows what lurks in offshore bank accounts, artwork, and jewelry, and then there's her collection of almost a thousand pairs of shoes. Reinaldo can always be counted on to be on great terms with the wives of despots, whom he inevitably finds extremely charming and much misunderstood.

Turns out he had stayed often with Imelda and Ferdinand Marcos in Manila and partied along with them and Colin Tennant on Mustique. He got Imelda's agreement for an interview and soon Nick was on his way to Hawaii with promised access to the Marcos hideout. He says he sat on his balcony at the

Kahala Hilton for four days, waiting for the call, until he decided, fuck it, and showed up uninvited at a local pro-Marcos Filipino-American community birthday celebration in Imelda's honor. He had the smarts to stay for the full five hours in the auditorium, then sidled over to introduce himself. That's what's great about Nick. He can hustle like a shoe-leather hack when he needs to, then charm his way to Imelda's three-bedroom rental. He said it was protected only by snoring guards and bustling domestics, a comedown, for sure, from the days when they owned twenty-nine presidential "rest houses" and a palace to host parties in by the sea. He got a three-hour interview with her of total unburdening that's gonna make so much news.

Monday, June 16, 1986
Quogue

We have had Cape publisher Tom Maschler in from London, staying with his girlfriend in Quogue. This house absorbs guests wonderfully. The sums Tom talked about paying his British authors seem ridiculously small after living in New York. Martin Amis was paid fifteen thousand pounds for his latest book! That seems pitifully small to me, given the size of his reputation. We are paying ten thousand dollars for an article.

And yet in London, where we were paid much less — Harry seventy thousand pounds and me eighteen thousand pounds a year — we seemed to never think about money at all. We felt we were living like kings at Ponsonby Terrace, minutes from the center of London, with four stories to roam around and our own studies with their creepered windows, the cats frisking along the wall I called the Cat Corridor dividing us from the neighbors. Here, with Harry paid two hundred thousand dollars and me paid a hundred and fifty-five thousand — astronomical sums! — we talk about very little else and live in a two-bedroom apartment. Quogue, of course, is where the money has gone, and we don't begrudge a dime of it. I wish I could cook in my new wonderful kitchen. I envy women like Julie Kavanagh, a domestic goddess with a chopping board who whips up amazing dishes so casually, then sits down and writes a brilliant book. I have zero confidence in the kitchen. I can executive-produce dinner, it seems, but not cook it.

Tuesday, June 17, 1986

Olivia Channon, the Guinness heiress and Oxford undergraduate, overdosed on heroin and died, and I am wondering whether I should get on a plane and try to re-create her story. Not sure why it haunts me so much. I always remember this as Oxford's magic time, of finals week and the greenness of the river, of gliding in a punt past the sweet-smelling banks with a bottle of cold white wine (in the days when I could still drink). Perhaps also because I devoured the riveting diaries of her American-born grandfather Henry "Chips" Channon, which chronicles with such a keen eye the world of London society before the war.

How could Olivia have wanted to dull her senses from the beauty of Oxford in June? Sarah Giles, who knows many of the people around Channon, is calling around, seeing if any of them would talk about it. I keep thinking about Olivia slumped in her heroin vomit in her room at Christchurch. Who let her down?

Monday, June 23, 1986

Came to Oxford. Immediately felt odd leaving Georgie for the first time. Brought Sarah Giles to help me connect with people. Ed Victor suggested I hire Willie Mostyn Owen's daughter, Allegra, who knew the Channon group and wants to be a journalist. Met with her today, a very beautiful third-year PPE [philosophy, politics, and economics] student at Trinity who exudes the usual low-energy blankness of upper-class youth. Was glad to shed her at a Boojums drinks party. The kids were a lot more friendly there. Liked the current editor of *Isis,* a sparky blonde in a very short skirt, and there were some sweet, pudgy old Etonians with open faces.

Gottfried von Bismarck, in whose room Olivia died, seems to have been a deeply bad influence, not just because of his drug habit. Beanpole thin, with a cadaverous stare, he was known for hanging around looking gaunt when he was not off in Gstaad or Verbier or Bavaria. The one quotable thing Allegra told me about Olivia was that she told her Gottfried had asked her "to feel his scalp because he knew it would repel me."

I had lunch with a bunch of posh students Allegra knows, including her boyfriend, a young fogey with a thatch of blond hair and a plummy voice called Boris Johnson. This group seemed more invested in the story not being told. I felt a ring of class loyalty and not enough time to penetrate. Frustration with being an editor on a short time frame instead of a reporter who can hang out.

Thursday, July 3, 1986
Quogue

Allegra Mostyn Owen turned out to be bad news. She wrote a really nasty piece about me in *The Sunday Telegraph,* even though she was supposed to be working as my paid researcher. The centerpiece was the lunch with Boris Johnson and co. But Allegra wasn't present, so Boris must have told her what to write — a snide, garbled version of what I said, because he took no notes and clearly recreated it, full of falsehoods, from memory — and then she put her byline on it. I was truly gobsmacked by the awfulness of it. God knows why smiling Boris would behave this way either. I wrote a letter to the *Telegraph,* pointing out the "author" Allegra wasn't actually at the lunch she described, which they are going to publish, and hopefully it will detract from any further career she may want to have in journalism. But Boris Johnson is an epic shit. I hope he ends badly.

G has been so lovably sweet since my return that I want to eat him toe by toe. And now we have another *VF* baby! The miraculous Pam McCarthy gave birth to an eight-pound boy, Joseph Winston McCarthy, on Wednesday night. Her first day of maternity leave! She closed the September issue, played in Chris Garrett (whom I had the brain wave of asking to come fill in for her for three months from her job as managing editor of *Tatler*), and dropped the baby. Her balancing skills are truly breathtaking.

I feel proud that we are managing these maternity exits with our own seamless organizational concepts — with the backing of PVZ, who helped me sell the idea to Si. We are just figuring it out on our own — bringing Chris

Garrett from London to shadow Pam so we don't skip a beat, and then when Pam comes back, Chris packs her bags and flies off with her umbrella. Why don't all big companies do this?

Heat wave continues. Chris Garrett's first day in the saddle greatly reassures me. I am lucky to know these two incredible women who understand how I work and are perfect counterbalances to my whirling ways.

Assigned a piece to a terrific new writer whom Sharon DeLano brought in — Alex Shoumatoff, shambolic, clever, Russian (by origin). I could tell from his endless circuitous storytelling in my office that he has a marvelous eye for detail. Writes sometimes for *The New Yorker.* Sharon felt he would be great for a story I am currently consumed by — the murder of the feminist primatologist Dian Fossey in Rwanda. This tale has it all. Mystery. Feminism. Gorillas. The village people called Fossey "Nyiramacibili" (the Woman Who Lives Alone in the Forest), which sounds immediately poetic and mysterious.

It's been a heavy lift to edit. Alex is one of those writers who needs to have it pulled from him in what he calls a "vomit draft." Once something's on the page, Sharon starts to shape it and it goes back and forth between us three. She often works all night and on the way home runs into Si arriving at four in the morning. Sharon's taste in writers is so good, it excuses all the tyrannical mayhem she introduces into the closing process. And her rigor is taking us to a new intellectual level. While Wayne is better at sentence polishing, Sharon is particularly good at structure, and when something is missing from a story's content, she — having been trained by Bob Silvers at *The New York Review* — obsessively researches new material to drop in. She got Alex to expand his purely naturalist bent to delve into why Fossey traveled so far to live on the edge, how from the days of her lonely childhood she seems to have disliked people as much as she loved animals, and how her rancor toward the poachers was actually deeper than her passion for conservation.

Shoumatoff is a new kind of writer for us and I am going to make him a contributing ed, listed on the masthead. We need more far-flung narratives, more exploration of topics like the environment, more windows into other cultures. The mag is now surpassing itself each month. It's like a living thing, competing with itself, straining its own boundaries.

Georgie's christening was a crazy delight, even though the turf went down literally the night before and we had three solid days of hammering, drilling, and frantic trucks back and forth. Not appreciated by Mum and Dad, whom I had brought out for a quiet rest after the jet lag, or by Georgie for that matter, who was cranky anyway after his TB jab. But it's all worth it! The new wooden floor on the porch, the lawn leading down to the pool — it looks fantastic!

The morning of the christening there was another sudden summer storm, which played havoc with the little tables all set up on the porch. It suddenly looked like the deck of the *Titanic,* lashed with wind and rain. The four-piece band that was supposed to play on the new brick terrace had to be relocated to the dry bit of the porch, a parking lot devised in all the mud. By the time we staggered off to the charming colonial Church of the Ascension with G swathed in his very royal-looking long christening robe, I was fit to be sedated. But sometimes a spontaneous disaster makes an occasion more memorable and that's what happened. And since it always rains in England for every outdoor event, it felt poignantly like home.

The Quogue church is 150 years old,

shingled and white-fenced and nestled in trees. In the rain it was woody-dark and damp and wonderful smelling. A car from New York disgorged Julie Kavanagh, Sarah Giles, Chris Garrett, and Bob and Victoria Hughes. Then came Dominick Dunne and Harry's DC friend, the young historian Michael Beschloss. Already in the church were the Clurmans, Miles, Marie, the Victors, the Janklows, the Hoges. The vicar, the Reverend Busler, was all-American and cheery; the service raced along with our chosen very British hymns — "Stand Up, Stand Up for Jesus," "All Things Bright and Beautiful," "To Be a Pilgrim." I held G, who was rapt throughout. Harry took him for the christening. G adores singing and being where the action is; he didn't cry once. After the rector had baptized him, Harry held him aloft and took him for a walk around the church to reintroduce him to the congregation. Then we all sloshed back to the house. The band bashed out thirties tunes, the champagne flowed, the balloons bobbed, the children ran about the house, and more guests started to arrive who hadn't got to the ceremony in the weather. With the wind and rain whipping around outside, it really was just like being on a boat.

When everyone had gone, Mum and I had some much needed mother-daughter time and walked to the beach barefoot in the rain, returning with frizzy hair and backaches but very happy. She has brought G a brilliant new toy he adores, a small plastic octopus with huge eyes (Mum says it looks just like him) and a squeaker. His new fave game is Mum holding it in front of him and then making it leap into the air as she chants, "Oh where, oh where is Octopi? He's in the sky! Oh where, oh where is Octo-pus! He's on a bus!" At this G bursts into a loud spontaneous gust of laughter. Life could not be more wonderful than now.

Sunday, July 20, 1986

I am in love with our August issue, starting with Herb Ritts's ultracool cover portrait of Jack Nicholson in a lemon shirt, pushing up his dark glasses, and a great Schiff piece to go with it. Then we have the knockout Imelda story by Nick Dunne, Gregor von Rezzori's Humbert journey, P. J. O'Rourke on my old taxi friend Dr. Ruth Westheimer, and John Richardson on Cecil Beaton's memorial service and what he meant as a society photographer. I defy anyone to produce a better combination of writers and subject matter. It's A-plus and I am madly proud.

Wednesday July 23, 1986
London, InterContinental hotel

Am in London to cover Prince Andrew and
Fergie's wedding for the *Today* show. I was
on with Di's brother, Viscount Althorp, who
has a pretty, sly face, a bit like Diana in drag.

I did my segment on the fearsome Fergie,
who represents the Dunkirk spirit to such a
degree that she has been able to triumph over
her naughty-knickers past. England, it seems,
has turned itself into a giant theme park. The
wedding coverage of Andrew and Sarah Fer-
guson is markedly more showbiz than it was
for Diana five years ago. Now the images of
beefeaters and ye olde taverns are slapped on
every artifact, and on the air I almost get the
sense that it's irrelevant if what I say is fact
or fiction.

Saw Bron Waugh for lunch and he was
oddly difficult. Then in the taxi he grabbed
my hand and kissed my hair and got very
emotional. I think he feels he has lost me now
to America and kept talking about how
London must seem to me "an inconsequen-
tial village." It's amazing to think that it's
only thirteen years since I was the English lit
student at Oxford he sponsored and men-
tored and fell in love with. He's changed very
little, but I feel that his sense of his own
limitations (and his awful marriage to the
dread Theresa) are more oppressive than

before. He is such a talent, such a voice, but so locked in his idea of what a Waugh should be. My picture of Georgie made him look so miserable that I put it quickly away.

The wedding was beautiful and flawless. The palace always manages to pull it off. The royal family are so much better dressed than they used to be. Not wishing to be outshone by Diana, they've all smartened up their act. Ironically, it was only Diana who didn't look so good. Maybe she's pregnant. Or more likely this wedding brought back memories of her own at St. Paul's and that made her sad because it's all been such a bitter disappointment. I don't believe the jealousy theory that's started to get traction. In fact, I think Fergie's presence in the royal family makes Diana feel less lonely. (I hear she said to the ballet dancer Wayne Sleep, "Fergie lightens the load.") Fergie is the perfect visual foil to Diana — the buxom figure, the hit-or-miss wardrobe, the exploding hair. If Diana wants to upstage Fergie, it's very easy to do so just by turning up at Ascot in a head-turning new outfit.

Susan Barrantes, Fergie's mum, was (as predicted by *VF*) the star of the show, looking ravishingly elegant. Like Diana's mother, she left home when Fergie was an overweight thirteen to go and live with her lover, the Argentinian polo player Hector Barrantes, on the other side of the world. That's another thing the two royal wives have in common — breathtakingly selfish mothers. Fergie, like Diana, was left to her own devices but without the Spencer grandeur, relegated to the care of neglectful housekeepers and tepid, low-caliber boarding schools in the shires.

One thing that has always fascinated me about upper-class Englishwomen is how, when required, they can effortlessly make the transition from dowdy old-shoe to staggering elegance. They are Cinderella artists, going from drab hair, shrunken cardigan, and beat-up brogues to tight, shining chignons, well-placed diamonds, and long racehorse legs. Even the Queen looked a treat in delphinium blue, and Princess Anne in vibrant yellow.

Fergie and Andrew were on TV last night. She, I predict, will fast get out of control and talk too much and lose the plot. And blonde sphinx Diana, currently her best friend, will become icy and have to remind her who's the star.

My cultural transplant to America has begun to take and I'm turned off by much about England now. I get an unsettling sense of malevolent claustrophobia, of a society obsessed with self-denigration. (How long will the Fergie honeymoon last? Not long before the trashing starts, I suspect.) On the subway it feels so weirdly homogenous, everyone white unlike in polyglot New York. I feel

England is decadent, insular, with the tabloid press a baying pack tearing itself and everyone else apart. But then at Sally Emerson's lovely house in North London I wandered with her on Highbury Fields and felt a whiff of longing to come home. It's wonderful how our friendship survives. I miss her spiritual wisdom in NYC.

Monday, July 28, 1986
NYC

Today there was a fairly ludicrous scene with Si, Doug Johnston, and the circulation director, Peter Armour. Doug hates the new *VF* TV commercial, which makes us look too cheap but happens to be working. I don't much like it either, but don't feel quite as exercised about it as Doug does, because I am increasingly browbeaten by how crass things have to be here to reach any kind of scale. Anyway, Si kept saying, "But it's working, Doug. I tried a classy commercial for *Gourmet* that actually described what the magazine did, as you want to do, and it bombed. Now we have to go back to what the audience likes — shots of big ice-cream desserts and people looking happy doing the dishes afterward." He started to giggle, which Doug didn't seem to notice as he suggested shots of readers calling each other up and saying, "Have YOU read *Vanity Fair* this month?" Sensing Si's boredom with this conversation, I said, probably unhelpfully but also with rising mirth, "Or maybe we could see a lot of museum directors calling each other up saying, "Have you read this month's culturally stimulating issue of *Vanity Fair*?" Si laughed so much he started to splutter. I felt treacherous to have said it.

Sometimes, though, Si can be very hard to get through to. He gets idées fixes and then is so hard to dissuade. Though he actually has very refined sensibilities himself, he bristles if he thinks you are appealing to them. He wants to be seen as a tough, crass business-man like his father, so the only way to win a point, I find, is to make those refined instincts of his think what they are hearing is a very pragmatic and commercial idea. It's a hard dance.

Monday, August 11, 1986

Excited about a half-edited piece by Barbara Goldsmith, who wrote the bestseller about Gloria Vanderbilt, *Little Gloria . . . Happy at Last.* It's about the rancorous probate battle between the children of J. Seward Johnson of Johnson & Johnson fame and his widow, Basia, a former Polish maid who moved in with the horrible Seward and wound up with a fortune of $350 million outright.

I have been coaxing along this delicious

rags-to-riches melodrama for months. Barbara Goldsmith is high maintenance. But she has both great access and a doggedness about breaking down doors. In a stunning interview with J. Seward's daughter, Mary Lea, Barbara learned she had been sexually abused by her father between the ages of nine and fifteen! By the end of her account we have learned not only that Seward was the great villain of this story, but also how he got that way. It turns the press's received gold-digger wisdom on its head and you can't help but cheer for Basia, who got the money. I am going to run it in two parts to give it room to breathe and have taken the risk of putting Basia's picture by Harry Benson on the cover. She sits coiffed and bejeweled under the headline "Dark Inheritance." Miles and I hammed up the cover lines: "A Widow's Spoils. A Father's Sins. The Children's Curse. Barbara Goldsmith investigates the Johnson & Johnson secrets and finds a billion dollars' worth of pain." Try not reading that, newsstand browsers!

Tuesday, August 12, 1986

Just got in from seeing Pam McCarthy's baby, Win. What a doll! It's wonderful how she and I have this new maternal complicity. The magazine has been so central to our life and partnership, but now we also have this

418

tacit understanding that as mothers, too, we will have each other's back. Harry's had enough of *US News and World Report*. My forebodings about Mort's volatility were right. He is wound up by the last person who speaks to him and gives mixed messages that create havoc with staff. I'd love to know what happened in his childhood to make him so untrusting. It's as if he only feels secure when everyone else around him isn't. For the sake of their friendship it's better if Harry doesn't work for him.

Now Si, in his mysterious and abrupt way, solved the problem by asking Harry to create a new travel magazine for Condé Nast! At first we both thought, travel? Harry, the consummate news guy? But then we both realized that news can be applied to any topic, even travel, and doing it brings him back to New York with us, which is a reason right there to say yes. Now, with all that's happened with Georgie, we just want to be together. I need him here with me so much.

Saturday, August 16, 1986

Reinaldo Herrera just called from Caracas. "Fearless Leader" — his new nickname for me — "I have got you Salvador Dalí!" For months since John Richardson planted it I've had Reinaldo negotiating with friends in the Spanish art world to get us an interview with

Dalí at his home in Figueres, the Catalan town where he was born and has now returned to die. It's such a scoop. Dalí hasn't really been seen since he set fire to his bedroom in the castle at Púbol. Most people have assumed him to be senile or comatose.

Helmut Newton has now got the pictures and is thrilled beyond measure with the results, which I won't see till next week. I told Reinaldo to start working to get Marie in to see Michele Duvalier, Baby Doc's wife. When it comes to art legends and kleptocrats, Reinaldo is really paying off in spades.

On Wednesday Sharon, Ruth, Jane, Charles, and I tramped off for a screening of *Sid and Nancy*, the movie about Sid Vicious and Nancy Spungen's murder-suicide, to see if they belonged in this year's Hall of Fame portfolio. It was hateful but brilliant. My instinct is to hold off and do Gary Oldman, who plays Sid, till March when he's cast as Joe Orton. I spent the weekend reading the Orton diaries, brilliantly edited by John Lahr. They're extraordinary, and through all the pre-AIDS promiscuity Orton's voice comes across as hard, cold, spare, honest, and so blackly funny that I laughed out loud. I found the lover Kenneth Halliwell's appearances so profoundly touching. One can hear his cries for help in the diaries getting louder and more desperate, offstage as it were. The brutality of the sex, knowing as we do it will end in Orton's murder, is chilling.

Monday, August 18, 1986

Bob Colacello told me Jonathan Lieberson has AIDS. I am extremely upset by this. Even though I have never liked him, I recognize his originality, his wit, his subversive energy. In conversation he always seemed antigay, which was confusing because I often suspected he was in the closet. I assumed if so he just had the odd affair, but now John Richardson tells me Jonathan used to hang out in hustler bars. It seemed painful and demeaning somehow for this cultured, refined man to have to go to these lengths to have a secret gay life. Now he's shut up in his mother's home in Connecticut, dying.

It's a plague, seeping through creative people. Way Bandy, the makeup artist we often used at *VF* shoots, died yesterday. I think of this lighthearted, truly talented, amiably gaudy individual, his love of celebrities, his dedication to making them look beautiful, and it's so sad he should have died so horribly, so young. I pray that Miles will be all right, and oh so many others we love and work with. It's not just the talents we are losing, but the people who enable and appreciate their gifts. Decoding the *Times* obituaries for cause of death has become a somber breakfast acrostic.

Tuesday, August 26, 1986

Scarcely has one's social nerves settled down after the Allegra Mostyn Owen–Boris Johnson ambush when I receive by Federal Express a postcard from Sally Quinn, disinviting me from Ben Bradlee's birthday party in East Hampton on Saturday because of Christopher Buckley's book review in the August *Vanity Fair*, describing her new novel *Regrets Only* as "cliterature." I have to say when I assigned this piece I did not regard it as an act of war, which she seemed to consider it to be (I just saw Chris as a great social eye), nor did I think the piece itself was a hatchet job. But that may be a cultural disconnect, because in England we are so much more iconoclastic in book reviews.

And even if I did, I couldn't have held it out of the magazine because of my friendship with her, or I would have no editorial credibility with writers. It's the downside of being an editor. Perhaps if I had seen it as negatively as she did, I would have taken the precaution of preparing her for it, but she's such a sharpshooter journalist herself, it didn't occur to me she would take it this way. That was clearly a mistake on my part. Anyway, she is wild with fury, apparently. I hope we can patch it up.

I fear the next flak attack is Bob Colacello's piece in the new issue about John-Roger, the new-age guru Arianna seems to have some weird partnership with. It's pretty hairy when the best stories right now are attached to a group I also socialize with. Perhaps I shouldn't. Bob Hughes just called and said the piece was a "major service to bullshit reduction." Wrestling with all this when Jim Wolcott announced that the next column he has just finished is about Gloria Steinem. Holy moly. All we need to add to my troubles is hatchet jobs of Barbara Walters and Lally Weymouth and I will have a full complement of furies lined up against me. Time to focus on captains of business or icons of archaeology (as long as none are Iris Love).

In nanny hell today, as a temp standing in for Juanita on vacation got another job, so I had to work from home when Georgie napped, and then when she came back I had to go in and process the whole November issue in one demonic day. I hurled pieces in and out, cut them or expanded them to the length they deserved, and reshaped the lackluster Vanities pages. Helmut's Salvador Dalí pics are sensational and outrageous and going to blow us out of the water with accusations of bad taste. He photographed Dalí posed in eye-rolling outrage, with the oxygen tube dangling out of his nose over his iconic mustache, and dressed in a flowing white satin robe, which Dalí had designed himself for the occasion. It's a great visual scoop.

"One must never conceal the truth," Dalí told Helmut, wanting the world to see him as he is now, so diminished. John Richardson came in to write extended captions, which are therefore superb.

H and I fell into the car with G at the end of the day and careened out to Quogue in time for a wedding anniversary dinner at the local inn. It's five years since we got married at the Bradlees' Grey Gardens. Well, the friendship may not have lasted, but the marriage did. We toasted the fact that yesterday Si officially hired Harry to conceive and launch a brand new monthly travel magazine. Sprung from *US News* in DC at last with a New York–based job. Hurrah! One of the many things that stuns me about Harry is the way he approaches every task, big or small, with the same level of intellectual intensity. I know friends are wondering what the fuck the guy who was London's most famous newspaper editor is doing editing a travel mag (*Condé Nast Traveler* launched in September 1987). But Harry never thinks about status, only about what excellence he can make out of whatever he's handed. The new job and its potential is what occupies him already. He started drawing the layout of an eight-page exposé of unsafe airlines on the paper napkin.

I finished working on the Dalí spreads with Alex, who was at his expansive best, and lunched with our new young fashion stylist, twenty-three-year-old Joe McKenna, who just arrived from London. He's very original — a bony nose, thin, freckled face, and black trilby on the side of his head. He reminds me of the characters in the current indie hit *My Beautiful Laundrette.* Joe is quintessential London *now,* and yet I can also imagine him shooting to fame back in the sixties, when the world suddenly opened up to pop culture. I think he will be a star.

He's found an apartment here and applied for a visa and is engagingly thrilled with his desk stuck out in the corridor. With Joe, Miles, Sarah Giles, and Chris Garrett now at *VF,* we are creating a bit of a Brit talent diaspora in the magazine world. I admire their willingness to join me in NYC, their flight from coziness, familiarity, and old friendships to make a stand somewhere new and tap into something more exciting, yes, but also harder and colder and less accessible than what they already know. And that, of course, is what makes them good.

Heavenly Labor Day weekend. The days have
the burnt glow of summer's end, the evenings
the cold edge of fall. We lit a fire and the
smell of wood smoke added to the delicious
melancholy sense that one season has ended
and another begun, the going-back-to-school
feeling of I must try harder! We've had a
perfect time with Georgie. He's not crawling
yet and the pediatrician says he ought to be.
Still bottom shuffling along the deck, which
worries us. Hoping the physical therapy will
get him there soon.

The waspish *Times* Style reporter John
Duka tried to suppress our piece on Halston
by Steve Gaines because he, Duka, is under
contract with Random House to do a book
on Halston and he thought our piece would
be a spoiler. Unfortunately Duka and Gaines
share the same agent, John Hawkins, who
called Howard Kaminsky at Random House
to use his influence with Si to try to get our
piece stopped! Then when that failed, Duka
called Si himself. Priceless Si immediately
called down to ask me what it was all about.
I told him that Duka had ripped off my idea
to write about Halston (I had approached
him first before Gaines) and he sold the idea
instead to Random House as a book. I asked
Si what he would say if he heard from Kamin-

sky. "I don't think I will hear," he replied after a brief laugh. "And anyway, I'd prefer not to have anything to do with it. You should go right on and act as separate companies." Actually I think he loves it when his executives vie over material.

Anyway, this plus the still-buzzing Sally Quinn fiasco made me take the bull by the horns about Bob's takedown on John-Roger in *VF* and call Arianna to warn her. She, of course, handled it with much more elegance than I would while professing "hurt" that it could appear in a mag edited by me. I did defuse it by calling her. A lesson well learned. I'd hate to lose her as a friend. Her heart is big, even if her ideas sometimes wacky. I should ask Clay Felker how he dealt with all this at *New York* mag when he did so many razor pieces about the society he moved in.

We saw the Clurmans last night. Dick thinks the flak I am getting is funny and inevitable for a good magazine. "Just pursue what's real, Tina," he said, which I found comforting.

Monday, September 8, 1986

Motherhood! It gives me brain fade when I have spent a few days retreated into playtime with G. His new fave thing is to loll across my body on the single bed in Harry's den, nibbling my nose and panting like a little hot

427

puppy. Occasionally he throws his head back and stares long and unflinchingly into my eyes, an exchange of pure love. We took him with us to a little drinks party hosted by Mrs. Hamish Maxwell, whose husband is a Philip Morris exec and is nominating us to the Quogue Field Club. Very WASPy crowd. We always look such a wreck on the weekends; Harry had his shirt hanging out and I was wearing some old cheesecloth wardrobe holdover, and clearly this snooty bunch are a floral-sundress-and-cherry-trousers crowd. But the club has wonderful swings and a tennis club and a kids' summer camp I know we will want. G was on his best behavior and charmed all with his instantaneously sunny smile.

I struggle through a few administrative goals as if through a mist. I am a cultural zombie, so locked in my Golden Books that I have zero clue what's on at the theater, the movies, what books I should read. Tonight on the way back to the city in the car I played a tape of Philip Larkin's poems, which thrilled me and chilled me and got my brain working again. "An Arundel Tomb": "Above their scrap of history, / Only an attitude remains."

Harry started with Condé Nast on Tuesday at *Traveler*. It was lovely and strange to have him there on the sixth floor.

Went to Malcolm Forbes's birthday on board his party yacht *The Highlander*. First regroup of power people after the summer and it was interesting to see them all refreshed from their Hamptons and Mediterranean renewal sojourns, women thinned down and younger, achieved in secret weeks at spas and clinics, men shiny and complacent from planning takeovers by the pool. As we purred down the Hudson River in Malcolm's pale mahogany floating crib, billions of dollars stroked each other's egos over lobster and champagne. There was the fleshy-faced Larry Tisch, who just captured CBS, with Bill Paley (temporarily no doubt) back at the helm. Barbara Walters (younger, in mailbox red), with Merv Adelson (richer, or behaving as if he is), Betsy Bloomingdale, sinuous and watchful with her tiny rich eyes and staccato shoulders, Pat Buckley, big-boned and noisier, Jim Hoge (handsomer) with Sharon (fraughter), David and Helen (Gurley) Brown (drunker), wearing a scarlet feather boa (her own interpretation of Reagan red?). *Architectural Digest* editor Paige Rense, squat and intractable, stalking rich people's houses. Mick Jagger and Jerry Hall — I've never seen them together and always found her off-puttingly trashy, but tonight I could see her appeal. The powdered pallor and long sliver of gold hair cascading over a black spaghetti-strapped evening gown with flashes of silver were extraordinarily effective. Mick in real life was also a surprise. He sat on Fran Lebowitz's knee, singing "Happy Birthday, Dear Malcolm" in that insanely famous croak. Being photographed so much, I am convinced, changes your actual face. There is a layer of legend to get through before you can pinpoint or believe in the familiar asymmetries of flesh. Standing together against the night skyline, Mick and Jerry looked like *Satyricon* creatures at a Venetian carnival with a whiff of decadence you only see as you get close.

Realize I am making it sound like a horrible party when it was actually an exceptionally good one. Perhaps I am overmelodramatic when I get these frissons of corrupt undercurrents, and not sure where I get my deeply moralizing instinct from or whether I should trust it. There were delicious moments such as when Malcolm's son, Steve, landed on the boat in a helicopter. We all went onto the upper deck to watch it come in, our hair whipped by its landing. The propellers whirled dangerously. "You go first," Harry said to Murdoch, and Rupert laughed. Malcolm's speech was very funny. "When my kids said we should all gather in the saloon, I thought, holy crow, it's a takeover, and I got on my satellite phone to check with my lawyer that I still owned the shares I thought I did!"

We've seen a dream apartment we want to buy desperately. Just off Sutton Place on Fifty-Seventh Street, $917,000, a crazy price but oh so beautiful, with high ceilings and gracious square rooms and a kitchen you can eat in. It's on the third floor of a 1929 building looking out over the art deco facade of Sutton Place and the wide corner where East Fifty-Seventh Street meets the East River. The apartment has only had one owner, a lady who lived to be ninety-nine, tended in her last years by a daughter in her seventies. Mercifully, it has therefore escaped modernization. The wood-block floors and the porcelain plumbing are all intact. What I love most are the big sash windows at the same level as the plane trees outside and the spaciousness of the eight high-ceilinged rooms. They flow into each other in a way that feels reassuringly European. After living in the shiny pornography apartment in the Solow tower, an aerial cigar box run by a mafia don on Central Park South and now on the faceless East Fifty-Sixth Street block with the Hollywood fountains, I am done with my modern experiments in living. Here when I look out the window and see a tiny park bustling with babies like mine, I know this could really be home at last. Now the chase to raise the money begins. Manhattan is the city of never-satisfied desire, but I want want want this beautiful apartment for the three of us.

Monday, September 15, 1986

Fall madness descends! My eyes burn with the stress of a day that begins at six, doing crunches with the thunder-thighed trainer, followed by an hour gurgling with G, an hour blowing out hair and getting dressed for the office, and then it's race race race to get through the day and home by five to walk G in his stroller and play with him (it's so damn tough to make the power woman–to–mommy switch), then on to his bath time and dosh up for one of the innumerable place-card dinners raining down.

Tonight was hosted by the socialite Louise Melhado and Henry Grunwald, now a couple, in a newly decorated Park Avenue apartment. The apartment is so freshly done, the cream carpet felt stiff and the chocolate-brown dining room gleamed with a disco shine. Henry, in his last year as a pooh-bah at Time Inc., where he was managing editor for so long, has become portly and somnolent in the recesses of his cigar. He was a subliminal host, if there is such a thing, perhaps not wholly at ease with the bargain he is striking with an elegant society woman to commandeer his creature comforts.

Harry and I were the first guests, unfortunately, because the second was the ballet legend and cultural impresario Lincoln Kirstein. In my first weeks on the *VF* job I stupidly rejected a piece inherited from Leo that Lincoln wrote about the New York City Ballet when I had not a clue who he was or that he actually founded it and nurtured Balanchine. The piece wasn't very good — typical of that period when great bylines gave *VF* their worst pieces — but it was pretty disrespectful of me to just toss it out with a perfunctory note. And I think he was so furious that there is no mending of it. His high nose and manic eyes give him the air of a haughty camel or the figurehead of a ship. He was immediately extremely difficult with me, repelling questions with knowing and contrary answers. With astonishing rudeness to our hosts he said to Harry, "Look at all these brand-new books! Pure set decoration for a woman who never reads." I went to recuperate in the powder room from all the social tension and on the way there ran into Henry and Louise pursuing Kirstein down the corridor.

"Is he leaving?" Henry was saying. "He's always doing this," Louise hissed back. And looking through the open front door, I now caught sight of Kirstein waiting for the elevator, wearing a festive expression and giving a little insouciant wave as the doors opened and he disappeared off into the night before

433

dinner was even served. I understand how he felt. If I was eighty I might also feel time is too short to be constrained by social form when you have decided the evening ahead will only yield pretension and a woman next to you one really doesn't want (in this case, me).

"You've just lost your dinner partner," Henry told me, much to my relief. Instead I sat next to Louise, whom I enjoyed so much more.

Tuesday September 16, 1986

Our dream apartment on Fifty-Seventh Street is becoming a reality. Si came through with a three-hundred-thousand-dollar loan as soon as I asked if he would consider it. I'm so grateful to him. I asked Nick Dunne for the name of a decorator and he suggested the former set designer who did his apartment so well, Chester Cleaver. He sounds perfect, because the last thing I want is some swanky taste baron who expects a million-dollar budget and the license to throw out all the furniture we have sitting in storage in London. I know exactly what I want, but would have no idea how to achieve it myself. My dream house remains Tony Lambton's in Siena. I want that casual, eclectic English charm with a dash of Visconti in its colors and hope this Chester guy can deliver it.

I've appointed Bob Hughes as *VF* food writer. Reinaldo is back from Caracas and is in full cry, organizing Spanish duchesses to dance the flamenco for our April issue. He is still hell-bent on getting us Michele Duvalier in exile for a profile. Her excesses will make a big, fat cover story for us if he pulls it off.

Monday, September 22, 1986

The effort of being superwoman is killing me. I was half-dead today after a weekend of agonizing transatlantic organization, getting ready for the sale of Brasted to underwrite the new apartment, and trying to plan a Christmas in London at Ponsonby Terrace with Mum and Dad between rentals because I just can't stand another characterless Christmas at a resort, and G needs his first English Christmas.

Today we did the Hall of Fame captions with Schiff, Miles, and Wolcott. Wolcott as always displaying his flashes of genius that mark him out. It was the usual scene of squashed Tab cans, Styrofoam cups, peach stones, apple cores, and cookie crumbs as we toiled over frantic alliterations. "Boris Becker. Because he's the sultan of serve, the kaiser of the court, the führer of forehand."

Miles: "The Nazi of the net . . ."
Me: "That's awful, Miles, and not sexy.

435

Boris is sexy."

    Schiff: "Because he's boom-boom Boris with a wiggle in his walk and . . ." (collapse of working group).

And so it went on. Tonight, Harry and I went to deposit the Brasted sale check into Citibank and plotted frantically how to con the 455 East Fifty-Seventh Street co-op board into thinking we have a vast bank account to support us taking the apartment. Everything in this city is about conspiring to keep everyone out except the superrich.

Friday, September 26, 1986

I defied a soaring temperature and went to a reception for Leonard Lauder, who was receiving the Order of Merit from the French government. I knew this occasion would draw all the advertisers and was right, so I hollowed out my ashen face with blusher, put on my skintight black two-piece, and hit the French consulate. I was set upon by every top retailer in NYC, showering plaudits on *VF!* Bill Ruben, the boss of Bonwit, Ira Neimark of Bergdorf's, Melvin Jacobs of Saks, Carol Phillips of Clinique. It was such a high after all the work, but I am dying to register all the praise as PROFIT.

    Then lurking in a corner, I saw Si, who had put in a call to me that morning. "I'm sorry I missed you," I said.

"I was just calling to say how wonderfully it all seems to be going," he said.

"I should miss such a phone call!" I laughed. "No, really," he said. And just then one of the retailers butted in and started to bang on about the glories of *VF* and Si just glowed happily. It was raining. "Let me give you a lift back," he said. I was happy with this unexpected treat of five minutes in the car with Si on his own. "Success," he said, settling into the shadows, "is mysterious. But I have learned not to question it when it arrives. Everyone . . . is talking about *Vanity Fair.*"

"I wish we could convert the talk into advertising dollars," I said. "We will," he said. "They're taking notice." We fell to talking about the other new mags that have started lately and he said what a pleasure it was now working with Harry at *Traveler.* "Where are you living these days?" he said, vaguely, as we approached my building. He had clearly forgotten he had just given me a three-hundred-thousand-dollar loan for Apartment IB, 455 East Fifty-Seventh Street. He got out of the car and walked me to my door, still glowing with secretive delight, and gave me a clumsy peck on the cheek when we reached the entrance.

There was something deeply touching about this encounter. I am so headlong, so driven, it's rare I allow myself to savor things in the here and now. Somehow I was reminded of a night five years ago just before Christmas when I had put *Tatler* to bed with Nick Coleridge and Miles and Gabé and walked down Piccadilly alone, delighting in the merry Christmas lights with a full heart.

What a pleasure collaborating can be. How much people miss out on by not working toward a common goal with a few close, believing colleagues.

Tonight the whole world dances at Barbara Walters's wedding party. I am fed up that I am unwell and in bed but maybe not. Lately I have found the competitive dressing and the rich gossip too much. I am sick of them all.

I had lunch last week with Ralph Lauren. We got on exceedingly well. He's more impressive when you drill deeper, with a shrewd, strategic mind. He tells me that he never goes to parties for the same reason they have palled so much for me. "Cut it out. It will kill you," said Ralph.

But I never will.

When we have our apartment on Fifty-Seventh I want to entertain in my own way! Not dinners where only the rich occupy the chairs like lead balloons. I want one Falstaff for every Hal, one pauper for every billionaire, one young Turk for every legendary old sacred cow.

Sarah Giles just called from France to say just when she and Marie had given up waiting and were packing their bags, Michele Duvalier's emissary showed up at the hotel! Another scoop in the bag for the Holiday issue of *Vanity Fair.*

Saturday, September 27, 1986

Still sick and didn't go to the fancy wedding of John Fairchild's daughter. Instead, G and I danced solemnly together to Whitney Houston on the radio, as I inhaled the milk-and-honey sweetness of his hair. When I was feeding him Marie phoned, back from the Duvalier scoop. G lay across my lap and looked at me with a deep, peaceful sweetness as I absorbed her news. Jerry Zipkin called to give me the download on the Fairchild wedding and left a message on my service. "You chose the wrong night to be ill." I had a brief fear-of-missing-out pang. Should I have forced myself into the high heels and gone?

I bought a huge quilt in Westhampton and am currently snuggled under it in my den in Quogue, listening uncharacteristically to Mozart's horn concerto, G asleep next door. The green check curtains I had made in a whirlwind of activity to distract me after G was born are hung, the central heating is on, a steaming cup of tea next to the bed, with Chips Channon's diary from 1939 to dip into. The New York carnival seems very far away. Together Harry and I throw out so much energy we sometimes wear each other out as well as everyone else. The thought of the city gives me herpes of the brain. The hairdressing! The breakneck showers. The seething limo rides! The shouting over noisy restaurants! The ceaseless clamor of thirsty egos! The umbrage and dudgeon and fencing and foiling. And yet I know that if I left all I'd want is to get it back.

Thursday, October 9, 1986

Took Harry to Alice Mason's, where he has never been, and it was fun to see it again this time through his eyes. He was fascinated by so many finger-jabbing takeover guys and their striving trophy wives under one roof. I had never noticed how bad the food was before — potted shrimps followed by a platter of German sausages and sauerkraut followed by a sherbet swan laced with Cointreau and topped off with Irish coffee. Horrendous. I was at Alice's table between Abe Rosenthal and NBC's Thornton Bradshaw. Then there was a babel of foreigners — a Mexican ambassador, a bejeweled brunette whose father, she said, founded Lebanon, some frenetic Italian, I guess all real estate prospects for Alice. The tables all packed in so close, the noise incredible with the hyperac-

tive publisher of *Avenue,* Judy Price, screaming into the small ears of Leonard Stern, who
recently bought *The Village Voice,* all watched
by an enigmatic Philip Johnson and eye-
rolling Linda Janklow. Through this tumult,
like a parody of the Marietta Tree–era hostess who actually knew how to deftly promote
general conversation, came the urgent scream
of Alice herself:

"Abe! Come on! You know about current
affairs! Get some general conversation going.
Let's not talk to one another, Abe, let's make
it general!" And Abe, with his rueful, cynical
look, would cup his hand over his ears and
howl, "I can't, Alice! The noise! The noise!"
Defeated by the effort to wrangle a common-
denominator topic, guests began to talk to
themselves. Abe talked about his love for
Shirley Lord, for whom he is getting divorced,
Thornton Bradshaw ground on about NBC
ratings, the Lebanese woman talked about
Beirut ("Home of my ruined hopes! Now I
am truly an orphan!"). The Mexican occasionally blew me a kiss and mouthed, "My
hearty con-gratulations on your *rebista Banity
Fair*! Iss truly fantastic!" while Gayfryd waxed
on about her education initiative for under-
privileged kids to which she's giving money:
"You see, Abe, if I can pick out the hundred
and fifty motivated kids, the one who will go
to violin practice, that's all I can deal with,"
and also her conversion to Judaism to please

Saul. We stumbled out of there at midnight, vibrating from German sausage.

Tuesday, October 21, 1986

Holiday issue gonna be great with Madonna on the cover photographed by Herb Ritts. He's done her with en brosse white-silver hair and heavy dark brows, skin gleaming with limelight. Compelling. For reporting juice there's Marie Brenner's Michele Duvalier–in exile scoop. She interviewed her at one of the Khashoggi villas in Mougins near Cannes, lured out of recalcitrance because, trapped in her gated villa, she had a cold and was bored. Otherwise she wasn't that eager to discuss how her corrupt, horrible husband has managed to steal between a hundred and five hundred million bucks from the luckless, poverty-stricken Haitian people. She told Marie every fifteen days she "gives Jean-Claude a manicure for his beautiful hands." Such a decadent little scene. What is it about dictators' wives that makes them so convinced the world is wrong, that they were saving their people from catastrophe, and are beloved by them even now that they have been chased and excoriated into exile? Duvalier told Marie her heroine is Eva Peron, who was so "liberal-minded and socially aware."

I had to fire Juanita tonight. Things had got very irritable because she gave G a cold, even though I told her not to come in sick. When G started to sneeze I said what a pity it was she came back early and she didn't speak to me for two days. Tonight, after a successful meeting with the 455 co-op board for the new apartment, I came back early and heard her on the phone in her room talking about me. Pausing at the door, what I heard appalled me. "I hate her. Georgie hates her. He loves me. She gave him a cold and then she accuses me. I want to choke her." It was scary. I have felt more and more concerned she's the wrong person for G lately, and at the physical therapy session last week, the therapist, Frances Sterne, took me aside and told me she thought he needed a change of nanny, that she keeps him too "inert" instead of moving and exercising his limbs. He is behind on his motor skills and still isn't crawling.

It's my fault. I kept her on too long. He needed more stimulation and cheeriness around him. I was just so insecure as a mother after his prematurity I depended on her "baby nurse" creds. But when I heard this torrent of bile, all my buried qualms about her rushed to the surface and I just wanted her OUT. I wrote a severance check, opened her door, and said, "Put down that phone, Juanita. Pack your bags and go," and handed her the envelope. She stared at me crazily for a moment. Then suppressed resentment gushed out and she started screaming at me, "I hate you. I hate working here. Georgie loves me more. You're awful, he hates you!" I called the doorman to come up with a cart and wait an hour while she packed, as she looked so nutty I didn't want a nail file between the eyes. She stuffed everything into paper bags, muttering and cursing. The funny thing was that G watched all this from his crib, shaking the bars and laughing and dancing around. Did he understand what was going on and wished her good riddance, too? I took him into my bed and we snuggled all night. I feel liberated! Even though now I need a new nanny, fast.

Saturday, November 8, 1986

Depressed week. I came down from the agitation of firing Juanita and felt a lot of guilt that I hadn't got her out of here before. I have found a jolly, plump American girl called Joanne to replace her temporarily. It's such a huge responsibility to pick the person who is going to be with your child all day.

Last night we went to Si's birthday party at their temporary new apartment. He was fifty-nine. The other guests were Donald and Sue, his two children, Sam and Pam, and their spouses, Alex and Tatiana, Leo and Gray, the Kaminskys, and a painter friend of Si's. I have grown enormously fond of Victoria. I like the tentative unfolding of her personality as she gradually surrenders her trust. When she finally decides in your favor it is, one feels, a commitment for life. Si was pink with happiness as he looked around the room.

I sat next to Alex after dinner on the sofa and we talked about Marlene Dietrich — there's a new film out about her by Maximilian Schell. He and Tatiana knew her well. He said her daughter resents her terribly because Marlene was always too caught up in her love affairs to pay her attention. "But you know," said Alex, "in the thirties, in Paris, people were really consumed by their erotic adventures. Children didn't count. I remember my own mother was always caught up with her lovers and abandoned me for months at a time. I didn't mind particularly. I understood the situation, which was always complicated. Francine, I know, has enormous resentments about a lack of attention from her mother, but you know, her mother was a sensation, an extraordinary vibrant creature, and really it was unrealistic to expect she could ever give more time to Francine than she did. Everything" — he paused to savor it — "was so much sexier at that time. Even Condé Nast himself was a great Lothario. Patcevitch [Iva

Patcevitch, his fellow Russian who was once president of Condé Nast in the old days] worked his way through every beautiful woman at *Vogue.* The magazine was chockablock with ravishing women like Babe Paley and Millicent Fenwick. Now, with yuppies and AIDS, I think New York is the unsexiest place on earth." And of course, he is entirely right.

Tonight I went to see the Dietrich film with Miles. It was an irritating piece of work and she is clearly a harrowingly, impregnable old Valkyrie today. But oh, how beautiful in her prime! I understand why she doesn't want to look at her old films. (Alex is the same, of course, and Tatiana, too, speaks in exactly the same vein about the past. Who cares? It's over and done with.) But for such a great beauty as Dietrich used to be, it must be agony to be reminded of what you were.

Thursday, November 27, 1986

November is the vibrant month when everyone hits town and the restaurants are decibels higher, with festive foghorn account executives blowing up their expense accounts.

The fall of Ivan Boesky has been the best sideshow anyone could hope for. The megamillionaire greenmailer has been busted for insider trading, and one by one his ilk will go down. I have felt as long as I have been here that the balloon had to burst eventually. I don't remember ever coming across Boesky, although I feel I must have in the shadowy crush of Alice Mason's drawing room. His slippery, avaricious face fascinates me, as do the reports of his insane working hours, his thirty telephones, his royal-sized estate in Connecticut stuffed with old masters. What we have been witnessing is money as cocaine. I long to know what Boesky is thinking and feeling now, a frenzy of lawyers bailing him out. And what does he say to his equally intriguing wife, Seema? Did she know? Does she hate him for the life he makes her lead? Or is greed her ruling passion, too? I want to know the answers to all these questions and hope to get a piece that does so for *VF.*

At a less sophisticated, nickel-dime level, Stanley Friedman, the Bronx Democratic leader, was convicted yesterday of running a squalid scheme to loot the NYC parking bureau. It's an old-time Boss Tweed–style corruption scandal and Friedman could be looking at decades in the big house. Meanwhile in Washington it looks like the era of Reagan excess is finally curdling. A scandal broke this week about secretly selling arms to Iran, of all places, and putting $30 million in a Swiss bank account for the Contras. Remains to be seen if Ronnie was complicit or just clueless. I'm betting on clueless, but then I've developed a soft spot for him since the

Harry Benson jaunt. Not his politics, just his disarming geniality and devotion to Nancy.

Meanwhile, I got into a ludicrous PR flak attack when I found Herb Ritts's cover picture of Debra Winger unacceptably dull and depressing. Ritts shot her for the February cover in a white terry bathrobe, looking morose. Since the shoot had gone quite well — only two hours late is a feat for her, I am told — we asked if we could do a second shoot to get a really good cover out of it. At this, Pat Kingsley, yes, the hypermanic, power-crazed PR from PMK, threw a tantrum. She called Jane Sarkin an "asshole" and a "fuckup" and suggested *VF* go screw itself. She'd probably spent a morning chewing the carpet at the feet of Winger and now felt she had to work off the humiliation on Jane. I was so furious I then wrote letters to all the people around Winger and the movie, saying that while we, in good faith, had tried to do a great cover, PMK was sabotaging our efforts to do so, demanding we kill the feature inside if it wasn't going to be the cover story. This created even more aggravation, including a call from Pat's lawyer claiming that I had slandered Winger and that if I wrote any more letters like that, she would sue me.

We pulled out our backup, an Annie picture of the hot Manhattan nightclub owner Nell, who looked exactly right for *VF* style. But let's face it, also unknown, and I knew with a sinking heart that Nell is not likely to be a circulation success. So we looked again at Winger in the beastly bathrobe. I said to the glum assembled staff, "Maybe we could save it with a clever cover line like we did with Joan Collins 'She Rhymes with Rich'?" From the back of the art room, Sharon's cynical voice pronounced, "How about she rhymes with punt?" I showed both covers to Alex, who, not having been involved in any of the manic ramifications, said immediately, "Winger has much more appeal. Who the hell is Nell?" Then he instructed that we blow up Winger further and load the image up with creative typeface. I knew he was probably right and that for the good of the mag it was my turn to eat crow and put her on the cover despite all our threats, which would be game, set, match for Pat Kingsley. So instead of calling Pat I called Larry Marks, producer of Winger's movie called, appropriately, *Black Widow,* and said, "Good news. We have turned up a more acceptable picture." To which he replied, "Well, I have to say you are a class act," but he probably thought, *This is why I pay Kingsley the big bucks.*

In the middle of all this, we closed on the new apartment at 455 East Fifty-Seventh Street. Tuesday, the decorator Chester Cleaver is moving in with his merry men. At the apartment closing, aside from our lawyer,

Jimmy Goodale, all the other legal eagles were women in their thirties. The realtor, an abrasive blonde, dealt and redealt the forms like a croupier for us to sign. Occasionally she went out and returned with Xeroxed copies of each document, and once chewed out the vendors' dude-like, macho lawyer for presenting a document that was wrongly dated. When he laughed nervously she snapped, "Stop turning this into a circus," which was hardly fair. Looking at all these tense New York women, a little frayed, a little underpaid, enough to keep them hooked on their career path but not enough to finance escape, I felt they are the new prisoners of the American dream, always working harder than the guys and dealing and redealing the paperwork.

Sunday, November 30, 1986
Quogue

Tonight we went for a drink with the Steinbergs. Saul was in a celebratory mood, buoyed up by the collapse of Ivan Boesky. He was offstage when we arrived but he soon entered in designer leisure wear, glowing pink after tennis. Immediately the volume was turned up — Saul plunges everything into quadraphonic sound. Of course I wanted to get him on Boesky and he repaid dividends. "Ivan," he honked, "was always a bad guy.

You know, he collects brass bulls. And a few years back Jacob Rothschild thought Ivan was the son of God and was going to make him millions. So to make nice to Ivan, he called him and told him about a great bronze bull he'd seen at some auction. Ivan says, terrific. Buy it. So Jacob lays out fifty thousand bucks for this bull and ships it. He hears nothing and calls me. Says, 'Saul, I haven't heard from Ivan and he ignores the bills for the bull. What shall I do?' I said, 'Jacob, get on the phone to Ivan and tell him he's got to pay.' So he gets through to Ivan and Ivan says, 'Sorry, I didn't like the bull, Jacob. It's too big.' And Jacob calls me and says, 'Can you believe what I just heard?' I said, 'Look, Jacob, I'll buy the bull.' And I did because I knew Ivan was never going to pay. It's fucking huge by the way — I put it in the conference room at Reliance." He also said that the first Seema Boesky knew of the crash was what she read in the papers. Also that Ivan has a boyfriend. Also, that despite what you read in the papers, he will in fact be ruined. "He'll be litigated to death. He'll be left with three mi-yun tops. He's going to be sued by everyone he's ever done business with. His legal fees will be forty mi-yun dollars! He'll go to jail for five years." Why do I find the Boesky story so compelling? Fear of falling is so central to the currents of New York life. I could see on Gayfryd's face the concern that must come from a private anxiety that Saul could somehow lose his own footing, not for something he's done, but for something unforeseen that could blow up their own high-rolling way of life. She went through it with her first husband, and I bet it worries her now. They all fly so fast and furious there has to be a fall.

We turned to Reagan and the arms-to-Iran scandal. "He should fire everybody," said Saul. "Only way he can get out of this now. Particularly Don Regan — he should have gone a long time ago, anyway. He should say, bye-bye, it's been great," and he whistled and jerked his thumb over his shoulder. "What I can't understand is why they didn't check with the lawyers. In business we do that all the time. It's a discipline, you know. I say it automatically. Hey, boys, sounds cute, but are we breaking the law?" Maybe so, but isn't the White House crawling with lawyers?

Sunday, December 21, 1986
In flight, New York to London

The year is over and we're off to London with our Georgie, his first Christmas! As I write he snoozes in his bassinet on the bulkhead tray. He was flashing huge cheesy grins at all the BA personnel as we boarded. Miles brought him a wonderful Christmas gift — a baby rocking horse with strapped seat. G rocked furiously all Saturday afternoon, waving a stick of celery in the air like a crop.

It was a cheery year's end at *Vanity Fair.* I spent time being Santa to all. Si's pug, Nero, is going with them to Vienna to be mated, so I sent him a prenup basket of treats, including a piece of blue velvet "in case things get a little wild." Around the office there was a spirit of warmth and achievement. I promoted Jane Sarkin to features editor and her delight was tangible. Even with the great curmudgeon, Sharon, there was a sense of esprit de corps. I love them all, my comrades in arms. After the office holiday party, a noise-intensive stand-up at Le Bilboquet, I brought Ruth, Charles, Miles, Jane, and poor Sarah Giles — her face still black and blue from being mugged last week — to Mortimer's for dinner and we made even more noise. Joan Buck was dining at a corner table with the critic Walter Clemons. Abe Rosenthal was at the bar with *Times* colleague Arthur Gelb. It all felt jolly and hectic as Christmas should. I want to savor the unfolding of next year instead of gulping it in fast bites. I met Chester in the new apartment, where he greeted me with two bags of chicly wrapped gifts and a little sack of swatches to "show my folks." I've decided he's like a marmalade cat with his ginger-blond hair and smiley face. The black and white kitchen tiles are down, the closets made, and the glass doors in the dining room installed to let the room breathe. It is all beautiful beyond my wildest hopes and I pray such happiness can last.

Friday, December 26, 1986
25 Ponsonby Terrrace, London

How unreal and nice it is to be back in this house where we haven't lived for three years! When I pause to turn my key in the lock and look back at the neat, white Regency houses with the railings in front and the secret lives of MPs inside, I feel the sense of walking out of one era and back into another.

I remember so well the last weeks of living here. The small bedroom on the third floor that had become my miniature office adorned with blown-up *Tatler* covers. Through the high window as I sat at my desk I could see the decaying cavern of the torn-down buildings below that marked the start of the "Crown improvements" behind Ponsonby Terrace. Incredibly, three years later, very little has changed, and the work and demolished buildings behind are still at the foundation stage, reminder of one of the maddening differences between England and America. In New York that building site would have long since become new apartments teeming with business action in the streets. Or Donald Trump would have taken it over and overcharged the city to turn it into a skating rink.

Tina and *Tatler* staff, London, 1979. Featured in these diaries: editorial enfant terrible Nicholas Coleridge (*far left*) next to deputy editor Georgina Howell. *At back:* Fashion editor Michael Roberts. *Right:* Cover girl punk rocker Paula Yates, 1982. *Left:* My husband-to-be, Sir Galahad *Sunday Times* editor Harry Evans, drawn by Mark Boxer.

Above: Literary heartthrob Martin Amis in 1980. *Right:* Tina with two of *Tatler*'s founding gang, Gabé Doppelt and Miles Chapman, reunited at Nicholas Coleridge's wedding, July 1989. *Left:* Tina snapped outside *Tatler*'s second office, Covent Garden, 1981.

Above: The people who made *Vanity Fair*'s pages, 350 Madison Avenue, circa 1988. *Front row, left to right*: Jane Sarkin, features editor; Charles Churchward, design director; TB; Pamela McCarthy, managing editor. *Second row*: Sarah Giles, editor at large; Sarah Lewis, assistant to TB; Elisabeth Biondi, photo director; David Kuhn, senior editor; Sharon Delano, senior editor. *Third row*: Ann Powell, assistant managing editor; Marina Schiano, style director; Miles Chapman, senior editor; Richard Sacks, research; Elise O'Shaughnessy, political editor. (Photo by Annie Leibovitz.)

Opposite: Tsar of all the Russias, Alexander Liberman, editorial director of Condé Nast Publications, combined deft political skills with sublime charm (photo by Arthur Elgort). *Above*: The Sun King, Condé Nast chairman S. I. Newhouse Jr, and his wife, Victoria.

TB's first *VF* cover, April 1984, showed Daryl Hannah shot by Helmut Newton with story by Dominick Dunne (*above*).

Fox-trot at the White House, June 1985.
The Harry Benson cover with the Reagans
and the kiss that ignited media mania. *Top
right*: TB says good-bye to the Reagans at
the White House; shot by Annie Leibovitz,
1989.

Top: Condé Nast legend Horst P. Horst (*above*) shot TB in classic black-and-white, 1985. *Right: VF* cartoonist Robert Risko's more irreverent portrait.

Opposite: VF's players. *Top row, left to right:* Michael Roberts, fashion/style director; executive editor Wayne Lawson with West Coast bureau chief, Caroline Graham; TB talking stories at the *VF* office with writers Dominick Dunne and Marie Brenner and art director Charles Churchward (standing). *Bottom row: VF*'s top gun critics James Wolcott and Stephen Schiff; design director Ruth Ansel.

TB's wedding to Harold Evans, August 1981, at Grey Gardens, the East Hampton home of *Washington Post* editor Benjamin C. Bradlee and his wife, Sally Quinn. *Left to right:* Anthony Holden, Marie Brenner, *Sunday Times* reporter writer David Blundy, Sally Quinn, the bride and groom, Joan Juliet Buck, Anna Blundy, and best man Ben Bradlee.

TB joyfully pregnant, August 1985, on the deck of the Evans-Brown oceanfront house at Quogue, Long Island, seen in watercolor above. *Right:* TB's mother, Bettina, with Georgie, age three. *Below:* TB and Harry backpacking eighteen-month-old Georgie.

Family portrait by
Annie Leibovitz,
1991. Thoughtful
Georgie in Bermuda,
1990.

Rock-a-bye Georgie, 1986, and
Georgie with baby Izzy

TB's parents, George and
Bettina, shot by George Lange
at Quogue, summer of 1988

Harry and TB at a
Manhattan fundraiser,
October 1985

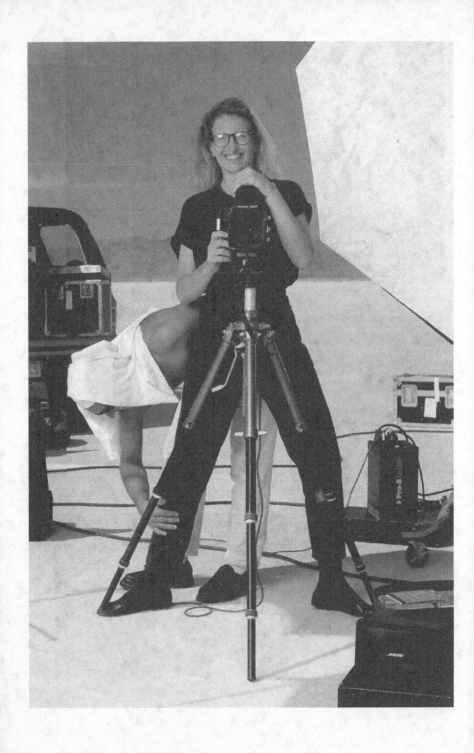

THE
Media
Decade

At the end of the eighties: Praise the Lord—and pass the treasure. Also the the Decade, it was the Media Decade. Satellites gave us deep-dish CDs made every living room a newsroom; MTVs made everyone a network programmer; and cable-based overseas into a supper-infinitesimal channels and still nothing to watch. The word got wired—PCs, faxes to offline networks and still nothing to read. Bored with the boardroom, CEOs became raiders. They bought the media, and became the message. Everyone had a book in them. Some, like Shirley MacLaine, had often bespoke books in them. And if they didn't do a book, they did a fragrance (their signature). And if they didn't do that, they did an advertorial. News was monitored. Image replaced reality. Lifestyle replaced life. Hype hijacked art. There was a media president, a media presence, a media pope, not a media Gorbachev who sowed the West. In the end of history, and the end of unrest. Who got out? Because its time for VF's big end-of-the-decade Hall of Fame.

Photographs by Annie Leibovitz

MEDIA
MAGICIAN
Michael Jackson
President, MJJ Productions

The new Lenny Bruce is somewhat different. She's black.
And she's cooking it softly.
JANET COLEMAN gets the Whoopi Goldberg variations.

Making
Whoopi

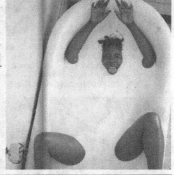

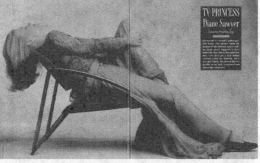

TV-PRINCESS
Diane Sawyer
Gets the Pixel for Lips

Opposite: Self-portrait of *VF*'s star photographer Annie Leibovitz, summer 1989. *Left from top:* Some hit Annie covers: Michael Jackson; Demi Moore—the iconic baby bump that launched two decades of replicas from other pregnant stars; the cultural charisma of ballet maestro Mikhail "Misha" Baryshnikov; and classic Cher. *Above:* Three quintessential Annie spreads: Hall of Fame opener Michael Jackson, Whoopi Goldberg, and a languid Diane Sawyer.

Vanity Fair's fifth-anniversary bash at Billy Rose's Diamond Horseshoe club, March 1988. *Above:* Saxing out with the blonde band. *Below:* TB steps out with one of the Carmen Mirandas; Donald J. Trump zooms S. I. Newhouse Jr. *Inset below:* Tom Wolfe tells TB a secret. *Right, from top:* Fashion designer Patrick Kelly and TB; the night's impresarios, Ian Schrager and Steve Rubell; *VF* writer Bob Colacello hits the floor with LA editor Wendy Stark.

Reinaldo Herrera, *VF*'s man-about-town editor, the indefatigable news source on foreign strongmen, art legends, and kleptocratic dictators.

Left: Helmut Newton's cover and inside shots of alleged murderer Claus von Bülow in black leather and spoofing Queen Victoria, that ran with the riveting report of the trial by Dominick Dunne, evoked astonishment and outrage, August 1985.

FATAL CHARM
THE SOCIAL WEB OF CLAUS VON BÜLOW

DOMINICK DUNNE is the one writer with access to all the tangled circles surrounding Claus von Bülow. During the second trial, Dunne was caught up among the dramatis personae—both sides chose him as their confidant. The children talked, servants talked, mistresses talked, duchesses talked. And von Bülow himself talked, answering the telling questions: Does he love Andrea? Did he ever really love Sunny? What made him cry when he went back to Clarendon Court? Claus von Bülow opened his door to *Vanity Fair*

TB and baby Izzy, two news junkies in Quogue, caught by Annie

The Princess Di cover story broke the news of royal marital discord, October 1985. Goldie Hawn, shot by Herb Ritts, was summer joy, September 1989. *Right:* Nightshirt editing.

The murder of zoologist Dian Fossey in Rwanda first brought naturalist writer Alex Shoumatoff (*near left*) to *VF*, September 1986. Many more compelling foreign reports followed.

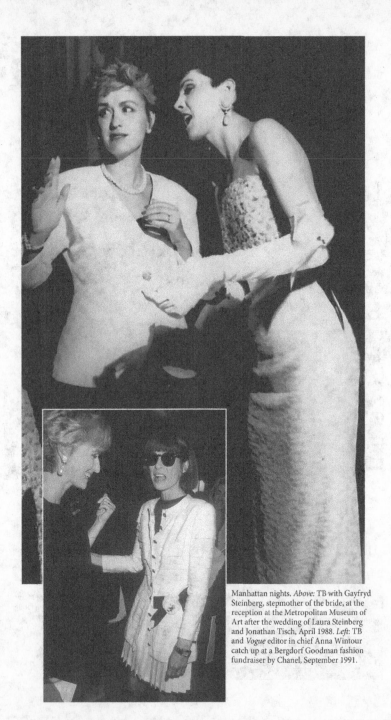

Manhattan nights. *Above*: TB with Gayfryd Steinberg, stepmother of the bride, at the reception at the Metropolitan Museum of Art after the wedding of Laura Steinberg and Jonathan Tisch, April 1988. *Left*: TB and *Vogue* editor in chief Anna Wintour catch up at a Bergdorf Goodman fashion fundraiser by Chanel, September 1991.

Party wizard Robert Isabell collaborated with Studio 54 founder Ian Schrager to transform the bare Culver Studio's soundstage in Culver City, California, for the *Vanity Fair* fundraiser for the Phoenix House rehab center, March 1990. *Left to right:* Bob Colacello, Ian Schrager, TB, and Dr. Mitchell Rosenthal, the founder of Phoenix House.

Next act: TB as editor in chief of *The New Yorker*. In 1994 Karl Lagerfeld dashed off this rendition of TB as the magazine's dandified symbol, Eustace Tilley, originated by graphic artist Rea Irvin on the first *New Yorker* cover in 1925.

For TB's first cover, the artist Ed Sorel's punk in a Central Park carriage evoked Old Guard anxiety about what the new editorial regime might bring, October 1992. Inspired by ethnic tensions between Jews and African Americans in Brooklyn's Crown Heights, Art Spiegelman's Valentine's Day 1993 cover was conceived as a dreamlike vision of comity and love, but it sparked a furor of heated debate. *Right:* TB at her desk at *The New Yorker*, 1998.

1987
SHAKE, RATTLE, AND ROLL

Saturday, January 3, 1987

Return to New York and suddenly feel the stark difference between rich and poor. There's a growing army of the homeless living on the streets. I see them propped up in doorways, lying half-conscious over gratings when I wheel Georgie down Fifty-Seventh Street in his stroller to the Palace Diner. Whatever the Reagan administration promised was supposed to "trickle down" hasn't. The hopelessness is such a contrast to the flash and shine of Condé Nast's world. Some of the new homeless aren't like others. They are New York's own version of Bombay's lepers: hollow eyed, hollowed out, on their way to the next world before they've entirely left this one. They are the AIDS sufferers, the ones who can't afford to hide and go quietly. Everyone in the universe of New York culture has friends who suddenly start to fade, whose paths have been horrifyingly diverted. I seem to always be at funerals. In December a dancer's death was reported every single day in one week, each with the same melancholy indicators — death at an early age after an unnamed illness, with parents and siblings listed as survivors.

I assigned a piece for the March issue on the toll of AIDS on the arts and fashion. No one has yet gathered up a gallery of faces of all those who have died and denuded us of their talent, and we have done it in a haunting double-page spread. I asked our new hire Michael Shnayerson, who was the editor of *Avenue,* to report it out. He's a young straight guy who lives in the West Village and who until this assignment was oblivious to AIDS. Now, reporting the piece, he says it's been like stepping into a war zone. He has done a slew of interviews with artists and arts leaders like Joe Papp who see the toll growing every day, and the doctors who recount stories from the front. Papp's tears rolled down his cheeks unabated as he talked to Michael about the loss. The most moving interview in the piece is with the makeup artist Way Bandy's lover, Maury Hopson, describing Way's last days. How dignified he was, how brave. "I mean, here was this person who was a makeup artist you might think would be some big sissy," Maury said. "And he went out like a fucking lion." It made me cry.

The piece has given me a chance in the editor's letter to write about the death of

Henry Post at *Tatler.* My shock when I visited him in New York–Presbyterian in the summer of 1982, his blond hair shaved off, his restless eyes raking the ward as if for explanation. "Your fashionable correspondent is dying of the fashionable disease," he said. Flippant to the last.

Collecting the pictures of the people who have died has been a real challenge. So many were in the closet or didn't want anyone to know they died from AIDS, or had hidden it from their families. Is it appropriate to run these pictures? We are going over each picture case by case, phone call by phone call. One difficult one has been Angelo Donghia, the interior decorator who died at fifty and never admitted what was wrong. Some of his business associates argued we should exclude his picture. But then the photo department reached a close friend of his who saw a lot of Donghia at the end. The friend was disturbed by the idea of including Angelo's face at first, but then called back and said he believed it was time to go public. "Angelo lived with his secret for two years," he said. "If only all of us had known, we could have nurtured him more and spared him, at least, a sense of shame."

I have wanted to do this piece for so long and feel at last I did something for Henry.

Sunday, January 11, 1987

Miles just called with a newsflash. Bob Gottlieb has been appointed editor of *The New Yorker.* It's been long rumored, but as always with Si, its timing was a total surprise. I wonder how he will set about it, and what it will mean for *VF* — absorb Si's attention more for a start. I hope Gottlieb doesn't go after Wolcott or Schiff. I would, if I were he. I am relieved to hear from Miles that Sharon doesn't get on with him, as she is the one editor I would be fearful of losing. In real terms his impact won't be felt for a while. I think Gottlieb will be superb for content, but I wonder how fast he will master magazine technique and effect all the format changes it requires. *The New Yorker* needs a refreshed layout, cover lines, more vibrant cover il-lustrations, blurbs introducing the stories, the introduction of photography, and shorter pieces to vary the length and tone. And a contents page! Just for a start. What I am not sure of is how reverential Gottlieb is of the magazine's look, because that's one thing that really needs to evolve. But then again, perhaps if he sharpens the content, readers can grit their teeth and hew their way through the density of the layout. Hmm.

Newsflash two. Doug Johnston just called to tell me Shawn didn't resign, he was fired. That Steve Florio said he'd been obstructive and was planning a successor who wasn't Gottlieb. Wow. That must have been tough for Si (not to mention tough for Shawn!). One of the most difficult scenes of Si's life, because he actually worshipped Shawn's *New Yorker.* His ability to flip chills the blood.

My life is so crazy, trying to juggle between the hunt for a nanny (Joanne moved on, other fish to fry), the pending move, G up four times a night. Harry has gone to Orlando to make a speech and G is asleep right now, which is a heady window of freedom that feels like a spa trip.

We had one of the daft roundtables with the ad department today about how hard they find it to sell *VF.* I am sick of hearing about how hard it is when there is such heat on the edit side. After three years it seems advertisers still don't know if we are a movie mag, a fashion mag, or a general-interest mag. Why should it matter?

Then I came down and stared morosely at seven different Molly Ringwald covers, trying to force my gut to choose one when I know none of them work. I took the best three down to the newsstand in the lobby and put them out among the commercial cacophony of faces and they all looked ineffably dreary.

In the middle of this, Peter Armour called me down from the circulation department and told me the February newsstand figures and just as I predicted at the time, the Debra Winger sales were a disappointment after the gains made by the Madonna cover, which was up 52,000 over the month before. I was right after all about that goddamn bathrobe picture of Winger, and no amount of jazzy type could make it appealing. It proves the irksome point that when I don't like something the readers usually agree with me. But sometimes there is no good alternative.

I sat down with Joe McKenna, Ruth, Charles, and Jane to do a postmortem of what went wrong on the Molly shoot so we can avoid it happening again and talk about why I felt it was about to be another turkey. I had told Ruth and Charles repeatedly: no Molly-just-standing-there-in-a-gust-from-a-wind-machine, please. So what do they do? Stand her there with a wind machine going, and let her gaze disconsolately out at us, wearing a dull black T dress and brown leather jacket. Nothing makes me more irritated than the art department telling me I don't understand how cool it really is and bombarding me with comments like "This skimpy sixties thing is where it's at now!" "But it's BORING," I insist. "Nothing is going ON in this picture." I pointed to the simplicity of the Herb Ritts cover of Jack Nicholson pushing sunglasses up the bridge of his nose, a small nuance that nonetheless suggested attitude. At which Ruth goes into her maddening offloading of responsibility onto Charles and Jane and Patrick Demarchelier (whose picture Molly is). I got home feeling cranky and thwarted and read about the scandal of the former (and first Jewish) Miss America Bess Myerson, caught up in a city bribery scandal to help out her lover, a married sewer contractor. That's a real story, perfect for Marie Brenner's zesty city insights. Maybe we should slap Bess on the cover instead.

I had lunch with Jean Stein, the heiress daughter of Jules Stein, to ask her how to crack the endless Warren Beatty tease, as they are close friends. She seemed a bit of a professional basket case, fluttering around in sixties disarray, exuding the recreational neuroses of the rich. Still, she seemed likable and might help. She said we should do it like her great *Edie* book [about the doomed Warhol superstar star Edie Sedgwick] as oral history but had to "find someone who would amuse Warren."

Today Isabelle Adjani stood up André Leon Talley at a shoot in Paris, so another cover bites the dust. I have now been told by Jane, who had it from the PR that Molly looked dreary because "she had stomach cramps." Stars are so damn ridiculous. That's one thing Bob Gottlieb doesn't have to deal with at *The New Yorker.* I long to just be able to think about the writing and the stories. One treat — our Dennis Hopper cover for April is wonderful. I wish Annie could do everything. She's caught the sly, wicked gleam in his eye as he looks out in semiprofile, a cigar burning between his fingers, the glimpse of a floppy black tie suggesting a loose-moraled night out. Ron Rosenbaum's profile of him is juicy. Newsstands need bad boys and women with a past, not drippy starlets with pious causes. The Joe Orton diaries inside are compulsive. The March issue, on the other hand, is way too artsy-craftsy. It's funny how issues develop their own personalities and mix. April, fiercely meaty; March, airily bohemian. The endless conundrum of how to get the mix perfect is what keeps me from getting bored. It's snowing and I have a passel of photographers out and about, trying to capture it for the next Christmas issue so we don't have to send them abroad.

Si hired the Indian publishing pasha Sonny Mehta from London to replace Gottlieb at Knopf. Clever appointment and one that's genial for us, as he and his wife, Gita, are already well disposed to Harry and me. Howard Kaminsky, for all his relentless bonhomie, has been getting too overbearing at Random House, very much exerting sway over Si. He is starting to replace Roy Cohn in Si's life. Si is a gangster of wishful thinking, always excited by the presence of swagger.

Tuesday, February 24, 1987
In flight, Chicago to New York

On the way back with the team from the opening of *The Art of Vanity Fair* show at Marshall Field's in Chicago, a great school outing. The show featured Steichen, Covarrubias, and Calder from the golden days, and Annie, the illustrator Robert Risko, and co from now. After the show reception, Philip Miller, aka the Robert Redford of Retail and the boss of Marshall Field's, hosted a three-table dinner party at the Racquet Club.

The obsession with shopping is one of the big differences between American and British women. Maureen Smith, a big, loud powerhouse lady who referred to a rich friend's first husband as her "starter" husband, was vocal on the subject. "You've heard the expression shop till you drop?" she shouted. "Well, that's me. I spend a hundred bucks just getting to the elevator."

"Me too," said Miller. "I've read somewhere that it's all about a need to control. That we have to own to get power."

"You're reading the wrong books," another

463

of the Chicago ladies said. "It's all about sex." And then we were off on why.

One thing I have learned is that the American compulsion to shop has nothing to do with having money. G's nanny Joanne couldn't leave the apartment without coming back loaded with merchandise, fired up with the illusion of "the bargain" that had made her spend the day pounding the streets of Queens. And at the other end of the scale is André Leon Talley, also madly questing a bargain but from very different stores. "Eighty-nine bucks, the topcoats in the I. Magnin sale," he shouts. "Adeney Brigg, same coat, five hundred!" What is this all about? Is the frenzy of acquisition a way to make up for the lack of history? Am going to assign an essay to explore it.

I decided I really like Chicago as a city. There is a structured, spacious feel to it, the sense of a forceful, virile past refusing to be swept aside by the less substantial present. There's also a big-time gusto, a sense of high stakes, and anything goes. So much less cautious than life in New York's petri dish, incubating viral successes and disasters. The TV anchorman Walter Jacobson, who interviewed us on his show, was better than anything on network TV. He had a great reckless spirit, impatient, risky, contrary, and real. "You've had enough airtime, powder puff," he suddenly yelled at a mayoral candidate who was blathering into the mike. Not for the first time, apparently. In 1983, I am told, he famously criticized Mayor Harold Washington for using city workers to paint and redecorate his apartment. Washington retaliated at a television academy luncheon, shouting, "Walter, you're the bottom of the barrel."

I could definitely live in Chicago.

Thursday, February 26, 1987
455 East Fifty-Seventh Street

We are here! In the apartment we have dreamed and schemed and screamed for! It's still awash with painters and missing bits, every room a turmoil, but the warm, comfortable glow of it still shines through and captivates me with a sense of HOME AT LAST. I marvel to be living in such a place on a block that is so secluded and so unbroken by modernity that it feels like a slice of Pimlico or Paris.

Armed with my Visconti–cum–Tony Lambton decor brief, Chester suggested each room should be a different color. He found some heavenly round-backed armchairs covered in dark green damask and a chintz sofa, and laid sisal on the floor. We've turned the little room off the dining room into a den for me, with a tapestry-covered Turkish bed flanked by brass reading lights where I can lie in the

465

evening with my hookah, reading manuscripts, lulled by the rotation of a wood-bladed ceiling fan.

But the real joy of the dining room is that it doubles as a library, the walls filled with our fifty cartons of books from London. Harry and I unpacked them ravenously, thumbing through our joyful old favorites as if they were long-lost friends. We spent the weekend hanging pictures with Chester. I came to realize that when he didn't like something he would say, with a nervous laugh, "This one would look great in Quogue." Our accumulated memorabilia is so eclectic that there's no point making sense of it, so we are playing up the differences with interesting juxtapositions: one wall in the living room features an oil painting of the Venetian countryside next to a scarlet pop-art caricature of me by Robert Risko, next to a gilt girandole mirror next to the sepia Lartigue. I love the way Chester shows up in his L.L.Bean rain shoes and cashmere overcoat, carrying a bag of coffee and bagels in one hand and three lavatory seats in the other.

We ate a delicious picnic when we had finished, sent over from Balducci's by Marie Brenner.

Saturday, February 28, 1987

Hectic few days. Andy Warhol died on Sunday

and it cried out for an electric *VF* package. At first, I tried to crash it into the lackluster June issue, but then everyone rebelled and we decided to do it big and properly for July. This afternoon, we sat around and hashed out the angles, with Bob Colacello on speakerphone in Gstaad. I had to lace my soothing condolences to Bob about the passing of his old mentor with the gentle but firm insistence that he write the "Behind the Mask" piece about Andy, because after all those years at the Factory, no one knew him better. John Richardson, meanwhile, said he would write the piece about Andy's voyeur energy, and Sarah Giles would get from his longtime business manager, promoter, and sidekick, Fred Hughes, the exclusive pictures of Andy's house and his last portrait. Fred has been named his sole executor, which perhaps disappointed Colacello. He's a cool customer, Fred, all slicked-back hair and invented pedigree. Richardson voiced the view that Warhol was a kind of saint, living a spinsterish existence, attending morning mass inside the whirlpool of weirdness around him. I couldn't let him get away with this notion, attractively counterintuitive though it may be as an editorial angle. I firmly believe that Warhol, along with Roy Cohn, was one of the two most amoral men of our times. Cohn was actively destructive, Warhol was the manipulative void, the dead star. Carolina Herrera told me that Andy was terrified of death and never attended a funeral his whole life (except his own in Pittsburgh tomorrow, along with the two perfectly normal middle-class brothers who've suddenly stepped out of the shadows to claim him).

Anyhow, I realize if we are to have Fred Hughes's cooperation, we can't portray Andy as the satanic figure I believe him to be, but we still have to suggest there was a dark side. John Richardson still says no, no, Fred Hughes totally cleaned up the Factory, and all the junkies who died around Andy were just an inevitable part of the "sixties scene," which I believe is pure sophistry. Andy was a devouring maw that had to be fed with decadence. Anyway. It's all very interesting and the debate was long and heated around my desk.

Wednesday, March 11, 1987

The Warhol package has turned out great. It was such a sweat to reel it in — took so much planning, wheedling, hustling, and pushing. The dramas raged for two weeks. Sarah and Reinaldo persuaded Fred Hughes to let us photograph Andy's house, which has never been seen. Then it was nearly snatched away by *House & Garden*. Lou Gropp, its sleepy editor, suddenly woke up and thought the Warhol house would drop into his lap out of droit du seigneur. Gropp wrote a letter to Fred Hughes that made him go wobbly about giving the exclusive to *VF,* and then, worse, told John Richardson that as part of his *House & Garden* contract he expected him to help him get it. Richardson, never Richard the Lionheart at the best of times, instead of fessing up and saying he was already writing it for us, got into a cowardly panic about his *House & Garden* contract and started blathering about how he could do both pieces and would indeed "raise it with Fred Hughes." What? I nearly had a heart attack. Sarah G had been sweet-talking Hughes at Nell's every night of the week to get this scoop. Richardson only got in on the act later, though having his name on it clearly helped. I sent John a stiff letter reminding him who was first in this story chase and Sarah, meanwhile, gate-crashed his à deux lunch with Fred Hughes to make quite sure John didn't mention *House & Garden*'s interest to Fred. So we managed to bag it. As I write, unbeknownst to Lou Gropp, who thinks we are all still discussing it, Evelyn Hofer is taking the pictures of Andy's house. As soon as the shoot is in our hot little hands, I will have to break it to Gropp. But that's showbiz, Lou. A scoop is a scoop.

I am playing hooky from the office and writing my editor's letter at home, with G playing happily next door. I am also waiting for the imminent delivery of Alex Shoumatoff's report of the trial in the Palais de Justice in Bangui of the Central African Republic's monstrous former emperor Jean-Bédel Bokassa — whose résumé includes the newsstand-friendly detail that he used to keep his enemies' corpses in his walk-in refrigerator. There is so little foreign feature writing in the US compared to London, and yet whenever we do such pieces there is a real audience for them. We have been trying to get a writer to Bangui for three months, then with ten days till the close of the June issue I at last got Shoumatoff to agree and crash it through. Three years ago I knew so few writers here, I would never know whom to reach for to do an ambitious story like this on deadline. But now the team plays their assigned roles so well. Sarah G hustling through the visa, Sharon waiting like a bulldog for the receipt of the rough copy she will wrestle into coherent shape, batting it back and forth to me for direction. Every issue this year has had at least one juicy, deeply reported narrative. With Sarah, Jane, Sharon, Elisabeth Biondi, we have the A-list writers' support team — without them we could never get the scoops or the access and the writers and photographers would fall through the cracks. It's a different system from that at most magazines, having people to help facilitate the writers, but it really works. I feel my professional life has never been more joyously productive. Over the weekend Chester said, "I've done a sketch of a little redesign of the nanny's area to create a tiny extra room in case Georgie has a sister." Dare I? The wail next door signifies that G again burrowed into the saucepan closet and fell on a frying pan. I love him so much I want to burst. Could there possibly be room in our hearts for two?

Wednesday, April 1, 1987

Wednesday was the PEN gala at the Metropolitan Club I vice-chaired with Gayfryd because Norman Mailer asked me to. Gayfryd had created decor that was totally over the top, with outsize flower arrangements you had to peer through like something out of *The Jungle Book.* She was wearing a shiny white satin gown with huge puffy leg o' mutton sleeves. The evening was fraught with comical seating disasters. I had invited Bob Hughes, John Richardson, DVF and Alain Elkann, Caroline Graham, and Jay McInerney to sit at my table, with the PEN host, Arthur Miller. The first crisis was Calvin Klein's assistant calling to say he had bought a ticket for the dinner but would come only if he sat at my table. I asked PEN if Miller could be moved to host another table, thus displacing America's greatest living playwright, which was hardly the spirit of the night. Worse followed. Carolina Herrera, for some reason, thought I had asked her and she turned up with Jerry Zipkin, only to discover, of course, there was no table allocation. Gayfryd and I had a heated powwow and I said I would ask Caroline to take one for the team and move off to an absentee slot, but where to find a place for Jay McInerney so we could seat Zipkin, whose poison if he had nowhere to sit was just too scary to contemplate? Jane Yeoman of PEN valiantly agreed to float until a seat came up and Jay was put at ITT CEO Rand Araskog's grand, dreary table, which didn't please Jay at all. All this switching meant that the balance of mine was now all thrown off and Bob Hughes was amazed to find his fellow PEN authors were Calvin Klein, Jerry Zipkin, Carolina Herrera, Jackie Rogers, and DVF. The Frocky Horror Show, from Bob's point of view.

Harry got into an altercation with the *New Yorker* fiction writer Jamaica Kincaid, who came over to Gayfryd and with an air of hoity-toity bemusement said, "I am puzzled by this event. Why are there so many rich people here?" (Because writers are the cheapest people in the world and don't care about other writers, so PEN has to be funded by rich people who don't care about writers either but at least are willing to pay for a dinner, Jamaica, that's why.) She'd had a bad evening because she sat next to Mort Janklow who told her that *The New Yorker* had never had an editor until now, which, given that Jamaica is married to Shawn's other son, Allen, didn't go over well. She also told Mort that she would never write for *Vanity Fair* because of the despicable way Si treated Shawn. What a cauldron of hot feuds.

Everyone was talking about Andy Warhol's memorial service. Two thousand people at St. Patrick's Cathedral. It was like paging through back issues of *Interview* over the decades — Halston, Liza Minnelli, Anne Bass, Claus von Bülow, Grace Jones, Yoko Ono, Tom Wolfe, Richard Gere, Prince Michael of Greece and his wife, Marina.

John Richardson got his opportunity to promote his Andy-as-saint angle, this time in the right setting at least, telling the crowd that Andy "fooled the world into believing that his only obsessions were money, fame, and glamour, and that he was cool to the point of callousness." But (here we go) he was, in fact, "more of a recording angel — the distance he established between the world and himself was above all a matter of innocence and of art." I still don't buy it, but the massive turnout of fashion, art, writing, and society was pretty extraordinary. Bianca Jagger looked so pretty and distressed in her little black hat. André Leon Talley was there in a bespoke suit as thin as a number two lead pencil with the young Brit fashion assistant Isabella Blow, wearing a couture suit and crazy hat. I couldn't quite take Claus von Bülow going up for communion, but it was full of vignettes in that genre. Andy would have loved it, there is no doubt about that.

Sunday, April 5, 1987

Spa break at the amazing Golden Door — I came with Ruth Ansel. It's unlike anything I have ever experienced at most other boring, airhead spas . . . a slice of Bel Air in the mountains, and the joy is the way they tailor everything to you personally, bringing exactly the right calorie amount for you by the pool. I particularly love the six a.m. hikes and the tiny muffins and coffee that await us, pre-hike, in the Wisteria Lounge. I chortled on the flight to San Diego at Bob Hughes's hysterical piece in *Time* about the van Gogh auction that last week netted $39 million for *Sunflowers,* which Bob called "the *Mona Lisa* of the vegetable world." I did have a sick moment on arrival at the Door when I spied

Park Avenue faces I know under sun hats, but they were also fleeing the city and melted away. Also sighted the extremely irritating *New Yorker* fashion writer, Kennedy Fraser, clearly basking in a freebie, going on about how appalling it was that Shawn had been removed. I said, given how advertisers were fleeing and readers averaging over sixty, what did she think the owner should do? "I really don't know," she exhaled, "except that he must understand that *The New Yorker* is a writer's magazine. We write about the things that interest us and what worries me about Gottlieb is he's assigning things. Mr. Shawn never assigned." Please! Surely what *The New Yorker* needs to be is not just a "writer's magazine" but a reader's magazine, because writers, unless guided and edited and lured out of their comfort zones, can go off-piste into dreary cul-de-sacs of introversion and excess and entirely forget about questions of content and pace.

Saturday, April 11, 1987

Came home a day early as I missed G too much to be apart anymore, but had a horrible stress attack on being back. Unless I am working, I am agitated. Hoped that the Golden Door would calm me down but the contrast makes me worse. I am hopeless with yoga; tried it at the Door and my head was always just full of articles I wanted to assign. I had a session with a maternal, milky-skinned woman named Anne-Harriet who is the Door's lifestyle therapist and she started by asking solicitously, "Is there a lot of stress in your life?" to which I could only laugh mirthlessly. But the stress is also self-inflicted and an addiction, and such remedies as breathing deeply and holding on to some smooth, spiritually imbued stone doesn't seem to work for me, folks. I am a vertical obsessive, unable to let go of any detail, not always the best thing for the mag. It ought to sort of run itself by now, but each issue also has its own unique requirement for one last thing to reach perfection and I always feel it's my job to search it out. Groan.

April 18, 1987

Came down with G and opened the house in Quogue. Glum weather but agita soon fled.

There has been a swirl of welcome to New York parties for Bernie Leser, who arrived from London Condé Nast. Yep, good old Bernie has fetched up in the Big Apple, having been made president of US Condé Nast to replace burly Bob Lapham, who has retired. I realize that Bernie, who was never a big player in London, where corporate titles don't mean much, could wind up as a hot ticket here with the status badge of president of CNP. And why not? He is much less preposterous than Carl Spielvogel, who looks like a pear with a permanent wave. He is more agreeable than Marvin Traub, the feted big-head who runs Bloomingdale's, and no more pompous than almost anyone I meet at Alice Mason's. I find myself rooting for him. Bernie is an affable man and his social climbing is only from insecurity. I was touched to recently learn from Lauder that his first language is actually German and that he fled Nazi Berlin as a child after being expelled from his Jewish boarding school on Kristallnacht and humiliated by jeering crowds. Once that fact about him is discovered, it changes one's whole view of him and I now see his life as a story of admirable and necessary adaptation and a survivor's social camouflage. I wish he would talk about it but he never does.

New York has so much more social mobility than London, and so many more histories like this. The Lesers are going to be in hog heaven. Exhibit A was Leonard Lauder's sit-down dinner for twenty in their honor, which had all of the above in attendance. Si also gave a dinner for him but did the minimum, which must have disappointed Bernie. To my slight consternation, the first person I saw when I walked in was Ed Kosner. One hour previously he had just learned that I've not only stolen Jesse Kornbluth from *New York* mag but also beaten him out to hire another great writer, Ron Rosenbaum, a double whammy. When Jesse broke it to him that he was leaving, Ed apparently said, "Oh, she's up to her old tricks again, is she?" Tee-hee.

Halfway through dinner Si asked Donald if he'd like to come into the bedroom and view his new Jasper Johns, *Out the Window,* for which he paid a staggering $3.63 million at Sotheby's in November, the highest price ever paid for a living artist. The two of them trotted off and when they came back I asked Si if I could see it, too. The Johns is hanging on the wall of a functional, unloved-looking bedroom with nothing much in it except a clock radio. I muttered something about the marvel of it and the interesting influence of Rauschenberg and took pleasure in Si's shy flush of pleasure as he gazed lovingly upon it. Seems like a ton of money to pay but maybe it will be worth more one day.

Sunday, May 3, 1987

I ran into Dick Snyder at a book launch and got an earful about the unraveling of his marriage to Joni Evans, a great modern saga of urban narcissism on steroids. It began, apparently, as the perfect two-career couple union at Simon & Schuster, romance on the job, both of them hungry killers working late together, sex on the desk, reading proofs in tandem, partners in all. She was his best editor at S & S, with a great batting average for hits. He wasn't bothered at first that Joni is even more undomesticated than he is. But then as time went by, claims he, her lifestyle demands seemed to keep growing. "Not one driver but two drivers. Not one chef but two. Before a dinner at our place Joni would get back from the office five minutes after me. I'd be there ten of eight. She'd be showering five of. Then we'd sit down and eat whatever the chef had ordered, she couldn't care less. She never made me so much as a tuna fish salad the whole time we were married." (A woman after my own heart.)

For a long time, Dick didn't miss the tuna fish salad, implication being because of other compensations (nothing makes a man miss good cooking less than good sex), but then he was promoted into the Gulf and Western stratosphere and he made Joni president of Simon & Schuster. That's when it started to go sour. As he mellowed into Mr. Big Shot of Broad Horizons, she turned into himself ten years earlier, but even more obsessed and more driven. "One evening I was sitting looking at the sun going down at our house in Westchester and Joni was talking shop as always and I suddenly thought, I might as well be married to Marty Davis [G&W's CEO]!" By the time the sun had disappeared

Dick had asked for a divorce and Joni eagerly agreed, or so he tells me. They separated and he is now madly in love with a twenty-nine-year-old S & S book editor much lower down the totem pole who loves to travel, have sex, and, I suppose, make tuna fish sandwiches. Joni — says Dick — has become financially vengeful in retaliation and is suing him for half his Gulf and Western stock, the Bedford house, and everything else besides, claiming "she made him." And yet they are still working together every day at S & S. The perennial irony here is that men still have all the cards. They can be driven bastards for years and ignore their kids. Then when they mellow out they can have a younger wife, a new family, and all the perks of a fresh start. The funny thing, though, was that Dick kept saying Joni had "blown it" in the marriage, but escaping from it sounds like the best thing she ever did.

Friday, May 8, 1987

I had a run-in with Al Taubman, the shopping-mall magnate and owner of Sotheby's, at some weird dinner for Paul Laxalt, a bland Republican senator from Nevada who just announced a presidential run the day before. God knows how we got on this dinner list. Taubman is a huge, halitotic dolphin with a big, hearty laugh and beady little eyes.

He was very unfriendly at first, though not to Harry, who had met him in DC and who was energetic on my behalf, trying to thaw Taubman out. Then Taubman suddenly turned to me and said, "Let me explain to you why I gave you that dirty look. In the current issue of your magazine you have horribly insulted my wife."

What could this be? "Please explain," I said solicitously.

"That piece on Madame Claude," he said ominously. "The paragraph that describes Madame Claude girls who've gone on to marry into society, including the wife of a New York auction house chief." Oh Jesus. James Fox's lethal piece about the celebrated Parisian madame did indeed have that paragraph and the former Miss Israel, aka Judy Mazor Taubman, was, without doubt, the lady James had in mind. "Are you aware how few auction house chiefs there are?" says Taubman with menace. "Do you think anyone thinks it's Mrs. Alsop of Christie's? The halls of Sotheby's are full of it! And my wife is being mortified by inquiries!"

Ouch. I realized we should have been a lot more careful with the disguising of identity, and now the more I learn about Judy Taubman, the daughter of a well-off jeweler who was married first to a clothing manufacturer, the more I also think James's supposition was highly unlikely. So I resorted to the old *Tatler* motto "there is no one I can't apologize to" and went into a twenty-minute charm offensive of shock, consternation, and puzzled innocence, saying how preposterous it was that anyone could level such allegations blah-blah until by the end he was saying, "You're so cute. I knew you wouldn't be mean, but people have got the wrong end of the stick and somehow we have to figure out how to put it right." More worryingly, he added, "My people will be calling you." Next day the Sotheby's PR man comes on the blower, firmly demanding reparations, and I come up with a brain wave. "What if," I said, "I could persuade a columnist like Suzy or Liz Smith to run a piece saying it wasn't true?" This would mean I didn't have to disavow our story, or James Fox, a writer I adore. The PR guy loved that idea and, fortunately, Aileen Mehle (Suzy) had been at the same table last night, so I called her and she was amenable, just told me to messenger a paragraph I wanted her to publish by four p.m. Bull's-eye. Taubman pacified, Fox protected, and no groveling required from *VF.*

Tuesday, May 12, 1987

The talk all week has been about Senator Gary Hart being caught with a racy blonde named Donna Rice aboard somebody's boat, deliciously named *Monkey Business,* in Bimini, Florida. What makes an obviously smart guy so firmly in the public eye with a presidential run risk everything for a weekend of sex frolics? JFK, Hart's role model, used to do this sort of thing, but Marlene Dietrich, Angie Dickinson, etc. etc. were the souls of discretion and anyhow decades ago the political press didn't regard fucking per se as part of All the News That's Fit to Print. I was torn whether a *VF* story would be too late by the time we could publish in two months, but there's the interesting and legitimately important angle of how much press exposure is kosher for a candidate's private life. So I asked Gail Sheehy to get on it ASAP. She's been doing well for us. At the moment she's on a Rudy Giuliani profile, digging to see if he's a latter-day Eliot Ness or just a media-hungry careerist. He took Gail to tool around John Gotti's haunts such as the Ravenite Social Club in Little Italy, and she says they came face-to-face with Gotti himself. Lucky Gail. Feel reporter envy.

I realize how I am now much more confident as an editor, and now have strong nerves in the job. Not just trusting my instincts more but failing to get hysterically rattled over flak on a story, because I now know I can handle it.

Came home and read Philip Larkin for soul food. I miss writing but I feel I shouldn't be competing for space with my own writers.

Am very proud of the June issue. Alex Shoumatoff's Bokassa piece is a tour de force thanks to Sharon's editing boot camp. He has a wonderful ability to capture the narrative juice, the regional atmosphere and the exotic details that keep you reading (e.g., the discovery of an alligator-infested pool and a collection of lions Bokassa allegedly kept to eat unwanted guests). He even interviewed pygmies who live in the forested part of the country Bokassa's family came from. It's an amazing tale of lust and greed and corruption. Plus we really got the pagination in the rest of the issue right. It's effective to go from the sinister, overpowering visual atmosphere of Bokassa to the crisp and vibrant Liza Minnelli pics by Annie that seem almost three-dimensional.

Sunday, May 17, 1987

We stayed in town for the weekend because on Friday night we had to attend a Front Page Awards dinner where Marie Brenner received one for her *VF* piece on Michele Duvalier. A proud moment for the mag. It's so different spending a spring weekend in town. Had a wonderful time. Sitting with G on the grass in Central Park in the sun after taking him to lunch at Rumpelmayer's, flopping in our mellow sitting room at home with the trees flourishing outside the windows. After the Friday awards dinner at the Waldorf, we walked home with Clay Felker and Gail Sheehy, who live three doors up across from us on Fifty-Seventh Street.

Clay is just about to accept the editorship of *Manhattan,inc.* He's been doing Harry's old job at *US News* in DC for the last eight months and now is also desperate to escape Mort's micromanaging. He's so happy to come back to NYC. Walking through the summery streets after the Waldorf dinner that featured an overpowering band we'd all felt obliged to dance to, H and I felt how civilized our life is now becoming, and how all the hustle and toil and pressure is bringing such great rewards. We are so lucky to be in America! In fact I feel my usual panic about life getting on an even keel. I even find myself daydreaming about taking a course on art at Columbia. (No, no, said Bob Hughes at lunch on Monday. "Just come to previews with me.")

We are worried, though, about Georgie's progress. I asked Anna Wintour if her husband, Dr. David Shaffer, who's a child psychiatrist, could come over for a drink and meet him. He noted G flaps and waves his hands when he moves his fingers in repose, which could be indicative of developmental issues. He spends hours standing at the window, obsessed with seeing garbage trucks. Nothing will break him away. He has such an amazing memory and the beginnings of a startling vocabulary, but mixing with other kids is hard for him. Shaffer recommended more medical follow-up. Feeling extra protective, I took him into our bed for mammoth cuddles.

Tuesday, May 19, 1987

The last two days have been perfect hell at the office with everyone at each other's throats. Annie brought in her pics of Diane Sawyer on Friday, telling me ahead of time she had grave misgivings because she hated the clothes André brought to the shoot. So I told her to bring the pics in to show me. As I walked into Ruth's office to look at them with Annie, Ruth and André were already at the light box, with Ruth crooning as we arrived, "Annie, these are spectacular. You really pulled it off!" which pleased Annie, obviously, and she and André then started congratulating each other about how great they turned out after all.

I looked at them myself and saw immediately that Annie's first misgivings were right. Low energy, low glamour, a rare flop. But in that atmosphere of festivity, it was now impossible to rain on the parade. Monday morning I arrive and Ruth has all the blowups on the desk. And now she's telling me Annie was the wrong person for these pictures. How the lighting was horrible. The clothes awful. "So why the hell did you tell Annie and André you loved them?" I said stonily. And Ruth just ignored that question and repeated how she was against it in the first place. Okay, I said, we just have to reshoot and I have to handle André on this one. I don't want him hearing it from anyone but me. Except it seems that Sarah Giles, the world's most indiscreet human, was lurking around in earshot. And she promptly went off and told André, who called Jane Sarkin, hysterical, and she came to see me in a total spin because she was the one who had fixed up the whole shoot and feared it was now in jeopardy, so I bawled out Sarah, who of course denied she'd been indiscreet, and she told André, who wrote a cover-your-ass note to me on her behalf, absolving her of any blame. Migraine.

It was so hard to switch into mummy gear when I got home. I was so wired that all I could do was make incendiary phone calls to everyone, making it worse, while G screamed in the background.

To cap it off, just as we are going to press with Gail's great Giuliani story, *New York* mag comes out with their own Giuliani cover and scoops us to death. So much for my crowing over Kosner. Chapeau, Ed. Another boomerang from hubris.

Wednesday, May 20, 1987

Ruth went to see Alex and he offered her a job at *Vogue*. We have to make the change because the art department confusion has become impossible. For Ruth, this could be the best and most dignified thing. This morning she called me, sounding very clearheaded and strong, and said she'd decided to accept the *Vogue* offer. Now that it's over I feel sad as well as relieved. Her sensibility is superb and she has certainly helped to raise my sights, visually. Better it end before it deteriorates. Charles is so good, and very excited to now lead. I hope his orderliness doesn't lack her magic.

Thursday, May 21, 1987
Quogue

Feel better after all the drama. The sun came out, and bicycling into Quogue village with G riding in a baby seat behind, wrinkling his nose to sniff the spring flowers and newly mown grass, was pretty nice, and so was sitting outside at the Quogue stationery, breakfasting on poached eggs. H and I walked along the beach, dissecting our week, with G snoozing on Harry's back. We came into that lovely seaside feeling of papers fluttering on the porch.

Bernie and Barbara Leser were out here

staying with friends for the weekend. Very pleasant. After tea we walked them back. It was a mind-blowing scene change. A gargantuan house on stilts with a hotel-sized swimming pool. The hosts, he some noisy guy in retail, had a family house party of twenty. Enormous bespectacled uncles wearing shorts with baggy crotches hinting at pendulous genitalia, overweight daughters shoveling onion crisps, beefy sons-in-law crashing around at a pool table. The wife kept dipping her huge mitt into troughs of Ritz Crackers and smearing them with caviar and chives. Collapsed on a recliner for the rest of the afternoon with social PTSD.

Tuesday, June 2, 1987

Jane Amsterdam, now out at *Manhattan,inc.*, and John Larsen asked us out to dinner. Jane is going through what Harry went through after leaving *The Times*. The syndrome he used to call Let'sHaveLunch, where everyone courts you but no one offers you anything. She said she's sent numerous messages to Bob Gottlieb about joining *The New Yorker* and he never calls back. He is crazy! She's an amazing editor. This is just another example of how he's not grasping the nettle! When he took over I thought he was a formidable choice, but now when I hear things like this, I wonder. He seems totally unresponsive to the pulse of the news. What is the point of *The New Yorker*'s weekly frequency if it doesn't respond? They should be able to do the ultimate profile of Ivan Boesky with all the deep texture of the era that other magazines don't have the talent pool to do. Or explain the Ollie North phenomenon with Iran-Contra. Of course it takes time to get good pieces, but we have shown it doesn't matter if it's late if it's full of new revelation, which is supposed to be *The New Yorker*'s mantra anyway. Still, if it doesn't work with Gottlieb, Si will give him a very long time to fail. Maybe one day I will read a piece about *TNY* folding into *VF,* instead of the other way around as I did in the past. But no doubt I will be long gone by then.

Took Reinaldo Herrera to lunch at Le Cirque, and he regressed into man-about-town mode and kept insisting on trying to pitch me a piece on Prince Michael of Greece, even though the prince is the most boring man in Athens. "Reinaldo," I said patiently, "can you suggest an angle on Prince Michael that would have, um, wider appeal for an American audience?" "You mean, which one of the family is on drugs, which one is facing financial ruin?" he said testily. (Well, it would help.)

Peter Duchin was at the next table. "Malcolm Forbes's party was a total bore," Reinaldo told him.

"I didn't play at it so it must have been," said Duchin.

"No, I mean, really a BORE," boomed Reinaldo, making the word so rich and reverberative it made people at other tables look our way. "Everyone was a tycoon or a CEO. It was the biggest BORE since the signing of the Constitution!"

"I didn't play at that one either," said Duchin.

Feeling antsy, or perhaps just wanting attention, I asked Si this morning what he would feel about my writing a book about the turnaround of *VF.* He look startled and discomfited. "That would be a bit like writing a biography of my grandchild," he said. "Don't you think a bit too soon?"

Wednesday, June 3, 1987

I flew on a bumpy Pan Am flight to Miami to talk to the Knight Ridder newspaper group about how to improve their Lifestyle sections. As I rattled on from the stage about the need to splash pictures, go after the big story of the day, cultivate writers with voice, I sensed I irritated all the Lifestyle section editors who made comments afterward to me like, "Of course, Tina here is not concerned with such pedestrian matters as service in her magazine," and one went as far as "Not that honesty and accuracy are the first thing on

Vanity Fair's agenda." Meow!

John Mack Carter, the brilliant editor of *Good Housekeeping,* stole the show with a preview of his new Hearst mag, *Victoria.* Without any market research he has crystallized the current longing for tradition and what he describes as the "lack of loveliness in the rootless, unbeautiful lives of the modern American woman who knows that deep down all the running is leading every day to a lesser life." Wow. How right he is about that and it's certainly what I feel myself every time I pause to take a breath. How interesting, though, that it has taken a man to articulate it.

Monday, June 8, 1987

I was Calvin Klein's date at the Fashion Institute of Technology benefit for Marvin Traub at the Waldorf. This made us coconspirators and put me next to Bloomingdale CEO Marvin Traub, whose ads we are still unable to get. Calvin is so much nicer when his guard is down. He is endearingly flaky, losing his keys, forgetting people's names, and desperate to get away from all the people hustling him for his business. I really liked his man Friday and PR guy, Paul Wilmot, impossibly stylish — greased-back blond hair and pale lemon dinner jacket, and yet relaxed and ironically funny about being Calvin's slave. He wasn't seated with us at dinner.

"Where was I sitting?" he asked rhetorically later. "Table nineteen. Right in the toilet with Patricia *Quelque Chose,* who designs horribly tacky costumes and kept telling me to put out my cigarette."

Calvin was incredulous that Marvin Feldman, the head of FIT, asked him if he could honor him for his ad campaign. "Doesn't he understand I wouldn't want to be honored for that!" (It was indeed a crass move that betrayed Feldman's real intent. "Let me honor you for your marketing budget!")

"Don't you decline, I'll handle it," said Paul, snapping his fingers to retrieve our limo from the line of others outside the Waldorf, and effortlessly getting Calvin ahead of everyone else. One could see in Calvin, whatever he said, how much he really loved the buzz and thrust of all those retailers paying court to him, how they now need him as much as he needs them.

I felt in the center of the humming commercial bazaar of the city. Skidding through the rain with Wilmot in the front seat drolly unpicking the evening, Calvin's lanky legs stretched out next to me with his feet shiny in patent shoes, along with Etta Froio, *W*'s fashion editor, who also got a ride, sharing retail gossip learned from her own end of the Waldorf ballroom, I felt happy to be on the inside of the city of hard surfaces.

On Monday morning Si called me in and said, "*Interview*, Tina. What's your response?" My heart sank. Clearly the rumors are true. "You are considering buying it?" I said.

"Yes."

"Well, the question is not whether you should buy it, but who would you have edit it?"

"You," he replied, giving me a look of intensity that said "checkmate." This was undoubtedly his way of saying, "If you have time on your hands to write a book, allow me to fill it." Serves me right for opening my big mouth last week. It felt a bit like when I made trouble at school and they'd try (at first) to move me up a class.

"Two magazines to run instead of one," he repeated firmly. I wonder if this has some of Alex's Machiavellian stamp on it. They clearly don't want a *VF* book written, and throwing me a new challenge is a good way to stop it. I said immediately that I foresaw only conflicts in having to do two titles at once. I counseled him not to get involved. "Fred Hughes is making such a mess of it there probably won't be an *Interview* in six months' time . . ."

"Think about it," he said implacably.

I spent Monday in a turmoil of angst. I suppose I should see it as an extension of the Condé Nast power base. I undoubtedly would if I were single, but all I could think was that it would add to the stress of spending enough time with G, who needs me more and more. Harry also saw complications of editorial conflict, as I do.

I decided to pitch Si the idea of folding the Warhol broadsheet into a *VF* supplement, and when I presented this notion he got excited, and brought in the circulation director, Peter Armour (who was totally confused, as he had been modeling out circulation figures for a sister publication), and barking "Get me Fred Hughes" on the phone to his assistant, Lillian.

I left him at it and went down to ask Doug Johnston what he thought. He told me to slow down and start thinking of how *Interview* could be a spin-off publication. He could sell it to advertisers as a dual package, and pointed out that a fold-in supplement might, in fact, have definite disadvantages to our more conservative advertisers, who would feel our own upscale image had been trivialized. Certainly, when I consider our meeting with the IBM account exec last week, Doug is probably right. Mr. IBM had spent a long time explaining to me why the company had fled *VF* in 1983. "It was the color spread on a bohemian theater group called Pina Bausch," he said somberly, as I dimly recalled the Helmut Newton pic of a huge red tongue in the ear of a horrific puppet in one of Leo's last issues, when he was trying to be avant garde. Mr. IBM said that although he liked *VF,* he "feared its element of surprise, its sudden flights into questionable taste" (i.e., the reason why people are buying it). I was about to urge him to in no way put his job on the line by buying into our magazine when he concluded, "So if we come back as I would like to, I need your assurance that we will be forewarned if someone like Claus von Bülow is on the cover." HOORAY! In other words, we are getting the IBM business, simply because they need to be present.

Anyway, coming off that success, I began to see that Doug might be right and ponder how *Interview* could somehow function as *VF*'s downtown sister, a place where the hip kids like Joe McKenna and Angela Janklow — the brilliant daughter of Mort and Linda, who's joined us — could spill over and seed a new farm team and we could operate it with a shared core production staff and an editorial leader like Gabé. I got quite excited and called Si to tell him so.

"Fred Hughes just called me," he said, sounding deflated. "He told me he doesn't want to sell for a year. So put your thoughts on paper." Which I have just done.

It all unsettled me and made me a bad mother all week.

Horrible few days. G is starting to hate my going to the office and it breaks my heart when he cries and says "ma ma ma" as I walk out the door. I want to be home with my baby! Our house is too turbulent for him. He needs a steadier environment. Knowing this makes me guilty.

I gave a good-bye dinner at home for Ruth and invited all the staff and some of her favorite photographers and contributors and friends. It was very jolly and convivial. Alex came early just for a drink before he left, as always, to look after Tatiana. He sat erect and composed on our sofa, observing the scene and radiating intelligence and precision. I felt huge affection, too, for Lloyd Ziff who seems to adore being Harry's art director at *Traveler*. Lloyd seems battered, though. So many are losing their friends to AIDS. When the photographer Robert Mapplethorpe appeared at the door looking so ravaged and thin, I had a renewed stab of anxiety about all my other gay friends. Miles is looking tired, too, and I pray he will be safe. There are times, and this is one of them, when I find the people I work with enormously touching. There's a tall, silent girl in the art department called Holland who's leaving *VF* after three years for a bigger job at *European Travel and Life*. Harry told me that yesterday

497

Murdoch, who owns it, called Si in the morning and offered to sell the magazine to Condé Nast, who would then fold it into *Traveler* and absorb the subscription list and advertising base. They are meeting on it this morning. As Holland spoke with excitement of her new job and how she was only taking one day off in between, when she would be accompanying her niece to the Bronx Zoo as a treat, I thought how sad for her it will be if Si does indeed buy her new job prospect and fold it just as she arrives. How crushing and careless these takeovers are. The big shots at the top never give any thought at all to the lives of the people caught up in them.

At the end of the party, the art department all struck rowdy poses and we took pictures. Lloyd Ziff seized two assistants from *VF,* shouting, "This one's for French *Vogue.*"

"You can't take this magazine anywhere," said Stephen Schiff as they all tramped out. Dear colleagues. Dear friends.

Friday, June 26, 1987

After my buzzing dining room all week I was happy to loll in bed tonight and watch TV. As I zapped between channels I landed on a new documentary about the 1979 murder of San Francisco's mayor Moscone and the gay rights activist Harvey Milk, narrated by Harvey Fierstein. I found it utterly gripping and important. The footage showed the excitable, exhibitionistic Harvey Milk ranting his freedom cry to "come out of the closet!," the pale, repressed face of the "family man" who slew him, and the streets full of candles as thousands tramped in a night vigil after the murder. All the passion of those days less than a decade ago! So much feeling, now cooled. All those messages of hope that now have been blighted by the advent of AIDS.

Tuesday, June 30, 1987

I'm on the Washington shuttle on the way to Kay Graham's seventieth birthday party. A more than six-hundred-strong black-tie thrash for the A list, or should I say, the Kay-list. I am sitting across from the Wall Street investor and CEO of CBS, Larry Tisch. He is somewhat more charming than the fleshy gargoyle face would suggest. And he was, I must say, very good humored when he asked me to reach up to the overhead compartment to get down his jacket and I tipped it upside down so all his money and pens and credit cards rained down on his bald head, and he had to grovel around under the seat and retrieve them. I was tempted to hang on to his Amex.

I walked out early from an office seething with problems, another high-horse outburst from André over a picture choice, Reinaldo

Herrera protesting a Farrah Fawcett photo shoot for being "dreadfully common," and Gail Sheehy suddenly wanting to be legally indemnified for her (explosive) Gary Hart story. The piece is Gail at her best. She's again proving the editorial point that just when the media pack has exhaustively trampled all over it, it's the very time to rereport it. She's gone deep into Hart's early life, talking to his sister, schoolmates, campaign aides, recreating his repressed childhood in a fundamentalist family that then gave way to a rebellion that pushed him to its farthest extremes. We've called it "The Road to Bimini" and it's shit hot.

Georgie is missing me a lot. "Quality time" is a myth. Babies want slow, wasted time together, not intense nose-to-nose "involvement." There is no comparison; G is much happier with me after a weekend of looking after him than during the wound-up hours we have when I return home after work for guilty play sessions on the floor. By the end of the week when I have been working, he's saved his best smiles and cuddles for the new nanny, Janet, a high-spirited, down-to-earth girl from Minnesota, which breaks my heart.

Wednesday, July 1, 1987

The Kay Graham birthday party was tremendous fun and groaning with clout . . . H and

I rendezvoused at the Hay-Adams hotel — so great to have some couple time. I am very much in love with my husband at the moment. Then on to the cavernous Departmental Hall Auditorium that the Graham kids, Lally, Bill, Steve, and Don Graham, had rented to toast their mother for the evening.

It was a massive assembly of big shots, including President Reagan and Nancy, all guests rejoicing at being handpicked to be there. There is nothing like the presence of the president to make everyone feel the Chosen Ones. I saw Nora Ephron give an extremely wide berth to Margaret Jay and vice versa, which is not surprising after *Heartburn* satirized Margaret's affair with Carl Bernstein so hilariously.

Harry had taken the wise precaution of going to the *Post* earlier and having tea with Ben Bradlee, to bury the hatchet over the "cliterature" debacle. Ben said he was sick of that fucking feud anyway, so when I saw Barbara Walters talking to Sally Quinn, I went over to Sally and said hi and gave her a hug and she responded with an acceptable amount of warmth, which felt a relief. Murdoch's face has degenerated to the melting rubber mask of a cartoon character, like Nixon's. He danced with Brooke Astor with his glasses dangling out of the corner of his mouth. Anna Murdoch seemed serene on whatever plane she lives on. Kay was wearing an oddly girlish white Oscar de la Renta polka-dot summer dress, nipped at the waist, which probably made her feel young but seemed a bit eccentric next to all the diamonds and pearls. You sense she is very self-conscious, and always hoping to get this clothes thing right. George Shultz looked like a twinkle-free Rex Harrison in a white moiré dinner jacket. His toast was bland but also quintessentially Washington in that it displayed the purely networking motivation of his friendship with Kay. "When I first came to Washington I was warned never to cross swords with Kay Graham, so I made a point of getting to know her under relaxed circumstances and now we cross tennis rackets instead." Ho. Ho.

Reagan looked much younger and fitter than on TV or in his current news pictures. Maybe he was just in a good mood. He described how he had been addressing a stag dinner out of town and Nancy got a call from Kay, asking if she was alone for dinner. "So my wife didn't spend a lonely evening because when she got to Kay's she found she was a guest of honor at a very lovely dinner party." Which to me said that Kay had read a news account of Ronnie being out of town and swiftly bagged Nancy to hot up her dinner. But perhaps I am a cynic. Or just am unfamiliar with Beltway etiquette. Art Buchwald at least was honest (and funny, which he has to be as a humor columnist). He had flown in for the dinner from Martha's Vineyard with William and Rose Styron. "The fantastic turnout tonight can only be attributed to one thing," he said in his remarks. "Fear." And then in a sly reference to the *Post*'s Watergate coverage: "Kay doesn't know how old she is because last month someone shredded her birth certificate."

I was thrilled to be seated next to Michael Kinsley, who now has the Steichen-era haircut, and transparent glasses. He's such a wit I can't get enough of him. "Does Leon Wieseltier still work for you at *The New Republic*?" I asked as we started our first course.

"Just because you fired him doesn't mean I have to," he shot back. (Leon's Vox column was a problem. His rant about Nora Ephron, calling *Heartburn* child abuse because of how it would one day be read by her son, Jacob, was too savage and I shouldn't have let it through. More important, if you're going to be rude about people, it has to be in your own name.)

Kinsley dragged me off to the dance floor for an overenthusiastic foxtrot, which allowed me to ogle Kay in the uneasy embrace of the president and get Kinsley's running commentary. Kay's expression was tentative as Reagan whirled her jauntily around the floor, and she kept glancing to the left and right as if to verify this crowd was really there for her.

It was all a bit like the dancing version of a state funeral. There were so many fired *Newsweek* editors on parade, Harry said the party was full of people rising above their own sense of dignity. Still, it was a glorious night of grande dame splendor that made everyone there feel in the biggest of big time.

Monday, July 20, 1987

Why are the mothers in the little park near our apartment so damn stuck up? There's a clique of them, very spoiled looking, with WASPy little purses and a lot of time on their hands, it seems. They never invite me and G to join them when we are down there in the evening, no doubt because I am from the enemy tribe of Working Moms. When I walk down the ramp into the park with G, another world takes over. The iron benches along the park's railings always feature at least one hollow-eyed wino. They form a sort of reproachful magic circle in the middle of which the offspring of Sutton Place's wealth, luck, and good health act out their charmed childhoods.

We bowled through problems at the office, except for one. Doug has demanded we eat into the usually unbroken run of feature pages with eight new ads that have to be adjacent to editorial. It ruins the layouts. So I marched up to Si to see if he would approve the extra cost of adding more pages. He was, as always lately, in a buoyant mood. He has framed the original artwork of the *Krazy Kat* comic strips to hang behind his desk and he was brandishing a yellow, lined pad featuring ominous breakdowns of the ad-page count in *New York* magazine, *Connoisseur,* and other competitors. All of which I knew meant that cost is on his mind, and he would turn me down, which he did.

"But you shouldn't eat into the feature run with ads," he said.

"We have to," I said, "or Doug will need to turn away the advertisers who are insisting on editorial adjacencies."

"That's his problem," said Si, amiably. "He should think of another way to sell ads."

"You know we can't bank up the ads together," I said. "Or we lose them."

"Then he better find a better way to bank ads," said Si, looking positively festive at this impasse. "They have to understand the rules of the game, otherwise it's economic chaos."

I saw the force of the argument but also knew that in the real world, which Si doesn't live in, there was no way Doug could go back to all the clients and swagger around and tell them to eat their adjacencies. So I returned to the art department and committed acts of violence on my own page count. Painful, and I had to do an apology tour to the ejected writers — but the honest truth was, it didn't hurt the overall issue.

A day of Quogue heaven! We sped off to Shelter Island to have lunch with Bob and Victoria Hughes, packing up an enormous beach bag for G including his box of Band-Aids to fiddle with, his barrel of monkeys, and his beach ball. By the time we arrived at Bob's modest shingled house it was raining. We sat out on the porch, talking about this week's issue of *The New Republic* with Leon (who seems to bear no ill will about Vox biting the dust) and Mahnaz Wieseltier, and the rain made everything smell heavenly. Bob was at his most pugnacious, strutting around in his baggy shorts and T-shirt, inveighing improbably against "pooftahs" like Charles Moore, who runs *The Spectator* in England, and the "Witches of Eastwick" as he calls Nora Ephron, Lally Weymouth, and the "other Southampton frightfuls" he dreads seeing if he ever goes out.

Leon and Mahnaz left, the sun came out, and Bob offered us a ride around the bay on his boat to show us the new house he's bought with his book advance ("Casa Fatal Shore," as he calls the house). We feared G would be scared of the boat, but he adored it, as Bob put it "prancing around like a dervish on the poop," jumping up and down in Harry's arms, eyes glowing, arms waving. On the way home we stopped for tea at a café that had a rocking horse; for twenty-five cents G had a wild ride.

Thursday, August 27, 1987

September *VF* is smoking-hot and the feedback is thrilling. It's juicy, it's meaty, and full of our best stuff in every category — Gail Sheehy's Gary Hart piece is making much news, the revamped Diane Sawyer cover story is glorious and gorgeous, and also making noise (Annie shot her languorously lolling back on the couch with her legs up, which has sparked a furor of is-this-appropriate-for-a-news-anchor?), the fascinating, sexy extract from Kathleen Tynan's memoir of her life with Ken, whose thrilling theater criticism is still unmatched anywhere. We've been able to use my favorite debonair David Bailey picture of Ken in a white suit, mid-drag on a deadly cigarette (smoking killed him in the end). It's such a great issue. I just hope we can keep it up.

The Four Seasons at lunch was full of media nabobs eating the grilled swordfish in their regular booths and plotting one another's downfall. John Fairchild of *W* was masticating on Anna Wintour news. She's coming back to New York to edit *House & Garden!*

After twenty months of kicking up the adrenaline of British *Vogue*, she has now had a second child and wants to get back here with David. Apparently he hates the commute as much as Harry did. She did a crackling job with *Vogue* but the British hacks were always on her case calling her "nuclear Wintour" and Gabé said she found it lonely with the two young babies. Plus London is definitely less good for ascendant women. She told me when we lunched on her last trip here that at her first *Vogue* features meeting she suggested a piece about all the women judges in England and was told there aren't any! Knowing Si's fierce competitiveness, she probably did what any intelligent person would do: deftly put out rumors that she was considering a move to Hearst.

Trouble is, Alex seems unwilling to fire Grace Mirabella and give Anna American *Vogue*, so to keep her at Condé Si has airlifted her into *House & Garden*, ejecting the luckless Lou Gropp, who knew none of this until his staff read the leak in *W*. When all hell broke loose, Si panicked his way downstairs to belatedly fire Lou in person, only to find he'd gone on vacation! So when Lou called in from a phone booth in LA Si gave him the news on the phone. What unholy frightfulness! Lou has been there forever. He probably needed to go but surely not in this manner. Reminds me yet again that with Si you never show vulnerability and always play tough. More chaos was caused because Marie-Paule Pellé, the stylish French editor of *Vogue Decoration,* has recently arrived to be Lou's creative director with the implicit understanding she would succeed him soon. There is no way that a fiercely independent taste baron like Marie-Paule would like being subservient to Anna, who would view her as foisted on her by Alex. So today, apparently, there was a big face-off with Alex, Si, Anna, and Marie-Paule to try to calm Marie-Paule down. I sent a message to her to come see me afterward since I could badly use her aesthetic for visual features on *VF.* Harry needs such a person, too, so I told her that if things didn't work at *H & G* she could get a joint deal with *Traveler* and *VF.* "I do not need thees drama! Eet is not what I was promised!" she said haughtily about her new situation. She was in too much of a huff to focus on my suggestion but the idea was planted and I will keep watering it. Condé Nast corporate politics are more intense than ever.

Tuesday, September 1, 1987

Condé drama continues. In one of her more brisk incursions, Anna offered André Leon Talley a job at *H & G* and he's taking it. She called me up and said, "Hi, how's Harry?

How's the baby? Just one thing, I'm taking André." There's supposed to be a taboo at Condé about internal poaching. It happens, of course, but usually with Alex as umpire. On the other hand, it's not really a surprise, especially after the run-ins with André lately. And he's so operatic, oh well. I am already eyeballing his replacement in the fashionista Marina Schiano, an Italian Morticia in cat's-eye sunglasses who I always see sitting in the front rows at the collections. She's a former model and muse of Yves Saint Laurent, famous for a ravishing black-lace back shot by Jeanloup Sieff. Warhol loved her, too, and put her on the cover of *Interview*. (It's an incestuous world. She briefly married Fred Hughes, apparently to get a green card.) She'd be a catch for *VF* and would likely bring fashion advertising with her. Change is often good. I am feeling pretty cocky at the moment because the July *VF* numbers just came in at 191,000 on the newsstand, an increase of over 38 percent compared to June.

One thing I have learned is that when one person leaves an organization, it destabilizes things and inevitably you lose someone else shortly after. It becomes a domino chain.

In more media fun and games, Fred Hughes fired Gail Love as editor of *Interview* and is making overtures to Sarah Giles. This is more rattling than André. Who could replace Sarah as a Rolodex jockey if she's stolen too, which

I strongly hope she won't be? Outside the tent she would be a crazed competitor.

Clay Felker wrote a brilliant editor's letter in his first issue of *Manhattan,inc.* He spoke of the "churning" of Manhattan power, the inevitable process of "irreplaceable people replacing each other all the time." Perhaps it was always thus in capitals of power, except in earlier times when status was predetermined by birth and station. New York is the essence of ego on the rise. In a way, I am enjoying the churn. Competition will keep us hot. And speaking of churn, Joni Evans has finally left S and S for her own imprint at Random House, a break made on the wings of her divorce from Dick Snyder. His quote in *The New York Times* was a chilling echo of the churn. "Joni Evans leaves with our respect, admiration and affection. S and S is a very strong company with considerable depth and resources and will remain so." And off the record, a person who was clearly Dick: "We're talking about one person. Joni contributed significantly to the trade division. We will replace her." Hard to believe, really, that he was talking about his recent wife.

Saturday, September 5, 1987

All the press on Anna's arrival is positioning her as a future ed of *Vogue,* which must make Grace Mirabella shake in her shoes. The press

511

is already hoping for rivalry between us. Anna is too frontal for feuds and *Vogue* has never interested me. I suppose catfights are the cliché that always dog (as it were) powerful women working in the same business. Actually her presence upstairs is a bit like suddenly having a sleek-haired race-horse pawing the other side of the fence.

Determined not to be distracted, I headed out to Quogue, emptied two boxes of manuscripts and read and extracted Donald Trump's autobiography, *The Art of the Deal*, which has a crassness I like. In the end, the only thing about self-serving books like this is, do they capture the true voice? Like Julian Schnabel's loudmouthed soliloquy I bought for the August issue, there is something authentic about Trump's bullshit. Anyway, it feels, when you have finished it, as if you've been nose to nose for four hours with an entertaining con man and I suspect the American public will like nothing better. Very glad I got it for the mag. Also read Marie Brenner's book on the Bingham newspaper dynasty and am very, very impressed. It's a fantastic family saga that will greatly lift an issue.

Sunday, September 13, 1987

Feeling cranky. Anna's André swipe is proving aggravating and it's difficult to find his combination of fashion know-how and celebrity people skills. I am still circling Marina, trying to decide if she's right, and interviewed Marian McEvoy, but she doesn't have the André flair. Anna has already launched into a full-throttle make-over at *House & Garden.* John Richardson, who is still on their payroll, came down after Anna's first staff meeting and gave a bitchy rendition of her new brief. "I need a Louise Brooks wig to do this properly," he warbled. Then he launched into " 'Biedermeier is out! Nothing old-fashioned! It's got to be fashion, fashion, fashion!' Apparently I am now working for *House & Closet!*" One good thing. Gabé is quitting British *Vogue* and moving to New York to join Anna at HG. I knew they'd hit it off.

I had dinner on Thursday with Nigel Dempster, visiting from London. Took him to Le Périgord with Sarah Giles and Christopher Sykes and had a riotous evening. He looks as dapper and pin-striped as ever. He told me a great story about how he had dinner here with Anthony Haden-Guest at Mortimer's, and Anthony was so liquored up he fell spread-eagled across the next-door table, where the historian Arthur Schlesinger, the grande dame Marietta Tree, and Lady Bird Johnson were having a quiet dinner. As he reared up with veal paillard pinned to his lapel, Anthony apparently said to the astonished Arthur Schlesinger, "I think somewhere along the line we are distantly related." This has to be the perfect transatlantic anecdote. Englishmen always feel that conjuring up class cousinage will get them through any crisis at home or abroad.

Wednesday, September 23, 1987

On Sunday night David and Patsy Puttnam came over for dinner to unload the backstory of his resignation from Columbia Pictures, where his tenure as CEO has been a disaster. His appointment from London as the incoming Mr. Class who produced *Chariots of Fire* (though he's actually a North London boy who was seen as the quintessential upstart in the sixties) created mayhem almost immediately and ended in disaster with his abrupt firing after only fifteen months. I have been bombarding David with telegrams and letters, requesting that he give us an exclusive as he hasn't talked yet. I want to write this one myself, as I have known him so long and understand all the people he went up against, especially the lethally powerful producer Ray Stark, who still calls the shots in Columbia Pictures politics and blesses or destroys any newcomer who comes to town. Stark's charisma derives not just from having produced hits such as *West Side Story* and *Funny Girl* and having discovered Barbra Streisand, but also because his mother-in-law was Fanny Brice and he is as loaded as he is legended. Puttnam needlessly offended him from the get-go. It's a classic tale of innocence abroad. Puttnam thought he was a swashbuckling Hollywood reformer, but turned out he was a babe in the woods when it came to the corporate Kabuki required to manage the brass at the Coca-Cola Company, who were his new bosses at Columbia. On the other side were the hostile tribal leaders of Hollywood self-interest led by Stark. As a British transplant into alien bear traps myself, I can't help but identify a bit.

Unsurprisingly, Ray phoned me Friday night and started sounding off about Puttnam. "Your compatriot, darling," he said in his soft, sinister voice, "is an asshole on a grand scale. He took over something that had everything going for it and royally fucked it up. That's the trouble, excuse me, darling, of English intellectuals. Puttnam should have been a professor, not a studio head." That's funny. I've heard Puttnam called a lot of things but never a professor! I guess in LA his British accent makes him "an intellectual."

"I'll talk to you, darling, and tell you everything," said Ray. "As long as you don't play 'Rule, Britannia' in the background." That's wonderful. If Ray gives me all the access to the corporates at Coca-Cola who own

515

Columbia — and other players — thinking I'm "his girl," that will be great copy. So I was full of anxiety to nail Puttnam when he rang the doorbell.

He looked white, taut, and red-eyed, as Harry was when he was in his *Times* crisis, and he kept plucking nervously at his two-tone beard. Patsy was, as always, the feisty sixties cockney, full of pent-up anger about how her man has been treated by Coca-Cola. "I tell you what," she said as she sagged down on the sofa, "I've got a new f-word, 'family.' The Coca-Cola family we were supposed to have joined at Columbia Pictures. I never want to hear that word again in my life." David said when he went to Atlanta for meetings with the Coke suits, it was all stroking and blandness.

He told them, "Are you sure you want me to run Columbia? I'm a hooligan. I offend people. I fire people." And they said, 'Yes, we need a person like you.' " He told them he was going to cut off Ray Stark's $1.8 million yearly retainer and they said, "Great, great, get rid of him."

"Yes, but why did you do that, David?" I couldn't help but ask. "Wouldn't it have been better just to keep him around until you were in a strong position?"

"I'd have had to take his phone calls every day," said David. I felt a lot of recognition with everything I felt myself when I was beginning at *VF.* My Ray Stark firing was Jonathan Lieberson. Like Puttnam, I went bullheaded at the cost wastage of having him around producing nothing, but I made a bad enemy who did a lot of poisoning of the well with the intellectual circles he moved in and they took a long time to woo back. Having political instincts is always underestimated as a requisite for hiring. In fact, calling someone "political" is usually pejorative, implying manipulation and distrust, but many jobs are impossible to succeed at without political skills.

Stark, a longtime power behind the throne at Columbia, allied with his friend the financier Herbert Allen, who's on the Coke board and helped to seal Puttnam's fate. It really is Shakespearian intrigue. "Have you ever looked at his ears?" David asked about Ray. "He's got funny, pointy ears. When he sat in front of the window all I could think about was his pointy ears." We talked till two in the morning, and only stopped when Janet opened the door and said there was a flood in the kitchen. The evening ended, Puttnam still talking, with the four of us swabbing the kitchen floor with bath towels.

Friday, September 25, 1987

I have just commissioned a profile of Ivana Trump to run at the time Donald's memoir

517

comes out, so I was amused to walk in the door at Ann Getty's and be introduced immediately to Trump himself. He was all over me, hoping to charm me into favorable presentation in the mag. So direct and candid that it's refreshing. At dinner, Ann, as weird and alienated as ever, put herself between Trump and Lewis Lapham, and Lapham was next to me. I had an Italian art dealer on the other side. Ann, for some reason, monopolized Lapham for two courses, leaving me and Trump both stranded, so he leaned over them and started bombarding me with interest. "Tina," he shouted, "what do you think of the *Newsweek* cover story on me?" "I haven't read it," I told him.

"You know, Tina, I could have had *Time*. They wanted me and I saw them, too. But *Newsweek* scooped them. Who do you think's better, Tina, *Newsweek* or *Time*?"

"*Time,*" I said mischievously.

"You really think so, Tina, you really think so?" His pouty Elvis face folded into a frown of self-castigation. "I guess it sells more," he said in a tormented tone. "I guess it does." Then he brightened. "You know how much Fawn Hall gets for a one-night appearance? Twenty-five thousand dollars! I've booked her for the night at Trump Tower. She can't sing. She can't dance. So what. She's so hot everyone's gonna come."

My Italian dinner partner and Tina Chow

on the other side of him listened with mounting disgust as I bounced it back and forth with Trump over the artichoke and shrimp. "You see this man, Trump," hissed the Italian on the other side of me. "He is trying to force you to think like him, and I think it's working."

"You know what?" Trump continued shouting across to me. "Went to the opening of the Met last night. *Ring Cycle.* Plácido Domingo. Five hours. Dinner started at twelve. Beat that. I said to Ivana, what, are you crazy? Never again."

"You know," hissed the Italian at me, "it is easy in America to take a very tiny sum like five hundred thousand dollars and turn it into three hundred million! So easy! But you know what? I don't want to. Because eet means raping those poor fuckers the American public even more than they are already. You know what ees the difference between the European peasant and the American peasant? The American peasant eats sheet, wears sheet, watches sheet on TV, looks out of his window at sheet! How can we go on raping them and giving them more sheet to buy!" And so it went on.

Saturday, October 10, 1987

Gave a *VF* cocktail party at Le Cirque for Helmut Newton and everyone came, the high-gloss women, the photographers and the weirdos and the retail kings and the high-energy cast of the best goer-outers I could muster to make Helmut happy. Alex made a pass-through appearance, which made Helmut feel thoroughly courted, which I want, or *Vogue* will steal him away.

Afterward I took a table for fourteen for dinner, having to enlarge it because Bernie Leser invited himself. Helmut said he once opened the door on Bernie in a hotel room in Sydney and he was wearing a hairnet, a character detail he seems to find definitive. I sat next to a wild-card friend of Helmut's, Robert Evans, the Hollywood producer. What a face. His aviator shades of course added to his sinister aspect, but when he took them off he looked so debauched I recoiled. For all his anecdotal charm, he's got to be the nearest thing to the devil of anyone I have encountered. I hope I never lose my barometer for good and evil. He went on to talk about Warren Beatty, which made me want to do that piece again if we could just reel the bastard in. According to Evans, Beatty is a health nut. He doesn't smoke or drink or take drugs and never has. "He has a pussy hair in his cerebellum. He will literally drive five hours for a fuck if he thinks there's competition for it." He said Beatty used to climb over his wall at night when Diane Keaton threw him out for having "phone disease." "He just couldn't stop talking on the phone."

I'm sitting in my suite at the Bel-Air in
Beverly Hills. Tomorrow we'll give a *VF* party
at Spago to woo Hollywood. If it goes well I
want to make a Hollywood party an annual
thing because our power base for covers is
here. Si might not understand what glamour
events can do for business, but I am convinced they work. The advertisers want to be
next to stars, and the Hollywood party will
be packed with everyone's business we want.
Social gatherings like this not only bring the
pages alive, they also make a statement about
our convening power. Clients want sizzle as
much as they want adjacencies. Pierre Bergé
at YSL understands that, but Condé Nast
doesn't. I wrote a long memo to Si, trying to
explain why we needed a real events department to do more of this, but he doesn't see
it. I had to twist Doug's arm to make this
one happen on his marketing budget.

The Bel-Air hotel is my idea of paradise. I
love its secretive paths and smell of jasmine.
Reminds me of Salto de Agua. We arrived at
lunchtime yesterday and I brought G with
me.

Before the *VF* party there was a seating
meeting in the hotel with the team. We as-

sembled to do the table-placing with a wall chart at six p.m. and it was still going on at two a.m. It was an insane task — 240 guests, half of whom we didn't know, in an L-shaped room, with fifty maybes and a power structure so fragile that one false place card would throw the whole thing out of whack. Too late we realized it was a futile idea to try to seat this at all. In the end we assigned each of the team to be a *VF* table host and built around that. The night began in chaos anyway because the seating frenzy was still going on after the first guests arrived or failed to do so. But the turnout was incredible. Two tables had to wait to be erected till the mob subsided, and since the mob never did, the tables never appeared. This meant we had a bunch of illustrious floaters, one of whom was the head of the LA County Museum. The other hazard we didn't expect was what turns out to be an absurd Hollywood custom — husbands and wives or people with their dates expecting to be seated together, and moving place cards when they weren't. At my table I put myself between the "superagent" Mike Ovitz — to romance him for covers — and Ray Stark, with Betsy Bloomingdale, Dick and Lili Zanuck, Liz Smith, Oliver Stone, and Dennis Hopper. However, Oliver's wife took one look at the table she wasn't at, made a scene, and insisted Oliver move to hers. Bob Colacello found chaos wreaked by some wannabe called Melissa Prophet who had to move her place card to be next to an equally illustrious nonentity named Craig Baumgarten who was seated somewhere else. Bob, forgetting he was supposed to be a table host, lost his temper and cried, "Well. This is sure not Europe. It's vulgar, pushy LA!" Then our cover subject, Farrah Fawcett, sent a note to say she had swollen glands.

"She really does," said Ovitz, who's her agent.

"Then she shoulda gargled and got over here," snarled Ray Stark. He told me he hadn't himself tried to seat a dinner since 1963, which was when social manners collapsed. But we battled on. I went to see him the next day to interview him and decided he's not the pure evil that Puttnam sees. He gave me breakfast seated by the window of his house in Bel Air, with the bronze Henry Moore of a cardinal outside. I realized that's really what Ray is — the profane cardinal of Hollywood to whom everyone must pay their respects. "Have you noticed Puttnam's teeth, Tina?" he suddenly asked. "Behind that beard are fangs! Fangs that haven't been to the dentist lately!" (He and Puttnam should make a werewolf movie.)

Swifty Lazar offered to give a dinner for me, which I later realized is a canny L.A. trap to siphon off half the stars from our event for his own VIP gathering with an invitation that sounds more exclusive. But then all was forgiven when I arrived at his house on Friday. I wore my new Carolina Herrera white dress with blue taffeta pouf skirt and immediately felt overdressed. The guests were super-casual Jack Nicholson and Anjelica Huston, Walter Matthau, Jack Lemmon, Farrah Fawcett and Ryan O'Neal, Joan Collins, Barry Diller, Alexander Godunov and Jackie Bisset, and Candy Bergen. Hard to beat that. The real delights for me were O'Neal and Nicholson. I had always seen O'Neal as a lout, but he's funny, self-mocking, full of wonderful colorful stories, and so outlandishly good-looking, with dazzling blue eyes and a thick mane of blond hair.

I realize I was inside the gated Hollywood few outsiders get to see — a distillation of screen glamour, presided over by the bizarre, doll-faced Mary Lazar, who's so stoned on tranquilizers that her head bobs all the time with a glassy smile. Ryan and Matthau told a rash of deathbed stories. Ryan told one about his own father. And Anjelica exclaimed, "Your father? Blackie? I saw him recently! I am so sorry!" Ryan clapped his hands over his eyes and wailed. "Oh God. I've been found out. Okay. He recovered! How did I know someone here would actually know my father?" Matthau said that on his deathbed

Freud had said, "Psychiatry is shit." And Mary Lazar rolled her stoned eyes upward to make her one comment of the evening. "Perhaps he said psychiatry turns you into a shit." And hovered away in her pencil-slim black and gold pants. Later I caught her popping pills out of a fake Bufferin bottle. Still, if she can produce a dinner like this stoned, maybe she's functioning somewhere in there. I realized in the middle of all this that the secret of Swifty's famous humor is that he has none. He just blurts out deals in a raspy voice and wears the ridiculous oversized glasses that make you assume he's funny. A stunt of self-invention for a tiny bald man. He didn't look well. He's deathly pale, like a skull in the desert, under the heavy black frames. His main obsession that night was pulling off the coup of selling Joan Collins's as-yet-unwritten book, *Prime Time,* to Century Hutchinson Publishers for a million dollars, and he said it's making her sister, Jackie, absolutely crazy that she has moved into her writer turf . . . What a night.

Sunday, October 18, 1987

Last week there was more roiling in the corridors of power. Howard Kaminsky is out as president of Random House! I had sensed he was out of favor at Si's court ever since the Joni Evans announcement that she was leaving S and S and joining Random House, as Howard seemed to have no part in her appointment. It was clearly a snub to him to move someone that senior into some vague new imprint position. Obviously Bob Bernstein, as Random House's longtime chairman, has been discomfited for a long time with Howard's obvious intimacy with Si — the dining club they share, their constant socializing, the conduit that kept cutting him out. Plus Alex also felt instinctively that Howard was bad news. He said to me at lunch once that he felt it was "time to plant the poison" about Howard, an unsettling insight into how he works. I knew Howard had lost his hold over Si in the last print order meeting when Si pounced on the piece I was telling them about, a story about an addict's downward spiral on crack cocaine, and said, "It might make a great book. I'll send it over to Joni Evans," when always before he said, "I'll send it over to Howard." Howard overplayed his closeness to Si. That was his prime mistake. And his delusion, too. Howard's downfall reinforces the need to maintain some distance from Si, however familial he feels. Keep the mysteries intact and one's talents in dignified service because, alas, he owns them.

Executive power is fragile in today's volatile marketplace, or perhaps it always was. Since Harry was unseated at *The Times* it's become more commonplace to be precipitously fired now than it was then, as the wheels turn ever faster. Just one of the stripes you wear if you're in the game and take risks as a hired gun. It all suggests the need for an entrepreneurial, financial independence so we are not at the mercy of the whims of our masters. I've always noted the chilling calculations of Si, how his interest withdraws instantly once usefulness ends. After Bernstein let him go, Howard apparently said he wanted to see Si. Bernstein replied, I am sure with some relish, that of course Si had been a party to the decision. Nonetheless Howard demanded to see Si and apparently Si gave him exactly three minutes. "He was gone," Howard told me woefully when I ran into him at a party. "Withdrawn as if I wasn't there." I know that expression. It's subterranean, veiled, that look he wears when he's about to perpetrate an act of pragmatic betrayal.

Now Howard has an interesting social problem. Whether to go to Si's sixtieth birthday party on November seventh, which he already accepted. He told me he was going to give Victoria the option, which seemed another blunder to me. He should gracefully recuse himself. Victoria, of course, being more socially sophisticated than Howard, elegantly pressed him and Susan to attend despite "the business." And with his usual tone-deafness, no doubt he will.

Harry and I threw a joint *VF* and *Traveler* party at Maxim's and a dinner afterward at Castel. It was a riotous and stylish evening, which made me feel as glamorous as we pretend to be. After a slow start, the new flamboyant fashion designer Patrick Kelly showed up with a posse of gorgeous African models wearing his short, tight cocktail dresses bedecked with gold buttons. It was so full of beautiful people surging in late, an A-list crowd of intellectual boulevardiers, fashionable artists, and opinionated media types; it was like surfing through the pages of French *Vogue.*

At the Castel dinner I sat between the old sparring partner photographers Helmut Newton and David Bailey. Helmut can be so deadly. Just when you're thinking he's a pussycat he hits you with some old grievance. "It takes a lot of ingenuity to lay out a portrait so the head of the subject disappears straight down the gutter of the magazine," he told me, swirling his white wine. "Chapeau, my dear!"

After dinner, Helmut pressured us to go back to the Hotel George V with him and June to show us some spreads from his own arthouse mag that might get him banned from every shoot we want to do with him for

VF — two obscene penis-in-mouth pictures aided by a hand wearing a pair of black gloves. The rest of the mag is typical Newton, *Cabaret*-esque decadence with sinister animal sex thrown in. Personally I find these spreads irritating. I think the journalistic work he does for us is so much better and more surprising. Ironic yellow journalism with us is a great departure for Helmut, much more cutting-edge than porn. June is now a bit worried that her name is on it as art director and it will jeopardize her own access. "I mean except for the cock-sucking it just looks like good, clean fun, doesn't it?" she asked me with a harried look. Good, clean fun is not what I would say about a beau monde woman giving a hand job to a sexually aroused horse, but never mind. Obviously, all Helmut wanted was for us to endorse his conviction, but none of us shared it. "Fuck it!" he exploded. "I'm sixty-seven on Halloween. What am I waiting for? To print cock-sucking when I am dead? To hell with it! I am paying for this myself." To which there is no answer really.

Tuesday, October 27, 1987

The stock market has crashed! Five hundred million in market cap evaporated from the Dow Jones in one mighty poof, or should I say pouf? It seems incredibly fitting it crashed at the same time as Christian Lacroix's New York opening! All the Marie Antoinettes who didn't see it coming. It was inevitable, foreseeable, but no one seems to have foreseen it. The blazing inequity of it all needed to be lanced. In a way it's a relief. The conversations I have been hearing at Alice Mason's and the Steinbergs were the decadent discourse of imminent decline even as they seem to be delivered from the glories of the top. What will this do to *VF*? Must respond with care. We have dined out on the decadence and now must deconstruct the collapse.

Monday, November 2, 1987

As soon as I got in today I was immediately hit with a message to go see Si because "something had come up." Oh fuck. Has the crash made him decide to close something? Us? But no, didn't even mention it, it was *Interview* again. Seems he has another crack at it. And thinks it needs to be taken "upmarket." I felt a rush of irritation. The market just cratered. Is he really in such a bubble? We are killing ourselves to get the ads. There's a chill atmosphere in the marketplace till people can see which way the wind is blowing. Brands are not buying. Restaurants are empty. Why take on another magazine that will compete in the same category as *VF*?

I decided not to respond verbally but with

a well-thought-out memo. I told him that a heated-up *Interview* would slice the *VF* cake to a life-threatening degree at a time when we face ever more copycat competition. Better just to let it die, as it likely will. I also said what I believe, that Fred has always wanted the class of an attachment to Condé, but his desire to fancy up *Interview* is exactly the wrong direction. It needs to go young, down-market for the summer movie crowd. And most important, we need to focus on how we can shore up *VF* from competitors. I whammed up the memo at eight a.m. before going to a breakfast at the Yale Club with the German publishing magnate Hubert Burda, who had asked George Weidenfeld to get a meeting with me. He seemed extremely pleasant and sane, but his idea is to start a *VF* kind of magazine in Germany and he wanted to pick my brains with no talk of partnership, just vacuuming my insights. It was like my memo to Si coming true. Everyone copying us, but what do we get out of it?

I was in a black mood by the time H and I joined Bernie Leser at a Condé Nast table at the annual B'nai B'rith dinner at the Grand Hyatt, this year honoring Ronald Lauder. Bernie, Bob Bernstein, and Si were on the dais in a chorus line of big Israel funders. New York social life is so deeply bizarre at times. To speed things up the chairman suggested after each name we give one clap, which only added to the glum, somber feeling of it all. Mr. Malcolm Forbes. [Clap.] Mr. Henry Grunwald. [Clap.] And so on. It felt like the ominous ceremony before the murder of Thomas Becket in Canterbury Cathedral. Ronald Lauder's speech was stem-windingly dull. How does he have the flaming nerve to even contemplate challenging Senator Moynihan's seat in NYC?

Wednesday, November 4, 1987
A day in the life of New York

Doug Johnston and I have an appointment with Paul Marciano, the marketing wiz behind the Guess Jeans ads. We get to the flashy office on Broadway and find Marciano, a round-faced Israeli teddy bear, in a flap about a hostile piece that just appeared in *Forbes,* claiming that the Marciano brothers, among other things, have bribed the IRS in their amassing of a $500 million fortune. Everyone is so jittery since the crash. He keeps jabbering and it's clearly not the moment to progress our pitch for his ad schedule. From there we go to Calvin Klein's show, a moment of fashion twittering I always enjoy. I sit next to Marina Schiano, whom I have succeeded in nailing as fashion director. She's going to be a great replacement for André, I think, if one can get past her sparkling malice.

She has a slightly crazed air behind the cat's-eye sunglasses, but there is no doubt she has an impeccable sense of style. On the way out of Calvin's show I collided with Oscar de la Renta, who said, "I am sorry you are not coming to my show."

"Oh dear, I hate to miss it," I said. "When is it?" "Now," he replied with steely eyes, and I felt, as I always do, Oscar Umbrage. Then it's on to the Yale Club, where Harry is hosting Juan Luis Cebrián, the Spanish founder of the great newspaper *El País.* I have always wanted to meet Ceb — he's such a hero of journalism and of Spanish democracy, rushing out a special issue of the paper during the army's attempted coup. He's much more fun than I expected, with an irresponsible laugh and a savvy political glint in his eye. We asked Jon Newhouse to encourage him to launch a new newspaper just like it here. Cebrián is best on the Spanish concept of honor, which he says bedeviled him as a newspaper editor. "My honor is not your honor," he explains, aspirating the *h.* "If I say someone is religious and his honor is that he is NOT religious, then I have offended that man's honor and he must be satisfied."

I get back to the office in time for an emissary from Dr. Mathilde Krim, who wants me to bring three tables full of rich and fashionable people to a benefit in aid of the Bailey Center Hospice. The two people who came to persuade me were a real estate man named Ronald English and the actor Andre Gregory, who sported a ragged beard because he's in the middle of rehearsing the role of John the Baptist in Scorsese's movie *The Last Temptation of Christ.* Ronald English reeled off all the dreadful AIDS stats and pitiful circumstances. "Of course," he concluded, "I have a selfish reason to be here. I am gay and have lost many friends and I have tested positive for the AIDS antibody." It was a melancholy kicker that I must obviously respond to. I thought what a strange world of contrasts I live in because right after these two, Patrick Kelly, the young designer I met in Paris, bowled in for a meeting, with his pale-faced Swedish manager and PA, about who should photograph his gold-button dresses for the March issue.

The evening found me at the Whitney Museum, gazing at the latest citrus-green plate paintings by Julian Schnabel, flanked by what the author of *VF*'s crack-addict memoir last month calls "the wide-eyed dead" of pale, social New York — Steve Rubell, Fred Hughes, et al. I told Steve about my uneasy encounter with Oscar. "Forget about Oscar," Steve said, grinning. "He will always lay some trip on you like that. That guy gives ice in winter."

As I tottered off to bed I heard from Wayne, who told me that Shelley Wanger is leaving

House & Garden to be editor of *Interview.*
More churn. Seems my memo stalled things
long enough to have Fred move ahead on his
own. Shelley is intellectually strong, brainy,
and has great taste but is way too languid to
turn a magazine around, unless Fred is smart
enough to balance her with an aggressive
journalist, which he wouldn't think of doing
because it's not at all where he lives or how
he thinks. But it's a loss for Condé because
Shelley had a Rolodex of upscale writers, and
in the literary world she is adored.

Saturday, November 7, 1987

Si's sixtieth birthday dinner at the UN Plaza
apartment was small and intimate. I was
seated next to Bob Gottlieb — haven't seen
him since I first arrived to take over *VF.* This
time he was immensely cordial, and yet I
warmed to him no more than before. He
spoke mostly of his intense dislike of a man I
adore, Brendan Gill at *The New Yorker,* his
intimidation by the "sinister" William Shawn,
and also how I as an English person could
never understand *The New Yorker.* He said
he had vetoed a travel piece John Updike offered to Harry to run because "it was far too
thoughtful for *Traveler."* What a preposterous
snob! He is so self-admiring and glib and yet
I see how he has got so far, especially with
Si, who is intellectually insecure himself.

There's no doubt Gottlieb is a skillful text editor from everything I've heard but the combination of carefully manufactured "eccentricity" and unassailable self-confidence allows him to be packaged as a "genius." He's probably now feeling insecure himself. Since the Kaminsky firing it's clear that Si goes by the numbers in the end, and the ads at *The New Yorker* are diving ever lower, despite the initial hype. Harry noticed that Victoria seemed very uneasy with Gottlieb, perhaps worried about more embarrassing musical chairs to come.

Tuesday, November 10, 1987

On the flight back from Detroit, where I went to talk to car advertisers and address a woman's club of *VF* subscribers. I went to the ad lunch straight from the airport, and as always with the ad department's brilliant deployment of me, I was seated between a client we already have and an empty chair. Doug left his pitch speech too late and by the time he started the room was half-empty. A reporter asked me which famous woman was my role model, a question that always leaves me stumped. I know it's the wrong feminist answer, but most of my role models have been men. They always had the lives I wanted.

More crash frisson. A quintessential New York evening — the screening of Oliver Stone's new movie *Wall Street*. A freezing night. A cinema line around the block churning with A-listers who want to be in on anything with rising buzz. In the line ahead of and behind me, the Mort Janklows, the investment guru Jim Wolfensohn, Mort Zuckerman. Janklow stabbing the air with his Manhattan forefinger, telling whoever would listen that the crime in New York is out of hand — both his cars had had their phones ripped out and cassette decks stolen within a week of each other.

"Who's screening this?" trilled Linda Janklow, who is always the custodian of how Social Things Should Be Done. "Fox? They need me to tell them how to run a screening!" Julian Schnabel floated like some predatory starfish on the outskirts of the line, looking for a familiar face to cut in behind. This was the heart of the zeitgeist, people! Finally the doors opened and we burst in and fought for seats, past Oliver Stone, wearing a red sweater and beaming his buccaneer's smile. As soon as the titles came up with the David Byrne soundtrack I was so glad I had fought to get Ken Auletta into the screening to write about it and only wished I'd had Michael Douglas on the next cover. It is going to be

537

such a monster hit: stylish, flashy, gripping but with that box-office edge of wish fulfillment. Gekko is the irresistible villain who everyone in that crowd knows is real. And as the credits went up I heard what we have all expected for so long as the decade nears its close: the sound of the tumbrels rolling for the Icahns, the Trumps, the Gutfreunds, and the horrible heavies of Wall Street. It's finally not fashionable to be them anymore. They are going down with the last days of the Reagan era. I have just finished reading the new Tom Wolfe masterpiece, *The Bonfire of the Vanities.* Thanks to his genius, we can all now make open fun of the Masters of the Universe. The new Caryl Churchill play *Serious Money* about the arbitrage world just opened at the Public. When art converges in this way and the stock market has just crashed, we are witnessing another major mood swing in America. I find it exciting, so much more interesting to cover and critique than the bloat that preceded it. Next Saturday is Donald Trump's book party at Trump Tower. I see it as the last party of the Reagan era. The gaudy postscript to an era's boom and crash.

Monday, December 7, 1987

Real departure for January issue. Have put Jesse Jackson and his presidential run on the cover with the great piece by Sheehy. Felt the right antidote to a year of glitz on the rocks. There's probably something in it to offend everybody, which is always promising. Jesse is an inspiration and a pioneer to so many and a symbol of danger to others — the anti-Semitic comments, the probably dodgy money, the womanizing — and yet no one is a more soaring or more galvanizing speaker. Circulation department says it will bomb on the newsstand, but sometimes an overall statement is more important.

Monday, December 14, 1987

A red-letter day! Si called me upstairs to give me a thirty-thousand-dollar raise! "What can I say, Tina. It's an extraordinary thing you have done. You do it very gracefully, too." That made me happy. Then he said, "I was surprised when I received the P and L on the November issue to see that, in fact, for the first time since its launch, *Vanity Fair* made a profit! A hundred and eighty-seven thousand dollars, to be exact. A year ahead of schedule." Ahead of schedule? Now he tells me what his real computations were. Awkwardly he clasped my hand. "Well done."

I felt as if a huge stone had rolled off my back. Out of the red. For four years I have lived in fear that losing money meant that in an act of Si's caprice as he sat in some holiday hot spot he would close us, whatever the succès d'estime *Vanity Fair* had become. There is no such thing as a succès d'estime in America. That's why it's a French phrase. There is only success. A hundred and eighty-seven thousand dollars' profit is nothing to write home about, but it's a hell of a lot better than the $30 million *VF* lost CNP in its first year. I look back at it now and see all the hard work, the turmoil, the effort to keep clarity as we pushed forward. With a bit of luck '88 will see us making real money. I felt proud, and grateful to Si, who took a chance on me. We have shared this great adventure.

Saturday, December 19, 1987

And so the year ends with the Night of a Thousand Trees, the AIDS benefit that Andre Gregory and Ronald English reeled me into. We took three tables for *VF* and then with three weeks to go before Christmas we had to twist, cajole, and blackmail a high-powered group to show up. Obviously knowing something I didn't, one by one on the day of the event they started to drop out. Sarah Giles and I sat by the phone for three hours, frantically trying to round up faithful seat fillers.

But first, in a fitting sayonara to the year, Donald Trump's book party for *The Art of the Deal*. We shared a car to Trump Tower with Barbara Walters, after another holiday bash. Barbara told me she was planning to go home in between and change out of her five-thousand-dollar Galanos cocktail dress into something "more formal with serious jewels because Ivana is sure to be dressed up." I told her I thought it would be a mob scene and not to bother. Hasn't she got the memo about the meaning of the crash?

I was right about the mob scene. It looked as if Trump had emptied out every croupier from his casinos and every gold digger who ever got into spaghetti straps. There was a crowd of squealing celebrity groupies on the sidewalk outside. Inside, the atrium was festooned with poinsettias and red balloons and the escalator glided up and down with cargos of gawking boldfaces. On the ground floor heaving arbitrageurs danced the night away to deafening pop hits. Donald Trump himself looked sleek and starry as a prosperous young seal in his tux and white evening scarf. "Can you believe this party!" he kept exclaiming. "No, seriously, can you believe it? Love your magazine! Beautiful piece on Ivana. Byoodiful!" It was indeed a great piece by Michael Shnayerson. He revealed that Ivana refers to her husband as "the Donald," which seems to be catching on.

At Ivana's Christmas lunch last week at the Grand Hyatt for the Ladies Who Count she made a toast exuding a lot of expressive body language, dipping and twisting like a downhill racer on the slalom slope in Gstaad. She threw back her glass and called out, "My goot friend, never minte the vicious rumor mill, my sister-in-law! [Blaine Trump] And my goot friend my mother-in-law, your very good health!"

The Night of a Thousand Trees at first seemed promising. It was held in a cavernous hangar on West Twenty-Third Street, and the inventive designer Christmas trees twinkled brightly. I knew that it was a mistake to ask Denise and Prentis Hale, but it was a mistake I didn't care about. I could see Prentis's eyes scouring the scene in the hangar with rising malignance. Cocktails were scheduled for seven thirty, but at nine thirty we still weren't sitting down for dinner. Then as we finally did so, the auction for the trees was announced. Colleen Dewhurst got up and in a slow, lugubrious voice intoned, "Death is your dinner partner tonight. [She was right in the case of Prentis.] Death is our dinner partner! AIDS is among us every day!"

We all stared at our plates. Dr. Ruth Westheimer (her again!) and the playwright and actor Harvey Fierstein got up and began a rasping banter that did not let up for a good forty minutes. Westheimer croaked about condoms and foreplay, Fierstein hurled abuse at the audience. "You think you've been asked here to have a good time?? You've been asked because you're RICH. Look at those dresses you're wearing. They could pay for a room for a boy eating garbage!" ("I could use some garbage myself," muttered Steve Rubell who, like me, was ravenous.) By ten thirty the auction for a hundred trees was at number eight. It began to dawn on us all that they were going to make us wait to eat till tree number one hundred had been sold. By now Denise Hale was lying back in her chair with a program over her head and Prentis was drumming his fingers and blaspheming. Steve Rubell was giving us a running commentary on other occasions he could remember that matched this one for torture, Reinaldo was eating everyone's bread roll. Susie Hayes, the lawyer Ed Hayes's wife, kept looking around in desperation, mouthing that she had a baby to breastfeed at home. Two hours in I stormed off in search of Ronald English, who had got me into this fiasco, furiously accosting waiters and bouncers till I found him. "Ronald, I am mortified," I hissed. "I've got thirty millionaires about to walk out instead of donating money to cure AIDS. They are starving to death and this evening is a fiasco! I am giving you eight minutes to feed us or we are outta here!" Thirty pairs of eyes watched me spinning with rage in the middle of the dance floor in my absurd pouf dress. As I stalked back to my seat they all clapped. The food at last arrived and we fell upon it.

Steve Rubell, by now in a melancholy mood, talked about the humiliation of meeting your mother in prison pajamas. He shelled out ten thousand for a tree and then donated it back. So did the French nightclub queen Regine, whom Reinaldo had persuaded to cancel a 7:30 p.m. flight to Chicago to be on *The Oprah Winfrey Show.* Whatever else one might say about them, New Yorkers are generous. Gradually, as the night wore on, a Dunkirk spirit took over, as they all got drunk and we felt we had been through something epic. Jackie Rogers slurred at me, "I haven't seen Denise Hale for ten years. Wow, whatta piece of work that woman is. Denise Hale is an animal, Tina, an animal." The auction was now at tree eighty. As I turned to flee with Harry I saw that at the next table were eight men holding hands. They were sitting with eyes closed in prayerful silence. It stopped me in my tracks. What are our spoiled concerns compared to the pain of all their loss?

1988
GOLD DUST

First day of the New Year and our last at the Elkhorn Ranch in Arizona, where we have had such a fine holiday, disconnected entirely from NYC's frantic pace. No phone in the cabin. No TV, no shops or places to visit. Meals are all in the big school hall with a roaring fire, huge Christmas tree and stuffed deer and a boar (G's favorite) gazing down at us from the wall. For Christmas I bought G a fur hat with a bear's face and fur ears and he looks so adorable in it. He has become obsessed with the clear, silver moon. Every time we set foot outside our cabin to walk to the big hall for supper the night air is riven by George mooing at the moon. MOOOON, he shouts, MOOOOON. He never sees the moon in New York, I realize. This holiday he has seen a real cow, many horses, two huge dogs, and the MOOON.

I'm entering my fifth year at *VF.* My New Year's resolutions are:

To get pregnant in the spring.

To strive for temperance, less speed.

To carve out more time with G.

To beware of Uncle Si as Mammon posing as a hamster.

Thursday, January 7, 1988

The year started with a bang — a gold-mine piece about *VF* in *Advertising Age* to mark our fifth anniversary. It showed a chart of our ad growth and great quotes from Doug and me about how we got there. It was a joy to see that graphics box of ascending ad figures. Better still, the anniversary issue we have toiled over with such intensity has come out well. We have Nick Dunne on the Collins sisters' rivalry (thanks for the tip, Swifty), accompanied by Annie Leibovitz's bold, brassy pics of the two of them in the back of a limo, plus Gabriel García Márquez in Cuba by Pete Hamill with pics by Helmut, profiles of Patrick Kelly and I. F. Stone, Al Gore on the couch by Gail Sheehy, and a juicy takeout on Clare Boothe Luce by Marie Brenner. It sizzles with bravado on every page.

Monday night we went to dinner with John Brademas, the president of NYU, for Harry's idol and former Brit home secretary Roy Jenkins, who was in town. Brademas is one of the dullest men in Manhattan and gave a total dud of a toast before he handed the floor to peerless Woy (as Roy pronounces it) Jenkins. As soon as the old orator started to speak I felt a wave of London longing. With no notes he riffed with such elegance, humor, erudition, and glancing self-parody that the room was mesmerized by the sheer casual virtuosity of it all. Afterward Harry and I and Roy and Jennifer (note to self: I want to be like her when I am seventy in brisk, comfortable walking shoes and stern silver hair) caught up over coffee. Roy is still exercised about David Owen's disastrous leadership of the Social Democratic Party, realizing now that their botched political experiment is the main reason we've got Mrs. Thatcher — and will keep her. The SDP's civility, education, and intellect, and, unfortunately, muddle were no match for Maggie's focused, primitive flair and it obviously burns Roy up. He so clearly was born to be prime minister. Or believes he was.

I feel how wildly foreign we Brits really are to Americans and how the gap is widening all the time. They see us as *Masterpiece Theatre,* to be briefly appreciated before zapping the channel to something more relevant. But who in American politics now can hold the floor like Woy?

Sunday, January 10, 1988

Si called me upstairs and said he wants to

buy *Details*. Whenever he comes back from vacation in Vienna he wants to buy something or fire someone, usually both. Ironically *Details* is now owned by Gary Bogard, and for a change I liked the idea of buying it. He was again assuming I would want to run it as well as *VF* and perhaps I should stop resisting that.

I have now been at *VF* for four years and do feel the call of expansion. I just can't risk it with G. I can see he is still not like other kids. For six months his only real play is the obsessional attachment to his small white garbage trucks that he runs back and forth across the window ledge. He is still so loving and funny, with his beyond-his-years vocabulary. He can recite long sections of *Winnie-the-Pooh* word perfect, but we are still looking for the doctor who can tell us what more we can do to bring him into normal play.

Meanwhile I am toiling to finish my piece on David Puttnam. If only it stays fresh — David is now talking to every damn outlet in sight. Harry helping me as he always used to do. I love working side by side with him again, his deft cuts and additions reminding me how in a class of his own he is as an editor. I can write good sentences, but his sense of structure is so great. He can create narrative pace, factual zingers, and write smooth segues that are somehow in my voice. The magus.

Much speculation at Condé about Anna's unveiling of the new *House & Garden* soon. John Richardson came down to our floor in a rage when he learned she was going to run his Gauguin essay through André Leon Talley's fashion pics of Azzedine Alaia's sackcloth dresses on native girls in Bora-Bora. Perhaps she will win him a new audience.

Monday, January 11, 1988

At Bob Colacello's suggestion, I spent the morning with Steve Rubell and his partner, Ian Schrager, planning the party for the fifth anniversary of *VF.* I want something really special and no one knows more about special than the creators of Studio 54. I know Steve, of course, but had never met his partner, Ian, and wasn't sure this was the right idea or that the white-powder flamboyance of 54 was the right way to go. Still, Bob persuaded me it couldn't hurt to consult. We met in the somewhat dingy office at the Century Plaza Hotel, which they are in the throes of renovating. Their idea of "boutique hotels" seems to be working. For the *VF* fifth, their immediate suggestion was that they open — just for the party — the defunct Billy Rose's Diamond Horseshoe club in the basement of the Paramount Hotel in Times Square, a run-down tourist joint they are about to transform with the help of Philippe Starck. The Diamond Horseshoe supper club opened in 1938 and closed in 1951 and hasn't been used since. I loved this idea, the period revival so excellent for *Vanity Fair*'s atmosphere and a conjured-up-just-for-one-night supper club had an instantly romantic flavor.

It's funny to see the dynamic between the two partners. Steve — with his whipped-cur smile, short attention span, and sudden flashes of flair — is all about the social energy. Ian, brooding, often silent, a bit Bob De Niro–like in appearance, is, I soon came to realize, the aesthetic genius, constantly flipping through art books, seeking visual references.

"Describe the feel you want," he said to me.

"Forties Hollywood," I replied dreamily. "Limos disgorging, flashbulbs popping."

"Yeah, we can do that," said Steve, drumming his fingers.

"Cigarette girls in short skirts!" I crooned.

"Yeah. Got that," said Ian.

"Saxophones wailing!" I cried.

"An all-girl band," said Ian carefully. "We can get Calvin to make the outfits. Blonde wigs. Matching." He made small notes like an accountant while Steve's eyes darted around, looking for new stimulus. He reminds me of Mosca, the flesh fly in Ben Jonson's *Volpone,* buzzing around feeding on fashionable people — the night porter of Manhattan who knows every secret and caters to any need. On Friday they asked me back and brought in a party designer they insist I work with, Robert Isabell. I disliked him on sight, with his unsmiling smile, pretty face, and slippery attitude to cost, but they said not to worry about cost, they would underwrite the whole thing (incredible news!), and that I must learn to trust them. I do trust Steve and Ian, who know more than anyone alive how to create a night to remember. So we shall see.

Sunday, January 17, 1988

The Council of Fashion Designers of America Awards at the Met gave *VF* this year's Magazine of the Year Award. I'd expected a low-key event, but it was full-on glitter and elegance. Wore the new black high-necked Patrick Kelly number and had a hair and makeup artist coif and paint me to the nines. Mrs. Reagan presented the lifetime achievement award to Brooke Astor. Calvin Klein received one for his last collection. Malcolm Forbes presented mine for bringing "high style, wit, and grace to photography and prose." Afterward there was a divine dinner in the Temple of Dendur and we bought a table for the team to celebrate. Halfway through the second course Mrs. Reagan's security guy came across and said the first lady wanted to see me. So I trotted across to her table, where she was dining with Oscar de la Renta, the Texan billionaire Sid Bass, et al. She looked like a fragile doll. "I want to tell you how much I love your magazine," she said. "I've still got three copies of the cover we did together. It's my favorite." I floated back to the table euphoric. I understood that this was a moment in the story to be savored. What people don't yet know is the impact *Vanity Fair*'s success has had on other magazines. By reversing the marketing bromides about how "general interest magazines don't work," we've allowed other outlets to get more imaginative, freed other editors to take risks.

Friday, February 12, 1988

G threw himself out of his high chair on a Sunday night and Harry heroically threw himself after him to catch him, and though he saved G, he cut his eye on the edge of the marble table, severing his tear duct. I rushed him to the ER at New York-Presbyterian with a screaming G, feeling so guilty as I know my work absorption has made G feel neglected and that's why he acted out. While we were sitting there in angst, H clasping his eye, I looked up and saw, of all people, Alex sitting waiting for a doctor, too. It was startling to see him in his Sunday attire. A pair of old jeans and a big gray sweater rather than his customary dark blue suit. He had brought in Genna, his Russian houseman who has AIDS and who had collapsed in the apartment. "My dearest, why are you here?" he cried, and put his arms around me as Genna was wheeled away. I felt such a connection to the real Alex at that moment. The old patrician Russian, taking care of his extended family, the close-knit émigrés, refugees as they still feel they are underneath. I realized for the millionth time how much he means to me.

H is okay now after his eye was sewn back together but it's been very upsetting.

Monday, February 15, 1988

I am spending many hours at the Rubell, Schrager office.

Steve is usually hunched with two telephones. Reinaldo has been roped in to help with planning the guest list. He said, "Madonna should come. She's been on our cover."

"Have you ever seen a grateful rock star?" said Steve, cupping one phone away from his mouth.

"Yeah, look at Cher," said Ian morosely.

"Right," agreed Steve. "Christmas Eve she leaves Morgan's after a six-week stay and I had to run around tipping all the staff."

Ian now has a pile of thirties picture books of Busby Berkeley routines to get the evening's decor completely right. "The floor," he suddenly says. "This" — he points at a picture — "is what we do with the floor. This is vinyl paint. Costs nothing." Sometimes I get confused because he's simultaneously looking at pictures for inspiration for the new Royalton Hotel they are renovating. "The toilets," he will suddenly exclaim. "This, this right here, is what we need to do with the fixtures."

Wednesday was the launch party for Anna's new *House & Garden* (now rechristened *HG*) at the New York Public Library. The revamp has panache but it's a bit too kinetic and derivative of *Vogue*. *House & Garden* always had a certain mellow savoring of the pleasures of living, banished in the new breakneck pagination. Still, it's hard to get it right straightaway. It's more difficult for Anna to be experimental because readers of the old *House & Garden* loved the magazine, whereas *VF*'s hated it.

I was surprised by the venue for the launch party at the library — black tie, placement, formal speeches. Si's been so leery of hype since the debacle of *VF*'s launch in 1983 that it's probably a mistake to have done this for a revamp of *H & G*. (I was seated between Calvin Klein and the British decorator Nicky Haslam, whom I haven't seen for years.)

His speech was a Si classic. He spoke in a slow, halting interior monologue, like Hamlet on the battlements. Bill Blass the next morning told me he half thought Si was going to produce a gun and shoot himself. "The new . . . *House . . . and Garden . . . HG . . .* is the product . . . of . . . the vision . . . of . . . a brilliant . . . and determined . . . editor . . . I am . . . in awe of her virtuosity." Then Anna got up and shrewdly threw bouquets at everyone who might be dangerous, like the editor of *Spy* magazine, Graydon Carter, and Ed Kosner, both seated at her table.

Wednesday, February 24, 1988

I've commissioned the novelist Joyce Johnson to write a piece about the horrific Hedda Nussbaum case, which has kept me up at night. Joyce is the perfect writer to get into the head of Nussbaum, herself a West Side intellectual in the publishing world.

Nussbaum was so battered by her lover, a vile lawyer called Joel Steinberg, that she failed to call emergency services when he beat their daughter, Lisa, to death. People see domestic abuse as a lower-class phenomenon. But it happens behind closed doors at every stratum. And women stay silent because of shame. It takes a novelist like Joyce to be able to humanize Nussbaum, who lost her sense of self so completely that she could abandon her own child. That's hard to empathize with on any level which is why we must do it. Everyone sees Nussbaum as a monster, but she was a victim, too, as Joyce will show.

Tuesday, March 1, 1988

Vanity Fair's fifth anniversary party! What a night! Maybe the best party in Manhattan since Truman Capote's Black and White Ball. It was the hit of hits, a risk that paid off better than we could have even dreamed.

I knew it from the moment joyful Patrick Kelly blew in from Paris like a fashion circus tumbler, bearing the dress he had been making for me all weekend, a skintight lace top and black taffeta skirt with his trademark buttons. Sunday all the *VF* top contributors met at the office to discuss how we would wrangle the guests. Reinaldo Herrera flew in from Mustique and promised to raise the energy by starting a conga line at midnight. Each contributor was assigned to look after, introduce, and shepherd a passel of three VIPs, one or two difficult oldsters and any potential troublemakers who badmouth when feeling neglected. We went over to the Diamond Horseshoe to look at the venue as it was being assembled. This was the moment when, at last, I understood what Ian and Steve meant about Robert Isabell. As we descended the stairs to the club in the basement, we saw a vision in the ecstasy of creation. Robert's passive-aggressive sullenness had utterly vanished. He was now shimmying up and down ladders like an agile circus performer, palm fronds in his mouth and a staple gun in his hand.

He had caused the shabby walls of the club to be painted gold. He had decreed that shiny black plastic garbage bags be laid on the floor (a cheaper, slicker solution than vinyl paint). Palm trees had been flown in from Miami and dipped in gold. Everywhere you looked, guys were hammering, painting, and draping at Robert's barked commands. Fifty small club tables, with pink tablecloths lit from below, glowed in anticipation. In two days Robert had transformed the dusty, shuttered old ballroom into a thrumming homage to the Age of Copacabana, tingling with energy and romance. And the genius of it, the sexiness of it, was that there was nothing Vegas or Trumpy or vulgar about it. The feeling instead was of improvised wit, of stylish theatricality, of glorious, naughty magic. One of the many innovative things about Studio 54, I have recently learned, was the movable theatrical sets and lights. It was Robert who created those replenishing nocturnal fantasies. I will never again do a big event without him.

By Monday, the day of the party, we were all in a fever. I showed up half an hour early to view the completed mise-en-scène. Down the stairs swiveled and sambaed the turbaned Carmen Miranda cigarette girls. Waiters in white gloves wafted by with trays. Stills from the old *Vanity Fair* adorned the walls of the foyer, bathed in colored lights. The backdrop to the stage was twenty enormous *VF* covers, in front of which a choir of sixteen girl saxophone players topped by gold Louise Brooks wigs (delivered up, as promised, by Ian) were blasting out their rehearsal moves. They swayed from side to side in unison, their long, black-stockinged legs flaunted in identical short black Calvin Klein dresses. Bouncers with walkie-talkies and paparazzi already thronged the street outside. Long, black limos with tinted glass were pulling up at the red carpet. Just as I had imagined.

Si arrived shortly after I did. He paced around, beaming and chuckling and flushing with delight as the *VF* contributors in their party getups, each more gorgeous than the last, descended the stairs. (Our Paris editor, the usually nondescript Tatiana de Rosnay, was now a French movie star in a silver-sequined strapless Patrick Kelly gown.)

Hilariously, the first four guests were Henry and Nancy Kissinger and Dennis Hopper and Jackie Collins: high-low on the hoof. Having expected a typical black-tie seated dinner, they looked dazed and amazed at finding themselves surrounded by gyrating Brazilian showgirls — another last-minute Steve Rubell touch. Si and I stood in the never-ending boldface receiving line, greeting a crocodile: the Norman Mailers, the Calvin Kleins, Lee Radziwill, Alexander Godunov and Jacqueline Bisset, Swifty Lazar, Marietta Tree, Liza Minnelli and Halston (arriving together in a blaze of TV lights), Anna Wintour and David. Behind them came Jerry Zipkin and behind him, Tom and Sheila Wolfe. Lurking next to a potted palm was the gossip scribe Billy Norwich with his notebook, looking exactly as I imagined my fictional character Quentin Wasp would look in *The Party Pack,* the play I will now never finish. The *Times'* elfin paparazzo Bill Cunningham leapt around, snapping his shutter like a maniac and squealing, "It's the end of the Reagan era! It's the beginning of the nineties!"

Whatever it was, it was certainly something. A new kind of social vaudeville, perhaps — part theater, part nightclub, part salon, part saloon. Isabell had been wonderfully right about the underlit pink tablecloths — a foolproof device, he explained, that makes every woman's complexion look great. And by casting the net wide to include all the young, hot, beautiful people, the models and the downtown crowd, we made jaded venerables like the Tisches and the Kissingers feel rejuvenated by new blood. As for the advertisers — who melted shyly but happily into the palm trees — they had at every turn a beautiful, fashionable, or famous person to gawp at. This would pay off with business in spades.

As Ian had constantly affirmed to me in the planning stages, in the end it's all about the crowd — and this one, culled from the multiple worlds *VF* lives in and covers, was a social classic. Our careful internal guest choreography of staff handlers worked like a charm. It allowed the old guard to feel looked after, which is what you always want from a party, comfort level for everyone, not just the supercool. Jerry Zipkin was thrilled that his was one of the six names with a card reserving a ringside table. "Why me?" he asked.

"Because I knew you'd bitch and moan and be unbearable if you didn't get one," I said with the reckless candor of the night. Zipkin was in seventh heaven, sitting Humpty-Dumpty–like on a banquette, surveying the swirl: the young German socialite Princess von Thurn und Taxis in a tiny minidress, pursued by Jerzy Kosinski; Donald and Ivana Trump; Ron and Claudia Perelman; Kurt Vonnegut and Bianca Jagger. An ecstatic Nick Dunne hollered at me that it was the best issue of *Vanity Fair* ever, but live! From the corner of my eye I saw Steve and Calvin heading off to the bathroom. Old Studio 54 habits die hard.

At nine thirty Si and I made our way to the

stage. I'd spent my afternoon rehearsing my speech with the speech coach Dorothy Sarnoff. Doug Johnston got up to introduce us and attempted to quiet the room — a lousy assignment, since everyone partied on at peak volume. But when money talks in a New York room, people listen. They shut up for Si, who was back in *HG* funeral oration mode. "Once in a decade," he began haltingly, "there's a [long pause] magazine like *Vanity Fair*. Once in a decade, there's an editor like [suspenseful silence] Tina Brown. Now . . . *Vanity Fair* fever is [five beats] sweeping America."

I felt dreamlike as I advanced toward the podium. This party, we all knew, was not just an anniversary party. It was a victory lap after all the toil and skepticism and bets against us. More than a turnaround. A resurrection.

As I spoke, I remembered Dorothy Sarnoff's exhortations. "Eyes sweep the room." "Don't rush it." "Throw it out." "Have a good time!"

I thanked all my team, searching them out with my eyes as they watched from their corners and bar perches. I smiled a lot. I got my last bit out with no mishap: "E. B. White once said no one should come to New York to live unless they're willing to be lucky. I've been more than willing, but also unbelievably lucky. Lucky to have such a brilliant team. Lucky to have you all here tonight.

"Now, as Harry Benson said to President

and Mrs. Reagan when we went to take their cover picture at the White House, 'Let's dance!' "

At this preplotted cue, the lights turned up and the saxophones wailed into a show-stopping rendering of "In the Mood," with the sixteen saxy blondes rocking out. The *VF* contributors hit the dance floor to encourage the rest. It was only then, just as the euphoria had begun to subside, that I realized with a sickening jolt that I had omitted Steve and Ian and Robert from my tribute. I'd been so focused on mentioning everyone at the office that my three muses had been left out. I saw the dashed look on Steve's face, and as soon as the first saxophone set was over I rushed back to the stage, grabbed the mike, and yelled out my thanks to the three master-minds. But by then the room was a hubbub, and I fear I didn't assuage their disappoint-ment — Steve's, anyway. Robert didn't give a damn. (Rooms, not people, are what he cares about. He loses interest as soon as the first guest arrives.) Ian was all right, too. He had already left the party, in his quiet, mysterious way, once he had, as he later told me, "checked that the magic was in place." Even so, Steve loves to be lauded, and I cursed myself. But I couldn't agonize for too long when it was all so glorious. I allowed myself to relax at a table and bask a bit with my Harry and the Mailers. Norman sat with his legs akimbo like a macho koala, eyes twinkling with satire as he cased the scene.

I ended the night congaing with Henry K and Patrick Kelly right behind. It was one thirty a.m. when Rubell, the eternal maître d', showed us out into the cold night, past the heavies with the walkie-talkies and a few dogged paparazzi waiting for the last guests.

"Billy Rose would have been happy," said Steve. "The club can go to sleep again now." I loved that imagery. The fact it would never be repeated made the magic even more potent.

As we left, Jerry Zipkin grabbed both my hands and said, "You didn't steal this success from anybody." That was a nice thing to say.

Tuesday, March 8, 1988

Fade to black. I heard from London that Mark Boxer has been diagnosed with a malignant brain tumor. I was stricken to hear it and wanted to fly immediately to see him. Witty, wonderful Mark! I loved asking him his opinion when he drew for us at *Tatler*. So contrary, so slyly amusing. He saw it all. He is the Alexander Pope of contemporary London. And no one has ever looked more debonair going out to bat at cricket. Last time I saw him for lunch when he visited NYC he was unusually testy. We had a bit of a rivalrous spar about our respective regimes at *Tatler*.

Perhaps incipient illness was why he was cranky. I think of his refined, droll face and hedgehog hair and weep. I can't bear to lose a great original like Mark, but the cancer sounds advanced and irreversible.

Wednesday, March 9, 1988

I want to record a day when everything went well in my whirling life.

1. Beat out the competition to extract Willie Shawcross's book on the Shah of Iran.
2. Got home to receive a call from Swifty. "How does two million dollars sound to you? If you can understand the power dynamics of Hollywood as well as you do in that Puttnam piece, that's what I can get for a novel by you."
3. Persuaded the terrific Sally Bedell Smith, who's writing a biography of Bill Paley, to break off and do a big piece about his last days for June (I am told he is dwindling). We struck a deal that if she did this piece, I would still extract the book when publication comes.
4. Pulled the missing elements for a dinner at home for Swifty, who's in town on his way to London, that was

proving hard to cast, by snagging Sid Bass and his Iranian seductress Mercedes Kellogg. Apparently Mercedes caught Sid's attention by throwing a dinner roll at him during a party in Southampton. Now Sid is so besotted he's prepared to pay Anne $200 million for his freedom to marry Mercedes. Anyway, on my night for Swifty, they had arranged to have dinner already with the David Nivens and the society financier Freddy Melhado, so I told Mercedes to "just bring them all." Mercedes laughed her throaty, courtesan's laugh. "Why not?" she said. That solved all my problems in one fell swoop. Best of all H and I took G to the park, and a *Daily News* photographer took a snap of Georgie eating a huge ice cream and it was splashed across the front page as a spring sunshine story. A moonstruck day in New York.

Sunday, March 13, 1988

Ahmet Ertegun was very, very funny at dinner, telling anecdotes about Sam Spiegel, the outsize film mogul who produced *Lawrence of Arabia*. (Spiegel is such a colorful character; will ask Sarah G, who knows him, to do an oral history, "Voices on Sam.") Once Sam told him there would be an actress on his boat with them named Bergen. "Candy?" said Ahmet. "Polly?" No to both of these. When they got on the boat there was the "actress," wearing a miniskirt, high-heeled shoes, and sockettes. "You can go downstairs and freshen up now, Ingrid, darling," said Sam. Whereupon she turned around and said, "How many more fucking times. My name is Camilla."

They all stayed till twelve thirty, with Mercedes laughing huskily at everything that Sid said. He told me they had spent a month in Aspen. Doing what? "Staying up all night beside the fire," he said. Mercedes is purring with good fortune. A billion dollars and all that sex to boot. Sarah Giles, who also joined us, said that she accepted an offer to go back with them for coffee afterward and saw the apartment in the Carlyle, which she described as a pure love nest. "Lots of Biedermeier and erotic curtains."

Thursday, March 17, 1988

Ray Stark is in a rage about my Puttnam piece. He hated me calling him the "profane cardinal of Hollywood," but his main fury stems from the fact that I quoted him saying, "Guy McElwaine is not exactly a rocket scientist," and Guy was his weekend guest at his ranch when *VF* landed! Herbert Allen is also irate about the way he is portrayed, according to the diplomat and man about town Dick Holbrooke, who lunched with him and Fay Vincent at La Côte Basque last week. Oh well! I don't regret a line. In fact, it behooves me to bite the balls of the establishment from time to time and sabotage excess coziness. I feel it's liberated me actually. Before we left I took Harry to an Alice Mason dinner, a bad addiction. Harry refused to come again. I now realize that that heinous dinner of tumescent gray sausage, sauerkraut, and Irish coffee is the only meal one will ever receive at her house. Doesn't she ever look around and see that every single woman leaves her plate untouched? As always she put me at her table bang opposite her, and between Mike Wallace and Jim Brady. On the other side of Jim was a Lebanese heiress wearing the incongruous dinnertime outfit of an outsize black mink hat with a huge diamond in the center of it. "Is it true," Mike Wallace asked, "that Arafat dresses up as a woman and fondles little boys?"

"I think not," she said. "However, that is his vocation." "What's he like really?" I asked. "Candidly?" she replied, her diamond winking fiercely over the tungsten sausage. "As a matter of fact I find him rather sneaky." I fell about laughing at that, to the puzzlement of everybody else. Sneaky is such a small-bore word.

I rethink my life for the millionth time. Why do I keep seeking out the very things I deride? Perhaps because I was born to chronicle them.

Friday, April 22, 1988

I found Philip Roth a bit of a disappointment at our dinner last night for Helmut Newton. I've always found him intriguing in pictures and on the page, but in reality he's like an accountant, although, granted, his mean, sparkling eyes suggest something more interesting. Norman Mailer also came. I felt he was slightly put out to see Roth in our house. Some literary feud I am too ignorant to remember? Or just two big dogs who need to be kept apart? Norman likes to be the only superstar writer swaggering around. It was a chaotic sprawling buffet, so I ushered Roth and Claire Bloom to a table (she is a high-minded, humorless bore) and Mailer joined us, riffing about whether God was a computer. They circled each other in conversation awkwardly all night. Steve Rubell and Ian Schrager slipped away, surmising, I am sure, that this was not their crowd. Some female producer Michael Cimino brought with him left in a rage when no one knew the movies she had made and I wrongly introduced her as Cimino's wife. As dinner parties go it was a total flop. Like a bad issue of the mag when I haven't paid enough attention.

Highlight of the week was the Tisch-Steinberg candlelit wedding at the Central Synagogue. Saul's daughter, Laura, was marrying Larry's nephew Jonathan, and it was as dynastic a coupling in new-money terms as if a Rockefeller married a Whitney or an Alsace hooked up with a Lorraine.

Laura is as porcelain as her father is porky. John is debonair and man-about-town-ish despite having inherited the Tisch family ears. It was a flabbergasting display of wealth, a riot of Arnold Scaasi tulle and bouffant skirts and white tie and tails for the men. According to *W,* the flower bill alone at the reception afterward at the Met came to a million dollars. Each gold-painted magnolia-leaf swag looked as if it was the price of a holiday in the South of France. Gayfryd had carpeted the Met dining room in white mohair and the tablecloths were gold thread. We were at her and Saul's table. I was between J. Carter Burden and Henry Kravis, which itself seemed symptomatic of the era. Old money ceding fast to new. Burden looked uncomfortable and had an unfortunate haircut that left his shiny, effete face overly exposed. He seems the quintessence of patrician indecision. Kravis, on the other hand, has a look of fierce mistrust that matches his barking, impatient manner. It was fortuitous my dress was designed by his wife, Carolyne Roehm, whose hungry face and anorexic evening shoulders were on the other side of Harry. Her eyes were starey with strain and the quest for perfection. She looked worn down by the French lessons and the piano lessons and the *cordon bleu* taster menus for every dinner party she hosts. She's a very, very talented designer, trained by Oscar, but that's not enough if you are the second Mrs. Kravis. One feels she never gets to collapse in her designer jeans in Connecticut and recuperate from her week competing. She has to go to Florida to shoot with the Kluges. To Mar-a-Lago to a house party of the Trumps. She has to look wonderful, have inventive sex with Kravis, and go to a black-tie dinner every night of the week. No wonder she looks like a zombie. Gayfryd does the same but seems to have more fun.

The irony that the trophy wives miss is that the husbands much prefer them as mistresses pure and simple, not the taste baronesses they become. I want to read (or write) an essay called "Sex and Decorating." The more decorating in a Park Avenue apartment, the less sex between the occupants. It's the Wall Street version of the Joni Evans and Dick Snyder tuna fish salad story all over again. Donald Trump apparently is loudly complaining wherever he can that he's sick of Ivana talking casino business when he gets home (instead of switching into geisha mode, as the Donald no doubt wants and expects). Gayfryd now sees her career as being chatelaine to Saul, with twenty phone lines to organize the staff. She has to ensure that whenever he wants one, a small coffee cup is delivered to him to drink in one fast gulp as the house factotum waits with the tray. (That's a status symbol, I have noticed, in Wall Street homes. The man of the house never swirls or lingers over his coffee cup. He knocks it back standing up, while someone waits.) Carolyne Roehm and Ivana Trump are playing the game as hard as their husbands, leaving them only voracious for more. More what? More everything: each course at the Tisch-Steinberg dinner — poached salmon with champagne aspic; trio of veal, lamb, chicken; and orzo with porcini — was interrupted by thirty minutes of wild dancing to the Hank Lane Orchestra. Vartan Gregorian swept me onto his cummerbund with the opener, "Do you enjoy original sin as much as I do?" As he twirled me around the slippery parquet, I kept seeing the pinched face of the Greek finance manager Alecko Papamarkou — once Arianna's entry-level patron — swirling by, humming "ay ay bamba." We made our escape as soon as it was polite, with money humming in our ears.

H and I have been fantasizing about starting a newspaper. *The New York Times* is pompous and badly laid out. Have a huge hankering to burst into Si with an amazing newspaper dummy and force and beg him to back it. *The New York Independent!* We have both been in a heart-racing mood, perhaps because it's spring, dying to give birth to some red-hot journalism.

Meanwhile we had the British theater producer Robert Fox and his wife, Natasha Richardson, over for dinner at the apartment. They are here for the opening of *Chess* on Broadway. A sulfurous row broke out between the playwright Peter Shaffer and the producer Joe Papp, who's producing a raft of celebrity Shakespeares. (The last was *Julius Caesar,* with Al Pacino as Mark Antony.) Papp started banging on about his totally fresh viewpoint, and how he's de-mothballing Shakespeare for Americans. Shaffer, a hilariously waspish old queen, listened to this in silence for about twenty minutes and then could take it no more. His fury erupted when Papp did a caricatural English rendition of Macbeth's "She should have died hereafter."

"Hold it right there!" erupted Shaffer. "Just hold it! I have been listening and suffering to your preposterous bullshit for the last half hour. You've clearly never been to a production at the RSC or the National. Didn't you ever see David Warner's Henry IV? Jonathan Pryce's Hamlet? Gielgud's second Hamlet?"

"I didn't know he did it twice," said Papp mildly.

"Of course you didn't know!" shouted Shaffer. "Because you are totally ignorant. Gielgud, my friend, did it four times. As anyone who pretends to know anything about producing Shakespeare is well aware. And nowhere, except at some ludicrous small repertory company, have I heard Shakespeare recited in the absurd way you have just performed." It was a splendid performance that mesmerized the table. Papp was so taken aback he fell silent, and Sidney Lumet's head went back and forth like at a Ping-Pong match. Shaffer teased him later, too. "On a film set," he declared, "the writer is way below the makeup man in status. If I wanted to change a ridiculous line in *Amadeus* that traduced Mozart's opinion of Handel, I was shooed off the set. But if the makeup man spotted a shiny nose, oh how the talcum powder flew!" I want him at every dinner party from now on.

More for the album . . .

Nick Coleridge is in town with his fiancé, a very beautiful young woman, Georgia Metcalfe, who looked ravishing in her long, black elbow gloves and feathery dress. His heart's desire was to meet Tom Wolfe, so I was thrilled Tom came to the reception we gave for them. I'd forgotten I was vice chairman of the PEN dinner and therefore had to take a table, so I had the brain wave of bundling it all, arranging for a car to ferry some of our guests over to PEN to join my table with the Polish journalist Ryszard Kapuściński, whom I was so excited to meet (and try to get a piece out of). I am obsessed with his book on Haile Selassie. The good thing about being vice chair is that you get to choose your PEN writer for the table, and I chose him. It was pretty hard to talk to him, however, since Gayfryd Steinberg's decor for the night was so over the top. There was a ton of obscuring foliage between us. It was all such a jungle of glitz you couldn't even see the speakers — Joseph Brodsky and Susan Sontag — on the podium. While Brodsky intoned heartbreaking stanzas about captive dissidents, guests peered through spray-painted ferns that looked like a hooker's idea of a harvest festival. Bob Hughes was in a lather about the foolishness of it all. We were packed in so tight we had to scream over the noise and plant life, which isn't easy when your dinner partner is Polish. I mourned all the insights and writerly observations that were drowned out. It was pouring rain when we disgorged from the Pierre, pouf dresses for Amnesty, as Harry called it, and I had swollen glands from the acoustics. Was so wiped out I could hardly be civil to Beverly Sills, who was in the seat next to me at the opening of *Chess* the next night. Maybe one day I can use the headline "Down and Out with Beverly Sills."

But guess where I am now? No, not sitting in a library reading Ryszard Kapuściński. Am on the Metroliner, speeding down to Washington to host a *VF* party for Gail Sheehy at the F Street Club.

Saturday, May 7, 1988

More spring fever. Classic Jerry Zipkin at a dinner after the American Ballet Theatre's *Romeo and Juliet,* as Nick Dunne's date. On the other side of Zipkin was Mrs. Asher Edelman (her husband was some Wall Street dude). Zipkin was in high-malice mode, which is always the most enjoyable. "Do you know when I last saw Makarova?" he cried. "At a dinner party twenty years ago. I was seated between her and a woman, some princess *"quelque-chose"* who took one look at me and vomited. I said, 'I am Jerome Zipkin. What's your name?'

"She said, 'Can't you read the place card?'

"So I said, 'Don't you know who you are?' And she rose and headed straight to the bathroom, never to return. So I turned to Makarova and she said, 'So you're a stinking capitalist!' And I said, 'You bet your ass I am! Born that way and bred that way!' And she

575

said, 'What do you do for sex?' My dear, I looked at her — this was my evening all right — and I said, 'Anything I can!' "

Monday, May 16, 1988

An interesting lunch with Si. Although one not wholly unexpected. I knew it had to be one of four things. The London company, *The New Yorker, HG* problems, or Alex's job. Turned out to be the latter.

The first course was his somewhat tortured ruminations about *HG*'s rejection by readers, but I tried not to get too drawn into that. It took me a year to get *VF* right (I still shudder at our 1984 Brooke Shields Thanksgiving cover, which looked as if she had a dead chicken on her head), and he should have learned the lesson of excess prehype from Locke's *VF.*

The second course arrived before we had got through the first. It sat at our elbows, cooling, as we galloped through mozzarella with tomatoes and basil.

"Well, I wondered," said Si shyly, "if you'd ever want the . . . the . . . . job."

"Which job?" I said carefully.

"Editorial director of Condé Nast," he said. Adding with the look of flushed hopelessness that often accompanies some outrageously golden opportunity he has just offered, "It's not much of a job in some ways." I realized that a lot of people would want to be in my shoes at that moment, but all I could think of was Georgie's sweet face and my need to have more freedom and time with him, and this additional responsibility would hardly provide it.

And yet, and yet . . . it could be pretty great to have all the magazines to play with and would be less line responsibility than *VF* — and therefore be less stress. "I would work with you," continued Si. "But the more I try to think of who to fill the role, I can't think of anyone else that would work." I had to play for time. "Well," I said, "when is Alex going to retire?"

"Not now. It could be three or four years. Alex has always been good at saying no to some of my worst ideas and I need that," he added with a grimace.

"I know that a large part of this job is to keep you in your basket," I said dryly, and he giggled again. I told Si I would be honored to do the job if he wanted me to (who knows what I will feel three years from now?) and he said he guessed he'd stop looking for the moment.

Wednesday, May 25, 1988

I'm on a flight from London. We arrived on Saturday to find the city under the spell of early-summer magic. The luscious greenness

577

of St. James's Park was enchanting. We got into London on the Concorde and headed straight for the park with G, who was enthralled with the ducks and all the pigeons to chase. I taxied to Chiswick to see Mark Boxer, whom I haven't seen since I learned of his illness. It was a melancholy scene. He was reclining on a sun bed in his beautiful garden, while his two curly-headed little girls gamboled around in their play house. His handsome face is now entirely misshapen from all the steroids, giving him the round, crooked countenance of a country squire, so odd for one of the best-looking men in London. His mind, though, is still intact and sharp and we gossiped about the New York company while his wife, Anna Ford, made tea, looking implacably cheerful. "I wish I could find a doctor who would tell me the truth," he told me, squinting into the sun. "If one hasn't got long, one would just like to know, that's all." We sat together for a while in silence.

Monday was the christening of Julie Kavanagh and Ross MacGibbon's baby, Joseph. Julie and I are now so close, closer than in our early London days when we first bonded after being dropped in quick succession by Martin Amis. His literary superiority irritated her so much that she left her job as London editor of *WWD,* went to Oxford, and got a first-class degree in English lit. She still looks like an adorable Mabel Lucie Attwell children's illustration with her round face and auburn ringlets. And Ross, a former principal dancer with the Royal Ballet, is such a heartthrob. Their little Cotswold stone house at Minster Lovell is my idea of heaven. H and I are godparents to Joseph. This is when I feel a great love and longing for England. Its low-key gentleness so entirely absent in NYC, where friendships often flare and burn themselves out. The other godfathers were the actor Peter Eyre and the writer Peter Conrad. Pat Kavanagh and Julian Barnes were there, of course, and many of Julie's rarefied literary protégés from *Harpers & Queen,* where she is now arts editor. Georgie babbled through the service and kept offering a stone pillar a drink. It was such a sweet day.

Afterward, we adjourned to Peter Eyre's wedding-cake house on South Street and had egg sandwiches served in the garden. I suppose it was the garden that made me homesick the most. I love that overwatered leafy smell of London greenness, the jungly, shabby intimacy. I love sitting in the slightly too cool early evening, with midges dancing over the fruit punch and women wandering in and out in polka-dot dresses as they descend the rusty little staircase from the sitting room down to the garden. It made me wistful for Ponsonby Terrace (which we visited to tell the tenants we are going to sell).

I missed those *Tatler* days, when Harry was editing *The Times* and we used to have breakfast outside with our papers while the two fat tabbies scampered along the cat corridor.

Tuesday was the memorial service for Sir Denis Hamilton, Harry's former chairman at Times Newspapers at St. Bride's Church — the reason we were in London, really. Harry was one of three readers at the service. The others being some cryptic brigadier and the former editor of the *Times* William Rees-Mogg, who preceded Harry in the job. I wouldn't have missed it for the world. Indeed, as I sat there at the end of a pew, with Rupert Murdoch at the other end, I thought it could be the perfect opening of an Anthony Powell novel. It was so rich in subtext.

There was Murdoch, who, having befriended and seduced Sir Denis Hamilton in order to secure Times Newspapers from the Thomson organization, then humiliated him by kicking him upstairs, excluding him from the running of the papers, and finally driving him out.

No one wanted Murdoch at the service, but he crassed it out and came anyway, arriving early at eleven thirty so he could get a good seat in the plum row right next to the speaker's podium where the cameras would catch him. Sprinkled around for moral support were his flunkeys from News International.

Facing the altar was the old chauffeur Harry and Hamilton shared, the garrulous Frank Bunson. He was seated beside cherubic Lord Altrincham, with his Dickensian flyaway hair. All the aging pooh-bahs of the British establishment were there, battleship-sized Lord Goodman, Lord Roll, and Lord Shawcross, a decaying eagle. Opposite were the bowed heads of the Hamilton family, the four somber mustached sons bearing up the neat, impeccably groomed widow, Olive. Such was the placement that she was diagonal to Rupert. As the thrilling strains of "I Vow to Thee My Country" soared to the rafters, her level gaze was able to meet the expressionless face of her husband's last tormentor.

The drama was heightened by the unbearable perfection of the choir, the sudden moment of theater as the trumpets of the Durham Light Infantry played the Last Post. William Rees-Mogg read from *Pilgrim's Progress,* his mellifluous whistling voice taking me back to all the dramas of the *Times* years. Thatcher has appointed him now to police the BBC's taste and morality standards. A real humbug job, the apotheosis of the Gentleman Hack. The next reading was by the old brigadier Sir Nigel Poett. "Death," he barked, "is nothing at all. I have only slipped away into the next room." Then Harry read Wordsworth's "Character of the Happy Warrior," which he's been practicing for weeks.

The church was held to attention as the words spoke to the glorious gain of the moral life. (Denis's daughter-in-law, Sandy, said the sight of Murdoch at one end of the pew and Harry at the other was like the scales of justice.)

Although I didn't know Hamilton except as the dry voice Harry used to speak to every Saturday night when *The Sunday Times* went to bed, I knew enough to be very moved by the implications of the service. The former Tory PM Edward Heath gave the address and spoke with a gravitas and solidity I admired. And he handled the Murdoch egregiousness brilliantly. He described how Denis had served first Lord Kemsley, then Lord Thomson with a tact and diplomacy that protected the editors from the caprice of their owners. Then he spoke of how Hamilton never allowed any newspaper he was associated with to let the news columns become dominated by opinion concealed as reporting. He spat out this last in Murdoch's direction. It was a great moment of political theater. I would love to retrace the paths of so many of us in this church. Because it really is the story of England, the process by which Great Britain became Fake Britain and the values of truth and courage gave way to mediocrity and materialism. Afterward at the lunch at Reuters, Murdoch stayed out on the balcony to avoid flak. Gordon Brunton, the managing

director of Times Newspapers, came barrel-
ing over with his big three-cornered head,
exuding bonhomie, and said, "You must do
another great newspaper, Harry." Yeah, right.
Great idea from the man who sold *The
Sunday Times* out from under Harry to the
beastly bully who fired him!

Everyone seemed much older and from a
different period, with noses like white straw-
berries and tufts of hair in ears and nostrils.

Friday May 27, 1988

Now I am in Spain, sitting on the terrace of
San Jorge, where I haven't sat for two years.
Despite the monstrous excrescences being
built all over the Salto de Agua, the jasmine-
scented oasis on this apron of green that darling Dad so tenderly cultivated and willed
into beauty through his Panglossian energy
and belief is still a paradise. But for how long?
Mum confessed they are pretty much stony
broke. No more movies have come in for
three years and despite Dad's Micawberism,
it's unlikely they ever will again. They can
manage okay in Spain, living on the invest-
ments made after the Little Marlow sale and
the odd royalty from the Miss Marple films.
But it's hard for Dad to accept that his
professional life may be over. He gets bron-
chitis a lot, which perhaps is psychosomatic.
Women are so much more flexible about the

change of circumstances. They are used to improvising because they've always had to. Mum is thriving. Has got herself a column in the local expat mag and is getting known as the social critic of the sangria set. But she has to spend so much time shoring up Dad's ego. She tells him he has such wonderful taste he could open an antique business, and he could, but his self-image is Movie Producer. Period. It makes me sad.

I hadn't expected Georgie to love it here so much, but the garden is an adventure playground, and he has toddled around all day, showing his treasures to Mum and Dad with such delight. Last night he sat on Mum's lap, enraptured by the enormous mooooooon.

Saturday, June 25, 1988

Ed Victor called to tell me that while staying with him in London Dick Snyder asked Ed if he thought I would ever be interested in coming to run Simon & Schuster for him. Whoa! I remember meeting him at my first ABA just five years ago in Dallas with Ed. He seemed so unbelievably powerful then, while I was this fringe groupie hired to help Leo fix up a faltering mag. America is such an accelerator.

I thought that again at Mort Zuckerman's brand-new Fifth Avenue apartment, high above Central Park, so high that the trees far below were like fluffy green clouds seen from an airplane window. The view must be one of the best in NYC and the space is so beautifully proportioned, even if the colors are mood-dampeningly taupe. Modern masterpieces lurk overlooked in dimly lit corners. But it clearly pleases Mort, who has adopted a new persona of sibilant low-key eminence, somewhat undercut by a Chinese takeout dinner of sweet-and-sour pork and chicken fried rice (actually served up by his Chinese manservant). This dinner was a charm offensive to get Harry back to edit *US News and World Report.* Therefore he danced around it for two hours, talking about how Harry belonged in DC, how he and I should do something together, etc. etc. I couldn't resist teasing him a bit. "But it's summer," I said. "You usually ask Harry to edit *US News* in the Russian Tea Room when it's snowing outside." He brushed this aside, but the evening ended with the typical Mortism of "We must have more conversations about this."

The next night we had dinner with Sally Bedell Smith and her husband, the hard-charging news-mag guy Steve Smith, at her urgent request. I have only met her briefly over the assigning of the Bill Paley piece, so it was obvious there was another agenda. Halfway through it was clear what the agenda was. "What's your take on Mort Zuckerman?" Steve asked Harry. "I mean he seems to be seriously trying to improve *US News,* which will never happen under Dave Gergen [the current occupant]." I couldn't look at Harry. It was too deliciously absurd. Mort up to his old tricks. Offering it to Steve on a Monday and Harry on a Tuesday or vice versa. We revealed nothing.

STOP PRESS.

There's a rumor going around that Anna was called upstairs and told that she is going to be editor of *Vogue* in September. An existing editor on the *HG* staff, Nancy Novogrod, is apparently being made editor of *HG* in her place. Makes sense because Si is clearly in a restless mood. Last week he called me up and asked me what I thought of making Nick Coleridge editorial director of London Condé. Nick could certainly do the job well but I said "interesting notion" and felt a bit of a butterfly attack. I had started to wonder if returning to the London company would not be a great move for me: slower pace and a small company to spruce up, less fraught than NYC. So I waited a week and asked him at the next opportunity. "What if I did the London job?"

He scowled. "What about *VF* if you left that? And *Traveler,* which is doing so well under Harry? That's a lousy idea. But I have found Nick is unacceptable to the editors there so I am putting in Robert Harling for a while." A bit of breathing time. Si is a constant instigator of staff musical chairs. I don't know what I want really. I feel adrift. Nick would probably be better suited than me to run London. I don't really want to go back. Would love to be pregnant again but am not. Now there's about to be more shake, rattle, and roll with Anna going to *Vogue.* Competition is coming from an ex-*Interview* employee, Gail Love, who is launching a new mag called *Fame* whose dummy is an outrageous knock-off of *VF.* Feeling the constant nag of New York ambition, mine and others. The churn.

Tuesday, July 5, 1988

An extraordinary week of turbulence in the CNP building. The Anna story broke on the evening news, throwing all the management announcement plans into rout. True to form, Condé hadn't bothered to tell Grace Mirabella that she was out. So she learned of her dismissal from a TV report. As it happens, I was giving a birthday party for Harry that night — Robert Hughes, Dick Holbrooke, Melvyn Bragg, Robert Caro, Peter Jennings, and many others. Si and Victoria were an hour late, no doubt because of red-hot phones. Si was very excitable, asked me what I thought of "the changes," and I said, diplomatically, that I thought Anna would do much better with *Vogue* than with *HG,* which

587

I do. Whereupon he shook his head and said he'd always rather liked the new *HG,* but no one else does, and it just goes to show you can't tamper too fast with a loyal readership. But the Condé building is all fired up about why the *HG* misfire now merits Anna's promotion to the company flagship and the Grace camp trying to put it out that Si has the hots for her. It's probably a smart move ultimately on Si's part. He moved too quickly to put her into *HG* but there is no one better than Anna for *Vogue.* If he lets her get too tarnished by the flak at *HG,* it could make it difficult to keep her mystique to advertisers at *Vogue.* Tough on Grace, though, to become the roadkill. Ironically, we ran into Lou Gropp, the ex–*House & Garden* ed, walking on the beach in Quogue yesterday. He said this was a Bernie maneuver to threaten Alex with someone stronger than Grace at *Vogue,* but that seems unlikely.

I feel rattled by the whole thing. Inevitably the manner of Grace's firing after such long service — thirty-some years at *Vogue,* seventeen as editor in chief — makes one feel like the disposable help. Surely there could have been a more elegant ascendance created for Grace if he wanted to move her out? It's lousy for Anna too, to begin a new job like this.

Retreated to Quogue for a long weekend to soothe nerves . . . I love the stolen quality of Sunday evenings. The air seems to smell even fresher on a late-afternoon bike ride, a time of peace when all the floating weekend population have left to travel in their nose-to-nose convoy back to the city. G cavorts around on the beach in a T-shirt with bare bottom like a madcap, silvery elf.

Tuesday, July 12, 1988

Bernie Leser asked Harry and me out to dinner with Helen Gurley and David Brown at La Grenouille. No sooner had we all sat down than Helen pitched into Bernie about Grace Mirabella's bum's rush, having just come from a grim good-bye celebration of Grace thrown by Dawn Mello at Bergdorf's. "How could Si be such a brute?" wailed Helen, while Bernie swiveled around uneasily in his chair. "Doesn't he realize how awful he looks?"

"Unfortunately, no!" blustered Bernie. "I wish I could get through to him on this." (Get through! One can imagine how Bernie has never stopped telling him he's done the right thing ever since it happened.) Anyway, in the middle of this sweaty moment, who should walk by but the Bergdorf party — Grace Mirabella with her husband, Dr. Bill Cahan, and Dawn Mello and her escort. Harry shot over and sat with Grace for twenty minutes, which made Bernie even shiftier.

"Doesn't Si care?" Helen pushed.

"He doesn't have to," I said recklessly. "No one ever tells you the truth when you are that rich." I knew that would be relayed by Bernie to Si.

And sure enough, at nine a.m. Si called and asked me to lunch. Felt a brief panic that I would be slammed for disloyalty but what the hell.

We settled into Si's booth at the Four Seasons, preposterously early as always, in an empty restaurant. Then after the usual breakneck first course he said, "Things are going very well at *Vanity Fair* and I think it's time for an . . . an adjustment."

"Adjustment?" I asked. Long pause.

"In your salary," he said. "Of . . . of . . . a hundred thousand dollars."

I hid my euphoria and looked vague. "That's very kind," I murmured. Clearly he felt he needed to spread snowflakes around after looking so bad to his employees, and I was now the happy recipient.

"Besides," he went on. "What about our talk? About, about, editorial director?"

"Yes," I said. "That was very flattering. But . . . you know Alex is at the height of his powers. He's so brilliant, you should get him to stay as long as you can."

He asked me what I thought of *The New Yorker.*

I do think of it a lot these days. How candid to be? The more I have pondered the edito-

590

rial director's job, the more I have thought reviving *The New Yorker* could be so much more satisfying, stretching me as an editor, raising my game with new writers. "I could modernize *The New Yorker,* Si," I said finally. "If it ever gets to be too much of a drain." This was a stake through his heart, as I saw his attraction to the idea fight with his resolve not to be seduced into doing it — yet. The two modes existed in his brief expression of panic. After a long silence, he said, "That, that's good to know." I was back in my office by one forty-five, feeling happy about the raise and recommitted to Si.

Saturday, July 23, 1988

But wait, a summons on Friday to Go Upstairs. Si is sitting at his desk, hurling balls of trash over his shoulder, as he does when he's looking for something on his desk. "Bimonthly," he says as I walk in, no warm smile for my sweet thank-you-for-the-raise note he probably perused at four a.m. "*Vanity Fair* is so hot, why not give people more of it, publish it twenty-four times a year? I've got Peter Armour looking at the figures." Groan. I understood immediately what this was about. Keep her busy until Alex retires. No thanks. I will scotch that one, and anyway I don't even know if I want Alex's job, which is such a political minefield. "Very, very interesting," I said. "Let me mull over what impact that would have on editorial." He looked at me without expression and threw another paper ball over his shoulder.

Tuesday, July 26, 1988

Mark Boxer died on Wednesday. He was fifty-seven. I can't shake off the melancholy. He's the first real friend I have lost. His picture over the *Times* obit, the quizzical expression under the hedgehog hair, made him seem so very much alive. I think of him on that May day in Chiswick with his two little girls and the gaunt-faced Anna. He bore his six months' death sentence so elegantly.

It makes me think about how I, like Anna Ford, married a much older man, who like Mark seems unquenchably alive. My darling HE, love of my life. Georgie is such a fragile, shy little boy, always hanging on a pause with other children. Will he, like Anna's beautiful little girls, suddenly be bereft? Harry is such a magical father, bringing imagination and gaiety into G's little world. Without him nothing would be right. Tonight, he went to London to finish sorting out Ponsonby Terrace and go to Mark's funeral. We held each other so tight when we said good-bye. We are so alike. We both feel the cold fingers of intrusive change that make us want to hold G fast in our loving cocoon.

I grieve for it all. For Mark. When he was in New York in February we all played a game at dinner, with Harry's old *Sunday Times* friends Clive Irving and Ron Hall, who were in town, about what we'd most want to be in a next act.

"Editor of a newspaper in New York," said Mark. "No. Not true. I'd like to be" — he gave that rueful whinny — "editor of *Vanity Fair*!"

I remember my brief stab of outrage. My job! Watch out for Mark!

Now, six months later, as I look at his obituary I feel ashamed.

Sunday, July 31, 1988

Had a wonderful time sitting next to Steve Rubell at a Reinaldo dinner. He went on about how much he wants to meet a girl and get married, which seems unlikely. Ian Schrager is now dating Carolina Herrera's receptionist and sharing him clearly threatens poor Steve's equilibrium. Steve has already lost Calvin Klein to Kelly, so maybe he thinks being gay isn't an obstacle. "Calvin's feeling the strain, Tina. That's why he's had to go into rehab. He loves her, but it's pressure." He told me that Mick Jagger and Jerry Hall are splitting up. Jerry's gone off with David Ogilvy, imagining it will make Mick jealous. "I once asked her how she stopped Mick playing around," said Steve. "And she said, 'I always give Mick a blow job before he goes out.' And I'm not even her friend!" marveled Steve. "I mean she knows I am going to tell at least three people!"

(Fashion note: What is the new affectation that makes rich women take their earrings off at dessert? I noticed at Oscar's and at other dinners in the last few weeks that both Nancy Kissinger and Mercedes Kellogg got their rocks off, as it were, with the arrival of the crème brûlée. Is it a sign that the earrings are so expensive they weigh down the earlobe? Definitely worthy of further study.)

I have been so glad that Mum and Dad are staying with us. It's been great cabaret for G and a blessing to me on the weekends, because he never seems to want to go to bed. I had a brain wave for their ruby wedding anniversary. As Christopher and Diana are here, too, I asked the photographer George Lange to come out to Quogue and take a generational shot of the whole family. Christopher in a big hat; his kids, Ben and Owen, in seersucker suits; G looking pensive in his little shorts; Dad jolly in a golf cap; Mum so vivacious in a colored Mexican skirt; me in my favorite red print cotton shirt. It captures all the freshness and spontaneity of a family day at the beach, something for all our scrapbooks, an occasion when my laborious planning seemed to work like a charm.

Monday, August 22, 1988

Liz Smith published a scorcher about Anna and all the Si rumors. But ever since she did, the feverish buzz has gone away. It's as if once printed the season's rumor fever was punctured. Perhaps it was just generated by the summer heat, the crazy-polluted steam of the city due to greenhouse gas, the humidity and hospital waste dumped into the ocean. Or just that the shelf-life of unconfirmed sex is never very long. The building has calmed down. Anna can now get on with being editor in chief of *Vogue* as she always wanted. Basta.

Gabé has moved upstairs with her to calm the troops and be her Features right hand.

Friday, August 26, 1988

Victory! I passed my driving test. I am finally a free woman! After two whole summers and thousands of dollars of lessons! The triumphant instructor, Bruce, was straight out of *Glengarry Glen Ross*. In the nineteen hours of driving around I got to know him intolerably well: his low opinion of high-tech managements, his Saturdays at Riverhead Raceway, his dissatisfaction with life at Yaphank. "Bye-bye, Brucie," Georgie used to intone forlornly as the Ford Fiesta nosed off down the drive.

On my way to a *Vanity Fair* sales meeting in Bermuda. Annie Leibovitz sent over the new pics she has taken of me for *Ad Age,* which has, thrillingly, named me Editor of the Year. Annie wanted me in a tight red dress — the exact opposite of anything I would ever wear, and for once I decided not to fight it and to discard my usual boring conservative attire. She and Marina Sciano picked out a scarlet thin wool wraparound dress, and banished my trademark goody-goody pearl earrings in favor of huge gold suns with pearls in the middle. Then added black stilettos, red lipstick, and professional makeup that turned me into Lana Turner playing Clare Luce, especially when Annie shot me from an angle that extended my legs by four inches. She's such a genius. Marina also produced a sea-green jacket and draped it over a black turtleneck, adding a black pencil skirt and three strings of fat Kenny Lane pearls. It made me want to trash all my sedate trouser suits and dress-for-success jackets and va-va-voom to the office every day. Except I'd never do it. True elegance is a real time suck, and flair misfires worse than being dull.

Editing *VF* gets to be more and more of a challenge now that we compete with ourselves. I feel the world and the news speeding up and we have to respond so carefully as a monthly has to be ahead of the curve, unless it's with deep new reporting that offers a distinctive counterview to the hack pack. The speed of news means a lot of last-minute tweaking and reangling headlines, loading up with attitude and injecting new context.

A slew of stories have had to be recast lately as we go to press:

A big Michael Milken profile — Jesse Kornbluth's piece was way too forgiving in the light of the SEC charges. Thank God there was time to reflect on it.

Mike Tyson suddenly admitted he was manic-depressive, so that perspective had to be darkened up and added to the story about him.

Murdoch pulled out of the bid for Hachette, which affected that boring-anyway business piece, and on the Dan Quayle saga everything is changing in the political circus every five minutes. *New York* mag scooped us on our death of Basquiat narrative so we had to repackage ours as if we had a new angle. The world seems to be competing with us on every story as the culture speeds faster and faster. I fear losing our edge. That's why I need Annie's glam pictures of me coming soon, announcing to the world I'm not slipping!

I'm enjoying my Bermuda limbo but am caught in a new emotional split. Harry keeps getting newspaper feelers from London, and I am vestigially haunted by *The New Yorker.* Alex suddenly threw me this week by asking, "Who could edit *The New Yorker?*" Alex never asks questions like that for nothing. Every article on Condé Nast lately tosses out my name as a putative replacement for Gottlieb. I can see he's floundering in the job . . . My agony is: Should I do it? The more I've brooded, the more I see that it could be done and the stakes are enormously high. The only thing that stops me pitching hard for it is, of course, Georgie's developmental challenges. And postponing another pregnancy. I am thirty-five. I want the agony taken out of my hands. I want Harry to accept a London paper. I want to find I am pregnant. But I am not and I am restless. When you have a small child, two days in a hotel is stunningly rejuvenating even in the theme park–like hotel of a sales retreat. A hot climate and a boat ride were just what I needed. This morning I gave my slide presentation to the sales force titled "Every Page Counts: How *VF* is Going to Stay Hot in the Coming Year." I babbled a bunch of bromides and was pretty bad, but this was the home team and they seemed to like it. Tonight a boat transported us all to a pirate's island. It was a beautiful night with a harvest moon and the muted backwash of reggae unwound me a bit. I liked the editorial director of German *Vogue,* who came as a guest, a stylish character full of office horror stories about his egomaniacal art director.

T. D. Allman was my editorial guest and he was very funny about the lousy band and a great raconteur about his reporting in Haiti. It's hard for me to believe that this army of people and the huge sales effort all hinges on me and the ideas our team tosses out and chases in random editorial meetings. It's amazing how solid our success has become on such improvised foundations. And yet I always feel half-unreal, like the pirate island.

Tuesday, October 4, 1988

On my way to Washington for the day to photograph President and Mrs. Reagan for the year-end Hall of Fame. Reinaldo called Nancy R. and persuaded her to do it. Annie's idea is to have them waving farewell on the cover, so I kicked Arnold Schwarzenegger off. He feels passé anyway. We will use a "Goodbye to All That" cover line for the Reagans, which is a great end-of-year idea. The issue has been madly volatile, with stories flying in and out as news changes them.

I feel the steadily moving iceberg of *The*

New Yorker looming . . . it's hard not to be intrigued. It would be the ultimate journalistic accolade, to be offered the crown jewel of American publishing after only five years in the US. On the other hand, it could be my undoing, as well as torpedo my efforts to be a good mother. I have a vivid recollection of the crazy stress of the first two years of *VF* before G arrived.

On Friday, Steve Florio, the president of *The New Yorker,* took me to lunch and made my heart beat with fear by saying that he'd walked into Si's office and demanded, "Give me Tina or give me something else to do." Apparently Si just kept pacing around and around, looking anguished. Florio seems to me hopelessly miscast at *The New Yorker.* He's big and boastful with a bonhomous mustache. I doubt he reads the magazine himself and was wildly indiscreet about his impatience with Gottlieb, regaling me with anecdotes of editorial cluelessness that always ended with "Seriously, you can't make this shit up" (which I mostly felt he had).

I go back and forth myself about the change. How to make these decisions? As Mike Ovitz told me when we met for a drink this week, "You try to do a life, Tina, in the round." That made me smile. Doing a life. A new Hollywoodism, I s'pose. Like doing coke.

Would a revamp of *The New Yorker* work? It doesn't have the intellectual heat of *The*

New Republic or *The New York Review of Books* that it could have, but those mags sell a tiny number of copies. Can an all-type medium like *TNY* without pictures achieve higher numbers? Are the six-hundred-thousand-odd subscribers only there because they forgot to cancel it? And it's such a masculine shop, I am told. If they learned the new editor was the lady in the red dress, would they revolt? These are questions I bet Si has not addressed and I don't know the answer to.

I commissioned a piece for fall from Tony Schwartz, a writer Marie knows — who was Trump's co-author — about the new, unmanageable pace of life. I am calling it "Acceleration Syndrome." Car phones and call waiting and home faxes are making everything so revved up. Tony's done great interviews with people like Bob Pittman, who intends to purchase a portable phone so he has no dead time walking between appointments, and a *USA Today* exec who takes a tape recorder for dictation to the pool. Great interview with Don Simpson about his exhaustive magazine reading list he's devouring while also watching TV. Trump, apparently, picks up every call very quickly but cuts you off midsentence as soon as his secretary brings a piece of paper announcing someone else. The trick is to call him back three minutes later just as he's got bored with whoever replaced you.

The piece has a great opening spread of Donna Karan in the back of a stretch — her mobile office and beauty salon — in her dark glasses, applying lipstick on the go.

Sunday, October 16, 1988

The Reagan shoot was great. So easy this time. I arrived thirty minutes early at the White House to converse with Annie and Marina, who had been shown into a room that led out to the Rose Garden, where they had set up their stuff. Annie was supertense. She had flown all night from Munich, where, ridiculously, we had only just pinned down Tom Wolfe for his Hall of Fame shoot. (The best, as it happens, in the whole Hall of Fame portfolio. I'd come up with the idea of photographing him against a blowup of a page of *Bonfire,* but Annie had added the brilliant touch of setting fire to the page. The result is Wolfe looking at his most debonair and electric against a blazing manuscript. She is such a wonder.)

The Reagans arrived promptly, as before, without any fanfare, impeccably groomed and holding hands. Nancy was in a floor-length red cashmere dress that clung to her youthful, pert body. The president seemed, as before, totally out of it, except on some level he must be present because as he sat and walked through the shoot, he kept quipping away with private jokes that caused her to laugh with such hilarity, it was as if she'd just heard them for the first time. (Mum used to say the secret of any successful marriage is continuing to laugh at your husband's jokes. When wives stop laughing, husbands get new wives, not new jokes.)

"Wave," Annie said.

"Who are we waving to?" Nancy asked.

"Congress, Nancy," the president replied.

Then they withdrew for a costume change and came back wearing matching red sweaters (who thought of that?) and sat down on a bench in the garden. I was struck again at how much of a unit they are, how they adore each other. In a deep sense, politics seems to utterly pass them by.

A few days later I dispatched Sarah Giles with the pictures for Nancy to look at, in case there was again any pushback. She loved them and asked for copies. Sarah said that as they stood in the map room where Churchill had met with Roosevelt, Mrs. Reagan was seeking approval for a pair of earrings she had bought for Betsy Bloomingdale for Christmas. Apparently, Barbara Bush is fit to be tied that Nancy has been zero help on the Bush campaign, but to me it seems entirely appropriate that Nancy, having no convictions nor commitments to anything except her husband, should, as his term in office ends, withdraw once again to the world of shopping for earrings.

Life is extremely complicated. G's nanny, Janet, left last Friday, which is traumatic for G. Fortunately, Harry's daughter, Kate, has been staying and has agreed to hang out while I find a new nanny, which makes the loss less great for G as he adores her. She's wonderful to have around and I love having her here. So fun and relaxed and practical, unlike his harried mother. I love sitting and catching up with her in the kitchen over tea. G hasn't mentioned Janet much but perhaps will when he knows she's not coming back. I also imported Mum and Dad for two weeks to distract him, about which he's ecstatic. It's so comforting the way family dynamics change with the arrival of children. When we first got together Kate was so resentful of Harry leaving her mother for me. That's all changed now. She is so over London and loves being with us in New York. Now I understand why in South Asia families live together in an interconnected commune. We are suddenly a real extended family. It's making Harry so happy to have her here.

Si called and asked me out to lunch next Thursday with Alex. It could just be a brain pick about who could edit *Glamour* or *Mademoiselle,* but the two of them have never asked me to lunch together since the day I was hired. As before, it has to be one of two things. *The New Yorker,* or Alex's job . . . last week the writer David Halberstam told me that all the *New Yorker* journalists are up in arms because they feel that no one cares about the nonfiction side of the magazine.

Sunday, October 30, 1988
Quogue

The lunch with Si and Alex was distinctly strange . . . It began with Si furtively brandishing a trashy-looking woman's mag called *Women* that he wants to buy. My heart sank. I don't particularly want to be consulted about that, though I s'pose I should be flattered by the consigliere role. "It sells five hundred thousand copies," says Si. "I think it would be for us like *New Woman* has been for Rupert." Obviously competition with Rupert is never far from Si's mind. At nearby tables at the Four Seasons, Clay Felker was lunching with Bernie Leser, and Ed Kosner was lunching with Geraldine Stutz. They both kept looking over, curious about what's going on in the musical chairs of CNP.

The day after the print order meeting, Si had said to me, "Lunch tomorrow . . . it's just a general conversation . . . on the other thing . . . *The New Yorker* . . . I'm still unsure. I don't know." I have now swung the other

605

way and am eager to dispel the idea I want it. G needs me to be calmer, not busier.

But after we had got past the ruminations of the *Woman* magazine idea, Alex suddenly exclaimed, "But Si, I believe your real project now must be *The New Yorker*. It must change or it will die! I would love to see you make the Brave Move." I see now that Alex fancies redoing *TNY* with me and thereby extending his own empire. And having fun. And he's egging Si on to do this. Si's brow furrowed. "To put Tina into *The New Yorker* would be a coup de théâtre . . . but I haven't solved the problem of the readership." He feels burned, I think by the *HG* reader insurrection. "My problem," he continued, "is I am damned if I do and damned if I don't."

To Alex's surprise, I think, I said I thought he should respect that instinct and wait for further developments. I hope he didn't feel I'd broken ranks with him. I haven't shared with him the ambivalence that sends me back and forth about *The New Yorker*'s attractions. Aside from my own private life issues with G, my objective assessment is Si should do nothing with *The New Yorker* at the moment. Right now, his problem is that he's five hundred ad pages down, but he has six hundred thousand subscribers, which is still a lot.

The quality of the ads is dismal — a few quarter pages of lugubrious crushable safari hats and dubious sterling silver jewelry. Clearly what has to happen is that *New Yorker* subscribers are turned back into active readers, as well as adding younger ones. ("Easier to praise than to read," as Tom Wolfe brilliantly put it.) Advertisers are bailing because of the rising age of readers and the lack of reader response they get. (The defection is not helped by the fact that Steve Florio clumsily fired all the top ad staff who had relationships, I am told, giving clients no reason to stick around for loyalty.)

What Florio hankers for is the quality of readership that *VF* has, the opinion formers and the conspicuous spenders who read us from cover to cover. I believe I could do it editorially, but the great insoluble problem right now is the PR. The perception of me is flashy, fast, and scandalous. The *New Yorker* staff and the media critics won't believe that high literary quality can coexist with visual excitement or be rendered more enticing by headlines and blurbs (and — heaven forfend! — cover lines), which make people want to start the safari into impenetrable type.

Given the caliber of writers I have attracted to *VF*, if I was some besuited beard in a red tie I would be hailed for my literary choices. But even in a report on this week's Editor of the Year citation in *Ad Age,* the writer calls my pointing up the magazine's journalistic chops as "a starlet wanting to play Juliet."

Which, when I think of the great work by Shoumatoff, T. D. Allman, Joyce Johnson, John Richardson, Marie Brenner, Barbara Goldsmith, and so many more, is fucking sexist crap. Women get stuck with being trivialized and just have to smile. If Si gives me *The New Yorker* now, the howls of "philistine!" would be very tough to overcome and might scare off more advertisers. Maybe in a year or more, the advertisers' perception will be more universally shared by the readership, and make it easier to update the magazine in the way it needs. At the moment, any dinner party is split fifty-fifty. The more intellectually confident people all agree that *TNY* is on a passport to doom. But the other 50 percent who actually don't really read it will always come to its defense and speak of a recent, definitive fifty-thousand-word piece on the Great Barrier Reef. Until this 50 percent also perceive *The New Yorker* is in decline, it would be very unwise to move Gottlieb.

I said all this, but did not agree with Alex that good quality writing is hard to find in a weekly. I cited *The New Republic* and *The New York Review of Books* and Bob Hughes's fantastic art criticism in *Time,* published weekly, and I did say that *The New Yorker* doesn't actually use its glittering writers — people such as John Updike and the baseball writer Roger Angell — in the way that it could and should. I guess the fact that we were discussing it means I am still the top candidate in his mind. Afterward, Alex got into a different limo and sped off to Connecticut. Si and I went back to the office together. "Alex is all for change," he said ruefully, as we purred along. "He's wonderful, isn't he?" He said it with the proud, adoring way of someone who knows he can share something with a fellow believer. I've always made my delight in Alex apparent to Si, whereas some Condé eds, like Art Cooper at *GQ,* just wish he was off their back (as they would me if I was editorial director). I think Si is grateful for that. "You should hang on to him as long as you possibly can," I said.

Over dinner at the Buckleys', Pat was very funny about the horror of a weekend at Mara-Lago as a guest of Ivana Trump for a "spa" weekend. Apparently they put her in the "conquistador suite" and she never found her way back for dinner. When she eventually relocated the party, she found Ivana and co dressed, not as Pat was, in a linen dress and bandanna but in full Carolyne Roehm black-tie regalia with commensurate diamonds. Pat is an amazing hostess. Presides over all the cooking herself, which is a rarity at the dinners I go to. "Did I put too much stock in the soup?" she asks. Or to Bill Blass, "I am trying out this new Sauternes but it's not nearly as nice as the one you serve."

"I'll send you over a case," said Blass, and

to me: "One of the nicest things about being as rich as I am is the ability to make these kinds of grand gestures."

Laugh-out-loud note. Park Avenue hostess Nan Kempner at a lunch last week discussing her estranged husband, Tommy. "I am feeling so good now that Tommy is back," she said. "Kicking him out after taking shit for thirty-seven years was the best thing I ever did."

"Where did he go when you kicked him out?" I asked.

"Downstairs to the guest room," Nan said. "It was time for him to know what it was like in the cold outside world. He had to give his own orders to the cook, make his own plans for dinner, give his own laundry to the maid. When I had a dinner party I left a note for him saying, 'Stay out tonight. I am having a dinner party for friends,' and he had to take himself on his own to a movie. Tina, it was the most salutary thing I ever did."

Monday, November 14, 1988

I am on my way to LA for a very quick trip. We're doing a promotion event for Sarah Giles's Fred Astaire oral history and afterward Wendy Stark, undeterred by her father's wrath, is giving a dinner for me. I decided to have Wendy do the dinner as a peacekeeping move. Why? Because my two contributing LA editors, Caroline Graham and Wendy, are locked in a bitter rivalry. The girls each want what the other has. Wendy has boyfriend famine but her daddy Ray Stark's power and millions behind her. Caroline is willowy and gorgeous and can't keep men away but is economically challenged. Hence a duel to the death.

On election night after a dinner with Bernie Leser, we went over to Diane von Furstenberg's suite at the Carlyle to watch the election returns with Susan Sontag and David Rieff, Carl Bernstein, Bianca Jagger, Harry Fane, and various other social types who sat shouting abuse at the TV in the bedroom. We all watched glumly as Dukakis said, "From this experience we have a lesson to learn." "You learn it, asshole," said Rieff. Joan Buck, always incorrigibly dramatic, came wearing a black mourning veil in anticipation of the foregone conclusion.

So it's to be President George Herbert Walker Bush and Vice President J. Danforth Quayle aka Dan. Like Batman and Robin except Bush as Bruce Wayne's goofy great-uncle and Quayle as a boy but not a wonder. Still, it's hard to mourn the rout of the Democrats yet again. Dukakis looked a shoo-in in July when he accepted the nomination to the strains of Neil Diamond singing "Coming to America." He was riding high in the polls. He was the duke, proud son of

Greek immigrants, successful governor, pragmatic policy guy who was all about getting things done. Then he took the rest of the summer off while Lee Atwater and co turned him into a flag-burning, pledge of allegiance–hating, murderer-coddling, elitist Harvard wimp. The debacle of the Snoopy impression on the tank in the ridiculous ill-fitting helmet. Why do the Democrats keep nominating stiffs? We went through this with Walter Mondale. But at least he had the excuse that he was running against a popular incumbent.

When I went to the White House to lunch with Barbara Bush and other lady editors a while back, she already seemed a doughty first lady with her Mount Rushmore head and imposing chest. A true Daughter of the American Revolution, a reassuring aunt who could outclass poor Kitty Dukakis with her neurotic drive and slimming pills. Oh dear.

American success. The rise and fall. There is nothing sweeter when you're up. Nothing glummer when you're down. I have a lot to thank God for this Thanksgiving.

Tuesday, November 15, 1988

I always feel serene and happy in LA, although for the first time I had doubts about living there. Perhaps it was just a little too much time discussing Oprah Winfrey's weight loss, a few too many programs on TV about

612

working out and looking good.

I sat between Barry Diller and Jeff Berg at Wendy's dinner. Diller was an insistent presence, hogging all the conversation from the ICM agent Jeff Berg, who is such a clever mind. Diller kept singing Rupert's praises; in Diller's universe having a billion dollars makes everything you do ultimately smart.

Wendy is so bright and funny she ought to be married to some big powerhouse who could take on her father instead of attracting one fortune hunter after another. She is still trying to lose weight, this time going to Oprah's diet doctor for special herbal vitamin pills. They cost her five hundred dollars and she dropped them all over the floor just before the party and the dog gobbled them up. "Oh my God," she screamed. "Should I take her to the ER? Should she have liposuction?" (A strange idea for a remedy.) It's amazing how Bel Air people do conform to their stereotypes.

Back at the hotel I spent an hour approving the last changes in T. D. Allman's remarkable Haiti piece in the next issue. The principal product of Haiti's government, he says, is kleptocracy. Tim has become a classic foreign correspondent in our pages, and this report captures the power of Haiti's magic and the nature of its pain. Like Nick Dunne, he always manages to collide with characters who define the strangeness of the atmosphere.

In his piece the latest oppressor, General Prosper Avril, suddenly appears at a beach party with mistress and retinue in tow. A strongman pays a courtesy call, in evening dress, to ensure his standing with the men who matter. The Haiti piece may be even better than the one he did for us on Panama's Iago, General "Tony" Noriega. So glad we have him.

Friday, November 25, 1988
Elkhorn Ranch, Arizona

I am a long, long way from all of the above. Last weekend we flew here to spend Thanksgiving on the ranch with G, back in the little stone-floored adobe cabin with the fireplace and the oil paintings of lone cowboys riding through snow and elks cantering around.

There's something enormously appealing about the people here. Not just the sure, sturdy wranglers and the Miller family who own it, but the guests young and old. They seem so sunny and uncomplicated compared to the tortured souls we all know "back East" as they say. G is alarmed by windmills, so Harry is teaching him how they work and he likes to act it out after dinner in the dining room, when we sit beside the fire having our coffee. Yesterday as a storm gathered he kept talking about the storm "biting the mountains," which was so poetic.

After Thanksgiving lunch on the terrace we climbed into the ranch van and drove the two hours to a Tucson medical center to have G's earache looked at before we fly. We have conquered G's fear of doctors from his preemie days by asking this one to examine each of our ears first. A nurse helped matters by giving him a green donkey. "A nice green donkey!" he kept saying with his best grin. Then we went to find a place for tea and the only thing open was some overluxe hotel and in the meantime G had soiled his diaper and Harry burst into the posh dining room, waving a smelly diaper, followed by G waving his green donkey and shouting for some reason, "I don't want my dinosaur boots!"

After the beauty of the ranch the Tucson mall was disorienting and depressing, a sprawling, characterless mess of Kmarts and gas stations and drugstores. As we drove around in the blinding rain, or cruised down the fluorescent-lit aisles of throbbing products in the gigantic pharmacy where we went to collect G's prescriptions, I thought how this is an America I will never warm to, America as a huge, vacant, product-filled, centerless, culturally sterile parking lot. It's fiercely alien to me and in a way I'm glad that it is. If it weren't, I'm not sure I'd be able to successfully edit *Vanity Fair.* I might not have the confidence to choose with uninhibited focus what interests me to read about.

615

The soulless, anonymous America of shopping malls and strip malls, of chain stores, Dunkin' Donuts, Walmarts, Drug Fairs . . . whenever I roam those aisles I feel dispossessed yet enclosed by them. I wonder if my tight little European soul will ever expand enough to fit. I fear it won't but that it will never shrink back down enough to fit England again. My home is now Transatlantica. That place between England and America is the only world where I can be happy now.

PS, on the way back to NYC, a humorous (to me) press release came out, announcing that Grace Mirabella has been hired by Rupert to launch *Mirabella,* a new fashion mag for the over-fifties. What a swivet that must be sending Si into, his archrival scooping up Grace. She is sure to steal some staff and has so much support on Seventh Avenue. Also every talk show Grace goes on will start with the manner of her firing. Nothing can touch *Vogue* and Anna will win. But it's still good for Si to understand that firing people boorishly does have business as well as social implications. The launch of *Mirabella* is a delicious Judith Krantz touch in the media soap opera.

Saturday, December 3, 1988

Coming back from DC after a Man Ray exhibit at the National Museum of Art in

Washington. Sitting between Ben Bradlee and Ambassador Gottlieb of Canada last night, I felt relaxed and jolly as I do in London. It was civilized and warm. Not the high-key hysteria that the new-money barons inject into NYC with the crazy upping of the ante that makes social life so tense.

Back in NYC, on Monday night, Brooke Astor gave a dinner for us in her apartment. This seemed puzzling until it became clear she wants to be contributing editor of either *VF* or *Traveler* now that she is chucking in *HG,* where she used to offer pieces about grand houses. I sat between her son, Anthony Marshall, a gloomy bore, and the British actor Peter Glenville, whom I've never seen the point of before but was amusing on this occasion. I got him reminiscing about Larry Olivier and he riveted me by saying that what tied him to Joan Plowright was "very dirty sex." When pressed he explained that Vivien Leigh was a porcelain romantic beauty that he could never get down and dirty with, but Plowright, "a runty gamine," was up for "anything bestial." This was so outlandish it paid the price of admission, as far as I was concerned.

Pat Buckley tried to get up and found that the sequins on her evening pants had locked together and she couldn't move. I thought Jason Epstein's pumpkin head was finally going to explode with mirth.

A new writer I like, John Seabrook, came in to talk about stories. Wants to do Barbara Bush. "Why should she say yes when we have trashed her husband twice?" I said.

"You could always tell her I am an idiot savant," he replied suavely, "who learned to read and write thanks to her literacy program."

I had to host a lunch for the director Barry Levinson and his new movie *Rain Man* at CAA's request. When I went to the screening I felt rising unease. Rain Man's insistent preoccupations remind me very much of Georgie. Could there be any element of Rain Man's autism in the way G rocks and repeats things and doesn't want to play with others?

Monday, December 5, 1988

This afternoon in the art-planning room I looked at the layout for Nick Dunne's piece on the last days of Robert Mapplethorpe. The final picture is Robert's self-portrait, probably the last before he died of AIDS, and it's haunting. The image that packs the most punch, though, is a paparazzi picture, not one of his own, taken recently at the opening of the Whitney. It shows what Mapplethorpe had really become at the end — hollowed out, wheelchair bound, surrounded by groupies and hangers-on. The leather loop of a woman's handbag nearby looks like a whip.

An incredible Dorian Gray picture of the end of the life he chose to lead and the death he doesn't deserve to die. Sharon felt it was important to use only Mapplethorpe's own portraits but the news picture makes a more powerful statement. I argued first with her, then with myself, feeling it was perhaps too raw. But then I decided, it's also the truth, hard to look at though it may be. I used it as the opener to the story, in black and white as a double-page spread.

1989
ART OF THE DEAL

Thursday, January 5, 1989

Hooray! I love my job! I love *Vanity Fair*! The crazed two-week Christmas holiday in London nearly put me away! Office life is a doddle after the chaos of uninterrupted family life. Bam bam bam! In the last three days I have persuaded Ryszard Kapuściński to write about Pope John Paul, dispatched Alex Shoumatoff to Brazil to write about the murder of the rain-forest activist Chico Mendes, aimed T. D. Allman at a profile of Qaddafi, and entertained Diana Ross for afternoon tea. In the middle of all this I am interviewing a weekend nanny. I was trying to decide between spreads of Catherine Deneuve and of Emperor Hirohito to lead off an issue when the first candidate showed up. I asked Sarah Lewis to go and chat with her first (a crazy idea, since Sarah always believes in everybody). G chose that moment to come on the line, wailing, "I want to be cozy with Mummy! I want to be cozy!"

What is the candidate like, I shouted through the door to Sarah. "She seems great," said Sarah. "She's Irish. She can cook. She can clean. She's a trained accountant and has just finished a computer-training course."

"Jesus! Does she do a shampoo and blow dry, too?" I had a sudden vision of the "wife" of my dreams, when in walks the most glowering individual I have ever entertained in my office. She radiated ill feeling as her left hand drummed neurotically on the side of her handbag. I would have been scared to be in the same room with her myself, let alone allow her to babysit G.

Today I reworked the March issue four times. It's still not as good as the February issue about to hit the newsstands, which has the Arafat interview scoop by T. D. Allman, Michelle Pfeiffer on the cover in a killer gold strapless dress, Dunne on Robert Mapplethorpe, and Peter Boyer's great story on the firing of the editor of *The Atlanta Constitution.* But it does have the new emperor of Japan, the new movie about the London prostitute Christine Keeler, and Anthony Haden-Guest on the last days of Christina Onassis. (It sounds like the lyrics for a Cole Porter song. Which it sort of is, really, the magazine version of it anyway.)

I feel the happy sense that we are flying! The sales of *VF* continue to get higher and the quality better and better. Average paid subscriptions for 1988 now 429,737 and newsstand 194,909, in total up 16 percent over 1987. The sky's the limit, I feel, and I have no desire to leave. We are starting to become indispensable reading for our current affairs and foreign coverage. People are loving Tim's Haiti piece and they will love his Arafat, too. It lifts my spirits when he barrels into the office, wheezing on his foreign correspondent cigarettes.

Sunday, January 22, 1989

On Thursday I went to lunch at Hearst at the invitation of the CEO, Frank Bennack.

Sane, solid, all-American, decent and humane, and very shrewd, I thought. I didn't like his bow-tied sidekick, Gil Maurer much. After a drink in the anteroom they took me into the executive dining room, the theme of the chat being all the opportunities offered by Hearst newspapers, TV stations, magazines, and, as Howard Kaminsky puts it, "a shitload of real estate." This company sell went on all through both courses and I tried to be bright-eyed and perky and suitably impressed. As coffee came, Bennack pushed back his chair and said, "Miss Brown, there are very few real stars in the editing world. They come along once every twenty-five years. And you are editing the best and the hottest book in America today. You have reached the top of the ladder very young. We at Hearst would like to offer you an Aladdin's lamp. What would you like from us? Any existing magazine in the company? Any magazine you would like to start? We would like to give you what you want."

I gulped. A pretty glamorous opening gambit.

It also felt ridiculous that I couldn't think of anything to want. I said I would think about that kind suggestion but that I am still under the sway of the genie of *Vanity Fair.*

Descending in the elevator, I felt high as a kite. But I also suspect that anything Hearst offered me Si would offer, too. And Si, I realize, has one great advantage. He doesn't have to please any board, or any shareholders. Bennack is a smart and impressive CEO, but Hearst is a family trust. He doesn't have the freedom of spending money that's his own.

I decided to tell Si of the approach, not to hit him up — it's dangerous to bluff if you don't plan to go — but because I may have been seen by some gossiper in the elevator coming down. Also I am trying to get Chris Garrett again, who is still working at *Tatler,* to come from London at additional expense to fill in for Pam's second maternity leave. It would make life so much smoother than trying to fill in with people who don't know how

I work. And this little Hearst overture may make him inclined to say yes. When I started to tell Si about Hearst, it was gratifying to see the expression of intense pain that crossed his face before he jumped up and ran around my side of the desk even as I reassured him I am not interested. Some of his fear, I am sure, is how much talent I could steal if I left. Chris Garrett's three-month sojourn is now safely approved if I can get her to agree.

This weekend was the first since we winterized Quogue and I have hired a warm, kindly woman from St. Vincent, Cynthia Knights, from the agency to help out with G on the weekends so I can work. She is so generous and sweet to G. It was a treat having her here and I had time to compose passionate, pleading faxes to Chris Garrett and her husband, persuading them to figure out how to come to America. Judging by the going-wobbly replies, I think I have succeeded.

Gabé called to tell me that the *Times* style writer John Duka died today. AIDS. No one knew he had it. It was incredibly swift: three months or so. Bruce Chatwin died on Monday. It goes on and on. Our Mapplethorpe piece has caused a storm. Including an irate letter from Dr. Mathilde Krim, who, unfairly in my view, accuses me of linking "the plague" to homoerotic behavior rather than to just being "in the wrong place at the wrong time in New York in the eighties." I can see how the impulse behind this distortion is probably well intentioned, because after all there is still so much homophobic bigotry out there. But it shouldn't require pretending AIDS has nothing to do with gay life to make it a cruel and tragic disease we have to stamp out.

The worst thing about Duka's end was how attached he was to all things ephemeral. Such sadness.

Wednesday, January 25, 1989

The cover of the February issue is making waves. That Herb Ritts photograph of Michelle Pfeiffer bathed in warm California sunlight, wearing the gold strapless, striped lace dress by Calvin Klein, has been a fashion sensation. Calvin's people say it is flying off the racks. Now other designers are calling Marina, saying they want their crack at getting a piece on the *VF* cover that becomes The Dress. Herb can be so difficult, such a control freak, but this cover, this dress is box-office gold. Charles Churchward is very happy, as Herb is his guy and he runs him as well as Jane manages Annie.

Thursday, January 26, 1989

G turned three. When he woke he looked around, blinked, and said, "Do you know,

Mummee, I am THREE!" We let him unwrap his present — a Playmobil zoo — and as he did it he kept grinning and saying, "It's so nice to be three!" He loved his party this year with all his friends and Marsha the Musical Moose, who was a much bigger hit than Silly Billy the clown last year. I think back to that snowy day when I opened my eyes at New York–Presbyterian and the morning I saw the *Challenger* space shuttle explode. My fragile darling boy.

Saturday, February 18, 1989

Newsweek called up yesterday and told me they are doing a "major piece on *Vanity Fair*" just as Doug and I were wondering how we could get some more thoughtful press about what we do.

They assigned Annie to take the pictures and Marina Schiano is going to town on the clothes.

On Tuesday I gave a book party for Melvyn Bragg for his Richard Burton biography. Great theater/film crowd of Stephen Sondheim, Martin Scorsese, the Mailers, plus Quentin Crisp and the whole *VF* stage army. Afterward we took Melvyn to dinner at Petaluma with Scorsese, James Ivory, and Ismail Merchant. Scorsese talks even faster than I do, with a demented laugh. He is like a mad priest full of torment and focused intent.

I invited the *Newsweek* writer Tom
Mathews to come to a features meeting,
which was full of good copy. Reinaldo rushing in shouting, "Stroessner has fallen!
Paraguay is in uproar!" (I dispatched Shoumatoff.) Annie appearing with her Don
Johnson shoot from Miami and Marina waft-
ing in, trailing a red scarf and dark glasses,
jabbering about what a "beeech Melanie
Griffith was for refusing to wear the white
suit."

Frank Bennack asked me back for another
lunch. I am pretty sure I don't want anything
from Hearst, but he's so gracious and I don't
want to offend him.

Saturday, March 4, 1989

There's no time for reflection. I feel changes
in the air.

On Tuesday Si gave a dinner party for
Nancy Reagan, whose book he's publishing
with Random House. It was vintage Si oddity. And even odder is the way Victoria seems
to play no part in improving it. Si even went
home early to oversee the arrangements. I arrived to find most of the Random House
brass milling around the living room, waiting
for Mrs. Reagan. I asked where I was sitting
and was told it's a buffet. Which seems a bit
off for the former first lady. I look around for
anyone Mrs. R knows, like Bill Blass or Zip-

kin, but the other guests are all male publishing suits — so many of them, it looks like a KGB convention. Mrs. Reagan arrives in cordial style, chats with her editor and the only people she knows, i.e., the Janklows. Then Si suddenly vanishes downstairs. I say to Victoria, "Um, are we going to dinner?" And she looks vague and startled and says, "Oh yes! In fact, why don't you follow Si. We thought it would be very nice if you sat with Mrs. Reagan in the first group." I helped myself to a plate of lamb and rice and blundered off down the wrong corridor. When I found them they were all seated with Leo, who apparently knows Nancy from the old days, on a sofa with ten-foot gaps between them. Every so often someone would come over and be waved into a gap. Plus Leo is too deaf to hear anything so conversation was spasmodic. Si said almost nothing, just kept leaping up to wave people in. Philip Johnson whispered to me. "Oh dear, oh dear, what is one to say?" The next day Alex told me it was one of the most excruciating evenings he had ever attended. He said the only thing worse was Bernie's thirty-years-at-the-company party, at which Si had decided he would only have the business side and no wives, so it was another KGB buffet.

I still had a headache the next morning when Si called. I said, "Thank you for the . . . interesting evening with Nancy." And Si said,

"She's awful, really, isn't she? Victoria and I were surprised how many people wanted to be introduced to her."

Meanwhile, as I feel less serious the magazine only gets more so. If you told me five years ago I'd be running a piece on the death of a Brazilian rubber tapper by a New Yorker naturalist and selling a combined seven hundred thousand copies in newsstand and subs [up from 275,000 in average paid circulation in 1984], I would never have believed you.

PS: We took G to the St. Patrick's parade in Westhampton. "What's Jesus up to?" he asked me suddenly. I didn't have the heart to tell him Jesus was about to have a very bad Easter.

Friday, March 24, 1989

We're off to LA for the Oscars! I feel like Cher, traveling with a cavalcade of suitcases stuffed with Marina's borrowings from Oscar de la Renta (he's coming around), Carolyne Roehm, and Calvin Klein. G is with me and we are taking over a suite at the Bel-Air. What a lark. But I feel as if I may as well take advantage of Condé's richesse. I suspect this is very different from the corporate culture of Hearst.

Alex took me to lunch at La Grenouille

yesterday and confided that *Vogue* sales are down for the last two issues and he's worried Anna is going too "downtown." She has sacked one of his favorites, Amy Gross, who was the literary "nose" there, and installed another Brit, James Truman, as features ed. I guess after all the years of Grace Mirabella, maybe *Vogue* is so bland and mainstream it can't move this fast. James is very clever, though, and knows how to come up with angles and headlines like Miles does. *Vogue* needs to be less safe and he will help Anna get it done.

Saturday, March 25, 1989
Bel-Air hotel, LA

Just came back from Swifty's dinner for Michael Caine: the Sean Connerys, the Johnny Carsons, Ryan O'Neal and Farrah Fawcett, George Hamilton, Alana Stewart, Cybill Shepherd, Jackie Collins and Oscar Lerman, and John Bowes-Lyon. Quite a lineup. The only snag was that I had Bowes-Lyon, a dim and boring English toff, on one side, but never mind, on the other side was Michael Caine and opposite me were Johnny Carson and George Hamilton.

George Hamilton was the major surprise. He really is hilarious and I understood at last why he's so popular. He was full of raffish stories about gambling with Kerry Packer and losing two hundred thousand dollars on his way from dinner at Aspinall's. Carson was much less deadpan than on TV. There was twinkle and a tinge of preoccupied warmth, though still an aura of cool self-control. Michael Caine just free-associates fun. "Farrah, why do you and Ryan keep that place in Malibu? Any stray sod can wander up the beach, like I did, and see you and Ryan sitting there in your cozzies [bathing suits]." Carson said he had to move away from the beach because the telephoto lenses and the fans rummaging through his garbage were too intense. His glamorous wife, Joanne, had a very peculiar, complicated dress on. She seemed to have a latent sense of humor. Jackie Collins said that her hairdresser, Wally, had gone off for a year with David Bowie. "Oh dear," said Mrs. Carson. "That's a long time to wait to get your bangs cut." Cybill Shepherd turned up very late with a friend in tow. Swifty was seething at her rudeness. "What can you expect?" he hissed at me. "Hick girl with hick manners. Brings her friend who goes and messes up the whole fucking seating plan!" Cybill was indeed a strange sight. She wore steel-framed specs, flat brogues, no makeup, and what looked like a Bonwit Teller navy-blue business suit. I kinda loved her for it. "Who's her friend?" I asked Ryan O'Neal. "Her wardrobe mistress," he replied. "Couldn't you tell from what she's got on?" Hollywood. Just as bitchy as NYC.

Saturday, April 1, 1989
In flight, LA to NYC

Caroline Graham introduced me to a very amusing CAA agent, Bob Bookman, a self-deprecating, ironic, Woody Allen–ish type very different from the rest of Ovitz's hit men. "No one at the agency is threatened by me," he said. "I represent books, so that means I must be an intellectual, and therefore ineffectual. When people at the agency introduce me they say, this is Bob Bookman. He reads." He said if you are an agent, your whole life is business to an intolerable degree. He said Irwin Winkler came back in despair from a ski holiday in Aspen with the Ovitzes and said a typical incident was one morning he wanted to go out on a run with Mike and Judy. Judy said, "Come back in an hour. We might have friends joining." When he came back there was Jane Fonda and Tom Hayden, Tom Cruise and Mimi, and Sally Field and her husband, and Ovitz had hired private instructors for them all.

I'm crazy about the producers Don Simpson and Jerry Bruckheimer, who took me to Morton's with Jesse Kornbluth and Jane Sarkin. Simpson talked about the rise of Madame Alex, the Hollywood Madame Claude. Also has a dark view of Michael Eisner.

"Here's the deal. Here's how it plays out. No one has done the book on Eisner. It's Barry Diller who's the good guy, not Michael Eisner. Diller is stuck as the bad hat, but it's Eisner who dissembles without a second thought. Diller is the smartest guy in Hollywood. He's got the best head. When Barry and I were at Paramount and we'd come to him with a ton of problems, it was fun. Because he's so smart, we could work through them and solve them all because of Barry." Bruckheimer has a thin, intense face and big black eyes and doesn't say much. Don has a wide, expressive face and a shock of blond hair like Don Johnson and he does all the talking. They both *LOVE Vanity Fair.* "Here's the deal," said Don. "I read every single piece. And I start to feel anxious when it doesn't arrive." He said the only way to judge whether a movie will be a hit is the "parking lot" theory. What's that? "You're both walking out of the movie house to the car, telling each other it was a pretty good movie. Then you get to the parking lot, look at each other and shrug, and go, 'Meh!' "

Monday April 3, 1989

I am deeply content with the May cover. Helmut Newton's divine shot of Kevin Costner in black-tie deshabille, dress shirt open, black tie dangling, whiskey tumbler in hand.

It's so hard to get the cover that defines the mood of the magazine inside and this one does. Sophistication, devil may care, the promise of surprise. Hallelujah. Inside, Myra MacPherson's "Anatomy of a Serial Killer" about Ted Bundy is top class. Myra did an amazing reporting job, talking to his mother, aunt, investigators, and — a major coup — got an exclusive with the New York psychiatrist Dr. Dorothy Otnow Lewis, who was one of Bundy's last confessors. Harry Benson's photograph for us of Ted's mother, Louise, clutching Ted's Boy Scout uniform, is agonizing. In the attention to victims, no one thinks about the pain of being the mother of a killer. The last and only person who thinks of him as human.

Sunday, April 16, 1989

Frank Bennack asked me to come in to Hearst again on Thursday. The third time. He wanted to focus discussions on *Harper's Bazaar.* The truth is I rarely look at the current incarnation, which feels like a humdrum fashion magazine. To me the excitement of *Bazaar* is in reinventing its distant past of the late thirties, forties, and early fifties, when Carmel Snow and Brodovitch reigned. It was always cleverer than *Vogue,* a magazine for "well-dressed women with well-dressed minds," as Snow put it. She brought cutting-edge fiction writers and art and reporting as well as iconic photography. She discovered everyone good from Vreeland to Avedon to Jean Cocteau to Truman Capote to Warhol. That's a legacy I could get my teeth into, as juicy as *Vanity Fair*'s.

I was snapped out of these musings by Bennack's financial pivot. He talked about a profit-linked bonus that was impressive, so good it made me quite miserable. I am also starting to really like and respect Bennack, and the time and patience he is putting into this courtship. He is a real gentleman. Since the meeting my mind keeps returning to *Bazaar*'s potential.

On Friday Bernie Leser called me up to tell me the close-held secret that year to date, *VF* January to March has made a profit of $1.4 million! Si always mumbles about the "chimera of meaningful profit" when I ask him how we are doing. Now I feel that a piece of that chimera as we grow ought to be for me. To compound all this, the persistent reporter Albert Scardino from *The New York Times* called me about a piece they are writing for tomorrow about *VF*'s writers getting top rate, and requested a graph of our rising revenue. Also, *Newsweek* is busy fact-checking their next week's piece on me. ("Fire and Ice" is one of the lines Annie Leibovitz saw on the cover dummy, if it makes the cut, which depends on the news.) It seems I am having a "moment" here. So what does all this point to? A big fucking quantum-leap change-your-life-forever raise, that's what. Now or never. Howard Kaminsky, who from contacts at Hearst has been privy to Bennack's interest in me, said that when I went in to Hearst I should say to him, "I've got only two words to say to you, Mr. Bennack: San Simeon."

The lawyer who was the model for Tommy Killian in *The Bonfire of the Vanities*, Ed Hayes, has become another consigliere on the matter. He thinks I should leave Condé. Why? "Because no one can ever crack the Newhouse barrier at Condé. You've always got the midget family Robinson one step ahead. You go to Hearst and you could end up as Kay Graham."

And Dick Holbrooke's ten cents: "Anything south of one mil is inadequate for what you've done for Si." He volunteered this not in the context of my confiding in him, but over dinner at the news anchor Peter Jennings's apartment, when salaries in general were being discussed. I was seated next to the financier Felix Rohatyn, whom I found extremely entertaining on the subject of who has the biggest golden parachute on Wall Street. At the same table was Jennings's boss at Capital Cities, Tom Murphy, a media suit with a conical head. He looked aghast when Holbrooke, whom I hadn't seen for a while, came roaring over, grabbed me, and slobbered over my exposed shoulder.

Anyway, bottom line, I need real professional advice on all this. Tomorrow morning I am having breakfast with Mort Janklow and I am going to ask him to represent me with Si. If I do it myself, Si will just throw me something incremental and I will wimp out and accept it. This time I want real acknowledgment that I took a money-hemorrhaging disaster story, invented a new magazine brand, and took it into profit that will only build over the next ten years. We are already on our way to being the company flagship just as much as *Vogue*. And if he doesn't want to do it, I will hightail it to *Harper's Bazaar*.

Sunday, April 30, 1989

The New York Times ran a piece on *VF* calling me "the gold-dust fairy" (which I assuredly wish they hadn't; *Spy* will have a field day). Said I have upped the ante on writers' payments, changed the literary marketplace, signed up all the available talent, and as a result (they printed two beautiful graphs to prove it) the circulation and ads are on a straight upward climb. Ed Kosner was quoted as saying that in the 1980s *Playboy* paid more than anyone else, "and then Tina came along and began throwing money around like crazy. She escalated everything." I love the way he says "throwing money around" as if I am some ditzy girl run amok with the budget, rather than operating with a budget blessed by Si and targeted strategically at top talent we get to do their best work. The *Times* graph shows it pays off. Scardino cites our 63 percent rise in circulation and tripling of ad pages from 431 in 1985 to 1,193 today. So fuck all the naysayers. I am so over being patronized by know-all guys.

On the wings of this I had my breakfast with Janklow. You only understand what's behind a celebrity reputation when you experience its force field of expertise first-hand. It turns out he knows Bennack. Thinks the world of him. Sees Hearst as I do — a sleeping beauty . . . was shocked by what I am paid (now $225,000) comparative to others he reps, especially when I told him that a month ago Dick Snyder had ruminated to Ed Victor about the S and S job that pays a lot more. Agrees with me completely that in an era when magazines are changing hands for as much as 150 mil, we need to explore all with Bennack, and then talk to Si. "You may still decide to leave, whatever Si counter-offers," he said. The thought of this discussion scares me witless. I sent a note to Bennack, holding him off for a few days while "I talk to my advisers." Back came a nice note mentioning financial "participation" in future success, something Si would never, ever do because of the wholly owned family situation. I would so much rather have stock options, or phantom stock (I am learning a lot from Mort), than perks and lifestyle treats. With phantom stock, a future payday tied to the performance of the magazine could turn out to be extremely valuable, especially if he ever sells it.

Then a weekend of tension. *Newsweek* kept coming back with fact-checking queries, clearly about to run. I bounced on and off the cover and finally lost it to a news piece on abortion, but with a cover strap line that read, "High-gloss news. Tina Brown revives *Vanity Fair.*" The blurb says, "A fresh eye, an advanced sense of mischief, and fingertips sensitive to the arrhythmic pulse of the eighties." Yippee. A timing bonanza. The last paragraph describes me as "a brightly polished red Porsche cruising down the highway." Jesus. First a gold-dust fairy. Now a red Porsche. Let's hope it doesn't crash on the expressway. All I had hoped for was a positive business story on the numbers that also noted we do good journalism, not just celebrity stuff. Good thing I wasn't on the cover — as it was, at the Waldorf the next day for the ASME magazine awards I could see the editorial gritted teeth at every table. Just in time, my skin broke out in a rash so everyone can say I am nothing like my picture (and indeed I am not, all thanks to Annie's brilliant retouching).

Byron Dobell, who is on the ASME awards board, had told me I would be "well pleased" with the result. So I kept it to myself but took three tables and made sure I was next to Si. I had Reinaldo on the other side of me. He deserves it. Has brought in so many scoops. He had just got off the phone with the Libyan ambassador, trying to nail Qaddafi for T. D. Allman. "If I eat one more plate of couscous for this story I will scream," he told me.

As awards began, the first unexpected bonus was Harry winning a reporting award for *Traveler.* Si was thrilled, as was Harry. *The New Yorker* won two awards, but Gottlieb was too much of a snob to show, so Steve Florio lumbered up to collect. Then the big one — the mag equivalent of Best Picture in our category, magazines with a circulation over four hundred thousand. And the winner is . . . *VANITY FAIR*! Si was so excited, he jumped up from his chair and whooped. The applause was so loud that *The Washington Post* later called it "the most popular award of the day." I shot from my seat and bounded up onto the platform before I was supposed to, and stumbled across to the craggy face at the podium for my trophy, the bronze Ellie elephant. I felt so emotional as I did all the thank-yous. I was happy we took three tables so many of the staff could come. When I got back to the table, Jane, Pam, Wayne, all of them, even tough, cynical Sharon, were so excited and tearful. (Okay, Sharon was not tearful, but she had a look of pure satisfaction.) Si was flushed with pride: "I can leave now, Tina. I am so thrilled."

But how thrilled? I wish he would show real trust and give me some real stake in the ongoing success. It would mean more to me than any raise. The true luxury of early success is it allows you to be conceptual about the rest of your career. (If not the rest of your life. A year ago Mark Boxer was dreaming of New York. Now his children are learning to forget him.)

I retreat to Quogue to think about it all. The power life roars along with all real thoughts, fears buried or put indefinitely on hold. I want more time to contemplate, but I can't seem to live any other way. I feel panic when I stop. I am an action junkie. My best hope for peace is when I am with G.

At the PEN dinner Vartan Gregorian grabbed Harry and urged him to come teach at Brown. "It's so wonderful," he said to Harry, "to be safe with my books in academia instead of watching ladies not eat their lunch at Le Cirque." I am sure he's right, but journalists like us find it hard to be out of the arena.

I am upstairs in the sitting room, writing this in front of the window that looks out on the dunes. I can hear the splashing and arguing of Harry and Georgie in the bath together. John Lennon on the radio — "Mother, you had me but I never had you." My legs ache after an afternoon of pursuing G around the playground, where he kept escaping me, crying, "You can't stop me! I'm the gingerbread man!" It was sunny but still cold. I can feel the tantalizing whiff of summer to come. This morning when I woke up with G in my bed he said, "Mummy, I love you with all my tummy." His new dear joke.

Last week in the wake of *Newsweek*'s encomium I feel the need to outperform. Pam McCarthy had lunch with an editor who runs a section in *Newsweek* and was taken aback when she opened the first course with "Well! Tom Mathews [who wrote the piece on me] will never work again! His career is over! And Steve Smith who pushed it through! He's over, too! What a puff piece! Everyone knows it's because Steve's wife wants to work for *Vanity Fair*!" Pam was stunned and surprised, which I wasn't. They are all gunning for me beneath their polite smiles at ASME. And I am fully aware at some point they will eat me for lunch.

On Tuesday night, Anna Wintour asked us to join her table at a Lifesavers dinner at the Puck Building, at which her husband, Dr. David Shaffer, was being honored for his life's work counseling and medicating teens who want to commit suicide. Wanted to go to show appreciation for David, who has been helpful with G. I like him. He has a wonderful, droll sense of humor. All the speakers had suicides in their families, from Joan Rivers to Mariette Hartley. The most affecting and surprising was the novelist William Styron, who suddenly got up from where he sat and spoke about the night he tried to kill himself. In between courses I went to tell him how powerful it was and asked if he would consider turning it into a piece for *Vanity Fair.* He was still moved from speaking so personally, but to my delight he said he would like to and asked me to call him tomorrow. It would be incredible personal history if he will do it. It would help so many people who live in shame, believing depression is a weakness instead of a disease. And he has never gone public before except in this circle of fellow sufferers. It would be news and literature combined. If I hadn't gone to this weird-sounding dinner, I would never have heard Styron or had the chance to approach him. Good for David for doing this suicide work, such a radical contrast to the life Anna leads at *Vogue,* which perhaps is why their partnership works.

I wondered what Anna herself thinks of all this? Clearly it was her night to support David. She looked wonderful as always in a tight dress and shiny bob and impassive face. David made the best speech, short and British in its crispness.

James and Toni Goodale had a wedding anniversary party the next night at Doubles that made me really see the point of Tom Brokaw. Toni Goodale had given Tom the task of handing out joke awards to guests, such as the couple who'd been married the longest and the couple who had been married the most times. Brokaw watched the proceedings coolly, murmured that Toni had given him a speech to make at the end that he felt "needed help, so if you'll excuse me . . ." He took out three index cards from his pocket and made small notes on them for five minutes, with the occasional pause to think. Then he got up and did a stunning tour de force riff about marriage that brought the house down.

This morning I followed up with Styron and he has agreed to do the essay on depression. Have asked Wayne to edit it and am praying it's as good as what he said about his ordeals at the Lifesaver dinner.

Thursday, May 18, 1989

Mort Janklow looks better and better the

more time I spend with him on the Bennack business. Part of my dilemma right now is that Bennack keeps throwing out numbers that make it impossible to turn him down, but I am so torn.

Last Thursday Mort went in to see him for a meeting that went on for two hours. When he came out he called from the car. "If this is the opening of a negotiation, it's unbelievable," he said. "It's something you seriously have to think about." Bennack is offering phantom stock, newsstand bonuses, and a huge pay hike. He also made it clear to Mort he is thinking of me as his successor. That after three years or less, if I turn around *Harper's Bazaar* I could move into the movie division, or the newspaper division, or the TV division. Now I am seriously thinking about *Bazaar* and its lustrous intellectual and visual pedigree. Commercially it is still a power in the market. It already has a circulation of seven hundred thousand but is number four with advertisers, hence Bennack's frustration. I have been dreaming up ways I could revive it and make it exciting. But I would be sacrificing my baby, *VF. Bazaar* would take two years to get right and its strong fashion element would not be as appealing to writers to contribute or opinion formers to buy. Plus, fashion doesn't interest me. Anna would be impossible to beat there. She lives and breathes it.

Last night at a dinner at Janklow's house, Si was there at another table and I felt more agony about my conversations with Hearst. But maybe I am being a drip.

"I can't stand a guy that's cheap with the help," Mort said to Harry and me after dinner. "And as far as Si is concerned, you are the help."

It's all true. Though I hate to hear it. And not wholly fair. Si took a chance on me, for which I will forever be grateful. And the chance he took paid off. Hugely. But then again, Mort's intelligence tells him I get paid less than Art Cooper at *GQ*. I feel men handle these pay discussions so much better, but it also pisses me off they get away with it.

I am musing on all this at the Bonaventure Resort and Spa over four days of bouncing in the pool with G. This afternoon I took him on an expedition to Ocean World to look at the dolphins play and realized with a pang this was the first time for many weeks I have felt unrushed and able to enjoy time with him. His welfare is another major consideration. Harry thinks I should stick with Condé. After what he went through in the change from Thomson ownership to Murdoch, he feels that these situations that look so good can often turn out to be a minefield. Plus Si would fight back, with a bigger budget for whoever succeeded me. And a new job at Hearst equals new demands, as I'll have to prove myself again. But for someone as restless as me, there is great appeal in starting over, armed with what I now know about dusting off another legend. Mort, of course, is looking at this as a business opportunity that has to be rationally assessed. Which is what I have engaged him to do.

Sunday, May 21, 1989
NYC

Wonderful spring weather. I got up early on Thursday morning for breakfast at the Knickerbocker Club with Derry Moore, the photographer who shot so many beautiful house interiors for us at *Tatler.* Then I sped downtown with Jane Sarkin to see Annie Leibovitz's new studio. When we walked into Annie's huge, white, empty loft with concrete floor and the bright sun streaming through the empty windows, I felt a stomach lurch of new pages yet to come. "It's so bright, isn't it?" Annie whooped, looking like a great eagle in her black slacks and turtleneck. She is happy at the moment, in a torrid affair with Susan Sontag. "All my new portraits, the subjects will be looking like this." She screwed up her eyes against the light. Over the speakers the music was dreamy and subaqueous, like in the aquarium at Ocean World. I stood in the middle of the white studio and spun around with joy. We are making publishing history here, and perhaps this is what people will write about someday. I felt a rush of affection for Annie. We have had so many fights and disputes, but only in the quest for perfection. I have come to trust her so much.

I feel at a strange slant to time and place. At breakfast with old-world Derry, I'd been thrown back to the London of *Tatler,* of Bruton Street, of Vogue House. Derry and I took so many great trips together for shoots, my favorite the series on the Wiltshire set's stately homes and manors as a way of capturing a look at Camilla Parker Bowles's house right before the royal wedding. That time now feels a different planet or century, one of small ads in *Harpers and Queen* for Gloucestershire antique shops, maternity smocks on Beauchamp Place, cookery schools in Belgravia, small farms in Wiltshire with paddock and converted barn. I suddenly thought how I must look to Derry, misleadingly sharp and metropolitan, in my sharp red shoulders and frosted hair that demands three hundred blowouts a year. I confided in him about Bennack and *Harper's Bazaar.* "I'd do it," said Derry in his Gielgudy voice, "like a shot. You know how ghastly Condé Nast is to its editors."

Jane Sarkin arrived to pick me up to go see Annie. "Who goes to the Knickerbocker anyway?" Jane screamed as we tore downtown in a Manhattan limo. "He's a peer," I said.

"His father is Lord Drogheda." "I knew it had to be somebody weird," said Jane.

It's strange to live between two cultures in my head. When I left Thatcher's England I had a jaded vision of its future — the widening schism between the classes and the coming of a new, moneyed yahooism, nihilistic and coarse, not meritocratic and aspirational as it is here. I don't know the names and the faces of the new England to really judge if that's true. Here I can penetrate into the subtext of what I see, but I don't know enough about American history or politics yet to be able to contextualize it against the past as I can at home. Here I live in a permanent red-hot present, fascinated, appalled, thrilled, amused, enraged — but never ultimately touched, because in the end I am always a spectator and a foreigner.

Monday, May 22, 1989

Bennack called me on Friday and asked me to come back in to Hearst. This time we cut through the social chat and I asked a lot of questions about the kind of freedom I would have editorially were I to do *Bazaar,* and the kind of budget I would have to operate with. He said it's true there had always been a bottom-line culture at Hearst, but he intended to break that rule with *Harper's Bazaar.* That each editor has a different style;

649

for example, John Mack Carter of *Good Housekeeping,* who's always operated with a lavish budget and been very competitive with acquisitions. I said I didn't want to be all front lawn, an expensive line item myself while presiding over a cramped budget. That if I hoped to attract a team as good as at *VF* and compete with Condé, the editorial budget would have to allow it. The only thing he didn't seem to like was my saying I would hire a top fashion editor rather than go to every fashion collection myself. I don't want to leave G for a week at a time four times a year. I see Anna constantly flying off to the collections and the boredom of that would be torture. Bennack's unease on the topic made me wonder if his own vision for *Bazaar* is at odds with mine. I would want to make a fashion director a star in his or her own right as Carmel Snow did with Diana Vreeland. He may have a more Seventh Avenue view of the mag (cf. Sam Spiegel — make sure you are both making the same movie; something to nail down). Still, as we parted, I felt exhilarated and high, thinking of the fun of creating something new again, of bringing back Michael Roberts, who I hear is getting bored again with *Tatler,* and Marina and co, adding substance and wit to this overpopulated fashion field. I went straight to Janklow's office to discuss it.

I have come to view Mort as a genial

Lucifer. By which I mean he is the quintessence of capitalism and undiluted worldliness. He would have been irresistible to Jesus when He looked down on a mirage of worldly rewards from the top of the mountain — a tall, self-possessed man with pointed ears and huge black eyes behind intimidating glasses, burning with the righteousness of market value. He sat with his long legs extended as I told my Hearst story and I asked if he thought a note from me to Si, asking him to talk to Mort, was a good idea.

"I've thought about that," he replied, "and you know? I think it's a lousy idea." He said he has breakfast with Si regularly to talk about Random House, and he would just bring it up then. "Or you could just go in and say, 'Si, for the last three years I've been paid well below my market value. I don't feel you've been terribly forthcoming about it so I have sought professional advice.' " I started to laugh at the way Mort said this, shooting his striped cuff with the expensive watch on it. It sounded so wonderful and convincing. But I would never be able to say it and sound like him. I'm too English and too female to blare these confident words at Si as he crouches behind his desk, flushed and astounded. The mere thought of it terrifies me. No. Mort will have to broach it. And if Si says no, then I will know I will go to *Harper's Bazaar.*

All this has been raging on while we're trying to put out a hot issue of *VF.* Si has agreed to give us a later-closing satellite capability so deadlines don't extend so ridiculously long, which has never been an issue for the fashion magazines, but has been agony for news, which is what we now are. He understands the news gene in *VF* and how it's the key to its heat. The late close will be expensive and I wonder if Bennack would do the same. I am trying to crash out Marie Brenner's Michael Milken piece in four days when the edit needs ten, and outbid *Time* on the Nancy Reagan memoirs. All this talk with Hearst and with Janklow makes me want to extend the range of the magazine, expand its appeal, make it even more international. If *Vanity Fair* is, as Si keeps saying, powerful, we need to make the power have a wider reach.

To help my courtship of the Nancy memoirs along, Reinaldo had a dinner for her in his narrow Upper East Side town house. He had one long table set up in his dressing room, under a tented canopy like Henry V's on the eve of the Battle of Agincourt. I could listen to the rise and fall of Zipkin's wailing cadences all night. "Boat trips? The most glamorous boat trip today is the Circle Line. I mean, if you'd sailed like me on Charles Revson's boat every summer, you'd know what it was like to be on a real boat! I'm talking grande luxe! I'm talking pistachio ice cream served on a silver tray! And a fleet of limos at every port! That's what I call being on a boat!"

Nancy Reagan looked better than I have seen her look in a long while. Dressed in a white Carolina Herrera dress with very sparkling eyes. She got on best talking politics with Harry, who had never met her. I realize she has a deeper grasp of things than we knew at the time. Harry said she was shrewd and knowledgeable, especially on foreign affairs. I got the sense she was thrilled to be in New York. Whatever relief it must be to be out of the White House, she now lives a rich, boring life in California, which must seem terribly limited after the role she has played for so long as Ronnie's consigliere. No one ever writes about that. How the wives grow, too, beside the man in office. I hope she does in her book, which I am trying to extract sight unseen.

Sunday, June 4, 1989
Quogue

I took Chester, who is staying with us, to the Steinbergs for a barbecue lunch. Saul was at his most exuberant. Bulldozers and cranes had torn up the front drive. In their place, discernible through Battle of the Somme mud, were Blenheim-like parterres, giant fountains. On the ocean side huge earth

653

movements had taken place and there was an enormous concrete hollow on the beach beneath the deck. "What's that," I said, "a giant's armchair?"

"Who knows?" bellowed Saul proudly. "I have no idea what Gayfryd is creating here. She's torn up the dune so we can get more of an ocean view. Only trouble is, she forgot about drainage."

"What do you care?" I said. "You're right," he said. "What do I care?" As we spoke, Gayfryd's thin ankle and wedge heel were surreptitiously moving a towel back and forth to dry the seeping shallows of the deck. I thought of Caroline Graham's shrewd observation that certain men love having "impossible" wives. It makes them feel powerful — "Do you know what she's done now?" "She kept me waiting two hours in Bergdorf," etc. etc. Saul is in that category. The more bulldozers in the driveway, the more mystified he plays it. As we walked into the dining room for lunch we stumbled over two gold Italian mirrors on the floor. "I got them for a hundred dollars each," she told us, implausibly. Everywhere one turned there were stray indications of acquisition frenzy: swatches of fabric on side tables, a twizzle of thin iron hanging from the ceiling — "a chandelier by this incredible artist you should do a piece about." In the kitchen no fewer than six people were preparing the hamburger and spaghetti lunch for the four of us plus the dreaded frock meister Arnold Scaasi, who has a house in Quogue, and their friend Danny Hersch, a heavy, genial businessman whom I last saw at their house when he was trying to start a new magazine called *Divorce*. Two years later he seems to have solved his problem. He arrived with a frisky forty-five-year-old model for *Lear's* magazine who had gunmetal hair in a ponytail. "We're engaged," he announced.

"Oh my God! The champagne," bellowed Saul. "Sheila, I don't want you to think we are not prepared for this event. We still go and visit the last two girls he said this to in rehab."

"Where did you propose?" Gayfryd said.

"Exit thirty-one," Sheila said, "and he never slowed down from ninety miles an hour."

"I would have knelt down," said Hersch, "except that we'd have been a bloody pulp on the expressway."

"Pour the best we've got, Jose," Saul told the waiter, and proceeded to tell funny, derogatory stories about Ronald Lauder's candidacy for mayor of New York.

"He's not a bad guy," said Saul. "Took it nicely when I said I propose to give him no money at all for his campaign."

"But I'm going to Jo Carole's luncheon tomorrow!" Gayfryd wailed. "I'm doing the renovation on our apartment without telling

the co-op board and she's in the next apartment!"

"Have you bought the ring yet?" Saul asked
Sheila.

"This week," said Hersch. "It will be done."

"Make sure it's so big that it's too much of
an investment to call off the wedding," said
Gayfryd, still mopping the deck with her right
foot. A telling aside, I thought.

Tuesday, June 6, 1989

Today Peter Guber, the producer of the movies *Rain Man, Batman,* and soon *The Bonfire
of the Vanities,* asked me to breakfast. I got to
the Regency early and recognized him as the
Hollywood guy as soon as he walked in —
the sloppy linen suit, ponytail, and all-even
tan, definitely not the NYC power-breakfast
look. "Tina," he said after briskly introducing
himself and ordering a California healthy
fruit plate, "what you have to understand is,
Hollywood is ruled by its dick. Men are ruled
by their dicks. Mine against yours. Excuse
me, I know you're a woman, but you understand what I'm saying. This business, movies,
is all about two things — power and sex. And
guess what, they're the same thing."

"I think I'll have an English muffin with
marmalade," I told the waiter.

"You're English!" marveled Guber. "I heard
so much about you from everyone in Califor-

nia! People I like, people I hate. I thought you'd be sixty years old and want to break my balls!"

"That comes later," I said. (What the fuck did he want?)

He moved swiftly to Puttnam. "That guy had a real dick problem, I tell you. Had to show it was bigger than Ray Stark's. Bigger than Ovitz's." He tucked into his fruit salad. "You should own your own magazine because you know how to create brands. But you know, when you go out on your own, it's sweet, because the guy you made all the money for, he's the guy who'll want to dance with you again."

Speeding back to the office with a Batman badge he gave me pinned to my lapel and still no idea what Guber had wanted to meet me about, I felt how lucky I am to be born in this era and working in New York City. Thirty years ago I would never have had this opportunity. I'd have probably, after Oxford, settled into being a nervy wife, writing stories in the Thames Valley instead of sitting in the Regency hotel over breakfast, hearing about the size of Hollywood's dick.

When I got back to the office, Janklow had left a message: "I've got breakfast with Si on Thursday. Leave it to me."

I had lunch in the Four Seasons with Diane von Furstenberg, who told me Barry Diller would love to give me Fox Studios to run. I had a brief surge of fascination when she said it, but had disqualified the notion by the time I was back in the car. I know nothing about that business and wouldn't survive six months. And after one week of not being the editor of *Vanity Fair* I'd be a nonperson. Reputations fade there with stellar speed. Take my new seer Peter Guber's comment about the director Alan Parker: "He said to me the other day after a row with somebody big, 'I'm finished in this town.' I said, 'Alan, to be finished you have to have been somebody first.'"

Wednesday, June 7, 1989

The difference in two days. Today's breakfast was with a Soviet journalist preparing "some explorations about the US media." I agreed to meet to get background for a Soviet Union piece and possibly help Gail Sheehy get access to Gorbachev. I wanted to say, "In Moscow, is everything about the size of your dick?"

It's now midnight and I am back from Alice Mason's dinner. I haven't been in nine months, but every so often I have to accept, just to take the pulse. It was the usual swirl of social mountaineers and fringe celebrities. The only interesting new face to me was Arthur Carter, owner of *The New York Observer,* whom I've read about and never met. He has rather scary, piercing black eyes in which you can see the whites all the way around, a sure index of megalomania. Unfortunately I wasn't next to him. Instead I was between the deadly bore John Weitz and some gnomish turnaround tycoon called Fred Adler. He painted such a picture of spiritual anesthesia that I asked him what he did care about.

"The smell of coffee in the morning," he said. "The taste of raspberries. Irish oatmeal. Walking in the rain. What the hell!"

"It's not a bad list," I said, warming to him somewhat.

"The brighter a person is," he continued, "the less he's satisfied. No one at this table has any satisfaction. They are all too bright."

I looked around the table where Alice Mason, Frances Lear, Carl Spielvogel, and Aileen Mehle were all taking bets on when Peter Kalikow would sell the New York Post. Being smart didn't seem to be what they had in common. Being rich did, except for Aileen, who so wants to be. Looking down at the sorbets on my zodiac plate, I felt the sterility of Adler's world. Sex provides the only edge when money is no longer a problem. Every time I looked up, Arthur Carter's black eyes burned a hole in my profile. "You are the bright shiny talent in this town," he told me after dessert. "And no one can touch you." I have started to feel a separation from these judgments and who I actually am. Tomorrow is Janklow's breakfast with Si. I have a sinking feeling it will not go well.

Thursday, June 8, 1989

I am reeling. Reeling.

At nine o'clock this morning my stock went into play and the price is careening up so fast that it's hard to think straight.

Mort met Si for breakfast at the Plaza Athénée hotel, where they often meet to discuss publishing matters. I, meanwhile, roamed up and down Madison Avenue under an umbrella, waiting for ten o'clock to go to Mort's office and hear the news.

Mort told me he pitched right in. Said how I had consulted him in some confusion about the offers, how he had gone to see Frank Bennack and "just listened." Apparently the moment he mentioned Bennack, Si looked stricken.

He told Mort he wanted to think about how he would respond. It didn't take long. Mort was back in his office ten minutes before I got there. "You'll have twenty messages from him when you get back," Mort said.

There was just one, "Mr. Newhouse called," and I found myself very keyed up when I went to his office. But the best decision I ever made was to ask Mort to help me. Why? Because when I walked into Si's office he was able to put on a mask of paternalism and sureness. Had I approached him directly, I would have seen the disarray of his reaction and it would have damaged his self-esteem to the point of lasting resentment. As it is, now he could be in control.

He wore a faux-jocular mien when he came around to my side of the desk. "Well, we have something to talk about!" he said. "I don't want to have to use Mort Janklow as a middleman."

"There was no other way I could bring this up," I said, resolving to stay very calm and remember how many editors he had unceremoniously bounced out the door when he tired of them.

"I've put some numbers down off the top of my head," he said. "But they are by no means set in granite." I did his conversation trick. I said nothing. He continued uneasily and set out a scheme that gave me another salary hike, not matching Bennack's, but he also said he would forgive his three-hundred-thousand-dollar loan for our apartment. Nice. What I really want is phantom stock in *VF* but still, this was a great gesture and I wanted immediately to say yes. But Mort had told me on no account to do that, so I still said nothing. Then I replied, "Thank you for that response, Si. I'm going to have to think about it." He gave another jocular smile but his eyes looked worried. "I want to make it clear that . . . I don't want you to leave. I hope you feel that working here has its advantages whether it's Camelot [as I once described it to him] or Krakatoa! And that Hearst may not have these same advantages."

"Well, you know, Si," I said. "The fact that Hearst is offering me a magazine title that is so ripe for revival is attractive. *Bazaar* is a sleeping beauty. I read the books about Alexey Brodovitch and Carmel Snow and realized here was a legend waiting to be revamped, and you know that's what I love to do."

"Yes," he croaked, jovial and ashen at the same time.

"And I feel," I went on merrily, "that in eighteen months I could take *Bazaar* from number four to number one, and that would give me the satisfaction that would compensate for the loss of the narrative journalism I love at *Vanity Fair.*"

"I don't doubt it," he said hoarsely.

"But I'll think about what you suggest," I said. And left his office, knowing he was catching the Concorde to London at lunchtime to cement the purchase of Century Hutchinson Publishers.

Within thirty minutes Alex was in my office.

"May I close the door?" he said conspiratorially. "My dear, I'm distraught. Si has just told me. I'm appalled by this. Appalled. You don't know how much you'd give up by going to a fashion magazine. It would trivialize you permanently. I have even suffered from it myself in my career. You can't leave the intelligence of this journalistic endeavor for the gross obsession of commerce." There was an edge of suspicion to Alex's look that made me sense his deepest fear beneath all this apparent concern. "I have been to Si and offered to step aside," he said. "My job is yours if you want it."

"Alex!" I said. "Please don't ever say that. This is not a power play. There is no such thing as 'your job.' There is you and when you choose to leave it, it will melt away. Si will just have strong editors and grow into running the show himself. But Alex, I have to think of me now. No one else is going to. I look around and see how editors end up at Condé Nast and it's not pretty." He winced.

"I have a great many family responsibilities. My father is not able to provide for their last years." I got emotional at this point, mentioning Mum and Dad. Doctors are such a disaster in Malaga. When their health fails they won't be able to stay for much longer. Their house in Salto de Agua will never sell for the kind of money they would need to buy a place in London. I'd love to be able to solve that problem.

"My dear!" he said, embracing me. "This is terrible. I had no idea you had such worries. Let me talk to Si and intervene!" (I didn't mention Si's proposed deal. Who knows what Alex himself is paid? And he's not called the Silver Fox for nothing. This could all have been about sussing out what I had been offered by Si to stay.) He left and I headed out to the Four Seasons to have lunch with Shirley Clurman. When I got there, Julian, the maître d', said, "Mr. Newhouse is trying to reach you. I'll bring a phone to the table. I gather he's at the airport."

"Let me take this at the desk," I said, as the other lunchers were casting me curious looks.

"Tina!" Si said as I huddled over the maître d's desk. "Alex told me all about your family problems. Let me assume those responsibilities. Let me take on the burden of helping with your parents' apartment and any medical expenses in the future." This was beyond belief. It was so personal, so kind, that it swept away all my efforts to keep seeing this move as a business opportunity. I thought of the joy and relief it would offer to Mum and Dad to be able not to worry anymore about money or medical crises, so they aren't just dependent on the NHS when they go back to live in England, as they eventually must.

I had never expected this and I doubt very much that Hearst, which is a trust, could ever do something this unusual for a person they care about, or rather I couldn't possibly ask it. Of course, with the way the magazine is growing, a piece of *Vanity Fair* would mean I could well afford to help my parents very handsomely without Si's moving gesture. Perhaps this was Alex and Si's ultimate brilliance, as the suggestion was so out of the box and appealed so much to my heart, it blew everything else out of consideration. On the way to Kennedy Airport Si must have sat there fully marinating what my departure to *HB* would mean to him, not just in losing me at *VF* but in gaining a horrible competitor for *Vogue.* I tried to stay calm.

"That's very, very kind, Si," I said. "And I appreciate it very much. I need to discuss this with Mort."

When I told Mort, he whistled and then laughed. "Now," he said. "Let me take care of the rest."

Friday, June 9, 1989

This morning Mort told me I should come over and see him.

As I hopped out of the town car to see "my lawyer," I felt the thrill of the big time. Mort had done some further negotiations with salary parity with Hearst and was poring over a pocket calculator. He told me Si had asked for a five-year contract but I should only do three. "If you let me loose in the marketplace, I could call Pete Peterson at Blackstone [the private equity group] and raise fifty million in ten minutes for a start-up. I'll get this

665

typed up and get it around to Si." I left Mort's office in an altered state. In the evening, with H still in California, I went to a movie with my dear Gary Bogard, who was in town. It had a symmetry. It's almost exactly ten years since he hired me to be editor of *Tatler* at twenty-five. And somehow, for old time's sake, it felt right to talk it all through with the man who started off my editing career. Gary was proud and full of admiration and not a bit wistful.

Si got off the Concorde at nine thirty a.m. By ten twenty he and Mort had talked. At ten thirty Mort called me and said, "It's a done deal. He also said you're eligible for a Condé Nast dress allowance. You're home, baby."

So this is the day I will never forget as long as I live, the day I made my quantum leap. The day I joined the boys club. Head spinning so much I haven't even called Mum and Dad yet to tell them their money worries are over.

I waited for the call from Si and when it came I went up and hugged him. I wanted this to be emotional, but in fact by this time I already felt something new — a more independent woman. A confidence that wasn't here before. Thanks to Mort, five years in I am now paid six hundred thousand a year on a three-year contract with a million-dollar bonus at the end, plus my parents taken care of and no debt on our apartment. It is better than my wildest dreams. It feels good that I got it through hard work, strong nerves, careful strategy, and an eye to the future. Those crazy dinner parties where the game of money and value is so vociferously discussed by the men turned out to be my listening tour of the way deals get done.

Si was affable. His self-possession recovered. He is smart enough to know he had made a good business decision himself. He hadn't just stopped me from leaving. He'd stopped me from revamping *Bazaar* and thereby damaging *Vogue.* Had I done that, it would have cost him a lot more, so it was worth it to Condé Nast. I am sure he discussed it with his shrewd brother.

"I'm sorry you had to be surprised by all this," I said. "I guess whenever you see Janklow, you know it's trouble."

"I rather like Mort," said Si indifferently. "You were right to go to him. It was the right thing to do."

I felt I have won more respect by pressing him to compete. No one but mega-Mort would have made him do it and still had us emerge on good terms. "The bad news is you've got ten pages fewer in your next issue," he said.

"Screw the next issue," I said.

"Is that the spirit of our new arrangement?" he said, with some amusement.

I didn't reach Frank Bennack till today in Lake Tahoe. I told him the truth, that it was mainly personal. The demands of Georgie, making another turnaround too disruptive to family life. I didn't feel I could tell him about Mum and Dad. He was disappointed, but very gracious as he always is. "I'll give you peace now," he said, "but not for long. I hope we can work together later on, Tina."

"Frank," I said. "So do I."

But I feel happy and calm. I know in my heart I belong with Condé Nast. Si annoys me, exasperates me, but he never bores me. When I came out of his office Alex rushed out of his.

"Darling!" he exclaimed. "Never lose you. Never."

So a new chapter begins. Harry came in from LA and we had a romantic dinner together in Quogue on the deck outside. He teased me about how he will now throw his cape in front of me to walk on like Sir Walter Raleigh with Elizabeth I. I told him I couldn't have achieved any of this without his belief in me. And it's true. We toasted our good fortune and went for a long, happy walk on the beach like we did the night before we got married.

I called Mum and Dad in Spain and told them they should stop worrying about what happens when they can't manage San Jorge anymore. Mum was jubilant and Dad was almost too moved to speak. I realized how much it's been worrying him. "I don't know what to say," he finally said. There was a tinge of ruefulness. Despite his relief, accepting this from his daughter is hard for his masculine pride. I stressed there was no need to move until they are ready. But the fact is, if this windfall hadn't happened, when their own money runs out in Spain they'd be on their way to a studio apartment in Hounslow. It's wonderful to be able to help get them something they deserve to live in when the time comes.

Sunday, July 2, 1989

Georgie today was so ineffably sweet, so delicious, I've loved him more than I can bear. Harry took him off for a walk on the beach on his shoulders, before bath splashing, high tea, and blissful bedtime with the sunset and the murmuring sea outside the window of his little room. Occasionally we could hear the distant bump of Pumpkin and Bagel, the two cats — who now come out with us every weekend — pursuing insects and imaginary creatures around the porch and colliding with the furniture.

I spoke to Mum and Dad in Spain, preparing to go over to London for a trip, and found to my consternation that Dad has had a dizzy spell and was told he needs a pacemaker. It's as if my psychic brain knew this was coming and propelled me into the Condé Nast mega-deal. I have gone from the euphoria of success to the sadness of times changing. I hope, I hope he gets some more years before the good times end.

On Monday I went to a memorial service for poor Jonathan Lieberson. He finally, at forty, lost his fight against AIDS. It's another tragic culling of a man so many thought was special. His memorial reflected it. In front of me was a freshly face-lifted Jackie O in a white schoolgirl shirt and black skirt, along with the Duchins, Brooke Astor, Richard Avedon, John Gregory Dunne and Joan Didion, Susan Sontag, the actor Peter Eyre, Diane von Furstenberg, etc. etc. And of course a stricken Bob Silvers of *The New York Review of Books,* who always saw Jonathan as his successor. It was Bob who choreographed the short tributes by the Nobel laureate Torsten Wiesel, Shelley Wanger, Elizabeth Hardwick, Jason Epstein, and Brooke Astor. As at all memorial services, the most interesting things were what was unsaid. How beneath the array of speakers' claims for his talents as philosopher, editor, and critic, "his essay on Wagner that could stand next to Shaw's," Jonathan was ultimately a thwarted soul, his verbal brilliance undermined by his incapacitating self-hatred that perhaps came from a distaste for his own homosexuality, which he always kept implacably hidden. It's tragic that he felt such shame. He never uttered the word "AIDS" to anyone, and the obituary said "cardiac arrest." In the end it's the bitterest irony that he had a slow, agonizing, and public death that finally proclaimed to everyone what he had kept hidden for so long.

All week I've woken up in the night, thinking with vague panic about Jonathan. Why, I'm not quite sure. He wasn't a special friend. Our relationship began horribly. I fired him and he was bitter about me in the drawing rooms in which I now thrive. But somehow despite all this rancor we came to like each other, or at least appreciate each other. I could see that his wit was pretty rare in the irony-free corporate world I have to spend too much time in, and, starved as I am of European magpie-ism, I was always entertained and refreshed by his eclectic range. And he came to respect *Vanity Fair*'s success if not me.

Brooke Astor was the best speaker because she didn't laud his braininess. Instead she remembered a day just before Christmas when he came to lunch and simply amused her and gave her "oh, the most wonderful gift, his company, for three solid hours." Standing behind the lectern in her ladylike hat and white gloves, the only one in such an outfit, enunciating clearly into the close summer afternoon, she brought such understanding and clarity to the meaning of social value. She lent an air almost of defiance, as if emphasizing that being an intellectual who wrote good book reviews was not the point of Jonathan at all. Because she was right, she was by far the most memorable.

Thursday, July 6, 1989
Quogue

I love how New York changes so completely in the summer. It's my favorite time of year here, sitting at my wooden desk before the open window with the cool sea breeze.

The August issue arrived by FedEx. The Jackie O cover story, and Michael Milken's rise and fall by Marie, is a much more commercial combo than July. To generate some summer heat I assigned Ed Klein to do Jackie to mark her sixtieth birthday. I asked him because he was always going on about how she liked him when he edited *The New York Times Magazine.* "What did she say when you called her?" I'd asked.

"She said, 'Oh, Ed, give me a break,' " he replied. Ed is so totally impervious to social temperature that he took that as his cue to barrel ahead. But then again that's probably his value. Jackie has every writer in such a stranglehold of sycophancy and terror, it takes a journalistic Clouseau like Ed Klein to get a cover story that everyone nonetheless will want to read at the beach. Just before we were going to press I glimpsed the *Life* August issue and was dismayed to see they had a very similar cover image of Jackie and it was too late to change ours. But not too late to change our cover line. Originally we wrote, "The Other Jackie O," which was such a lazy, predictable effort I don't know how it survived our critical disgust. The tension of necessity can often produce more creative solutions. In a surge of irritation with all the Jackie hagiography, I changed it to "Jackie, Yo! You're rich, you're gorgeous, and along comes Maurice!" (Tempelsman, her boyfriend.) It leapt out of the FedEx bag with good attitude.

Monday, July 10, 1989
NYC

Shoumatoff's piece on the end of Stroessner in Paraguay, "The Fall of the Tyrannosaur," is A-plus, an incredible lead for the all-important September issue we are working on now. It's amazing how little America cares about what happens in this region. Harry says James Reston once commented that people will do anything for Latin America except read about it. And yet the stories are numerous, rich, and crazy. Stroessner had Paraguay in his grip for thirty-four years but no one paid much attention to the fact that his paranoid witch hunts of "communists" gave Paraguay the highest number of unsentenced prisoners in the Western hemisphere, many of them subject to terrifyingly inventive torture. Shoumatoff has collected such chilling stuff, getting into the walled Arabian palaces of Asunción's elite and the expat Nazi communities in Nuevo Germania. It's full of sinister echoes. He calls Paraguay "the most refined culture of deceit on the planet except possibly Hollywood."

I was up till four in the morning on Sunday rewriting Kevin Sessums's story on the Rolling Stones wives for the same issue. It had to be as good in its way as Shoumatoff is on the fall of Stroessner. Unless low is as strong as high in *VF,* we blow the intelligence pact with readers. The Stones piece was my brainchild, all because of a cover line that hit me in the bath: "The Women Who Still Sleep with the Rolling Stones" (it's the "Still" that makes it great), and then I had to assign a story to match it. I loved the idea of revisiting the old rock-and-roll chicks who have stuck around, with Annie's wonderful pictures.

The computer and fax machine in my study were humming all weekend.

In the middle of it all, Georgie, being spookily sensitive to atmosphere in the house, sensed I'd shut him out to work and kept waking up every ten minutes and screaming. In the end I had to lay him on the floor next to my desk where he could watch me working, no doubt a resentful memory he will harbor long into adolescence.

Tuesday, July 25, 1989

On our way back from London to New York after a troubled week. Dad had another vertigo spell and was told he had to have a pacemaker op immediately. He had it done on Wednesday and went back yesterday — his birthday — to have his stitches out. While he was out, Mum got a call from Dr. Stuttaford about another test. A urine sample for his prostate check. To our chagrin Stuttaford told us the change in his enzyme in the blood indicated "further prostatic activity," meaning there is very likely a malignancy. Poor dear Dad, after thinking he was over his ordeal and feeling so excited about the new freedom from money worries, now finds everything cloudy and frightening. It was an awful seventy-sixth birthday. He, of course, was brave and jovial as he could be.

"Unsettling" is the word for the whole trip. The best part of the seventieth birthday party for Frank Giles, Harry's deputy at *The Times,* was talking to the historian Asa Briggs about Richard Nixon. "I think he will be like Richard III," said Briggs. "Nixon will have his demonology. But also his admirers in every century." As Harry works on the weekends on his new book of political history, *The American Century,* and as books get written about his years at *The Times,* I have come to realize that history is only point-of-view journalism about dead people. There is no objective truth about anything. This is what Nixon meant when Henry Kissinger in *White House Years* says, "History will treat you differently, Mr. President." And Nixon replies, "It depends who writes it."

I brought Miles with me as an excuse to give him a trip to London for a vacation. I am very worried about him. He's had sudden inexplicable rashes all over, which alarm me. In the middle of Nicholas Coleridge's wedding he broke it to me that he wants to leave *VF* and return to London. This news would make my heart stop except I am so worried about him. I think he should leave New York. There is no future for him alone in a burnout environment, going to funerals every week. It's perilous for his health and I will do everything I can to help him move.

Felt blue on return to Quogue. G was very contrary all afternoon as I dutifully accompanied him with H to feed the ducks, go to the playground, etc. Felt the burden of relentless good mummy–dom and ached to be reading my Doctorow novel.

Wednesday, July 26, 1989

On my way to work when Wayne called to
say that Steve Rubell had died the night
before. Died! I felt so stricken. All my memories of planning *VF*'s fifth anniversary with
him flooded back. The last time I saw him at
the now gloriously revamped Royalton I was
struck by how tiny and thin he looked. And a
year ago, at Reinaldo's birthday party, I
thought his arms looked like breadsticks,
ready to snap. I guessed at imminent AIDS
but thought somehow he'd be with us for a
few more years, like Jonathan.

But it seems Steve was much sicker than
any of us knew. And in his obituary, sadly, as
with Jonathan, no one is saying the word
"AIDS." Barry Diller told me that Calvin
Klein's grief for Rubell was exacerbated by
the fact that they hadn't spoken in a year,
Calvin wanting to distance himself from
Steve's night-owl allure. And who can blame
him. AIDS has made Steve's kind of carousing a life, not a lifestyle, choice.

It was a packed and very Jewish funeral a
few days later at Riverside Memorial. Unbearable to think of Steve's speedy little body
subdued forever in that oak box. In the hall
outside, a pale Ian Schrager, in his yarmulke,
moved among the mourners with the same
purposeful management as when policing the
throngs outside Studio 54. Calvin looked

distraught. David Geffen was unrecognizably straight in an Armani suit, Diller in black with white shoes and a cane, implacably tough, his face betraying tragic lines but his stance daring anyone to make him a member of a slowly decimating circle.

I wish Reinaldo hadn't worn a yarmulke. With his dark glasses it made him look like a hit man for a Colombian drug cartel. Bianca Jagger, she who had once ridden into Studio 54 astride a white horse in the glory days of 1977, looked for the first time old, while in his distress, Jann Wenner, whose *Rolling Stone* was so much a part of that era, looked very young. The funeral was Steve's last party. You could almost imagine him urging us from the coffin to heat up the action. Robert Isabell looked the most traumatized. He was puffy-faced with despair.

The most moving speaker was Steve's nephew, who remembered Steve last summer downing Cokes and playing Madonna's "True Blue" over and over again. It was the funeral of the private Steve, the striving guy from Brooklyn whose father was a postal worker, and who worked his way up from owning steak houses in Queens, the man none of the celebrities ever knew. No boldface names got up. Perhaps Ian just felt this was one happening that didn't need the publicity value, one where the real Steve could at last admit who he really was.

I've lost my voice from screaming over the band at Saul Steinberg's fiftieth birthday party last night for 250 heavy hitters at the beach. Well. Gayfryd certainly decided to put Quogue on the map. When I heard Robert Isabell was doing the tent like a seventeenth-century living room, I expected extravagance, but nothing like this. Fifty peons had worked for three weeks on what the architect Charles Gwathmey told me was a feat much more difficult than simply building a room. Extending the entire length and breadth of the tennis court, the tent was a baronial seventeenth-century Flemish eating and drinking house to the last detail. You approached from the road on a long, carpeted corridor flanked by a million votive candles in terra cotta pots, a marine corps of valet parkers stationed outside. On the walls of the tent hung replicas of Saul's old masters in real frames. From the ceiling shone an enormous brass chandelier with a star-emblazoned ball matched by the star in the middle of the black-and-white checkerboard dance floor. Alcoves along the sides featured actors hired for the night posing in tableaux vivants of famous paintings by Rembrandt and Vermeer, including a real nude from Rembrandt's masterpiece *Danaë*. Tapestry tablecloths, Rembrandt tile place mats, "oak" beamed ceilings, antique china. Out by the pool it was Gatsby time. Identical twins posed as mermaids. It was the Park Avenue answer to Charles de Beistegui's Venetian costume parties in the fifties and confirmed that Robert Isabell is a kind of genius (or perhaps that Gayfryd is a kind of lunatic).

Watching her flit and flash about the dance floor, wearing a huge movie-star diamond and sapphire bracelet and a strapless, cobalt-blue gown that skinny-fitted her like steel piping — appropriately, perhaps, since in her past marriage she was the owner of a steel-pipe company — I realized that Gayfryd has the generalship of a social Napoleon. She should be running IBM, not birthday parties. Saul toasted her with "This may be a bit of history. Honey, if this moment were a stock I'd short it."

As always a ton of dull Steinberg relatives mixed in with the big players. "I feel icky in this blue suit," Ron Perelman hissed at Claudia as a white-suited Mort Janklow and a white-panted Steve Ross, the entertainment mogul cruised by. "Honey, you look just great. There are lots of blue suits here," said his wife. "I said I feel icky," he hit back. It's a serious business marrying megabucks like Ron — the obeisance, the grooming, the tireless upkeep of the spouse's ego. Watch the Texan commerce secretary's wife, Georgette

Mosbacher, and Gayfryd fall on their husbands with compliments after they've made
their toasts and you see the twenty-four-hour
vigilance required, the unflagging stroking.

I was seated between the decorator Mark
Hampton and Saul's brother, Bob, a less
charismatic version of himself. "What happens to this tent tomorrow?" I asked.

"The A-list party," he replied.

Gayfryd seated herself between Robert
Mosbacher, in recognition no doubt of the
social rise of Georgette in DC, and J. Carter
Burden, plus the Henry Kravises. This is the
fourth time, I note, that she has chosen handsome, WASPy Carter to sit next to . . . He is
certainly the antithesis of Saul.

"My brother is brilliant, he's innovative.
He's full of shit," said Bob Steinberg as first
Saul, then Gayfryd, then Laura Tisch, then
Vartan Gregorian, then Robert Mosbacher
made their elaborate toasts to the munifi-
cence of Saul.

In my ear the decorator Mark Hampton
said, "Most extravagance is obnoxious because it's devoid of humor, but this is really
very amusing!" Since Gayfryd herself is un-
susceptible to humor, the touches of whimsy
must be Robert Isabell's knowing eye.

"Well!" said Gayfryd when she got up to
make the toast, not a glint of sweat on her
shiny shoulders. "What do you all think?"

This was a glimpse of the unfinished learning curve — seeking guest feedback in the moment from the women who compete with her — and I couldn't help liking her the more for it. Saul's daughter Laura Tisch's speech thanked her for uniting the children of Saul's three marriages. The muscles in Gayfryd's back rippled almost imperceptibly in satisfaction. Smart trophy wives don't fight with the kids. They unite, the better to forestall later arguments about the will. As Mort Janklow put it, as we tried an aerobic fox-trot to a series of sixties numbers that were clearly Saul's golden hits, "Gayfryd understands the big picture."

Does she? Or is it tempting fate to do something this extravagant now? I suspect the ghost of Michael Milken and the fall of Drexel may have been on the minds of many guests as they quaffed the vintage vino. It certainly was on mine. "Milken is the Dr. Strangelove of Wall Street," Hampton said. "Why did we strive to admire him so? Shudder. Shudder. Shudder."

But decorators such as Mark and everyone in that tent were happy to feast at the boom trough.

Wednesday, August 9, 1989

I'm pregnant!

Two weeks late, with a bout of laryngitis, I told the doctor before he gave me antibiotics that perhaps we should do the test. Subliminally, I suppose, the feeling had been growing, the feeling of bloatedness and breast tinglings. I called Harry with the news and he sounded as stunned about it as I feel. But I am so happy, grateful to God for blessing me again just when I had started to long for it. Have been feeling a pang every time I see G alone at the window. Now he'll get a brother or sister and I am walking on air! It's been hard to concentrate with my expanding secret.

The Styron piece about his depression is in, and it's magnificent. He talks about how his lifelong battle with the disease became so agonizing that suicide became seductive. Even though there has been so much written on depression, no one with his kind of profile has written so candidly about what it's like to live with the real pain and darkness of something, light-years away from just "the blues." We are running the piece at twenty thousand words with a powerful headline I stole from Milton in *Paradise Lost:*

No light, but rather darkness visible
Served only to discover sights of woe,
Regions of sorrow, doleful shades, where
   peace
And rest can never dwell, hope never
   comes
That comes to all.

Darkness visible. That seems to describe Styron's pain so well. Strange how poetry hangs around in the mind so long.

Thursday, August 10, 1989

Was invited out by Aline, Countess of Romanones, who has finished her next memoir, *The Spy Went Dancing,* another romanticized account of her life in the OSS. Since Luis died she has dropped twenty years, with an incredible face-lift that has given her back the oval-shaped face of her youth, set off by a cracking-great sapphire and diamond necklace. A cobalt-blue (clearly this season's color) culotte suit clung to her iron-pumped form.

The evening was what Nancy Mitford used to call "dinner for the dug-ups," an uneasy mix of return social matches with many hidden mines — Harold Brodkey, whose last novel Jim Wolcott brilliantly took apart in *VF* last year; Lynn Nesbit, whom Brodkey had just acrimoniously left for Andrew Wylie, the literary agent stealing everyone's clients; Marife Hernandez, the Puerto Rican socialite on the board of every museum, whom Michael Shnayerson assassinated in *VF* three Christmas issues ago; John Shad, the new head of Drexel who pretended not to have read Marie Brenner's talked-about-everywhere piece on Milken; and, thank God,

Reinaldo to oil the wheels. Far from harboring grudges, Brodkey spent the whole evening romancing me about *VF*. "The voice of Anglo-Saxon intelligence," he gushed. "You are the only editor not afraid of it. No magazine has ever had this influence before."

"What about Harold Hayes's *Esquire*?" I said suspiciously.

"It was never influential," said Brodkey, which is so untrue. And what about Felker and Wenner? What about William Shawn, for whom he wrote at *The New Yorker* for so many years? Brodkey is so full of shit, but the question is, why?

Friday, August 18, 1989

What a terrible week. I miscarried. On Monday night I started to have cramps and bleed. All through Tuesday the bleeding continued. I went for a blood test and an ultrasound. Looking at the screen, the technician said, "This doesn't look right at all." Dr. Thornton told me on Wednesday that the blood test figures were flat and she would end the pregnancy. Yesterday I went into New York Presbyterian for a D&C and woke up in the ghostly cold recovery room feeling as if I had awoken in a mortuary, which in a way I had. How do some women cavalierly have abortions? I feel so distressed and knocked over. Harry is devastated and keeps saying he didn't protect me enough, which isn't true.

I can't believe this has happened. Except to view it as divine retribution for the sin of thinking I am in control. I thought I had it taped — the new Condé Nast money, looking after the family, the new phase of job security, and then I would "allow" myself a baby. Not happening. I should not imagine I can play God in this way.

It has left me feeling strangely dead and precarious. Now I have to add miscarriage as well as premature birth to my anxieties about a second pregnancy. I feel terribly bereft.

Saturday, August 26, 1989

Gray fingers of anxiety. Worried about G. He has been so difficult, going into what I think of as his Rain Man mode, getting stuck on one activity, in this case building "dark tunnels" (what awful Freudian terror does this signify?) and refusing to be deflected. Took him to an optometrist at the suggestion of his UN preschool, where they say he has difficulty with visual tasks. Doc said his cognitive functioning is erratic, able to duplicate a block design — a square with a triangle on top — but unable to do it diagonally. He has difficulty keeping balance and manipulating a pencil. Said his gross, fine, and graph motor function need further training, so we will step up the physical therapy. He is much calmer in Quogue. I know we should spirit him away out of the stress of New York City.

The fax machine keeps remorselessly chugging and spitting out bits of office data. I feel trapped. It's funny how our new freedom from money concerns is quickly replaced by other anxieties. Now all I think about is the health of family and friends. I suppose I am crazy to want another child, but I feel such a chasm where the second one should be.

Tuesday, September 26, 1989

I hardly know how to describe this last month. It's been a tunnel of blood, the crazy collision of planets. Dad went to London for a bone-cancer scan and was told it was positive until a second trip three weeks later registered it was negative and he was reprieved. Then, weirdly, uncannily, on his way back from his pacemaker checkup, he had a stroke! For three days when his condition didn't stabilize, it really looked as if he might die. I found myself starting to lose control. As I left on the plane to London, G developed a raging fever that I learned when I landed had turned out to be pneumonia. Mum has had an agonizing time shuttling between hotels and Chris and Diana's basement. I felt my prime role was to keep her spirits up. Dad was so happy to see me, though he looked so pale and reduced in the hospital bed. Hard to see him like this instead of how I always think of him, so big and ebullient with his huge laugh.

Miraculously he quickly plateaued and has suffered only slight damage to his left leg and arm, which are already improving with physical therapy. The voice therapist came this morning to work on his slightly slurry speech. "Now, Mr. Brown. Let's have a little bit of Gilbert and Sullivan, shall we?"

"I am the very model of . . . a model — major general," my dear dad said heavily, and I thought of his vaudeville mother, who sang Gilbert and Sullivan to him in the costume hamper, where he slept as she went onstage, and the Kipling man he always wanted to be. It seemed so poignantly right for the epitaph on his life. He was the very model till his health and the career he loved gave out. I told the nurses, to show them he wasn't always like this, about his great producing days, his derring-do war years filming the action in the Western Desert for the Air Ministry and stealing away the Krupp archives in Essen before the Allies got there, how he was married first to Maureen O'Hara, eloping with her when she was only seventeen. They were fascinated by all this dashing stuff and I could see that growing in their estimation made him feel better. I cried a lot of tears on the plane home.

The best thing in all this was being able to

spend time alone with Mum for the first time in so long. After visiting Dad we would adjourn to a café in St. John's Wood and gorge on croissants. She is still so funny and wonderful, telling me about their comical ex-pat community in Spain and their new social life full of retired tycoons with Swedish models and "the adorable train robbers who live up the hill." She and Dad haven't stopped giving their colorful parties. She knows they can't continue to live in Spain much longer. She will find that crushing.

Saturday, September 30, 1989

All this distraction hasn't helped the mag. For the important November issue we had a great Baryshnikov cover story by Stephen Schiff only to find again (is there an office mole?) that *Life* has one, too. Then, just as I was trying to figure out how to make ours different, we find Misha has now quit the American Ballet Theatre after a huge row and said fuck you to the fiftieth anniversary gala, which *VF* is, by the way, cosponsoring, and which is a huge ballet-world story not cap-tured in Schiff's piece. Six hours to go before press so I raced into the office to strip in new copy. Labored with Sharon and Stephen on inserts that covered the political row at ABT and choose different pics with Charles and wrote new captions and blurbs that sounded like we had the red-hot dope we didn't. Damn damn damnsky all aroundsky.

One of my fave quotes from Misha defending himself for doing Amex ads and his own perfume lines is, "What is life if you can't be cheap and vulgar sometimes? It makes you better appreciate the good things. Sometimes I do cheap things and why not? I don't give a shit." Misha understands high-low entirely. I should be as defiant as he when I get the dreary old rap about what *VF* should and shouldn't do (currently being killed for running the pics of the "vulgar" Steinberg party). As a woman, however, I could never get away with a quote like that.

In the middle of all this a blast from the past showed up, Stephen Glover, my old Oxford flame, who's launching with others a new English daily paper called, damn it, *The Independent.* So jealous! He always had such a dreamy, poetic air when we were students, this dynamism surprised me.

Friday, October 6, 1989

Have decided to give this year's Hall of Fame a theme. The Media Decade. There have been twenty-five hundred new magazines in the eighties. Within the media *Spy* is making the most impact because the media is what it's all about. It flatters media people by bothering to take them down. It treats ink-stained wretches like movie stars or politicians or business moguls, important enough to be mercilessly ridiculed. It's not as funny as *Private Eye* in its heyday, but its relentless branding of foibles, e.g., Trump as a "short-fingered vulgarian" are pretty inspired.

The explosion of media in the last ten years is not just about volume. Media is invading media. With the Time Warner merger we've got Batman scaling the walls of Time Inc. Art romping with commerce — Joan Didion posing for a Gap ad, CEOs becoming performers and performers becoming CEOs. It's not enough anymore to be Oprah Winfrey. You have to be Oprah Winfrey, president of Harpo Productions and Harpo Studios.

The image makers are now as important as the stars themselves, and certainly more interesting. Maybe because their power is our need. The more fragmented we become as a culture, the more the media holds us together. Americans have less and less in common as a people, but we all watch the same TV shows and the same movies.

We've picked the biggest media influencers for the Annie portraits, some obvious, some not so. There's Steve Ross and Mike Ovitz and Ted Turner and Diane Sawyer, but also some less expected such as the huge pear-shaped political manipulator Roger Ailes, the trashy biographer Kitty Kelley, photographed by Annie with lookalikes of Liz Taylor, Frank

Sinatra, etc. — all the celebrities she's dished on (a megaproduction that took a week). She's done *W*'s John Fairchild at a fashion show, quizzically gazing out between the striding couture legs and stilettos of a runway model, Spielberg asleep on a child's bed full of toys, Andy Warhol's headstone in Pittsburgh (RIP media decade). Even persuaded Murdoch to pose. Why not? He may be a shit but he belongs there. I'm giving this a massive forty-page run, Annie's biggest extravaganza yet. It's pretty glorious and has taken three months to complete.

And what for the cover? Seemed only one possibility. We took it to the last minute of deadline but Jane and I were determined to reel it in. Michael Jackson, midmoonwalk on his toes, legs bent, white Errol Flynn shirt billowing behind him. Locks flowing. Such a Thriller, an Annie pièce de résistance.

Wolcott came in, back from travels, plus Schiff, Miles, and Kornbluth, and we stayed late writing the twenty Hall of Fame two-hundred-word blurbs. Took us all day and late into the evening, with many empty Coke cans, but it turned out well.

Loved Wolcott's caption for the MTV girls of Robert Palmer's rock videos, who looked just like the *VF* anniversary saxophone band. "It began as radio for the eyeballs and soon became the postmodern trash-masher."

All through the session Charles Churchward kept barging into my office with a flushed face, carrying the unwieldy layout board and shouting, "The color has to go out NOW. If we don't do it now there will be NO RETOUCHING. We need to clean up Kim Basinger's TEETH. The hair on her top lip has to GO!"

Nights like these at the mag make it all worthwhile.

I realized tonight as I hung around, waiting for my car in the crisp fall air, that these are the memories we will cherish, our own convivial version of the Algonquin Round Table. On my way out I picked up a copy of the snappy new mag *7 Days,* edited by Adam Moss. It's so good. It has a big feature on Wolcott as a terror and a tastemaker on a level with Mencken and Mailer. We're very lucky to have Jim with us and feel good that in *VF* he's becoming more and more of a star. The roster of talents takes so much nurturing and protecting and shaping, but I know that task is my most important priority as an editor, bar none.

Saturday, October 28, 1989
Bonaventure Resort and Spa, Florida

Escaped here with G because the Holiday Issue close was such a BRUTE. The Hall of Fame so late to go to press that even Pam McCarthy was on the verge of quitting. We figured out the portfolio took fifteen hundred rolls of film, forty-one thousand miles of air travel, and the photo of Malcolm Forbes posing with twelve working paparazzi took 250 calls to set up. Obeisance to Jane Sarkin. I took her out to lunch.

Now that Miles is about to leave for England he is in a vile mood. "New York's loss is London's loss," commented Jesse Kornbluth after yet another Miles tantrum. The close was so late I even missed the end-of-the-year sales conference in Nantucket. (Silly sodding place to have it, and reports of the tiny bouncing plane made me very happy I wasn't there.) Instead I did a video like the Queen's speech at Christmas to register my cheerleading from the office. Then I had to leave for Naples for the annual ASME magazine conference, where I was doing a panel on celebrity covers.

I was so beat by the closing of the December issue that I was really lame on the panel. Plus I put on five pounds in two weeks from eating chocolate, thanks to the stress of late-night calls to harangue writers, trying to whip up a journalistic January cover story since all the celebrities that month are duds. The good thing to hang on to is that the sales figures of the mag are so great. That September issue — with the Rolling Stones women, Stroessner, and the Goldie Hawn in cobalt-blue minidress with feathers cover — sold 312,948 copies on the newsstand, which is so prodigious and a record to date. Winning is an addiction.

When I got back I breakfasted with Dr. Mitch Rosenthal, the founder of Phoenix House drug rehab center, which has been abandoned by Nancy Reagan in their fundraising drive. So much for her Just Say No campaign. Now that she's out of office, it's Just Say Whatever. I am trying to decide whether to step in there and help him raise the money. Want him to show me the PH facility and the work they are doing with kids. He's almost too good-looking to be credible. What's the flaw? Is he a Dr. Lydgate figure who succumbs to society or is he the real thing?

Monday, October 30, 1989

Received such a tortured letter from Auberon Waugh, who hasn't written in two years. Three pages on both sides of *Literary Review* writing paper from his spidery pen. Much of it spent telling me why he has never come to New York to see me because he so hates everything about it and Americans in general. "Where you see zippy, zesty lesbian Jewesses bubbling with new ideas, I see plodding, ill-mannered, bottomlessly earnest boobies." Jesus. Bron has become so archaic in social attitude, he's turning into Evelyn.

He is upset by the *VF* success that he feels has driven us apart. And reading this letter upset me, too. "When I think of you, which I do quite often," he writes, "I do not scowl or sneer. It is brilliant of you to have conquered New York and I am terrifically proud. Your hair was extremely poignant when I last saw you because you were wearing it very short, almost en brosse, and when I left you outside that ghastly American hotel we had lunch in I ran my hand through it and felt an unbearable pang which is with me now, although the Duchess of York is expecting her second baby since that event and we have not seen each other since." A bitter serenade to return to England with asides that told me how bored I would be if I did. It was so raw it made me want to jump on a plane and let him cry in my arms in Bertorelli's, en brosse hair or not.

Sunday, November 5, 1989

Actually, Bron's letter unsettled me. I am split in two trying to be Mother of the Year as well as an editor! The weekend was hard, with G being very difficult and Harry chained to his computer as bloody always, writing his *American Century* book. Two workaholics don't make a rightaholic, particularly when it comes to raising kids. I long to read a book, write, get drunk (if only I could drink!), do anything other than live in this work-dominated monotone we have inflicted on each other. Mum and Dad marvel at how boring our lives are. Nothing like their marriage, where they always had their special hour of a gin and tonic together and their glamorous trips together to film festivals in Venice and Argentina. G never seems to go to bed till ten forty-five, leaving me with no evening. Tonight I got in to a sleeping G and H working and thought maybe, maybe! I could write this diary, play some music, allow myself to dream of another life of wanderlust and hedonism, but then G woke up and I had to spend an hour getting him back to sleep. I felt like throwing myself out the window. I just need three months of freedom, then I swear I will return to the goody-goody track of purposeful achievement and maternal quality time. Fuck.

Friday, November 10, 1989

History is made! Was working at home and had CNN on in the background all day, as the world was being turned on its head right before our eyes. Last night, amid the unrest in East Germany, some Communist Party spokesman was giving a completely boring press conference, and a journalist asked him when the new law allowing more freedom of travel from East to West would go into effect,

697

and the spokesman said, more or less, "Immediately, I guess." And suddenly all of East Berlin was flowing toward the wall. The guards didn't know what was going on and held them off for three hours, while traffic jammed the street and crowds got angrier and angrier. And then the guards relented, and suddenly the gates were being opened. People flowed through them all night, and all day today, and now it's night again in Berlin and people are standing on the wall, singing and dancing in front of it, pulling East Germans up to freedom on top of it, the Brandenburg Gate brooding in the background. Young people with hammers and chisels have been pounding at the cement, and there are throngs of deliriously happy people moving through the night, waving, shaking banners, singing, weeping, tearing up their passports, embracing strangers, dancing in conga lines — all while the Stasi, killers to a man, watch placidly, their stony faces masking what must be complete confusion and astonishment. On NBC, Tom Brokaw has been fronting an incredible scene. The West German police are actually trying to protect the wall so that the East German police can dismantle it peacefully, one slab at a time. NBC calls it Freedom Night. It all seems surreal, unbelievable. Brokaw is saying it's like New Year's Eve, only better because that holiday hasn't been celebrated there for so many years. "It's as if all the energy put toward isolation now is being spent on joy and a new beginning." Does this mean the end of the Cold War? I feel breathless at the pace all this has happened.

Monday, November 13, 1989

The December issue arrived and it's truly beautiful. The Media Decade Hall of Fame is wonderful — every bit as spectacular and funny as we hoped. The extra forty pages I stole from the page count of the next four issues was worth it, though I know I will be bleating at paying off the page debt next year. The Styron piece is still getting an enormous reaction. We have been flooded with letters from readers sharing their own experiences and telling us they no longer feel ashamed of suffering from depression. Makes us all proud. I will publish them.

Barry Diller took me to lunch and suggested I make movies as well as edit *Vanity Fair*. I fail to see how I could be a serious editor and do both. The writers need my attention and when I do other stuff they all get restive. Plus I am sure Si wouldn't allow it, and shouldn't, the amount he's paying. In the boardroom chill of the Four Seasons it briefly seemed possible. Probably because Barry is so persuasive that he makes everything sound easy. We have a great chemistry.

He makes me feel very much myself and I make him laugh and vice versa. There is a well-disguised insecurity beneath his tough persona I find endearing. He wants to seem in charge all the time. When we waited too long to order, it was "Julian, are we here for the day!"

We spent the whole of the first course discussing the latest Ovitz fracas in Hollywood. (Ovitz reportedly threatening to ruin the career of Joe Eszterhas, a screenwriter who wanted to leave CAA. Eszterhas then wrote a letter to Ovitz, recapping all his threats, and then faxed copies to everyone who mattered in Hollywood.) "Is he damaged by this?" ruminated Barry, a keen student of rises and falls. "All I know is that right now a big window has opened at CAA and I've told all my people at Fox to dive right into it. Once someone cracks open that little game, the power's lost."

"Is Ovitz upset?" I said.

"He has to be," said Barry. "Last week I was in my office at seven thirty in the morning and there was a message that Ovitz had called me at seven. I called him back and he didn't say anything. I said, 'Michael, did you call?' There was a little pause. And he said, 'Barry, this is the worst thing that's ever happened to me.' And I said, 'Michael, what can I tell you? The dogs bark and the caravan moves on.' "

Si, meanwhile, tossed out another trusted executive this week — Bob Bernstein, the president of Random House. Twenty-two years of honorable service. And much admired for his campaigns over the years for human rights. Slice. Off with his head. For a week it looked like another Grace Mirabella horror show, except Si then redeemed his gracelessness a bit by putting in the well-regarded Alberto Vitale, the much more commercial strongman CEO of Bantam Doubleday Dell, whom I think he met first at my dinner party for Ed Victor.

Si does seem, alas, to get a kick out of the brutal unceremoniousness of these topplings. After my print-order meeting for *VF* he called me in and said, "Well? Well?" eagerly. "What's everyone saying about Bob?" Perhaps it makes him feel part of the action from which his wealth really excludes him. Or is it the one way he can truly be seen to exercise power, since, as he once said to me, he feels he doesn't really have any? Each firing seems to lead to another, like a serial killing. The truth is, in the five years I have worked for him his style has gone from Caesar Augustus to Caligula.

Friday, November 17, 1989

In the midst of life we are in death. Last week I was having lunch at the Royalton with

Howard Kaminsky when a phone call came from the office to say Henry Porter had called from London with the news that David Blundy had been shot covering the rebel uprising in El Salvador for *The Sunday Correspondent.* His heart stopped twice on the operating table, but there was hope he would make it. The next call said he was dead.

Blundy! Not you, too! Why is it always the vivid, brave people who seem to be dying before their time! I can see him so clearly in the old *Sunday Times* days, his chaotic, long-limbed body, his self-parodic, emphatic way of talking, the quivering tip of his ceaseless cigarettes. His teasing bright blue eyes. I think of him sitting on the edge of my Murphy bed in Gloucester Terrace in that tiny studio, pulling on his jeans, smoking, laughing helplessly as I mimicked a North London feminist, whining, "Dave, Dave, I'm a person first and a woman second." He was a foreign correspondent of the legendary school. When I was younger I didn't understand how good he was or his obsession with "boring" places like Belfast. It's only since I have evolved as an editor, handling more and more reported pieces at *VF,* that I see how his values were the true ones, his obsession to get it right and tell it with clarity, precision, and detail. No amount of style is better than the heart of a story plucked out and dispatched with deadly aim. He died because he went out of his hotel room, as always, to get one last fact before he filed. He was hit by a sniper's bullet.

We never talked about the fashionable success of *The Sunday Independent,* but I bet he found it too writerly. I know he longed for Harry's kind of newspaper that would expose the truth with a cool eye and a passionate heart. Now he's on his way home from El Salvador in a box. What possible way to remember him except with a newspaper that honors his reporting values? Harry is so devastated.

RIP beloved Blundy. That sarcastic laugh. Those sentences. I weep.

Sunday, November 19, 1989

What a funny and enjoyable week. I cohosted a dinner with Anna Wintour for Nigel Dempster. Doing this with her made me understand and like her better. She is all business, clip clip clip. She does her side of things very well and efficiently. Progressing things immediately without second thoughts or self-doubt. We had breakfast two days running at the Royalton with Gabé, who had done a very good rough draft of the eighty place-cards to show us. On the last day I suggested to Anna we do a final revision in the lunch hour.

"I'm going to the hairdresser," she said.

"So am I," I said.

"Which one?"

"Louis Licari."

"So am I!"

So the final seating meeting took place as the tinfoil was folded into our highlights in the teeming beauty scene at Madison and Sixty-Fifth. It was perfect power-woman time economy. The salon was full of our guest list, all the alpha ladies being frothed and crimped and coiffed as they marked up manuscripts, rearranged dinner lists, or muttered into their little tape recorders for their secretaries to type up. Licari, with his pale face and intense stare, was a focused machine, moving at warp speed among all the tinfoil heads with masterly comb and scissors. Anna was having her bob minked. I was having my streaks bleached. When I left she was furiously scribbling notes for her toast to Nigel, with long, thin legs stretched out for a pedicure. As I raced out of the salon with my new frosted locks I collided with a glut of crew members, trailers, and Winnebagos setting up the next shots for Woody Allen's new movie.

The dinner for Nigel at 150 Wooster in Soho, Brian McNally's new hot spot, was funny for quite other reasons. I love Brian. He always forgets to make money with his restaurants because he loves talking to the customers. He's such a philosopher and brain box, much more interested in books than gnocchi. The dinner was a very hot ticket.

Ten tables of media heavies and Brit luminaries. What we hadn't bargained for was Nigel's speech, a wild bad-taste salvo about Christina Onassis. Nothing showed more the sensibility gap between London and New York. I am so used to the difference now, I have learned to recalibrate. America is less barbed, more bland, more decorous, completely unused to such asides from Nigel as "Stand up, Luis Basualdo! The only man who didn't sleep with Christina for her money!" with Luis shouting back, "I'll sue you, you fool." Out of the corner of my eye I saw *New York* mag's Julie Baumgold's appalled expression, and sneaking my chair around I saw the ramrod back of Anne Bass, and the dark brows of Diane von Furstenberg, who was probably a friend of Onassis.

It was like a Charles Addams cartoon, the pockets of laughter in the room coming only from the Brits — Brian McNally, Chris Hitchens, Anthony Haden-Guest, Gully Wells, David Shaffer, Sarah Giles, Anna, John Heilpern, and Miles — against the utter silence and scowls of everybody else. Suddenly there was a snort and the painter Jennifer Bartlett shot out of the restaurant in disgust. After Nigel finished there was a long pause and then a buzz of disbelief. The Brits gathered in a corner together in solidarity against American censoriousness. Brian McNally vented cockney rage: "What the fuck's

Jennifer Bartlett's problem?" he shouted. "Whatever happened to the fucking avant-garde! Whoever said you 'ad to 'ave good tiste! I never said Good Tiste was on the menu!"

Nigel himself seemed as impervious as always. Anna shrugged and said maybe Nigel's humor doesn't travel.

I am pissed off today because the *Times* ran a piece titled "How to Fix the *New Yorker*" and the lead-off item counseled against "short articles" and "light jazzy material like *Vanity Fair.*" Maybe they should take a look at Harold Ross's *New Yorker* in the thirties. Talk of the Town was telegram snippets. There was visual gaiety on every page. The *Times* always patronizes the *VF* achievement. Styron's twenty thousand words on depression is hardly "light jazzy material." Nor is Alex Shoumatoff on Chico Mendes. We have so many outstanding writers contributing and wanting to contribute and not enough space to publish them. It blows my mind that the stiffs at the *Times* still don't get the concept of mix even now. It reawakens my desire to storm the *New Yorker* citadel, awaken it from its slumbers, and steal some of the *Times'* best writers. Already started by nabbing *NYT*'s writer Peter Boyer and Leslie Bennetts, ace reporter.

Liz Smith, as expected, wrote a dyspeptic column about the Nigel dinner picked up by the *LA Times* as "British Humor Rankles the Hoity-Toity in New York," full of sententious finger-wagging about how Americans just don't find this kind of thing funny.

Now on the plane to LA. I decided after G's flu last week that it wouldn't be fair to drag him on and off planes, but it's the first time I have left him as long as five days. Our favorite thing to do is to go to Story Hour at the Quogue Library, where a soppy redhead with big legs and a woolen dirndl reads children's books to a small circle of tots who listen on beanbags on the floor. I love the smell of the library in the afternoon, as it starts to get dark outside. It reminds me of being the undergrad in the Bodleian, huddling serene and sexless in a big sweater with Jane Austen books strewn around. When do I set free my inner Quogue Library lady? A few weeks without my trainer dragging me out of bed at six, a few forgotten visits to Louis Licari, in two months I would be a big girl in thick glasses with a bushy ponytail. How lovely that sounds.

But instead, like for Leonard Lauder, it's onward and upward with the id.

I am now thirty-six. A serious age. Or rather an age to be serious. "You'll find," said Bob

Hughes, "you'll be able to be more and more yourself from now on. That's the blessing of precocity. You'll be able to shed so many fears and self-censorings that youth inflicts, yet have the wisdom early success brings." The Philip Larkin thought: "Someone will always be discovering in himself the hunger to be more serious." I feel that now. I am getting impatient with the things that don't count at work, the lightweight elements in the mag are not what I want to focus on. I want to publish the best piece from the Prague Spring, the best piece from El Salvador, to honor David Blundy. Would *The New Yorker* be more intellectually satisfying? These feelings are compounded by the grimness as well as the headiness of our times. The thrill of the developments in Eastern Europe makes me hanker to be there. East Berlin is falling away. German reunification is inevitable. Soon stifling Soviet repression on half a country will feel like inconceivable sepia history. There's no doubt in my mind that Europe in the nineties is going to be the most alive place to be, and we will see a huge rejection of the America of the eighties.

Monday, November 27, 1989

My chameleon self arrives in LA. I brought Peter Boyer with me so he could infiltrate my contacts. He's a fantastic hire and will beef up our media coverage a lot. He's a southern boy, the son of a preacher (not just a Dusty Springfield song as it turns out) who feels he's always battling the conspiracy of liberal media, which is a bit of a laugh given where he worked and where he works now. I've got him on the Sony story, to which I have solemnly donated the size-of-one's-dick comment from Peter Guber, in the hopes Peter can get him to say it again on the record. He was deeply satisfied to meet all the people who try to avoid his calls, and now that I have introduced him to them in person, they have to talk to him.

Tuesday, November 28, 1989

Ovitz asked me in to see the new CAA I. M. Pei building in Beverly Hills. Sitting in the lobby, gazing at the enormous Lichtenstein mural waiting to go up, was like being in a Florentine square in the afternoon. It has a kind of clean serenity with the bustle of work in the beehive levels above. Every so often an agent comes out to the gallery and leans over like Romeo, casing the lobby.

I had dinner with Barry Diller, who keeps up the Fox interest. He is still fulminating about Fox president Leonard Goldberg's work ethic, saying that every morning at eight fifteen as he drives to the studio he passes Leonard and his wife, Wendy, going the other way on their morning health walk. "It says it all for me," said Barry. "Going in the wrong fucking direction! And by the time he has showered and shaved he won't be in the office until ten, while my film company is going up in flames!" A nice whiff of what it's like to work for Barry. He took every opportunity to defenestrate Si as an untrustworthy boss: "He's like Herbie Allen, who recently talked in an interview about the 'hired hands' who work for him. It made me crazy! But it's true of all second-generation billionaires. And mark my words, these ugly Condé Nast firings are all about anger, anger at being short and unworthy and trying to show control after years of having none." Well, Barry is working for a dynastic billionaire, too. Wonder how long he will survive with Rupert Murdoch. I know whom I would rather work for.

Back at the Bel-Air, I saw through the half-open door of Suite 118 Ted Turner and Kirk Kerkorian, locked in negotiations about MGM. Ted hollered through the door at a hovering flunky, "Bring me that fax!" This morning as I came out of the breakfast room with Caroline Graham and Jane, I whipped around and saw Ted striding by to the exit, his coat over his shoulders, a fierce light in his eye. "Ted!" I shouted. "Thanks for posing for the Hall of Fame!" "You look great," he said with a girl-appraising look as he kept walking.

This was a glamorous day by any standards. It began with a meeting with Michael Jackson and ended with sitting next to Clint Eastwood at dinner.

I couldn't believe the Jackson meeting came through. When he posed for Annie for the Hall of Fame, I had romanced the hell out of his middleman, Bob Jones, during our pursuit. David Geffen also put a word in.

Sure enough at two o'clock today, Jane Sarkin and I were on our way to an anonymous apartment block on Wilshire Boulevard where Michael sometimes hides out. I am sure Michael had motives for seeing me other than delivering for Jones — feeling perhaps it's time he made an appearance outside his current elephant-man facade to show to someone influential that he is a compos mentis star. Combined with curiosity perhaps. My good terms with the producer Berry Gordy had afforded me the original connection to Michael, which would generate some trust. And the press is so predatory and tormenting to him, he must have felt the Hall of Fame tribute was something that at least honored his art.

Jane and I were let into a half-empty highrise apartment, which had a train set and a

711

stuffed lion on the floor. We sat doing small talk with Bob Jones when someone slipped in, someone tall with a fast, stooping walk, wearing a cowboy hat. He slid onto the sofa in front of us. "Hi," a high voice said. We were looking at Michael Jackson, wearing full makeup, with long tendrils of black hair and two curling locks stuck to each cheek with masking tape, and a huge round Band-Aid on the side of his nose. He kept looking away as he talked but was chattering affably, which astonished me because I had expected a mute weirdo who signed an autograph and vanished. "I just wanted to meet a very kind lady," he said in his high, soft voice. "What you did, putting me in the Hall of Fame, I was so honored." He stayed with us for an hour. In fact it was I who had to leave.

I got him to talk about composing.

" 'Billie Jean' came to me when I was driving down Ventura and suddenly the opening bars, the arrangement, the words, all of it, all together, came like a gift. All at once. That's why I don't understand arrogance. A gift is from God. I don't have anything to do with that gift choosing me. It could have been someone else." It didn't sound sappy or faux humble. I think he's a Mozartian kind of genius. A weird innocent with the combined power of both otherworldliness and utter worldliness. "I'm thinkin' of doing a movie. I like to watch Steven Spielberg. He lets me watch and he's thinkin' of somethin' for me . . . with Disney." (Michael Eisner said that when Michael calls up and says in that child's voice, "Hi!" he can't help falling into the same voice with a waiflike "hi" in return. At which Jacko shoots back, in a very different, and normal tone, "Don't talk in my voice!") He told us he's trying to find the modern way to do a musical that isn't MTV and isn't the old-fashioned segue-into-song that contemporary audiences find ridiculous. I asked him how he comes down to earth after his incredible live performances. "I read," he said, "in my hotel room. O. Henry sometimes. Frank O'Hara." Not exactly the world's image of him. But strangely gratifying at the same time.

A talent as enormous as his is bound to be strange after so many years of supercelebrity, where all the boundaries of how you are expected to behave disappear. His gift, like that of anyone world-class, is fostered by lonely discipline, obliterating obsession, and the desperate drive for the extinction of ego by the gift itself.

But here's the paradox. In some ways Michael is less weird than people want him to be. Not just his surprising literary tastes. During the course of this trip I learned he talks to Geffen and Ovitz and the entertainment lawyer John Branca as well as Eisner about his career and his projects. For someone supposedly a whacky naïf, those are canny advisers to seek out. There's a lot of shrewdness to his intuitions.

Wendy Stark's dinner followed this epic encounter.

Clint as a dinner partner — quiet, watchful, instinctive. Also hard work. Long, taciturn silences. A kind of heavy chivalry, calling me ma'am. Said nothing memorable. How could one be bored after one course with the world's biggest heartthrob? I was. I was glad to switch places to sit with the profane, volcanic Ray Stark. We had a rapprochement after our Puttnam feud. Actually feuds are the stuff of life for Ray. His latest vendetta is against Siskel and Ebert for their review of *Steel Magnolias.* Apparently one of them said on TV, "I moon this movie," with a thumbs-down.

"I am going to write him a three-page letter," fumed Ray, "and say, anyone who moons this movie is an asshole." I was glad we mended our feud.

My favorite guest at dinner was the *Lethal Weapon* producer Joel Silver. What a character, with his black leather trousers and thrusting beard. "I read nothing anymore," he shouted. "Only coverage. Maître d' gives me a menu and I tell him, bring me the coverage!" When I fall into bed in my Bel-Air room, apricot sheets turned back, two chocolate mints at the bedside, another wicker basket with hot tea on a tray, I feel free and happy in a way I rarely do in New York.

The only thing missing is my darling, curly-haired G breathing softly at my side.

Tuesday, December 19, 1989

Sharon is becoming hard to handle. The carnage of weeping copy editors and fuming art assistants after she has closed a piece suggests it may be time for one of PVZ's deftly choreographed "conversations." But I continue to value her. She has the best intellect and judgment on a story when she's not trying to wage some personal war against someone else's. Plus she has strong bonds with some of the best writers, such as Richardson, Shoumatoff, and Schiff. (Though I sense Stephen is getting weary of the drama.) I took her to lunch at the UN Plaza and suggested a sabbatical. She was thrilled.

Thursday, December 21, 1989

Finally escaping for Christmas! What a pantomime of an exit! We were supposed to go to London for three days first, but just before leaving heard of a flu epidemic that's hospitalizing half the country, so G and I are flying direct to Spain to see Mum and Dad and Harry is going to London to deliver presents to his kids and then join us. We need a break. All he does is work on his book, and I am so overscheduled we are both on short fuses.

I had a sad evening this week when Anna Wintour and I had a good-bye party at the Royalton for Gabé and Miles, who are both leaving New York. Miles to get a life back and then look for something. Gabé has found New York too tough and accepted a job from Nick Coleridge back at *Tatler*. I sat between Miles and Gary Bogard, who was in town. A real *Tatler* reunion and very nostalgic for days that seem so long ago. I am going to miss Miles so much. And Gabé. Miles is one of my best and real friends, we have been through so much together. It was such a funny, touching party after a frenetic week, closing the issue with Gail Sheehy's fantastic piece on Gorbachev, and Boyer's Sony piece that will bring me untold flak.

There was a fiery office debate about whether to risk sales and enrage the PR by dumping the Ellen Barkin cover in favor of Gorbachev. The circulation department was dead against Gorby. I went with it anyway. It feels exactly the right moment to catch the wave. Gorby said at the Malta summit with Bush, "The characteristics of the Cold War should be abandoned." Which is pretty epic stuff. Gorby is the man of the hour. I want to see that charismatic birthmark on our cover. Plus it's a good political pivot for us, choosing the man who ended the Soviet Union over this month's flavor of the month. This is the direction I want to take *VF* into now, news in its broadest sense. Found a strong, compelling head shot of Gorby and never felt better about a cover decision.

Miles and Gabé's party was full of love. Miles always moaned and groaned about having no friends, but the Royalton filled up fast with his world, downtown fashion stars and scrappy number twos in art departments, all the talented comers who get squeezed out sometimes from the pages of big, booming *VF* and are the rising stars at hipper shops. It was fun to hang with them. I get sick of big shots. Gabé wrote me a fond good-bye letter on *Vogue* scrap paper. "I too am sorry I never made it to *VF* but I look forward to running Tina Brown productions." Dear Gabé, dear Miles! *Tatler* was such a permanent bonding for all of us.

Chris Garrett has moved here permanently and is working for Harry at *Traveler*. Sarah Giles is now being interviewed for a senior job in features at *Harper's Bazaar*. Scary if she takes it. They are a crack squad, and the core of them are the *Tatler* Brits. Soon they will be competing with me all over town. But this night we were all just joined by the past. It made me cry.

At the annual Condé Nast holiday lunch party at the Four Seasons, Si was in classic form. He got up and started on a metaphor about mountain climbing and how there were more mountains ahead, and there were rocky foothills, until after a bit he realized he was in a total muddle and could never sustain it and abruptly sat down. Then he came over to my table, where I was sitting with Alex, and he banged his head on the hanging poinsettia. Bernie Leser's speech was some genial blather about corporate spirit. In the middle Alex started to giggle because he decided that Bernie looked like Paganini. This was my sixth Condé holiday lunch. I saw the new editor at *Self,* Alexandra Penney, staring around in a perplexed way, unsure how to handle a corporate culture so full of eccentrics. Anna looked particularly gorgeous in a red suit and very high heels. She has such powerful allure, such a presence. We traveled in the car together to lunch. Looking at her, wrapped unapologetically in a Fendi fur, exuding the expensive halo of Chanel perfume, and talking in her terse, businesslike voice, I could see why she casts a spell.

Thursday, December 28, 1989
Spain

What an odd Christmas. Mum and Dad had told me of the incredible rain in Spain not staying in the plain but swamping the coast. Somehow I had not fully appreciated the degree. Their unwinterized holiday villa is totally unfit for these storms. The creeping discomfort of it has been compounded by the freak weather into something fearfully bad for Dad's health. He should have stayed in London and not come back here. A few days of sun cheered it all up, but at nightfall the house was chilly, and the huge gas fires that they wheel about from room to room, saying brightly, "So much cozier than central heating," cannot take the dank feel from the house. Towels are always slightly wet, the kitchen, always Mum's disastrous blind spot, is now something out of Madame Tussaud's Chamber of Horrors, with its ancient toasted sandwich machine and cracked coffee cups. I felt I have become an American snob, over-used to creature comforts. I reminded myself Brits are always freezing in drafty houses. None of it would have really mattered, however, if the pipes hadn't burst, creating a river straight into the village and making Dad the subject of a denunciamento to the local police.

All this stress is causing Dad to deteriorate. I fear that stubbornly continuing to live here is now shortening his life a good deal and now that we can afford it, it's time to make the big move back to London. The place is a nightmare of daily hassles, and he is half out of it. He got quieter and quieter during the course of the week, a faded version of his usual vigor.

Mum is locked into her usual "All's well" facade. I honestly believe that when Dad is in the terminal ward she will refer to it as an "exciting new phase." When the heavens opened on day four, seeping into one's very bone marrow, she said, "Of course London is so much colder, darling. New York is so freezing, too, and a little bit of rain is nothing!" A little bit of rain? The house is slowly sliding down the hill! One especially poignant moment from this holiday from hell: the sight of Dad in his tweed Little Marlow hat, standing outside with two workmen with pickaxes. In his hand I can see something that looks like a vacuum cleaner he is waving over the muddy ground. I realize it's the metal detector Mum bought him for his birthday thirty years ago when we were obsessed with the notion that there was an Anglo-Saxon burial ground in the field behind us in Little Marlow, full of silver buckles and shoulder clasps. Now the treasure he seeks is broken sewage pipes. I doubt San Jorge will fetch more than seventy-five thousand at this point. I feel a certain rage that they kept from me the dilapidated state of the house. What if I hadn't got the money from Si?

Mum and Dad's systematic denial of the truth all my life is perhaps where I get my savage realism. I still can't believe Mum told me only five years ago that Dad's father was not, as we were always told, Christopher Brown, my brother's namesake and the manager of the Vaudeville Theatre in the Strand. Dad's real father was a musical comedy star named George Layton, who had an affair with our grandmother when she was eighteen. That's why as a baby Dad slept in the hamper in her dressing room — there was no one home to mind him.

I would so love to have heard about Granny's struggles and her shame, which must have been profound in that censorious era, but Mum uncharacteristically forbade me to raise it with him or, she insisted, marital mayhem would have ensued. Her own family history is really just as unexplored. When her sister, Sonje, died, Chris was going through her private papers and was gobsmacked to find that her German grandfather's name was Fekkel Kohr and he was Jewish! Is that why he fled to England just before the First World War? Escaping rising anti-Semitism? Perhaps the anti-Semitism followed him, because he shot himself in the garden shed, according to the death certificate. Why had we never heard about this from Mum?

Mum loved talking about her crazy family. Her eccentric Irish mother's obsession with moving house, and the succession of Catholic schools she attended, tyrannized by crafty, punitive nuns, but we hadn't heard a word about her half-Jewish roots until Fekkel's birth certificate showed up. When confronted she just went vague and didn't want to be drawn out. To me, it explains the feeling she always had of being an outsider. Maybe this is what bound Dad and her together so tightly, the family secrets they shared.

As I write this now I can hear the rise and fall of their complicit laughter from the patio as they sit out under the stars, and I feel, as I used to do as a child, a pang of exclusion from the depths of their bond. Perhaps it's why, when I detect facades, the lashing words begin to form.

1990
WE ARE FOUR

Wednesday, January 10, 1990

A new decade! It's amazing how fast the eighties recedes in the back mirror. *Dynasty* finally bit the dust at the end of last year and it now feels as antique as ancient Rome. What will the nineties bring? Schiff has done a great essay in the mag on the Particle People, which we're all becoming — splintered apart by the inequity of wealth, by the seventies counterculture before it, the youth boom, the changing demographics, isolated by our camcorders and fax machines and home computer modems on the desk. That's why we like Roseanne, because she's so old-school and overweight. How do particles not become alienated? By feeling part of a mass wave that technology will deliver. Jason Epstein at Random House has produced a telephone directory–sized tome called the Reader's Catalog that makes forty-nine thousand different books available, a personalized book-store that gives you backlist as well as current. According to Schiff, by the mid-nineties computer owners will be able to buy everything from their home offices and retail marketing will become a dinosaur. Who will then advertise in *Vanity Fair*? Happily, he doesn't address that question.

Thursday, January 12, 1990

Stricken to learn that the fashion designer Patrick Kelly has died of AIDS. He was only thirty-five! He lived in such a joyful, colorful world. I remember the thrill of opening the box containing my *VF* fifth-anniversary dress, buried in rustling tissue paper, which he brought to New York from Paris himself. His ribbons and buttons had such innocent whimsy. He was always in motion in his baggy overalls as he tucked and pinned and flourished his spools of vibrant fabrics. I grieve that so many bright lights like Patrick, one by one, continue to be stolen from us by AIDS. It's not only a heartbreaking loss but more depletion of talent, more decimation of creativity that's going to have an unimaginable impact on the future of taste. RIP, dear Patrick.

Monday, January 22, 1990
In flight, New York to London

Feeling combative.

The "relaunched" *Tatler* under Nick Coleridge's editorial directorship arrived, and I was taken aback to see that the typeface and many other design features are a direct ripoff of *VF.* Fuck that! We were scheduled to go to dinner at the Newhouses the same night and I was so annoyed that I avoided talking to him. Julie Kavanagh has been in from London and staying with me and she said, why not start a London edition of *VF* to block all the copycats? After sleeping on it, I loved the idea. And a much better response than bitching about something that's not going to change. Same editorial except a few regional tweaks and different ads, therefore very little overhead for a new magazine. It's a score on every front. So instead of adding — as Si clearly expected by his nervous expression — to his day's pain when I walked into his office first thing in the morning, I hit him with my new idea. And suggested we could test-market it by upping our newsstand circulation in the UK right now. He seemed intrigued by the idea, perhaps because he felt joyful that he wasn't about to get a diva attack. He promised an instant market study of the notion.

Had spats with a lot of the editors this week. Sharon seems more and more entwined with her Baader-Meinhof/Bloomsbury group of Susan Sontag, Barbara Epstein from *The New York Review,* Shelley Wanger, and the

King of the Scorpions, John Richardson. Individually I like them all. Together they are a lethal band. She's going to take the two months off in Europe and let's hope it improves the mood. One good thing in all this flux — I rehired Michael Roberts! He's been living in Paris, where he's been much happier, doing illustrations for French *Vogue* and taking pictures for *The Independent.* I called him there on the off chance he was available and asked him to be our new Paris bureau chief. He immediately agreed in the same tone as if I only saw him last week rather than four years ago, when he melted off to London. So happy to have him back in the fold.

Tuesday, January 23, 1990

Today I had a tragic meeting with the young editor Duncan Stalker, who had been at *VF* when I first arrived as a Leo hire and whom I let go because he never seemed to get on board with what I was trying to do. But he has proved in the years since to be so talented at *Manhattan,inc.* and then at *Traveler* that I realized I'd been wrong. I rehired him as a senior editor in November, five years after we first parted company, knowing he was HIV positive but hoping for the best. Now he came to tell me he has been going through hell with his dying boyfriend and feels he can't cope anymore and has to quit. I felt stricken as I looked at him. He's suddenly so pale and insubstantial. His head has become a strange bulbous shape and his shoulders look as if they could crumple like paper. I told him he could be paid for as long as . . . And both our eyes filled with tears. Duncan, this promising young editor of thirty-two, began to speak of himself in the past tense. "I wanted so much to have a magazine myself," he said. "Now I never will." He broke down and we wept together. He asked me to look after the writers he's been nurturing. I told him to look after himself, to use the office whenever he wants it.

Wednesday, January 31, 1990

Gail Sheehy's Gorby piece is a big hit. People seem to love the surprise of slapping him on the cover under the banner headline "Red Star." Next issue good, too. A piece on the last days of Alfred Herrhausen, the CEO of Deutsche Bank who was blown up in Bad Homburg by some splinter group of the Red Army Faction, Mort Rosenblum on the Honduran drug connection, Marie Brenner on a gay modeling cult, and a hysterical piece by John Seabrook about the gossip columnist Cindy Adams, who rose from being Miss Bagel to a confidante of Noriega. What's not to like here?

A comic encounter with the Italian *Vanity Fair* crowd. What Italian *Vanity Fair*? Yes, in typical Newhouse fashion, the first Doug and I heard of its existence was when I got a fax from Italian Condé Nast, asking me to send the artwork for the logo! Meanwhile Doug was getting his own bombardments re dispatching to Milan *VF* promotional T-shirts, pencils, notebooks, etc. Si is clearly trying to make the point that *VF* is his franchise and my participation is irrelevant. Why aren't I put in charge of it? Now that I am launching UK *VF* I don't care as much, but I will care if *VF* Italy is crap and damages the mother ship.

Next I learn that Si's nephew, Jonathan Newhouse, who has been put in charge of the European company, was in town and wanted me to have lunch with Mr. Pietroni, the editorial director of European Condé, and his photo director. We all trooped to the Four Seasons. Unfortunately Mr. Pietroni speaks not one word of English. Jonathan at this point speaks Berlitz French and the female photo editor no language anyone could recognize. Pietroni was a mournful figure with a five o'clock shadow and an outsize Borsalino. Every so often there was a long burst of rapid-fire Italian that I assumed was an effort to understand the philosophy of the magazine until the gamine photo director would say, "Mr. Pietroni, he ask, when please can he have the Madonna pictures?" The Four Seasons service was impossibly slow and by the end of it I was desperate, trying not to look wistfully into the next booth, where Ed Victor was lunching with Richard Saul Wurman from TED and others. Downstairs in the coat check I tried to be expansive to the Italian contingent as the Victor party assembled there. "Ed," I said, flailing, "may I introduce you to the most distinguished editor in all of Italy, Mr. Pietroni?" But I hadn't noticed that the lineup behind me had changed and a voice said, "I am not Mr. Pietroni. I am Jonathan Newhouse." Turns out that Jonathan, perhaps in an effort to look as cosmopolitan as his new role dictates, was also now sporting an enormous Borsalino. Ed Victor said he laughed about this all afternoon.

On Thursday Mike Ovitz came in to see us at *VF* for a change. He was transfixed by my wall of past covers, immediately wanting to know how many each had sold. He seemed happier, liberated from his LA woes, and launched into an immediate brainstorm session about the next cover, which was a glimpse of the fun he must be at the office on a good day. "Robin Williams?" Me: "Nah." Ovitz: "Fantastic movie. Bill Murray?" Me: "Won't show up." Ovitz: "This time I can deliver him. He'll do it. I'll tell him. Sean Connery?" Me: "Too old!" Ovitz: "Okay. Pin that."

"I'd like Warren Beatty but I've given up," I said. "Don't," he said, "I'll make him do it. That's what I'll do for you." Now he's come up with a favor that in due course he will call in. Shortly after he left, Jane Sarkin's phone was red-hot with CAA agents pitching their stars for covers, which must have meant that Mike, always enjoying internal competition, had told each one of them there was a *VF* cover going if they could strike now. It was a good indicator of why he is so successful. Parachuting into my office, putting himself in the middle of my problem of the moment, and then trying to solve it to his own advantage. Regarding my own multiple courtships, he offered, "Diversify, but never leave your power base," which felt like very good free career advice from the person who charges more for it than anyone currently operating in Hollywood. I felt again that I made the right decision about not leaving *Vanity Fair.*

Thursday, February 22, 1990

I have avoided Alice Mason's Nights of the Living Dead for a year, but she was persistent this time. Arthur Carter, who was there as usual, looking mysterious, said the nineties are already over and it's only six weeks into the decade. The combination of events, he says, makes it almost too easy for journalists and historians. There's the Trump divorce (Marla's brazen confrontation with Ivana on the ski slopes in Aspen over Donald was a moment worthy of a Movie of the Week), the dissolution of Drexel Burnham Lambert, the pollution and retrieval of Perrier water, and the release of Nelson Mandela from prison as the world went crazy with cries of FREE-DOM. All that is now required is for Alice herself to go up in a puff of smoke. I couldn't wait to escape and give a ride to Nick Dunne to plot out his definitive story on Donald and Ivana's life and times. He told me that Marla Maples is a red herring and that Donald has been having a fling with a well-known New York socialite. Wow. That would be a head-liner and is hard to believe. Though this could give Trump what money can't buy — the silver edge of class. They all fall for class in the end.

Friday, March 2, 1990

A memorial service at St. Bart's Church for Malcolm Forbes. Another nineties cataclysm — all the great movers and shakers are going down. It was very sudden, and there are whispers of suicide because of illness. And there is only one illness that people whisper about, and that is AIDS. Could Malcolm have decided he couldn't face being outed at last? He was of a generation that couldn't bear it, and always feigned masculinity so strenuously, with the gruff voice and motorbikes. It would have been so great if he could have declared the truth and turned away the shame so many others feel, too, but he chose this way instead. Or that's how I read it. The service was another boldface ecclesiastical blowout such as I am getting used to attending, with Sirio from Le Cirque standing outside, serving as a sort of funeral maître d'. It was as over the top as Malcolm would have loved, with Scottish kilts and cabinet ministers and Gallic players performing on the hunting horn that used to be at Malcolm's French château. I half expected him to float over in one of his beloved balloons.

The Phoenix House fund-raiser for drug rehab has been preoccupying my time. The TV producer Grant Tinker, who's donating the soundstage in Hollywood, insists we ought to have entertainment. I have never been a fan of entertainment at parties. It just stops you from talking, but this of course is not a party. It's a ticket-buying fund-raiser so we have to offer something more than rubber chicken and chat. But what? For the most blasé crowd of Hollywood A list who know more about entertainment than any other crowd on earth? I called an emergency caucus of Ian Schrager, Reinaldo, and Colacello. As I hoped, as soon as Ian's head was engaged, my panic began to abate. "Don't try to do Hollywood," said Ian. "You've got to bring out New York sheen. We'll get Anita Sarko to do the disco. I'll pay for it. What about two white pianos like *Fabulous Baker Boys*? What about getting Liza to do the Michelle Pfeiffer bit?" Now I am excited myself.

"We're flying out on Thursday to look at the space," I said.

"I'll come," said Ian. "I'll get the red-eye back. I'll look at the space with you and I'll bring Robert Isabell. Then we'll figure out the theme." Hooray! But the next day anxiety returned when we found Liza is booked that night to perform with Frank Sinatra, and Harry Connick — another suggestion — did Lilly Tartikoff's benefit two weeks before.

I called Ian to get plan B.

"Well, let's just think," said Ian in his methodical way. "New York. What does it mean to LA? [pause]. Statue of Liberty . . . Rockettes . . . Truman Capote . . ."

"Capote! Robert Morse!" I shout. Morse is currently getting raves in a one-man show about Truman on Broadway. What could be more New York than Capote? We both knew immediately this was pay dirt. "Twenty minutes," said Schrager, already editing it down. "We gotta bring him out and get him to do twenty minutes as Truman."

Turns out David Brown is the show's

producer and I call him immediately. Would he close the theater for the night and have Morse fly to LA and perform Truman for Hollywood? I could almost see his mustache light up. "I LOVE the idea!" he crowed. "If the logistics work and I can shuffle the tickets to a dark night, I'll do it. Give me till tomorrow at four." I love these creative producers. The Schragers and the David Browns who get the idea, say yes, and make it happen.

Wednesday, March 7, 1990
Four Seasons, LA

The *Tru* coup was achieved with a bit of brinkmanship. The management of the Booth Theatre had agreed, but on Friday night Robert Morse hadn't. David Brown said, "Look, Tina, he doesn't want to do it. There's only one hope. Tomorrow night is the hundredth performance. We're giving a little cocktail party for him between shows. Why don't you turn up and bat your blue eyes at him." I called the office and got ahold of Charles Churchward, who was just locking up. "Remember that great cartoon of Capote at a table with all the Park Avenue women at La Côte Basque that's now hanging on my wall?" We had assigned it to go with the extract of Gerald Clarke's biography of Truman two years ago. "Take it down, gift-wrap it, and send it over to me." Then I called

Nick Dunne, who is an old carousing friend of Robert Morse, and Bob Colacello, who knew Truman so well. We watched the last ten chilling moments (I had seen it before), then David Brown scooped us up and took us downstairs to await Morse in the bar. He came out, so unbelievably different from his stage persona, and embraced Nick right away. There were choruses of goodwill and I gave him the wrapped cartoon gift.

"Oh, my goodness, how wonderful!" he cried when he opened it.

"Bobby," said David, "Tina was hoping you'd reconsider her little proposal, which would get such great press for the show." I went down on my knees, literally. "Please do this, Mr. Morse," I began, and Nick gave him the intimate, back-knowledge smile that I think clinched it.

My new favorite person is Jay Presson Allen, the writer/producer of *Tru*. She's sixty-eight, a silver-haired lady of the theater in appearance, but utterly direct and candid in her approach.

"You know, Tina," she said, "old age sucks. A few years ago, I'd get a cold and bounce back. Now the cold turns into some asshole virus that lays me low for weeks." It was unexpected dialogue coming from this grande dame in a silver bob and pearls.

All the way to LA to check out the Culver Studios soundstage our group swapped seats and plotted different aspects of the evening. Ian is getting married in two weeks to Carolina Herrera's publicist, Deborah Hughes, and is consumed with anxiety about it. When not working with me, he and Reinaldo were planning his stag party. A detail I overheard was a white limo rolling up to collect Ian with a female driver who, when she stepped out to open the door, would be naked from the waist down. (That will make Ahmet Ertegun happy at least.) Our project was a distraction for Ian. When we got to Culver City, he and Robert wanted time alone on the soundstage to conceive the visuals and we went off for lunch.

The plan they came up with sounds so great. It has the cavernous soundstage enclosed with a cyclorama on which enormous images will be projected at specific moments in the evening. It's great to bring our social buzz to raise the profiles of efforts like Phoenix House. Drug-addicted kids have zero appeal to vanity donors who want their names on a building — until their own kids succumb.

Tuesday, March 20, 1990

Unexpected hiccup. All the guests were assembled on the lawn of Ian's house in Southampton on Friday with the rabbi waiting, while upstairs Ian and Deborah fumed in different rooms about the telephone directory–sized prenup agreement that she had second thoughts about. Reinaldo and Carolina waited at the heliport with the Perelmans for the signal to take off and finally did so anyway, arriving just in time to be told the wedding is off.

The unhappy debacle has of course messed a lot with Ian's concentration on Phoenix House. I took off for LA again on Saturday, not knowing if he was coming or not. To compound difficulties, Robert and Ian had brought in someone they describe as a "lighting genius," Arthur Weinstein. He's another of their weirdo nightlife kings, a former fashion photographer who turned to creating sexy ambience in after-hours clubs like the World. No one asked me about bringing him into the mix but there he was, already dipping candelabra bulbs into tubs of magenta dye, his arrival threatening to take us fifteen thousand over budget. The *VF* team adjourned to a nearby hotel bar to rethink. Clearly we were going to have to raise more money. We had to ensure we hit our million-dollar fund-raising target.

"I could try Phyllis McGuire again," said Sarah Giles, conjuring up the old gangster's moll Nick Dunne had profiled in Las Vegas. "I could ask her who else could cough up." (Phyllis's suggestion was Meshulam Riklis, who said he'd give us fifty thousand if his wife, Pia Zadora, could be the cabaret. We passed.) "Don't worry, fearless," said Reinaldo, "I will call my friend Al Taubman."

"Al Taubman?" I squeaked. "Remember we called his wife a Madame Claude girl and how long it took to get him over it?"

"Well, but Alfred is a friend," said Reinaldo, getting suaver by the minute as he hyped himself for the pitch. "I can just call him and say, 'Hallo, this is Reinaldo, I'm in a bit of a bind. I've asked five hundred people for dinner on Thursday and find I have no lighting. Can you give me fifty thousand dollars for the cause?' " I loved imagining Taubman's face on the other end of the phone when he heard this request, but the imperturbable Reinaldo went off to make the call (and came back very quickly, I might add, with suspiciously little to report). Incredibly, it was Sarah who scored the biggest. Phyllis McGuire was so disgusted by Riklis's quid pro quo that she coughed up another thirty thousand of Sam Giancana's mob money. That should do it.

I was supposed to have dinner with the producer Larry Gordon at Morton's but I was too stretched to go. Instead I asked if he would come to me at the Bel-Air. I got a call from his PR person shortly afterward, asking, "Mr. Gordon would like to know, is this a power play?" Imagine retaining someone to make a call like that? No, it's not a fucking power play. I just have a migraine and don't want to slog over to Morton's. Anyway, he showed up: another wild-man producer in the Joel Silver genre, produces big action movies like *Predator* and *Die Hard*. "Wanna know who has the balls in this town?" was his opening riff. Here we go . . . What is it about this crew? Ovitz asked me the other day, "Wanna know how big are the balls of Akio Morita at Sony?" NO, ACTUALLY. "They are YAY big."

Tuesday, March 27, 1990

Phoenix House gala. When I arrived at the soundstage at two o'clock for the dress rehearsal I gasped. The magic wasn't just in evidence, it pervaded every luminous, beautiful corner. Robert's crew were testing the slide shows on the cyclorama and when I walked in the ten-foot-high *Vanity Fair* covers, a visual feast of Annie and Helmut's best work, glowed and pulsed from every wall with Force 5 celebrity glamour. The magenta chandelier bulb, the rosy underlit fuchsia tablecloths, the rich glory of poppies, the blue mystery lights in the gantry, the stage at the back — yes! I felt the spine tingle of perfection . . . It was even more beautiful than the *VF* fifth-anniversary room, until now Robert and Ian's pièce de résistance.

From the moment the first guests arrived it

became clear this night was going to reinvent the charity gala in LA, because every single star, expected or not, showed up. Limos disgorged Arnold Schwarzenegger, Bruce Willis, Anjelica Huston, Isabelle Adjani, Paula Abdul, Elton John, Joan Rivers, Milli Vanilli. David Kuhn came with Daryl Hannah, who whispered "What the hell is this all about?" to him before the cameras descended, and, fed by David, she said, "Phoenix House is the most important drug rehab center in California and it needs FUNDS," which was a gold-dust sound bite for Mitch. Along with the stars came all the major power players, studio heads, network honchos. *Tru* was the hit of hits. LA loved getting twenty priceless minutes that meant they didn't have to see the show. (I won't tell David Brown that bit.) My table was Ovitz, Geffen, Berry Gordy, Carrie Fisher, the producer Suzanne de Passe, Reinaldo, and Helmut Newton.

After Mitch spoke so movingly about his work, David Geffen told me he would send him a check the next day for fifty thousand dollars. Many others said they would dig deep. Mitch was deeply content, which made me feel good.

I looked around for Robert Isabell as the crowd began to thin. He had vanished, as he always does, along with Arthur Weinstein and his magic elves. I did see Ian, who only had time for a brief, businesslike hug. He was walking out of the backstage to catch the red-eye, carrying his suit bag, maybe getting married, maybe not.

Looking in the mirror in the ladies' room, I patted the gentle bulge under my black Giorgio di Sant'Angelo jersey tube and allowed myself to admit a fact I have been hiding from myself and everyone else till this was over: that I am pregnant. This is a pleasure, a gift, a reward that outweighs any other and I feel bathed in happiness.

Monday, May 28, 1990
Memorial Day, NYC

Waiting for my trainer, Richard, he of the enormous thighs and high-pitched laugh, to come to take me to the gym. He still knocks on my door three times a week and drags me, snarling, into the street for an aerobic walk or I'd never do it. Probably the only reason I haven't put on fifty pounds like I did the last pregnancy. I am fat but still hidably so. This is the day that the London Condé Nast contingents arrive to talk about the UK launch. Tonight I am having dinner with them to try to ensure all goes well. The prospects are good. Si has done his usual trick and hired the publisher without letting me meet her first. I just don't understand him. Thankfully, I think she may be okay, but it makes me crazy that she is already giving interviews

741

about *VF* in London without ever having talked to the editor about how to interpret the magazine. Anyway, I am getting used to it and trying to shortstop it by meeting her today.

Spoke to Gabé in London. She hates being back at *Tat* and said she made a huge mistake returning to England. She's asked Anna for her old job back and Anna's trying to make it happen. Very hard to go back to the UK after living in New York. The pace here is so intense it shaves off all patience with a ten o'clock start to the day and phone calls not instantly returned.

Monday, July 2, 1990
Quogue

Well, hooray. The visit from the British *VF* group was terrific. I am crazy about the publisher, Sarah Vincent, so kudos to Si this time for appointing her. Wish I had her over here. She is very good-looking and tough and experienced, a go-getting meritocrat, not some lame procrastinating Sloane Ranger from Condé of old. I also love the Brit circulation director, Vivien Matthews, another toughie with a Buster Brown haircut and Jean Muir suit. These are girls after my own heart and we bonded fast.

Have been closing Marie Brenner's terrific piece on Donald and Ivana Trump. We

wanted to capture their fascinating repositioning now that they are divorcing and Ivana
has been upgraded to superstar victim of a
brutish, philandering husband, which she is
playing to the hilt. Toiling with Marie and
Wayne to get the copy right. Wayne is so
remarkable, the way he can enable writers to
be their best. He's a seamless tailor, sewing
and stitching and cutting. Marie has been
able to establish such a pattern of lying and
loudmouthing in Trump that it's incredible
he still prospers and gets banks to loan him
money. Great quote where his brother says
Donald was the kid who threw cake at the
birthday party. He's like some monstrous id
creation of his father, a cartoon assemblage
of all his worst characteristics mixed with the
particular excesses of the new media age. And
the portrait of Ivana as a Stockholm syndrome enabler, reconstructing her whole face
and body to try to win favor, absorbing all
his delusions and adding her own striving,
desperate pretensions is really great stuff. The
revelation that he has a collection of Hitler's
speeches at the office is going to make a lot
of news.

I feel more and more pregnant, which has
been awkward as *60 Minutes* has been filming
in the office for a piece about us, a coup for
VF. Will be incredible exposure that could
drive up circulation exponentially. I am
nervous about the footage they have got. I re-

alize I called Sly Stallone's fiancée a bimbo in the art department when they were filming and am praying they don't use it (as I would for sure if I'd been the reporter!).

Wednesday, August 22, 1990

So long between entries. Have had the whole family to stay at Quogue. Heaven having the cousins here for Georgie.

When not with the kids have been glued to CNN, watching the developments in the crisis in the Gulf since Saddam Hussein invaded Kuwait. He's such a preposterous figure, with the backward beret and huge chimney-sweep mustache, but clearly much more dangerous than anyone gave him credit for. No one took Hitler seriously either. It seems to be the hallmark of the most dangerous dictators that no one considers them a threat until too late.

Now I am in NYC to progress the November issue and have to figure out how to respond to it when events are changing so fast. The September issue is a news storm with the Trump piece and the Hitler speeches revelation. Happily, Trump trashed us to Barbara Walters on her show, and that spun another column from Liz Smith. We are promoting the hell out of it. Marie is such a huge asset to *VF*, with the tenacity of her reporting and eye for the killer detail.

Tonight had the underwater feel of summer in the city. A strange social group for the dog days of August assembled at Le Cirque at the behest of Swifty Lazar — the Erteguns, the social decorator Chessy Rayner, etc. Mary Lazar was more noticeably sozzled than in colder months. Ahmet was somewhat drunk as well and in nostalgic vein with Swifty, punch-lining his stories with cries of "Well, fuck you, Daddy!" Chessy in her new looser, post-husband-Billy-dumping-her mode, Mica Ertegun her usual impeccable, patent-haired self. At one point everyone was talking about hair and Chessy commented: "There's nothing worse in life than a small head." That's one to remember. Throughout the long, rich, somnolent dinner, the rise and fall of laughter from the next table felt like a distant liner at sea. Swifty kept up his usual repertoire of ancient anecdotes. "Dino De Laurentiis. Now, there's a man who was truly ignorant. He wanted to make a movie out of *War and Peace.* He's never read it in English. He's never read it in Russian, and sure as hell he's never read it in Italian . . . ANYway . . ."

"Daddy," said a gently slurry Ahmet, "do you remember that awful night on Sam Spiegel's boat in Cannes?" And so on and so on. No one mentioned the crisis in the Middle East except when Mica and Ahmet argued about what Henry Kissinger had said at a dinner the night before, which no one in the alcohol haze seemed to be entirely sure about. Stepped outside into a blast of hot air like Delhi, feeling that the world is blowing up all around us and no one seems to notice — dancing on the lip of a volcano, as Julie Baumgold put it in her wonderful piece on Lacroix in *New York* mag.

Tuesday, August 28, 1990
Quogue

The coming of fall is always poignant. The winds at night picking up speed. G has been so loving and sweet, as if he senses this is our last summer on our own together. The house is full of inflatable whales, big and small, that he drags up and down stairs. He enjoyed camp at the Quogue Field Club, though I find all those stuck-up WASPs impossible. But I could see with a lurch of anxiety how very different he is from the other kids, not just the nervous fiddling with his fingers but the daydreaming introversion that makes him check out and refuse to either concentrate or properly participate in the games. He is helped by his glowing beauty and sweetness, which make everyone want to support him. At the International Preschool, where he is with a nice motley crew of UN kids, they love him. And his cleverness with words is a godsend. Anyway, when we splash around the pool with Monstro the whale, with him calling me Mummy Mermaid and me calling him Georgie Shark, I love him so much that I would lie down and die for him. I dread the coming of September turbulence and fear he will feel displaced by the coming sibling.

Monday, September 17, 1990

A lot of stuff happening as I wait for baby X, who we now know, to my wild joy, is a girl. G is getting excited, too. I find myself thinking about her all the time. Will we be as close as I have always been to my own mother? I never had rebellious years with Mum. All my rebellion was focused on school. It's a wonderfully soothing feeling, the notion of a best friend coming whom I haven't even met.

VF sales have been punished by Iraq and Desert Storm. There's an ad recession we didn't expect. The war is bad for a magazine with a title like *Vanity Fair,* just as the thirties were bad for it before. *VF* suggests glamour and levity and that's not the mood of the times. I am moving the editorial in a more serious direction by choice as much as need, but perception will lag behind the reality of what's now in our pages. The split identity we have evolved of the movie star on the cover and the grit inside has worked well for us until this moment, but it's hard to judge how much to change in the news direction without also alienating the huge audience who love that high-low balance that we do. October has the come-hither smile of Debra Winger (a big improvement on the last time) for the newsstand sale, but inside are powerful stories, such as the strong piece on President Bush confronting the encroachment of Saddam, Winnie Mandela and upheavals in South Africa, the Menendez murder, which gives a classic Dunne portrait of California affluence and amorality, and Ralph Nader, the scold on the rise.

Meanwhile Harry's had an amazing offer that couldn't have come at a more difficult moment, just as I am about to give birth and want him more at my side. Alberto Vitale has asked him to be the editorial boss of Random House, as president/publisher, which is a fantastic opportunity and restores him to the top of the tree, where he belongs. I have admired so much his creativity and brio in his four inventive years at *Traveler.* Everyone said behind his back the job was too small, but he never felt or behaved that way, he just threw himself into founding a brilliant new magazine — in profit faster than any Condé Nast mag before, says Si. Most men of his age and stature would have "held out" for some big board seat or top CEO position that wouldn't have come. A classic mistake when people at the top are fired. When you have been a big star in a job and lose it, everyone dances with you, but everyone is too threatened to hire you. It's very, very hard to get a commensurate power base back. So he has been smart as well as creative to take *Traveler* and make it a hit. Success in America is a brand in and of itself. Truth is, he's happier than he's been for years playing the mentor role to a young staff, with time to work on his *American Century* history and be home early with us. Now the big time wants him back. If Harry does Random House, that locks us into NYC for another five years. I will have to stop imagining there could still be an alternate reality in London. The decision was brought into nerve-racking relief when, on his way out to Quogue from the Hunterspoint Avenue train station, a menacing thug in a beanie leapt out of nowhere, pointed a gun at him, and demanded all his money. Took it and fled. It rattled us both. I kept thinking of how he could have become one of those news stories we devour in the *Post.* The three of us, me, H, and G, sat on the little seat at the end of the boardwalk at Quogue, holding one another tight, soothed by the ocean. G, holding his penguin, had no idea what his dad had been through.

Tuesday, September 25, 1990

I received an anonymous typed note today in interoffice mail. "You are going to have a staff insurrection on your hands," it read, "if you don't fire Sharon DeLano." Jesus. Wonder who wrote it. Sharon, back from her European jaunt, is again making waves of static. Conferring with Pam about how to handle it. I can't create another sabbatical. But it's an awkward moment with the baby due in October.

How did we get to the Holiday Issue with no cover again? Just when I am about to go off for maternity leave? And no good lead either. I got cold feet about putting Trump's new squeeze, Marla Maples, on the November cover, though there was a strong lobby to do so. So I slapped on Cher, who had been destined for December. I should have left it alone as I now have no cover when I am out with the baby. Instead, in a spirit of reinventing the cultural mood, I am using an insane Annie pic of Roseanne Barr on top of her husband, Tom Arnold, her huge bosoms squeezing out of a swimsuit, with inside photos of them mud wrestling half-naked. Proletarian chic is all the rage. Nothing could be sexier at the moment than a fat guy in a wife-beater vest, frolicking around with a roly-poly wife. Ralph Lauren will have a heart attack, but I will be on leave so won't have to hear the flak. Fuck fuck fuck, as Madonna shouts in her new crotch-grabbing video. I am reeling from all the combined pressures. The construction on the apartment across the landing we have annexed to ours to make room for baby's arrival was supposed to be completed this week, but has fallen months behind. Why is it always like this in our house? (Answer: because we live here.)

On Friday night we were unable to slink out of town because Si and Victoria asked us to join them for dinner for the opening night of the New York Film Festival. The two other guests were Joan Didion and John Gregory Dunne, who I find are always a struggle. Not helped by the fact that Wolcott just savaged John's new novel in one of his best columns lately. But there were only six of us, so we all had to behave.

At dinner, John Dunne was maddeningly contrary. Joan and John have always seen everything first and have a view on it. The festival movie was *Miller's Crossing,* which was flawed, but Gabriel Byrne was very good in it, I thought. "I like Byrne," said John, "but not in this movie. He was much, much better in that little David Puttnam movie four years ago." It was like that all the way through. John always disagreeing on the basis of some prior inside intelligence. Joan's tiny voice is impossible to hear. She is redeemed of course by the amazing talent I love and revere. Si sat most of the time in silence, except when he suddenly got exercised by an idea that seized him about California — that it had only ever produced marginal art. And that only metropolitan centers can produce art at all. (Dunne was able to counter that by talking about how there was no good art being produced any-where, period.) I longed to be eating a baked potato in Quogue.

It was incredible to be sitting around a table again with Wolcott, Schiff, and Jesse Korn-bluth writing the captions for this year's Hall of Fame. It's the first time Miles wasn't here to berate us. Wolcott says the least until the rhythms trouble him into speaking out, and then he offers something perfect. But it's less good than the Media Decade last year. Seri-ous heroes are less compliant with outrageous Annie pictures. And yet this year we have two major real ones — Nelson Mandela and Vá-clav Havel, leader of the Velvet Revolution. We threw in some baddies for contrast, Andrew Dice Clay and John Gotti. Jim had the brain wave of writing the Clay caption in his own voice. "So I pissed off a few fruits and scags. Is that any reason to crucify me?"

Tuesday, October 16, 1990

Waiting for baby D-day! My Caesarian is scheduled for October twenty-second. Dr. Thornton thinks that with the prematurity of G and the miscarriage, I should not risk natural birth. Oddly, I have never felt more energized and focused, ballooning around the office and getting work cleared so I can soon disappear. Roseanne will be much reviled, but I think it is a great conversation starter and I love adding comedy and comedians to shake up movie-star blandery. Jim Wolcott came in again to help with cover lines. ("Roseanne in Fat City"?) T. D. Allman turned in an excellent, deeply reported piece on Helmut Kohl and German reunification. I couldn't help laughing when I thought of how Kohl would feel when the issue arrived with Roseanne cavorting half-naked. I know it will crush Tim Allman, who was so happy to be able to send Kohl the Gorby cover to reassure him we are serious, and that did give me pause. When he saw it, he said grimly, "One day I hope we will solve our cover problems." "You never know," said Wolcott. "Roseanne probably looks just like Frau Kohl."

We have some staff swings and round-abouts, which will actually energize the mag. Sharon is going. When I called her in to talk about staff complaints again she called me a cunt, which was a bit excessive, even for her. Seems to want to work on projects with Son-tag. Still, I will miss her dogged ability to restructure a "vomit draft" piece. Then in the usual way one exit causes another, over breakfast photo director, Elisabeth Biondi, who has been so stellar for so long, said she had accepted a job to go back to Germany and work at Stern. I told her she would hate boring Hamburg. No one can leave NYC once they have lived here for long. She knows it's true but wants a life.

So we have lost Sharon and Biondi but gained Mike Caruso as an editor, and I hired as a new promotions director Hamilton South, lured away from Barney's. He has such style and charm, he can be the missing link between ad clients and editorial we so much need. Since neither Si nor Doug understand nor value the need for social skills with luxury clients, I managed to slip Hamilton in on the editorial budget. Only anxiety before the baby is *60 Minutes,* which airs this Sunday, on baby eve.

G is finally getting excited about the baby and decided to name her tonight. We had been thinking Daisy, but G was adamant. "Let's call her Isabel," he said. It felt unfamiliar until I said it aloud. Isabel Evans. I love the two together. And suddenly felt I knew who she is, serious and calm and clever and sweet.

Tuesday, October 23, 1990

Lying in my New York hospital bed feeling wonderfully quiet and serene. My darling little baby Isabel Harriet has just been wheeled back to the nursery. She is so tiny, with bright alert blue eyes and a lovely big mouth. The amazing thing is there is something about the shape of her beautiful brow that is just like my mother, and she is dark,

754

too, like Mum, her peach-fuzz hair dark brown.

She was born yesterday morning. As the nurses stuck me up with needles and an anesthesiologist shot me up with the epidural, I felt the huge weight of being a woman. Giving birth is something only we can do and it is full of pain and fear. Next door a woman in labor moaned and wailed with cries from the Middle Ages while I held Harry's hand tight and quailed in my cubicle over the imminence of the knife. Dr. Thornton was so reassuring, though. Gone was the power woman in pink heels and fuchsia dress. Now she was all doctorly seriousness in her blue paper cap. At eight thirty a.m., when my waist had begun to freeze, they wheeled me into the OR, placed a curtain between me and my bottom half, and began to work away at me. Harry was squeezing my hand like mad and was more agitated than I was. After about six minutes I felt a strange pressure on my tummy. "Her head is coming out!" cried Thornton. "Her shoulders!" It was like a painting emerging from invisible ink. Harry was weeping and shouting, "The darling! The darling!" and suddenly my stomach felt empty and I heard a raspy little cry. When the nurse parted the curtain, I saw her, my tiny, mottled, dark-haired little sweetheart baby girl, Isabel! They brought her up to my face so I could kiss her and look into the brightest, beadiest little pair of blue eyes.

"She's so alert!" everyone chorused, and they took her off to swaddle and clean her, then laid her gently on my breast. She grasped the nipple firmly and eagerly in her questing mouth, and I felt the purest love for my daughter, who is mine forever, the deepest love of my deepest self.

Lying here cut off from the world is wonderful peace from my jagged life beyond. Harry spent the weekend before Operation Isabel negotiating with Vitale down to the wire, when Alberto suddenly got cold feet about removing Joni Evans as president of Random House entirely. In the end it was solved graciously with her taking her own imprint instead. It was bedlam trying to get the space ready for the baby and baby nurse, with the half-completed apartment addition in builder's chaos and G agitated by all the turbulence, racing around the dining room like a train, frantically calling up *Little Mermaid* characters on the phone. Where does he get it from? Then as the mad weekend drew to a close we all sat around the TV for *60 Minutes.*

It was fabulous. They really showed the mix of journalism and celebrity in the mag, made it seem alive and important, and it's going to be an incredible boost to *VF* sales. A thrilling way to put one phase of my life to bed and drive in serenity to the hospital to give birth the next morning. The great upside of a Caesarian is that you can shoot up with Demerol and float out to sea. Isabel spent most of yesterday snuggling at my breast so peacefully. Now I can stare at her for hours and see the full sweetness of her big mouth and smooth, round cheeks. My new little stranger for whom I feel such stirrings of crazy love. G came to visit and suddenly seemed so huge and bouncy. I had ensured there would be a gift at home for him, a set of tiny Little Mermaids, and he brought Ariel to see me and kissed her and me with equal gusto. He's such an affectionate soul, I think he surely must love Isabel. My dear little family! I feel now the circle is complete and all the real things in life can surround me in peace. What an amazing few days. But all pales beside the gorgeous, sweet-smelling bundle nestling beside me.

Friday, November 2, 1990

After a quiet weekend at home with the new arrival, all hell let loose when G suddenly realized Isabel is not going back. His sweet interest was replaced with vengeful imprecations. "Let's flush her down the toilet!" Then he was back to sweet again, waving his magic wand over her bassinet and saying, "You must be a brave, truthful, and true baby sister!"

Whenever I pick her up for a feed, he tries to grab me away for a cuddle. I suppose such jealousy is normal, but it's been a roller coaster. Meanwhile, Isabel has been developing her own real face — strong nose, bright, curious eyes, kissable pink mouth. I feel she will be more down-to-earth than Georgie. "Come on, Mummy, let's get real," I can hear her say as G drifts off into the ether with poetry and Edgar Allan Poe stories. It's heavenly to be around my home, however chaotic, instead of racing out with a pile of manuscripts spilling out of my bag. Heavenly to take my own children to the pediatrician instead of calling the doctor from the office for an update. Was just savoring my domesticity when news of Harry's new job as president and publisher of Random House broke. "Too much cultural power centered on one living room," Leon Wieseltier put it darkly when he called me to "congratulate." *The New York Times* went crazy, putting the story on page one, with a two-column turn to the business section, with a three-column "golden couple" sidebar on the new baby, etc. Feel ominous when I read such hyperbole and can only imagine Nora Ephron's fangs out.

What is great, though, is how much pleasure there is for Harry around town, where he is so popular. So much backbiting about my having "outstripped" him, and this really rights that gallingly sexist perception, unimaginable the other way around. A delicious irony is that two weeks ago Random House bought Rupert Murdoch's autobiography, so Harry is now his publisher. All the papers made note of that.

Friday, November 30, 1990

Caroline Graham calls to say I have to apologize to the CAA agent Ron Meyer, who is livid about the remarks I made on *60 Minutes* about his most important client and friend, Sly Stallone, whose girlfriend I unhappily called a "bimbo" on camera. (Yup, of course they used it. I should have guessed and warned him, but it slipped my mind while giving birth.) Apparently he was on his car phone and kept cutting in and out so that all Caroline could get was "How could Tina stab . . . who does Tina think she . . . mired me in shit by . . ." Finally Caroline said, "Look. I am sure Tina didn't realize what she was doing to Sly," and Meyer bawled, "Don't bullshit me! Tina Brown went to Oxford! She always knows what she's doing!"

Being here with my snoozy, snuffly little baby with the hammering and banging of the apartment extension is unbelievable. Why did we do this extension? The place suddenly feels too big. I feel I need roller skates like Princess Di to elude the cacophony of builders, and nannies, and faxes and phone calls and packages from the office, interrupted by Isabel's hunger pangs or Georgie climbing onto my bed to demand "a big, fat kiss." Tonight he told me, "Your cheeks smell of blueberry muffins." It's been lovely for G having my parents around, but hellish for me because of their oxygen-eating neediness. I feel an emotional wreck, not ready at all to face the office as my slim maternity leave is whittled away. I am worried that G will always be so demanding, it will squeeze out Isabel, my dear pink worm, and she will get the short end of it.

With his usual exquisite timing, Si suddenly fired Doug Johnston and appointed Ron Galotti as *VF* publisher. Ron is a fantastic choice, as I saw how brilliantly he launched *Traveler* for Harry. But couldn't Si have waited for me to get back? I felt bad for Doug but did warn him that he had less time than he thought. Ron is very swaggery, a creative business guy. A player. Compared to Doug's preppy affability, Ron's dialogue is right out of *Goodfellas,* which is pretty entertaining. He absolutely despises Bernie Leser, unfortunately, which won't help corporate relations. We met to get to know each other better at the Small Café, a block from me, and I grilled him on what he would do for *VF.* His slicked-back hair shone with "product" and his necktie was man-of-the-world dapper. He immediately launched into a Bernie Leser offense.

"That guy's so full of it, it's incredible," he told me. "The other day we were standing outside Condé Nast and he was giving me some story about how his vacation in Australia was no vacation because of all the clients he saw, and I started to stare at my feet. Bernie says, 'Why are you looking down, Ron,' and I say, 'Because I am up to my knees in bullshit, Bernie, and it just keeps raining down.'"

Bernie keeps trying to get between him and Si to try to wield control over Condé's most successful, and therefore threatening, publisher. "I say, look, Bernie. When the Man calls down from the fourteenth floor, am I going to hang up on him? Put him on hold and check it out with you? Give me a break here. Stop haunting my house. It's beyond belief, Tina. It's beyond belief." If this dialogue keeps up, I will for sure be happy.

Saturday, December 1, 1990

Gail Sheehy came over to talk about a new piece she wants to write about menopause. Two women at opposite ends of the fertility spectrum confronting each other over a cup of tea.

It was nice to talk stories after six weeks of cotton head. We sat in the living room while I nursed Izzy and she laid the piece out. I love the idea of tackling menopause. Women always feel they have to hide it, or treat it like some secret disease instead of part of a natural cycle. And then when we're through it, we're made to feel discarded and reduced. Gail said, on the contrary, she wants to write about the incredible "postmenopausal rush" when women are at their most confident and productive. Yippee. I can't wait. Must be so liberating to be done with the need to be attractive and focus instead on fulfillment and power. I can't wait to be a grand old trout making influential decisions. I told Gail absolutely, do it. Let's call it "The Secret Passage," referencing back to her old bestseller, *Passages,* and amplifying the taboo angle. It's good to turn Gail back to personal life after a long winning streak on politics. Writers need constant refreshment and change of direction. Nothing worse than being stuck on a "beat."

Hollywood people are unbelievable. Jeffrey Katzenberg called me up a week ago and asked if I would do a screening for his new movie *Green Card* with Gerard Depardieu. I told him I just had a baby and was on leave. He totally ignored me and told me I must do this for him because I owed him. (For what?) It's a great movie, he insisted, that's what friends are for, etc. I should have told him to take a hike, then of course succumbed. But I really didn't feel ready for it, like a deep-sea diver as I swam around the faces I didn't want to see, with baby-head making me forgetful and vague. I had forgotten how terrifyingly tough NYC is, what an hourly battering it is to stay on top. I was in such a sensitive mood that I felt I had gone out stark naked.

It was the first time I have faced people since I put Roseanne Barr on the mag's cover, which has, as expected, been universally reviled. Nick Dunne said he has been aggressed about it everywhere he's been, with "Trust me, she's gone too far this time" as the most common response. Still, they are all still reading it. And our *Tatler* motto of "the magazine that bites the hand that reads you" is still my mantra.

Sunday, December 2, 1990

Today I had an unsettling visit from Georgie's physical therapist at the hospital, who told me, to my sadness, she does not think G can go to a mainstream school. And as she itemized all the preschool things he has trouble with — his lack of participation, she says, is due to neurological processing problems — I realize the way he perseverates, the way he can't do puzzles or stick things on paper or cut out and make things like other children, is due to delays from the prematurity she now

763

painfully points out. It breaks my heart to have it confirmed but I only love him all the more, determined to get him all the support he needs to overcome it. He's so brilliant with words and so original, I know he will find his own path. He loves preschool so much, arriving with the other kids and bustling in, but I do see more and more the difference between him and them. If only he had come to full term. Was it my fault for working too hard and long? I worry so much about what the cruel world has in store when he has so many challenges. I told Harry tonight and he was deeply upset. We sat on the sofa together and cried. We have been to so many doctors and none of them have come up with a label to hang on to. It only makes us both more deeply connected to him. He surprises us all the time with new things he can do. My task is now to find a school that will really help him. I am even more glad to have a second child, who, when she grows up, will always be there for G.

We resolved to make this the best, the happiest Christmas he has ever had.

1991
NATURAL BORN WOMAN

Monday, January 7, 1991

New York is so cold after our Florida idyll with G and Izzy. It was bliss pulling Iz around the pool in her rubber ring at the Ritz-Carlton in Naples, her tiny feet splashing, while Harry took G off on speedboat rides.

People may think I want to go off and run the world, but my stubborn dream is being the mistress of an Oxford college, living in my own personal Garsington Manor, and summering in Tuscany with my teetering pile of books on British history. Yet whenever I go to an expat Oxford alum event I am reminded of how genially hilarious Oxford is, pure Alan Bennett. The vice-chancellor of Oxford, Sir Richard Southwood, showed up in town for a huge fund-raising drive, but it's all done in the amateurish, apologetic way of the English that is so hopelessly ineffectual in New York, capital of capital. Southwood's résumé for a start: he's a zoology professor specializing in exotic beetles. As he started to speak I realized how long it was since I'd heard anyone say "I hasten to assure you" or refer to "donkey's years."

"Oxford!" Southwood proclaimed to the listening circle of putative American donors. "Home of such important international influences . . . *Winnie-the-Pooh* . . . *Alice in Wonderland*!" (This sly whimsy was lost on the group, who looked puzzled and shifted in their seats.) "Scholarship today is not [raising a finger] what you might think! A matter of a notebook and a pencil. Heavens, no! It requires computers! Highly complex technical aids to further our researches. These are expensive! Let me tell you a little story! A friend of mine is an ancient historian at Magdalen. For the last five years he has been trying to ascertain the precise date of the opening of the silk route and has been stumped. Now, however, there exists an intricate piece of technology that can take the remnant of silk and tell us exactly when it was produced! But the technology is expensive and that, my friends, is why I'm here."

Watching the unimpressed faces at the four tables, I realized how American I have become. Coaching him, I would have said, "Look, Dick, that résumé won't fly in New York. How about Soviet studies? They always love that." "I'm a zoologist!" he would protest, but, sadly, silk routes, beetles, and "hastens to assure us" are not going to raise Oxford a dime. Everyone shuffled off into the elevator afterward, looking puzzled and somewhat drunk.

Wednesday, January 16, 1991

War broke out with Iraq just as we were on our way to a dinner with, of all people, Henry and Nancy Kissinger at the River House. With CNN's reports of the aerial bombing campaign of military targets blazing in the background, we milled (inevitably) with Rupert and Anna Murdoch. (Oh, the wheel of fortune. Rupert's huge papier-mâché face has imploded with debt crunch. Anna is tight around the eyes with pretending not to worry.) TVs were on in every room. And all attempts to talk about anything else were abandoned. Dinner was postponed till after Bush and Cheney spoke at nine o'clock. When the TV set in the living room had too many people watching it, Henry K, Harry, Chessy Rayner, the TV journalist Barbara Howar, and I went upstairs and plunked on Henry and Nancy's huge orthopedic bed with a view of books and a dog basket. Henry was in charge of the remote. "NBC's analysis is superior, but CNN for the news breaks," he rumbled, flipping back and forth. "*Nightline* keeps calling," he added to Nancy. "Shall I go on?"

"Will they put Cheney on by ten thirty?" fretted Nancy in her long drawl. "The meat will spoil."

"Put it on a slow gas," growled Henry. And as Gerald Ford came on, he added, "I hear there's a great movie on at eleven. Heh-heh."

Harry sensed tension between Murdoch and Barry Diller, doing such an amazing job running Fox. No doubt it's because Barry got the stock up with the network success, and then Rupert's *TV Guide* blunder and Sky Channel madness have forced it down again. Diller expresses himself so well and colorfully, whatever the gravitas of the situation it makes me smile. "Did that terrible *Bonfire of the Vanities* movie make any money?" John Gutfreund asked him. "Fifty million dollars gone Venezuela," Barry replied with an urbane smile. His judgment of our Lew Wasserman piece was one to remember for a tombstone epitaph . . . "There was great dust in his wake." So was another epigram about the changes Harry needs to make at Random House: "There is nothing to protect except going out of business."

He and Diane von Furstenberg kept exchanging knowing looks across the table. They have a *Les liaisons dangereuses* bond, it seems — today's Valmont and Merteuil. A complicity of past secrets now mellowed into worldly friendship that continues to advance both.

It was surreal having dinner with this lot as bombs exploded on the multiple screens. Arguments at the table over who is best — Rather, Brokaw, or Jennings — but CNN wins hands down. (I am addicted to Peter Arnett.)

We commented on the commentators, on who was ahead and who behind, as though they were players on a sports team. That was part of the unreality, too. There we were, watching this massive attack as if it were a movie or a game, some strange new form of entertainment. I realized nothing like this had ever happened on TV before, not in real time. Real people were dying, six thousand miles away from the River House, and what we felt was mainly excitement at the spectacle. I looked around at these titans of media, government, and society. None of them was at risk here. None of them had a son or daughter over there, or any real skin in the game — and game it was to them, and even to me. Is this what war feels like now to all of us who don't serve — remote and weirdly beautiful, with only the reassuringly familiar faces of our favorite news stars to connect us to this distant, enormous event?

On such a night of high points and subtext I love my job, which allows me to be there and then walk away and assign what I learned. We were home early as the River House is so close, and then it was back to more CNN, more Gulf War in our pajamas.

On my way back from launching *Vanity Fair* in London. Hated leaving my darling baby girl so much and am still pumping breast milk — a horrible wrench. I love holding her in my arms late at night and staring at her sweet, plump mouth and happy smile. Now that they've sold the house in Spain, Mum and Dad are settled into their elegant new apartment in St. John's Wood. So the only consoling thing in having to leave Isabel was that it enabled me to bring Mum the very latest pictures of her new granddaughter.

Because of the Gulf War, the plane was entirely empty except for Barbara Walters. That was a girl-power statement. Everyone else chickened out of flying, but we didn't. She was going over to get some scoop interview. There is a reason she is on top.

In the office, we talked at first about canceling the *VF* launch event. Everything is in such panic and disarray with travel plans and doubt about "what's appropriate." Then we thought, fuck it, Dunkirk spirit, we won't do a big launch event, but a series of small things to say *VF* has arrived in London. I took the usual indefatigable team of *VF* talents who are such great promoters and ambassadors

and now work so well together, it's like the
Rockettes on a school outing. We divided and
conquered with a series of promotion parties
in London (all paid for by the hosts, which
was better still in austere times). As I raced
through empty streets in a black taxi, I felt
like Pamela Harriman in the blitz on my way
to see Edward R. Murrow. I half expected to
see handsome young airmen in uniform kissing backlit blondes good-bye in doorways.

One of the things I always forget about
London is how wonderfully louche it is
compared to NYC. Brits get to the restaurant
for lunch at one and leave at three forty-five,
slightly drunk and wreathed in cigarette
smoke, instead of, as in Manhattan, bolting
from the restaurant at two o'clock, leaving
half a Caesar salad and a glass of Perrier.
Nigel Dempster's "Who's Saddam fucking?"
was the closest anyone got to the Gulf crisis
during the hack lunch, which actually was
the best of all the occasions because writers
are the best tribe, bar none, especially these
— Auberon Waugh, Margaret Drabble, Michael Holroyd, Angela Huth, Melvyn Bragg,
Tony Holden, Michael Roberts, and dear
Martin (Amis), in thoughtful mood.

When I read the London coverage I was
thrilled but also depressed, as I scarcely
recognized who they were writing about, viz
my "frosty professional patina," my "power
mask," my "chilly charm," etc. It reminded

me how loose and informal the Brits are and how I have to play against that acquired American buttoned-up image all the time (even though it's taken so long to put in place). Most Americans don't realize there are two ways to answer a question. Question: "With the recession and the war, is this a good time to launch a new glossy magazine called *Vanity Fair*?" American answer: "Well, it may look inauspicious, but all the market trends are nonetheless in our favor. There's a definite niche for a blah-blah-blah." English answer: "No. It's a perfectly awful moment. In fact, when I read about the snowstorm I thought, my God, we scored a hat trick." I knew I would get asked about the embarrassment of *Spy* publishing the suck-up letter I wrote to Ovitz, trying to get him to sit down for a profile with Jesse Kornbluth. The leaking thing is a drag. I have received so many similar gushing letters myself, requesting interviews, that pretend to care about my literary taste rather than asking for the glitz piece they really want, and TV bookers write them all the time. But it's sweaty, as Martin would say, to see it leaked. And I was dopey to send it under my name. At least I was ready for the question. When the cocky Jonathan Ross asked me about it, I just said I sent the same letter to Saddam Hussein.

We did a lunch for the fashion crowd, who were such a funny bunch en masse — Bruce

Oldfield, Manolo Blahnik, Roberto Devorik, Hardy Amies all bitching and moaning about business being bad instead of, as we do in NYC, pretending it's good. Roberto Devorik kept shouting: "Let's face it, business is sheet! It is sheet!"

"This blotty George Bush," Manolo postured. "His Hollywood war! His Mary Quant bombs that are supposed to smell nice and not kill any-botty. I think he is a mass murderer and that is final!" (The next day we read about the US bombing of four hundred civilians in an Iraq air raid and Manolo's joke looked horribly prescient.) Hoary old Hardy Amies was at first mystified as to who Reinaldo was, because in Europe Reinaldo uses his operatic Venezuelan title of marqués de Torre Casa.

"I just met someone called the count of Torremolinos," he told me. "I thought I was the only titled queen here." I told him that that was, in fact, Reinaldo Herrera. "Ooh," he said, "I think I know his mother. I KNOW YOUR MOTHER!" he mouthed across the table, not at Reinaldo but at a baffled Joseph Ettedgui, the designer who was sitting next to him. By week's end the buzz on the new *VF* was deafening and the first newsstand check showed a sell-through of 60 percent, which is pretty incredible. The big question now that we're launched is, will they come back for more?

Harry's been in LA to try to sign up Marlon Brando's memoir. I called him at the Bel-Air hotel last night and he didn't answer — even at midnight, which started to make me angsty. Some gorgeous girl he encountered in the Bel-Air lobby? Turns out he couldn't get away from Brando after a bizarre evening of his ranting about Native Americans and how the writer Peter Matthiessen is a CIA agent, while Harry kept delicately trying to get him back around to the memoir. Apparently he is totally paranoid, so Harry omitted to tell him he's married to the person who published the piece in *Vanity Fair* he hated by Peter Manso about his son Christian's murder of his sister's boyfriend.

They played a two-hour chess game in which Marlon avoided the only thing Harry wanted to talk about: the content of a possible book. When he was again about to leave, Marlon energetically insisted he join him for a midnight swim. His huge bulk floated in the deep end for an hour in pitch darkness with only the sound of Japanese chimes, declaiming Shakespeare as Harry trod water — Mark Anthony's funeral oration: "*Lend me your ears!* Emphasis on the 'lend,' not the 'ears,' Harry." Then he wanted Harry to stay for a bonding sauna, still declaiming (at 1:30 a.m. and wearing tentlike underpants in the steaming heat) "O what a rogue and peasant slave am I." At the end of this bizarre publishing quest, NO book agreed, but a promise of "more such congenial conversational occasions, Harry."

Friday, March 22, 1991
Sonesta Spa, Fort Lauderdale

Snatched up the kids and fled town to Florida. Harry's Random House sales conference was well timed and we tagged along and stayed after he left. Isabel is the most glorious, affable baby I have ever met. She gurgles and gurgles all day, with her vast satellite-dish eyes and rosebud mouth that eats your arm and slobbers into your neck. She gazes at Georgie in total fascination and he is much more connected to her now. (He kissed her yesterday and when I exclaimed, "How sweet to kiss your sister!" he replied darkly, "I'm giving Isabel my cold.")

In between I struggle to keep the magazine on its high wire. We did an incredible April issue with Madonna on the cover, shot by Steven Meisel; inside was Marie Brenner on Oscar Wyatt, T. D. Allman on Arafat and the PLO. Meaty, newsy stuff. But then the May issue fell apart and it was like back to the worst old times when we had no lead and wound up having to buy a Marilyn Monroe book extract. This is the endless dice roll of monthly magazines, the dependence on quality that sometimes just does not arrive or disappoints.

I am also brooding how I can make a definitive editorial statement that will distance us from the eighties. A new adrenaline shot. Without explicitly saying so we need to make a turn that's decisive or we will be defined by the passé Reagan era of glitz and Park Avenue. The nineties is about divestment. About shedding old social structures and pretenses. There's a lust for a reckoning, too, after all the Wall Street malfeasance. We need to get deeper, darker, more expansive while keeping the joy factor. I am looking for a cover that will do that and have talked about it a lot with Annie.

Harry's Random House job has added a whole lot of turmoil to our domestic lives. (Turmoil he adores, I have to say.) I forgot it would mean there is a book launch every night that he has to go to, even if I refuse. He did finally, after two more meetings, corral Brando's memoir. There was a brief crisis last week when Marlon connected that he was married to me and nearly pulled out. "And now comes a large cloud of black crows," he wheezed down the phone to Harry from LA. "Your wife, I learn, is Tina Brown." But Harry performed the feat of somehow distancing himself from his wife of ten years and the deal was signed for a mighty $5 million.

Si gave a dinner for David Geffen to try to appease his wrath over Art Cooper's *GQ* profile, which had incensed Geffen into taking Paul Marciano to lunch and convincing him to pull all his Guess ads from *GQ*. (A low blow. Geffen knows how to stick the knife.) I sat between him and Dick Snyder, who is in the middle of a fight for his life at S and S that he probably will not win. It is now obvious that he was destined to implode. I will always be fond of him, perhaps because he was the first publishing power I ever met at that first ABA in Dallas with Ed Victor. I will never forget the image of him walking into the hotel lobby flanked by his S and S court of leggy senior editors and glitzy PR girls. He was such a king. He now has an entirely perpendicular blow-dry and a lobster-tinged complexion. The iconoclastic wit has a destructive edge. It will be bad for him when he is eventually fired, which I sense will not be long.

Tuesday, April 30, 1991

Just back from the wake for Tatiana Liberman at Frank Campbell's memorial home. Poor Alex! It finally happened. The end of his great love. Her tyranny. The absorption with *her.* Oscar de la Renta told me, "Two months ago I saw Alex. Tatiana was bed-ridden, demanding even more than usual. And Alex said to me, 'If only I could just keep her like this, I'd be so happy.' "

But in the last months as his own health has been failing, the strain has exhausted him. He is waxen. Tonight, in the group of murmuring friends assembled — Pierre Bergé flown in from Paris, Annalee Newman, the widow of the painter Barnett, Joan Buck, Si and Victoria, etc. — Alex sat on a sofa with that stiff, dignified smile he wears when his mind is somewhere else. He took both my hands. "Dear friend," he said sorrowfully.

How true and real a bereavement makes people become. Francine du Plessix Gray, who has always, I felt, disliked me, and who only two weeks ago snubbed me at the PEN dinner, was animated with grief. "Alex loved your note," she said with emotion. And we both teared up and talked about how stupid and inadequate the *New York Times* obituary of Tatiana was, making her sound like a frivolous socialite who only made hats instead of the woman of culture she was and an artist's muse.

Alex, noble ruin, has seen so much history come and go in the last fifty years.

We went to a fiftieth birthday party for the diplomat Dick Holbrooke last week at the 21 Club, which was social torture, with three toasts before the first course, three before the second, and three before dessert. Actually they were roasts, not toasts, an American tradition that I very much dislike. All the remarks were borderline offensive in a heavy, power-people kind of way. Dick's son went on about what it was to be the son of a man who'd force Pete Peterson and his wife, Joan Ganz Cooney, to host such a gathering as this. Dick laughed somewhat hollowly throughout as he was described again and again as an egregious social climber. It may be true, but I also love him for his brilliance and bigness of temperament in a smaller and smaller world.

Pondering on why it was such a discomforting night: there's a new social trend that seems to be about marketing your private life. Every birthday, every anniversary, every baby shower, every wedding is just the excuse for a positioning statement. I knew what we were in for as soon as we entered that big, sententious room at 21 and I saw the podium and the place cards and the microphone waiting ominously. Dick lusts to be secretary of state at some point, so maybe I am wrong and this is what he wanted.

I am now on my way to Vancouver to speak to the American Newspaper Publishers Association at the request of Donald Newhouse. Amazingly, he's had me picked up in a private plane. They want me to go tell them what's wrong with American newspapers (where do

I start?). It's a bit of an uncomfortable role as the outsider magazine editor from the UK. According to Steve Newhouse, whom Harry just saw at his Arizona sales conference, they expect me to come in and "kick butt." Have spent many hours prepping for it.

It's been interesting to think about why American newspapers are so much less potent than England's. It's fashionable here to sneer at the British tabloids, but I grew up on the wit and buoyancy of those headlines and sorely miss them. There's so much talent on the back bench of British papers, even though often put to such hopelessly meretricious ends. The press vitality there is unbeatable, the flamboyant sense of design, the picture choices, the cropping, the sharp captions. *The New York Times* is so self-important and badly laid out. *The Washington Post* is so much better — the Style section has all the flair of European journalism — but what I miss here is the surprise of a Hollywood splash lighting up a news page or an irreverent headline undercutting a pompous public moment. What's great about Fleet Street is that literary talents like Kingsley Amis or Keith Waterhouse or Auberon Waugh don't feel above writing both for the popular press and the high-minded or literary press. There is huge snobbery and hand-wringing here about what "serious" papers "should" publish and where writers "should" write. Plus I am always shocked how crappy local American papers *look*. There needs to be a total overhaul of visual approach and a willingness to entertain popular culture, a more flexible sense of inclusion that doesn't mean being trashy or they will lose their audiences and die. And they have to get rid of the concept of "women's pages" and understand women are half their audience and emotional content needs to pervade throughout. The *Daily Mail* in England has been sensational at that, ruthless and amoral though they may be. Their human angles make every single story, even when about people I don't give a damn about, totally irresistible to read. Which is what I plan to tell them!

Si warned me that once I sampled it, I'd never want to travel any other way than on a private plane, and how right he was. It was due to take off from Newark at eleven, but it was pouring rain and I arrived at five after, having been told it would take off whenever I got there. Yan, my fave driver from Manhattan Limo, drives me through the electric gates after murmuring my "tail" number (the number on the tail wing; the cats would like that). A smiling stewardess then waves me, and only me, aboard an empty ten-seater Gulfstream with plushy beige leather seats and writing tables and a cornucopia of the day's papers I am about to trash in Vancouver. Just as we are about to take off, the pilot comes out and says, "Brenda Phipps [my invaluable executive assistant] needs to speak to you." So I trot downstairs again and into the little private terminal to the phone booth and call her. "I wanted to know," she says, "what kind of skunk would you like to get for Georgie at FAO Schwarz? The fourteen-dollar one or the sixty-five-dollar one?" "What's furrier?" I demand. "The sixty-five." "Go for it," I said. Returning to my creamy seat on the plane, I tell the crew, "Just a small office crisis," settling down after takeoff with piping coffee that appears from nowhere. And soon, I am rehearsing my speech at top volume to an invisible audience, only stopping for a reclining nap and to feast alone on chicken and angel-hair pasta, until we reach Vancouver.

Tuesday, May 7, 1991
In flight, Vancouver to New York

Delivery of speech was a B but the content must have scored, as there were a bunch of reporters afterward asking for copies. Last night Sue and Donald gave a dinner for all the newspaper big shots. Frank Bennack was there with his wife, Luella. I felt a pang because I do really like him and he was very nice with no hint of resentment. I felt great affection, though, for my own dear New-houses. For a family of gerbils they have a dash of style. It was very cool of them to lay on the plane.

As I socked it to the audience about how boring their newspapers are, it occurred to me that if I was offered one to edit, I would certainly accept. I still find newspapers way sexier than magazines. I am bored with the world of Ralph Lauren and Polo. My dream would be to do it with Harry, but he's now ensconced in the even slower world of books. Steve Newhouse, Donald's son who runs the New Jersey paper, was very thrilled and sparkly-eyed about my speech. Perhaps he will be the one who shakes it all up.

Friday, May 17, 1991

The lead of the July issue collapsed. I lost confidence for the fourteenth time in Gail Sheehy's Saddam Hussein piece. She hasn't nailed it this time, it needs more deep Middle East knowledge. It's been a curse. Or as Gail would write, a black cloud, a brooding threat, a dark imprecation. Pam McCarthy has been locked in the office with Gail half the week, trying to nail down her sourcing, at one point emitting the desperate cry "But Gail, how do you know what Saddam's mother was thinking?"

Being stuck in this position showed the weakness in our system at the moment. I need a greater variety in lead writers to tackle these pieces or I ask too much of the great ones I already have. And we have to have backups for when things flame out. I have been doing too many extracurricular things and it's making the staff irritable. It was thus a flak-filled day, arguing on the phone with Gail, Elise O'Shaughnessy, who was editing the piece, and Pam for denying us more deadline time, and forcing the fact-checking department to go over it again, while at the same time having to get the backup piece on the Agnelli empire, which is the only available (but unremarkable) substitute ready for publication in case we can't make it work. At one comical moment I had a raging Gail Sheehy on one line, Norman Mailer on another, trying to talk more about my involvement with the Actors Studio gala, and Si wanting to read over the phone to me the speech he's written for the FIT tribute to Condé Nast.

Saturday, May 18, 1991

Gave a book publishing dinner for Clark Clifford's memoir, cowritten with Dick Holbrooke, that Harry is publishing at Random House. Twenty years from now I will look back on it with fascination.

The whole atmosphere of the dinner was glowing with dated power. Here was Clifford, in his eighties — one of the most distinguished figures in American politics, patrician wise man to Presidents Truman, John F. Kennedy, LBJ, and Jimmy Carter, publishing a book that should be his legacy victory lap, and instead he's in the middle of the BCCI banking scandal, facing charges of fraud, conspiracy, and taking bribes, a furore that has broken over his head at the same time as the pub date of this long-awaited book. He claims he was "duped" by his partners over BCCI, but the reality was probably a rare error of judgment fueled by latent character weakness, a love of power and reward that has increased as he loses relevance and believes his own legend.

An extraordinary assembly of mostly Camelot survivors convened to celebrate this ancient, elegant politico who's right out of one of Gore Vidal's novels. ("Will there be re-marks?" he inquired as we sat down to eat.) And his own "re-marks" were some of the best I have heard, a reenactment of a party thrown by a "dry" senator twenty years ago at which "those who usually had one drink before they got there had four, those who usually had six had eight," the result being that all the senator's guests arrived half-drunk, and Clifford proceeded to act out each of the half-drunk senators' toasts — with full body-movement and speech content — to such a hilarious degree that the entire room was howling. It's probably a routine he's done many times but it was astounding! A good thing the DA wasn't here, given his BCCI defense is that he can't remember.

The arrangement of this dinner had given me much anxiety. Holbrooke, in his incorrigibly pushy way, kept inviting extra people and our dining room only seats sixteen for a seated dinner of two tables of eight, or at most thirty if we do buffet and five tables of six. This clearly was not a buffet crowd. Octogenarian Camelotters and the most famous first lady in history have to be properly respected. But as guest after guest accepted, it seemed a buffet for thirty would be unavoidable (though I still place-carded it). Was particularly worried about Jackie Onassis, who has never been to our house. I knew after the *VF* cover story "Jackie, Yo!" she would ruminate long and hard about accepting this, and would only do so for Clifford. Our piece, although very "pro" her, was pretty vulgar and intrusive. There is no doubt she hated it. And only two issues ago we ran the juicy Marilyn Monroe extract from the Peter Lawford bio, which had pull-quotes about JFK having sex with Marilyn.

How would she react to me after the gracious introductions? I would find out in a wonderful, subtle put-down she aimed at me, unforgettable in its deft and understated malice.

In person Jackie has an enormous head and

a fragile presence. At dinner she and I sat close to each other because we were on either side of Clifford. The rest of the table was the historian Arthur Schlesinger, whom I sat beside her for the comfort of an old friend in a strange house, Victoria Newhouse, Ambassador Philip Habib, and the fabled speech writer Ted Sorensen. Watching Jackie close up was mesmerizing. Her face is always slightly out of whack with her expression, as if they are two separate entities at work. She has perfected a fascinated stare. Sitting finishing-school upright in a fuchsia Carolina Herrera jacket over a dark sheath, she looks into your face, not your eyes, and not mine, I hasten to say. In fact, "crazed" is what I decided about Jackie by the end of the evening. I felt if you cleared the room and left her alone, she'd be in front of a mirror, screaming. Her responses are so out of kilter. After thirteen minutes of a rapt stare, she suddenly claps her hands and cries in that breathy little voice, "Oh, Clark! You sly fox, you! The way you, the way you . . . dispatched Eisenhower! In that sly, slinky, oh, Cliffordy way! All the, all the, revisionism about Eisenhower! Oh, Clark, I don't know about it! You know how we all . . . when we leave office . . . we're dumped on. And then we, then we come back and it's all written over again! Oh, Clark! What you wrote was so, so perfect!"

These disjointed outbursts came like a rush

of animation from a puppet. It's as if somebody jerks the strings, the body lurches to
life, then she gradually sinks back into starey-
eyed repose. But on to the put-down. Halfway
through dinner, Arthur Schlesinger began to
praise our Mrs. Thatcher profile by Maureen
Orth. He was telling Habib he should read it,
and Clifford, who amazed me by being a solid
VF reader from all his references, agreed that
it was first-rate. Jackie listened to all this,
then suddenly turned to Clifford and said,
"Oh, Clark! There's a wonderful piece in this
week's *New Republic* you must, must read!" I
knew instantly what she was referring to; the
savaging of Gail Sheehy's Gorbachev book
by Tatyana Tolstaya, ridiculing all the alleged
inaccuracies. Everyone knows that Sheehy's
Gorbachev book derives from her hit cover
story in *Vanity Fair.* She went on, "Clark,
Clark, I will send you this piece because
you'll die laughing. It's about this, this naive
American girl journalist, who's oh so culturally ignorant about the Soviet Union that she
applies her, her limited, silly Western views
and logic to all the mysteries of the modern
Soviet state!" As soon as I saw her game I
broke away into a conversation with Habib
while listening to her with one ear and catching her delicate sideways look to me across
the salmon puff pastry, a look that registered
she knew I knew she was shafting me and
why. It was masterful.

Still the evening was a magical one, the casualness of it, the small tables and the careful seating worked so well. I shall never forget the vignette of Clifford sprawled on our big green round club chair after dinner with his long, spindly legs extended and Jackie kneeling at his feet, looking up at him. A nice surprise was her longtime escort Maurice Tempelsman, whom I had always filed as plodding and dull but who on this night was enormously warm and charming. After (delicious) rhubarb pie and coffee, Jackie floated around the room to stare into other faces and for a time sat nose to nose on a sofa with Clark's wife, Marnie Clifford, who Harry said was divine. She seemed as happy as she is likely to get.

The next day Holbrooke told me Jackie called and said, "Oh, Dick, wasn't it the most wonderful night! It was like the evenings Jack and I used to have at the White House! Distinguished and powerful men! Beautiful women of accomplishment! Dick, Dick. It was just like an evening at Versailles!" Which compensated for the fact that she tellingly and, I am sure with considered forethought, didn't write me a thank-you note.

America, as with everything else, makes you more professional about entertaining. In London we just threw fun parties. Here one sees what works and formats it, so that each dinner is the dress rehearsal for the next one.

In our case, the small tables, the long cocktail hour, the fast service, and the mobile dessert and coffee mean no one is stuck with anyone too long. I can't talk to a dinner partner for more than twenty-five minutes a side without desperation setting in. No one has more than that to give, in my view, unless they are having an affair with the person next to them. And the guests seem to love it. Plus, having the dining room double as the library, books floor to ceiling, makes it all feel much cozier and more intimate.

I reflected afterward that had Jack Kennedy been alive, Clifford would have been the man Jackie turned to to handle her divorce from Jack.

Maybe some of these thoughts were in Jackie's head as she carried her strange, tight stare away into the spring night.

Monday, June 10, 1991

I have been in hell with a screw-up on the Mrs. Thatcher profile that was entirely self-inflicted. Have been really whipped for it, not without justification. In the press release that went out with Maureen Orth's piece, our London PR Belinda Harley pulled out and hyped up Maggie's quote about Dennis Thatcher: "Home is where you go when you have nothing better to do." It sparked a huge media reaction in England, with numerous pieces by loudmouthed Fleet Street women columnists sounding off about the low priority of marriage and domestic life on Mrs. T's agenda, and on the other side her supporters were calling us purveyors of trash. In fact, the full Mrs. T quote in Orth's piece was much less damning than the release's truncated version. But, despite my inept attempts to explain that, the UK media kept confusing the two. I went off on vacation with the family to Bermuda, having fired off an unwise letter to *The Spectator* (who had pummeled me the worst), calling my most savage attacker, the Tory historian Paul Johnson, an "empurpled blowhard."

I returned to the seaside cottage where we were staying after a perfect day at the beach to receive a frantic call from Pam McCarthy. It seems Mrs. Thatcher's press office had been taping the interview as well and now released the whole transcript to *The Times*. It showed her quotes had been shamelessly truncated by us in the release, thereby giving a totally incorrect gloss to what Thatcher meant. In the *Times* script we could see that Mrs. Thatcher was not being dismissive about home — quite the contrary. She was talking about its place in the minds of grown-up children who have left it: "We are a very close family even though we do our own thing. That is what family life is about. This [home] is where you come to with your problems.

This is from where you go, to do whatever you wish. And sometimes if something happens and we don't see the family as often as we would wish, and they go off, I say: 'Well, look, home is where you come when you haven't anything better to do. We are always there.' "

Fuck. Why did I write that over-the-top blowhard note about Paul Johnson? The transcript should not really have been a problem because it's what Orth had more or less quoted in the piece, but with my being marooned on vacation, my efforts to differentiate what we published in the magazine from what we put out in the release only seemed to make it worse. The UK news narrative was now that we had falsely quoted the prime minister with malicious intent.

The Bermuda phone was red-hot with press calls from London. I tried to get Harry out of the ocean to advise me, but he had just been stung by a jellyfish. To my consternation I could view him from the porch, peeing on his own leg, while Izzy screamed from her stroller on the deck, Georgie was drubbing me about going to the beach, and the credibility of the magazine's reporting was imploding on the other side of the Atlantic.

Worse was to come. The released Maggie tape got me flayed anew in every British paper. I should have convened a conference call between Pam, Belinda, and Orth and made a coherent full-throated apology, but this whole debacle was ruining the kids' vacation and I kept dealing with it too quickly. "Empurpled blowhard" was now the ubiquitous quote of the week. Johnson wrote a follow-up column in *The Spectator,* saying I should be "horsewhipped." The worst was Simon Jenkins, as editor of *The Times,* writing a signed editorial, something he never does, calling out my disgraceful journalistic ethics. *VF* was now totally in the penalty box after all the great work we have been doing this year. All because of rushing. No doubt Jackie Onassis, remembering Arthur Schlesinger urging Philip Habib to read the piece, will be thoroughly gratified, and it's so frustrating because the piece itself is so good and quoted Thatcher accurately. I have let Orth down. She is pissed and I am mortified and must be MUCH MUCH more careful in the future AND BE LESS IMPULSIVE AND NEVER RESPOND WITHOUT FULL MEETING OF ALL PLAYERS INVOLVED AND CAREFUL LANGUAGE AND APOLOGIZING PROPERLY AT THE RIGHT MOMENT WHEN WE FUCK UP.

Sunday, July 7, 1991

Nervous about going to England after the Thatcher debacle but had to do so for the fund-raiser the British edition is doing for the Bodleian Library in Oxford. I walked into Harry's Bar for lunch and there was Princess Margaret at a table full of grand wrinklies, and they all stopped talking when they saw me. "You are notorious," George Weidenfeld told me. Ouch.

I can't even remember how we got into this Oxford thing, or why, perhaps outreach from the beetle prof, but we took fifty guests to a Haydn concert at the Sheldonian Theatre followed by a magnificent dinner cooked by Raymond Blanc at Convocation House.

Actually, a bit of history was a soothing relief after my Thatcher shaming. The beauty of the Sheldonian was breathtaking. When I was an undergrad we took it all so much for granted. The magnificent concert, played on sixteenth-century instruments, made me feel as if we had time traveled to a small party for James II's court. And when Prince Charles arrived in a sudden blaze of royal glamour, that sense of another time enveloped us all the more. I felt we should all be bowing our bewigged heads like in *The Madness of King George.*

I've met Prince Charles on numerous occasions and never thought him the least bit charismatic. But this time one felt the full force of the HRH effect. As he strode by in his red gown with white ermine collar, followed by the slithery quiet of ceremonial proctors, the rush of history swirled up to the Christopher Wren ceiling. We got a whiff of what Diana fell for in the first place, the jet-set tan, the bright blue eyes, and the flash of impeccable tailoring beneath the academic gown.

Suddenly, all the gossip about the royal marriage fell into a new, constitutional perspective, a rending of social fabric that was more than just a tabloid affair. The Charles-Di rift we all feast on is not just a problem marriage. The crown is in crisis. The prince looked desperately unhappy all through the soaring strains of *The Creation*. He had a face of real tragedy, as if in deep spiritual torment, which he couldn't hide from all the sideways peeking of the guests. Having felt so sympathetic to Diana until now, I suddenly had an intuition that perhaps he is being set up. The outcry in all the Sunday papers about his not giving a thirtieth birthday party for Diana is suspect. She was, no doubt, the one who leaked the melancholy information that she drove the children back to London alone the night of her birthday. She is playing the press like a fiddle, and since Charles cannot answer or explain, he's coming off as the villain. As Sir Charles Mackerras led the choir in "God Save the Queen," I had an impending sense of great national pain if they were to throw it all away.

Tuesday, July 23, 1991

After the three-week-long persecution of the Thatcher affair comes the happy distraction of the Demi Moore cover on the August issue. When Annie and I first discussed doing Demi, I thought how great it would be to show her pregnant instead of doing the normal thing with stars who are over three months gone and cheat the cover with a head shot or some other disguise. But being Annie, she went one better. She did Demi in profile, yes, full body, yes, but also . . . naked! She unveiled it after first showing me the shots of Demi in brief summer dress, explaining she had just done these others privately. But as soon as I saw that warm, golden image of the utterly naked, enormously pregnant, totally glorious Demi, I knew this was the shot we had to have. I felt retrospectively liberated from a long 1990 trying to hide the expanding Izzy, the vicarious shout of joy of showing Demi's bump to the world. Women need this, dammit! Annie was the persuasive genius who got on the phone and got Demi to agree to make this private picture public. But kudos to Demi too for her bravery and willingness to go out on the edge.

We have wanted so much to do a story that moved *Vanity Fair* decisively on from the eighties, that made a statement of modernity, progressiveness, freshness, openness, after the heavy Trumpy glitz of that decade. I have been beating my brains out looking for the social commentary that would achieve it. And now, in one simple, dazzling image, Annie has the home run. This is it. This is what a celebrity looks like in the nineties. Not just natural but au naturel! And it's a wonderful feminist statement at the same time.

Now I was afraid I would be stopped from doing it by the circulation department, after Walmart went batshit with the Roseanne Barr cover. So I took the precaution of showing first Alex, then Si. Alex just looked quizzical and said, "Are you sure, my dear?" and shrugged. And Si did his pensive gerbil face and finally said, "Why not?" This, in the end, is the joy of working at Condé Nast, particularly when Ron Galotti showed buyers at the big chains to ensure they didn't reject it — and they did. So, resourceful Ron has had the issue shrink-wrapped for the newsstand like a porno mag. Makes it feel even more like forbidden fruit.

I told Hamilton South to try to get the *Today* show to use the image. Which now seems a joke, because this cover has immediately gone into the stratosphere. I expected some buzz, but not what is unfolding — a media orgy that uses the cover on TV eight straight nights in a row — every network news show, *Primetime Live, Entertainment Tonight, Good Morning America,* plus Annie as

Woman of the Week with Peter Jennings on ABC and umpteen references to it by Johnny Carson, Arsenio Hall, David Brinkley, and on and on. The shrink-wrap stunt makes it hotter. It has ignited a million nationwide talk radio shows and newspaper opinion polls about whether or not we should have shown a pregnant belly without clothing. (*The Atlanta Constitution* is running a front-page poll asking if the newsstand should have banned the picture and five thousand readers have responded. Most in favor of publication.) It seems we have broken the last visual taboo. And the perfection of it was that it was an unassailable platform for controversy. Who's ever managed to shock with family values before?

Seventy-five million in TV views so far, and fifty-nine newspapers, not including all the covers in Latin America, Europe, and India that have started to roll in. Plus a full page in *Magazine Week* hailing it as a "stroke of marketing genius." We should sell well over a million in total. Letters have poured in to me from all over the world from other editors saluting it. Pregnant women see it as a breakthrough image for them.

It's such a happy boost. Jane Sarkin, who was the point person for it all, is ecstatic, which is great since she takes so much crap from Hollywood flaks all day long. Pregnant Demi has been like a rebirth for us all. Hail

Annie! She did it again! I feel a surge of energy and creativity that will infuse the whole second half of the year, almost like being stuck in the mud, breaking free, and careening off at twice the speed.

Friday, August 16, 1991

Isabel's christening. Our divine daughter has turned into this unbelievably joyous bundle of protein. She is like a baby Olga Korbut, her tough, plump little legs, her ever-moving, agile little body. She has a special mummy smile that melts my heart, a big, wide smile with two teeth that makes me want to squash her with mad kisses.

We christened her last weekend on one of the nicest days we could have dreamed of, at the Church of the Atonement, Quogue's little clapboard church, as we did for G. It was a glorious day. We had all the friends over for a buffet lunch on the porch and a local band playing at the entrance. Izzy looked so adorable in her frothy little dress, with those huge eyes in her china doll face. She loved being swooped up and down by all the guests, grabbed the rector's cross from around his neck, and chomped on it happily. She has all Harry's power-packed energy and his equable temperament. Nothing fazes her as she moves from one passionate absorption to the next. How lucky I am.

Last week Si asked me to lunch out of the blue. He rarely does, so I knew something was afoot. The issue of What Next has suddenly become pressing. I sensed this lunch was part of some next fulfillment of a plan, which made me anxious.

Right after the Perrier water at the Four Seasons, Si launches into "So who do you think I should be considering to fill Alex's shoes?" (Alex has just come out of the hospital for the second time in two months.) "Who do YOU think, is surely more important?" I said.

"Well, there's Rochelle Udell," said Si. (Huh?) "She's done a wonderful job at *The New Yorker* and Random House."

"She's a good art director, yes," I said tersely, suddenly fatigued by this runaround.

"And then there's you." I wanted to throw a bread roll at his head. I said nothing.

He asked, "But would you find this job creative enough?"

I replied, "Perhaps yes, perhaps no. But clearly the time is drawing near when I have to think about the future." He hurriedly continued, "Well, let's talk some more about Alex's job." And painted it in terms of it being the sagacious role of his discreet consultant. (No thanks.) I said what I thought was a better idea, moving *VF* into other fields, widening it into media beyond just a magazine. Books. Movie production. Radio. A TV show like *60 Minutes*. Susan Mercandetti, a fantastic producer from ABC, came to see me this week about developing *VF* as a news show. She's so good I immediately thought about what she could also bring to the mag as another contributing editor. There could be cross-pollination, developing a show and stories for TV that could also work in the pages of *VF*. She totally sees that a magazine with the kind of fast potency we now have should be thinking laterally as well as vertically. If we lock ourselves into just being a magazine, it will be diminished returns, ultimately. We are a brand, and with the London edition launched, an international one, and should start producing other forms of media from our material. Si seemed a bit intrigued by this passionate riff from me and flushed in his rising-interest way. We adjourned our lunch and he went off for a week's vacation.

Tuesday, September 24, 1991

Si hasn't been in the Four Seasons for ten days. When Si is not in the Four Seasons it means something is up. He's hiring someone big or buying something. But whom or what? And will it affect me? In a moment of paranoia I thought he could be buying *Rolling*

Stone as he has long wanted to do and making Jann Wenner editorial director as part of the package. (Not a bad idea. At least he's brilliant.) I called Ovitz to suss it out. He said he'd check with Wenner but reported back that, after oblique discussions about other stuff, Wenner revealed he's not in selling mode or mood. So what's cooking in the hamster cage? Definitely something, and after the way the Coleridge move went down I don't like it.

The reaction to Demi Moore doesn't stop. Letters pour in from ecstatic women every day. We've sold 548,058 copies on the newsstand (an 82 percent increase on July newsstand sales), giving us a total sale of 1,127,521. It's phenomenal. And the joy of Ron Galotti as *VF* publisher knows no bounds. I finally feel I have a business partner who gets it and can leverage our heat. We're now the hottest book with advertisers as well as readers. Calvin Klein took a 116-page outsert (as it's called), which got us gold-dust business coverage everywhere and of course made every Condé editor of a fashion book green with envy. I feel a moment coming. Should I, after tea and cakes and ices, have the strength to force the moment to its crisis?

Someone is going to make a major play. But what is it to be?

Monday, November 25, 1991

Mick Jagger called me today in agitation about a Nancy Collins cover-story interview, something that's taken me two years to get. Nancy is a razzle-dazzle blonde famous for tell-all Q and As; she's a good addition to our cover-writer repertoire. Before the shoot Mike Caruso called and said, "I'm worried about Nancy. She seems to be flipping out. Think you should call her." But when I did I found she'd already left for London. Next thing we know, urgent faxes are arriving from Jagger's people, demanding we take Nancy off the story. Caruso told me Nancy had called him to say it was clear Mick hated women because of his denying mother, and that she had "let Mick have it" over his obvious desire only to be with women who don't answer back. Caruso reminded her we had three interview times with Jagger, two before Annie's shoot and one after, and that we had agreed she'd delay tough questions till the shoot was in the bag. I called the Stones people to try to keep the show on the road and they put Mick on the line.

"Look, it's like this," the loud, cockney voice of "Satisfaction" blurted from my speakerphone. "Nancy keeps on about me mum. She's just got this bee in her bonnet about me mum. Says she was my 'problem,' but you know, Tina, she wasn't a problem. It was me dad who was the problem. I mean," the foghorn voice continued, "I've done interviews before, you know. Quite a lot of interviews in my time. But she keeps on about me mum. So, Tina, finally, I said, 'Look, Nancy, I am trying as hard as I can to remember what it was like when I was three, but quite honestly, what's the point?' Then she seemed to get all pissed off at the end of lunch because I 'ad to go and try on all the clothes with Annie and Marina for your shoot. And I couldn't sit there talking any more about me mum. So, Tina, then she says that I only want to fuck bimbos! But, honest, I think my girls 'ave been a mixed bag. I've 'ad my share of bimbos, I s'pose, but some of 'em have been quite bright. I mean Bianca's quite bright. Anyway, can you sort it?" It was so surreal. The totally sane rock-and-roll star interviewed by a totally out-there journalist. I called Nancy to tell her to pedal back the mum assault till we got the pictures and she answered the phone in a "take no prisoners" voice. "You've been manipulated," she shouted. "Manipulated by a celebrity! This interview will see the light of day even if not in your magazine!" Slam. I dispatched Stephen Schiff to London to save the cover and write three thousand words on Mick fast.

Tuesday, November 26, 1991

Si called down and said he didn't want Ron Galotti supervising UK *VF* as had been promised, because it would mean discounting the quoted rate card, customary in the UK but a no-no here. US advertisers might hear of it, he said, and start expecting the same discount in the US edition. He's not necessarily wrong, but this question of Ron overseeing UK had all been settled a long time ago. Now Si's arbitrarily reneged on it. I am pissed. So many of my strategic editorial moves have turned to profit, then I'm left out of decisions and presented with a fait accompli. Feel dissed by his patriarchal bullshit. Consoled by Leslie Bennett's important piece in the new issue about pedophilia in the Catholic Church. She's exposed the cover-up of a New Orleans priest who exploited young men for sex and collected kiddie porn.

Sunday, December 8, 1991

I recruited the music-world lawyer Allen Grubman to cochair the next Phoenix House gala with me. The man is a rolling sound bite, I just want to sit in his office all day with a tape recorder on.

A few nuggets. On a phone call from Robert De Niro.

"Bobby calls me today and says, 'I'm at an

airport.' "

"Which airport?"

"What's the difference?"

"Which country?"

"What are you? A travel agent?"

Re my wish list for his help on Phoenix House entertainment: "What's this? Madonna? Bruce Springsteen? Want me to get you Gorbachev to make his resignation speech at Phoenix House?"

Instructed by me to raise money, he calls Jonathan Tisch on the speakerphone. "Jono, it's Allen. I want you to do something for me. Phoenix House twenty-fifth anniversary."

"Yeah, yeah. I heard from Tina Brown. I bought a table."

"No, Jono, I want you to sell another five."

"Oh, Jesus, Allen. I can't. I want people to say to me when we meet, 'Hi, Jonathan, how's Laura and Charles?' I don't want them to run when they see me coming."

"Jonathan, I want to ask you something."

"Yes?"

"How's Laura, how's Charles? Now buy five tables."

Grubman's first charity mistake — this is not his world — was asking the producer Mark Goodson, whose wife, Suzanne, left him for Mitch Rosenthal, to buy a table. "He told me this story about his wife!" said Allen. "I mean, how could this be? I thought Mitch Rosenthal was Albert Schweitzer or something. I mean humanitarians don't shtup, do they?"

And then: "Can anyone tell me why the rich are so cheap?"

Tuesday, December 10, 1991

Marie Brenner called to tell me an extraordinary incident that took place last night at the NYC Parks black-tie gala at Tavern on the Green after the opening of the Streisand movie *The Prince of Tides.* She was sitting demurely in her black dinner suit at the parks commissioner Betsy Gotbaum's table when she felt something cold and wet running down her back. Out of the corner of her eye she saw waiters with trays of wine moving around and assumed one of them had spilled the vino. Unwilling to embarrass the waiter, she didn't turn around. Until the other guests at the table started pointing and yelping, "Oh my God! Look what he just did!" The "he" in question was Donald Trump! She saw his familiar Elvis coif making off across the Crystal Room. The sneaky, petulant infant was clearly still stewing about her takedown in *VF* over a year ago and had taken a glass of wine from the tray and emptied it down her back! What a coward! He couldn't even confront her to her face! Marie was as outraged as she was incredulous but chose to ignore it. Everyone knows he's going broke and he spent most of the evening canoodling with his pouty blow-up doll, Marla Maples.

1992
RHAPSODY IN BLUE

Monday, January 20, 1992

Christmas with the kids at the Elkhorn Ranch already seems so long ago.

My contract is nearing expiration and I can't decide whether to renew. What else could I do? Can't go back to London as Harry's having a ball at Random House, minting bestsellers. The Alex job doesn't get more appealing. I would be frustrated to be out of the business of assigning stories and would miss working with writers. Editorial director may sound powerful but it's really just courtier work, and trying to improve the magazines incrementally without offending turf-warrior editors. Plus half the Condé mags don't even interest me — *Self*, *Brides*, *HG*, *Glamour*. Anna is making *Vogue* sizzle and I wouldn't want to interfere there, except on the features side, and if I did, that would just create icicle aggravation I don't need.

On Thursday Si came down to talk to me. I thought it was another run around the Alex succession track but it was about *The New Yorker.* It is, he told me, losing 19 million a year.

Immediately my head started to spin. The dual emotions of agony and excitement. The desire to raise my intellectual sights is like a thirst. But the struggle is that *TNY* would make me busier and given what G needs, life would be more difficult, not less. He cannot stand any alteration in my schedule if I promise to be there and then am late. He's on a good course at Stephen Gaynor School with all the personal attention but I can't kid myself. And then again, *VF* is on such a roll and making real money. I'd love the new challenge that would deploy my deeper skills as an editor and provide a more challenging outlet to raise my game. The joy of no more conversations about how to get Madonna for a photo shoot! Could I do it and still be a decent mother to G and Izzy?

I feel at sea about whether to trust Si. He keeps proving that he's in the bombshell business. In a recession that's killing three magazines a month, *VF* is now flying. We seem to be hanging on to the circulation gains with Demi Moore, holding at over a million in combined newsstand and subs. Ron's got the ads up substantially in the next quarter, a flaming miracle. But I know everything can change in a minute. I have been reading Robert Massie's fascinating book *Dreadnought* that Harry's publishing about the prelude to World War I. I realize there is a bit of the kaiser in Si's whims. For all his support of me these last years, it's been such a dance to head off his secretly cooked-up moves. The company needs outside input, not just family conferences. He blew me off when I raised again moving *VF* into new arenas. Wouldn't even consider it. I sat the ABC producer Susan Mercandetti next to him at a dinner to co-opt him on the TV idea, and he said, "Before you start to talk to me I want you to know I think a TV show is a terrible idea. Why would you dilute a great brand like *Vanity Fair* by putting it on air?" He's wrong.

There is something disturbing about the thought of all these nepotistic decision makers with the lives and jobs of others in their hands. This is what everyone warned me of when I turned down the move to Hearst. Bennack runs a professional shop. Condé Nast is a court, always dependent on the favor of the king. And yet.

The upside of a court is there is only one person who decides.

Thursday January 23, 1992

This morning Si called me upstairs and sat me down next to him in the chair near his desk. "Alex and I have been talking," he said. "How much do you read . . . *The New*

811

Yorker?" A long pause. "Not much lately," I said. A longer pause. It felt endless. Had I just disqualified myself? He behaved as if I said the opposite. "How would you go about it?" he said. My turn to pause. I thought about the issues of *The New Yorker* I do love, the ones from the Harold Ross period of the twenties and thirties. I bought a set of them at the Strand.

There's a crispness, variety, and pace in them that's vanished from the current model. The use of artists and cartoonists in the Ross days was bold, irreverent, sometimes full page. The covers were social commentary of the era. Nothing like the tepid, ornamental images we associate with *The New Yorker* now. In Ross's magazine, the vitality and varied lengths of pieces and deft use of spot art made it feel current and alive. You could feel a news edge, sense a metropolitan eyebrow raised. There was less of today's endless scrolls of print, the impenetrable absence of definition, the sense that you are in a word church. I told Si I could not edit Shawn's or Gottlieb's *New Yorker,* but Ross's *New Yorker* spoke to me as if it were published yesterday. He smiled when I said all this, then said we would talk again soon.

And now I am at home, waiting for Harry and pacing the apartment. *The New Yorker* is a weekly. I cannot do this to the kids unless — unless — Mum and Dad would come and live with us in New York. Mum has never failed me when I asked her to do something and perhaps they would. We miss each other more and more, and I sense since Izzy was born Mum longs to be more a part of the family. If Mum and Dad came, it would be a boon for G. They are so wonderful with him, playing endless, patient games. There are the critical three hours when G gets off the school bus from Stephen Gaynor before I can get home. How wonderful if his grandparents could be there to greet him.

I am deeply attached to the *VF* writers and would be sad to leave them, but there are others I see sporadically in the pages of *TNY* — Adam Gopnik, the art writer, ought to be doing more than art, he's clearly got expansive range, and Louis Menand, who's doing book reviews — I'd like to see him do longer essays. Janet Malcolm is a jewel to keep. So is Roger Angell. Then there are the talents I have spotted elsewhere and long to recruit, some from London. John Lahr, who did the Orton book. He might come over and do theater. I am loving the film pieces in *The Independent* by the young writer Julie Kavanagh knows, Anthony Lane. He's almost Waugh-like, and so witty. I could bring the critics section alive. I'd love to hire David Remnick, who writes so fluently about Russia at *The Washington Post*. He's been on book leave and we should grab him. I'd need a consigliere who knew the folkways at *The New Yorker.* Maybe Hendrik Hertzberg at *The New Republic,* who used to work there in Shawn's day and is such a brilliant editor as well as writer and still has a lot of friends there I've heard. I'd need Sharon DeLano back. She has the intellectual heft to wrestle the big pieces, and Kim Heron, who has come over to VF from *The New York Times* and is a superb editor. Her Mary McCarthy style would fit the culture, I'm sure. I love the idea of doing reported essays, getting the critics to engage with the world around them and the news, something *The New Yorker* has the brain power for but rarely does. Gopnik could do those. So could Henry Louis Gates, the black studies professor at Harvard who writes great op eds in the *Times.* Philip Gourevitch at *The Forward* is a huge talent I've noticed. There are so many fabulous writers out there and there is no more room at *VF* to publish them all. A weekly means four times as many writers each month! *TNY* needs to refresh the pool and find new talent just as good as the old. It would take me back to my literary roots at the *New Statesman* that lately I miss more and more. (Larkin again: the "hunger to be more serious.") My head is racing now. It would be thrilling to be able to work with John Updike. It would be a joy to work with Brendan Gill. But so much people management with a bigger staff and an apparently arcane system of payment and benefits. I would have to bring Pam McCarthy with me to help me strategize! *VF* (and I) would fall apart without her . . . Chris Garrett could take over her role so *VF* wouldn't miss a beat with whomever they picked to replace me. I can't believe I can even write those words, "replace me" . . . I expect Si will want to keep Nick Dunne and Marie at *VF.* They are the two defining voices of the mag and at least for a year or two would need to hold it steady.

I picked up a *New Yorker* on the way home. It would need to visually evolve while keeping its cool beauty. I'd want to bring the Harold Ross flavor and pace, with a today spin. The mag has no photography at the moment except some little tiny pictures in the Goings On About Town section. I would ask Richard Avedon (I have never managed to use him at *VF,* where he feels crowded out by splashy talents like Annie) to be the one photographer, just him, to open the magazine's windows. The clarity of his black-and-white images have the same purity as *The New Yorker*'s Caslon typeface. He could provide just a few pictures from his own archives and sometimes a new portrait, dropped into the text as punctuation points.

Covers! I know from *VF* there are throngs of untapped illustrators and cartoonists we could use. Art Spiegelman, Ed Sorel, Bruce

McCall. I wish Mark Boxer were still alive. He was born to draw for these pages. I need to find black-and-white line drawings that echo his sophistication. And I want to nurture and grow more cartoonists! They are the lifeblood of the mag. I could give them a Holiday Issue all to themselves. The Cartoon Issue. I love it already. And I would heat up the fiction. Not my area of passion, but I could raid *Granta* and see if its brilliant literary editor Bill Buford wants to move to NYC. He's a five-hundred-pound gorilla who would probably want my job, but also the kind of alpha talent *TNY* needs. One thing about the Ross *New Yorker* that had so much charm was the rubrics that recur: Annals of Personal History. Shouts and Murmurs. I will revive them. Shouts and Murmurs could be a back-page humor column.

My heart begins to race and I close my eyes. In the next room I can hear Izzy wake up and call out for me. But I also hear something else, something I can't resist: the sweet Gershwin strains of a new opportunity.

EPILOGUE:
WHAT HAPPENED LATER

Six months after I wrote that last entry, I walked a block and a half southwest from Condé Nast headquarters on Madison Avenue to a handsome 1920s Beaux Arts building on West Forty-Third Street overlooking Bryant Park. It was June 30, 1992, and as the new, thirty-eight-year-old editor of *The New Yorker* I was on my way to meet its senior editing staff for the first time.

I was the fourth editor in sixty-seven years and the first woman. It was a clear, sunny day. In a spirit of summer gaiety I wore a polka-dot silk wrap dress and, to boost my confidence, my highest Manolo heels. I didn't keep a diary of those first insanely hectic six months, but what I remember from that day is a group of about a dozen men — all men, all in horn-rimmed glasses and tweed jackets — sitting around a board table, eyeing me with poorly concealed mistrust. One participant looked different. A baleful, bony face glared from between curtains of Frank Zappa hair. "I suppose you'll want to cut down on cartoons?" This, I would soon discover, was Bob Mankoff, the cartoonist.

The next chapter of my editing adventures had begun — six and a half years of thrilling intellectual contentment. With the help of Pam McCarthy to clear the wilderness, I replaced seventy-one of the 120 *New Yorker* staff with fifty outstanding new talents, all from my original dream list and others we later identified: David Remnick and Henry Louis "Skip" Gates Jr. right off the bat, and over the next two years Malcolm Gladwell, Jane Mayer, Jeffrey Toobin, James B. Stewart, and Lawrence Wright. We added a sparkling trio of new critics who lit up the back of the book: Anthony Lane on movies, John Lahr on theater, and the British historian Simon Schama on art. As the explosion of media continued, Ken Auletta came aboard to write a column on communications. Skip Gates let us poach his precocious Du Bois Institute protégé, Henry Finder, an eclectic highbrow who would become our books editor and an all-around editorial influence. Far from cutting down on cartoons as Bob Mankoff feared, I promoted him to cartoon editor, gave him an annual all-cartoon holiday issue, and launched the *New Yorker* Cartoon Bank, which curated for sale the huge archive of cartoons, including thousands that were accepted but never published, producing income not only for the magazine but also for the (sometimes impecunious) cartoonists themselves.

There were other gems from the old guard who I wanted to stay. Nancy Franklin was an editor whose scalding memos about train-wreck pieces were so funny, I made her our second-string theater critic. The incumbent deputy editor, Charles "Chip" McGrath, proved to have one of the most sensitive set of copy eyes I'd ever encountered. (It was Chip who also wryly helped me translate such coded old-guard responses to an incoming article as "It's a useful piece," which meant, of course, the absolute opposite.) Greatest Generation jewels from the old *New Yorker* such as Lillian Ross and Roger Angell were reinvigorated, existing talent such as the dazzling art critic Adam Gopnik changed their beats (I sent him to Paris) or expanded their range (I harassed Mark Singer into profiling Donald Trump), and, thanks to the new art editor, Françoise Mouly, covers got a new vibrancy and energy (no more Central Park benches with autumn leaves). Her husband, the Pulitzer Prize–winning graphic novelist and artist Art Spiegelman, contributed cover images of incendiary intelligence. Through it all I was guided by the essential *New Yorker* alumnus, Hendrik Hertzberg, who returned from his post at *The New Republic* in Washington to run the Comment section and help me breathe life back into *The New Yorker*'s pages while keeping faith with its founding spirit and mission. (One of Rick Hertzberg's many benefactions was identifying a former *New Republic* colleague, Dorothy Wickenden, a fierce defender of editorial standards, who became my executive editor and still plays that role for David Remnick.)

None of this happened without tumult. My first three years were an uproar of indignant protests and apocalyptic doomsaying. The fury of not a few veteran ex-staffers coursed through the media, certain that I would sack the sepulcher.

One would think that putting bylines at the beginning of articles instead of at the end heralded the end of civilization. Garrison Keillor noisily quit as I arrived. George W. S. Trow called me "the girl in the wrong dress," a slur whose meaning, though not its malice, was unclear. To Jamaica Kincaid I was "Joseph Stalin in high heels." (Jamaica would later return to *The New Yorker* as our gardening columnist.)

These were the most vociferous responses to change, but they were by no means the most typical. Most of the old staff — some reluctantly, some eagerly — soon adjusted to the new rhythms, the new timeliness, the new visual energy, and their new colleagues. One of my most pleasing days on the job was in the summer of 1996 when the novelist and long-time *New Yorker* contributor John Updike was in my office for a sandwich. Unfailingly courteous and modest, Updike seldom came down from Massachusetts and didn't usually stay long. As it happened that week, Anthony Lane was in from London. Anthony, Cambridge-educated and still in his twenties, had quickly become one of the defining voices of the new *New Yorker* critic roster. He branched out from movie reviews to effervescent reassessments of Henry James and Edward Lear and other writers he referred to (though not in print, of course) as "sad old fucks." Updike was the literary hero Anthony most yearned to meet. I told him to knock on my door around lunchtime and I would introduce the new contributor to the old. As I did so, Updike rose from his chair and stopped me midflow. "Anthony Lane!" he exclaimed. "I have been wanting so much to meet you!"

At that moment I knew that the editorial graft had taken. There was no longer, as the press narrative usually went, a *New Yorker* "old guard" pitted against an upstart editor and her "new guard" hires. There was one magazine again — healthy, vital, regenerated, off the critical list. Advertisers returned. Circulation rose by a quarter of a million. The annual deficit steadily declined, going from a huge $18 million to a less huge $12 million (and would finally disappear altogether in 2002, under the business leadership of David Carey). Most important and gratifying, a new generation became readers. In April 1995 we won the Oscar of the magazine world, the General Excellence award, for the first time in *The New Yorker*'s history.

Something else happened. *The New Yorker* changed me as much as I changed *The New Yorker.* It made me more thoughtful, more rigorous, more addicted to excellence. It was satisfying to depart from my own determination to shrink excessively long pieces when the quality demanded something exceptional. Since David Blundy's death I had followed obsessively the conflict in El Salvador. On December 6, 1993, we devoted an entire issue of *The New Yorker* to one piece, a fifty-thousand-word investigative report by Mark Danner, "The Truth of El Mozote." Mark scrupulously revealed that the Salvadoran Army on December 11, 1981, had murdered nine hundred villagers and concealed the atrocity, burying the slaughtered in mass graves, and that the US colluded with the lie that the victims were all communist guerrillas.

All this took collaboration and judgment. I loved the hours of passionate debate in my office with Remnick and Hertzberg and Finder and Pam over the pros and cons of whether to publish a piece or a cover. (One that slipped through the net was my outlandish notion of asking Roseanne Barr to be a "guest editor" of a special issue on women that misfired spectacularly and was aborted by unanimous outrage before publication.)

Si Newhouse, who supported me through the whole raucous literary experiment, was over the moon.

My family life was joyful, too. My parents moved from London to the apartment across the corridor from ours on East Fifty-Seventh Street. That dream of the kids getting in from school and going over to play with their doting "gaga and gumpy" became reality.

In all my successes and misadventures since, the warm strength of family life has been behind every leap of faith I've taken. Georgie was finally diagnosed with Asperger's syndrome in 1995, when he was nine, astonishingly through an article by Oliver Sacks that came to me at *The New Yorker*. Dr. Sacks wrote about a fascinating, obsessional scientist named Temple Grandin. She manifested so many of our son's attributes that I knew we had finally found the answer to the riddle of his gifts and his struggles, even before a specialist whom Sacks recommended to us confirmed the medical label. A committed therapist, Dr. Anne Marie Albano, helped transform his ability to empathize, reduce his anxiety, and organize his thoughts. I am happy to report that after many challenges and much support from all who love him, Georgie is an independent, exuberant thirty-one-year-old, living in his own apartment in downtown Manhattan and working at a small nonprofit, where he's beloved for his quirky humor and affectionate heart. Izzy, meanwhile, flew through Harvard and now works as a news producer at Vice Media. She is as full of life and speed as her unstoppable father, who, at eighty-nine, swims a thousand yards daily, moderates public Newsmaker interviews at Reuters, and in June 2017 published his twelfth book, *Do I Make Myself Clear?* Now that the kids have left home, Harry and I savor our news-junkie breakfasts together at the local diner, where I get to have his rapid re-edit of the front-page agenda all to myself.

As I look back on the *Vanity Fair* years I realize that you never know you're living in a personal golden age until it's over. I shall always be grateful to Si Newhouse for following his instincts and hiring me, and allowing me, over seventeen years of working for him, to follow my own. Alexander Liberman, ever the improviser, unexpectedly thrived after the death of his wife, Tatiana, marrying her Filipina nurse, Melinda. (He died in 1999, at the age of eighty-seven, in Miami Beach, where he had moved after his remarriage and retirement.)

Miles Chapman continued his editing career in London until he was diagnosed with Parkinson's disease in 2002. While researching his illness he discovered at last who his real father was: a Cheshire chef named Cecil Jesse Proudlove. This has proved to him a source of considerable amusement. He now walks with a cane but is mostly unchanged. Sarah Giles died tragically early in 2014 at the age of sixty-three after a cardiac arrest and a stroke. Even though she was wheelchair-bound for her last five years, she held court for friends who came to visit from far and wide. Chris Garrett and Jane Sarkin remain at *Vanity Fair* still, twin pillars of its prosperity. Pam McCarthy continues, like Atlas, to hold together all the moving parts at *The New Yorker.* Sharon DeLano now works almost exclusively for Annie Leibovitz, whose worldwide renown requires constant text accompaniment and curation. Michael Roberts joined me as style director of *The New Yorker* and now continues a Cocteau-like transatlantic career as an acclaimed illustrator, photographer, and journalist. Ron Galotti enjoyed a pop-culture moment when it was revealed he was the real-life model for Mr. Big in Candace Bushnell's *Sex and the City.* He got out of the magazine business, moved to Vermont, and became a happy and successful farmer and volunteer fireman.

I've stayed in close touch with so many of

the writers, photographers, and editors I have worked with over the years that sometimes I forget which publication(s) we collaborated on. Some traveled with me on the whole bumpy journey. Gabé Doppelt — who also joined me as Features editor at *Talk* magazine in 1999 and as West Coast bureau chief at *The Daily Beast,* the digital news site I founded in 2008 — has reinvented herself in the hotel business in LA. I still rely on her high, clear voice on the phone to ruthlessly dissect a problem.

It makes me happy that my successors at *Vanity Fair* and *The New Yorker,* Graydon Carter and David Remnick respectively, flourished as editors in chief. David is a natural wonder. Besides editing and supervising a great magazine and its thriving website, he writes as much or more of its content than anyone on his staff and hosts *The New Yorker*'s popular weekly hour-long radio show. (Nowadays, when I listen to that show and the podcasts and when I see the success of *Vanity Fair*'s books and documentaries, I feel a certain satisfaction that Condé Nast has finally seen the potential of expanding their brands beyond print.)

Oh, and yes: Anna Wintour reigns forever as queen of Condé Nast.

The media has changed unrecognizably since the 1980s Valhalla of well-funded editorial confidence, when you could pursue excellence as well as profit in a profession marked by community as well as competition. Stephen Schiff — now executive producer and writer of the hit FX TV show *The Americans* — was prescient in a 1990 *Vanity Fair* essay when he suggested that we were all becoming unmoored, atomized "Particle People," but what he didn't predict was that media itself would splinter, proliferate, and cull so many of the creative talents on which algorithms depend. Writing brilliant sentences (and editing them) does not have the market value of writing brilliant code, even though, as we learn every day, critical thinking is the DNA of democracy. What no one could have predicted is that even as we are swept toward an unknown future we live in a strangely recurring past. The ultimate personification of the gilded grossness of the 1980s, Donald Trump, is president of the United States. And as a consequence of his excesses — and of the boom in Fake (and Fox) News — an appreciation of powerful independent journalism is reviving. We may even be at the start of a new golden age.

Meanwhile, I feel every day the stirring to tell new stories — and a recurring sensation in my life of new beginnings: restlessness.

ACKNOWLEDGMENTS

The entries in *The* Vanity Fair *Diaries,* written in the heat of the moment, were inevitably rife with errors, names half remembered, dates scrambled, relationships confused, professions and titles bollixed up. I enlisted some invaluable reading eyes to help clean up confusions. I hope that in this editing process we caught all or most of the flubs while leaving intact the immediacy of the original text.

I am deeply grateful in this endeavor to a trio of punctilious fact police: Jolene Lescio, Cindy Quillinan, and Brenda Phipps. They also provided invaluable administrative support. My daughter, Isabel, offered essential millennial bafflement about people I assumed everyone knew, but about whom, it turns out, no one under thirty has a clue. She encouraged me to add identifications of the characters who appear throughout as they are introduced. And I am so appreciative of Miles Chapman, who brought his beady eye to

829

catching errors and style points in late-stage galleys.

Annie Leibovitz, who figures so much in these pages, generously allowed reproduction of her pictures from *Vanity Fair* and of my family and me over the years; she was as passionately engaged as ever when I sought her advice on other issues. Karen Mulligan and Laura Cali from Annie's studio were remarkable in the swiftness and care with which they found the wonderful images we featured in the book.

Stephen Schiff, *Vanity Fair*'s brilliant critic and contributor, was always readily available to amplify certain cultural details — and I am indebted to Gabé Doppelt for her pointed suggestions.

The glorious photographic insert section was the result of miraculous teamwork by friends, helpers, and former colleagues. First, it was a pleasure to work with Henry Holt's remarkably talented design director, Meryl Levavi, who contributed so much creativity. I thank especially *VF*'s managing editor, my old friend Chris Garrett, along with Ivan Shaw, Allison Ingram, and Matthew Barad in Condé Nast Rights and Permissions, for speedily clearing multiple images for publications.

Tiggy Maconochie of Maconochie Photography was uncommonly helpful in securing Helmut Newton's pictures for publication, as was Arthur Elgort's agent, Marianne Houtenbos, when I set my heart on Arthur's masterly portrait of Alexander Liberman, caught in full charm mode at a Manhattan night out. (Thanks, too, to André Leon Talley, for urging me to use it full page, providing the "glory" that Alex would have urged on me in the past.) Roxanne Lowit, peerless snapper of Manhattan nights, was generous with her time in the dog days of summer, printing up all the evocative snaps she took of *Vanity Fair* guests and contributors, supported by assiduous work from Melanie Martinez and Lucky Singh at Lucky Visuals Inc.

A big, big thanks to the photographers and artists who were so kind about the inclusion of their work — Eric Boman, Harry Benson, Kathy Amerman, Tim Graham, Mark McKenna (on behalf of the late Herb Ritts), Ed Sorel, Art Spiegelman, and *The New Yorker*'s art editor, Françoise Mouly, who facilitated the reproduction of two of my favorite *New Yorker* covers. Elisabeth Biondi, *VF* and *TNY*'s former photo director, helped me reach many photographers no longer in my rolodex. And finally, Leigh Cafferty and Elena Adams at Tina Brown Live Media were a great support in their willingness to get this onerous task completed in record time.

I thank, too, the Alliance for Audited Media (formerly the Audit Bureau of Circulations) for digging out *Vanity Fair*'s accurate circulation numbers in its first eight years of life.

It could not be more of a pleasure to be published by Holt. The conviction and support of president and publisher Stephen Rubin has buoyed me up through the whole process, and it's been a pleasure to experience the dynamism and cool decisiveness of editor in chief Gillian Blake. Thanks to them, I was blessed to work with the extraordinary editor Courtney Hodell, whose sophisticated judgment and punctilious attention to detail were a great gift, as was the judicious attention of copy editor Jane Elias and the all-seeing eye of managing editor Kenn Russell. Thanks also to Holt's Rick Pracher, Maggie Richards, and Pat Eisemann for their energy and insights.

I would not have had the courage to publish the diaries at all without the encouragement, discernment, and keen judgment of my brilliant friend and former *New Yorker* colleague Hendrik Hertzberg.

And of course, as always, my guiding voice throughout has been the editor I turn to first and last, my husband, Harry.

This book is dedicated to my literary agent of thirty-five years, Ed Victor, who died last June after a long, difficult illness. Without his optimism, strength, and belief in me, *The* Vanity Fair *Diaries* would not exist. Thank you, dear Ed.

PS. Left to right: July 2000. After the Queen honored TB with a CBE (Commander of the British Empire) for services to journalism, TB and Harry celebrate in the courtyard of Buckingham Palace. Summer 2017: Holiday snaps of Georgie and Isabel. Right: Harry turns 89 and eats the words of his latest book with a Do I Make Myself Clear? birthday cake.

ILLUSTRATION ACKNOWLEDGMENTS

All images in this book are courtesy of the author's private collection with the exception of the following:

Dedication

Ed Victor, champion and beloved friend. © Carol Ryan Victor.

Insert

Tina and *Tatler* staff. Photograph by Graham Morris/Evening Standard/Getty Images.

Paula Yates *Tatler* cover. © Norman Parkinson.

Harold Evans drawing. © Mark Boxer.

Martin Amis in 1980. © Angela Gorgas.

Tina outside *Tatler's* second office. © Ken Sharp.

Alexander Liberman. © Arthur Elgort.

Staff group *VF,* 1992. © Annie Leibovitz.

Si Newhouse Jr. with his wife. © Roxanne Lowit.

Dominick Dunne. © Kathy Amerman.

VF cover, "Blonde Ambition." Photograph by Helmut Newton. © The Helmut Newton Estate / Maconochie Photography.

The Harry Benson Reagan cover. © Harry Benson.

Goodbye to Reagans at White House. © Annie Leibovitz.

Kiss that ignited media mania. © Harry Benson.

Michael Roberts. © Roxanne Lowit.

Wayne Lawson with Caroline Graham. © Roxanne Lowit.

Tina talking at *VF* office with Dominick Dunne and Marie Brenner. © Annie Leibovitz.

James Wolcott. © Gasper Tringale.

Stephen Schiff. © Roxanne Lowit.

Ruth Ansel. © Roxanne Lowit.

Tina in classic black-and-white. © Horst P. Horst.

Condé Nast legend Horst P. Horst. © Michael Auer.

Tina portrait by *VF* cartoonist Robert Risko. © Robert Risko.

Family portrait, 1991. © Annie Leibovitz.

Tina's parents, George and Bettina Brown, summer 1988. © George Lange.

Annie Leibovitz self-portrait. © Annie Leibovitz.

VF cover, Michael Jackson. © Annie Leibovitz.

VF cover, Demi Moore. © Annie Leibovitz.

Ballet maestro Mikhail (Misha) Baryshnikov. © Annie Leibovitz.

VF cover, Cher. © Annie Leibovitz.

VF spread, Michael Jackson. © Annie Leibovitz.

VF spread, Whoopi Goldberg. © Annie Leibovitz.

VF spread, Diane Sawyer. © Annie Leibovitz.

Saxing out with blonde band. © Roxanne Lowit.

Tina with one of the Carmen Mirandas. © Roxanne Lowit.

Donald J. Trump and S. I. Newhouse Jr. © Roxanne Lowit.

Tom Wolfe tells Tina a secret. © Roxanne Lowit.

Patrick Kelly and Tina. © Roxanne Lowit.

Ian Schrager with Steve Rubell. Photograph by Patrick McMullan/Contributor/Getty Images.

Bob Colacello dancing with Wendy Starke. © Roxanne Lowit.

Reinaldo Herrera. © Roxanne Lowit.

VF cover, "Fatal Charm." Photograph by Helmut Newton. © The Helmut Newton Estate / Maconochie Photography.

Claus von Bülow with bowl on head. Photograph by Helmut Newton. © The Helmut Newton Estate / Maconochie Photography.

Helmut Newton. © Roxanne Lowit.

VF spread, "Fatal Charm: The Social Web of

Claus von Bülow." Photograph by Helmut Newton. © The Helmut Newton Estate / Maconochie Photography.

Tina and baby Izzy in Quogue. © Annie Leibovitz.

VF cover, Princess Diana. © Tim Graham.

VF cover, Goldie Hawn. © Herb Ritts.

VF spread, "The Fatal Obsession of Dian Fossey." © Alan Root.

Alexander Shoumatoff. © David Holderness.

Tina and Anna Wintour. Photographer/Artist: Ron Galella, Ltd./Getty Images.

VF fundraiser for Phoenix House drug rehab center, March 1990. Courtesy of Mitchell Rosenthal's private album.

Bob Colacello, Ian Schrager, Tina, and Dr. Mitchell Rosenthal. Courtesy of Mitchell Rosenthal's private album.

Tina as *New Yorker* dandified symbol. © Rea Irvin.

New Yorker cover, October 1992. © Ed Sorel.

New Yorker cover, February 1993. © Art Spiegelman.

Tina at *New Yorker* desk, 1998. © Eric Boman.

Acknowledgments

The Queen pinning the medal on Tina and Harry in Buckingham Palace courtyard, July 2000. © British Ceremonial Arts Limited.

Tina and Harry in Buckingham Palace court-yard, July 2000. © PA Images / Alamy Stock Photo.

ABOUT THE AUTHOR

Tina Brown is an award-winning writer and editor and the founder of the Women in the World summits. Between 1979 and 2001 she was editor successively of *Tatler, Vanity Fair,* and *The New Yorker.* Her 2007 biography of the Princess of Wales, *The Diana Chronicles,* topped the *New York Times* bestseller list. In 2008 she founded *The Daily Beast,* which won the Webby Award for Best News Site in 2012 and 2013. Queen Elizabeth honored her in 2000 as a Commander of the Order of the British Empire (CBE) for her services to overseas journalism, and in 2007 she was inducted into the US Magazine Editors' Hall of Fame. She founded Tina Brown Live Media in 2014 to expand Women in the World internationally. She is married to the editor, publisher, and historian Sir Harold Evans and lives in New York City.